A TEXTBOOK OF CHRISTIAN ETHICS

IN

A TEXTBOOK OF CHRISTIAN ETHICS

BY
ROBIN GILL

T. & T. CLARK LIMITED
59 GEORGE STREET, EDINBURGH

Copyright © T. & T. Clark Ltd, 1985

Typeset by Pennart Typesetting (Edinburgh) Ltd,
Edinburgh, Scotland
printed in Great Britain at the University Press, Oxford

for

T. & T. CLARK LTD, EDINBURGH

First Printed 1985
Reprinted 1985

British Library Cataloguing in Publication Data
Gill, Robin
    A textbook of Christian ethics.
    1. Christian ethics
    I. Title
    241   BJ1251

ISBN   0-567-29127-8

CONTENTS

Section 4 HUMAN LIFE AND INTERPERSONAL RELATIONSHIPS

vii

ALAN MORTON GILL
1909–1985

paternus adjutor et doctus lector

ACKNOWLEDGEMENTS

Thanks are due to the following for permission to use copyright passages:

Penguin Books Ltd (*City of God* and Copleston: *Aquinas*)

Prior Provincial, O.P., St Dominics Priory, London (*Summa Theologica*)

Fortress Press (*Luther's Works* and Bonino: *Doing Theology in a Revolutionary Situation*)

Basil Blackwell (*Aquinas: Selected Political Writings*)

William B. Eerdmans (*Nicene and Post Nicene Fathers*)

Doubleday (*Summa Contra Gentiles*)

Macmillan and SCM Press (Bonhoeffer: *Ethics*)

Scottish Academic Press (Ramsey: *Scottish Journal of Theology Occasional Paper 11*)

Harper & Row (Little & Twiss; *Comparative Religious Ethics*)

Oxford University Press (Barth: *The Epistle to the Romans*)

Geoffrey Bles Ltd (Berdyaev: *Freedom and the Spirit*)

Charles Scribner's Sons (Niebuhr: *Moral Man and Immoral Society* and *The Nature and Destiny of Man*)

Shepheard-Walwyn & SPCK (Temple: *Christianity and the Social Order*)

Catholic Truth Society (*Pacem in Terris* and *Humanae Vitae*)

Orbis Books and SCM Press (Miranda: *Marx and the Bible*)

The Fellowship of Reconciliation (Raven: *The Theological Basis of Christian Pacifism*)

Verlag Herder (Welty: *Handbook of Christian Social Ethics*)

Council of Religion and International Affairs (Ramsey: *The Limits of Nuclear War*)

SCM Press (URC Group: *Non-Violent Action*)

Princeton University (Fletcher: *Morals and Medicine*)

Harvard University Press (ed. John T. Noonan; *The Morality of Abortion*)

Ecumenical Patriarchate, Geneva (Clément's article from *Episkepsis*)

Quaker Home Service (*Towards a Quaker View of Sex*)

Victor Gollancz Ltd (ed. Hall & Matthews: *Race: A Christian Symposium*)

Winston/Seabury Press (Ruether: *New Woman/New Earth*)

World Council of Churches (ed. William H. Lazareth; *The Lord of Life*)

The Westminster and SCM Press (Fletcher's *Situation Ethics*)

PREFACE

This textbook might have been given the subtitle 'Unity and Diversity in Christian Ethics'. Certainly diversity is evident at every point. The reader will soon be aware of the fact that Christian ethics is a highly pluralistic discipline. Fundamental differences are apparent in the presuppositions, methods, and conclusions of the various writers represented here. Future socio-historians may notice that it is currently a feature of a number of areas of theology to emphasise pluralism. Perhaps this is inescapable at a time when theologians have become more conscious of ecumenism, of non-Western Christian thought, and of secular pluralism. It might have been possible to produce a book on moral issues which ignored this pluralism and diversity – but not a serious textbook of Christian ethics. A mature understanding of the discipline cannot bypass diversity.

If diversity is admitted, where is the unity in Christian ethics to be found? A superficial reading of this textbook might reach the conclusion that it is wholly absent. The diversity appears overwhelming. But that would, I believe, be a superficial reading. At certain key points I will suggest that the unity of Christian ethics lies mainly in certain *biblically consonant values held in tension*. I will be highly critical of simplistic attempts to derive individual values from the Bible. At the same time I do believe that it is a feature of most of the exponents of Christian ethics represented in this textbook, that they seek to hold in creative tension values that are consonant with distinctively Christian, and particularly biblical, resources (recognising that these resources themselves represent a variety of tensions). Thus, on this understanding, 'love' (*agape*) as an isolated value is not a sufficient Christian resource, but 'love' in tension with 'justice' is. Differing exponents of Christian ethics will emphasise this particular tension in varying ways, but for most it is an essential, irreducible and creative tension. I believe that it is also a crucial point of unity in an otherwise diverse discipline. At various points I will indicate a number of these tensions –

xi

between 'peace' and 'justice', between 'compassion' and 'moral indignation', and finally between what I term in the final pages the adeodatic axiom and the agapistic axiom. That these tensions are essential and irreducible derives from the nature of Christianity itself. As theologians such as Augustine (with his notion of the two cities) and Luther (with his notion of the two kingdoms) were well aware, Christianity is always a mixture of the 'now' and the 'not yet'. Indeed, the Synoptic concept of the Kingdom of God seems to contain both present and future elements. To reflect this, a degree of creative tension will always be a crucial feature of an adequate understanding of Christian ethics. And, precisely because it is structured around essential but elusive tensions, Christian ethics will always be subject to popular misrepresentation and reduction. It is only too easy to present 'Christian values' simplistically and with scant regard to their role-in-tension in Christianity itself. I hope that this textbook is able to contribute to a more mature understanding of Christian ethics.

I have been struggling with the teaching methods in this book for thirteen years and actually writing it for five. It was begun on sabbatical in Zambia, continued whilst teaching at Dartmouth College, New Hampshire, and effectively finished whilst teaching at the United Theological College in Bangalore. These unique venues opened up new vistas in Christian ethics for me which I have tried to incorporate in the book. I am most grateful to colleagues in all of these places for their help and encouragement. However, it is to my colleagues and students at Edinburgh that I owe the most. Generations of students have acted as guinea-pigs on the various texts and extracts. Without them I would never have known which to discard and which to include. And my colleagues, Alastair Campbell, Duncan Forrester, and Ian McDonald have all given most generously of their time. I am sure that they will all be profoundly grateful that they are to be pestered no more (at least on this book!). Ian, in particular, undertook the heroic task of helping me to proof-read the whole text. David Cook of Oxford also very kindly commented on Section 3. I am sure that errors must remain and I have no doubt that future generations of students will point them out to me with great glee! Before they mention it, the spellings in the texts and extracts stick to the conventions of the books from which they have been drawn - sometimes British and sometimes American. But then the textbook *is* intended for both audiences.

Finally I would like to thank my family. I am always extremely relieved that most of them never read my books. Much more importantly they offer me an adeodatic context of *agape* – especially Jenny, Martin and Judy. However my late father not only read my books but meticulously corrected their grammar, spelling and sometimes logic. To him I owe a special debt.

INTRODUCTION

STRUCTURE

The structure of this textbook is built around a systematic comparison of texts with extracts. These two terms are used simply for convenience to distinguish between classical excerpts from Augustine, Aquinas and Luther and present-day (i.e. within the last 50 years) excerpts – the first being termed texts and the second extracts. This structure is an extension of a method developed at Edinburgh University over the last 15 years but here made more elaborate and systematic with most excerpts chosen *de novo*. It differs significantly from the historical approach of Waldo Beach and H. Richard Niebuhr's *Christian Ethics* and of Arthur F. Holmes' *War and Christian Ethics* in a number of ways: (a) it does not attempt to present a selection of historical writings in Christian ethics – an important undertaking successfully achieved in these two books, but one that does lead to the reproduction of material of little contemporary relevance; (b) it stresses the value of the comparative approach as an important means of learning; (c) it provides a systematic means of analysis for each text and extract, which in turn makes comparative study more possible; (d) it places an emphasis upon the contemporary relevance of the discipline. This last point is certainly a feature of a number of readers in Christian social ethics, but from the perspective of the theological teacher they often lack a serious historical dimension and are in any case readers and not textbooks.

This book is designed to be a textbook and, at the end of this introduction, a method of using it as such is suggested. The fact that it is a textbook and not simply a reader has determined the choice of texts and extracts. After many experiments it was decided to limit the texts to three key theologians in the belief that this gives more coherence to the four Sections and brings

1

out better the main options and variables within Christian ethics. Naturally, at times, references are made to Church Fathers earlier than Augustine (particularly Tertullian, Origen and Ambrose), to Scholastics other than Aquinas and to Reformers other than Luther (notably Calvin) and it was tempting to include texts from them all. But that would seriously have distorted the aims of this as a textbook and might have turned it instead into an historical reader. By confining the texts to these three key theologians, it is hoped that the student will be encouraged to focus clearly upon the differences between them and to distinguish their differing effects upon present-day Christian ethics. Not only do they represent three of the most powerful post-New Testament influences on Christian theology, but they also represent the three distinct phases of Western Christianity – the Undivided Catholic Church, the Medieval Roman Church and the Protestant/Reformed Church.

The extracts, too, have been chosen with the needs of a textbook and not simply of a reader in mind. They are not necessarily 'the best' from recent Christian ethics. For example, the Quakers' *Extract 22* would not generally be recognised as a distinguished work of theology (its authors never claimed to be professional theologians), but it does represent a position that has had a considerable influence upon the contemporary churches. It also raises important dilemmas for the exponent of Christian ethics. It has been our experience in teaching the subject that students can learn from weaker extracts as well as from those which are more intellectually sophisticated, although the balance is intended to be in favour of the latter. As will be explained presently, the extracts have been chosen to represent as wide a range as possible within and between differing Christian traditions.

The book is divided into four Sections with the three texts and at least six extracts in each. The first Section is concerned with methodological issues and the subsequent Sections with substantive issues in Christian ethics. Sections 2-3 are mainly concerned with issues in social ethics and Section 4 with personal ethics, although these divisions sometimes become somewhat arbitrary (e.g. marital issues are clearly personal issues, but, at least within the Judaeo-Christian tradition, they also have a relationship with society at large). The Sections are self-contained and contain many cross-references to other Sections and therefore can be studied in any order. Each Section is introduced by a summary of the main issues raised within it as they relate to Christian ethics. Each Text and group of Extracts is introduced by a six-fold system of analysis and at the end of each a critique is given.

SYSTEM OF ANALYSIS

The six-fold system of analysis introducing each Text and group of Extracts consists of (1) Background (2) Key Issues (3) Ethical Arguments (4) Bases of Christian Ethics (5) Social Determinants and (6) Social Significance. The critique at the end of each forms a seventh part. In more detail they are as follows:

I. BACKGROUND
This part of the analysis suggests relevant biographical details and identifies the document from which the Text or Extract has been taken. Since part of the present introduction is concerned with comparing Augustine, Aquinas and Luther it will not be necessary to repeat these biographical details every time a Text is introduced. Until the central differences between the three theologians become clearer, a student would be well advised to keep referring back to this part of the introduction. In this Textbook a strong assumption is that biographical details are, at times, directly relevant to an understanding of the thought of a particular theologian. Thus some knowledge of Berdyaev's life is considered to be essential for an adequate understanding of *Extract 8*.

2. KEY ISSUES
The overall introduction to each Section seeks to provide a summary of the main issues arising from the Texts and Extracts within it. But here secondary issues will also be raised and it will be indicated how the specific Text or Extract in question relates to the main issues. The aim of this part of the analysis is to help

students to isolate specific issues from the Text or Extract so that they can relate them to the other Texts or Extracts. One of the surprising features of examining, in detail, even quite a short excerpt from a given author, is to discover how many of his or her characteristic ideas occur within it. Thus, if examined thoroughly, even a short Text from a theologian as complex as Aquinas may contain quite a number of his assumptions and ideas. Again from experience of teaching Christian ethics, Texts or Extracts need not be lengthy to be instructive, they must merely be studied with care and attention.

3. ETHICAL ARGUMENTS

A vital feature of analysis in Christian ethics involves the identification of differing types of ethical argument. An important distinction must be made between moral decision-making and ethical analysis. In so far as it is an academic discipline, ethics, and with it Christian ethics, is usually considered to be concerned more with the second than with the first. It is concerned with examining the nature of prescriptive language, the grounds on which moral beliefs are held, the types of argument which those who hold them use to promote them, and the consequences that they involve. If decision-making is involved, this is usually achieved on the basis of a systematic or developed theory. Ethics, or moral philosophy, understood in this way is clearly related to intelligent moral decision-making, but is not identical with it. Similarly, Christian theology is not usually considered to be identical with Christian belief: it is an intellectual, theoretical and second-order discipline. So, whereas presumably all Christians make moral decisions and hold certain religious beliefs, only some are exponents of Christian ethics and of Christian theology. It is in this sense that the terms will be used here, even though elsewhere the terms 'theology' and 'ethics' are often used in a broader and less academic sense.

It would be inappropriate to attempt an outline of general ethics or moral philosophy. Instead good introductions can be found in the following:

ed. Phillippa Foot, *Theories of Ethics*
A. MacIntyre, *A Short History of Ethics*
P.H. Nowell-Smith, *Ethics*

G.J. Warnock, *Contemporary Moral Philosophy*
Mary Warnock, *Ethics Since 1900*

In addition, A.V. Campbell's *Moral Dilemmas in Medicine*
provides a clear and readable account of the classical approaches
to ethics using medical issues as case-studies. Ian C.M.
Fairweather & J.I.H. McDonald's, *The Quest for Christian Ethics*,
gives a more detailed account of the approaches.

For the purpose of this Textbook three basic types of ethical
arguments should be clearly identified – the deontological, the
consequential and the personalist:

(a) *Deontological ethical arguments*
It is a feature of deontological arguments – derived from the
Greek for 'necessary' or 'imperative' – that by nature they are
absolutist. One cannot argue beyond them. So, if one maintains
that murder is wrong and is asked to give a reason, a
deontological response would be:- 'Because it is against the law
of nature', or 'Because it is against God's will', or 'Because it
breaks the Sixth Commandment', or even 'Because it is simply
wrong'. Such responses merely refer the other person to some
norm or absolute beyond which there can be no further
argument (for a finer distinction between authoritarian and
formalistic types of deontology see *Extract 6.14-20*). There is no
attempt here to argue that it is the consequences of murder that
make it wrong; indeed, murder is seen as wrong regardless of its
consequences. Of course, there may be situations in which two
or more norms conflict (as in euthanasia – see *Extract 19*) and
further argument is then required in order to determine moral
priorities (sometimes termed 'casuistry'), but values, as such,
cannot be justified other than by reference to the norm from
which they are derived. Immanuel Kant's (1724-1803) concept
of the categorical imperative is a clear example of deontological
ethics, whereby morality is regarded as autonomous, categorical (in the sense that it is a 'given' of the human mind – it is not an
invention of man and requires no proof), imperative (it is to be
obeyed, not argued with) and universal. For Kant the categorical imperative of morality commands that we act only on the
maxim that we would wish our behaviour to become a
universal law: morality is an end in itself and not a means to

something else. As will be seen, it is quite different from utilitarianism which is essentially conditional and a means to a further end (e.g. pleasure or happiness). A more recent example of deontological ethics is the present use of the concept of 'rights', as in the 'right to life' or 'the right of the woman to choose' dicta, often used in opposite sides of the abortion debate.

Again, one can argue about whether or not a given situation really constitutes a clear-cut moral case. So, although murder might always be considered to be wrong, one might still argue about whether a particular situation does or does not involve murder. Thus, many of those who believe that murder is wrong but that killing in war can be justified, argue that the latter does not involve the former (e.g. since war does not involve privately motivated killing – see Aquinas' *Text VIII*). Others, using a conflict theory, might argue that although killing in war is wrong, it is overridden by the greater wrong of not defending one's country when called to do so. In both instances a deontological stance is still taken on the issue of murder.

It will be seen in the various Sections that both Augustine's and Luther's Scriptural arguments are predominantly deontological. Indeed deontology is also a feature of Aquinas' moral arguments, even though his commitment to Aristotle's maxim that 'happiness is the chief good' tends him also to consequentialism. Many would argue that, in some form, deontology is an essential feature of all Christian ethics. However, this is an issue which will be debated at length throughout this Textbook.

(b)   Consequential ethical arguments
It is a feature of consequential arguments – sometimes termed teleological arguments although the two can be distinct – that they treat morality, not as autonomous or as an end in itself, but as a means to something else. At its simplest, one is enjoined to be good so that one may receive some reward – either in the form of some present or near future state, such as 'pleasure' or 'happiness', or in the more distant form of an earthly utopia or of a transcendent eternal life. To return to reasons for believing that murder is wrong, consequential responses typically might be:- 'Because murder, if allowed, would destroy society', or

'Because murder does not contribute to general happiness'. In each response murder is thought to be wrong, not because it is wrong in itself, but because it leads to something else which is thought to be wrong or perhaps just undesirable – e.g. the break-down of society, the absence of general happiness, or the reception of eternal punishment. If this 'something else' is itself thought to be wrong, then clearly consequential arguments eventually do have a deontological basis. On the other hand, if this 'something else' is thought to be no more than undesirable, it may have no such basis (and for this reason some maintain that therefore it is not a moral argument at all). In addition to the object varying, in consequential arguments, the recipient envisaged also varies. In some forms of the argument, it is the agent himself whose ends are considered, in others it is those of society as a whole and, in others still, it is man only in some transcendent state (see further *Extract 6.21-7*). However, in all, moral conduct is judged in terms of its goals or consequences (teleological arguments stress more the first and consequential arguments more the second).

Various types of ethical utilitarianism and pragmatism constitute forms of consequential argument. For Jeremy Bentham (1748-1832) morality was concerned with attempting to increase the total pleasure of mankind and the avoidance of pain – an explicit form of hedonism, albeit not calculated on an individualistic basis (i.e. it concerns, not the specific pleasure of the agent, but the greatest amount of pleasure for the greatest number of people). For John Stuart Mill (1806-73) morality should be empirically based, ascertaining first what people really find 'desirable' and then arranging society so that as much as possible (quantitatively as well as qualitatively) of what people desire can be obtained, by as many as possible, in an orderly and co-operative way.

In some forms of the Christian tradition consequential arguments have assumed a strongly eschatological character. For example, in the 6th Century Rule of Benedict, monks were told, 'if we wish to escape the pains of hell and attain to eternal life we must hasten to do such things only as may profit us for eternity, now, while there is time for this and we are in this body and there is time to fulfill all these precepts by means of this light' (*The Rule of Benedict*, prologue, trans. W. K. Lowther Clarke, 1931).

A more immediate form of consequentialism, rooted clearly in deontology, is evident in the following paragraph from the Didache:

> 'My son, flee from all wickedness and from everything like it. Do not become angry, for anger leads to murder. Do not become jealous, or quarrelsome, or irritable, for it leads to fornication. And do not use obscene language, or let your eye wander, for from all these come adulteries. . . My child, do not be a liar, because a lie leads to theft; be not greedy of money or empty glory, for from all this come thefts. My child, do not be a grumbler, because it leads to blasphemy, do not be proud or malicious, for from all these arise blasphemies'
> (*Didache*, v, from *The Apostolic Fathers* – ed. Ludwig Schopp, The *Fathers of the Church*, Vol. 1).

Whatever is thought of the logic of the links in this very early (possibly early 2nd Century) document – anger leads to murder, jealousy leads to fornication, grumbling leads to blasphemies, and so forth – their consequential nature is evident. One thing is considered wrong because it leads to (or it might even derive from) something else which is already known to be wrong – in this instance because murder, adultery, stealing and blasphemy are known to be wrong from the Decalogue.

Consequential arguments will be seen alongside deontological arguments in a number of the Texts and Extracts. Utilitarianism in the more formal, philosophical sense will be seen to be present in Fletcher's *Extract 4*.

(c) *Personalist ethical arguments*
It is a feature of personalist arguments that they view morality, not as obedience to autonomous, absolute principles or as a means to something else, but as an expression of individual feeling, conscience or love. It is frequently argued by exponents of personalist ethics that moral dilemmas cannot be resolved in advance of particular situations. Thus, it makes no sense to

argue, as an abstract principle, about whether or not murder is wrong. Only in particular situations when the individual is confronted with the possibility of murder, can that individual determine whether or not it is wrong. Confronted with the prospect of murdering one's sister now, the personalist can reply that this murder is wrong:- 'Because I feel that it is wrong', or 'Because my conscience tells me that it is wrong', or 'Because it would contradict my love for her or my respect for her as a person'. In these responses it can be seen that there are elements of both deontology and consequentialism. Feelings, conscience, love and respect for persons are all treated as normative and only in relation to them are actions considered to be right or wrong. Nonetheless, the emphasis is individualistic and situational. It is conceivable that, given a change in the situation or in the persons involved, an individual might reach the verdict that to murder one's sister would be right. It might be war-time and the sister might be discovered to be working for the Gestapo. The deontologist could feel impelled to murder the sister in these circumstances, but would tend to argue, either that it was not really murder in this instance, or, that it was murder and was therefore wrong, but that it would be a greater wrong to allow one's country to be betrayed. The consequentialist, on the other hand, might argue that the happiness or well-being of society determines that the murder of all traitors is right. In contrast to the deontologist, the personalist may argue that this actual murder *is* right, even if it is still thought to be murder. In contrast to the consequentialist, the personalist argues that general pronouncements about traitors being murdered should not be made in advance of particular situations. This does not mean that society should not make laws on issues like this (in order to discourage traitors in war-time it may feel obliged to do so), but such laws should not be confused with moral laws. By definition, the latter cannot be codified. The positions of the deontologist and the consequentialist can be and frequently have been, codified (both Bentham and Mill sought to influence law-making as well as moral philosophy). But the most that the personalist can offer are general moral guide-lines, which can be overridden in particular situations.

Personalism, in one form or another, has proved to be very

attractive to a number of recent moral philosophers and theologians, There has been a widespread loss of confidence in Natural law theories and the more sophisticated forms of utilitarianism seem to many to involve tortuous and unrealistic moral calculations. Within moral philosophy emotive theories of ethics (criticised in Copleston's *Extract 3*) have been popular. It is interesting that even a critic of these theories like R.M. Hare bases his own theory on the Goldern Rule (do-as-you-would-be-done-by or, in more explicitly Christian terms, 'Love thy neighbour as thyself'). Theologians have additional reasons for finding personalist theories attractive: (i) the anti-legalism of Paul (and possibly Jesus) seems to conflict with some forms of deontology; (ii) personalism fits in well with the Dominical Commands to Love; (iii) the aims of some forms of utilitarianism seem distinctly un-Christian (e.g. the sole pursuit of 'pleasure', as distinct from 'happiness' in Aquinas' sense).

In the Extracts, Fletcher's theory of Situations Ethics in *Extract 4*, and implicit in *Extract 19*, seeks to combine a general personalist ethical theory with a specifically Christian one around the concept of *agape*. Although Bonhoeffer's *Extract 1* explicitly rejects secular ethics, his ethic based solely on the Call of Christ does have similarities to Fletcher's position (see *above* p. 61), as does the position based upon the Quaker notion of the 'inner light' in *Extract 22*.

Fletcher's position has been the subject of considerable debate in recent Christian ethics (see Ramsey's *Extract 5*, which also adds important distinctions to the way *agape* is used in Christian ethics). Arguments about its strengths and weaknesses will occur at several points in this Textbook. However, it is important to note here that, although Augustine's overall position was undoubtedly deontological, there was also a strong stress upon love in his writings. To claim that he was actually a situationist would be to claim far too much. Nonetheless, his celebrated dictum 'Love God, and do what you want' sums up at least a part of what be believed. His sermons also reveal a repeated stress upon love:

'If deeds deny him, without doubt deeds also declare him. No man, therefore, says, 'Jesus is Lord', whether with mind, word, deed, heart, mouth, or work, no man says, 'Jesus is Lord', but in the Holy Spirit; and no man says so but he who loves him. . . What therefore we have now to learn is that he who loves already has the Holy Spirit, and that his present possession entitles him to a larger possession and the larger possession to a larger love' (*Joh.Ev. Tractatus* 74. 1-2).

It will be evident that these three approaches to ethics – the deontological, the consequential and the personalist – are not entirely separable. It might be more accurate to describe them as emphases rather than as discrete theories. But, however inter-related, an ability to distinguish their differing characteristics is important for the analysis necessary in Christian ethics.

4. BASES OF CHRISTIAN ETHICS

The question 'In what way is Christian ethics different from general ethics?' is one that is central to Christian ethics and, as a result, recurs frequently in this Textbook. Apart from the Extracts cited a number of books will be found useful in this context:

Peter Baelz, *Ethics and Belief*
James M. Gustafson, *Can Ethics be Christian?* and *Theology and Ethics*
Paul Lehmann, *Ethics in a Christian Context*
Edward LeRoy Long, Jr., *A Survey of Christian Ethics* and *A Survey of Recent Christian Ethics*
Enda McDonagh, *Invitation and Response* and *Gift and Call*
ed. I.T. Ramsey, *Christian Ethics and Contemporary Philosophy*
G.F. Thomas, *Christian Ethics and Moral Philosophy*
Keith Ward, *Ethics and Christianity* and *The Divine Image*.

If the question is asked at the empirical level, the answer, at least in the West, may be that the two hardly differ at all. In all three Substantive Sections here a considerable amount of disagreement between Christians is evident – almost as much, it might be maintained, as contemporary disagreements between non-Christians. This point can be exaggerated (Sections 2-4 will each conclude with points that unite Christians), but, granted a transposition theory, it may have some basis. According to this theory, Western values are still largely the product of a Christian past: even though they may no longer be formally nourished by the churches, values in society at large have been mainly transposed from Christianity. Not surprisingly then, it is argued, the results of Christian ethics and moral philosophy in the West often still coincide (see further my *Prophecy and Praxis*). Certainly, Miranda's *Extract 12* and Bonino's *Extract 17* see an affinity between Christian and explicitly Marxist values, an affinity that some see as related to the indirect influence of Christian values on Marx himself.

However, if the question 'In what way is Christian ethics different from general ethics?' is asked at a more theoretical level a number of answers are possible. These range from the near identification of the two in Fletcher's *Extract 4* to the denial of any similarity between them in Bonhoeffer's *Extract 1*. However, Bonhoeffer's position is difficult to maintain and it will be seen that there are reasons for doubting whether, in fact, he does maintain it consistently. At the very least, it is evident that the three ethical approaches outlined above occur in both disciplines.

One way of approaching the question is to isolate the specifically Christian appeals that are characteristically made within Christian ethics. Of these, four in particular can be isolated (although, in practice, they are often made together): appeals to the Bible, to Christian tradition, to Christian experience and to Christian belief:

(a) *Appeals to the Bible*
Of all the specifically Christian appeals, within Christian ethics, this has become the most complex. Whilst all Christians afford the Bible an important role, the combined disputes generated, first in the 16th Century by the Reformation and then in the 19th Century by the advent of Biblical Criticism, have ensured that the relationship between Christianity and the Bible is now considerably more varied than, for example, the relationship between Islam and the Koran. Appeals to the Bible, within Christian ethics, now face a number of serious problems – of

which the following have been suggested in the literature referred to at the end of this sub-section:

(i)   It has always been evident that many passages in the Bible can be interpreted in more than one way. It will be seen presently that Augustine varied in his interpretation of Genesis 3, his earlier allegorical interpretations giving way to literalistic ones. Section 3 will show that Tertullian gave a thoroughgoing pacifist interpretation of Matthew 5.39 ('turn the other cheek'), whereas Augustine repudiated this interpretation with the claim that 'what is here required is not a bodily action, but an inward disposition' (see *Text VII.8*). However, Biblical Criticism increased this problem enormously. Redaction Criticism, for example, requires one to recognise that the Gospel is a multi-layered phenomenon and is considerably more pluralistic than was generally realised in the past (e.g. see James D.G. Dunn's *Unity and Diversity in the New Testament*)

(ii)   Debates about the authority of the Bible are amongst the most vexed in Christian theology. The problems raised by the Reformation have proved particularly serious. Whilst before Luther most Christians would have assumed the infallibility of the Bible, particular tension was caused by his stress on the Bible as the *sole* source of authority for Christian ethics and belief. This tension is still evident in the Extracts that follow, as is also the question as to whether or not Christian tradition and/or experience should be allowed in Christian ethics as separate sources of authority in addition to the Bible. For most Roman Catholic theologians, and for many Anglican theologians (following in the tradition of Hooker, who insisted that God's law is operative, not only in the Bible, but also in man's reason and conscience), Luther's *sola Scriptura* stress, however understandable in the context of 16th Century Europe, is too theologically restrictive. Again, Biblical Criticism has further aggravated this situation. Once the literal infallibility of every verse in the Bible is rejected, and contradictions, factual and moral errors, anachronisms and inconsistencies are claimed, the exponent of Christian ethics can no longer adequately base moral claims on particular proof-texts in the manner of Augustine, Luther and, even at times, Aquinas. As a result, differing concepts of the authority of the Bible will be evident in the various Extracts. It would, of course, be ridiculous to criticise Augustine, Aquinas or Luther themselves for treating the Bible in a pre-critical manner. But, once the changed social context brought about by the advent of Biblical Criticism is taken into account, the exponent of Christian ethics is confronted with formidable problems. It is not the aim of this introduction to resolve these problems, but rather to point to the various ways they have changed the present-day discipline.

(iii) It is difficult for even the most literalistic biblicist not to be operating *de facto* a 'canon within the Canon'. That is, it is difficult to treat all parts of the Bible with equal seriousness and attention and not to be biblically selective. It will be seen later that, in this sense, Luther was selective. An over-view of the history of Christian theology might suggest that each age 'rediscovers' some aspect of the Gospel and forgets others. In the 20th Century, through the stimulus of Weiss and Schweitzer, theologians have 'rediscovered' the concept of the Kingdom of God and the eschatological notions associated with it, and rejected the 'lives of Jesus' of the previous Century. Doubtless future Centuries will judge our own as guilty of neglecting other aspects of the Gospel. Again, when the diversity of the Bible generally and of the Gospels, in particular, is accepted, some degree of selectivity seems inevitable – if only the sort of selectivity involved in isolating 'the central message of Jesus'or the 'Gospel'. Yet this clearly creates problems, since many forms of selectivity, themselves based on extra-biblical criteria, are possible. The Index shows a stress on Matthew and Romans.

(iv) A major difficulty for Christian ethics has always resided in determining the degree to which the Old Testament is taken as seriously as is the New. Tensions between Old Testament moral precepts and Christian teaching are already present in the New Testament (e.g. on the issues of fasting or retribution) and continue today. In section 3 it will be seen that attitudes to the issue of war are affected by the relative weight given to the Old Testament or to the New, since pacifism is clearly not envisaged in the former whereas, in the latter, arguably it is. Nowhere is this issue more crucial than in the role given in Christian ethics to the Decalogue. Differences of attitude to the Ten Commandments will be noted in the Texts between Aquinas and Luther.

And today, despite their continued use in many liturgies and their place in Western folk religion, some theologians would maintain that they are largely irrelevant to present-day Christian ethics. For them the discipline cannot be based upon a series of largely negative moral injuctions, which do not envisage many of the most important modern moral dilemmas (such as war in a nuclear age or the problems created by technology and medicine), which are too closely related to a traditional Jewish culture (e.g. not pronouncing the name of God and keeping the Jewish sabbath), and which have been 'superseded' by the Dominical Commands. Again this is an issue which will recur in this Textbook.

(v) Related to this, is the problem of how much weight should be afforded to the words of Jesus himself. Most Christians might agree, in principle, that the words and ideas of Jesus, once established, should be given a central place in Christian ethics. So, there has been considerable discussion over the Centuries on whether Matthew 5.32 permits divorce – with the Roman Catholic, Orthodox and Anglican Churches reaching a wide variety of conclusions. However, Biblical Criticism again greatly complicates the issue. The so-called 'quest for the historical Jesus', even after more than one hundred years, shows few signs of ending, and the construction of an account of Jesus', as distinct from the early church's, thought has become one of the most difficult and risky undertakings in New Testament studies. Thus, whilst there is now a good deal of agreement about Jesus' use of the concept of the Kingdom of God, there is little agreement about his use of the equally crucial concept of the the Son of Man. The depth of research necessary and the tentativeness of the eventual conclusions, is well illustrated by a study of attitudes to wealth and poverty in the Gospels, David Mealand's *Poverty and Expectation in the Gospels*. Mealand outlines four layers – redaction, sources, oral tradition and Jesus' own teaching and action – in the Synoptic Gospels, each with a different attitude towards wealth and poverty and each related to a different socio-political context. Alongside such research, the Biblical claims of the Texts and some of the Extracts may appear highly simplistic. In addition, the christ-clogical assumptions of the exponent of Christian ethics will affect the relative weight he or she affords to Jesus' own words and ideas. It will be seen that in Raven's *Extract 13* the more importance one attaches to the manhood of Christ, the more inclined one may be to see him as an example for other men: on the other hand, a relatively 'high' christology may be more inclined to see Christ as the law-giver (the position more of the Texts).

(vi) During the 19th and 20th Centuries there has been considerable debate amongst New Testament theologians about how far the teaching of Paul can be reconciled with what can be known about the teaching of Jesus. Since Paul, as will be seen, played such an important role in the writings of both Augustine and Luther, this question cannot be ignored. This issue was particularly important for a theologian like Schweitzer. His detailed studies, first of the eschatological teaching of Jesus and then of the mystical world of Paul's concept of *en Christo*, led him to conclude that they were difficult to reconcile, both with each other and with the modern world. Some of the present differences between Reformed and Catholic theologians may be due to the relative importance the former give to Paul.

(vii) Finally, a number of the most crucial present-day moral dilemmas – particularly in the areas of technology and medicine, as will be seen in section 4 – were never envisaged in biblical times. Of course, we can make inferences from injunctions that do exist in the Bible, but such inferences are notoriously hazardous. Further, if, as is widely accepted by New Testament scholars, it is believed that Jesus and his most immediate followers confidently expected the *parousia* to arrive very soon, it is hardly surprising that they apparently showed little interest in social ethics. As a result, Augustine, faced with a radical change in the socio-political status of Christianity, was confronted with a new moral situation for which the New Testament provided few clear answers. The problem here is a double one; in the New Testament some issues are treated, but only ambiguously and fleetingly, as befits those living in a soon-to-be-destroyed world, whereas others are ignored or simply not envisaged. Together they present serious difficulties for a form of ethics based upon the Bible alone.

Stated so baldly this may appear excessively negative. There have in fact been a number of important attempts to face these various problems in Christian ethics. It is worth mentioning Ian C. M. Fairweather and J. I. H. McDonald's *The Quest for Christian Ethics*. These seven sets of problems should be studied carefully in relation to each of the Texts and Extracts. Whilst an overview of the latter demonstrates that the Bible still plays a vital role in most traditions of Christian ethics, this role is now extremely complex and varied. A study of the ethics of the New Testament itself reveals some of this complexity: see particularly:

J.L. Houlden, *Ethics and the New Testament*
John Knox, *The Ethics of Jesus in the Teaching of the Church*
Barnabas Lindars, 'The Bible and Christian Ethics', *Theology*, 76, 1973.
T.W. Manson, *Ethics and the Gospel*
Jack T. Sanders, *Ethics in the New Testament.*, SCM 1975

It is compounded further by a study of the way in which the Bible is used by Christians: for this see:

James Barr, *The Bible in the Modern World*
C.H. Dodd, *The Authority of the Bible*
D.E. Nineham, *The Use and Abuse of the Bible*

(b) Appeals to Christian Tradition
The ways in which Churches appeal to Christian tradition reveal some of the most important historical differences between them. In very broad terms, Orthodox appeal only to the decisions of the historical Ecumenical Councils, Roman Catholics include appeals even to the most recent Papal Encyclicals, Anglicans make only a general appeal to Christian tradition and Lutherans subordinate all such appeals to the principle of *sola Scriptura*. However, today these generalisations can be made with less accuracy. Internal opposition to a strict interpretation of papal infallibility in present-day Roman Catholicism, Anglican divisions between Anglo-Catholics and Evangelicals, and an increased catholicity amongst many Reformed theologians, have made traditional divisions less clear-cut than they might once have appeared. A study of the

Texts and Extracts reveals many of these differences and areas of overlap.

In the Texts, Aquinas' *Text VIII* shows his use of Augustine as an authority. The latter also had a profound influence on Luther. But *Text III* shows the extent of Luther's acceptance of the notion of justification by faith alone and his radical rejection of papal authority, papal councils and long-accepted traditions of Catholic piety.

In the Extracts, Welty's *Extract 14* shows the traditional approach of Roman Catholics to papal authority. In contrast, Miranda's *Extract 12* and Hastings' *Extract 24* show far more radical Roman Catholic approaches. The issue of papal authority has been most seriously tested for many Roman Catholics today by Paul VI's *Extract 23*. The traditional Orthodox appeal to Christian tradition is seen in Clément's *Extract 21* , whereas a more independent voice is raised in Berdyaev's *Extract 8*. A comparison of Fletcher's *Extract 19* with Temple's *Extract 10* and Raven's *Extract 13* reveals very different Anglican assumptions about the authority of tradition. Finally, a comparison of Bonhoeffer's *Extract 1* with Niebuhr's *Extract 2* also reveals very different assumptions within the Reformed tradition, with Bonhoeffer appearing as the traditionalist and Niebuhr suggesting a new form of catholicity.

A number of questions can be isolated under this heading: what constitutes Christian tradition?; is Christian tradition self-authenticating?; what happens if Christian tradition conflicts with itself or with biblical evidence?; is Christian tradition still in formation today? The Extracts show that, on all of these questions, there is disagreement amongst Christians. In addition, the following books show something of the range of this disagreement:

G. R. Dunstan, *The Artifice of Ethics* and *Duty and Discernment*
James M. Gustafson, *Protestant and Roman Catholic Ethics*
V. T. Istavridis, *Orthodoxy and Anglicanism*
Hans Küng, *Infallible?*
Paul Lehmann, *Ethics in a Christian Context*
Edward LeRoy Long, Jr., *A Survey of Christian Ethics*
Paul Ramsey, *Who Speaks for the Church?*

(c)   Appeals to Christian Experience

The Quakers' *Extract 22* represents, in the form of conscience, the clearest appeal to experience. An appeal to conscience, in some form, constitutes an element in many types of Christian ethics, including those of Luther (see *Texts VI* and *IX*) and Aquinas (see Coppleston's *Extract 3*). At least four attitudes towards conscience are evident in the discipline:

(i) An appeal to the conscience of all men, whether Christian or not. At times, this seems to be the position of the Quakers – i.e. if only they will listen carefully to the voice of conscience, all men have the truth already in their hearts.

(ii) An appeal to specifically Christian conscience. This appears to have been the position of George Fox himself. His *Journal* suggests that he believed in a literal understanding of Genesis 3 and therefore, apart from Christ, in the sinfulness of man. To the jury at Lancaster Assizes in 1664 he said, 'I was a man of tender conscience, and if they had any sense of a tender conscience, they would consider that it was in obedience to Christ's commands that I could not swear' (p.231). Yet there was also a universal element in his christology and, with it, in his radical appeal to conscience. In 1653 he wrote, 'To that God in your consciences I speak; declare or write your dissatisfactions to any one of them whom you call Quakers, that Truth may be exalted, and all may come to the light, with which Christ has enlightened every one that cometh into the world' (p.90). This seems nearer to position (i).

(iii) A belief that conscience is but one important element of the moral life of the individual, provided that this conscience is instructed by other elements, such as the Bible or Christian tradition. This is the position of Coppleston's *Extract 3*, of Roman Catholicism generally, and of those sections of Anglicanism which follow in the Hooker tradition (see, for example, Kenneth E. Kirk's *Some Principles of Moral Theology*). Exponents of this position often insist that, for a number of reasons, individual conscience cannot be treated as the sole source of authority for Christian ethics: (a) conscience is affected by sin and thus it is often distorted, (b) it is influenced by psychological and sociological factors and therefore cannot be regarded as fully independent, (c) it can too easily be confused with prejudice or convention, so that individuals can have 'consciences' about trivial matters, such as the length of their hair, (d) consciences are often ambivalent and, on that account, unable adequately to judge what is right in particular situations. On the other hand, usually these exponents insist that without individual free-will and conscience the moral life would not be moral. In short, it is a *sine qua non* of morality in Christianity, but it is not its sole base.

(iv) A radical rejection of conscience. This is apparently the position of Bonhoeffer's *Extract 1*: conscience is seen as an element of secular ethics which is rejected by the radical call of Christ to the individual. The Christian moral life is seen, not as as an attempt to distinguish right from wrong and then to follow right, but rather as a life obedient to the Call of Christ. Again, it will be argued later that Bonhoeffer's position was not thoroughly consistent: it is even possible that his understanding of life in Christ was similar to position (ii).

Appeals to Christian experience may also appear in other forms. For example, some forms of agapism may be generated by an initial experience in Christ of *agape* (see the distinctions in Ramsey's *Extract 5*); mystical experience may be linked with morality in Christianity (see Berdyaev's *Extract 8*); and, in religious ethics generally, numinous experience, involving as it does a mixture of attraction, awe and fear, has obvious relevance (see Rudolf Otto's *The Idea of the Holy*). In addition, most understandings of Christian ethics today would regard existential commitment, on the part of the individual, as an essential element of the moral life: that is, an individual is regarded as moral, not simply because of acting morally, but also because of intending to act morally.

One concept that is particularly relevant in this context is that of 'vision'. Under the influence of writers such as Iris Murdoch (see her *The Sovereignty of the Good* and also articles by her and Ronald Hepburn in ed. I. T. Ramsey, *Christian Ethics and Contemporary Philosophy*) morality is seen primarily in terms of vision: the individual is invited to 'see' or 'perceive' the world and social relationships in a particular way. This idea has been imaginatively employed in Christian ethics by Stanley Hauerwas and David Harned. The following books are useful:

ed. James Gustafson and J. T. Lamey, *On Being Responsible*
David B. Harned, *Grace and Common Life* and *Faith and Virtue*
Stanley Hauerwas, *Vision and Virtue* and *Character and the Christian Life*
C. A. Pierce, *Conscience in the New Testament*
In addition, the difficulties faced by classical theories of conscience are usefully discussed in A. V. Campbell's *Moral Dilemmas in Medicine* and H. D. Lewis' article in *Christian Ethics and Contemporary Philosophy*.

(d) Appeals to Christian Belief
There is a real danger in a Textbook of Christian ethics of giving the impression that it is a thoroughly pluralistic discipline, with disagreements evident in all its aspects. Indeed, an important feature of analysis in any academic discipline *should* involve an appreciation of the range of disagreements within it. Appeals to Christian tradition and to individual conscience tend to divide, rather than unite, Christians. However, appeals to the Bible and to Christian beliefs in principle should unite them, even if in practice different understandings of the Bible and of Christian belief abound within Christianity. Nonetheless, a number of exponents of Christian ethics have argued that, however internally varied, these latter appeals do differentiate Christians from non-Christians. So, Keith Ward has argued, in his *The Divine Image*, that the doctrine of Creation gives Christians grounds for taking ethics more seriously than non-believers, since they are given grounds for believing that the moral life and the life of the world generally are not fortuitous, but the products of a loving God. For the theist, morality and cosmology are necessarily related to each other.

Sometimes this contention has been used as the basis for Christian apologetics, as it is in the following passage from A.E. Taylor's 1926 Gifford Lectures, *The Faith of a Moralist (Vol. I)*:

'I should infer that. . . the moral life itself, at its best, points to something which, because it transcends the separation of "ought" from "is", must be called definitely religion and not morality, as the source and inspiration of what is best in morality itself, and that the connection between practical good living and belief in God is much

more direct than Kant was willing to allow. I cannot doubt
that morality may *exist* without religion. An atheist who
has been taught not to steal or lie or fornicate or the like is,
probably, no more nor less likely, in average situations, to
earn his living honestly, to speak the truth and to live
cleanly, than a believer in God. But if the atheist is logical
and in earnest in his professed view of the world, and the
believer equally so with his, I think I know which of the
two is more likely to make irreparable and "unmerited"
grievous calamity a means to the purification and enrich-
ment of personality' (pp.155-6).

In different ways, Temple's *Extract 10*, Raven's *Extract 13*,
Gregorios' *Extract 18*, Gustafson's *Extract 20* and Hastings'
Extract 24 illustrate this approach. The method of deriving
Christian ethics systematically from the Christian doctrine of
Creation, which is a feature, to some extent, of all these
Extracts, raises important possibilities which go well beyond
their own premises. After all, a doctrine of Creation unites
Christians, Jews and Muslims, and a system of ethics derived
from it might be highly relevant to inter-religious dialogue and
cooperation. However, a central difficulty is raised by Temple;
the particularization of general ethical principles, themselves
derived from general Christian beliefs, notoriously divides,
rather than unites Christians – as can be seen from any of the
Substantive Sections. In order to overcome this problem, he
develops the notion of 'middle axioms' used in the Life and
Work Movement. The difficulties confronting this notion will
be discussed in relation to *Extract 10*.

Clearly, Christian beliefs cannot be regarded as the only
source of Christian ethics, since they themselves are dependent
on other sources – such as the Bible, Christian tradition and
even Christian experience. Yet, it is possible that they form the
parameters of the discipline, parameters that give it a degree of
unity – a unity of general attitude rather than specific content
(although, occasionally, even a specific content can be isolated).
The term 'moral theology', frequently used in the past by
Roman Catholic and by Anglican theologians, served to
emphasise this, but is little used here, since its scope was often

regarded as including, in addition to ethics, pastoral theology and ecclesiastical practice.

However, this approach to Christian ethics must face an important criticism. If ethical prescriptions are derived, even in part, from Christian doctrines, it might seem that an 'ought' is being derived from an 'is'. This criticism should be raised in relation to specific Extracts, even if it is initially conceded that the 'ought' and the 'is' are not always wholly separable (see Helen Oppenheimer, 'Ought and Is', *Theology*, 76, 1973).

5 *SOCIAL DETERMINANTS*

It has already been claimed that, at times, biographical details are relevant to an understanding of the thought of a particular theologian. However, an analysis of the social determinants of theological positions (and a subsequent analysis of their social significance), goes beyond this claim. It assumes that ideas can be related to social structures – an assumption which is central to the sociology of knowledge. That is, that theological and ethical ideas may be influenced by society (i.e. socially determined) and may, in their turn, have an influence upon society (i.e. socially significant). Within highly cognitive approaches to theology and philosophy, it is often assumed that ideas from one social or historical context can straightforwardly be compared with those from another. So, ideas from the Texts can be compared directly with ideas from the Extracts. But, for a more sociologically-minded approach, such direct comparisons ignore the degree to which specific ideas are related to specific social contexts. According to this approach, comparisons should be made only after social analysis. It is this approach which this Textbook aims to encourage by including an examination, first, of social determinants and then of social significance, in its system of analysis.

A number of theologians have attempted to apply social analysis to ideas in theology and Christian ethics. In this respect, Ernst Troeltsch's *The Social Teaching of the Christian Churches* and H.R. Niebuhr's *The Social Sources of Denominationalism* have proved to be of abiding interest, not only to theologians, but also to sociologists of religion. Dietrich Bonhoeffer's very early work, *Sanctorum Communio*, also demonstrated an interest in sociology. Amongst sociologists, Max Weber, particularly in his seminal *The Protestant Ethic and the 'Spirit' of Capitalism*, showed a considerable interest in and knowledge of, theology, as do present-day sociologists such as Peter Berger and David Martin. Recent examinations of the methodological problems facing attempts to analyse theology sociologically can be found in the following:

Gregory Baum, *Religion and Alienation: A Theological Reading of Sociology*

Robin Gill, *The Social Context of Theology* and *Theology and Social Structure*

ed. D. Martin, J. Orme-Mills, & W.S.F. Pickering, *Theology and Sociology: Alliance and Conflict*

In addition, David Martin's article 'Ethical Commentary and Political Decision' (*Theology*, May 1973) makes important points about the relation between sociology and ethics. Specifically in relation to Christian ethics and their social determinants, a number of points must be made:

(a) An analysis of social determinants too easily gives rise to a suspicion of an overall social determination. It would be false to assume that all those who attempt to ascertain the social determinants of something are committed to a position of thoroughgoing and mechanistic determinism. However, it will be argued in Section 1 that the latter would probably be disastrous to all but the most strictly 'Lutheran' understandings of Christian ethics. If free-will in some form is essential to Christian ethics (see especially Augustine's *Text I*), a thoroughgoing sociological, psychological or biological determinsm would appear particularly destructive. Indeed, it will be seen that theological determinism, based, for example, on a rigid predestinarianism, faces the same problem. Some of the serious logical difficulties involved in thoroughgoing theories of social determinism are amusingly isolated in Peter Berger's *A Rumour of Angels*. Most obviously, there is the status of the theories themselves – presumably they are themselves socially determined – and on this account Berger suggests the task of 'relativising the relativisers'. It should emphatically be stressed that in this Textbook social determinism is not consciously assumed.

(b) Social scientists are nonetheless committed to providing as total explanations of social phenomena as possible. Just as 'god of the gaps' arguments are discouraged in the physical sciences, so social scientists, in so far as they are acting as social scientists, should not be expected to account for religious phenomena in anything other than social terms. After all, it is their task to do so, even if they happen to be religious people in their private life. Berger, in his *The Social Reality of Religion*, has termed this attitude *methodological* atheism (although I prefer the term 'as if' methodology – see *The Social Context of Theology*). This should not be confused with actual or ontological atheism or with sociological imperialism. Rather, it assumes that separate and seemingly self-contained accounts of human behaviour can be built up from a variety of perspectives – sociological, psychological, physiological, bio-chemical, theological, etc. Whereas it might be difficult to form any overall picture of particular moments of interpersonal behaviour using all the perspectives simultaneously, at the same time, it would be wrong to assume that only one of the perspectives may provide a 'legitimate' explanation. In the past it was the theologian who tended to be imperialistic in this way, but today it is more likely to be the physical or social scientist. Again, it should be underlined that this Textbook does not intentionally subscribe to any such imperialism.

(c) Related to this point, a confusion is sometimes made between 'explaining something' and 'explaining something away'. The fact that Marx, Durkheim or Freud explained religious phenomena in social terms does not necessarily mean that they were 'explaining away' these phenomena. Durkheim and Freud, at least, were usually aware of this distinction (a point missed in the, otherwise very useful, book of D.W.D. Shaw, *The Dissuaders*). An exposure of the origins of particular ideas tells us nothing logically about their validity (the genetic fallacy), although, of course, they may be psychologically distressing to believers. Thus, even if it is agreed that religious belief may be the product of a neurotic perpetuation of childhood fantasies, it is still open to the believer to claim that God acts through these fantasies. However, if one always sees religious claims as linked to these fantasies, *psychologically* one might find it difficult to remain convinced of their truth. Such a Freudian explanation may well appear as a threat to the believer, but it is not strictly a logical threat: indeed, an element in Christian theology has always stressed the 'oddness' or even absurdity of Christian belief. It is important that this point should be kept in mind, especially when examining the social determinants of the ideas of people as psychologically interesting as Augustine or Luther.

(d) Behind the attempt in this Textbook to isolate the social determinants of particular ideas and positions, is the belief that such analysis produces a sharper critical understanding of the Texts and Extracts. Thus, it will be maintained that it is important to know that Augustine's theological understanding of the relation between Church and State was developed at a time of very considerable political upheaval, or that his concept of the 'just war' coincided with a newly established political status for Christianity. Again, it should be clearly understood that such analysis does not thereby invalidate Augustine's ideas, or render them anachronistic for present-day Christian ethics. But it does entail that they should be compared point-for-point with the latter only with caution.

(e) A full appreciation of the social determinants of any of the Texts and Extracts would be beyond the scope of this Textbook, but it is hoped that the student will be encouraged to develop them further. Considerable selectivity is inevitable. In relation to the Texts, different points will be raised in the context of the various contributions from each of the three authors. Further, it is usually easier to suggest the social determinants of such much-studied authors than it is of the Extracts of recent authors. A complete understanding of their social determinants would involve a consideration, at one end of the spectrum, of the psychological peculiarities of particular authors, their family, early training, socialisation and later development and, at the other end of the spectrum, of the overall political structure and culture of the age in which they lived. In addition, the various levels of influence of these differing factors would have to be recorded in terms ranging, from the loosest coincidence, to the tightest causal relationship. Even if such an ideal version of the sociology of knowledge could be achieved, it is clearly not appropriate here. However, as the following demonstrate, this task has already begun in ethics generally:

John H. Barnsley, *The Social Reality of Ethics*

J. Habermas, *Knowledge and Human Interests*

Alasdair MacIntyre, *A Short History of Ethics* and *Against the Self-Images of the Age*

Maria Ossowska, *Social Determinants of Moral Ideas*

and accounts of the sociology of knowledge are summarised in my *Theology and Social Structure* and can be studied in:

ed. J.E.Curtis & J.W. Petras, *The Sociology of Knowledge: A Reader*

Peter Hamilton, *Knowledge and Social Structure*

Werner Stark's *The Sociology of Knowledge* and Peter L. Berger and Thomas Luckmann's *The Social Construction of Reality* give interesting, but more partial, accounts of the discipline.

6. SOCIAL SIGNIFICANCE

An interactionist account of knowledge requires an examination, not just of the social determinants of particular ideas, but also of their social significance. It maintains that ideas may act, both as dependent and as independent variables, within society – both being shaped by society and, in turn, helping to shape society. The fact that a particular idea or position has been structured by society does not prevent it from having a subsequent influence upon that society, or indeed upon a quite different society. One has only to think of the influence of the Nicene Creed, in order to realise this. Church historians have no difficulty in showing, that some of the central terms used in this Creed owe their existence to a particular social context and to the polemics of the Fourth Century Church. However, once accepted by the Church, the Creed soon had, and, indeed, still has, a very considerable influence upon the way in which christological issues were debated.

A two-way process is thus presupposed. Ideas, influenced by a number of social factors, may also be seen to have their own influence in a variety of ways. Clearly, this is the case with the Texts. Whichever social determinants may be identified, the ideas of Augustine, Aquinas and Luther have obviously had a profound effect upon theologians, upon the churches and upon Western ideas in general. By systematically comparing the Texts with the Extracts, some of this profound influence should become evident. Naturally, it will often be more difficult to assess the social significance of the Extracts, but even here some immediate points are possible.

A number of qualifications must be made:

(a) The interactionist analysis required will sometimes be extraordinarily complex. Thus, whilst Luther's influence upon the Reformation may be relatively clear, his relationship to the Renaissance is not. It has proved extremely difficult to assess to what extent the Reformation was influenced by the Renaissance and what was the relative influence of each upon subsequent Western culture. It is even difficult to determine their relative influence upon the churches.

(b) A full analysis of the social significance of particular Texts or Extracts would also be a very lengthy undertaking, requiring several levels of analysis and a range of causal terms. At least four levels of analysis can be isolated – the influence of particular ideas and positions upon theologians in an academic context, their influence upon those who preach or teach in a more popular context, their influence upon lay Christians who listen directly to the preachers or teachers, and their influence upon society at large. It is too easy to assume that these levels of influence will always be broadly similar (in *Theology and Social Structure*, for example, I have argued that different levels of influence can be detected in the differing responses to *Honest to God* in the early 1960's). Considerable selection is again inevitable.

(c) It is important to underline that an analysis of the social significance of ideas in Christian ethics is not an attempt to belittle the theological importance of these ideas. For example, if Weber's contentions are accepted, that Luther's concepts of election and predestination and his attack on monastic asceticism had a profound influence upon the rise of the spirit necessary for the development of Western Capitalism, it does not follow that Luther's theology is thereby necessarily belittled. It could still be maintained, that the theological significance of these ideas was even greater than their socio-economic significance. The former is not, of necessity, enhanced or belittled by the latter (although in *Prophecy and Praxis* I maintain that theologians ought to be considerably more aware of the latter than they are at present). However, Weber's analysis might give a theologian like Bonino, in *Extract 17*, additional reason for distrusting traditional Lutheranism – but this would stem from his own prior political and theological commitments.

7. *CRITIQUE*

At the end of each Text and group of Extracts a brief critique is appended. This position is deliberate, not because critique is considered unimportant, but rather because analysis must be as full and informed as possible before a serious critique is made. Of course, students should be encouraged to make their own critique. It is an essential part of learning. In each case an attempt is made to suggest some of the strengths and weaknesses of the particular excerpt, not only in relation to the internal ideas of the work from which it is taken, but also in relation to the ideas and theories of other exponents of Christian ethics.

FURTHER READING

Books suggested as further reading, in relation to each Text and set of Extracts, are intended to provide a stimulus to the student. Although a fairly full biography (which includes all the publishing details of books cited earlier) is supplied as an Appendix, no attempt has been made to supply an exhaustive reading list. Since repetition of suggested reading would have been tedious, as for instance in relation to the Texts, reference should constantly be made back to this Introduction. Naturally, the Texts and Extracts should never be regarded as substitutes for referring back to the original books, but, ideally, they should provoke enough interest in students to do this for themselves. The further reading suggested consists, first, of relevant books by the author himself or herself and, then, of bibliographical or theological books about the author or about the issue in question.

THE TEXTS: AUGUSTINE, AQUINAS AND LUTHER

In any understanding of Christian theology or ethics, Augustine, Aquinas and Luther are three of the most important figures. Each stood at a pivotal moment in Christian history and each has had an abiding influence upon Christian thought. Together, they cover a very broad spectrum of possibilities within Christian ethics and, an analysis of the differences between them reveals many of the central differences that still are apparent today amongst exponents of the discipline.

Of course, there is a real danger in comparing the ideas of these theologians, especially in the light of the type of social analysis already discussed. Each stood within a radically different social context, each presupposed a different political situation and each one has influenced different sections of the churches – although it will be seen that, in a more ecumenical age, their influences are now less clear-cut than they were in the past. Since it has already been insisted that socio-political differences should never be ignored, it would obviously be wrong to compare these three theologians' ideas point-for-point, as if they were always writing about the same things, albeit from different perspectives. Nonetheless, the very fact that their primary writings are still widely used in contemporary ethical decision-making by Christians makes some comparison inevitable, if only sometimes to reveal the differences between their situations and our own. Most obviously, as seen in Sections 2 and 3, the political and economic views of Augustine, Aquinas and Luther have had a major influence upon Christian thought and continue to shape attitudes today: but, at the same time, it is soon realised that their thoughts were developed in political and economic contexts which bear little relation to present-day, Western, industrial society. In this situation, the task of distinguishing between perennial and ephemeral problems in Christian ethics, can be seen to be highly important.

AUGUSTINE (c. 354–430) was born at Thagaste, a small inland town in Proconsular Numidia in North Africa (the modern Tunisia and eastern Algeria). His mother was a devout and somewhat ascetic 'Catholic' Christian, but his father, a relatively impoverished citizen of curial rank, remained a 'pagan' for most of his life. Augustine was a catechumen in his youth, but was not baptised until he was 33. He became a student at Carthage at 16 and a follower of Manichaeism at 19. He remained a follower for 9 years, wrestling for much of this time with the problem of evil, which the radical dualism of Manichaeism seemed to solve. He finally abandoned this form of religion when the celebrated Manichaean bishop, Faustus, failed to answer his questions to his satisfaction. Subsequently, he became increasingly impressed with the sermons and arguments of the Catholic bishop of Milan, Ambrose. He had a son, Adeodatus, but despite a long-standing relationship with the boy's mother, he never married her. Brilliant at debate, rhetoric and logic he became a professor of rhetoric, founding his own school at Rome in 383. After his break with Manichaeism and a period of contact with Ambrose, he finally became a 'Catholic' Christian after a conversion experience at Milan. He was profoundly influenced by neo-Platonism and was baptised by Ambrose in 387. He returned, with a small group of family and friends, to lead a monastic life in Africa, but, with great reluctance, was soon ordained priest and then elected a bishop of Hippo in 396. He remained there as bishop for 34 years, living in community and writing extensively. He died as the Vandals were laying siege to Hippo. Indeed, he lived at a crucial stage in the break-up of the Roman Empire, albeit in the relative isolation of North Africa. He wrote *The City of God* in order to rebuff the charge, that the official adoption of Christianity by Constantine was the reason for this break-up. He was forced to work out afresh the implications of this adoption for Christianity and felt impelled, at various stages, to defend 'Catholic' Christianity against Manichaeans, Donatists and Pelagians – even enlisting the help of the civil authorities to supress the latter. Through his many writings he gave Christianity a new intellectual depth and status and had a profound influence upon both Aquinas and Luther.

AQUINAS (c. 1225–74) was born at the castle of Roccasecca at Aquino, between Naples and Rome. The son of a count, he was sent to the abbey of Monte Cassino for his elementary schooling and in 1239 went to university at Naples. There, much against the wishes of his father, he entered the Dominican Order. He studied under the Dominican, Albert the Great, at Paris and then at Cologne and, in 1252, returned to Paris as a lecturer, becoming a regular professor of theology in 1256. From 1259 to 1269 he taught successively at Amagni, Orvieto, Rome and Viterbo, before again returning to Paris. In 1272 he went to Naples and in 1274 he was summoned by Pope Gregory X to take part in the Council of Lyons, but on the way there he died. Towards the end of his life he had a number of mystical experiences and, four months before his death, after an experience whilst saying Mass, he stopped work on his *Summa Theologica*, saying that 'all I have written seems to me like so much straw compared with what I have seen and with what has been revealed to me'. He wrote this monumental work as a systematic expositon of theology for 'novices'. His other most important work, *Summa Contra Gentiles*, was written earlier, in order to combat the 'naturalistic' thinking of Graeco-Islamic philosophy. In both works he was concerned to show that the Christian faith rests upon a rational foundation and that philosophy (largely in the form of newly rediscovered Aristotelianism) and theology are not mutually exclusive types of activity. Aquinas lived at the time of the greatest power and influence of the Catholic Church in the West. At this stage of medieval history, the Catholic Church came nearest to being a Universal Church – a phenomenon that can be traced back to the age of Augustine. Aquinas has continued to have a profound effect upon Roman Catholic moral and systematic theology, re-inforced by Pope Leo XIII's encyclical letter, *Aeterni Patris*, 1879, declaring his to be the 'perennial philosophy'.

LUTHER (1483-1546) was born at Eisleben in Saxony. A miner's son, he went to school at Mansfeld, Magdeberg and Eisenach and entered university at Erfurt in 1501 to study law. However, after a profound experience during a thunder-storm, he abandoned his legal studies at the age of 21 and, despite parental disapproval, entered an Augustinian monastery at

Erfurt. There he led an extremely ascetic life. He was sent to the University of Wittenberg and eventually became professor of biblical studies there. Convinced of the necessity of seeking his own salvation by keeping the biblical commandments, he became gradually persuaded of his own inability to do this. In 1507 he underwent a conversion experience, reputedly whilst climbing the Scala Santa at Rome and, in 1517, posted his celebrated 95 Theses against the abuses created by the Church's sale of indulgences (authorised by Pope Leo X, in part to pay for the building of St. Peter's in Rome) on the door of the Castle Church in Wittenberg. He refused to retract to the papal legate, Cardinal Cajetan, and appealed directly to the Pope and then in 1519 to the new Emperor, Charles V, who was himself of German extraction. Excommunicated by Leo X in 1520 and tried by Charles V at Worms, Luther was placed under imperial ban by the Edict of Worms of 1521. His break with Rome was now complete and he spent the rest of his life (albeit with the vital support of a number of German princes) translating the Bible, revising the liturgy, writing hymns, preaching and writing books on many aspects of the Christian life, and reorganising churches in defiance of Rome. Luther lived in an age of very considerable social and political change, which saw the break-up of medieval Christendom and the rise of capitalism and of new forms of nationalism, in Europe. He witnessed a major rebellion of the German peasants in 1525 and died in the year in which war broke out between Reformers and Catholics – a war that ended only with the Treaty of Augsburg, 1555, which allowed the German princes to choose to follow Catholicism or Lutheranism and to coerce their subjects accordingly. Himself a highly influential figure in all these changes, he has continued to be one of the most significant theologians within Reformed or Protestant forms of Christianity.

From these brief biographies, a number of key points of contrast can be drawn. Each theologian represented widely different cultures – North African, Italian and German – in radically different ages. And, even though both Aquinas and Luther were deeply influenced by Augustine, temperamentally they were very different from each other and tended to emphasise different elements in his writings. It is sometimes held that, whereas Aquinas was heir more to the ecclesiastical side of Augustine's writings, Luther, with his rejection of Augustinian monasticism, was heir more to Augustine's Pauline theology. Nonetheless, it is possible to make some comparisons between them, finding similarities, now between Augustine and Aquinas, now between Augustine and Luther and sometimes between Aquinas and Luther – provided, of course, that their radically different social, political and cultural contexts are kept in mind:

(1) Both Augustine and Luther lived in ages of revolution. Augustine witnessed the gradual break-up of the Roman Empire, dying as Hippo itself was under siege. Luther witnessed the break-up of medieval Catholic Europe and also died surrounded by war. Yet neither man was himself a revolutionary. Augustine wrote to defend Christians against the charge that they were responsible for Rome's collapse and remained a Roman in much of his thinking. He even enunciated a just-war theory, in contrast with the pacifism of previous generations of Christians (see *Text VII*). And Luther, to their amazement, bitterly rejected the cause of the revolutionary peasants (see *Text IX*). Aquinas lived at what might, at first, appear to have been one of the most settled ages in European history. But the seeds of the Renaissance were already present in the 13th Century, with the art of Giotto (c. 1266-1337), celebrating the life of Francis of Assisi, and the poetry of Dante (1265-1321), reflecting parts of Aquinas' *Summa Theologica*, soon to change man's understanding of himself – an understanding clearly relevant to the Reformation. By looking forward to the Renaissance and even to the Reformation and backwards to the newly established relationship between the Church and State in the 4th and 5th Centuries, Aquinas stands naturally as a pivot between the two.

(2) In terms of class or social stratification, the origins of the three men were quite distinct. Aquinas' origins were clearly the most aristocratic, Augustine's were those of a relatively impoverished middle-class in an age of rapid inflation, and Luther's, although by no means totally impoverished, were unmistakably working-class. Viewed from a more dynamic perspective, only Luther's family was upwardly socially mobile,

moving from a situation of working as miners, actually to owning mines and then being in a position to be able to send their son to university to study law. Whilst all three belonged to the minority of university-educated writers and thinkers, Luther's socially mobile background made him the most suitable to be an agent of radical social change, while Aquinas' comparatively static social background made him the least suitable. Amongst the upwardly socially mobile it is also not uncommon to find an antipathy towards those belonging to the class of their origins: a tendency to radical innovation can be combined with a dismissiveness of those of a lower social class. It is possible that Luther's rejection of the writings and actions of the revolutionary peasants may have owed something to this factor. His tendency to side, at times, with the rulers over-and-against the ruled, is seen particularly in the way he, like Augustine before him, enlisted the help of the rulers to supress dissension and even 'heresy'. However, the fact that all three men went to university and became monastic Catholic priests means that there is also a strong similarity of socialisation which they held in common.

(3) All three experienced celibacy and some form of ascetic monasticism. Nonetheless, their experiences here were distinct. Aquinas, highly cerebral and evidently rather corpulent, became a Dominican as a young man and remained one until his death. Augustine, having rejected Christianity for so long, became extremely ascetic only after his conversion – although there can be little doubt that he was always serious-minded and intense and by no means the sensual youth he is sometimes thought to have been: even his celebrated relationship was long-standing, apparently faithful, loving and in accord with contemporary Roman moral practice. In contrast, Luther was fiercely ascetic only before his radical break with monasticism and Rome. Both Augustine and Luther were fathers, but only Luther married – Augustine painfully broke off his relationship, whilst Luther married a former nun, seemingly out of duty, though he soon discovered great happiness in marriage.

(4) In terms of religious psychology, both Augustine and Luther had what is sometimes called a 'twice-born' and Aquinas a 'once-born' type of religious temperament. Augustine and

Luther had almost classic Pauline conversion experiences and, not surprisingly, thereafter showed a particular affinity for the Pauline epistles. Like Paul, Luther was 'converted' from a life of legalistic pietism to one of entire dependence upon grace. Augustine, on the other hand, was 'converted' from a relatively free-thinking attachment to Manichaeism to ascetic 'Catholic' Christianity. Before their 'conversions', both men experienced a considerable period of emotional and psychological turmoil – displaying what some psychologists would undoubtedly identify as obsessive religious personalities, and, after these conversions, comparative calm. A number of psychological and sociological studies of conversion would suggest that this comparative calm hid a good deal of continuing doubt, uncertainty and marginality/liminality – and this may be another point of contrast between these two men and Aquinas. Certainly, whilst Aquinas was concerned to defend 'orthodoxy' against 'heresy' (as, for example, in the *Summa Contra Gentiles*, see *below*, p. 203), there is little in his writings to equal the polemics, scorn and, sometimes, vitriol, particularly of the later Augustine and Luther (see *Text XII*). Of the three, Aquinas was by far the most conciliatory in style, appealing more consistently to reason than to emotion, although, as has been seen, his life was not without mystical experience. Indeed, the very rationality of Aquinas has given offence to some. In contrast, Book VIII of Augustine's *Confessions*, written twelve years after the event, gives his classic, and highly influential, account of conversion, containing many of the key features of a conversion experience, as it might be recognised empirically: extreme anxiety, voices, a sense of the 'numinous', a random opening of the Bible, an instrumental text (in this case Rmns. 13, 13-14), sexual remorse, catharsis and withdrawal.

These four sets of psychological and sociological variables – political context, social stratification, marital status and religious psychology – are all vital to an adequate understanding of the differences between the three theologians and should be examined carefully in relation to the Texts. Again it should be stressed that a preparedness to take them seriously does not necessarily reduce the significance given to internal theological factors determining their thought. In addition, three other points of contrast can be made from the biographical sketches:

(5) It is often pointed out that whereas Augustine did much to relate Platonic or neo-Platonic ideas (such was the scarcity of books in his day that he only knew of Plato's ideas through the work of Plotinus) to 'Catholic' orthodoxy and thereby rendered Christianity more intellectually respectable to his contemporaries, Aquinas achieved a similar correlation with the newly rediscovered Aristotelian ideas of his time. Luther, on the other hand, might have regarded any such undertaking with strong suspicion: for him it was the Scriptures which must form the main axiom for theology. But, as so often in his writings, Augustine was ambivalent in this correlation, simultaneously being attracted by some Platonic notions and repelled by others, such as polytheism (e.g. see *City of God* VIII.9f). It will be seen from the Texts, that Aquinas' understanding of the relationship between philosophy and theology is more consistent than that of Augustine and it was he who was instrumental in the eventual triumph, in Roman Catholic theology, of Aristotelianism over Platonism. The more naturalistic Aristotelianism seems to have provided him with a more congruous rational/ natural basis, than transcendental Platonism, for the supernatural overlay of Christian belief. Precisely because Platonism locates the 'really real' in a transcendent realm, outside everyday experience and the everyday world, it presents those following Aquinas with a potentially more damaging challenge than Aristotclianism: if Platonic transcendentalism and biblical revelation conflict, any real correlation between them breaks down, since the conflict appears as a conflict between two supernatural views of the world. In contrast, a correlation between Aristotelian naturalism and Christian supernaturalism considerably reduces this risk of conflict.

(6) Both Augustine and Luther were church leaders of very considerable contemporary influence. As a bishop of Hippo for 34 years, Augustine's pastoral, as well as his theological, influence extended far beyond the provincial confines of North Africa. And Luther's contemporary fame and influence were even greater. Apart from his key role in sparking the Reformation, for over 25 years he was engaged in an astonishing range of

activities aimed at reforming the German churches. It is difficult to find another church leader with a comparable range of gifts and versatility. Only Aquinas remained the academic that the other two had once been and took very little part in ecclesiastical politics. Ironically, he died on his way to a church council. Regarded as a dangerous theological innovator by some of his contemporaries, his work gradually became established in the Roman Catholic Church, receiving its final endorsement in 1879. However, as the 'perennial philosopher' of his Church, his work has had, until very recently, a position of primacy afforded to few in other Churches.

(7) All three were voluminous writers and even present-day collections of their work require multi-volume editions. For Augustine alone there are extant 113 books and over 200 letters and 500 sermons. Amongst present-day theologians only Barth is comparable. But, perhaps inevitably, volume fits uneasily with consistency. Of the three, Aquinas was by far the most consistent and systematic, but even in some of his ideas, changes can be traced. Generalisations about their ideas must usually be carefully qualified and, with Augustine and Luther, it is often important to relate their ideas to the particular point in their lives in which they were expressed. As writers, however, their overall tasks were distinct. Augustine wrote extensively to defend the Catholic Christianity to which he returned against attacks from 'pagans' and from 'heretical' Christians. Aquinas wrote his *Summa Theologica* as a systematic exposition of Christianity for 'novices' within Catholicism. Luther wrote many of his books to restate the Gospel in contrast to what he regarded as the corruptions of contemporary Catholicism. Of course, in other respects there are similarities between their writings. Aquinas wrote his *Summa Contra Gentiles* as well as his *Summa Theologica* and, in this respect, appears like Augustine. And, both Augustine and Luther have bequeathed to us volumes of sermons. Yet their overall distinctiveness as writers remains.

With these seven points of contrast in mind, a number of key theological comparisons between their respective theological notions can be made. Others will emerge from a detailed study of the Texts, but, in view of their importance for Christian ethics, the following deserve special attention:

8. *THEIR USE OF THE BIBLE*

In comparison to many of the Extracts, Augustine, Aquinas and Luther have much in common with each other, since (a) their ethical prescriptions are regularly related to biblical texts, (b) the Bible is regarded by them as normative in Christian ethics and theology and (c) the Bible is used in a pre-critical, literalistic and sometimes eisegetical manner. So, in contrast to Niebuhr's *Extract 2*, all three might have understood Genesis 3 to be literal history (even though Augustine, in his early writings, attempted an allegorical interpretation of this passage - see *de Genesi ad Manichaeos* 2.15). And, in contrast to Fletcher's *Extract 4*, they would all have stressed the normative role of the Bible in Christian ethics. The contrast, in this respect, between present-day Christian ethics and that of the Texts, is well illustrated by the attitude of Augustine and of Luther to polygamy (see *below*, pp. 422ff.). In parts of the Old Testament, polygamy is clearly accepted, so Augustine could not bring himself to say that it was ethically wrong and even Luther, at one point, concluded that it would be better for Philip of Hesse to take a second wife, like the Old Testament patriarchs, rather than go against the Matthean prohibition of divorce. In this respect Augustine's arguments are particularly interesting. In seeking to defend the Bible against Faustus' attacks he wrote:

'Jacob the son of Isaac is charged with having committed a great crime because he had four wives. But here there is no ground for a criminal accusation: for a plurality of wives was no crime when it was the custom; and it is a crime now, because it is no longer the custom. There are sins against nature, and sins against custom, and sins against the law. In which, then of these senses did Jacob sin in having a plurality of wives? As regards nature, he used women not for sensual gratification, but for the procreation of children. For custom, this was the common practice at that time in those countries. And for the laws, no prohibition existed. The only reason of its being a crime now to do this, is because custom and the laws forbid it.' (*Reply to Faustus the Manichean*, XXII.47)

Aquinas would not have seen polygamy as consonant with nature (see *Text XI*), but, in spite of its offence to their contemporary sensitivities, the fact that it is condoned in parts of the Old Testament, led both Augustine and Luther to view it as ethically neutral.

Despite this overall agreement, Augustine, Aquinas and Luther might have disagreed with each other about the extent to which the Bible is to be used as *the* arbiter within Christian ethics. Luther might have been the more emphatic: the Bible is the only arbiter of Christian faith (his stress on *sola Scriptura*, which was to act as one of the guiding principles of the Reformation). The importance he gave to translating and expounding the Bible naturally follows from this emphasis. Even though it will be noted that, at times, there are appeals to conscience and Natural law evident in his Texts, his intended *sola Sriptura* stress remains. It is important to emphasise the word 'intended': occasions will be noted when Luther's position goes clearly beyond the biblical evidence. Nevertheless, in his mind, he was always attempting to be faithful to the Bible – in contrast to the Roman Catholic Church which had, in his view, constructed an entirely extra-biblical, and therefore illegitimate, structure. Augustine, too, was emphatic about the key role of the Bible in the Christian life, as his sermons clearly demonstrate. Nonetheless, he made frequent appeals to Church tradition, saw convergences, at times, between neo-Platonic and Christian values and even sometimes (as will be seen in Section 3) borrowed from pagan philosophy when the Bible failed positively to resolve moral dilemmas. A *sola Scriptura* stress might perhaps have made least sense to Aquinas. Given his understanding of Natural law (see *Text II*), reason is able to ascertain moral truths which can also be known through biblical Revelation. Aquinas' method of using the Bible is seen very clearly in *Texts XI*: his argument is based upon Natural law and logical reasoning and biblical evidence is only quoted once that argument is completed – thus, the Bible is seen to confirm what can already be known through a proper use of reason. As a result of this method and understanding, he was able to borrow freely from Aristotle, Augustine, and Church tradition generally, provided, of course that such borrowings did not seem to conflict with the Bible. In overall, and perhaps too schematic terms, whereas Luther intended normally to start from the Bible and use other evidence only if it was congruent with it, Aquinas tended to start from man's natural reason and demonstrate that it was in accord with, or, at least, did not conflict with, the Bible. It will be seen that these different methods derived from their different understandings of grace.

It is possible that there is another tendency which Augustine and Luther had in common. Both had a strong disposition towards the Pauline Epistles. In the light of what has already been suggested concerning their 'twice-born' religious temperaments, this disposition is very understandable. Further, the early Luther was suspicious of the theology implicit in James and Revelation. As a result, some have claimed that their use of the Bible was unwittingly determined by some 'canon within the canon' – a permanent difficulty facing all emphatically Biblical approaches to Christian ethics. The same difficulty will have to be raised in the context of some of the present-day Extracts, such as Miranda's *Extract 12* and Raven's *Extract 13*. The more pluralistic the Bible is thought to be in the light of modern critical scholarship, the more this difficulty is increased.

9. THEIR THEOLOGICAL ANTHROPOLOGIES
Augustine, Aquinas and Luther might have agreed on several points that differentiate them from a number of the Extracts; (a) they assumed that the Fall was (to use an anachronism for the moment) an 'historical event', (b) as a result, apart from Christ, man is in a state of original sin, (c) original sin is, not simply a propensity towards sin, but involves concupiscence which itself involves actual guilt, (d) as result, apart from Christ, none can be saved. However, their theological anthropologies can be differentiated from each other by the way in which these points were interpreted by them. In Augustine, there is a stress upon the 'original righteousness' of Adam: he is sometimes portrayed, before the Fall, as an ideal athlete, philosopher and saint.

But, in Aquinas, Adam's original righteousness consists, quite explicitly, in supernatural qualities (*donum supernaturale* or sometimes *donum superadditum*), so the Fall represents a fall from a supernatural to a natural level: Adam, and through him man subsequently, is still man and not a beast, he is still rational and possesses the properties belonging properly to human nature (*pura naturalia*). For him, then, the Fall is a privation rather than a deprivation.

There is considerable debate about how far these scholastic notions of Aquinas can be applied to Augustine, whose theological anthropology often appears somewhat ambivalent, but they certainly cannot be attributed to Luther. Luther rejected the notion of *donum supernaturale* and tended to see the Fall rather as a fall from the human to the sub-human. Not surprisingly, he tended to mistrust man's independent rational abilities, his capacity to know God apart from revelation and even his free-will in moral decision-making – three characteristics of man that Aquinas would have considered essential.

The ambivalence of Augustine is demonstrated by his belief that mankind constitutes a single 'lump of sin' (*massa peccati* or *massa perditionis*) which lacks freedom (*libertas*) but still possesses free-will (*liberum arbitrium*) – an extraordinarily difficult distinction that he sometimes made. In *Text I* it will be seen that he combined a strong stress upon the prescience of God with a belief that sinful man does have genuine free-will. However, he does little to resolve the tension between these two positions – perhaps some degree of tension here is inevitable in all serious theological discussion.

There is a growing recognition today that assumptions about theological anthropology have a profound effect upon the rest of theology. If this is so in theology, it must be the case *par excellence* in Christian ethics. The differences here between Augustine, Aquinas and Luther are still of considerable relevance to the Extracts and help to explain some of the crucial differences between such Extracts as Raven's *Extract 13* and Welty's *Extract 14* and between Barth's *Extract 7*, Berdyaev's *Extract 8* and Niebuhr's *Extracts 2 & 9*.

10. *THEIR SOTERIOLOGIES*

All three might have agreed that; (a) God's revelation in Jesus Christ is essential to salvation, (b) God's laws can be known, in part at least, from an inspection of the natural world, but that knowledge of these laws does not of itself lead to salvation and (c) those who reject Jesus Christ are damned. Yet, when these points are elaborated, difference between them immediately arise, and again, some of the Extracts would dissent even from these general points. So, Bonhoeffer's *Extract 1* seems to deny the initial assumption in (b) that the natural world can reveal anything about God and many might feel uneasy about taking (c) as literally as do the Texts. Even on (a) there is an evident difference between the exclusive christologies of Barth and Bonhoeffer and the more inclusive christologies of Raven, Temple and Hastings.

Aquinas and Luther present the clearest and most sharply differentiated accounts of the relations between nature and grace and between reason and revelation. If, for the former, these relations were continuous, for the latter they were discontinuous. For Aquinas, 'natural' religion and morality were crowned by revelation: natural reason could establish the existence and some of the attributes of God, but only revelation could establish the Triune nature of God: in short, grace completes or crowns nature and revelation adds to what can be known through reason and makes us fit for salvation. Thus, faith is not a contradiction of reason, as it appears to be, at times, in a theologian like Kierkegaard, but rather is a stage beyond reason, albeit a necessary stage for salvation. However, for Luther, what can be established through reason or Natural law can, at best, simply show us the impossibility of achieving moral perfection through our own efforts. Man is so embedded in original sin and through this concupiscence is such a powerful force in the world, that, at worst, the apparent 'good deeds' of non-Christians are really sins. Even the Ten Commandments can do little more on their own than convict us of our sinfulness:

> 'We have in the Ten Commandments a summary of divine teaching. They tell us what we are to do to make our lives pleasing to God. They show us the true fountain from which, and the true channel in which, all good works must

flow. No deed, no conduct can be good and pleasing to God, however worthy or precious it be in the eyes of the world, unless it accord with the Ten Commandments. Now let us see what our noted saints find to boast in their holy orders and the great and difficult tasks they have invented for themselves, at the same time neglecting the commandments as if they were too trivial or had long ago been fulfilled. My opinion is that we shall have our hands full in keeping these commandments – in practising gentleness, patience, love towards our enemies, chastity, kindness, and whatever other virtues they may include... Poor, blind people! they do not see that no one can perfectly observe even so much as one of the Ten Commandments; but the Creed and the Lord's Prayer must help us. Through them we must seek and beseech the grace of obedience, and receive it continually.'
(from *The Large Catechism*, conclusion to the Ten Commandments, trans. John Nicholas Lenker, *Luther On Christian Education: Luther's Catechetical Writings*).

For Luther, then, salvation is achieved emphatically not through man's efforts, but solely through God's action. The notions of election and justification by faith were central to this position and, indeed, to the Reformation as a whole. God alone chooses whom he will save and men in turn are saved, not through any works of their own, but solely by faith, that is, by faith itself given to man by God. For Luther, God 'foresees, determines and actually does all things, by his unchangeable, eternal and infallible will. By this thunderbolt the whole idea of free-will is smitten down and ground to powder' (*De Servo Arbitrio* 1.10). He would have flatly denied the advice of *The Rule of Benedict* that, 'if our wish be to have a dwelling place in his Kingdom, let us remember it can by no means be attained unless one run thither by good deeds' (from the prologue, trans. W.K. Lowther Clarke, 1931). Yet Luther refrained from the, more strictly logical, Calvinist doctrine of double predestination, according to which the lot of both the saved *and* those to be eternally damned are predestined by God.

In Augustine, many of these ideas sat together uneasily. He

held a doctrine of predestination, but it was relatively uninfluential compared with Luther's doctrine, being known mainly, not to ordinary church-goers, but to scholars. He frequently emphasised grace and maintained that his own efforts to find God through the gnosis of Manichaeism had been disastrous. He knew and used Paul's notion of justification by faith and, like Luther, was convinced that all those who were not justified, even unbaptised infants who died, were damned. In contrast, Aquinas argued that unbaptised infants go to Limbo, where they certainly would not be punished. On the other hand, it has already been seen that Augustine did not reject free-will or rational/philosophical argument and that he used Natural law positively, although not as systematically as Aquinas. Further, he did write, at times, about the Christian seeking moral perfection – but then, even Paul, despite his stress on grace, could also say that God 'will render to every man according to his works' (Rmns 2.6). If the bias of Augustine's soteriology is in Luther's direction, it is not a consistent bias.

Most complicated of all is Augustine's concept of 'grace'. For him, grace was essential, both to enable man to act rightly in the first place, and to allow him to continue to act rightly (cf. the scholastic distinction between prevenient and co-operant grace). Grace appears to be irresistible but, at the same time, it does not destroy free-will. Further, through its operations some, who are still damned, are enabled to do certain good works (i.e. Jews, 'heretics' and schismatics, but not complete 'pagans'), some are fore-ordained to become Christians through baptism, but backslide and are also damned, and others are elected, not just to be Christians, but also to receive the gift of final perseverance and, eventually, that of eternal life in heaven (cf. the scholastic distinction between sufficient and efficacious grace).

The issues raised here go to the very heart of some of the present-day differences within Christian ethics and constitute some of the most intractable problems facing the discipline. They also have strong resemblances to some of the key problems facing moral philosophy generally, notably those concerned with the issue of free-will *versus* biological or social determinism, that of reason *versus* emotion and that of subjectivism *versus* objectivism within ethical analysis.

11. THEIR DOCTRINES OF CHURCH AND STATE

It is often held that their doctrines of Church and State are readily distinguishable, since Augustine regarded Church and State as entirely separate realms, with the Church, as a temporary and, somewhat uneasy, resident in the State, Aquinas regarded them simply as different spheres of a single society, with the Church having primacy of authority, while Luther regarded the Church as always subordinate to the authority of the State. These positions are then frequently compared with Calvin's concept of theocracy and the Anabaptists' radical rejection of the State. But these superficial contrasts (which are well in evidence in *Texts IV – VI*) disguise more subtle differences and similarities between their positions. In relation to their socio-political contexts, Aquinas and Luther were closer to each other than to Augustine. Augustine was writing at the beginning of the attempt by Christians to come to terms with the State and to make sense of the moral problems confronting, not just the individual within the State, but the State itself. Constantine's adoption of Christianity – for whatever personal motives – presented Christians with new problems, or problems from a new perspective, which Ambrose alone, before Augustine, had begun seriously to tackle. It is hardly surprising that Augustine did not present a thoroughly consistent theory of the State, or of the relation between Church and State. Nor is it surprising that, in view of the State's pagan and sometimes anti-Christian past, he remained wary of identifying the Church too closely with the State. Yet, despite his sometimes vivid contrasts between the earthly and heavenly cities, *Text IV* shows that he did see a relationship between earthly and heavenly peace, while *Text VII* shows how, at the risk of contradicting centuries of Christian pacifism, he adapted to the moral perspective created by the changed Church/State relations.

The socio-political contexts of Aquinas and Luther were quite different from that of Augustine. The 13th Century witnessed the climax of the close relationship between the State and the Catholic Church, and Aquinas never appeared to regard the overall relationship as problematic. The boundaries between the two were boundaries of power and authority, not of opposing aims, values and social orders and even Luther's challenge was concerned primarily with the former, rather than the latter. Neither Aquinas nor Luther conceived of anything resembling the 19th and 20th Century concepts of the 'secular State'. From this perspective, Calvin's Geneva and Rome in Aquinas' time appear remarkably similar. It is significant too that Luther, in *Text VI*, is still basically a medieval in his underlying economic assumptions–despite the possibility that he may have been instrumental in undermining these assumptions.

If these socio-political factors are taken seriously – and in this area of Christian ethics, at least, they surely must be taken seriously – it is dangerous to assume that when Barth appealed to Romans 13, as in *Extract 7*, his presuppositions, ideas and language were the same as those of Luther or Augustine when they appealed to the same passage. And none of them may have had much in common with the eschatalogically fragile world of Paul himself. The task of distinguishing between these various socio-political factors and the underlying Christian principles essential to an adequate theological understanding of Church/ State relationships today, is one of the most difficult, but important, facing exponents of Christian ethics. It is also a task that directly affects one's understanding of the problems raised in the Extracts in Sections 2-4. In this sense, these are, indeed, perennial problems.

Students of Augustine, Aquinas and Luther are well served by these readable and authoritative studies:

Peter Brown, *Augustine of Hippo: A Biography* (his *Religion and Society in the Age of Saint Augustine* is also very useful)
F.C. Copleston, *Aquinas* (see also his *History of Philosophy*)
Roland H. Bainton, *Here I Stand: A Life of Martin Luther*

Although there is no substitute for going back to their primary writings, other books will be recommended in relation to particular Texts. In attempting to make comparisons between their theological concepts of grace and original sin, it is worth recalling the important works of Williams:

N.P. Williams, *The Ideas of the Fall and of Original Sin*, the 1924 Bampton Lectures, and *The Grace of God*, a much slighter, but still readable, book.

THE EXTRACTS

The Extracts have been chosen to represent a wide spectrum of approaches within recent Christian ethics. So each substantive Section (2–4) contains at least one Extract from the Roman Catholic, Orthodox, Anglican and Reformed traditions. In addition, the Extracts from each of these traditions have been chosen to represent differing internal emphases (themselves sometimes as great as differences between traditions).

Thus, the Roman Catholic Extracts contain parts of two papal encyclicals, John XXIII's *Pacem in Terris* and Paul VI's *Humanae Vitae*, *Extracts 11 and 23* (themselves of very different emphasis), a traditionalist passage from Welty, *Extract 14*, a somewhat more radical passage from Hastings, *Extract 24*, and the still more radical Miranda's *Extract 12*. The contribution of Hastings is, indeed, radical, but is still recognisably within the Thomist tradition. That of Miranda is more evidently influenced by the Reformed tradition and, possibly, has more in common with non-Roman Catholic Liberation theology than it does with traditional Roman Catholic Moral theology. Certainly it compares interestingly with the Methodist Bonino's *Extract 17*.

The Anglican Extracts vary from the modified Natural law position of Temple in *Extract 10*, through the theologically and biblically oriented approach of Raven's *Extract 13*, to the iconoclasm of Fletcher's *Extracts 4 and 19*. Anglican 'comprehensiveness' is well in evidence in these Extracts.

However, the Reformed Extracts show, perhaps, the greatest variety and the greatest internal divisions. At one end of the spectrum, Niebuhr's *Extracts 2 & 9*, Ramsey's *Extracts 5 & 15* and Gustafson's *Extract 20*, have similarities in style to the modified Natural law approach of Temple. Together, they represent some of the most important thinkers in 20th century Christian ethics. At the other end of the spectrum, is the radical rejection of secular ethics of Bonhoeffer's *Extract 1* and of Barth's *Extract 7*. A combination of Reformed Christian ethics and radical politics is to be found in Bonino's *Extract 17*.

The Quakers' position in *Extract 22* cannot be identified straightforwardly with any of these traditions, but serves to represent, both the radical Quaker stress on individual conscience and the changing attitudes towards sexuality characteristic of the 20th Century.

The Orthodox tradition is represented in each of the substantive Sections, in Berdyaev's *Extract 8*, Gregorios' *Extract 18* and Clément's *Extract 21*. Clément represents a traditionalist approach to abortion, whereas Gregorios' offers a unique Indian/Orthodox approach to war. Berdyaev was clearly influenced by his Russian Orthodoxy, but he was always too independent a philosopher to rest firmly in any single tradition. His mystical individualism was most evident in his understanding of sexuality. For him, the sexual act 'shackles man to that decadent order of nature, where reigns the endless relay of birth and death'; true love is 'a tormenting search for the androgynous image, for cosmic harmony', with male and female natures mystically fused into the androgynous image of God (*The Meaning of the Creative Act*, p. 193). Overall, the strong Orthodox stress upon the Spirit and the spiritual is apparent in all three Extracts.

The internal variations apparent within these traditions, make inappropriate any simplistic identification of particular ethical approaches or stances with particular Churches. Naturally, there always have been internal differences within the Roman Catholic, Orthodox, Anglican or Reformed Churches. However, ecumenism and, with it, the growing tendency of professional theologians to read widely in traditions other than their own, make these differences considerably more complicated to analyse. At the same time, they make comparative analysis all the more interesting and exciting. Aquinas and Luther can no longer be described as the property of particular Churches.

METHOD OF STUDY

The fact that this is a textbook and not simply a reader, requires that it should be used systematically. The System of Analysis, already outlined, requires particular attention and the description of it should be re-read as study of the Texts and Extracts progresses. There are three vital phases of a systematic study of these Texts and Extracts – comprehension, comparison, and critique – which should always be undertaken in that order:

1. COMPREHENSION

A student should read each Text and Extract several times carefully, first, to understand the general argument and, then, to be able to comprehend it in terms of the System of Analysis. At this stage, there is often a danger of becoming too involved in the substantive issues in question, or of making premature comparisons or criticisms. Comprehension must take priority.

2. COMPARISON

The main comparison, around which this Textbook has been constructed, is that between Texts and Extracts. The System of Analysis is designed to make this comparison easier. In addition, the introduction to each section makes a number of overall comparisons between the Texts and the Extracts within it. It has already been thoroughly emphasised, that comparisons between documents coming from very different ages and socio-political contexts, should only be made with caution. Further, it should be stressed, that the thoughts of one theologian should only be compared with those of another, *in all their complexity*. It is precisely this that has caused some of the greatest difficulties already in comparing the ideas of Augustine, Aquinas and Luther. Their views on a given issue were not always consistent throughout their writings. For example, Augustine's views on sexuality were, at some stages, more Manichaean and dualist than at other stages and Luther may have become more anti-Semitic as he grew older. Comparisons between Texts and Extracts, should keep in mind comparisons between the Texts or Extracts of a single author, represented elsewhere in this book.

A third type of comparison can also be made, i.e. that between the various Extracts. This can be done in three separate ways; by comparing differing views on the substantive issue in question, by comparing the approaches of different traditions or by comparing approaches from the same tradition but from different Sections of the book. All these comparisons will be made, at times, in the System of Analysis accompanying the various Texts and Extracts.

3. CRITIQUE

This is the most important phase, but it should be the last. An attempt should be made to assess the strengths and weaknesses of particular Texts and Extracts. Reference should be made, both to the method used and to the substantive issues raised and should be concerned, both with the internal consistency of an author's arguments and with their external consistency with the arguments of other authors. It will also be important, sometimes, to raise questions about the social effects of a particular author's ideas.

As already mentioned, the four Sections of this Textbook can be studied in any order. Nonetheless, these three phases of study and their relative order should always be used in whichever Section is to be studied.

SECTION 1

METHODOLOGY

SECTION I

METHODOLOGY

Fundamental differences are evident amongst exponents of Christian ethics on both external and internal questions about the nature of their discipline. And the following Texts and Extracts have been chosen to illustrate some of them. These differences are evident on *the external question* of the distinctiveness of Christian ethics vis-à-vis secular forms of ethics. They are also evident on *the internal question* of the relative importance to be given, within the discipline, to the distinctively Christian appeals to the Bible, to Christian tradition, to Christian experience and/or to Christian belief. Yet answers to these questions have a crucial effect upon the way the discipline of Christian ethics is conceived and practised. It will be the object of this introduction to focus upon these two questions.

The external question about the distinctiveness of Christian ethics vis-a-vis moral philosophy is, in part, a modern problem. It was Kant, after all, who insisted so emphatically that ethics is an autonomous discipline (even though he subsequently advanced a moral argument for the existence of God). And the separate attacks of Kant and Hume on an assumed bond between Christian ethics and Christian dogma did more than anything else to produce the present-day gulf between Christian ethics and moral philosophy. Our 20th Century assumption that moral philosophy can, in principle, be conducted without reference to God, is a clear product of 18th Century rationalism and a sharp departure from the medieval assumptions of Aquinas or from those of Luther. Even Augustine was primarily concerned with contrasting Christian ethics with 'heresy' and 'paganism' rather than with atheism (although see *Text I.8*).

Nonetheless, the fact that Aquinas was so concerned to explore correlations between Aristotelian ethics and Christian ethics makes his work highly relevant to a discussion of the external question. It does, at least, provide a clear answer to the problem of the relationship between Christian ethics and moral philosophy (as presented in Copleston's *Extract 3*). For Aquinas, there was no inherent conflict between Aristotelianism and Christianity, since the first was primarily concerned with what could be known through natural reason, whereas the second relied, in addition, upon supernatural revelation. As it was the same God who created the natural world, established its laws and then revealed himself in Jesus Christ, there could be no *inherent* conflict between reason and revelation and thus, surely, no inherent conflict between Christian ethics and moral philosophy. Of course, particular moral philosophers might make mistakes in their reasoning, or they might even be wilfully perverse in their reasoning, and this, in turn, might lead to a conflict between the two disciplines. But, inherently, on Aquinas' presumptions, there need be no conflict.

In terms of the presuppositions derived from Luther, conflict appears distinctly more likely. Bonhoeffer's sharp contrast between ethics and Christian ethics, whilst owing something, as will be argued, to his particular social context, is consistent with his Lutheranism. Any individual quest for moral perfection, especially one guaranteed by the ministrations of the clergy or of the papacy, was rejected by Luther in favour of the doctrine of justification by faith. Morality is essentially a product of faith, not a means to faith, and certainly not an autonomous entity apart from faith. Whilst Luther clearly recognised the need for society to make laws in moral areas, and, indeed, as Niebuhr points out, continued to make appeals to Natural law and to conscience when it suited his argument, his overall position was quite different from that of Aquinas, (see *above*, pp

43-5). Human nature is far too corrupted by sin for it to be a reliable source of ethical judgments. By somewhat extending Luther's position, Bonhoeffer maintains that even evidence of human conscience, is, in fact, evidence of man's disunion with God. When man aspires to be a moral person, whilst ignoring Christ, he is at his very worst. However, for Niebuhr, such a conclusion would be quite untenable. Although his Extracts show a frequent stress upon sin and an attack on what he regards as unrealistic Christian utopianism, nonetheless he believes that man does have, naturally, some knowledge of the good and, indeed, that without this, 'faith in Christ could find no lodging place in the human soul' (*Extract 2.2*).

In relation to the external question, both of these overall positions can find echoes in Augustine's writings. In *Text I* he emphatically insisted upon the reality of man's free-will, despite its evident conflict with God's prescience. But, elsewhere he was not so consistent. For example, when expositing Romans 9.10f., he wrote that, 'in this enquiry we laboured indeed on behalf of human free-will: but the grace of God won the day' (*Retractions* 2.1). More illuminatingly, elsewhere he could write that, 'to will or not to will is in the power of the man who wills or wills not, only in such a way that it does not impede God's will or vanquish his power' (*De corr. et grat.* 14.43.). But, even here, he could disconcertingly add that, 'God has men's wills more in his power than they themselves have their wills in their own power' (*ibid.* 14.45). Since the reality of man's free-will is a prerequisite of Aquinas' understanding of moral decision-making, but seems irrelevant to that of Luther, this ambivalence is highly significant. It is also an ambivalence which still affects contemporary exponents of Christian ethics.

Serious doubts about the reality of man's free-will stem from three distinct, although frequently interrelated, considerations. The first concerns the omniscience and omnipotence of God. This was one of Augustine's main problems: if God knows everything in advance and indeed created everything that exists, how is it that man can be said to choose anything on the basis of human volition, since even man's will to choose has been created by God and all its contents are known to him at the moment of creating? The second concerns the corruption of man and it was this which was one of the central focuses of Luther's thinking. If man, through Adam, lives in a constant state of sin, so that even the 'best' aspirations are corrupted by sin, it is difficult to see how, in any real sense, the human will remains 'free'. Indeed, from this perspective (viewing the Fall as a deprivation and not simply as a privation – see *above* p.42), an insistence upon free-will raises suspicions of Pelagianism. The third concerns social and physical determinism. If full account is taken of the sociological, psychological, biological and genetic factors determining man's behaviour, it becomes notoriously difficult to maintain nonetheless that man does possess free-will. By the time that these various factors have been taken into consideration, in relation to an individual's act of moral decision-making in a concrete situation, little room may have been left for free-will. In fact, even those philosophers who still claim that man does possess free-will tend to admit that it is considerably more restricted than is popularly imagined (e.g. H.D Lewis in *Philosophy of Religion*). In most situations one acts in one way, rather than another, because one has been brought up to do so, because one is expected to do so by others and etc. – not because one consciously and freely chooses to do so. Although, naturally, he knew nothing of Freudian or Weberian analysis, Augustine's critique of astrology shows that he knew something of these various factors (see *City of God* V.2).

There are obvious connections here with other highly intractable problems in theology and philosophy. The problem of evil, in the context of Christianity, is intensified by an insistence upon the ominipotence and omniscience of God. And one of the 'solutions' offered by Christian theodicy is precisely that, if God were to give man free-will, then he must also have allowed man the possibility of moral evil as well as moral good – since the second makes no sense without the first (a point that distinguishes Bonhoeffer's from Niebuhr's account of the Genesis 3 myth). In this respect 'the problem of evil' and 'the problem of good' are inter-connected, though equally intract-able. Again, if a Lutheran, such as Bonhoeffer, is tempted to distinguish 'better' secular regimes from others (as he appears to do elsewhere in *Ethics*) he may be in danger of re-introducing -secular ethical categories that he has methodologically rejected.

If a tension is often felt, in theology, between God's omnipotence and omniscience and man's free-will and moral evil, the tension in philosophy generally between free-will, self-determination and physical and social determinism is just as severe. Recently, a number of philosophers, sometimes termed Compatibilists, have argued that free-will and thorough going determinism are compatible. In various ways, they maintain that, the fact men can reason and then act morally is sufficient evidence of free-will, even if their moral decisions are entirely predictable. So an ability to predict accurately the moral behaviour of particular individuals, or an ability to identify the antecedent causes of their moral reasoning, do not belittle the reality of their moral decison-making. Indeed, there is a clear difference, between an individual such as a psychopath who is incapable of moral reasoning, and an individual who is so capable, even if it is entirely predictable how both will behave.

An adapted version of Compatibilism could also be used to resolve some of the tension between God's omnipotence and omniscience and man's free-will. So, it could be maintained that, the fact that God has created individuals whose actions are already known to him before their birth, does not of itself invalidate their moral reasoning. The key difference, here, between this version of Compatibilism and philosophical Compatibilism, is that the determinant (God) is himself aware of what he determines. But this, in itself, is a very crucial difference and is considerably complicated by the fact that terms like 'know' and even 'create' are used of God only analogically. If man could understand, in any literal sense, what it means for God to 'know' everything in advance, he would, of course, be God and not man.

Both versions of Compatibilism will seem unsatisfactory to some. The notion of free-will offered by Compatibilists is, clearly, not strong, particularly if the act of moral reasoning itself is thought to be determined. And in philosophical Compatibilism it might seem that an ontological, rather than simply methodological, determinism is too often assumed (see *above*, pp. 24-5). In most recent understandings of Christian ethics, a rather stronger notion of free-will would seem to be required. It might even be possible for the Christian apologist to argue that, it is the fact that one believes in a created, rather than fortuitous, world and in a man, within that world, who is created in the image of a loving God, who himself possesses free-will, that one is given grounds for belief that man does have real free-will. Thus, without this creationist belief one might find it difficult to escape the conclusion that man's actions are wholly determined by an ultimately fortuitous world. It is not necessary to draw from this argument the additional conclusion that secular ethics is a worthless undertaking, as Bonhoeffer might. The creationist can still maintain that the free-will thought to be necessary by some secular moralists, is made possible by a loving God – whether or not the non-theist knows this.

The internal question concerning the relative importance to be given to the distinctively Christian appeals to the bible, Christian tradition, Christian experience and Christian belief, reveals just as many differences between the Texts and the Extracts in this Section. The single-minded focus upon the Bible in Luther is apparent in all his Texts. In contrast, there are more appeals to tradition and to Aristotle than to the Bible in Aquinas' *Text II*. Interestingly, though, Luther's *Text III* opens with the criterion that if one finds one's 'heart confident that it pleases God, then the work is good' (*III.1*). Augustine, in *Text I*, is more philosophical than exegetical. However, their differing approaches to the Bible have already been discussed (see *above*, pp. 39-41).

Within the Extracts, one of the most important differences is caused by the claims of Situation ethics. Fletcher's book *Situation Ethics*, coinciding with the radical writings and utterances of Bishop John Robinson in Britain and of Bishop Pike and others in the States, proved remarkably influential in the 1960's and early 1970's. Its somewhat anecdotal and superficial style reads oddly in comparison with the other Extracts, but its position cannot be ignored. Indeed, few works in Christian ethics have been written, since its publication, without making some reference to it. Its iconoclasm has irritated many and soon it will be observed that its criticisms of 'legalism' fail to take fully into account Aquinas' complex theory of exceptions. Further, many have argued that Fletcher's characteristic method of arguing from irregular paradigms (see

4.18f) distorts Christian ethics – just as, at the secular level, no nation can construct a legal system on the basis of exceptions. Fletcher tends to write as if no one had ever thought seriously about exceptions before him. However, when all these points have been made, his thoroughgoing stress upon *agape* and his overall personalist approach to Christian ethics, have undoubtedly found important sympathisers. For them, personalism and agapism accord more fully with present-day consciousness than Aquinas' theory of Natural law.

It is at this point that Ramsey's *Extract 5* is so important. After a long critique of a number of personalists, he offers his understanding of agapism. In relation to Fletcher's account, it is considerably more complex and subtle. Further, the position that he adopts as his own, involving Rule-Agapism, as well as simply Act-Agapism (see *5.8f*) allows him to accept a modified form of Natural law theory similar to that of Niebuhr. It is particularly interesting that, just when a number of radical Roman Catholics (e.g. Miranda in *Extract 12*) are moving away from traditional Thomism, a number of Reformed theologians should show fresh, if modified, interest in Natural law theory. This becomes even clearer in Ramsey's discussion of war: he chides other Reformed theologians for failing to take traditional just-war theory seriously in their pronouncements on nuclear weapons (cf *Extract 15*).

There are also obvious similarities between Fletcher's and Bonhoeffer's accounts of Christian ethics. For Bonhoeffer, too, the discipline is predominantly personalist (see *1.13f*) and it is based upon a single criterion, the 'Call of Christ'. Further, both men justify their positions in relation to what they take to be the central thrust of the New Testament (see *4.9-10*). But, in relation to the external question, mentioned earlier, they are quite different. Bonhoeffer sees a sharp divide between ethics and Christian ethics, whereas, for Fletcher, Christian and non-Christian Situation ethics differ only in the *summum bonum* regarded as their standard (see *4.11*) and, in practice, he moves almost imperceptibly from one discipline to the other (see *Extract 19*). Fletcher's approving quotation from Bonhoeffer (*4.5*) ignores this crucial difference between them.

Fletcher's differences with other Anglicans also emerge in

Extract 4. He specifically rejects the notion of 'middle axioms' that Temple and others within the Life and Work Movement in the 1930's believed to be so important. In part, his rejection is based upon a semantic quibble (*4.13*), but, in part, it may be based upon a correct realisation that the notion of 'middle axioms' assumes a modified Natural law theory – itself, of course, assumed by Temple. The Church of Scotland's wartime 'Baillie Commission' accurately described this notion:

> 'It is . . . the duty of the Church in our day and place to guide the individual, within . . . limits of its competence. ., what to do with his vote and in what directions to exercise his influence. The requisite principles for the implementing of this duty are fully available to us in the New Testament. No new principles are necessary or are permissible, but only the application of the dominical and apostolic teaching to a situation different from that in which our Lord and His first disciples were ever called upon to stand. . . It is clear, however, that the carrying out of such a task will involve the formulation, in each case, of certain secondary and more specialised principles to the particular field of action in which guidance is needed. "Middle axioms" they have been called. . . They are not such as to be appropriate to every time and place and situation, but they are offered as legitimate and necessary applications of the Christian rule of faith and life to the special circumstances in which we now stand'
> (*God's Will for Church and Nation*, pp.44-5).

This understanding of Christian ethics adheres, more strictly, to a use only of those principles that can be derived from the Bible, than do traditional understandings of Natural law theory. It clearly wishes to avoid the sort of casuistry and complex theory of exceptions also associated with the latter. Nonetheless, it seeks to take both general principles and the exigencies of particular situations seriously, by developing, admittedly fallible, secondary principles for these exigencies. It is in this sense that it can be identified as a modified Natural law theory and it is probably in this aspect that it is most sharply differentiated from Fletcher's Situation ethics.

Finally, Fletcher's case-study on abortion can be compared with Paul VI's *Extract 23* and Clément's *Extract 21*. The substantive issues will be discussed in Section 4. but, for the moment, it is worth comparing Fletcher's suppositions about 'legalist' positions on abortion with these two extracts (written, as they are, from the 'legalist' positions of traditional Catholicism and Orthodoxy). Again, it appears that he has blurred distinctions and oversimplified positions. Nonetheless, it is perhaps, his position on abortion which more nearly represents the position of many Christians today. In contrast, his position on euthanasia in *Extract 19* may be more radical than that of many Christians.

With an increasing interest in world religions in the West, the comparative study of various forms of religious ethics is likely to become more important in academic circles. It is for this reason that an Extract from Little and Twiss' *Comparative Religious Ethics* has been included in this Textbook. The new-style discipline is still in its infancy and it would be inappropriate in a specifically Christian Ethics Textbook to give it too central a position. Nonetheless, the virtue of Little and Twiss' study is that it does demonstrate that comparative religious ethics has insights to offer even those working only in one religious tradition.

A Reading List on the methodological issues raised in this Section will be found on p.11 *above*.

TEXT I
AUGUSTINE
God's foreknowledge and man's free-will

I. BACKGROUND

This Text comes from *The City of God* V. 9-11 (Pelican Classics, trans. Henry Bettenson and ed. David Knowles, Penguin, 1972, pp 190-6) Consisting altogether of 22 books, *The City of God* was Augustine's most substantial work and a vital source for his mature theology. It was inspired by Alaric's sacking of Rome in 410 and in it he set out to demonstrate that this event was a punishment for Rome's paganism and not the result (as 'pagans' claimed) of the Emperor's adoption of Christianity. To achieve this demonstration he attempted to expose a number of key 'pagan' notions (e.g. 'fate') and to ridicule the whole idea that the 'pagan gods' had, in any way, protected Rome from her enemies. In contrast to this, Augustine elaborated the concept of the heavenly city, founded and ruled alone by God revealed in Jesus Christ (see further, *Text IV*). He started the work in 413, but did not finish it until 426, writing Book V in about 416. He later described it as follows: 'The first five books refute those who attribute prosperity and adversity to the cult of the gods or to the prohibition of this cult. The next five are against those who hold that ills are never wanting to men, but that worship of the gods helps towards the future life after death. The second part of the work contains twelve books. The first four describe the birth of the two cities, one of God, the other of this world. The second four continue their story, and the third four depict their final destiny' (*Retractions* 2, 43, 2). In relation to the following Text, it is important to realise that the Pelagian controversy was taking place then, but, despite its obvious relevance to the theme of free-will, it is seldom mentioned in the work. Cicero's *On the Nature of the Gods*, which had been an important influence on Augustine in his Manichaean phase, however, is explicitly attacked here.

2. KEY ISSUES

Augustine is concerned in this Text to defend both God's prescience and man's free-will. He is fully aware of a potential conflict between the two, but rejects Cicero's resolution of this conflict in terms of denying God's prescience (I.2-3). For Augustine, God 'knows all things before they happen', but this does not imply either a notion of 'fate' or a denial of man's free-will (I.4). Distinguishing between 'natural' and 'voluntary' causes, he regards God as the author of the first, but insists that God still allows man the second (I.6-8). So man's will has 'only as much power as God has willed and foreknown' (I.9). Augustine also seeks to refute the Stoic understanding of 'necessity' as a limitation which abolishes freedom for God or man (I.10-11). Free-will is not invalidated by God's foreknowledge, but rather, the very fact that God does foreknow man's free-will, demonstrates its genuine existence – since otherwise there would be nothing to foreknow (I.12-13). God has indeed created man free (I.14).

3. ETHICAL ARGUMENTS

There is a strong deontological emphasis throughout his refutation of Cicero and the Stoics. Augustine treats both God's prescience and man's free-will as given and simply accuses his opponents of 'profanity' and 'impudence'(I.4), potential atheism (I.8) and 'blasphemy' (I.12). For him, their position is manifestly wrong and it is sufficient to demonstrate that they deny either prescience or free-will. Natural law assumptions are also apparent in the Text, notably in his claim that 'evil wills do not proceed from him because they are contrary to the nature which proceeds from him': the natural, for Natural law theory, in itself is always good (I.7). A more consequential argument is introduced in 1.12-13: the reality of man's free-will, prayer, exhortations and sin can be derived from the fact that God foresees them, since, if they did not exist, he could not foresee them.

4. BASES OF CHRISTIAN ETHICS

Augustine's two uses of the Psalms in this Text illustrate two different uses of the Bible. In 1.4 the Psalms play a central role in his argument, but in 1.8 they merely provide a flourish at the end of the argument. However, it is the doctrine of creation which provides the central basis of Augustine's position (especially in I.14). He is particularly offended by Cicero, since he believes that his contentions undermine the very basis of God as Creator (I.8). In his defence of the latter, he is convinced that 'pagan' notions, such as fate, must be refuted by the Christian as 'profane and irreverent impudence' (I.4).

5. SOCIAL DETERMINANTS

Various facets of Augustine's pre-Christian life have influenced the argument in this Text. Cicero's notions are singled out for particular attack and Augustine's own previous interest in, and subsequent rejection of, astrology is evident. Free-will is defended, but, above all, he stresses the power of God: his own rejection of Pelagianism is evident, as is the strong conviction of the convert that it is God who is triumphant. Augustine, the former rhetorician, is also strongly in evidence (although this is even more the case in his much earlier *On the Free Choice of the Will*). It might even be claimed that a defence of free-will comes more naturally to one from the middle-classes than one, like Luther, who has known, at first hand, the social constraints upon the agrarian working-classes. In addition, in his arguments about the very notions of 'prescience' and 'free-will', Augustine shows that he was heir, more to the Graeco-Roman world, than to the Hebraic world: even his declaration of faith (in *1.14*) uses the un-biblical notions of 'omnipotence' and 'soul' (see further, p.306, *below*).

6. SOCIAL SIGNIFICANCE

Augustine's twin stresses upon the prescience/omnipotence of God and the free-will of man had a very considerable effect upon subsequent theology and upon Western thought. His correlation between neo-Platonic and biblical notions proved enormously influential and served to give Christianity a new intellectual credibility. He also bequeathed a, sometimes puzzling, combination of Graeco-Roman and Hebraic notions, particularly in the areas of Christian anthropology and eschatology.

FURTHER READING

In addition to the primary reading from *On the Free Choice of the Will* and from *The City of God* and the secondary reading suggested in the Introduction on Augustine, N.P. Williams' *The Ideas of the Fall and of Original Sin* is particulary important.

TEXT I

AUGUSTINE

God's foreknowledge and man's free-will

I.1   For our part, whatever may be the twists and turns of philosophical dispute and debate, we recognize a God who is supreme and true and therefore we confess his supreme power and foreknowledge. We are not afraid that what we do by an act of will may not be a voluntary act, because God, with his infallible prescience, knew that we should do it. This was the fear that led Cicero to oppose foreknowledge and the Stoics to deny that everything happens by necessity, although they maintained that everything happens according to fate.

I.2   Now what was it that Cicero so dreaded in prescience of the future, that he struggled to demolish the idea by so execrable a line of argument? He reasoned that if all events are foreknown, they will happen in the precise order of that foreknowledge; if so, the order is determined in the prescience of God. If the order of events is determined, so is the causal order; for nothing can happen unless preceded by an efficient cause. If the causal order is fixed, determining all events, then all events, he concluded, are ordered by destiny. If this is true, nothing depends on us and there is no such thing as free will. 'Once we allow this,' he says, 'all human life is overthrown. There is no point in making laws, no purpose in expressing reprimand or approbation, censure or encouragement; there is no justice in establishing rewards for the good and penalties for the evil.'

I.3   It is to avoid those consequences, discreditable and absurd as they are, and perilous to human life, that Cicero refuses to allow any foreknowledge. And he constrains the religious soul to this dilemma, forcing it to choose between those propositions: either there is some scope for our will, or there is foreknowledge. He thinks that both cannot be true; to affirm one is to deny the other. If we choose foreknowledge, free-will is annihilated; if we choose free-will, prescience is abolished. And so, being a man of eminent learning, a counsellor of wide experience and practiced skill in matters affecting human life, Cicero chooses free will. To support this, he denies foreknowledge and thus, in seeking to make men free,he makes them irreverent. For the religious mind chooses both, foreknowledge as well as liberty; it acknowledges both, and supports both in pious faith. 'How?' asks Cicero. If there is prescience of the future, the logical consequences entailed lead to the conclusion that nothing depends on our free will. And further, if anything does so depend, then, by the converse logical process, we reach the position that there is no foreknowledge. The argument proceeds thus: if there is free will, everything does not happen by fate; if everything does not happen by fate, there is not a fixed order of all causes; if there is not a fixed order of all causes, there is not a fixed order of events for the divine prescience, for these events cannot take place unless preceded by efficient causes; if there is not a fixed order for God's prescience, everything does not happen as he has foreknown them as due to happen. Thus, he concludes, if everything does not happen as foreknown by God, then there is in him no foreknowledge of all the future.

I.4   Against such profane and irreverent impudence we assert both that God knows all things before they happen and that we do by our free will everything that we feel and know would not happen without our volition. We do not say that everything is fated; in fact we deny that anything happens by destiny. For we have shown that the notion of destiny, in the accepted sense, referring to conjunction of stars at the time of conception or birth, has no validity, since it asserts something which has no reality. It is not that we deny a causal order where the will of God prevails; but we do not describe it by the word 'fate', unless perhaps if we understand fate to be derived from *fari* (speak), that is from the act of speaking. We cannot in fact deny that it is written in Scripture, 'God has spoken once, and I have heard those two things: that the power belongs to God; and that mercy belongs to you, Lord, and you render to each in accordance with his works' (Psm. 61.11f). The words 'has spoken *once*' mean 'he has spoken *immovably*', that is, unalterably, just as he knows unalterably all that is to happen and what he himself is going to do. For this reason we should be able to use the work 'fate', deriving it from *fari*, except that this word is generally used in a different sense, a sense to which we should not wish men's hearts to be directed.

I.5   Now if there is for God a fixed order of all causes, it does not follow that nothing depends on our free choice. Our wills themselves are in the order of causes, which is, for God, fixed, and is contained in his foreknowledge, since human acts of will are the causes of human activities. Therefore he who had prescience of the causes of all events certainly could not be ignorant of our decisions, which he foreknows as the causes of our actions.

I.6   Cicero's own concession that nothing happens unless preceded by an efficient cause is enough to refute him in the present question. It does not help his case to assert that while no event is causeless, not every cause is the work of destiny, since there are fortuitous causes, natural, and voluntary causes. It is enough that he admits that every event must be preceded by a cause. For our part, we do not deny the existence of causes called 'fortuitous' (from the same root as the word 'fortune');only we say that they are hidden causes and attribute them to the will, either of the true God, or of spirits of some kind. The 'natural' causes we do not detach from the will of God, the author and creator of all nature. The 'voluntary' causes come from God, or from angels, or men, or animals – if indeed one can apply the notion of will to the movements of beings devoid of reason, which carry out actions in accordance with their nature, to achieve some desire or to avoid some danger. By the wills of angels I mean both the wills of the good angels of God, as we call them, and of the evil 'angels of the devil', or even 'demons'. The same applies to the wills of men; there are those of good men, and those of evil.

I.7   This implies that the only efficient causes of events are voluntary causes, that is, they proceed from that nature which is the 'breath of life'. ('Breath' also refers to the air or the wind; but since that is corporeal, it is not the 'breath of life'.) The breath of life, which gives life to everything, and is the creator of every body and every created spirit (breath), is God himself, the uncreated spirit. In his will rests the supreme power, which assists the good wills of created spirits, sits in judgement on the evil wills, orders all wills, granting the power of achievement to some and denying it to others. Just as he is the creator of all natures, so he is the giver of all power of achievement, but not of all acts of will. Evil wills do not proceed from him because they are contrary to the nature which proceeds from him. Bodies are mostly subject to wills, some to our wills – that is to the wills of mortal beings, the wills of men rather than of animals – the others to the wills of angels. But all bodies are subject above all to the will of God, and to him all wills also are subject, because the only power they have is the power that God allows them.

I.8   Thus the cause which is cause only, and not effect, is God. But other causes are also effects, as are all created spirits and in particular the rational spirits. Corporeal causes, which are more acted upon than active, are not be counted among efficient causes, since all they can achieve is what is achieved through them by the wills of spirits. How then does the order of causes, which is fixed in the prescience of God, result in the withdrawal of everything from dependence on our will, when our acts of will play an important part in that causal order? Let Cicero dispute with those who assert that this causal order is decided by destiny, or rather who give that order the name of destiny, or fate – a position which shocks us particularly because of that word 'fate', which is generally understood in a way which corresponds to nothing in the real world. But when Cicero denies that the order of all causes is completely fixed and perfectly known to God's fore-knowledge we execrate his opinion even more than do the Stoics. For either he denies the existence of God, which indeed he has been at pains to do, in the person of a disputant in his treatise *On the Nature of the Gods*; or else, if he acknowledges God's existence while denying his foreknowledge, he is even so saying, in effect, exactly what 'the fool has said in his heart'; for he is saying, 'God does not exist' (Psm. 14.1). For a being who does not know all the future is certainly not God.

I.9   Thus our wills have only as much power as God has willed and foreknown; God, whose foreknowledge is infallible, has foreknown the strength of our wills and their achievements, and it is for that reason that their future strength is completely determined and their future achievements utterly assured. That is why, if I had decided to apply the term 'destiny' at all, I should be more ready to say that the destiny of the weak is the will of the stronger, who has the weak in his power, than to admit that destiny, in the Stoic sense of 'the causal order' (a use peculiar to Stoics, in conflict with the generally accepted one) does away with the free decision of our will.

I.10   There is no need, then, to dread that 'necessity', through fear of which the Stoics took such pains to distinguish between the causes of things, withdrawing some of them from the sway of necessity, subjecting others to it, and classing our wills among the causes they wished to emancipate from necessity, for fear, I suppose, that they would not be free if subject to it. Now if, in our case, 'necessity' is to be used of what is not in our control, of what achieves its purpose whether we will or no – the 'necessity' of death, for example – then it is obvious that our wills, by the exercise of which we lead a good life or a bad, are not subject to a necessity of this kind. We do a great many things which we should not have done if we had not wished to. In the first place, our willing belongs to this class of acts. If we so wish, it exists; if we do not so wish, it does not; for we should not will, if we did not so wish.

I.11   If, on the other hand, we define 'necessity' in the sense implied when we say that it is necessary a thing should be thus, or should happen thus, I see no reason to fear that this would rob us of free will. We do not subject the life and the foreknowledge of God to necessity, if we say that it is 'necessary' for God to be eternal and to have complete foreknowledge; nor is his power diminished by saying that he cannot die or make a mistake. The reason why he cannot is that, if he could, his power would certainly be less; and he is rightly called 'all-powerful', although he has not the power to die, or to be mistaken. 'All-powerful' means that he does what he wills, and does not suffer what he does not will; otherwise he would be by no means all-powerful. It is just because he is all-powerful that there are some things he cannot do. The same applies when we say that it is 'necessary' that when we will, we will by free choice. That statement is undisputable; and it does not mean that we are subjecting our free will to a necessity which abolishes freedom. Our wills are ours and it is our wills that affect all that we do by willing, and which would not have happened if we had not willed. But when anyone has something done to him against his will, here, again, the effective power is will, not his own will, but another's. But the power of achievement comes from God. For if there was only the will without the power of realization, that will would have been thwarted by a more powerful will. Even so, that will would have been a will, and the will not of another, but of him who willed, although it was incapable of realization. Hence, whatever happens to man against his will is to be attributed not to the wills of men, or angels, or any created spirits, but to the will of him who gives the power of realization.

I.12   It does not follow, then, that there is nothing in our will because God foreknew what was going to be in our will; for if he foreknew this, it was not nothing that he foreknew. Further, if, in foreknowing what would be in our will, he foreknew something, and not nonentity, it follows immediately that there is something in our will, even if God foreknows it. Hence we are in no way compelled either to preserve God's prescience by abolishing our free will, or to safeguard our free will by denying (blasphemously) the divine foreknowledge. We embrace both truths, and acknowledge them in faith and sincerity, the one for a right belief, the other for a right life. And yet a man's life cannot be right without a right belief about God. Therefore, let us never dream of denying his foreknowledge in the interests of our freedom; for it is with his help that we are, or shall be, free.

I.13   By the same token, it is not true that reprimands, exhortations, praise and blame are useless, because God has knowledge of them before; they are of the greatest efficacy in so far as he has foreknown that they would be effective. And prayers are effectual in obtaining all that God foreknew that he would grant in answer to them; and it is with justice that rewards are appointed for good actions and punishments for sins. The fact that God foreknew that a man would sin does not make a man sin; on the contrary, it cannot be doubted that it is the man himself who sins just because he whose prescience cannot be mistaken has foreseen that the man himself would sin. A man does not sin unless he wills to sin; and if he had willed not to sin, then God would have foreseen that refusal.

I.14   Thus God is the supreme reality, with his Word and the Holy Spirit – three who are one. He is the God omnipotent, creator and maker of every soul and every body; participation in him brings happiness to all who are happy in truth and not in illusion; he has made man a rational animal, consisting of soul and body; and when man sins he does not let him go unpunished, nor does he abandon him without pity. He has given, to good men and bad alike, the existence they share with the stones; he has given man reproductive life which he shares with the plants, the life of the senses, which he shares with the animals, and the life of the intellect, shared only the with the angels. From him derives every mode of being, every species, every order, all measure, number, and weight. He is the source of all that exists in nature, whatever its kind, whatsoever its value, and of the seeds of forms, and the forms of seeds, and the motions of seeds and forms. He has given to flesh its origin, beauty, health, fertility in propagation, the arrangement of the bodily organs, and the health that comes from their harmony. He has endowed even the soul of irrational creatures with memory, sense, and appetite, but above all this, he has given to the rational soul thought, intelligence, and will. He has not abandoned even the inner parts of the smallest and lowliest creature, or the bird's feather (to say nothing of the heavens and the earth, the angels and mankind) – he has not left them without a harmony of their constituent parts, a kind of peace. It is beyond anything incredible that he should have willed the kingdoms of men, their dominations and their servitudes, to be outside the range of the laws of his providence.

CRITIQUE

It has already been seen that the tension between ascribing prescience/omnipotence to God and free-will to man is a serious one – in Christianity, Judaism and Islam. If God is seen as all-powerful, all-knowing and all-loving, then it is difficult to see why there is evil in the world and how man is really able to have free-will. Augustine solved neither problem.

At one level, his argument in I.12-13 appears to work. If George is able to fore-tell what Stephen is going to will in a particular situation, this fact does not diminish Stephen's free-will. It might imply a notion of 'fate' apparently incompatible with real free-will, but his own foreknowledge as such does not do so. But the difference between George and God is that one is creature and the other Creator. If it is the Creator, who has given existence to all that is, including Stephen's very will, who is the one to know, in advance, what Stephen is to will, his free-will appears considerably more problematic. The greater the stress on the power of God, the more man appears as an automaton created by him. Further, Augustine only vaguely considers the possibility that, whilst God may know of all the millions of man's potential choices at the moment of creation, nevertheless, in his loving condescension, he might allow man to make the actual choices.

Naturally, it is no criticism of Augustine to say that he did not fully resolve all of these major problems. Many exponents of ethics, whether Christian or not, would insist that free-will is a prerequisite of moral behaviour and, as a result, they are forced into the tensions mentioned earlier. Indeed, there is something curiously circular and nonsensical about thoroughgoing theories of social, biological or even theological, determinism: for, if they are true, then we cannot necessarily know them to be true, since presumably, both they and our perceptions of them, are themselves completely determined and possibly thereby distorted.

TEXT II
AQUINAS
Natural law

I. BACKGROUND

This Text comes from *Summa Theologica*, 1a2ae, 96, 4-6 (Vol. XXVIII of the English Dominican translation, Blackfriars with Eyre & Spottiswoode, London, and McGraw-Hill, New York, 1966). Aquinas wrote this, his major but unfinished work, from 1265 until his mystical experience of December 1273, shortly before his death. It is designed as a textbook for theological 'novices' – hence its style of starting with a question, raising objections and counter-objections and then giving a reply and conclusions. As befits a textbook, *Summa Theologica* is liberally sprinkled with quotations, from Aristotle (e.g. *Ethics* in II.1.2), the Bible, Cicero, the early Fathers, Augustine (see particularly *Text VIII*), Isidore (of Seville, d.636, whose *Etymologies* was the main encyclopedia of classical learning for the Middle Ages, in II.1 & 8.3) and more recent authorities like Gratian (whose *Decretum* of 1141, reviewing existing legislation in the Western Church, was regarded as seminal in the Middle Ages, along with Lombard's *Sentences* in theology, in II.1.1, 7.1 & 8). The text comes from the major section in *Summa Theologica*, *Prima Secundae*, which, together with *Secunda Secundae*, deals with Christian ethics. The initial section, *Prima Pars* (cited in II.11.2), is mainly concerned with the existence and attributes of God, while the last section, *Tertia Pars*, deals with christology and ecclesiology. Aquinas has distinguished four types of law – eternal, natural, human and divine. For him 'law is nothing but a dictate of practical reason issued by a sovereign who governs a complete community'. God is indeed a sovereign and it can be held that 'the whole community of the universe is governed by God's mind'. This governance is eternal law. However, this law can be known properly only to God and those who have seen God. As intelligent creatures, men can join in and make this eternal law their own and, in so far as they do, this is natural law: 'natural law is nothing other than the sharing in the eternal law by intelligent creatures'. Human laws, themselves derived from natural law, are also necessary, because of the limitations of human reason. And finally, divine law is essential for salvation: men have been designed for 'an eternal happiness out of proportion to their natural resources.. and therefore must need be directed by a divinely given law above natural and human law... Although through natural law the eternal law is shared in according to the capacity of human nature, nevertheless in order to be directed to their ultimate supernatural end men have to be lifted up' (S.T. 1a2ae 91). So the need for revelation. Thus, grace can be seen to crown, nature and faith can be seen to crown reason (see *above*, pp. 43-5).

2. KEY ISSUES

In this Text, Aquinas focuses specifically upon Natural law and responds to three questions:

(*a*) Is Natural law the same for all? Despite empirical indications to the contrary (see further Copleston's *Extract 3*), Aquinas is convinced that Natural law is ubiquitous in man. Following Aristotle, he believes that man has a natural tendency towards happiness or well-being (*eudaimonia*), leading ultimately, for the Christian, to the beatific vision of God himself. This is the 'end' of man (in both senses) and is the main spur for morality in all men. Morality is to be discerned through the use of 'practical reason', whereas 'science' is to be discerned through theoretic reason. But, of course, men are fallible in their use of practical reason – even more fallible than in their use of theoretic reason (II.4). But the general principles of both types of reason remain the same for all men, whether they actually recognise them or not. Secondary principles, derived from the general principles of morality, are also the same for most people. But here, error, sin or bad customs may distort these secondary principles (II.6).

(*b*) Can Natural law be changed? General principles are unalterable, but secondary principles may occasionally be altered. Like Augustine, (see *above*, p.39), Aquinas believed, on the basis of the Old Testament, that God can sometimes go against Natural law (II.11.2). In addition, although *men* cannot contradict Natural law, they can sometimes add to it (II.11.3).

(*c*) Can Natural law be abolished from the human heart? Again, general principles cannot be destroyed in any man, although, in particular situations, lust and passion can over-ride them (II.13). Secondary principles, in contrast, can be effectively destroyed by error, sin and bad customs.

3. ETHICAL ARGUMENTS

The Aristotelian frame-work to Aquinas' theory of ethics tends to give it a consequential bias. The *telos, finis* or 'end' of natural man provides the spur for morality and, as will be seen in the substantive Texts, ultimately directs his ethical analysis of particular issues. Thus, for him, 'the objects to which men have a natural tendency are the concern of Natural law, and among such tendencies it is proper to man to act according to reason' (II.2). But, as can also be seen from this quotation, there is a strong deontological assumption underlying it: an understanding of man's nature reveals man's moral obligations. An identification is made between description and prescription: man 'is' created thus and also 'ought' to behave thus. Further, the precepts of Natural law are also contained (prescriptively) in Divine law (II.7.1).

4. BASES OF CHRISTIAN ETHICS

The Bible is seen to be in keeping with Natural law, although, of course, it adds to it (II.7.1) and, sometimes, produces exceptions to it (II.11.2). Significantly and, perhaps erroneously, he views Romans 2 in the light of Natural law theory (II.12.1). As already noted, he characteristically refers to a large body of Christian and pre-Christian tradition and, through Aristotle, to the natural rational 'experience' of man. Further, just as man perceives the general principles of theoretic reason through *intellectus*, man perceives the general principles of practical reason through *synderesis* (not quite 'conscience', but still an innate human faculty).

5. SOCIAL DETERMINANTS

Aquinas derived this theory of Natural law from a number of

classical and Christian sources (see P.M. Farrell, 'Sources of St.Thomas' Concept of Natural Law', *The Thomist*, 20,3,1957). Aristotle distinguished between natural justice and conventional, or written, law and Aquinas extensively used and adapted his theory of knowledge. In addition, he used Roman legal thinking, often mediated through Cicero, and Augustine's concept of Eternal law. The whole balance that he achieved between the four types of law may well reflect the confidence and felt-balance of medieval Christendom. Certainly, it is far removed from the radical discontinuities of Augustine and of Luther, in their ages of revolutionary change. In addition, the 'once born' religious personality of Aquinas might possibly be compared with the liminality of Augustine and Luther's convert personalities. Correlation and inclusiveness characterised both his theoretical position and his personality.

6. SOCIAL SIGNIFICANCE

Through modern Thomism and neo-Thomism, Aquinas' theory of Natural law has continued to have an enormous effect upon theology. Even Reformed theologians (see Niebuhr's *Extract 2*) have been significantly influenced by it. There are signs, too, that his work continues to be of interest among some moral philosophers. Although he borrowed extensively from previous sources, his achievement in producing a system of moral, theological and metaphysical concepts is unique. In this respect, he both reflected and surpassed the ambitions of 13th Century Catholicism.

FURTHER READING

S.T. la2ae 90-7 is the basic primary source for Aquinas' Natural law theory. Copleston (*Extract 3*) is one of the best sympathetic guides to his theory and D.J.O'Connor's *Aquinas and Natural Law* provides an excellent critical account of it in the light of present-day moral philosophy. N.D.O'Donoghue's article 'Towards a Theory of Exceptions', *Irish Theological Quarterly*, Sept, 1968, provides a clear account of Aquinas' theory of exceptions in the light of the Situation ethics debate – there will be further discussion of this in relation to *Extract 3, Text VIII* and *Text XI*. For an analysis of the wider legal, political and ethical aspects of

Natural law theory, see A.P. d'Entrèves' *Natural Law: An Introduction to Legal Philosophy.*

TEXT II
AQUINAS
Natural law

Is natural law the same for all?

II.1.   OBJECTIONS: 1. Apparently natural law is not the same for everybody. It is stated in the Decretum that 'the natural law is that contained in the Law and the Gospel'. Taken so it is not common to everybody; it is said in Romans, 'All do not obey the Gospel'(Rmns 10.16). Therefore natural law is not the same for everybody.

2. According to the Ethics, 'All lawful acts are said to be just acts'. Yet in the same work it is remarked that nothing is so just for all as not to vary for some. Natural law, then, is not identical for all.

3. Or put the matter like this, it has been said that objectives sought because of man's very constitution belong to natural law. These are different in different men, for by their constitution some are moved by desire for pleasure, others by ambition for honour, and others by other incentives. Therefore there is not one natural law for all.

ON THE OTHER HAND Isidore says, Natural right is common to all nations.

II.2   REPLY: As we have shown, the objects to which men have a natural tendency are the concern of natural law, and among such tendencies it is proper to man to act according to reason. Now a characteristic of reason is to proceed from common principles to particular conclusions: this is remarked in the *Physics.* However the theoretic reason and the practical reason set about this somewhat differently. The business of the theoretic reason is with natural truths that cannot be otherwise, and so without mistake it finds truth in the particular conclusions it draws as in the premises it starts from. Whereas the business of the practical reason is with contingent matters which are the domain of human acts, and although there is some necessity in general principles the more we get down to particular cases the more we can be mistaken.

II.3 So then in questions of theory, truth is the same for everybody, both as to principles and to conclusions, though admittedly all do not recognise truth in the conclusions, but only in those principles which are called 'common conceptions'. In questions of action, however, practical truth and goodwill are not the same for everybody with respect to particular decisions, but only with respect to common principles; and even those who are equally in the right on some particular course of action are not equally aware of how right they are.

II.4 So then it is evident that with respect to general principles of both theory and practice what is true or right is the same for all and is equally recognized. With respect to specific conclusions of theory the truth is the same for all, though all do not equally recognize it, for instance some are not aware that the angles of a triangle together equal two right angles. With respect to particular conclusions come to by the practical reason there is no general unanimity about what is true or right, and even when there is agreement there is not the same degree of recognition.

II.5 All hold that it is true and right that we should act intelligently. From this starting point it is possible to advance the specific conclusion, that goods held in trust are to be restored to their owners. This is true in the majority of cases, yet a case can crop up when to return the deposit would be injurious, and consequently unreasonable, as for instance were it to be required in order to attack one's country. The more you descend into the detail the more it appears how the general rule admits of exceptions, so that you have to hedge it with cautions and qualifications. The greater the number of conditions accumulated the greater the number of ways in which the principle is seen to fall short, so that all by itself it cannot tell you whether it be right to return a deposit or not.

II.6   To sum up: as for its first common principles, here natural law is the same for all in requiring a right attitude towards it as well as recognition. As for particular specific points, which are like conclusions drawn from common principles, here also natural law is the same for most people in their feeling for and awareness of what is right. Nevertheless in fewer cases either the desire or the information may be wanting. The desire to do right may be blocked by particular factors – so also with physical things that come to be and die away there are occasional anomalies and failures due to some obstruction – and the knowledge also of what is right may be distorted by passion or bad custom or even by racial proclivity; for instance, as Julius Caesar narrates, the Germans did not consider robbery wicked, though it is expressly against natural law.

II.7   Hence: 1. The text should not be taken to mean that everything in the Old and New Laws is of natural law, since many things there imparted are above our nature. It means that natural law precepts are there fully covered. So when *Gratian* says that 'natural right is what is contained in the Old and New Laws' he explains himself at once, and adds: 'By which everyone is commanded to do to others what he would have done to himself, and forbidden to do to others what he would not have done to himself'.

2. Aristotle's statement should be understood to refer to things which are naturally just, not merely according to general principles, but also according to certain conclusions drawn from them. In most cases these are rightful, yet in a few cases they fail to meet the situation.

3. Since mind in man dominates and rules his other powers, so their natural urges should be subordinated to mind. Hence it is generally held that it is right for all

human tendencies to be directed according to intelligence.

Can Natural law be changed?

II.8   OBJECTIONS: 1. It seems that natural law can be changed. For on the text of Ecclesiasticus, 'He gave instructions and the law of life' (17.9). The Gloss comments, 'He willed the document of the Law to be written in order to correct natural law. Now what is corrected is changed. Therefore natural law can be changed'.

2. Moreover, the killing of the innocent is against natural law, and so is adultery and theft. Yet you find God changing these rules, as when he commanded Abraham to put his son to death, the people of Israel to spoil the Egyptians, and Hosea to take a wife of harlotry. Natural law, then, can be altered.

3. Furthermore, Isidore says that 'common ownership of property and the same liberty for all are of natural law'. Human law seems to change all this, and therefore natural law can be changed.

ON THE OTHER HAND it is said in the *Decretum*, 'Natural law dates from the rise of rational creation, and does not vary according to period, but remains unchangeable'.

II.9   REPLY: A change can be understood to mean either addition or subtraction. As for the first, there is nothing against natural law being changed, for many things over and above natural law have been added, by divine law as well as by human laws, which are beneficial to social life.

II.10   As for change by subtraction, meaning that something that once was of natural law later ceases to be so, here there is room for a distinction. The first principles of natural law are altogether unalterable. But its secondary precepts, which we have described as being like particular conclusions close to first principles, though not alterable in the majority of cases where they are right as they stand, can nevertheless be changed on some particular and rare occasions, as we have mentioned in the preceding article, because of some special cause preventing their unqualified observance.

II.11   Hence: 1. The written Law is said to have been for the correction of natural law because it supplied what was wanting there, or because parts of natural law were decayed in the hearts of those who reckoned that some things were good which by nature are evil. This called for correction.

2. All men without exception, guilty and innocent alike, have to suffer the sentence of natural death from divine power because of original sin, according to the words, 'The Lord kills and brings to life' (1 Sam. 2.6). Consequently without injustice God's command can inflict death on anybody whether he be guilty or innocent. Adultery is intercourse with a woman to whom you are not married in accordance with divinely given law; nevertheless to go unto any woman by divine command is neither adultery nor fornication. The same applies to theft, the taking of what belongs to another, for what is taken by God's command, who is the owner of the universe, is not against the owner's will, and this is of the essence of theft. Nor is it only in human affairs that whatever God commands is just, but also in the world of nature, for as stated in the *Prima Pars*, whatever God does there in effect is natural.

3. You speak of something being according to natural right in two ways. The first is because nature is set that way; thus the command that no harm should be done to another. The second is because nature does not bid the contrary; thus we might say that it is of natural law for man to be naked, for nature does not give him clothes; these he has to make by art. In this way common ownership and universal liberty are said to be of natural law, because private property and slavery exist by human contrivance for the convenience of social life, and not by natural law. This does not change the law of nature except by addition.

Can natural law be abolished from the human heart?

II.12   Objections: 1. It would seem that natural law can be abolished from the human heart, for a text in Romans speaks of the Gentiles 'who have not the law' (2.14). The Gloss comments, 'The law of justice blotted out by fault is engraved on man's heart when he is restored by grace'. The law of justice is natural law, and this, therefore, can be abolished.

2. Again, the law of grace is more powerful than the law of nature. Yet it can be wiped away by sin, and this therefore, and with all the more reason, can happen to natural law.

3. Besides, what is established by law is set forth as being just. Now many human statutes have been enacted against natural law. Therefore natural law can be destroyed in men's hearts.

ON THE OTHER HAND Augustine says, 'Thy law is written in men's hearts, and no wickedness can efface it'. This is natural law, and it cannot be effaced.

II.13.   REPLY: As we noticed when speaking of what belongs to natural law, to begin with there are certain most general precepts known to all; and next, certain secondary and more specific precepts which are like conclusions lying close to the premises. As for these first common principles in their universal meaning, natural law cannot be cancelled in the human heart, nevertheless it can be missing from a particular course of action when the reason is stopped from applying the general principle there, because of lust or some other passion, as we have pointed out.

II.14   As for its other and secondary precepts, natural law can be effaced, either by wrong persuasions – thus also errors occur in theoretical matters concerning demonstrable conclusions – or by perverse customs and corrupt habits; for instance robbery was not reputed to be wrong among some people, nor even, as the Apostle mentions, some unnatural sins (i.e. Rmns. 1.24).

II.15   Hence: 1. Sin cancels natural law on some specific point, not as to its general principles, unless perhaps with regard to secondary precepts in the manner we have touched on.
2. Though grace is more powerful than nature, nevertheless nature is more essential to man, and therefore more permanent.
3. This argument is true of secondary precepts of natural law, against which human legislators have sometimes passed wrongful enactments.

CRITIQUE

In view of the historical and modern importance of Aquinas' Natural law theory it is not suprising that it has generated extensive analyses and critiques (see further on *Text XI*, which provides a striking illustration of the theory). Serious criticisms can be made of each of the replies he gives to the three questions in the Text:

(*a*) Is Natural law the same for all? Both the existence of an ubiquitous Natural law and the moral use to which Aquinas puts it, have been questioned. In view of the extraordinary moral differences between groups of men revealed by social anthropology, it may be more difficult today to maintain that these differences are simply due to the distortions caused by error, sin or bad custom (though see *Extract 3*). Further, as D.J.O'Connor asks, 'what is there in common between a human being of the capacity of Newton or Shakespeare and the brief sub-animal existence of a monstrous birth?' (*Aquinas and Natural Law*, p.30). But, even if such a Natural law is accepted, can one derive, as Aquinas does, man's moral end legitimately from man's natural tendencies? For many, this seems a pre-Humean confusion of the 'ought' with the 'is': description is conflated with prescription. This is still a particularly contentious area in moral philosophy, but it raises important issues in Christian ethics (see *above*, p.21). For, example, if ethical precepts are derived from the theory of evolution, as they are in some forms of Evolutionary ethics, this criticism clearly applies:

evolutionary 'development' is not simplistically to be identified with moral 'progress', unless a category error is to be made (see A.G.N. Flew, *Evolutionary Ethics*). But, if such an undertaking were to be made from the explicit perspective of a world created by God, it is not so clear that a category error would be involved. Granted a belief in the Christian God, it might well be assumed that natural human tendencies accord with the way God wishes man to behave – unless, of course, one accepts Luther's (and especially Calvin's) position that these tendencies have become thoroughly distorted by sin (see further, *below* p.195).

(*b*) Can Natural law be changed? Aquinas' distinction between general and secondary principles raises many problems. The relationship between them is by no means always clearly specified and many have found the general principles to be so general as to be vacuous (e.g. the principle that good ought to be done and evil avoided). The question of whether general principles can be usefully specified will recur in Section 3 in relation to just-war theory. Furthermore, the notion that man can sometimes add to Natural law, in II.11.3, now seems particularly dangerous in view of the way Aquinas used it to justify the existence of slavery. Again, as O'Connor asks, 'if slavery can be excused in this way, why not contraception or abortion or euthanasia?' (p.64). Nonetheless, Niebuhr's *Extract 2* and Ramsey's *Extract 5* suggest, in different ways, that attempts to isolate general principles simply cannot be avoided in Christian ethics.

(*c*) Can Natural law be abolished from the human heart? For Aquinas, it is *synderesis* which enables men to apprehend general principles; it is reason that they must use to derive secondary principles from them and it is conscience (*conscientia*) that prompts them to act on these principles. The nature and existence of this innate disposition, *synderesis*, able infallibly to apprehend general principles, has been the subject of debate amongst Thomist scholars and moral philosophers. Clearly, this has similarities to the debate about conscience in Christian ethics (see *above*, pp.19-21). Further, Luther (and again especially

Calvin) might have responded that sin and the Fall have radically reduced the significance of Natural law and that, in any case, the whole attempt to build a system of morality from it distorts the doctrine of justification by faith. This point leads naturally to the next Text.

TEXT III
LUTHER
Treatise on good works

I. BACKGROUND

This Text comes from the *Treatise on Good Works* of 1520 (from *Luther's Works*, Vol. 44, Fortress Press, Philadelphia, 1966, trans. W.A. Lambert and rev. James Atkinson, sections 4-6,8,12,13-14 & 16). This year was a crucial one for Luther, coming between the Leipzig Disputation of 1519 (when he debated his new radical position in public with John Eck, appealing in the same year unsuccessfully to the Pope and then, later, to the Emperor) and the Diet of Worms of 1521, which finally placed Luther under the Imperial ban and forbade the publication of his works, or the proclamation, or defence, of his opinions. Luther spent the respite (between Leipzig and the arrival of Pope Leo X's Bull excommunicating him, in the October of 1520) writing in great haste. Believing himself to be a doomed man, he was determined to write as much as possible. Both the *Treatise on Good Works* and *The Appeal to the German Nobility* come from this period, as do *The Papacy at Rome*, *The Babylonian Captivity* and *The Freedom of the Christian Man*. Together, they sealed Luther's decisive break with Rome.

Begun as sermon material for his congregation, *Treatise on Good Works* soon grew into a small book. In it, Luther was particularly concerned to refute the criticism, that a stress upon justification by faith alone leads to a neglect of good works and to general antinomianism. He elaborated his argument in the context of a discussion of the Decalogue – this Text comes from the opening sections on the first Commandment. In the work as a whole, the medieval distinction between 'religious' good works (fasting, prayer recitations, attendance at mass, almsgiving and etc.) and 'secular' good works, is challenged. For Luther, it was just as important that an individual should be a good father, in faith, as that he should do 'religious' works, in faith: however trivial it might seem to others, whatever is done in faith is pleasing to God. It is faith alone that is vital.

2. KEY ISSUES

Luther's central argument, the very touch-stone of the Reformation, comes out clearly in this Text. It is faith alone that matters: 'good' works, without faith, are worse than worthless, they are actually sin: monasteries and the church generally, are deeply implicated in this sin. Paul's notion of justification by faith is seen to refute conventional understandings of morality and piety. In the sequence presented here, the argument is as follows:- Work without faith is sin (III.1). Faith has been turned into just another virtue and even a work (III.2). But really, in faith all works become equal (III.3). Faith needs no instruction (III.4), but is rather like the spontaneity of love in marriage, which is destroyed by efforts to win favour (III.5). The Christian does things that need to be done, not to gather merit, but simply to please God (III.6), so no amount of fasting, confession, intercessions, or monasteries or churches can function without faith in God (III.7). Outward works, without faith, lead only to idolatry and hypocrisy (III.8) and of such are the papal bulls, seals, flags and indulgences (III.9). But, of course, faith does not forbid good works: the vital thing is that it should always come first (III.10). Indeed, if everyone lived by faith, there would be no need for laws or ceremonies (III.11 – see further *Text VI*). Faith can eliminate all sins – even the most deadly (III.12).

3. ETHICAL ARGUMENTS

In one sense, Luther's position is strongly anti-ethical. The moral calculations of his contemporaries are condemned as the following of 'blind reason and heathen ways of thinking' (III.2): an unequivocally theological stance is taken against ethical argument. But, in another sense, there is an evident personalism involved in his position, both in his initial appeal to the inspection of an individual's feelings (III.1) and in the analogy of married love (III.5). Indeed, the claim that 'a Christian man living in this faith has no need of a teacher of good works, but he does whatever the occasion calls for' (III.4) is characteristically personalist. It is even possible that Natural law has influenced his analogy in III.5 (cf VI.5). The example of married love (he did not marry himself for another five years) gains greater strength if there is actually an *analogia entis* – that is, if the affinity between husband-and-wife love and God-and-man love actually results from the way the world is created by God.

4. BASES OF CHRISITAN ETHICS

The principle of *sola Scriptura* is well in evidence: all but four of the paragraphs contain direct biblical quotations. Not surprisingly, a strong affinity for Paul is apparent, but there are also several quotations from the Old Testament and from the Gospels. In contrast to Aquinas, no reference is made to Christian tradition, other than to disparage contemporary papal practices. His appeal to the feelings of the individual Christian have already been noted and the whole Text is clearly dominated by a theological concern for faith.

5. SOCIAL DETERMINANTS

At the psychological level, Luther's debt to Paul (possibly through Augustine – see *above*, p.45) is apparent in his central notion of justification by faith. But, as with Paul, it is important to see his stress upon this in the context of his personal experience of the failure of 'legalism'. He came to identify his own struggles, as a monk, with Paul's life, as a Pharisee: increased 'works' served only to precipitate their crises of faith. And, as with Augustine, the converted Luther characteristically despised his pre-conversion life. At the more strictly social level, the undoubted excesses of the 16th Century Catholic Church, with its sometimes astonishingly corrupt papacy, both provoked and confirmed Luther's rejection of contemporary practices and beliefs. As his personal rift with Rome deepened, so his animosity towards it and his identification of the Pope with the 'anti-Christ' increased. At the political level, it is often argued that a growing German nationalism was also relevant to this rift.

6. SOCIAL SIGNIFICANCE

Luther's writings of 1520 were crucial to the subsequent development of the Reformation. In attacking papal indulgencies and insisting so forcefully on individual faith, Luther was instrumental in effecting a radical change in church structure and in Western consciousness. Few theologians can even approximate to the vast influence he has had upon both the Western Church and Western society. The challenge to papal authority, evident in this Text, caused lasting repercussions in the West: the already ailing power of Rome would never again be able to dominate Europe. And the 'new' understanding of Christian living, vocation and faith would encourage a new consciousness which Weber saw as related to the rise of Western Capitalism (see *above*, p. 28). The consequences of Luther's understanding of faith are that 'all works become equal' (III.3) and that the man of faith 'has no need of a teacher' (III.4), of ecclesiastical intermediaries or even 'of the laws of the church and of the state' (III.11): in short, the new European man must work out his or her own individual relationship to God and man. The individualistic, business entrepreneur is but one product of this radical shift of consciousness.

FURTHER READING

In addition to this primary source and to the secondary sources referred to in the Introduction, a number of books will be found useful. Max Weber's theory is found in *The Protestant Ethic and the 'Spirit' of Capitalism* and in his *Sociology of Religion*. Criticisms of this theory are numerous, but see, especially, Michael Hill's *A Sociology of Religion* for a review of some of the recent sociological discussion of it. For interpretations of Luther's theological notions here, see George W. Forell's *Faith Active in Love* and *History of Christian Ethics* and Gustav Wingreen's *Luther on Vocation* and *The Christian's Calling*.

TEXT III

LUTHER

Treatise on good works

III.1   Now everyone can notice and feel for himself when he does what is good and what is not good. If he finds his heart confident that it pleases God, then the work is good, even if it were so small a thing as picking up a straw. If the confidence is not there, or if he has any doubt about it, then the work is not good, even if the work were to raise all the dead and if the man were to give his body to be burned. This is the teaching of St. Paul in Romans 14 (.23), "Whatsoever is not done of faith or in faith is sin." It is from faith as the chief work and from no other work that we are called believers in Christ. A heathen, a Jew, a Turk, a sinner may also do all other works; but to trust firmly that he pleases God is possible only for a Christian who is enlightened and strengthened by grace.

III.2   That these words seem strange, and that some people call me a heretic because of them, is due to the fact that they have followed blind reason and heathen ways of thinking. They have set faith not above but beside other virtues. They have made faith into a kind of work of its own, separated from all works of the other virtues, although faith alone makes all other works good, acceptable, and worthy because it trusts God and never doubts that everything a man does in faith is well done in God's sight. In fact, they have not let faith remain a work but have made it a *habitus*, as they call it, although the whole of Scripture gives the name good, divine work to no work except to faith alone. Therefore, it is no wonder that they have become blind and leaders of the blind. And this faith soon brings along with it love, peace, joy, and hope. For God gives his spirit immediately to him who trusts him, as St. Paul says to the Galatians, "You have received the spirit not from your good works but because you have believed the work of God" (Gal. 3.2).

III.3   In this faith all works become equal, and one work is like the other; all distinctions between works fall away, whether they be great, small, short, long, many, or few. For the works are acceptable not for their own sake but because of faith, which is always the same and lives and works in each and every work without distinction, however numerous and varied these works always are, just as all the members of the body live, work, and take their name from the head, and without the head no member can live, work, or have a name.

III.4   It further follows from this that a Christian man living in this faith has no need of a teacher of good works, but he does whatever the occasion calls for, and all is well done. As Samuel said to Saul, "You shall become another man when the spirit enters you; do whatever your hand finds to do, for God is with you" (I Sam. 10.8–7). So also we read of St. Anna, Samuel's mother. When she believed the priest Eli, who promised her God's grace, she went home in joy and peace (I Sam. 1.17–18), and from that time paced the floor no longer: this means that whatever happened to her was all the same to her. St. Paul also says, "Where the Spirit of Christ is, there all is free"(Rom. 8.2). For faith does not permit itself to be bound to any work or to refuse any work, but, as the first Psalm says, "it yields its fruit in its season" (Ps. 1.3), that is, in the normal course of events.

III.5   We may see this in an everyday example. When a husband and wife really love one another, have pleasure in each other, and thoroughly believe in their love, who teaches them how they are to behave one to another, what they are to do or not to do, say or not to say, what they are to think? Confidence alone teaches them all this, and even more than is necessary. For such a man there is no distinction in works. He does the great and the important as gladly as the small and the unimportant, and vice versa. Moreover, he does them all in a glad, peaceful, and confident heart, and is an absolutely willing companion to the woman. But where there is any doubt, he searches within himself for the best thing to do; then a distinction of works arises by which he imagines he may win favor. And yet he goes about it with a heavy heart and great disinclination. He is like a prisoner, more than half in despair, and often makes a fool of himself.

III.6   Thus a Christian man who lives in this confidence toward God knows all things, can do all things, ventures everything that needs to be done, and does everything gladly and willingly, not that he may gather merits and good works, but because it is a pleasure for him to please God in doing these things. He simply serves God with no thought of reward, content that his service pleases God. On the other hand, he who is not at one with God, or is in a state of doubt, worries and starts looking about for ways and means to do enough and to influence God with his many good works. He runs off to St. James, to Rome, to Jerusalem, hither and thither; he prays St. Bridget's prayer, this prayer and that prayer; he fasts on this day and that day; he makes confession here and makes confession there; he questions this man and that man, and yet he finds no peace. He does all this with great effort and with a doubting and unwilling heart, so that the Scriptures rightly call such works in Hebrew *aven amal*, that is, labor and sorrow. And even then they are not good works and are in vain. Many people have gone quite crazy with them and their anxiety has brought them into all kinds of misery. Of these it is written in Wisdom (of Solomon) 5 (.6). "We have wearied ourselves in the wrong way and have followed a hard and bitter road; but God's way we have not acknowledged and the sun of righteousness has not risen upon us". . .

III.7 As I have already said, I have always praised faith and rejected all works which are done without such faith in this way in order to lead men from the false, pretentious, pharisaic good works done without faith, with which all monasteries, churches, homes, and the upper and lower classes are overfilled, and to lead them to the right, true, genuine, real works of faith. Nobody strives against me in this except the unclean beasts who do not part the hoof (as the law of Moses decrees) and who will tolerate no distinction of any kind between good works, but go lumbering along. If only they pray, fast, establish endowments, go to confession, and do enough, everything is supposed to be all right, although in all this they have had no faith in the grace of God and no certainty of his approval. In fact, they regard these works most highly when they have done a great many major ones for a long time, without any such confidence, and they look for good only after the works have been performed. And so they build their confidence not on God's favor, but on the works they have done. That is building on sand and water, and in the end they must fall, as Christ said in Matthew 7 (.26-27). This good will and favor, on which our confidence rests, was proclaimed by the angels from heaven when they sang on Christmas morn, "Glory be to God on high, peace on earth, good will to men" (Luke 2.14). . . .

III. 8   See for yourself what a difference there is between the fulfilment of the first commandment with outward works and fulfilment with inward trust. For it is the latter which makes true, living children of God; the former makes for a wretched idolatry and the most pernicious hypocrites on earth, who with their great show of righteousness lead countless folk into their way, yet they leave them without faith. So these folk are led astray pitiably and bogged down in external wailing and show. Christ speaks of their kind when he said in Matthew 24 (.23), "Beware then if any one says to you, 'Lo, here is the Christ!' or 'There he is!'" Or again, John 4 (.21-23), "I say to you, the time will come when you shall not worship God either on this mountain or in Jerusalem, for the Father seeks spiritual worshippers."

III.9   These and passages like them have moved me (and ought to move everybody else) to repudiate the ostentatious display of bulls, seals, flags, and indulgences, by which the poor people are led to build churches, to give, endow, and pray. Even then faith is not mentioned at all and is even suppressed, for since faith makes not distinction among works, then where faith is present such trumpeting and urging of one kind of work above another cannot exist. Faith desires to be the only way of serving God, and will allow this name and honor to no other work, except in so far as faith imparts it, as it does when the work is done in and by faith. This perversion is indicated in the Old Testament when the Jews left the

Temple and sacrificed at other places, in gardens and on the mountains (Isa. 65.3, 66.17). These men do exactly the same. They are zealous to do all works, but this chief work of faith they never have any regard for at all. . .

III.10   Therefore, when some people say, as they do, that when we preach faith alone good works are forbidden, it is as if I were to say to a sick man, "If you had health you would have the full use of all your limbs, but without health the works of all your limbs are nothing", and from this he wanted to infer that I had forbidden the works of his limbs. Whereas on the contrary I meant that the health must first be there to work all the works of all his limbs. In the same way faith must be the master-workman and captain in all the works, or they are nothing at all.

III.11   You might ask, if faith does everything through the first commandment, why then do we have so many laws of the church and of the state, and so many ceremonies of churches, monasteries, and holy places, which urge and tempt men to do good works through them? The answer: Simply because we do not all have or heed faith. If every man had faith we would need no more laws. Everyone would of himself do good works all the time, as his faith shows him. . .

III.12   But you say, how can I be absolutely sure that all my works are pleasing to God, when at times I fall, talk, eat, drink, and sleep too much, or otherwise transgress in ways I cannot avoid? Answer: This question shows that you still regard faith as a work among other works and do not set it above all works. It is the highest work because it blots out these everyday sins and still stands fast by never doubting that God is so favorably disposed toward you that he overlooks such everyday failures and offences. Yes, even if a deadly sin should arise (which, however, never or rarely happens to those who live in faith and trust in God), nonetheless faith always rises again and does not doubt that its sin is already gone. As it is written in I John 2 (.1-2), "My dear children, I am writing this to you so that you may not sin; but if any one does sin, we have an advocate before God, Jesus Christ, who is the forgiveness for our sins". And Wisdom (of Solomon) 15(.2), "And though we have already sinned, we are still thine, and know that thou are great." And Proverbs 24 (.16), "A righteous man may fall seven times, but he always rises up as many times." Yes, this confidence and faith must be so high and strong that a man knows that all his life and works are nothing but damnable sins in the judgment of God, as it says in Psalm 143 (.2), "For no man living is found righteous before thee." He must despair entirely of his works, and believe that they cannot be good except through this faith which expects no judgment but only pure grace, favor, kindness, and mercy.

CRITIQUE

There are elements in Luther's understanding of the doctrine of justification by faith which almost all Christians today might accept. Most would agree that the Christian life is primarily about pleasing God and not seeking to gather merit (III.6) and that for the Christian, faith should be regarded as primary and works as secondary (III.10). They might even agree that if everyone lived by faith there would be no need for laws (II.11 – see further, *below*, pp. 207-8).

However, it is important to recognise that Aquinas would also have accepted these propositions. So, just because Luther's contemporaries appeared to reject them and were, in a number of cases, highly corrupt, an acceptance of them does not commit one to a rejection of Catholicism as such. Arguments against a corrupt papacy and a corrupt church, are, not necessarily, arguments against papacy and Catholicism as such – a point that Luther sometimes appeared to forget, particularly as, in later life, his writings became more irascible. Aquinas would have insisted that good works do not on their own achieve salvation – grace being essential for that – but, nonetheless, they are still important prerequisites for salvation: works are necessary, but not sufficient, for salvation. Whatever merits are achieved by works, salvation, as such, most certainly is not. Nor would Augustine have accepted such a Pelagian position: for him, grace was essential, both to enable men to act rightly in the first place and to allow them to continue to act rightly (see *above*, p.44).

Further, many have argued that there is a dangerous antinomianism inherent in Luther's arguments. At first, Augustine's dictum 'love God, and do what you want' might seem to have similarities to Luther's position, particularly when it is used in conjunction with Paul's notion of justification by faith. But Augustine's position was less single-minded than that of Luther: like Paul himself, he could still talk about 'merit' (see *above*, p. 45). It is possible that the sort of single-minded stress of Luther, Bonhoeffer in *Extract 1*, or Fletcher in *Extract 4*, less than justice to Christian ethics. In the case of all three, it will be seen later that they may bring more presuppositions to moral decision-making than they realise (for Luther, see the analysis of *Text IX*, and the comments of Niebuhr in *Extract 2*).

Finally, there may be a dangerous exclusivism inherent in Luther's position. For him, all good works without faith in Christ, are nothing but sin. The shocking attitude he adopted towards the Jews in *Text XII*, in later life, was consistent with this position. Indeed, there always may be a danger in drawing negative conclusions from a positive position on faith. So, to claim that, for the Christian, faith is primary and works only secondary, or even that works only flow from faith, it is not necessary to claim, at the same time, that the good works of those who do not share this faith are entirely without virtue. Augustine shrank from this negative conclusion, in at least some of his works (see *Text IV*). And, clearly, it would not accord with Aquinas' theory of Natural law. Whereas the notions of 'empty works' and hypocrisy are obviously important for Christians today (thanks in part to Luther), the complete denigration of the moral actions of all but explicit Christians, might be accepted by comparatively few.

EXTRACTS 1-6

Bonhoeffer, Niebuhr, Copleston, Fletcher,
Ramsey and Little and Twiss

I. *BACKGROUND*

Dietrich Bonhoeffer's Extract 1 comes from *Ethics* (SCM, 1978,
pp. 3-6 & 9-13), Reinhold Niebuhr's *Extract 2* from his 1939
Edinburgh University Gifford Lectures, *The Nature and Destiny
of Man* (Vol. 1, *Human Nature*, Nisbet, 1941, pp.281-9, 313-4, &
315-6), F.C. Copleston's *Extract 3* from his *Aquinas* (Harper &
Row and Search, 1976, pp. 226-35), Joseph Fletcher's *Extract 4*
from his *Situation Ethics*, (SCM, 1966, pp.26-30, 30-3 & 37-9).
Paul Ramsey's *Extract 5* from his *Deeds and Rules in Christian
Ethics (Scottish Journal of Theology Occasional Papers* No 11,
Oliver & Boyd, 1965, pp. 93-6, 98-102, 105-6 & 109-10) and
David Little & Sumner B. Twiss' *Extract 6* from *Comparative
Religious Ethics: A New Method* (Harper & Row, 1978, pp.96-7,
98-101, 101-103, 103-106, 106-107, 107-109, 111-113, & 113-
114).

The chapter in *Ethics* from which the Bonhoeffer Extract
comes, 'The Love of God and the Decay of the World', can be
dated to the period 1939-40 and is thus almost contemporary
with his *The Cost of Discipleship* of 1937 and with Niebuhr's
Extract. Obviously, this was an extremely turbulent period for
both theologians. Niebuhr wrote in his preface that 'these
lectures were given in April and May of 1939 when the clouds of
war were already hovering ominously over Europe'. Bonhoeffer had already joined the Confessing Church and had returned
in 1935 from America to Hitler's Germany. Whilst in America,
Bonhoeffer (1906-45) studied at the Union Theological Seminary, where Niebuhr (1892-1971) had been Professor of
Christian Ethics since 1928. Niebuhr later recollected that
Bonhoeffer had said at this critical stage in his life, 'I shall have
no right to participate in the reconstruction of Christian life in

Germany after the war if I do not share the trials of this time with my people' (quoted in the preface to *The Cost of Discipleship*, SCM, 1978, P.11). At the time of writing this Extract, he was still head of the College of the Confessing Church at Finkenwalde. By 1955, when he first published *Aquinas*, Copleston, a Jesuit and Oxford trained philosopher, was Professor of Metaphysics in the doctorate course at the Gregorian University, Rome. He was appointed Professor of the History of Philosophy at Heythrop College, in 1939 at the age of 28, retired in 1974 from a chair in London University and is author of the multi-volume *History of Philosophy*. Joseph Fletcher, (1905-81) like both Niebuhr and Bonhoeffer, was a pastor before he became an academic, was appointed as Professor of Social Ethics at the Episcopal Theological School, Cambridge, Massachusetts, in 1944 (from where he wrote *Situation Ethics*) and finally went to the University of Virginia. Paul Ramsey (b.1913) was, until his retirement in 1982, Professor of Religion at Princeton University. Like Fletcher (see Section 4), he has a major interest in medical ethics – writing *The Patient as Person* and *Fabricated Man*, amongst other books, after being a visiting professor of genetic ethics at Georgetown University Medical School – and in the ethics of war. *Extract 5* was written in direct response to the Quaker Report (*Extract 22*), John Robinson's *Honest to God* (1963) and Paul Lehmann's *Ethics in a Christian Context* (1963) and then expanded as a book, *Deeds and Rules in Christian Ethics* (1967), in response to *Situation Ethics*. Between these two versions he also wrote his influential critique of the World Council of Churches, *Who Speaks for the Church?*. David Little is Professor of Religion and Sociology at the University of Virginia and Sumner B. Twiss Associate Professor of Religious Studies at Brown University. *Comparative Religious Ethics* is the product of more than a decade of collaboration and attempts to advance a new and wholly empirical method of analysing religious and secular ethical claims.

2. KEY ISSUES
Bonhoeffer highlights the difference between ethics and Christian ethics: man's unaided ethical deliberations and conscience

merely reflect a disunion with God. Man was originally created in the image of God, with a knowledge of an origin in God, but, through the Fall, this knowledge has been reversed, so that man now is thought to be man's own creator and the originator of good and evil (1.1-4). Man's conscience (1.10) and quest for self-knowledge (1.11) both illustrate this reversal, since they falsely try to reach God through interpersonal relationships: in contrast, Jesus' ethics start from his unity with God (1.15).

Niebuhr, however, insists upon a view of man's nature apart from God which *does* know something of good and evil, but which is nonetheless still subject to sin. Even those deeply involved in sin retain this knowledge (2.1) – although Christ is necessary to restore it fully (2.2). On this basis, he rejects a Calvinist doctrine of the total depravity of man (2.4) and a literalist version of the Fall (2.5-7): nothing can change the essential nature and structure of man, but, through a misuse of their God-given freedom, men can destroy the proper function of their nature (2.8). It is through this misuse that man is tempted to seek self-sufficiency and self-mastery (2.12): but, through love, the other self ceases to be a mere object (2.13): through love, made possible only by faith, the vicious circle of egocentricity can be broken (2.13-4). Thus, Niebuhr attempts to combine, a (modified) Catholic appreciation of Natural law against modern utopianism, with a stress on faith and sin (2.16f).

Copleston's concerns in *Extract 3* are more philosophical than theological. He is concerned to clarify Aquinas' Natural law theory in the light of modern relativist and emotive theories of ethics (3.13). In contrast to relativist objections to a theory of unalterable moral precepts, he points out that empirical differences on moral issues between men, do not, of themselves, disprove Aquinas' theory (3.3-5). With emotivists, he agrees that Aquinas' theory is not simply rationalistic – moral decision-making involves rational and prudential reflection on human nature as *known in experience* (3.8: an important point to compare with Fletcher's criticisms of 'legalism'). Against emotivists, however, he points out that Aquinas' position assumes an objective moral relationship: whilst feelings are important in moral decision-making, they are too subjective to form the *basis* of morality (3.12).

Fletcher has criticised legalist and antinomian approaches to Christian ethics earlier in his book and now, in *Extract 4*, seeks to defend a third approach, that of Situation ethics. In this, ethical maxims are treated as illuminators (but not as rules or laws) in particular situations: if love is better served, they can be compromised or set aside (4.1 & 12). Like Natural law, Situation ethics accepts reason in moral decision-making (4.2) and even involves rational calculation (4.12f: elsewhere in *Situation Ethics* he accepts the term 'utilitarianism' to describe this function). But it rejects the 'objectivity' of Natural law (4.2) and accepts only one *summum bonum* as law (4.10-11). For the Christian situationist, this *summum bonum* is *agape* (4.10): only the commandment to love, for the Christian, is categorically good (4.2): and only general 'principles', not rules or laws, can be derived from this *summum bonum* (4.3-9).

Ramsey, too, lays emphasis upon *agape* in Christian ethics, but nevertheless he insists that some form of Rule-Agapism is necessary in addition to Fletcher's Act-Agapism. Using the philosopher Frankena's distinctions between Pure Agapism and Mixed Agapism and distinguishing, in the first, between Pure Act-Agapism (5.4), Modified Act-Agapism (5.5) and Pure Rule-Agapism (5.6), he defends a view of Christian ethics which treats *agape* as involving rules, as well as acts (5.8f). Even though the Christian starts with people and not with rules in his moral behaviour, this behaviour still ought not to be 'unruly' (5.16) and, in this respect, the New Testament does seem to offer rules or principles (5.17). Christians can know something about the requirements of *agape*, requirements which can be related to differing situations and which can, indeed, be known in advance of these situations.

In sharp contrast to the other Extracts, Little and Twiss' concerns are solely analytic. In their introduction they disavow any apologetic motives, being concerned instead to compare and analyse value-judgments from a variety of religious and secular contexts. In this Extract they set out their overall method and subsequently test it by examining three different religious traditions – that among the Navajo Indians, that of early Christianity as represented by the Gospel of Matthew and that of Theravada Buddhism in some of its basic texts. Clearly they believe (in contrast to Bonhoeffer) that there are continuities of structure in various religious and secular moral contexts, despite real differences of substance.

3. ETHICAL ARGUMENTS

It has already been argued that there are obvious similarities and differences between the personalism of Bonhoeffer and the situationism of Fletcher (see *above*, p.61) Bonhoeffer's personalism is evident also in his earlier writings. As an assistant minister in Barcelona, he wrote in 1929 that, 'there are not and cannot be Christian norms and principles of a moral nature; the concepts of 'good' and 'evil' exist only in the performance of an action, i.e. at any specific present, and hence any attempt to lay down principles is like trying to draw a bird in flight' (*No Rusty Swords*, Fontana, 1970, p. 36): and again, 'there are no actions which are bad in themselves – even murder can be justified – there is only faithfulness to God's will or deviation from it' (p.41). Thus, 'we can give no generally valid decisions which we might then hold out to be the only Christian one, because in so doing we are only setting out new principles and coming into conflict with the law of freedom. Rather can we only seek to be brought into the concrete situation of the decision and to show one of the possibilities of decision which present themselves at that point' (p.42). Affinities with Pure Act-Agapism and Situation ethics are evident here. But, in the same lecture, there is also evident his radical division between ethics and Christian ethics. In addition, unlike Fletcher, it is the 'will of God', rather than *agape*, that he regards as central in Christian ethics: for him 'there is no other law than the law of freedom' (p.40): *agape* cannot be treated as law: 'the new commandments of Jesus can never be regarded merely as ethical principles' (p.41). Clearly this position is different from both that of Fletcher in 4.10 and of Ramsey in 5.17.

The Extracts of Niebuhr, Copleston and Ramsey differ from those of Bonhoeffer and Fletcher in that they postulate some form of deontology. Ramsey's position is most clearly linked to *agape*, derived from the teaching of Jesus (though see *Extract 15*), but a strong stress upon love is also present in Niebuhr. Interestingly, Copleston concluded a critical review of *Situation Ethics*, by insisting that 'belief that in Christian ethics love is the supreme value seems to me unquestionably valid' (quoted in the third impression of *Situation Ethics*). However, Ramsey's concluding concept of 'love transforming natural justice' (a concept which can be traced back to his *Basic Christian Ethics* of 1950) seems to bring his position closer to that of Niebuhr. It will be seen in Niebuhr's *Extract 9* that there is often a tension in his writings between the concepts of love and justice and, undoubtedly, he would have regarded Fletcher's avoidance of this tension, by stressing only love, as a form of 'Christian utopianism' (2.18). For neither Niebuhr nor Ramsey is *agape* a sufficient basis for Christian ethics: both, whilst remaining critical of traditional Natural law theory, wish to affirm the objective existence of other additional principles (cf Gustafson in *Extract 20*). But, as Reformed theologians, they might wish their positions to be more systematically related to the New Testament and to Luther's notions of sin and faith, than the understanding of ethics that Copleston clarifies.

4. BASES OF CHRISTIAN ETHICS

This point leads naturally to the next part of analysis. Only in Bonhoeffer's *Extract 1* is the Bible used as *the* basic resource of Christian ethics. Fletcher also makes (rather uncharacteristic – see *Extract 19*) use of the New Testament in 4.9, as does Niebuhr in 2.9. Yet the discussion, in both of these Extracts, is mainly dictated by appeals to Christian tradition. In both Copleston's *Extract 3* and Ramsey's *Extract 5* the discussion is rather dictated by philosophy (except 5.17): indeed, Copleston wrote his *Aquinas* primarily, 'to make it easier for the reader to consider sympathetically his style of philosophizing and his interpretation of the world' (p.17), not to defend his theology as such. Despite his early interest in sociology and psychology (e.g. in *Sanctorum Communio*), it is doubtful whether Bonhoeffer would have considered such philosophical concerns to be worthwhile undertakings in Christian ethics. They belong more to the tradition of Augustine and Aquinas than to that of Luther.

Appeals to Christian experience are made, at times, by all five theologians. In *Extract 1* Bonhoeffer appears to reject conscience, but later in *Ethics*, he claims that 'it can never be advisable to act against one's own conscience' (p.211). This, it would seem, is conscience which has already been informed by Christian faith, rather than an innate faculty of man. In contrast, Niebuhr in 2.2 does seem to be referring to the latter and even Fletcher has a puzzling reference to 'problems of conscience' in 4.8. However, Bonhoeffer's rejection of secular conscience is complicated by the fact that, as the German Church became increasingly divided in the war and a number of secular liberals started to stand out against Hitler, he began to note an affinity of 'consciousness' of values between their position and that of his own. It became clear to him that 'it was not the Church that was seeking the protection and alliance of these concepts; but, on the contrary, it was the concepts that had somehow become homeless and now sought refuge in the Christian sphere... The children of the Church, who had become independent and gone their own ways, now in the hour of danger returned to their mother' (*Ethics* pp. 38-9). However, this 'consciousness' may still not be an innate faculty or tendency of man: it may, instead, be better understood in terms of a transposition theory (see *above*, p.12). In terms of Christian belief, Bonhoeffer's and Niebuhr's Extracts (the two most theological Extracts) also differ from each other – most notably in their Christian anthropologies and in their interpretations of the doctrine of the Fall (i.e. in 1.4f and in 2.5f).

5.   SOCIAL DETERMINANTS

These Extracts represent three distinct phrases of Western theology; the late-1930's, the mid-1950's and the period since the mid-1960's. The first phase was dominated by the neo-orthodox reaction of Barth and others against theological liberalism and by impending world war. The second was a period of some optimism and attempts at theological construction. And the third was characterised by theological ferment and radical self-criticism. Both Niebuhr and Bonhoeffer were heirs to the Barthian theological revolution. The early Niebuhr rejected theological liberalism and he always remained critical of

'Christian utopianism'. His pastorate in industrial Detroit led him to a strong sympathy with Marxism, which can be detected in *Extract 9*, but later he became more critical of Russian Communism and his attitude towards American politics became distinctly less radical. His mature theological writings also show a considerable hostility towards a rigidly neo-orthodox approach to Christian ethics. Bonhoeffer, in contrast, remained firmly attached to this approach and shows the considerable influence of Barth in *Extract 1*. In some respects, both he and Barth are more Lutheran than Luther: for instance, residual elements of Natural law theory (present in Luther's own writings) are consciously denied by them. Their negative understanding of mankind apart from Christ and Niebuhr's negative understanding of 'Christian utopianism', may owe much to their experience of political collapse and of chaos in the 1920's and 1930's. Indeed, their suspicion of Natural law may owe something to their observations of its misuse in Nazi Germany. This contrasts with the tentative attempt at reconstruction offered by Copleston in the 1950's. His tentativeness is, doubtless, a response to the severe strictures of English philosophy in the 1930's and 1940's against theology and metaphysics and, characteristically, he seeks to 'clarify' rather than defend. In contrast again, the radical innovations of the 1960's, in the West, are strongly reflected in Fletcher's iconoclasm (see further *Extract 19*). Some have suggested that there is a strong middle-class, Western intellectual assumption in *Situation Ethics* (as in Harvey Cox's *Secular City*), that the individual is capable of making unstructured moral decisions from one situation to the next. In part, Paul VI's *Extract 23* was a reaction against this assumption. A further reaction is seen in *Extract 6*: the growth of the religious studies movement, in Western academic circles, has tended to view religion as a pluriform phenomenon, to be analysed in disinterested and detached terms. Here the concern is to analyse, rather than prescribe, and to compare, rather than criticise.

6. SOCIAL SIGNIFICANCE
All five theologians have had a profound influence upon Christian ethics. Interest in Bonhoeffer's writings was inevit-

ably sharpened by his martyrdom, but in their own right his books remain important for theology. Niebuhr's social influence was perhaps greater than any of the others and few recent theologians can match his influence upon political policy-making. *Extract 2* was written at the height of this influence and shows a maturity of thought denied to Bonhoeffer. Copleston has established himself, through his *History of Philosophy*, as the most influential Roman Catholic philosopher in England. His *Aquinas* successfully presented his subject as one to be taken seriously by present-day philosophers, who might otherwise deny his theological and biblical presuppositions. Fletcher's *Situation Ethics*, as already noted, has had a major effect upon Christian ethics and few within the discipline fail to take it into account (if only to deny its premises). And Ramsey is, perhaps, the most influential modern exponent of Christian war ethics and medical ethics in America. However, in relation to Western society as a whole, they may, together, reflect a declining influence of the discipline of Christian ethics. Today, it is difficult to imagine a theologian such as Niebuhr having as profound an influence as he did in America during the 1930's and 1940's, or even the comparable influence of William Temple (see *Extract 10*) in Britain. Certainly, it is too early to offer any predictions about the future social significance of the sort of religious studies analysis represented in *Extract 6*.

FURTHER READING
Bonhoeffer has been the subject of many studies, but, amongst these, Eberhard Bethge's *Dietrich Bonhoeffer* and John D. Godsey's *The Theology of Dietrich Bonhoeffer* are still amongst the most important. Studies of Niebuhr are less available, but see ed. C.W. Kegley and R.W. Bretall, *Reinhold Niebuhr, His Political, Social and Religious Thought* and D. Meyer's *The Protestant Search for Political Realism*. Important comparisons of Niebuhr's, Bonhoeffer's and Ramsey's ethical methods are contained in Edward LeRoy Long, Jr.'s. *A Survey of Christian Ethics*. Suggested reading on Natural law theory has already been given in relation to Aquinas' *Text II*. Fletcher's *Situation Ethics* has been subjected to considerable criticism, including ed. J.C.Bennett, *Storm Over Ethics*, G.R. Dunstan, *The Artifice of*

Ethics, and Stanley Hauerwas, *Vision and Virtue*. Fletcher responded to some of the early criticism in his *Moral Responsibility*. Ronald M. Green's *Religious Reason: The Rational and Moral Basis of Religious Belief* presents an interesting, critical, but heavily Kantian, alternative approach to comparative religious ethics.

EXTRACT I

BONHOEFFER

Ethics and Christian ethics

1.1   The knowledge of good and evil seems to be the aim of all ethical reflection. The first task of Christian ethics is to invalidate this knowledge. In launching this attack on the underlying assumptions of all other ethics, Christian ethics stands so completely alone that it becomes questionable whether there is any purpose in speaking of Christian ethics at all. But if one does so notwithstanding, that can only mean that Christian ethics claims to discuss the origin of the whole problem of ethics, and thus professes to be a critique of all ethics simply as ethics.

1.2   Already in the possibility of the knowledge of good and evil Christian ethics discerns a falling away from the origin. Man at his origin knows only one thing: God. It is only in the unity of his knowledge of God that he knows of other men, of things, and of himself. He knows all things only in God, and God in all things. The knowledge of good and evil shows that he is no longer at one with this origin.

1.3   In the knowledge of good and evil man does not understand himself in the reality of the destiny appointed in his origin, but rather in his own possibilities, his possibility of being good or evil. He knows himself now as something apart from God, outside God, and this means that he now knows only himself and no longer knows God at all; for he can know God only if he knows only God. The knowledge of good and evil is therefore separation from God. Only against God can men know good and evil.

1.4   But man cannot be rid of his origin. Instead of knowing himself in the origin of God, he must now know himself as an origin. He interprets himself according to his possibilities, his possibilities of being good or evil, and he therefore conceives himself to be the origin of good and evil. *Eritis sicut deus*. 'The man is become as one of us, to know good and evil', says God (Gen. 3.22).

1.5   Originally man was made in the image of God, but now his likeness to God is a stolen one. As the image of God man draws his life entirely from his origin in God, but the man who has become like God has forgotten how he was at his origin and has made himself his own creator and judge. What God had given man to be, man now desired to be through himself. But God's gift is essentially *God's* gift. It is the origin that consititutes this gift. If the origin changes, the gift changes. Indeed the gift consists solely in its origin. Man as the image of God draws his life from the origin of God, but the man who has become like God draws his life from his own origin. In appropriating the origin to himself man took to himself a secret of God which proved his undoing. The Bible describes this event with the eating of the forbidden fruit. Man now knows good and evil. This does not mean that he has acquired new knowledge in addition to what he knew before, but the knowledge of good and evil signifies the complete reversal of man's knowledge, which hitherto had been solely knowledge of God as his origin. In knowing good and evil he knows what only the origin, God Himself, can know and ought to know. It is only with extreme reserve that even the Bible indicates to us that God is the One who knows of good and evil. It is the first indication of the mystery of predestination, the mystery of an eternal dichotomy which has its origin in the eternally One, the mystery of an eternal choice and election by Him in whom there is no darkness but only light. To know good and evil is to know oneself as the origin of good and evil, as the origin of an eternal choice and election. How this is possible remains the secret of Him in whom there is no disunion because He is Himself the one and eternal origin and the overcoming of all disunion. This secret has been stolen from God by man in his desire to be an origin on his own account. Instead of knowing only the God who is good to him and instead of knowing all things in Him, he now knows himself as the origin of good and evil. Instead of accepting the choice and election of God, man himself desires to choose, to be the origin of the election. And so, in a certain sense, he bears within himself the secret of predestination. Instead of knowing himself solely in the reality of being chosen and loved by God, he must now know himself in the possibility of choosing and of being the origin of good and evil. He has become like God, but against God. Herein lies the serpent's deceit. Man knows good and evil, but because he is not the origin, because he acquires this knowledge only at the price of estrangement from the origin, the good and evil that he knows are not the good and evil of God but good and evil against God. They are good and evil of man's own choosing, in opposition to the eternal election of God. In becoming like God man has become a god against God.

1.6   This finds its expression in the fact that man, knowing of good and evil, has finally torn himself loose from life, that is to say from the eternal life which proceeds from the choice of God. 'And now, lest he put forth his hand, and take also of the tree of life, and eat, and live for ever … he drove out the man; and he placed at the east of the garden of Eden Cherubims, and a flaming sword which turned every way, to keep the way of the tree of life' (Gen. 3.22 and 24). Man knows good and evil, against God, against his origin, godlessly and of his own choice, understanding himself according to his own contrary possibilities; and he is cut off from the unifying, reconciling life in God, and is delivered over to death. The secret which man has stolen from God is bringing about man's downfall.

1.7   Man's life is now disunion with God, with men, with things, and with himself.

1.8   Instead of seeing God man sees himself. 'Their eyes were opened' (Gen. 3.7). Man perceives himself in his disunion with God and with men. He perceives that he is naked. Lacking the protection, the covering, which God and his fellow-man afforded him, he finds himself laid bare. Hence there arises shame. Shame is man's ineffaceable recollection of his estrangement from the origin; it is grief for this estrangement, and the powerless longing to return to unity with the origin. Man is ashamed because he has lost something which is essential to his original character, to himself as a whole; he is ashamed of his nakedness. Just as in the fairy-story the tree is ashamed of its lack of adornment, so, too, man is ashamed of the loss of his unity with God and with other men. Shame and remorse are generally mistaken for one another. Man feels remorse when he has been at fault; and he feels shame because he lacks something. Shame is more original than remorse. The peculiar fact that we lower our eyes when a stranger's eye meets our gaze is not a sign of remorse for a fault, but a sign of that shame which, when it knows that it is seen, is reminded of something that it lacks, namely, the lost wholeness of life, its own nakedness. To meet a stranger's gaze directly, as is required, for example, in making a declaration of personal loyalty, is a kind of act of violence, and in love, when the gaze of the other is sought, it is a kind of yearning. In both cases it is the painful endeavour to recover the lost unity by either a conscious and resolute or else a passionate and devoted inward overcoming of shame as the sign of disunion. . .

1.9   In shame man is reminded of his disunion with God and with other men; conscience is the sign of man's disunion with himself. Conscience is farther from the origin than shame, it presupposes disunion with God and with man and marks only the disunion with himself of the man who is already disunited from the origin. It is the voice of apostate life which desires at least to remain one with itself. It is the call to the unity of man with himself. This is evident already from the fact that the call of conscience is always a prohibition 'Thou shalt not.' 'You ought not to have.' Conscience is satisfied when the prohibition is not disobeyed. Whatever is not forbidden is permitted. For conscience life falls into two parts: what is permitted and what is forbidden. There is no positive commandment. For conscience permitted is identical with good, and conscience does not register the fact, that even in this, man is in a state of disunion with his origin. It follows from this also that conscience does not, like shame, embrace the whole of life; it reacts only to certain definite actions. In one sense it is inexorable; in forbidden actions it sees a peril to life as a whole, that is to say, disunion with oneself; it recalls what is long past and represents this disunion as something which is already accomplished and irreparable, but the final criterion remains precisely that unity with oneself which is imperilled only in the particular instances in which the prohibition is disobeyed. The range of experience of conscience does not extend to the fact that this unity itself presupposes disunion with God and with men and that consequently, beyond the disobedience to the prohibition, the prohibition itself, as the call of conscience, arises from disunion with the origin. This means that conscience is concerned not with man's relation to God and to other men but with man's relation to himself. But a relation of man to himself, in detachment from his relation to God and to other men, can arise only through man's becoming like God in the disunion.

1.10 Conscience itself reverses this relation. It derives the relation to God and to men from the relation of man to himself. Conscience pretends to be the voice of God and the standard for the relation to other men. It is therefore from his right relation to himself that man is to recover the right relation to God and to other men. This reversal is the claim of the man who has become like God in his knowledge of good and evil. Man has become the origin of good and evil. He does not deny his evil; but in conscience man summons himself, who has become evil, back to his proper, better self, to good. This good, which consists in the unity of man with himself, is now to be the origin of all good. It is the good of God, and it is the good for one's neighbour. Bearing within himself the knowledge of good and evil, man has become judge over God and men, just as he is judge over himself.

1.11   Knowing of good and evil in disunion with the origin, man begins to reflect upon himself. His life is now his understanding of himself, whereas at the origin it was his knowledge of God. Self-knowledge is now the measure and the goal of life. This holds true even when man presses out beyond the bounds of his own self. Self-knowledge is man's interminable striving to overcome his disunion with himself by thought; by unceasingly distinguishing himself from himself he endeavours to achieve unity with himself.

1.12   All knowledge is now based upon self-knowledge. Instead of the original comprehension of God and of men and of things there is now a taking in vain of God and of men and of things. Everything now is drawn in into the process of disunion. Knowledge now means the establishment of the relationship to oneself; it means the recognition in all things of oneself and of oneself in all things. And thus, for man who is in disunion with God, all things are in disunion, what is and what should be, life and law, knowledge and action, idea and reality, reason and instinct, duty and inclination, conviction and advantage, necessity and freedom, exertion and genius, universal and concrete, individual and collective; even truth, justice, beauty and love come into opposition with one another, just as do pleasure and displeasure, happiness and sorrow. One could prolong the list still further and the course of human history adds to it constantly. All these disunions are varieties of the disunion in the knowledge of good and evil. 'The point of decision of the specifically ethical experience is always conflict.' But in conflict the judge is invoked; and the judge is the knowledge of good and evil; he is man.

1.13   Now anyone who reads the New Testament even superficially cannot but notice the complete absence of this world of disunion, conflict and ethical problems. Not man's falling apart from God, from men, from things and from himself, but rather the rediscovered unity, reconciliation, is now the basis of the discussion and the 'point of decision of the specifically ethical experience'. The life and activity of men is not at all problematic or tormented or dark: it is self-evident, joyful, sure and clear.

1.14   It is in Jesus's meeting with the Pharisee that the old and the new are most clearly contrasted. The correct understanding of this meeting is of the greatest significance for the understanding of the gospel as a whole. The Pharisee is not an adventitious historical phenomenon of a particular time. He is the man to whom only the knowledge of good and evil has come to be of importance in his entire life; in other words, he is simply the man of disunion. Any distorted picture of the Pharisees robs Jesus's argument with them of its gravity and its importance. The Pharisee is that extremely admirable man who subordinates his entire life to his knowledge of good and evil and is as severe a judge of himself as of his neighbor to the honour of God, whom he humbly thanks for this knowledge. For the Pharisee every moment of life becomes a situation of conflict in which he has to choose between good and evil. For the sake of avoiding any lapse his entire thought is strenuously devoted night and day to the anticipation of the whole immense range of possible conflicts, to the reaching of a decision in these conflicts, and to the determination of his own choice. There are innumerable factors to be observed, guarded against and distinguished. The finer the distinctions the surer will be the correct decision. This observation extends to the whole of life in all its manifold aspects. The Pharisee is not opinionated; special situations and emergencies receive special consideration; forbearance and generosity are not excluded by the gravity of the knowledge of good and evil; they are rather an expression of this gravity. And there is no rash presumption here, or arrogance or unverified self-esteem. The Pharisee is fully conscious of his own faults and of his duty of humility and thankfulness towards God. But, of course, there are differences, which for God's sake must not be disregarded, between the sinner and the man who strives towards good, between the man who becomes a breaker of the law out of a situation of wickedness and the man who does so out of necessity. If anyone disregards these differences, if he fails to take every factor into account in each of the innumerable cases of conflict, he sins agains the knowledge of good and evil.

1.15   These men with the incorruptibly impartial and distrustful vision cannot confront any man in any other way than by examining him with regard to his decisions in the conflicts of life. And so, even when they come face to face with Jesus, they cannot do otherwise than attempt to force Him, too, into conflicts and into decisions in order to see how He will conduct Himself in them. It is this that constitutes their temptation of Jesus. One need only read the twenty-second chapter of St. Matthew, with the questions about the tribute money, the resurrection of the dead and the first and great commandment, and then the story of the good Samaritan (Luke 10.25) and the discussions about the keeping of the Sabbath (Matt. 12.11), and one will be most intensely impressed by this fact. The crucial point about all these arguments is that Jesus does not allow Himself to be drawn in into a single one of these conflicts and decisions. With each of His answers He simply leaves the case of conflict beneath Him. When it is a matter of conscious malice on the part of the Pharisees Jesus's answer is the still cleverer avoidance of a cleverly laid trap, and as such it may well have caused the Pharisees to smile. But that is not essential. Just as the Pharisees cannot do otherwise than confront Jesus with situations of conflict, so, too, Jesus cannot do otherwise than refuse to accept these situations. Just as the Pharisees' question and temptation arises from the disunion of the knowledge of good and evil, so, too, Jesus's answer arises from unity with God, with the origin, and from the overcoming of the disunion of man with God. The Pharisees and Jesus are speaking on totally different levels. That is why their words so strikingly fail to make contact, and that is why Jesus's answers do not appear to be answers at all, but rather attacks of His own against the Pharisees, which is what they, in fact, are.

EXTRACT 2
NIEBUHR
Christian ethics and man's nature

2.1   "The greatness of man", declares Pascal, "is so evident that it is even proved by his wretchedness. For what in animals is called nature we call wretchedness in man; by which we recognize that, his nature now being like that of animals, he has fallen from a better nature which once was his. For who is unhappy at not being a king except a deposed king? .. Who is unhappy at having only one mouth? And who is not unhappy at having only one eye? Probably no man ever ventured to mourn at not having three eyes. But any one is inconsolable at having none" (*Pensées*, par. 409). No man, however as normal. Some memory of a previous condition of blessedness seems to linger in his soul; some echo of the law which he has violated seems to resound in his conscience. Every effort to give the habits of sin the appearance of normality betrays something of the frenzy of an uneasy conscience. The contrast between what man is truly and essentially and what he has become is apparent even to those who do not understand that this contrast is to be found in every human being and has its seat in the will of man himself. Those who do not understand the real nature of sin sometimes portray the contrast in terms of various levels of human culture. "The superman built the aeroplane", declared a modern scientist recently, "but the ape-man got a hold of it". Or sometimes they regard the contrast as one between the good man and his lagging and imperfect institutions. The sense of a conflict between what man is and ought to be finds universal expression, even though the explanations of the conflict are usually contradictory and confused.

2.2   This universal testimony of human experience is the most persuasive refutation of any theory of human depravity which denies that man has any knowledge of the good which sin has destroyed. It is true of course, as Christian faith declares, that any human statements of the blessedness and perfection which are man's proper state and nature are themselves coloured by sin, so that Christ, as the second Adam, is required to restore the image of the first Adam as he was before the Fall. The reason why there is a heightened sense of sin in Christianity is that the vision of Christ heightens the contrast between what man is truly and what he has become, and destroys the prestige of normality which sinful forms of life periodically achieve in the world. Yet faith in Christ could find no lodging place in the human soul, were it not uneasy about the contrast between its true and its present state; though this same faith in Christ also clarifies that contrast. Men who have fallen deeply into the wretchedness of sin are never easy in their minds; but their uneasiness is frequently increased by some vivid reminder of the innocency of their childhood or the aspirations of their youth.

2.3   There are no forms of disease or corruption, short of death, which do not reveal something of the healthful structure which they have corrupted. The blind eye is still an eye, though it may be completely sightless. The aberrations of an insane mind betray coherences in the very welter of incoherences which only a human and not an animal mind could conceive. The disorder of war would not be an evil did it not operate within and against some kind of harmony and interdependence of nations; and it could not be evil if it could not avail itself of the good of internal and domestic peace, from which it draws the capacity of conquest. "Even the thieves themselves that molest the world beside them," declared Augustine, "are at peace amongst themselves" (*City of God* IV 12).

2.4   Though Christian theology has frequently expressed the idea of the total depravity of man in extravagant terms, it has never been without witnesses to the fact that human sin cannot destroy the essential character of man to such a degree that it would cease being implied in, and furnishing a contrast to, what he had become. It is not surprising to find this emphasis in Thomas Aquinas, who does not hold to the doctrine of total depravity. Yet even Luther, who believes that nothing but the name of the "image of God" is left to sinful man, animadverts upon the significance of man's uneasy conscience, a phenomenon which can be understood only as the protest of man's essential nature against his present state. Augustine is very explicit in his affirmation that the evil of sin cannot completely destroy the goodness of what God has created in man: "And it was manifested unto me that those things be good which yet are corrupted; which neither were they sovereignly good nor, unless they were good, could be corrupted: for if sovereignly good, they were incorruptible; if not good at all there is nothing in them to be corrupted . . . But if they be deprived of all good they would cease to be . . . So long therefore as they are, they are good: therefore whatsoever is, is good" (*Confessions*, VII, 12).

2.5   The problem of the relation of man's essential nature to his sinful state has unfortunately been confused in the history of Christian thought by a difficulty which we have previously observed in the doctrine of original sin: Christian theology has found it difficult to refute the rationalistic rejection of the myth of the Fall without falling into the literalistic error of insisting upon the Fall as an historical event. One of the consequences of this literalism, which has seriously affected the thought of the church upon the problem of man's essential nature, is the assumption that the perfection from which man fell is to be assigned to a particular historical period, i.e. the paradisaical period before the Fall. This chronological interpretation of a relation which cannot be expressed in terms of time without being falsified must not be attributed to the authority of the Biblical myth alone. The Stoics, after all, also believed in a golden age of innocency at the beginning of the world, and thought that the equality and liberty which their natural law enjoined, but which were beyond the possibilities of actual history, were realities of that blessed period. Furthermore every individual is inclined to give a chronological and historical version of the contrast between what he is and what he ought to be; for he regards the innocency of his childhood as a symbol and a reminder of his true nature. Yet the Biblical myth must be regarded as the primary source of the Christian belief in a chronological period in which man had a perfection which he has since lost.

2.6   The effect of this literalism has been to bring confusion into Christian thought on the relation of man's essential nature to his sinful condition. In Protestant thought it aggravated the tendency toward extravagant statements of man's depravity, and confused the effort to moderate such statements by the admission that some little power of justice remained to man. For the remnant of original perfection which was conceded to man was falsely identified with the capacity for "civil justice", a capacity which is as obviously corrupted by sin as any other human capacity. In Catholic thought, chronological literalism encouraged the definition of the state of original righteousness as a special supernatural gift, a *donum supernaturale* which was added to the *pura naturalia*, this is to the essential humanity which Adam had as man. In consequence the paradox – that sin is a corruption of man's true essence but not its destruction – is obscured in both Protestant and Catholic thought. In Catholicism the Fall means the loss of something which is not essential to man and does not therefore represent a corruption of his essence. In radical Protestantism the very image of God in man is believed to be destroyed. And when Protestant thought recoils from such extravagance, it looks for the remnant of man's original goodness in insignificant aspects of human behaviour.

2.7   The relation of man's essential nature to his sinful state cannot be solved within terms of the chronological version of the perfection before the Fall. It is, as it were, a vertical rather than horizontal relation. When the Fall is made an event in history rather than a symbol of an aspect of every historical moment in the life of man, the relation of evil to goodness in that moment is obscured.

2.8   It is impossible to do justice to the concept of the image of God and to the perfection of that image before the Fall without making a distinction between the essential nature of man and the virtue of conformity to that nature. Nothing can change the essential nature and structure, just as blindness of the eye does not remove the eye from the human anatomy. Not even the destruction of the eye can change the fact that the human anatomy requires two eyes. On the other hand the freedom of man creates the possibility of actions which are contrary to, and in defiance of, the requirements of this essential nature. This fact justifies the distinction between the essential struc-ture and nature, and the virtue of conformity to it. Man may lose this virtue and destroy the proper function of his nature, but he can do so only by availing himself of one of the elements in that nature, namely this freedom.

2.9   This fact prompted Irenaeus to distinguish between the image and the likeness of God upon the basis of Genesis I, 26, a distinction which persisted in Christian tradition until the Reformation questioned its exegetical validity. According to Irenaeus the Fall destroyed the likeness but not the image of God. (In Greek the homoiosis but not the eikon: in Latin the *similtudo* but not the *imago*). Luther was quite right in rejecting the theory from the stand-point of exegesis. The original text, "Let us make man in our image, after our likeness" represents no more than a common Hebraic parallelism. It certainly does not justify the later Catholic distinction between the *pura naturalia* and a *donum supernaturale*, the latter a special gift which God gave to man in addition to his natural endowment, a distinction which was reared upon Irenaeus' original differentiation. Nevertheless the distinction, properly limited and safeguarded, is helpful and even necessary.

2.10   It is important to distinguish between the essential nature of man and the virtue and perfection which would represent the normal expression of that nature. The essential nature of man contains two elements; and there are correspondingly two elements in the original perfection of man. To the essential nature of man belong, on the one hand, all his natural endowments and determinations, his physical and social impulses, his sexual and racial differentiations – in short his character as a creature imbedded in the natural order. On the other hand, his essential nature also includes the freedom of his spirit, his transcendence over natural process and finally his self-transcendence.

2.11   The virtue and perfection which correspond to the first element of his nature are usually designated as the natural law. It is the law which defines the proper performance of his functions, the normal harmony of his impulses and the normal social relation between himself and his fellows within the limitations of the natural order. Since every natural function of man is qualified by his freedom and since a "law" defining normality is necessary only because of his freedom, there is always an element of confusion in thus outlining a law of nature. It has nevertheless a tentative validity; for it distinguishes the obvious requirements of his nature as a creature in the natural order from the special requirements of his nature as free spirit.

2.12   The virtues which correspond to the second element in his nature, that is, to the freedom of his spirit, are analogous to the "theological virtues" of Catholic thought, namely faith, hope and love . . . Faith in the providence of God is a necessity of freedom because, without it, the anxiety of freedom tempts man to seek a self-sufficiency and self-mastery incompatible with his dependence upon forces which he does not control. Hope is a particular form of that faith. It deals with the future as a realm where infinite possibilities are realized, and which must be a realm of terror if it is not under the providence of God; for in that case it would stand under either a blind fate or pure caprice. The knowledge of God is thus not a supernatural grace which is a "further gift" beyond man's essential nature. It is the requirement of his nature as free spirit.

2.13   Love is both an independent requirement of this same freedom and a derivative of faith. Love is a requirement of freedom because the community to which man in impelled by his social nature is not possible to him merely upon the basis of his gregarious impulse. In his freedom and uniqueness each man stands outside of, and transcends, the cohesions of nature and the uniformities of mind which bind life to life. Since men are separated from one another by the uniqueness and individuality of each spirit, however closely they may be bound together by ties of nature, they cannot relate themselves to one another in terms which will do justice to both the bonds of nature and the freedom of their spirit if they are not related in terms of love. In love spirit meets spirit in the depth of the innermost essence of each. The cohesions of nature are qualified and transmuted by this relationship, for the other self ceases to be merely an object, serviceable to the self because of affinities of nature and reason. It is recognized as not merely object but as itself a subject, as a unique centre of life and purpose. This "I" and "Thou" relationship is impossible without the presupposition of faith for two reasons: (1) Without freedom from anxiety man is so enmeshed in the vicious circle of egocentricity, so concerned about himself, that he cannot release himself for the adventure of love. (2) Without relation to God, the world of freedom in which spirit must meet spirit is so obscured that human beings constantly sink to the level of things in the human imagination. The injunction, "love thy neighbour as thyself", is therefore properly preceded both by the commandment, "love the Lord thy God", and by the injunction, "be not anxious".

2.14   These ultimate requirements of the Christian ethic are
therefore not counsels of perfection or theological virtues
of the sort which merely completes an otherwise incom-
plete natural goodness or virtue. Nor can they be
subtracted from man without making his freedom a
source of sinful infection. They are indeed counsels of
perfection in the sense that sinful man lacks them and is
incapable of achieving them. But they are basic and not
supplementary requirements of his freedom.

2.15   This analysis of the matter leads to the conclusion that
sin neither destroys the structure by virtue of which man
is man, nor yet eliminates the sense of obligation towards
the essential nature of man, which is the remnant of his
perfection . . .

2.16   Against pessimistic theories of human nature which
affirm the total depravity of man it is important to assert
the continued presence in man of the *justitia originalis*, of
the law of love, as law and requirement. It is equally
important, in refutation of modern secular and Christian
forms of utopianism, to recognize that the fulfilment of
the law of love is no simple possibility. Love is the law of
freedom; but man is not completely free; and such
freedom as he has is corrupted by sin. All historic
schemes and structures of justice must take the contingencies of nature and history and the fact of sin into
consideration . . .

2.17   Just as Catholic rationalism makes too complete a
distinction between natural law and the *justitia originalis*,
it also tends to differentiate too completely between a
relative and absolute natural law. Nevertheless these
distinctions correspond to actual realities in the moral
experience, which modern secular and Christian utopianism disregards. The distinctions are too absolute because
it is never possible to define the limits of the force of sin
or of the ideal possibilities which transcend sin. One
cannot, by definition, determine where and when an inequality of nature or history must be accepted as ineluctable
fate and where it must be defied. Nor can one determine in
advance where and when tyranny and injustice must be

resisted, even if such resistance results in overt conflict. If the distinction between relative and absolute natural law is made too sharp (as it is in mediaeval theory) the inequality and conflict which the relative law allows are accepted too complacently. There are no precise distinctions either between relative and absolute natural law, as there are none between natural law and the law of love, for the simple reason that the freedom of spirit is so enmeshed in the necessities of nature, and the health and sickness of that freedom are so involved in each other, that it is not possible to make rules isolating certain aspects of nature and sin without having them disturbed by the claims of the law of love as the requirement of freedom.

2.18   Yet it is better to make these distinctions, however arbitrary, than to dispense with them entirely as modern utopians do. The Christian utopians think they can dispense with all stuctures and rules of justice simply by fulfilling the law of love. They do not realize that the law of love stands on the edge of history and not in history; that it represents an ultimate and not an immediate possibility. They think they might usher in the Kingdom of God if only they could persuade men not to resist tyranny and thus avoid conflict. They do not recognize to what degree justice in a sinful world is actually maintained by a tension of competitive forces, which is always in danger of degenerating into overt conflict, but without which there would be only the despotic peace of the subordination of the will of the weak to the will of the strong.

2.19   The secular utopians of the eighteenth century added the love which transcends all law to the liberty and equality of a transcendent and absolute natural law, and fondly imagined that 'liberty, equality and fraternity' constituted the law of 'nature' in the exact sense of the word. They thought that these ultimate possibilities of human freedom transcending all history were not only simple possibilities of history but that they were actualities of nature as given. The combined influence of religious and secular utopianism has brought confusion into the whole problem of justice in the modern bourgeois-liberal world, and incidentally complicated the problem of defending the genuine values of this world against the peril of a barbarism which has grown out of the decadence of our civilization.

2.20   Since Christianity measures the stature of man in terms of a freedom which transcends the necessities of nature but also finds that freedom corrupted by sin, it obviously has no simple answer to the question, whether the original righteousness, the perfection before the Fall, which sinful man retains as law, can finally become a realized fact of history.

EXTRACT 3

COPLESTON

Objections to natural law

3.1   Aquinas' theory of the natural moral law gives rise to a number of questions. I can comment, however, only very briefly on a few selected questions. And I begin with the one which is perhaps most likely to present itself to the reader's mind.

3.2   Aquinas believed that actions which are contrary to the natural moral law are not wrong simply because God prohibits them; they are prohibited by God because they are wrong. Suicide is wrong and eating meat on Friday when one is bound by the ecclesiastical law of abstinence is also wrong. But while there is nothing wrong in itself in eating meat on Friday, so that to do so is wrong only when and because it is forbidden, suicide is contrary to the natural moral law and so is wrong in itself. Ecclesiastical precepts like the law of abstinence on Fridays can be suspended or changed, but the natural moral law in unalterable. It is true that Aquinas distinguishes between primary and secondary precepts, derived from the first, and says that the last can be 'changed' for special reasons in a few particular cases. But what he means is that in some particular cases the circumstances of an act may be such that it no longer falls under the class of actions prohibited by the precept. For instance, we can say in general that if someone entrusts his property to us for safe keeping and asks for it back we ought to return it. But no sensible man would say that if someone entrusts us with a knife or a revolver and asks for it back when he is in a state of homicidal mania we are obliged to return it. In its general form, however, the precept remains valid. And we can say with truth that Aquinas believed in a set of unalterable moral precepts.

3.3 The question arises, however, whether this theory is compatible with the empirical fact that different people and different social groups have held divergent moral convictions. Do not the empirical facts suggest that the moral law is not unalterable but changeable? Or, to use the value-language, do not the empirical facts suggest that values are historically relative and that there are no universal and absolute values? Believing in a human nature which is constant Aquinas was led to postulate an unchangeable moral law; but some of the precepts which he regarded as forming part of its content have not been regarded by many people in the past and are not now regarded by many people as moral precepts at all. Is it not reasonable to conclude that Aquinas simply canonized, as it were, the moral convictions and standards of his time or at least of the society to which he belonged?

3.4 This is a far-reaching problem, and I must content myself with making the following relevant point, namely that differences in moral convictions do not by them-selves constitute a disproof of the theory that there is an unchangeable moral law. For there might be an un-changeable moral law and at the same time varying degrees of insight into the content of this law, these differences being explicable in terms of the influence of a variety of empirical factors. To use the value-language, there might be objective and absolute values and at the same time different degrees of insight into these values. I do not mean to imply either that the existence of an unchanging moral law was for Aquinas an uncertain hypothesis or that the explicability of differences in moral conviction on the theory that there is such a law proves of itself that the theory is true. My point is that differences of opinion about moral precepts and moral values do not constitute a proof of the relativist position. And this point is one that should be taken into consideration in any discussion of the problem.

3.5   Aquinas himself was not ignorant of the fact that different groups have held different moral convictions. According to him all men are aware of the most fundamental principles in their most general form. All men would agree that in some sense good is to be pursued and evil avoided. If a man denies this principle he is probably denying not the principle itself but that what another man or a given society calls good is good. But when we come to less general and more particular conclusions, derived from the fundamental principles, ignorance is certainly possible. 'In the case of some the reason is blinded by passion or by bad habits or by physical conditions. For example, according the Julius Caesar robbery used not to be considered wrong among the Germans, although it is expressly against the natural law'. (i.e. II.6 *above*). A *fortiori* there can be differences of opinion about the application of precepts to particular cases. Conscience may be erroneous, whether through our own fault or through some cause for which we are not responsible. And if our conscience tells us that we ought to perform a particular act, it is our moral duty to perform it. 'Every conscience, whether it is right or wrong, whether it concerns things evil in themselves or things morally indifferent, obliges us to act in such a way that he who acts against his conscience sins' (*Quodlibetum*, 3, 27). This does not mean that there is no such thing as right reason and no such thing as an objectively correct moral conscience; but ignorance and mistakes are possible in moral matters, and the nearer we come to particulars the greater is the field for error.

3.6 But though the reader may be prepared to admit that differences in moral convictions do not by themselves alone constitute a disproof of Aquinas' theory of an unalterable moral law, he may easily feel that the latter's whole approach to the subject of moral precepts is extremely artificial and excessively rationalistic. For Aquinas talks as though people derive or deduce less general from more general moral precepts and then proceed to apply these precepts to particular actions. But surely, it may be said, this picture does not represent the facts. Moral precepts seem to be ultimately reducible to the expression of feelings of approval or disapproval of certain actions or of certain types of action. True, we do enunicate general moral precepts; and moral philosophers have not unnaturally tried to rationalize their own moral convictions or those of the group or society to which they belonged. But feeling comes first: it is the whole basis of ethics. It may indeed appear that ethical disputes can be settled by rational argument, and in a certain sense they can sometimes be so settled. For example, if two men can agree on a definition of murder they can discuss in a rational manner whether the action of killing someone who is dying from a painful and incurable disease falls under the definition or not. Each man points out to the other features of the action in question which he thinks that the other has overlooked, and it is at any rate possible that in the end one will succeed in convincing the other. But rational argument is possible only when there is already a certain measure of moral agreement. Is it not a notorious fact that if two people disagree about fundamental moral issues or defend sharply opposed sets of values, neither can be convinced simply by the arguments advanced by the other? They will either agree to differ or they will end in anger and even abuse. Moreover, the function of any arguments which may be advanced by one of them seems to be that of facilitating a change of feeling or of emotional attitude. And perhaps the same can be said of discussions concerning the moral quality of particular actions or types of action when these discussions cannot be reduced to a quasi-logical problem of classification. If two men discuss the question whether so-called 'mercy killing' is right or wrong, the one maintaining that it is right, the other that it is wrong, the function of drawing attention to aspects of the action which the one man believes to have been overlooked by the other seems to be that of facilitating a change of emotive reaction in the other. The one man desires to substitute in the other man a feeling of approval for a feeling of disapproval or *vice versa*, as the case may be; and the arguments and appeals to reason which are employed are techniques used to facilitate this change of emotive response. *In fine*, morality is 'more properly felt than judged of', to use Hume's words (*Treatise*, 3, 1, 2).

3.7   It can hardly be denied that Aquinas' language sometimes seems to imply an extremely rationalistic interpretation of the way in which people form their moral judgements. But we have to look at what he means by the statements which he makes. He compares, for example, the precept that good is to be pursued and evil avoided with the propositon that the whole is greater than any one of its parts. And while he thought that this proposition is known to all human beings once they have had experience of material things he did not mean to say that every human being explicitly enunciates it to himself in so many words, even though he would certainly assent to it if it were proposed to him. 'In the cognitive powers there can be inchoate habits ... And the understanding of (firšt) principles is termed a natural habit. For it is owing to the very nature of the intellectual soul that once a man knows what is a whole and what is a part he knows that every whole is greater than any one of its parts, though he cannot know what is a whole and what is a part except through ideas derived from images' (*S. T.*, Ia, IIae, 51,1). Directly a human being has experience of material wholes he recognizes immediately the relation between whole and part, and that he knows this can be seen by the fact that he never assumes that any part is greater than the whole of which it is a part. But it does not necessarily follow that he ever says to himself in so many words that a whole is greater than any one of its parts. Similarly, a human being obtains the idea of good, of a thing considered as perfecting or as satisfying his nature in some way, only through experience of actual objects of desire and sources of satisfaction. But because of his innate inclinations to the good in this sense he immediately apprehends it as something to be pursued, while he apprehends evil, considered as that which is opposed to his nature and natural inclinations, as something to be avoided. The fact that he does apprehend the good or the perfection as something to be pursued and the evil, that which is opposed to or thwarts his natural inclinations, as something to be shunned and avoided is shown by the whole of his conduct. For every human being naturally shuns whatever appears to him as opposed to his nature. But it does not necessarily follow that he ever explicitly enunciates to himself the proposition that good is to be pursued and evil avoided. One may be tempted to say that all this belongs to the instinctive level and the level of feeling rather than the level of rational apprehension. But Aquinas would doubtless comment that a man does not shun death, for example, simply in the same way that an animal can be said to do so. For he shuns it not only instinctively but because and in so far as he apprehends it with his reason as destructive of his nature. And since he shuns it and avoids it as evil, knowledge that evil is to be shunned and avoided is implicitly presupposed. Though we could have no idea of evil except through experience of things opposed to our natural inclinations, apprehension of the principle that evil is to be avoided is logically presupposed by recognition of the fact that this particular thing is to be avoided because it is evil.

3.8   As regards deduction, Aquinas did not think that we can deduce the propositon that to have sexual intercourse with someone else's wife is wrong from the precept that good is to be pursued and evil avoided simply by contemplating, as it were, this latter precept. We can no

more do this than we can deduce from the principle of
non-contradiction the proposition that a thing which is
white all over cannot at the same time be red all over. We
obtain our ideas of whiteness and redness from other
sources than an analysis of the principle of non-
contradiction. At the same time we reject the proposition
that a thing can be simultaneousely white all over and red
all over precisely because it involves a contradiction.
Similarly, we do not obtain our ideas of other people and
of wives and of sexual intercourse simply by analysing
the precept that good is to be pursued and evil avoided.
But once we have obtained those ideas we reject, if we do
reject, the proposition that it is right to have sexual
intercourse with someone else's wife because we
apprehend actions of this sort as being evil. The word
'deduction', therefore, can be very misleading; and what
Aquinas actually says is that other precepts of the natural
law are 'founded on' or 'based on' the precept that good is
to be done and evil avoided. The concrete good for man
can be known only by reflection on human nature as
known in experience.

3.9   It has been said above that we reject, 'if we do reject',
the proposition that it is right to have sexual intercourse
with someone else's wife because we apprehend actions
of this sort as being evil. As we have seen, Aquinas
thought that the nearer we come to particulars the more
possible becomes ignorance or error concerning the
objective good for man, and so concerning the particular
precepts of the natural moral law. But some particular
types of action are practically always apprehended as evil,
as opposed in some way or other to human nature. For
example, even at the lowest level of civilization some acts
will be immediately 'felt' to be destructive of social
cohesion in the group and so opposed to human nature
considered under its social aspect. And they will awaken
disapprobation in a quasi-instinctive manner. I have put
the word 'felt' in inverted commas and I have spoken of a
'quasi-instinctive' manner because I think that while
Aquinas might agree that the term 'feel' has a use in

drawing attention to the difference between, say, a primitive man's apprehension of an act as evil and a moral philosopher's reflective appreciation of its moral quality he would still maintain that the primitive man mentally apprehends the act as evil and that the term 'feel' is inappropriate in so far as it suggests the absence of any mental activity.

3.10 One can put the matter in this way perhaps. Aquinas thought that all men share some very vague ideas about the good for man, precisely because they are men and possess certain natural tendencies and inclinations in common. For instance, men see that knowledge of the truths required for life should be sought for. And if one wishes to draw attention to the immediacy of the perception one might perhaps say that they 'feel' this. But Aquinas would doubtless insist that mental activity is involved and that some word like 'apprehend' or 'understand' is more appropriate.

3.11 But when it comes to apprehending what are the truths necessary for life and, in general, to determining in a concrete way what is the good for man and to forming moral judgements which are less general than what Aquinas calls the primary principles of the natural law in their widest form, there is room for prolonged reflection and discussion. There is room also for the intervention of a variety of factors other than rational reflection, which can exercise an important influence in the formation of man's moral outlook and set of determinate values. And these factors can be internal, physiological and psychological, as well as external, like upbringing and social environment.

3.12 Finally, when there is question of applying principles to individual cases, of deciding whether a given action belongs to this class or that class, and is right or wrong, Aquinas recognizes (cf. his commentary on the *Ethics*, 2, c.2, *lectio* 2) that though the moral philosopher can provide some help, by drawing attention, for example, to different features of the action, he cannot settle a person's perplexity by a process of sheer logical deduction.

Ultimately a man has to make his own decision. And Aquinas observes that a man's actual decision may be perfectly correct even though the abstract problem has not been satisfactorily settled. Perhaps we might say that in such cases the man 'feels' that the action is right or wrong, as the case may be, in order to emphasize the difference between the immediacy of the judgement and a piece of logical or mathematical deduction. But Aquinas would doubtless say that the virtue of 'prudence' often enables a man to discern the objective moral quality of an action even when he is unable to give adequate reasons, which would satisfy a moral philosopher, for saying that the action is right or wrong. An action is right or wrong for Aquinas in virtue of its relation to the good for man, and this relation is discerned by the mind, even though the immediacy of the discerning may be such as to incline one to use the word 'feeling'. And the (or at least a) fundamental difference between Aquinas' theory and a purely emotive moral theory is that the former asserts an objective and determinable relationship in virtue of which actions are good or bad, right or wrong, whereas the latter does not.

3.13   In this section I have mentioned ideas suggested by the relativist and emotive theories of ethics. My purpose in doing so, however, was clarificatory rather than polemical, and to avoid misunderstanding I want to explain this point. It was not my intention to 'expound' these theories; and therefore I have carefully avoided mentioning the name of any philosopher save that of Hume, who was mentioned as the author of a proposition which it is usual to quote on these occasions. Nor was it my intention to refute the theories by means of Aquinas' philosophy. My purpose was simply that of using some ideas suggested by these theories to clarify the latter's position. The chief plank on which the relativistic theory of morals rests is probably the empirical fact that different people have held divergent views about moral matters. And as facts are facts whatever conclusions may be drawn from them, it is important to ask whether Aquinas had any idea of these facts and whether his ethical theory is capable of accounting for them or of allowing for them. Similarly, in the moral life of ordinary people deduction, as this is understood in logic and mathematics, does not seem to play any very conspicuous role, whereas something that might plausibly be described as 'feeling' appears to be an important factor. It is therefore a pertinent question to ask whether Aquinas thought that everyone forms his or her moral convictions by a process of logical deduction and whether his theory can account for the factor of immediacy in our moral and valuational judgements. In other words, my purpose was simply that of making a brief contribution to the clarification of Aquinas' position with the aid of ideas suggested by later ethical theories.

EXTRACT 4

FLETCHER

Situation ethics

4.1   A third approach, in between legalism and antinomian unprincipledness, is situation ethics. (To jump from one polarity to the other would be only to go from the frying pan to the fire). The situationist enters into every decision-making situation fully armed with the ethical maxims of his community and its heritage, and he treats them with respect as illuminators of his problems. Just the same he is prepared in any situation to compromise them or set them aside *in the situation* if love seems better served by doing so.

4.2   Situation ethics goes part of the way with natural law, by accepting reason as the instrument of moral judgement, while rejecting the notion that the good is 'given' in the nature of things, objectively. It goes part of the way with Scriptural law by accepting revelation as the source of the norm while rejecting all 'revealed' norms or laws but the one command – to love God in the neighbor. The situationist follows a moral law or violates it

according to love's need. For example, "Almsgiving is a
good thing *if*. . ." The situationist never says, "Almsgiving is a good thing. Period!" His decisions are hypothetical, not categorical. Only the commandment to love is categorically good. "Owe no one anything, except to love one another." (Rom. 13:8). If help to an indigent only pauperizes and degrades him, the situationist refuses a handout and finds some other way. He makes no law out of Jesus' "Give to every one who begs from you." It is only one step from that kind of Biblicist literalism to the kind that causes women in certain sects to refuse blood transfusions even if death results – even if they are carrying a quickened fetus that will be lost too. The legalist says that even if he tells a man escaped from an asylum where his intended victim is, if he finds and murders him, at least only one sin has been committed (murder), not two (lying as well)!

4.3   As Brunner puts it, "The basis of the Divine Command is always the same, but its content varies with varying circumstances." Therefore, the "error of casuistry does not lie in the fact that it indicates the infinite variety of forms which the Command of love may assume; its error consists in deducing particular laws from a universal law . . . as though all could be arranged beforehand . . . Love, however, is free from all this predefinition" (*The Divine Imperative*, pp. 132ff.). We might say, from the situationist's perspective, that it is possible to derive general "principles" from whatever is the one and only universal law (*agape* for Christians, something else for others), but not laws or rules. We cannot milk universals from a universal!

4.4   William Temple put it this way: "Universal obligation attaches not to particular judgments of conscience but to conscientiousness. What acts are right may depend on circumstances . . . but there is an absolute obligation to will whatever may on each occasion be right". (*Nature, Man and God*, p.405). Our obligation is relative *to* the situation, but obligation *in* the situation is absolute. We are only "obliged" to tell the truth, for example, if the situation calls for it; if a murderer asks us his victim's whereabouts, our duty might be to lie. There is in situation ethics an absolute element and an element of calculation, as Alexander Miller once pointed out. But it would be better to say it has an absolute *norm* and a calculating method. There is weight in the old saying that what is needed is "faith, hope and charity". We have to find out what is "fitting" to be truly ethical, to use H.R. Niebuhr's word for it in his *The Responsible Self.* Situation ethics aims at a contextual appropriateness – not the "good" or the "right" but the *fitting.*

4.5   A cartoon in a fundamentalist magazine once showed Moses scowling, holding his stone tablet with its graven laws, all ten, and an eager stonecutter saying to him, "Aaron said perhaps you'd let us reduce them to 'Act responsibly in love.'" This was meant as a dig at the situationists and the new morality, but the legalistic humour in it merely states exactly what situation ethics calls for! With Dietrich Bonhoeffer we say, "Principles are only tools in God's hands, soon to be thrown away as unserviceable". (*Ethics*, p.51).

4.6   One competent situationist, speaking to students, explained the position this way. Rules are "like 'Punt on fourth down,' or 'Take a pitch when the count is three balls.' These rules are part of the wise player's know-how, and distinguish him from the novice. But they are not unbreakable. The best players are those who know when to ignore them. In the game of bridge, for example, there is a useful rule which says 'Second hand low'. But have you ever played with anyone who followed the rule slavishly? You say to him (in exasperation), 'Partner, why didn't you play your ace? We could have set the hand'. And he replies, unperturbed, 'Second hand low!' What is wrong? The same thing that was wrong when Kant gave information to the murderer. He forgot the purpose of the game . . . He no longer thought of winning the hand, but of being able to justify himself by invoking the rule."

4.7   This practical temper of the activist or *verb-minded* decision maker, versus contemplative *noun-mindedness*, is a major Biblical rather than Hellenistic trait. In Abraham Heschel's view, "The insistence upon generalization at the price of a total disregard of the particular and concrete is something which would be alien to prophetic thinking. Prophetic words are never detached from the concrete, historic situation. Theirs is not a timeless, abstract message; it always refers to an actual situation. The general is given in the particular and the verification of the abstract is in the concrete." (*God in Search of Man: A Philosophy of Judaism*, p. 204). A "leap of faith" is an action decision rather than a leap of thought, for a man's faith is a hypothesis that he takes seriously enough to act on and live by.

4.8   There are various names for this approach: situationism, contextualism, occasionalism, circumstantialism, even actualism. These labels indicate, of course, that the core of the ethic they describe is a healthy and primary awareness that 'circumstances alter cases' – i.e., that in actual problems of conscience the situational variables are to be weighed as heavily as the normative or 'general' constants.

4.9   The situational factors are so primary that we may even say "circumstances alter rules and principles." It is said that when Gertrude Stein lay dying she declared, "It is better to ask questions than to give answers, even good answers." This is the temper of situation ethics. It is empirical, fact-minded, data conscious, inquiring. It is antimoralistic as well as antilegalistic, for it is sensitive to variety and complexity. It is neither simplistic nor perfectionist. It is "casuistry" (case-based) in a constructive and nonpejorative sense of the word. We should perhaps call it "neocasuistry". Like classical casuistry, it is case-focused and concrete, concerned to bring Christian imperatives into practical operation. But unlike classical casuistry, this neocasuistry repudiates any attempt to anticipate or prescribe real-life decisions in their existential particularity. It works with two guidelines from Paul: "The written code kills, but the Spirit gives life" (II Cor.

3:6), and "For the whole law is fulfilled in one word,'You shall love your neighbour as yourself'" (Gal.; 5:14). . .

4.10   *Christian* situation ethics has only one norm or principle or law (call it what you will) that is binding and unexceptionable, always good and right regardless of the circumstances. That is "love" – the *agape* of the summary commandment to love God and the neighbor. Everything else without exception, all laws and rules and principles and ideals and norms, are only *contingent,* only valid *if they happen* to serve love in any situation. Christian situation ethics is not a system or program of living according to a code, but an effort to relate love to a world of relativities through a casuistry obedient to love. It is the strategy of love. This strategy denies that there are, as Sophocles thought, any unwritten immutable laws of heaven, agreeing with Bultmann that all such notions are idolatrous and a demonic pretension.

4.11   In non-Christian situation ethics some other highest good or *summum bonum* will, of course, take love's place as the one and only standard – such as self-realization in the ethics of Aristotle. But the *Christian* is neighbor-centered first and last. Love is for people, not for principles; i.e., it is personal – and therefore when the impersonal universal conflicts with the personal particular, the latter prevails in situation ethics. Because of its mediating position, prepared to act on moral laws or in spite of them, the antinomians will call situationists soft legalists, and legalists will call them cryptoantinomians.

4.12   It is necessary to insist that situation ethics is willing to make full and respectful use of principles, to be treated as maxims but not as laws or precepts. We might call it "principled relativism". To repeat the term used above, principles or maxims or general rules are *illuminators*. But they are not *directors*. The classic rule of moral theology has been to follow laws but to do it *as much as possible* according to love and according to reason (*secundum caritatem et secundum rationem*). Situation ethics, on the other hand, calls upon us to keep law in a subservient place, so that *only* love and reason really count when the chips are down!

4.13   Situationists have no invariable obligation to what are sometimes called "middle axioms", logically derived as normative propositions based on love. An example of what is meant is the proposition that love of the neighbor in practice *usually* means putting human rights before property rights. The term "middle axiom", first used used by J.H. Oldham and William Temple, and notably by John C. Bennett in America, is well-meant but unfortunate, since an axiom is a self-validating, nonderivative proposition and it cannot stand in the "middle" between something logically prior to it and a subsequent derivative. Middle-axiom theorists must beware lest they, too, slip into the error of deriving universals from universals.

4.14   There are usually two rules of reason used in moral inquiry. One is "internal consistency", and nobody has any quarrel with it – a proposition ought not to contradict itself. The other is "external consistence" (analogy), the principle that what applies in one case should apply in all similar cases. It is around this second canon that the differences arise. Antinomians reject analogy altogether, with their doctrine of radical particularity. Situationists ask, very seriously, if there ever are enough cases enough alike to validate a law or to support anything more than a cautious generalisation. In Edmond Cahn's puckish phrase, "Every case is like every other case, and no two cases are alike."

4.15   There is no real quarrel here between situationism and an ethic of principles, unless the principles are hardened into laws. Bishop Robinson says: "Such an ethic [situationism] cannot but rely, in deep humility, upon guiding rules, upon the cumulative experience of one's own and other people's obedience. It is this bank of experience which gives us our working rules of 'right' and 'wrong', and without them we could not but flounder." (*Honest to God*, pp. 119-120). Nevertheless, in situation ethics even the most revered principles may be thrown aside if they conflict in any concrete case with love. Even Karl Barth, who writes vehemently of "absolutely wrong" actions, allows for what he calls the *ultima ratio*, the outside chance that love in a particular situation might override the absolute. The instance he gives is abortion.

4.16   Using terms made popular by Tillich and others, we may say that Christian situationism is a method that proceeds, so to speak, from (1) its one and only law, *agape* (love), to (2) the *sophia* (wisdom) of the church and culture, containing many "general rules" of more or less reliability, to (3) the *kairos* (moment of decision, the fullness of time) in which *the responsible self in the situation* decides whether the *sophia* can serve love there, or not. This is the situational strategy in capsule form. To legalists it will seem to treat the *sophia* without enough reverence and obedience; to antinomians it will appear befuddled and "inhibited" by the *sophia*.

4.17   Legalists make an idol of the *sophia*, antinomians repudiate it, situationists *use* it. They cannot give to any principle less than love more than tentative consideration, for they know, with Dietrich Bonhoeffer, "The question of the good is posed and is decided in the midst of each definite, yet unconcluded, unique and transient situation of our lives, in the midst of our living relationships with men, things, institutions and powers, in other words in their midst of our historical existence." (*Ethics*, p.185) And Bonhoeffer, of course, is a modern Christian ethicist who was himself executed for trying to kill, even *murder*, Adolf Hitler – so far did he go as a situationist...

ABORTION: A SITUATION

4.18   In 1962 a patient in a state mental hospital raped a fellow patient, an unmarried girl ill with a radical schizophrenic psychosis. The victim's father, learning what had happened, charged the hospital with culpable negligence and requested that an abortion to end the unwanted pregnancy be performed at once, in an early stage of the embryo. The staff and administrators of the hospital refused to do so, on the ground that the criminal law forbids all abortion except "therapeutic" ones when the mother's life is at stake – because the *moral* law, it is supposed, holds that any interference with an embryo after fertilization is murder, i.e., the taking of an innocent human being's life.

4.19   Let's relate the three ethical approaches to this situation. The rape has occurred and the decisional question is: May we rightly (licitly) terminate this pregnancy, begun in act of force and violence by a mentally unbalanced rapist upon a frightened, mentally sick girl? Mother and embryo are apparently healthy on all the usual counts.

4.20   The legalists would say NO. Their position is that killing is absolutely wrong, inherently evil. It is permissible only as self-defence and in military service, which is held to be presumptive self-defense or justifiable homicide. If the mother's life is threatened, abortion is therefore justified, but for no other reasons. (Many doctors take an elastic view of "life" and thereby justify abortions to save a patients *mental* life as well as physical.) Even in cases where they justify it, it is only *excused* – it is still held to be inherently evil. Many Protestants hold this view, and some humanists.

4.21   Catholic moral theology goes far beyond even the rigid legalism of the criminal law, absolutizing their prohibition of abortion *absolutely*, by denying all exceptions and calling even therapeutic abortion wrong. (They allow killing in self-defense against malicious, i.e. deliberate, aggressors but not in self-defense against innocent, i.e., unintentional aggressors.) Thus, if it is a tragic choice of the mother's life or the baby's, as can happen in rare cases, neither can be saved.

4.22   To this ethical nightmare legalism replies: "It is here that the Church appears merciless, but she is not. It is her logic which is merciless; and she promises that if the logic is followed the woman will receive a reward far greater than a number of years of life." Inexplicably, shockingly, Dietrich Bonhoeffer says the same thing: "The life of the mother is in the hand of God, but the life of the child is arbitrarily extinguished. The question whether the life of the mother or the life of the child is of greater value can hardly be a matter for human decision." (*Ethics*, p.150)

4.23 The antinomians – but who can predict what *they* would say? Their ethic is by its nature and definition outside the reach of even generalities. We can only guess, not unreasonably, that if the antinomian lives by a love norm, he will be apt to favor abortion in this case.

4.24 The situationists, if their norm is the Christian commandment to love the neighbor, would almost certainly *in this case*, favor abortion and support the girl's father's request. (Many purely humanistic decision makers are of the same mind about abortion following rape, and after incest too.) They would in all likelihood favor abortion for the sake of the patient's physical and mental health, not only if it were needed to save her life. It is even likely they would favor abortion for the sake of the victim's self-respect or reputation or happiness or simply on the ground that no *unwanted and unintended* baby should ever be born.

4.25 They would, one hopes, reason that it is *not* killing because there is no person or human life in an embryo at an early stage of pregnancy (Aristotle and St. Thomas held that opinion), or even if it *were* killing, it would not be murder because it is self-defense against, in this case, not one but *two* aggressors. First there is the rapist, who being insane was morally and legally innocent, and then there is the "innocent" embryo which is continuing the ravisher's original aggression! Even self-defense legalism would have allowed the girl to kill her attacker, no matter that he was innocent in the forum of conscience because of his madness. The embryo is no more innocent, no less an aggressor or unwelcome invader! Is not the most loving thing possible (the right thing) in this case a responsible decision to terminate the pregnancy?

4.26 What think ye?

EXTRACT 5

RAMSEY

Agapism beyond situation ethics

5.1   William K. Frankena (*Faith and Philosophy* ed. Alvin
Plantinga) chides theologians for failing to say clearly
what they mean by Christian normative ethics. He
believes that 'its theological proponents may be selling
Christian ethics short by their manner of expounding and
defending it' (p. 204). A philosopher, he writes, reading
in the literature of Christian ethics, 'is bound to be struck,
not only by the topics discussed and the claims made,
but by the relative absence of careful definition, clear
statement, or cogent and rigorous argument, as these are
judged by the standards with which he is familiar in his
own field (even if he does not himself always conform to
them)' (p. 203). Frankena wants to do something toward
remedying the situation. He proposes to do this by again
indicating positions 'that are possible'. With a number of
wry comments about his own proclivity for multiplying
categories and upon the fact that like all mankind he 'has
sought out many inventions', he proposes a dozen or
more types when you take account of the combinations
that are possible. . . a somewhat simplified review of his
suggestions may assist us in identifying or projecting an
unfinished agenda for Christian normative ethics. . .

5.2   (1.) *Pure Agapism*
This general position 'assigns to the "law of love" the
same position that utilitarianism assigns to the principle
of utility; it allows no *basic* ethical principles other than or
independent of "the law of love" ' (p. 205.) In order that
the point of Frankena's suggestions for the doing of
constructive Christian ethics be not blunted, it should be
noted that his typology sits loose within the terminology
he employs, and would be repeated if a Christian ethicist
judges that it is better to use some other root word in
place of *agape*. Someone may object to using love as the
'primitive idea' in Christian ethics; or someone may

object to calling love a 'principle'. To them Frankena replies: '. . . What interests me here is not so much the question whether love or the love-command is itself a rule or principle as the question whether there are *other* rules or principles which do not mention love, what their status is, and how they are related to love (whether this is conceived as a principle or not). . . Some take faith or commitment to God as the basic virtue or posture of Christian ethics, rather than love, but even then most of what I say will hold with "faith" or "commitment to God" substituted where I say "love"' (p. 206).

5.3   *Pure Agapism*, which allows no *basic* ethical principles other than or independent of love, may take four forms:

5.4   (a) *Pure Act-Agapism.* This view holds that 'one is to discover or decide what one's right or duty in a particular situation is solely by confronting one's loving will with the facts of that situation. . .' (p.211). The facts of other similar situations, or generalisations drawn from such situations, or from previous moments of loving obedience, are simply irrelevant or misleading. This is 'circumstance' or 'situational' ethics in its purest form. This view, of course, may be formulated without using '*agape*': it holds that 'each moral decision about what to do is to be a direct function of faith,... or the experience of God together with a knowledge of the facts of the case, with no other ethical principles coming into the matter' (p. 205).

5.5   (b) *Summary Rule Agapism* or *Modified Act-Agapism.* Here I deliberately reverse the sequence of Frankena's two expressions for this position, in order to emphasise and make more prominent its reliance on 'summary rules'. This view holds that there are rules of conduct. These rules are summaries of past experience, perhaps of past acts of loving obedience; but 'it cannot allow that a rule (or principle) may ever be followed in a situation when it seems to conflict with what love dictates in that situation. For, if rules are to be followed only in so far as they are helpful as aids to love, they cannot constrain or constrict love in any way' (p. 212). We have had an example of this position under scrutiny in so far as Robinson modifies his act-agapism to include a considerable concern for 'working rules' or in so far as his 'working rules' are not intended and cannot be shown to be rules that have general validity. Frankena himself says that perhaps some of the so-called contextualists or 'circumstance' moralists actually belong in this category; and he cites Joseph Sittler's *The Structure of Christian Ethics* as an example.

5.6   (c) *Pure Rule-Agapism.* This view maintains that 'we are always to tell what we are to do in particular situations by referring to a set of rules, and that what rules are to prevail and be followed is to be determined by seeing what rules (not what acts) best or most fully embody love'. (p. 212).

5.7   To these three types of pure agapism it should at once be added that there is a fourth classification:

5.8   (d) *Combinations* of Act-Agapism and Rule-Agapism; or combinations of Act-Agapism, Summary Rule Agapism and Rule-Agapism. *Vide*: John A.T. Robinson. This final type of pure agapism arises from the fact that Act-Agapism may be believed to apply in certain kinds of particular cases or situations while Rule-Agapism applies to other kinds of situations or moral problems. (Someone *might* say, for example, that Act-Agapism or its modification into Summary Rule Agapism govern private morality, while Pure Rule Agapism to a very great extent governs public morality or social ethics.) Combinations also arise from the fact that Summary Rule Agapism may be believed to be the correct interpretation of certain principles of conduct, while Pure Rule Agapism is required for an adequate understanding of certain other principles. It would seem, in fact, that if a Christian ethicist is going to be a Pure Agapist he would find this fourth possibility to be the most fruitful one, and most in accord with the freedom of *agape* both to act through the firmest principles and to act if need be without them...

5.9   A set of basic questions that should be raised concerns the nature of the decision in Christian ethics (if choice must be made) between Summary Rule and Pure Rule Agapism. If one takes the latter viewpoint, he must say, for example:

5.10   'Keeping-promises-always is love-fulfilling'. This will be a principle that has general validity even if it is a derived or secondary principle. It is one of those 'classes of things' of which Bishop Robinson said that it is so inconceivable they could ever express love that for the Christian they can never by right. Breaking-promises is wrong however, *for this reason*, that it is never love-fulfilling. Moreover, love itself has entered and will continue to enter into the determination of the meaning of the promise-keeping that is enjoined because this will always be love-fulfilling, even as it helps to define the meaning of the prohibited breaches of promise which can never express love.

5.11   In contrast, Summary Rule Agapism will say: 'Keeping promises is "generally" love-fulfilling.' The difference, according to Frankena, is that according to Pure Rule Agapism 'we may and sometimes must obey a rule in a particular situation even though the action it calls for is seen not to be what love itself would directly require'; while proponents of Summary Rule Agapism 'cannot allow that a rule may ever be followed in a particular situation when following it is known not to have the best possible (or love-fulfilling) consequences in this particular case'. (pp. 212 & 208).

5.12   This draws the contrast too sharply, and in a way that would require a Christian to govern his actions if by rules at all by summary rules only, since he should always do what love requires. Perhaps those Christian ethicists who endorse acts or summary rules only have a similar if inarticulate understanding of the nature of Pure Rule Agapism. To correct Frankena will be to correct them also. It will be to join the issue where it should be joined, and possibly in some combination of Summary and Pure Rule Agapism, to establish the fact that *Pure Agapism* may take two possible forms each of which *equally* may be expressions of love in that very decision to be made, i.e.

in the novel and exceptional or in the ruled action to be performed. There may be kinds of situations or kinds of principles in which love implies rules summarising love's past obedience or experience and there may be situations or principles in which love implies rules that have general validity. The discussion is prejudiced from the very beginning if Pure Rule Agapism is defined in such fashion that this means that a Christian should obey a rule 'even though the action it calls for is seen not to be what love itself would directly require'. That would be to do less or something other than love requires.

5.13   I cannot speak for the pure rule utilitarian, or for how philosophers are accustomed to speak about rules. But the Christian does not believe that he lives in a world populated by rules, or that there is a 'general subject' of moral agency acting in accord with these rules, or that he should tell what he should do in particular situations (as Frankena seems to suggest) *by referring to a set of rules* and choosing from among them those that are to be followed by seeing what rules best or most fully embody love.

5.14   The Pure Rule Agapist does not follow the rule thus selected even when he knows very well that this leads to particular actions that do not embody love as well as would other actions that he might have performed.

5.15   Pure Rule Agapism, if there is such a position in Christian normative ethics, proceeds rather the other way around. It begins with persons and then devolves or discerns the rules. And yet, I believe, it can and may and must arrive at more than summary rules. There is such a thing as Pure Rule Agapism, and this covers a good part of the moral decisions and problems in the midst of which the Christian life must find its direction. The Christian – and this includes the Pure Rule Agapist – starts with people and not rules. He starts with the multiple claims and needs of his neighbours for whom Christ died. If then, among the directives in which love manifests its direction and service there are any that are discovered to have general validity, this would precisely mean that when a man omits to act in accord with these rules or principles or when he acts contrary to them he would fail to do what love requires in that situation and would act contrary to the requirement of love in that situation. Starting with persons in all the actuality of their concrete beings (but without the blinkers of momentalism on his eyes), a Christian with unswerving compassion asks: What does love require? It is indifferent whether this leads to particular acts and summary rules only or also to general principles of conduct. If love leads to them, it leads to them. A Christian should still do what love requires.

5.16   If it could be shown that to act in accord with one of these love-formed principles of conduct is in a particular situation not what love itself directly requires, then that was not a general principle of conduct but a summary rule only. A Christian, however, will be particularly careful lest for 'what love directly requires' he has put 'what love (or sentiment) *immediately* requires'; and he foreknows that such unruly behaviour may not be what love requires.

5.17   This is the only way to *join* the issue between Summary Rule and Pure Rule Agapism; and it is the only way for there to be any collaboration between them in the whole of Christian ethics. The question is simply whether there *are* any general rules or principles or virtues or styles of life that embody love, and if so what these may be? Answers that have been given to this question include the characteristics of love peerlessly set forth in I Corinthians 13 (which are all, so far as I can see, *universal* statements about what *agape* requires); the qualities called the 'fruits' or 'works' and 'gifts' of the Spirit by St. Paul; the qualities called theological virtues, infused moral virtues, gifts, fruits and Beatitudes in Thomistic ethics; what Christ teaches us concerning the broadest and deepest meaning of justice; the bond of marriage tempered to the meaning and strength indicated in Ephesians 5; order or the orders in dialectical relation with justice and with love; truth-telling and promise-keeping; and (as the floor below which love can and may and must not fall) those works of sin in the flesh listed in Scripture, the more or less than seven more or less deadly sins, or those 'classes of things' like murder, theft, rape, promiscuity, pillage, adultery and sexual relations that are genuinely and therefore irresponsibly pre-marital. Some of these things may not be quite general, and there may be more to be added that will always and everywhere form the conscience and the life of the Christian man. But the point to be made in an essay on the methods of ethics is simply that Pure Rule Agapism cannot be ruled out once its definition is corrected as I have suggested. To do so, or to accept Frankena's definition it (which is that of a legalism that does less than love requires) would be like saying that love cannot will in every situation what in fact it does will to do or not to do. Doubtless what *agape* requires can always be resolved into what love finds itself required to do, and what is pleasing to love can be resolved into what love ever finds it pleasing to do (if that is proper speaking). But to rule out from this any concern for general principles of conduct (or to say that in following these rules love's concrete requirements are violated) arbitrarily limits the freedom of love in determining the right. It says that 'Love, and do as you *then* please' can mean almost anything, *except* that it *cannot* mean that anything will be found to be generally pleasing. Of course, the Rule Agapist says that one ought not act wide of the rule *for this reason*, because of the love that is in it and which would be violated by any departure from it. But this is only for him to invoke or fall back upon his most basic theory of normative ethics. This does not make him a situationalist who does not know beforehand this much, and very much else, about the requirements of love. Nor does he expect ever to support action in accord with rules even though they can be 'seen' to mean doing in a particular situation less than love requires. *He sees no such thing,* and that is why he is a proponent of Pure Rule Agapism in some matters...

5.18.   (2). *Mixed Agapism*
There may be theologians who regard love as one of

the principles to be used in the elaboration of Christian ethics, but not as the only basic one. Such a normative theory of ethics Frankena calls 'mixed agapism', in contrast to the types of pure agapism that we have so far considered. For views of this second sort there are judgments about right and wrong which are independent of love and of love derived rules or acts. It is important that Mixed Agapism not be restricted to theories that combine agapism with natural or rational morality. This type says only that there *are* principles or precepts that are *not* derived from the law of love in any such way as pure agapists believed to be the nature and source of all their principles. Such non-agapistic norms may be known to us from *revelation* no less than there may be norms that are naturally known. The conclusion that either is also basic within Christian ethics would produce an instance of Mixed Agapism. Frankena takes C. H. Dodd's *Gospel and Law* to illustrate this; and he is correct if Dodd believes that there are 'ethical precepts' in the Gospels which are neither the summary nor the general rules of love but which still govern the Christian life. The conservative Christian ethics written in America by Carl F.H. Henry would be another example. So also would Bonhoeffer's doctrine of the biblical 'mandates' (even if one would never gain this impression from the purveyors of Bonhoeffer in the English speaking world). Thus, theories of divine law as well as theories of Christian natural law may be classified under Mixed Agapism. . .

5.19   As for myself, I have already indicated that if one is going to be a proponent of Pure Agapism, it would seem that some combination (I (d) above) of Act-Agapism, Summary Rule and Pure Rule Agapism will prove the most fruitful procedure and theory to explore in regard to the situations, moral problems or principles that may turn out to be corrigible to adequate interpretation by one or another of these procedures within the normative ethic of Pure Agapism.

5.20   It remains for me to say that, on account of the diversity in the practical wisdom that may be needed for the guidance of moral and political action, it seems to me that if a Christian ethicist is going to be so far a Pure Agapist, and as far as this will take him in throwing light upon the path of action, still there can be no sufficient reason for him programmatically to exclude the possibility that there may be rules, principles or precepts whose source is man's natural competence to make moral judgments. An inhabitant of Jerusalem need not rely on messages from Athens, but he should not refuse them; and he might even go to see if there are any. This would be Mixed Agapism – a combination of *agape* with man's sense of natural justice or injustice which, however, contains an internal asymmetry that I indicate by the expression 'love transforming natural justice'.

EXTRACT 6

LITTLE AND TWISS

Comparative religious ethics

6.1   Our respective definitions of "morality" ("moral action-guide") and "religion" ("religious actionguide") – not to mention "law" ("legal action-guide") – demonstrate the centrality of practical justification for these phenomena as we conceive them. We understand the concept of practical justification as an activity that involves *the giving of authorizing reasons for the performance of an action*. For example, we defined a "moral statement" as one "expressing the acceptance of an action-guide that claims superiority, and that is considered *legitimate*, in that it is *justifiable* and *other-regarding*" (note italics). Correspondingly, we defined a "religious statement" as one "expressing acceptance of a set of beliefs, attitudes, and practices based on a notion of sacred authority that functions to resolve the ontological problems of interpretability." We are most interested in religious statements as they function to *support or warrant* actions and practices, or what we call "religious action-guides."

6.2   At the outset we wish to emphasize something that we tried to make clear in our discussions of definitions, namely, the autonomy of moral and religious justifications. Reasons can be given for acting in particular ways – like those given by Jeremy Bentham in support of utilitarianism – that meet the conditions of moral legitimacy or justification, but that are not in any sense religious reasons, according to our definition. In contrast, actions can be supported by authoritarian reasons, such as are found in early Christian literature, or by "mystical" reasons, such as are found in classical Theravada Buddhism, that are grounded in conceptions of sacred authority, in our sense of the notion. These reasons meet our conditions for religious legitimacy, but need not, for example, be other-regarding, as we specify this condition for moral legitimacy. They would not, in other words, meet our special conditions of moral legitimacy. Of course there can be complex interweavings of religious and moral justifications in specific empirical cases. Nevertheless, for analytical purposes it is important to keep our distinction clearly in mind. . .

6.3   It is necessary to make an initial distinction between the *content* and the *structure* of a code of conduct, whether the code be moral, religious, or legal, or whether it be some combination of these. The content of a code is the substantive beliefs and action-guides that comprise it. The structure is the way in which the code is logically arranged so as to provide authorizing reasons that aim to induce acceptance of the action-guides of the code and, indeed, the code as a whole. In short, the structure comprises the pattern of justification inherent in a code of conduct.

6.4   We propose that although the specific content of practical codes varies, the structure of justification among all codes involves several formal features that exist in a fixed relationship with each other. There are three general features of justification: situational application, validation, and vindication. As the conceptual diagram in Figure 1. indicates, these features are related to each other in an appellate fashion; that is, they constitute three ascending levels of appeal in the process of providing justification.

SITUATIONAL APPLICATION

6.5   The action-guides contained in a code of conduct must be applied to concrete situations. Application involves specifying (1) the character of the act and (2) the condition of the actor or agent. With respect to the character of the act, a specific action-guide indicates what is to be done, to whom, in what way, under what circumstances. With respect to the condition of the agent, codes of conduct, especially moral and religious codes, specify certain attitudes, dispositions, motivations, virtues, and traits of character an agent ought to manifest in performing prescribed actions.

6.6   For example, in the case of Theravada Buddhism, Winston King cites the following five conditions as indications for determining the application of the moral prohibition against killing:

(1) It must be a living being (that is destroyed); (2) it must be known (by the killer) that it is a living being; (3) there must be a desire or an intention (*cetana*) to kill that living being; (4) an endeavor must be made to kill that living being; and (5) that living being must be killed through the efforts made (by the would-be killer). A person who commits an act of killing, fulfilling all the above conditions, may be said to be guilty of killing (King, *In the Hope of Nibbana*, p.120).

Note that conditions 1, 4 and 5 describe in general terms the character of the prohibited act of killing. These conditions identify the victim (a living being), what must be done to it (it must, in one way or another, be destroyed), and the killer (the agent directly causing death). Conditions 2 and 3 describe the conditions of the agent. He must be cognizant of what he is doing, and he must intend to kill the living being. Insofar as all these conditions are met, the perpetrator is guilty of an immoral act; that is, he has specifically violated a central action-guide in the Theravada Buddhist moral code.

6.7   The distinction between the character of the act and the condition of the agent can be heightened, as in the following example from the New Testament of Christianity:

'You have heard that it was said, "You shall not commit adultery." But I say to you that every one who looks at a woman lustfully has already committed adultery with her in his heart' (Matthew 5:27-8).

Here reference is made both to the character of the proscribed act, namely, performing adultery, and to the intention and disposition of the agent, namely, that he not even desire to engage in adultery, whether or not he actually performs it. The distinction between the character of the act and the condition of the agent is particularly emphatic. There are, in early Christianity, certain motivations, certain dispositions, certain attitudes that are considered wrong in themselves, regardless of whether they are carried out in practice or exhibited in overt behaviour. Religious and moral literature is full of similar examples. . .

VALIDATION

As we have just suggested, action-guides must be applied situation by situation. They must also be capable of being justified on request. Practical justification involves two general steps: validating and vindicating.

6.8   To illustrate how the procedure works, let us imagine an incident in which a teenage boy, who is a member of a hypothetical religious community, gives evidence that he is about to strike his father. A bystander intervenes and reminds the boy that he ought not to hit his father in these circumstances. What has the bystander done? In the first place, the bystander has applied situationally what he understands to be the "fitting" action-guide: He has identified the father and son as the relevant parties and he has pointed out the restrictions concerning the action. In the second place, the bystander, were he a "good" member of the hypothetical religious community – that is, one who knew well the details of the prescribed code of conduct and also understood it or grasped "how it worked" – would be prepared to give reasons why the boy ought not to strike his father.

6.9   These reasons would be arranged in an appellate pattern, moving from the more specific to the more general. As in a well-developed legal system, where a specific application of the law is appealed from a lower court of restricted jurisdication to an ascending series of higher courts with expanding jurisdiction, so the bystander would be prepared to appeal to a series of "higher" and "more general" levels of reasons to support his original prescription to the boy, "Do not strike your father".

6.10   On the first level, the bystander might simply appeal to a rule like, "One ought not strike one's parents." In support of that rule, he might point out that the act of striking a parent is prohibited because it constitutes incontrovertible proof of the repudiation of parental authority. Repudiation of parental authority, in turn, is always condemned because it is a violation of a general imperative, "Never dishonor your parents," an imperative that is regarded as highly stringent by our hypothetical community.

6.11   "Never dishonor your parents" is to be unconditionally obeyed because it is taken as a direct commandment uttered by the god of the community. And direct commandments of God are to be obeyed because the community has accepted as its underlying prescriptive premise, "Whoever has the power to create man has a right to have what he commands obeyed and what he forbids avoided by his creatures." With this appeal to the "rights of the Creator," we have reached the logical end of the validating procedure. We have uncovered the community's basic norm and the sequence of subsidiary norms that establish the validity of the original action-guide, "Do not strike your father". . .

6.12   It is possible to conceive of several types of basic norm, and part of the task of the student of comparative religious ethics is to identify which type of basic norm characterizes a given religious and/or moral code. In proposing the particular types we do, we emphasize two things. First, only after specific case analysis can it be determined whether the relevant type of basic norm is religious or moral in character. In other words, the types may apply to both religious and moral codes. Second, our list of proposed types is not assumed to be exhaustive. It will undoubtedly need to be extended and refined, although at the present stage of our investigations, it is sufficient to cover what seem to be the prominent types of basic norm.

6.13   Following philosophical convention, we divide the types of basic norm into two major classes, *deontological* and *teleological*. Deontological norms specify certain general characteristics or conditions according to which the rightness (or wrongness) of actions is determined, without regard to the consequences produced by performing such actions. By contrast, teleological norms specify general characteristics and conditions according to which the rightness (or wrongness) of actions is determined on the basis of the consequences produced by performing these actions.

6.14   Deontological basic norms may, in turn, be subdivided into *authoritarian* and *formalistic* norms. Authoritarian norms denote that actions are right and ought to be obeyed if they are commanded or required by a competent authority – that is, actions are justified by the source or origin from which they come, rather than by their intrinsic characteristics. Moreover, authoritarian norms may be personalized, as in the case of a human or supernatural figure who is acknowledged as entitled to direct action. Our previous hypothetical illustration of practical reasoning yields a clear example of an authoritarian basic norm. In that case, as we saw, the emphasis was on the source of the command, not on the character of the command itself.

Figure 1. The structure of Practical Justification

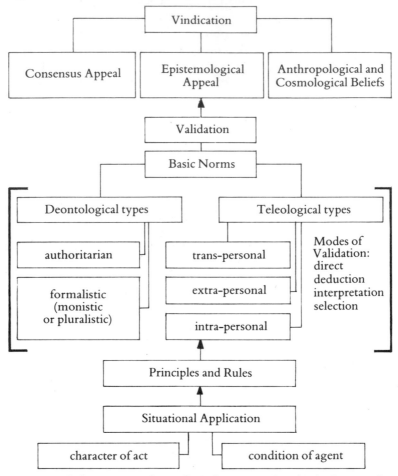

6.15   Other examples of at least an implied form of a personalized authoritarian basic norm can be found in the New Testament, and particularly in the Synoptic Gospels, though such examples frequently compete with other types of basic norm.

6.16   Authoritarian norms may also be impersonalized, as in the case of traditionalistic prescriptions – insofar as actions are authorized by custom and by antiquity, they are to be obeyed. The Anglican theologian Richard Hooker gives voice to a traditionalistic form of authoritarianism when he writes:

'And to be commanded we do consent, when that society whereof we are part hath at any time before consented, without revoking the same after by the like universal agreement. Wherefore as any man's dead past is good as long as he himself continueth; so the act of a public society of men done five hundred years (ago) standeth as theirs who presently are of the same societies' (Hooker, *Laws of Ecclesiastical Polity*)

6.17   Formalistic basic norms, in contrast to authoritarian ones, emphasize the intrinisic characteristics and conditions – the "form" – of actions as determinative of their rightness, rather than the origin or source from which an action-guide emanates. So far as moral justification goes, Immanuel Kant's basic norm, or "supreme principle of morality," as he calls it, is formalistic in our sense of the term. The conditions of "pure practical reason", such as consistency, universality, respect for persons, and the like, are those conditions according to which the rightness of acts is validated.

6.18   Similarly, one of the basic norms, implied in the Letters of St. Paul is formalistic. When, in the early chapters of Romans, Paul argues that men ought to have given thanks to God for the blessings of creation, and later when he contends that men ought to be grateful for God's mercy and saving grace, which was freely given despite man's lack of appreciation and respect, Paul is trading on the following basic norm, along with appropriate inferences:

1. Beneficiaries ought to show thanks for blessings received, by attending to the requests and interests of the benefactor.
2. God is a benefactor and man a beneficiary.
3. Therefore, man ought to attend to the requests and interests of God.

In this argument, the basic norm (1) constitutes a set of criteria stipulating what sort of acts are considered right.

It specifies that when one agent (a benefactor) acts in a certain way (beneficially) towards a recipient (a benefici-ary), the recipient is thereby obligated to requite the benefactor in certain ways (by attending to the benefac-tor's requests and interests). Accordingly, actions com-plying with this "form" are subject to its prescriptive implications.

6.19   While Kant's "supreme principle" and the preceding illustration from St. Paul are examples of basic norms that are moral, by our definition, it is also possible to construct a purely religious example of a formalistic basic norm. A religion might stipulate that actions are valid according to whether they are motivated by certain sacred dispositions, such as "piety" or "blessed uncon-cern", as in the Buddhist tradition, dispositions that are understood as excluding all regard for the "material" welfare of others.

6.20   Whether they are moral or religious, formalistic basic norms can be *monistic* or *pluralistic* in character. In spite of his various formulations, Kant pictured his basic norm in monistic terms, which means that he thought of it as providing one unified criterion for validating moral action: "The three aforementioned ways of presenting the principle of morality are fundamentally only so many formulas of the very same law, and each of them unites the others in itself" (Kant *Foundations of the Metaphysics of Morals*). A philosopher like W. D. Ross, however, posits several basic norms, which he calls "prima facie duties", from which selections must be made in particular cases, that is, from among the duties of fidelity, reparation, gratitude, justice, beneficence, self-improvement, and nonmaleficence. In the same way, a religion might indicate one unique and ideal attribute, like love, for validating action, or it might posit several basic attributes that do not all come to the same thing, and among which choices must be made in specific cases.

6.21   *Teleological basic norms*, or those that specify the sort of consequences that render actions right or wrong, may be subdivided three ways, depending on who is affected by the specified consequences, and how that person is affected. An *intrapersonal* basic norm is essentially an egoistic norm. Accordingly, a state of affairs is designated as desirable from the agent's point of view, exclusive of all reference to the desires or welfare of others. To the degree that the actions achieve the agent's interests, as defined, they are valid. Thomas Hobbes seemed to propound this sort of basic norm, though, as in the case of most egoists, he advanced a *modified* form of (ethical) egoism. In the pursuit of each agent's own maximum pleasure, Hobbes believed, it is usually expedient to take the interests of others into account. This is a factual condition that does modify, in practice, Hobbes's otherwise consistent egoism. . .

6.22   It is difficult to know with certainty whether the apparently egoistic or intrapersonal references in religious traditions like Theravada Buddhism and Christianity can be construed as implying an intrapersonal basic validating norm. The more complex the tradition, the more complex the set of basic norms operative in the practical reasoning of that tradition, and the more difficult it is to sort out the different strands of appeal in each tradition. Along with the clear evidence in Christianity of deontological basic norms of both the authoritarian and formalistic types, it is possible that there is also a teleological intrapersonal norm, in which the end or good of the self is defined in other-worldly terms. The references in the teachings of Jesus to supernatural rewards and punishments for individual deeds and misdeeds lend some plausibility to this idea. It is also possible, though, that the allusions to rewards and punishments in the New Testament are more in the nature of "motivating" or "exciting" reasons, rather than of validating reasons, or reasons that establish the rightness of an action. The appeal to personal interest may do nothing more than prompt the believer to do his duty, a duty determined on other grounds, such as by the command of God. . .

6.23   In the case of Theravada Buddhism, the matter is somewhat clearer, though it is not completely free of ambiguity. There the references to the self's materialistic gratification do appear to come closer than in early Christianity to constituting one sort of basic validating norm, among others, in Buddhist practical life – namely, a teleological intrapersonal norm. This norm applies to only one segment of life, which is governed by "karmic reality." Nevertheless, in the appropriate range of behaviour, morally good or right action is very near to being determined according to the yield of hedonistic satisfaction (beauty, health, prosperity) for the self. . .

6.24   An *extrapersonal* basic norm includes a concern for the welfare of others in addition to the self-concern of the agent. With respect to moral justification, the version of utilitarianism articulated by Jeremy Bentham presents a clear example. The basic validating principle, "the greatest happiness for the greatest number," designates that while hedonistic satisfaction is the end to be maximized by all correct actions, it must be produced aggregatively. Unlike the intrapersonal norm, regard for the welfare of others is built into the basic norm itself.

6.25   Alexander MacBeath gives an illustration of what may be an extrapersonal basic norm among the Bantu:

'It is their conception of the good of the group, as that good is embodied in their institutions, that sets them their duties and prescribes their obligations. It requires of them that they subordinate their personal advantage and private inclinations to the larger good, the good of the group as a whole, a good which they also recognize as their own'(MacBeath, *Experiments in Living*, p. 189).

If MacBeath is right, the Bantu notion of "the interest of the clan" is itself the validating principle of Bantu action-guides. In this case the conception of "good" is obviously collective.

6.26   A *transpersonal* basic norm designates a state of fulfillment above and beyond the typical consciousness of the acting person. While an other-worldly intrapersonal norm also identifies a state of satisfaction that is "transcendental," so to speak, and thus beyond everyday experiences, it nonetheless assumes the notion of a self-conscious agent who himself succeeds in experiencing the desired form of bliss. By contrast, actions that are validated by means of a transpersonal norm have, as their final end, the "extinction of the self," at least as the concept of self is ordinarily understood. Mystical religious traditions, such as forms of Buddhism, Hinduism, and Taoism, clearly espouse this kind of basic norm.

6.27   Transpersonal norms are, by definition, non-moral, although they may be religious in character. The concept of morality, as we understand it, presupposes conscious selves in relation to each other, who consider, up to a point, the "effects of the action of one person on the material welfare of others". Obviously, transpersonal states do not involve such presuppositions. The concepts of self and of others are themselves problematical in regard to such transpersonal states, as in the notion of regarding the material welfare of others. Transpersonal norms, however, may be religious according to our definition. They may imply, as they do in Buddhism, Hinduism and Taoism, "a set of beliefs, attitudes, and practices based on a notion of sacred authority that functions to resolve the ontological problems of interpretability". . . .

VINDICATION

6.28   In discussing the next, and last, aspect of practical justification, let us recall once more our example of the rebellious boy and the bystander. We carried the process of justification up to the basic validating norm – "Whoever has the power to create human beings has the right to have what he commands obeyed. . . ," – and we saw that this basic norm was the end of the line as far as validation is concerned.

6.29   Nevertheless, it is apparent that even though no further validating reason can be requested (on pain of an infinite regress), it is still intelligible to ask why one should accept this sort of authoritarian norm (or any other norm) as basic, and be disposed to act on it. The answer the bystander would give to this question is: We should do it for *vindicatory* reasons, that is, reasons that are "suggestive considerations" (rather than logically compelling ones), intended to persuade the boy to accept and act on the recommended action-guide and the related practical code. For example, the bystander might first suggest empirical evidence for the existence of God and for his creative power. Then, he might go on to ask the boy whether he does not find the prospect of such a God to be awesome, to be something that inspires in him a disposition to obedience. He might add to these vindicatory maneuvers what he believes is the common acceptance of a close connection between the concept of author and the concept of authority.

6.30   When we are concerned with vindication, we are operating on what might be called the "metapractical" level. In respect to moral discourse, we turn, on this level, to metaethical matters, namely to a discussion of those salient considerations that might persuade one to adopt one kind of basic ethical norm and one particular mode of validation, rather than another. Formally speaking, the same sort of concerns are addressed in regard to the metapractical aspects of religious or legal discourse, or any other form of practical discourse for that matter.

6.31   *Consensus appeal*:   Whenever an author claims that the Ten Commandments, for example, ought to form the foundation of a moral code because they 'have the weight of mankind behind them,' he is resorting to a consensus appeal. While this was an important appeal in certain historical periods, it seems, for better or for worse, to have fallen on hard times under the impact of 'cultural relativism,' among other things. . .

6.32   *Epistemological appeal*:   In attempting to vindicate a basic norm, someone might appeal to one or another epistemological theory. For example, he could, along with certain intuitionists, hold that the basic norms for practical judgements are self-evident, and thus readily available to any right-thinking or right-feeling human being. Some intuitionists believe that we 'know' the basic norms, as well as how to apply them, in the same way that we know the first principles of mathematical or logical systems and the procedures for working the systems. For others, such as those of the moral sense school, we perceive the basic norms as well as the procedures for applying them, in the same way we perceive other sensations.

6.33   Religious thinkers, on occasion, make an appeal to self-evidence, as when Jesus refers his hearers to 'the signs of the times,' and suggests that those who do not perceive what is going on before their eyes are willfully blind. Similarly, St. Paul seems to be offering a related sort of appeal when he writes: "[The Gentiles'] conduct shows that what the law commands is written on their hearts. Their consciences also show that this is true, since their thoughts sometimes accuse them and sometimes defend them" (Romans 2:15)

6.34   *General anthropological and cosmological beliefs*: When Jeremy Bentham and John Stuart Mill attempt to vindicate a basic norm like "Always seek the greatest happiness of the greatest number," they make claims of the following sort. Man is so constituted, they argue, that he naturally and inevitably seeks happiness in the form of pleasure, and the recommended norm is only a generalization of that fact. Consequently, for them the basic practical norm is rooted in the nature of man. Thomas Hobbes's maneuver would be exactly the same. It would be easy to list any number of psychological and sociological theories about the nature of man that might be used to persuade people regarding one or another basic norm.

6.35   Similarly, religious theories about man and about the universe have again and again been employed to vindicate one or another religiously oriented basic practical norm. For example, the Buddhist cosmological conception of *karma*, as the law of cause and effect that governs all natural and human events, supplies backing for at least some of the action-guides put forward by Buddhism.

CRITIQUE

An internal comparison of the Extracts will generate a number of important criticisms – e.g. by comparing Bonhoeffer's and Niebuhr's understandings of the Fall or Copleston's and Fletcher's theories of exceptions (the last sentence in 4.2 is clearly an over-simplification). In addition, a number of specific criticisms can be isolated:

Bonhoeffer's Extract must face crucial questions: (1) If we have no prior knowledge of God or of morality, how do we accept the truth of Christianity in the first place? (2) Does Bonhoeffer altogether avoid general ethical categories? At various points in his life he appeared to hold deontological views on such issues as pacifism and abortion. Further he shared these views with some non-Christians over-and-against other Christians (see, particularly, *Ethics*, chapt.3). (3) In their stand against Hitler, does he sometimes allow secular moralists some relative value? A parallel point will arise in relation to Augustine's *Text 1V* and all these questions must be addressed to Barth's *Extract 7*.

Niebuhr's thesis in *Extract 9* raises the most crucial problems, but some of these are also present in *Extract 2*. In his writings it is always difficult to know how effective Christian *agape* is in society and to ascertain the balance between it and the concepts of 'justice' and 'freedom'. It would be unrealistic to expect a balance free from all tension. Indeed, Niebuhr's dialectical method seems to require some tension. But it will be seen later that the balance he does achieve creates problems in political decision-making.

Copleston's Extract does not answer some of the most serious problems already raised in relation to Aquinas' *Text II*. So, even allowing for human error, custom or sin, he does not specify the positive evidence needed to suggest that there are moral precepts common to man as man. Whilst evidence of empirical differences, on moral issues between men, may not actually disprove Aquinas' theory, unless there is also some positive evidence in its favour, it must undermine our confidence in it.

Most exponents of Christian ethics might agree that *agape* is a central concept, but few might agree with Fletcher that it is a sufficient concept (see *below*, pp. 547-9). Empirically, it can be asked whether many of us are sufficiently free or strong to make continuous moral decisions, without knowing, in advance, any of the requirements of *agape*. And, at the theoretical level, it would seem that Fletcher himself does, at times, assume criteria other than *agape* in his examples of moral decision-making. For example, in 4.24 he suggests the ground that 'no unwanted and unintended baby should ever be born': but, clearly, many 'unwanted and unintended' babies are still loved, so some other factor seems to be contributing to this ground. And, in 4.25, the force of his argument depends upon the prior belief that 'murder' is wrong and that 'insanity' relieves the individual of moral responsibility.

In Ramsey's Extract some of the subtler distinctions between Pure Act-Agapism, Modified Act-Agapism and Pure Rule-Agapism may, in practice, be unnecessarily complex and difficult to apply. Further, in pointing to the rules required by *agape*, he does not appear wholly to resolve their relationship to Natural law theory. At times, he prefers to refer to 'natural justice' rather than Natural law, but even this distinction may not resolve the issue. This remained an issue of contention between Ramsey and Niebuhr. In response to Ramsey's contribution to the collection edited by Charles W. Kegley and Robert W. Bretall, *Reinhold Niebuhr: His Religious, Social, and Political Thought* in 1956, Niebuhr wrote:

'Ramsey . . . thinks that I do not do justice to "natural law" concepts as defining the essential structure of human existence. I may have been too critical of natural law concepts, but I do not think that Professor Ramsey really deals, except by implication, with the two main points of my criticisms of classical, catholic, and modern natural-law concepts. The one point is that these concepts do not allow for the historical character of human existence. They are rooted in a classical rationalism which did not understand history. They therefore do not understand the uniqueness of historical occasion or the historical biases which creep into the definitions of natural law . . . The other point . . is the tendency to make the law of love an addendum to natural law, so that the one defines the determinate possibilities and the other the indeterminate possibilities of good. My point is that it is not possible to draw a neat line between determinate and indeterminate possibilities. Justice is an application of the law of love. The rules are not absolute but relative. They are applications of the law of love and do not have independence apart from it. They would be independent only if they were founded in an "essential" social structure. If the illusions of classical rationalism are dispelled, it will be seen that it is not possible to define an essential structure of community except the law of love' (pp. 435-6).

Here, in contrast to *Extract 2*, Niebuhr's position appears wholly personalist and anti-deontological.

Because it does not intend to advance a substantive position, any criticisms of *Extract 6* must be somewhat different from those of the other Extracts. Little and Twiss are usually careful to make only limited claims about their work: 'we are sensitive to the variations in practical reasoning within different religious traditions, and, for that reason, have restricted our analysis, particularly in the case of literate traditions. Therefore, we make no attempt to typify the whole religious tradition . . . While our method may still not be delicate enough to do full justice to the range of variation within Christianity and Buddhism, for example, it does make a start in the right direction' (p. 19). Nonetheless, they are forced to make working definitions of 'religion' and 'morality' in general (6.1) that adopt such sociologically contentious concepts as 'sacred authority', which are, arguably, still confined to Western conceptualization. Again, as with Ramsey, some of their finer distinctions may be difficult to apply in practice. Finally, from the perspective of Christian ethics, the discipline of comparative religious ethics, however fruitful and interesting, can only be regarded as a prelude to ethical understanding. The individual working from within a particular religious tradition will, perhaps inevitably, find a continuous limitation to anlaysis and value-free comparison too restricting. Certainly, in the present Textbook, critique is seen as an essential part of the method of Christian ethics – although, of course, only critique which follows careful analysis.

SECTION 2

POLITICS AND SOCIAL JUSTICE

SECTION 2

POLITICS AND SOCIAL JUSTICE

Within recent Christian ethics the cluster of issues surrounding the overall theme of politics and social justice has proved particularly important. The rise of Liberation theology, especially, has made apparent some of the differences within the discipline, just as the inter-war political crisis revealed crucial theological differences for a previous generation. The problem of the relationship of Christianity to the political order and to the issues of social and economic justice, is not simply of theoretical interest, but of considerable practical importance. At the individual level, the Christian attempts to arrive at an understanding of the implications of his or her faith for involvement in political realities. At the corporate level, ecclesiastical institutions attempt to decide how far they are to be involved in specifically political institutions and in detailed political decision-making. The focus of this Section will sometimes be on the individual level and sometimes on the corporate one. In some of the Texts and Extracts attention is given to overall political structures, whereas in others it is the specific issues of economic or social justice which are of primary concern. However, it must be stressed firmly at the outset, that each of the Texts or Extracts must be set in its own socio-political context before it is (anachronistically) related to others within the Section. It must not be assumed, too readily, that the various authors all attach the same meaning to their social or political terms.

171

One way of demonstrating the variety of positions open to the exponent of Christian ethics in this area is to compare possible answers to the following questions:

(1) Can specific political structures, ideals or programmes be derived unambiguously from the Gospel?

(2) How far can the Church be identified with specific political regimes, ideals or programmes?

(3) Should the individual Christian be totally obedient to specific political regimes, ideals or programmes?

If a positive response is given to (1), the two other questions may appear relatively unproblematic: the Church can identify fully with such political regimes, ideals or programmes and, likewise, the individual Christian clearly should be obedient to them. But, of course, even for those who would accept (1), most might acknowledge that actual politicians or political regimes seldom adopt unsullied Christian ideals or programmes. Even if they disagree with the dichotomy that Niebuhr advanced, between individual Christian ethics and political moral practice, they might still agree that Christian ethics makes demands upon politicians and political regimes which are frequently ignored. If, however, a negative response is given to (1), either because the Gospel is thought to be too ambiguous on many political issues, or because it is thought to be uninterested in them, any close identification of the Church with specific political regimes, ideals or programmes would seem to be precluded. For many, total obedience of the individual Christian to specific political regimes, ideals or programmes would also be thereby precluded. But to some, as will be seen, it would still be required, on the grounds that political regimes are always divinely appointed, even when they conflict with Christian ideals and principles.

Within this broad framework it is possible to locate the overall positions of the authors of the Texts and Extracts in this Section. A very broad acceptance of (1) is evident in Aquinas and John XXIII. In very different ways, it is also evident in Miranda. A rejection of (1), on the grounds of the lack of interest of the Gospel in specific political matters, is evident at times in Augustine and Berdyaev. And an extreme wariness of

(1), combined with a rejection of (2), but an insistence on (3), is evident in Luther and Barth. These three clusters of possibilities must each be examined separately: like all such clusters, they may reveal similarities, but blur real differences.

Aquinas' use of Natural law is very evident here: 'it would seem best to deduce the duties of a king from the examples of government in nature' (V.1). He believed that from nature he could both justify and understand monarchical, hierarchical government. But, as always, the Bible was thought to accord with this justification and understanding; the latter could be derived from direct analogical argument from Genesis 1 (V.3). If this position is accepted, it might seem to follow that the Church *can* be identified with specific political regimes, ideals and programmes and, that the individual Christian does have a general duty to be obedient to them. Naturally, this position is further re-inforced by the peculiarities of the Church/State relationship in 13th Century Europe. It has already been noted (see *above*, p. 46) that this consisted of boundaries of power and authority, not of opposing aims, values and social orders. Indeed, only in the Extracts is the concept of the secular state assumed.

Aquinas' derivation of political monarchy, from Natural law and from Biblical bases, compares interestingly with Calvin's justification (albeit in the changed context of 16th Century middle Europe) of democracy. Calvin's *Institutes* declared emphatically, that some form of government was essential and he was sharply critical of any form of Christian anarchism: 'some fanatics who are pleased with nothing but liberty, or rather licentiousness without any restraint, do indeed boast and vociferate, that since we are dead with Christ to the elements of this world and, being translated into the kingdom of God, sit among the celestials, it is a degradation to us and far beneath our dignity to be occupied with those secular and pure cares which relate to things altogether uninteresting to a Christian man' (*Institutes* III.2). In contrast, he maintained that political government and the reign of Christ 'are in no respect at variance with each other'. He even admitted that, if one compares differing types of government – monarchy, aristocracy or democracy – 'their advantages are so nearly equal that it will not be easy to discover of which the utility preponderates'. Nonetheless, once he had analysed them in terms of their dysfunctions, he did decide for democracy:

'It is true that the transition is easy from monarchy to despotism; it is not much more difficult from aristocracy to oligarchy, or the faction of a few; but it is most easy of all from democracy to sedition. Indeed, if these three forms of government which are stated by philosophers be considered in themselves, I shall by no means deny that either aristocracy or a mixture of aristocracy and democracy far excels all others; and that indeed not of itself, but because it very rarely happens that kings regulate themselves so that their will is never at variance with justice and rectitude . . . The vice or imperfection of men therefore renders it safer and more tolerable for the government to be in the hands of many, that they may afford each other mutual assistance and admonition, and that if anyone arrogate to himself more than is right, the many may act as censors and masters to restrain his ambition. This has always been proved by experience, and the Lord confirmed it by his authority when he established a government of this kind among the people of Israel, with a view to preserve them in the most desirable condition till he exhibited in David a type of Christ' (*Institutes* III.8).

The differences between Calvin and Aquinas (separated by differing cultures and centuries) are instructive. On face-value, Aquinas might have agreed with the opening sentence of this quotation, but from it he would have derived the conviction that monarchy accords most closely with Natural law. He might also have agreed with the last sentence: natural experience accords with biblical revelation. However, the central section of the quotation clearly differentiates their positions. Calvin's support for democracy appears here as a negative support: it is the least dysfunctional form of government and offers the greatest hope of checking sin. Nonetheless, from this position he did then go on to insist that a properly functioning government does require the obedient support of the individual Christian.

Variants of Aquinas' position can be seen in John XXIII and Temple's Extracts. Both are written from the 20th Century perspective of the secular state and, in this sense, differ radically from Aquinas. Yet, both also contain a mixture of Natural law and biblically based arguments: both believe that the Gospel does imply specific political structures, ideals and programmes and that, as a result, the Church should be identified with them: and both believe that this confronts the individual Christian with specific duties. Pope John's *Pacem in Terris* is a detailed exposition of the rights and duties (both of the individual and of the state) on the major issues threatening the peace of the world. Unlike Niebuhr, he apparently sees no difficulty in moving from the individual to the social level on ethical issues. The fascinating and important challenge of John's Extract is that it enlarges categories usually used in theological debate, in order to justify the right of individual nations to survival and self-determination and in order to argue for the necessity of some form of world government. Temple's canvas is smaller and less directly dependent on Aquinas, seeking to distinguish between general political principles, which can and ought to be adopted, both by the Church and by the individual Christian, and particular political policies, which will be more divisive and are more subject to specialist judgment.

The positions of Luther and Barth, in relation to these central political questions, differ sharply from those already mentioned. Luther's *To The Christian Nobility* of 1520 was a passionate attack on the medieval concept of the relationship between Church and State and specifically on the control of the former over the latter. In advancing his positive theory of the relative autonomy of the political order (though not, of course, the concept of the secular state), he frequently insisted that it is the individual Christian who should be obedient to the state and not the state that should be obedient to the individual Christian or to the Church. In the next Section it will be seen that, for Luther, obedience to the appointed ruler was crucial, even if the latter was a tyrant and thoroughly un-Christian (see IX.11f). Luther was resigned to the belief that there would sometimes be a very considerable gap between the moral behaviour of the Christian and that either of the ruler or of the majority of people in society (see VI.23f). His notion of the Two Kingdoms – the spiritual and the temporal Kingdoms of God – sometimes accentuated this gap still further. Nonetheless, the obedience of the individual Christian was always required – as indeed it seems to be in Barth's early writings.

Here again there is a crucial difference from Calvin. The latter's overall position was similar to that of Luther and Barth: government is essential to society, is appointed by God and should be obeyed by the individual. So, in his exegesis of Romans 13, Calvin argued: 'The reason why we ought to be subject to magistrates is because they are constituted by God's ordination. For since it pleases God thus to govern the world, he who attempts to invert the order of God, and thus to resist God himself, despises his power; since to despise the providence of him who is the founder of civil power is to carry on war with him' (*Commentary on the Epistle to the Romans* 13.1). This differs from Barth's analysis of the same passage only in its reference to 16th Century magistrates. But, crucially, Calvin believed that there *were* circumstances when authorities should be resisted, particularly when what they were doing was inimical to the Gospel. For example, in commenting on Daniel's civil disobedience, he wrote:

'We must remember that passage of Peter, "Fear God, honour the king" (1 Peter 2.17). The two commands are connected together, and cannot be separated from one another. The fear of God ought to precede, that kings may obtain their authority. For if anyone begins his reverence of an earthly prince by rejecting that of God, he will act preposterously, since this is a complete perversion of the order of nature... For earthly princes lay aside all their power when they rise up against God, and are unworthy of being reckoned in the number of mankind. We ought rather utterly to defy than to obey them whenever they are so restive and wish to spoil God of his rights, and, as it were, to seize upon his throne and draw him down from heaven' (*Commentary on Daniel*, Lecture 30).

In the *Institutes* the emphasis is somewhat different: private individuals must be obedient and suffer unjust rulers, but magistrates have a positive duty to oppose them. Indeed, there, Calvin insisted that, if magistrates 'connive at kings in their oppression of their people, such forbearance involves the most nefarious perfidy because they fraudulently betray the liberty of the people, of which they know that they have been appointed protectors by the ordination of God' (*Institutes* III.31).

Ironically, despite this crucial difference between Calvin and Luther, the latter was not particularly obedient, in practice, to civil authorities. Luther spent a life of constant strife with a number of civil and ecclesiastical authorities: his civil obedience was at best selective. Interestingly, too, the growth of Nazism presented Barth with both a personal and a theological crisis: the sharp contrasts of *Romans* became more ambivalent as the 1930's proceeded. Here, *par excellence*, the influence of socio-political realities upon theological positions is evident.

Many of these issues and positions can be found in the very varied writings of Augustine. More than most other theologians Augustine was forced, in an age of immense transition in the social status of Christianity, to agonise over the position of Christianity in relation to political realities. Confronted by the confusion created by Christianity, on the one hand having been adopted in the previous century as the state religion and, on the other, by it being attacked as the cause of the state's present demise, Augustine's views were highly ambivalent. On the issue of war, he came to accept (albeit reluctantly) a defence of the state's position (see Text VII): on that of sexuality, his views usually diverged sharply from the dominant ethos of Roman culture (see Section 4). Within the *City of God*, his understanding of the relationship between the two cities – the earthly and the heavenly – often appears strained. He was always emphatic that the heavenly city is by far and away the most important, but he appears to oscillate between regarding the earthly city as a source of relative good and seeing it simply as a painful necessity. Neo-Platonic and Manichaean tendencies were never entirely eliminated from his writings.

An emphatic stress upon the primacy of the spiritual and the consequent relative unimportance of the political, is also found (in a somewhat different form) in Berdyaev. Despite living through momentous political upheavals, first in revolutionary Russia and then in German occupied Paris, his writings were often remarkably apolitical. Even when he considered explicitly Marxist themes (which had been particularly important to him as a young man), this generally remained the case. Describing himself as a 'Christian theosophist' and even as a gnostic, the spiritual always takes considerable precedence over the temporal and, in this ·respect, he appears even more Platonic than Augustine.

Quite apart from differences in socio-political context (which, obviously, must be given especial attention in this Section), a number of theological factors appear to affect the response of particular theologians to political issues. The relative balance given to the spiritual and the temporal (or however this is to be expressed in less Hellenistic terms) is clearly crucial. The acceptance or rejection of some notion of 'natural law' or 'natural order', is also crucial. The extent to which political realities are seen as inherently sinful is also a factor. Biblical exegesis is also very important and has become considerably more complex in the light of recent critical scholarship. For many it has become increasingly difficult to derive detailed and unambiguous structures, ideals or programmes from the New Testament. Sections 3 and 4 should serve to reinforce this point. However, it is perhaps in Liberation theology, and in recent responses to Liberation theology, that these differences have now become most crucial. As an approach to theology it is unified in its attempt to adopt a position alongside all those who are deemed to be oppressed, but it is less unified in the actual methods or policies that it adopts. In addition, it is an approach which interestingly cuts across divisions between churches, as the Extracts from the Methodist Bonino, in the next Section, and the Roman Catholic Miranda, in this Section, demonstrate.

TEXT IV
AUGUSTINE
The earthly and heavenly cities

I. BACKGROUND

This Text comes from *The City of God* XIX. 14-17 (Pelican Classics, trans. Henry Bettenson and ed. David Knowles, Penguin, 1972, pp. 872-9). Book XIX opens the fifth and final section of *The City of God* and was thus written in the period, of A.D. 420-6 (see *above*, p.64) – well over 20 years after *Text VII*. At last Augustine could set out what he saw as the destinies of the earthly and heavenly cities. Against 'pagan' critics of Christianity, such as Porphyry, Augustine insisted that *his* was not a narrow, parochial religion which was incapable of making sense of world history. To the cultured Roman 'pagan', Christianity appeared to be just that: it lacked any serious historical and cultural roots and, since its adoption a century before by Constantine, had demonstrably contributed to the demise of Rome. However, Augustine saw the concept of the two cities as one which could not only make sense of history, but also give clarity to the extraordinarily difficult relationship of Church to State. For both personal and intellectual reasons, he could neither totally identify Church with State nor totally separate them. The concept of the two cities was used to clarify this relationship, but it was not identical with it – it was much broader and more far-reaching:

'Although there are many great peoples throughout the world, living under different customs in religion and morality and distinguished by a complex variety of languages, arms, and dress, it is still true that there have come into being only two main divisions, as we may call them, in human society: and we are justified in following the lead of our Scriptures and calling them two cities. There is, in fact, one city of men who choose to live by the standard of the flesh, another of those who choose to live by the standard of the spirit. The citizens of each of these desire their own kind of peace, and when they achieve their aim, that is the kind of peace in which they live' (*City of God*, XIV, 1).

Here the concept of the 'cities' (*civitates*) represents, not particular institutions or locations, but rather basic human divisions and differentiating loyalities. Whatever points of contact undoubtedly exist between the two cities, their ultimate aims and aspirations are thoroughly distinct: the one concerned with the temporal and even demonic and the other with the divine.

2. KEY ISSUES
This passage expresses very clearly the quite different aspirations and aims of the two cities. The end of the earthly city is earthly peace, consisting of concord between body and soul and an ordered life and health, whereas that of the heavenly city is eternal peace (IV.1). In so far as he has a rational soul, mortal man is in need of divine direction and assistance (IV.2). The latter is evident in the two chief precepts, love of God and love of neighbour. Specifically, earthly peace and ordered harmony involve obeying the rules of not harming anyone and helping everyone whenever possible (IV.3). Ordered harmony at the domestic level, however, is not to be confused with domination. Man's dominion applies to a dominion over the natural world and not over fellow man: slavery, for example, results mainly from sin or is a punishment for sin (IV. 4 & 5). Domestic harmony or peace – between members of a family and between master and slave – ought to contribute to the peace of the city (IV.7). Yet all these versions of peace, domestic or social, appear in the context of faith as relative to heavenly peace. The person of faith is like a pilgrim in a foreign land: earthly peace has some use, but is still a temporary and passing phenomenon (IV.8). Indeed, there are polytheistic and pagan elements in the earthly city which are antithetical to the heavenly city, so that the laws of religion, particularly, cannot be the same in the two cities (IV.9). The heavenly city does not annul earthly laws, but

follows them in so far as they do not hinder the Christian religion. The pilgrim of the heavenly city makes use of earthly peace and laws, but regards heavenly peace as the only form of peace that really deserves the name of peace (IV.10).

3. ETHICAL ARGUMENTS

Augustine's understanding of the value of earthly peace seems to oscillate between consequentialism and deontology. Consequentialism is particularly evident in IV.8. Here Augustine maintains that the heavenly city 'must needs make use of ' earthly peace 'until this mortal state, for which this kind of peace is essential, passes away', not only because it provides for an ordered society, but also because it provides for a 'harmony' between the two cities. On this understanding, earthly peace is not accorded any merit for itself, but only for its usefulness to the heavenly city. Other paragraphs, however, seem to imply a more deontological or Natural law understanding of earthly peace – particularly IV.1 & 2 and explicitly in the first sentence of IV.4. And there does appear to be a relationship between the dominical commands or precepts at the beginning of IV.3 and the two rules for social order given in the middle of the same paragraph. Set against this, there is a typical Augustinian stress upon sin in his understanding of slavery in IV.4 & 5. This stress always makes it difficult simply to interpret Augustine in terms of a Natural law theory: the more wholly corrupt men are thought to be, the less one can identify their natural propensities or ends.

4. BASES OF CHRISTIAN ETHICS

The Bible is used here more frequently and pivotally than in Text I, with two direct OT quotations, three direct NT quotations and several indirect allusions. Further, the use of the Bible in IV.3, 4 & 5 is prescriptive and crucial to the argument. The issue of slavery, particularly, presents Augustine with a dilemma and his uneasiness with it is apparent in his discussion in IV.4 & 5. His derivation of *servus* is in fact mistaken – although it was widely accepted by his contemporaries. And he avoids the obvious point that nowhere in the Bible is slavery actually condemned. However, his overall aim, of attempting to show that his understanding of the two cities accords with the Bible and makes sense of human history, is clear.

5. SOCIAL DETERMINANTS

The influence of the transition of Christianity from a sectarian to a more church-type position in society is evident (see further, on *Text VII*). Given the radically changed socio-political status of Christianity since Constantine, and given the criticisms from traditionalist non-Christians, Augustine felt constrained to articulate an understanding of the relationship between Church and State. However, as a result of both his neo-Platonic modes of thought and his indebtedness to the Bible (see *above*, p.66) he made his articulation in the somewhat ethereal terms of the concept of the two cities. So, the earthly city cannot be identified with 'secular' society or with the State and the heavenly city certainly cannot be equated with the extant institutional Church. The overall concept of the two cities also reflects Augustine's background in African Christianity. In that context, it was already so commonplace that he could refer to it at one point as that 'which everyone brought up in the traditions of the holy church should know' (*Enarr. in Ps.* 136.1).

6.   SOCIAL SIGNIFICANCE

It would be difficult to exaggerate the importance of Augustine's position here. His *City of God*, written in old age, represented a major achievement and presented the late classical world with its most sustained and cultured Christian apologetic. In view of the precarious position of Christianity in the early 5th Century Roman world, the social significance of such an apologetic is evident. Even if his particular understanding of political realities (it cannot be claimed that he actually advanced a political theory) proved to be too firmly located in the social context of the late Roman Empire, his overall conception of the tension between the Christian vision and political actualities has remained important in much contemporary theology. The ways he resolved this tension varied considerably in his writings, but it is always apparent.

FURTHER READING

Important discussions of the *City of God* will be found in David
Knowles' Introduction to the Pelican translation of the *City of
God*, in Peter Brown's *Augustine of Hippo* and in R.W. Barrow's
Introduction to St. Augustine, 'The City of God'. Augustine's
discussions of the concept of the two cities occur particularly in
Books XIV-XV and XVIII-XIX of the *City of God*.

TEXT IV

AUGUSTINE

The earthly and heavenly cities

IV.1   We see, then, that all man's use of temporal things is
related to the enjoyment of earthly peace in the earthly
city; whereas in the Heavenly City it is related to the
enjoyment of eternal peace. Thus, if we were irrational
animals, our only aim would be the adjustment of the
parts of the body in due proportion, and the quieting of
appetites – only, that is, the repose of the flesh, and an
adequate supply of pleasures, so that bodily peace might
promote the peace of the soul. For if bodily peace is
lacking, the peace of the irrational soul is also hindered,
because it cannot achieve the quieting of its appetites. But
the two together promote that peace which is a mutual
concord between soul and body, the peace of an ordered
life and of health. For living creatures show their love of
bodily peace by their avoidance of pain, and by their
pursuit of pleasure to satisfy the demands of their
appetites they demonstrate their love of peace and soul.
In just the same way, by shunning death they indicate
quite clearly how great is their love of the peace in which
soul and body are harmoniously united.

IV.2   But because there is in man a rational soul, he
subordinates to the peace of the rational soul all that part
of his nature which he shares with the beasts, so that he
may engage in deliberate thought and act in accordance
with this thought, so that he may thus exhibit that
ordered agreement of cognition and action which we

called the peace of the rational soul. For with this end in view he ought to wish to be spared the distress of pain and grief, the disturbances of desire, the dissolution of death, so that he may come to some profitable knowledge and may order his life and his moral standards in accordance with this knowledge. But he needs. divine direction, which he may obey with resolution, and divine assistance that he may obey it freely, to prevent him from falling, in his enthusiasm for knowledge, a victim to some fatal error, through the weakness of the human mind. And so long as he is in this mortal body, he is a pilgrim in a foreign land, away from God; therefore he walks by faith, not by sight. That is why he views all peace, of body or of soul, or of both, in relation to that peace which exists between mortal man and immortal God, so that he may exhibit an ordered obedience in faith in subjection to the everlasting God.

IV.3   Now God, our master, teaches two chief precepts, love of God and love of neighbour; and in them man finds three objects for his love: God, himself, and his neighbour; and a man who loves God is not wrong in loving himself. It follows, therefore, that he should be concerned also that his neighbour should love God, since he is told to love his neighbour as himself; and the same is true of his concern for his wife, his children, for the members of his household, and for all other men, so far as is possible. And, for the same end, he will wish his neighbour to be concerned for him, if he happens to need that concern. For this reason he will be at peace, as far as lies in him, with all men, in that peace among men, that ordered harmony; and the basis of this order is the observance of two rules: first, to do no harm to anyone, and, secondly, to help everyone whenever possible. To begin with, therefore, a man has a responsibility for his own household – obviously, both in the order of nature and in the framework of human society, he has easier and more immediate contact with them; he can exercise his concern for them. That is why the Apostle says, 'Anyone who does not take care of his own people, especially

those in his own household, is worse than an unbeliever –
he is a renegade.'(1 Tim. 5.8) This is where domestic
peace starts, the ordered harmony about giving and
obeying orders among those who live in the same house.
For the orders are given by those who are concerned for
the interests of others; thus the husband gives orders to
the wife, parents to children, masters to servants. While
those who are the objects of this concern obey orders; for
example, wives obey husbands, the children obey their
parents, the servants their masters. But in the household
of the just man who 'lives on the basis of faith' and who is
still on pilgrimage, far from that Heavenly City, even
those who give orders are the servants of those whom
they appear to command. For they do not give orders
because of a lust for domination but from a dutiful
concern for the interests of others, not with pride in
taking precedence over others, but with compassion in
taking care of others.

Man's natural freedom; and the slavery caused by sin

IV.4   This relationship is prescribed by the order of nature,
and it is in this situation that God created man. For he
says, 'Let him have lordship over the fish of the sea, the
birds of the sky. . . and all the reptiles that crawl on the
earth.' (Gen. 1.26). He did not wish the rational being,
made in his own image, to have dominion over any but
irrational creatures, not man over man, but man over the
beasts. Hence the first just men were set up as shepherds
of flocks, rather than as kings of men, so that in this way
also God might convey the message of what was required
by the order of nature, and what was demanded by the
deserts of sinners – for it is understood, of course, that the
condition of slavery is justly imposed on the sinner. That
is why we do not hear of a slave anywhere in the
Scriptures until Noah, the just man, punished his son's
sin with this word; and so that son deserved this name
because of his misdeed, not because of his nature. The
origin of the Latin word for slave, *servus*, is believed to be
derived from the fact that those who by the laws of war

could rightly be put to death by the conquerors, became *servi*, slaves, when they were preserved, receiving this name from their preservation. But even this enslavement could not have happened, if it were not for the deserts of sin. For even when a just war is fought it is in defence of his sin that the other side is contending; and victory, even when the victory falls to the wicked, is a humiliation visited on the conquered by divine judgement, either to correct or to punish their sins. We have a witness to this in Daniel, a man of God, who in captivity confesses to God his own sins and the sins of his people, and in devout grief testifies that they are the cause of that captivity. The first cause of slavery, then, is sin, whereby man was subjected to man in the condition of bondage; and this can only happen by the judgement of God, with whom there is no injustice, and who knows how to allot different punishments according to the deserts of the offenders.

IV.5   Now, as our Lord above says, 'Everyone who commits sin is sin's slave', (Jhn. 8.34), and that is why, though many devout men are slaves to unrighteous masters, yet the masters they serve are not themselves free men; 'for when a man is conquered by another he is also bound as a slave to his conqueror' (2 Ptr. 2.19). And obviously it is a happier lot to be slave to a human being than to a lust; and, in fact, the most pitiless domination that devastates the hearts of men, is that exercised by this very lust for domination, to mention no others. However, in that order of peace in which men are subordinate to other men, humility is as salutary for the servants as pride is harmful to the masters. And yet by nature, in the condition in which God created man, no man is the slave either of man or of sin. But it remains true that slavery as a punishment is also ordained by that law which enjoins the preservation of the order of nature, and forbids its disturbance; in fact, if nothing had been done to contravene that law, there would have been nothing to require the discipline of slavery as a punishment. That explains also the Apostle's admonition to slaves, that they should be subject to their masters, and serve them loyally and willingly (cf. Eph. 6.5). What he means is that if they cannot be set free by their masters, they themselves may thus make their slavery, in a sense, free, by serving not with the slyness of fear, but with the fidelity of affection, until all injustice disappears and all human lordship and power is annihilated, and God is all in all.

Equity in the relation of master and slave

IV.6   This being so, even though our righteous fathers had slaves, they so managed the peace of their households as to make a distinction between the situation of children and the condition of slaves in respect of the temporal goods of this life; and yet in the matter of the worship of God – in whom we must place our hope of everlasting goods – they were concerned, with equal affection, for all the members of their household. This is what the order of nature prescribes, so that this is the source of the name *paterfamilias*, a name that has become so generally used that even those who exercise unjust rule rejoice to be called by this title. On the other hand, those who are genuine 'fathers of their household' are concerned for the welfare of all in their households in respect of the worship and service of God, as if they were all their children, longing and praying that they may come to the heavenly home, where it will not be a necessary duty to give order to men, because it will no longer be a necessary duty to be concerned for the welfare of those who are already in the felicity of that immortal state. But until that home is reached, the fathers have an obligation to exercise the authority of masters greater than the duty of slaves to put up with their condition as servants.

IV.7   However, if anyone in the household is, through his disobedience, an enemy to the domestic peace, he is reproved by a word, or by a blow, or any other kind of punishment that is just and legitimate, to the extent allowed by human society; but this is for the benefit of the offender, intended to readjust him to the domestic peace from which he had broken away. For just as it is not an act of kindness to help a man, when the effect of the help is to make him lose a greater good, so it is not a blameless act to spare a man, when by so doing you let him fall into a greater sin. Hence the duty of anyone who would be blameless includes not only doing no harm to anyone but also restraining a man from sin or punishing his sin, so that either the man who is chastised may be corrected by his experience, or others may be deterred by his example. Now a man's house ought to be the beginning, or rather a small component part of the city, and every beginning is directed to some end of its own kind, and every component part contributes to the completeness of the whole of which it forms a part. The implication is quite apparent, that domestic peace contributes to the peace of the city – that is, the ordered harmony of those who live together in a house in the matter of giving and obeying orders, contributes to the ordered harmony concerning authority and obedience obtaining among the citizens. Consequently it is fitting that the father of a household should take his rules from the law of the city, and govern his household in such a way that it fits in with the peace of the city.

The origin of peace between the heavenly society and the earthly city, and of discord between them.

IV.8   But a household of human beings whose life is not based on faith is in pursuit of an earthly peace based on the things belonging to this temporal life, and on its advantages, whereas a household of human beings whose life is based on faith looks forward to the blessings which are promised as eternal in the future, making use of earthly and temporal things like a pilgrim in a foreign land, who does not let himself be taken in by them or distracted from his course towards God, but rather treats them as supports which help him more easily to bear the burdens of 'the corruptible body which weighs heavy on the soul' (Wisd. 9.15), they must on no account be allowed to increase the load. Thus both kinds of men and both kinds of households alike make use of the things essential for this mortal life; but each has its own very different end in making use of them. So also the earthly city, whose life is not based on faith, aims at an earthly peace, and it limits the harmonious agreement of citizens concerning the giving and obeying of orders to the establishment of a kind of compromise between human wills about the things relevant to mortal life. In contrast, the Heavenly City – or rather that part of it which is on pilgrimage in this condition of mortality, and which lives on the basis of faith – must needs make use of this peace also, until this mortal state, for which this kind of peace is essential, passes away. And therefore, it leads what we may call a life of captivity in this earthly city as in a foreign land, although it has already received the promise of redemption, and the gift of the Spirit as a kind of pledge of it; and yet it does not hesitate to obey the laws of the earthly city by which those things which are designed for the support of this mortal life are regulated; and the purpose of this obedience is that, since this mortal condition is shared by both cities, a harmony may be preserved between them in things that are relevant to this condition.

IV.9   But this earthly city has had some philosophers belonging to it whose theories are rejected by the teaching inspired by God. Either led astray by their own speculation or deluded by demons, these thinkers reached the belief that there are many gods who must be won over to serve human ends, and also that they have, as it were, different departments with different responsibilities attached. Thus the body is the department of one god, the mind that of another; and within the body itself, one god is in charge of the head, another of the neck and so on with each of the separate members. Similarly, within the mind, one is responsible for natural ability, another for learning, another for anger, another for lust; and in the accessories of life there are separate gods over the departments of flocks, grain, wine, oil, forests, coinage, navigation, war and victory, marriage, birth, fertility, and so on. The Heavenly City, in contrast, knows only one God as the object of worship, and decrees, with faithful devotion, that he only is to be served with that service which the Greeks call *latreia*, which is due to God alone. And the result of this difference has been that the Heavenly City could not have laws of religion common with the earthly city, and in defence of her religious laws she was bound to dissent from those who thought differently and to prove a burdensome nuisance to them. Thus she had to endure their anger and hatred, and the assaults of persecution; until at length that City shattered the morale of her adversaries by the terror inspired by her numbers, and by the help she continually received from God.

IV.10   While this Heavenly City, therefore, is on pilgrimage in this world, she calls out citizens from all nations and so collects a society of aliens, speaking all languages. She takes no account of any difference in customs, laws, and institutions, by which earthly peace is achieved and preserved – not that she annuls or abolishes any of those, rather, she maintains them and follows them (for whatever divergences there are among the diverse nations, those institutions have one single aim – earthly peace), provided that no hindrance is presented thereby to the religion which teaches that the one supreme and true God is to be worshipped. Thus even the Heavenly City in her pilgrimage here on earth makes use of the earthly peace and defends and seeks the compromise between human wills in respect of the provisions relevant to the mortal nature of man, so far as may be permitted without detriment to true religion and piety. In fact, that City relates the earthly peace to the heavenly peace, which is so truly peaceful that it should be regarded as the only peace deserving the name, at least in respect of the rational creation; for this peace is the perfectly ordered and completely harmonious fellowship in the enjoyment of God, and of each other in God. When we arrive at that state of peace, there will be no longer a life that ends in death, but a life that is life in sure and sober truth; there will be no animal body to 'weigh down the soul' in its process of corruption; there will be a spiritual body with no cravings, a body subdued in every part to the will. This peace the Heavenly City possesses in faith while on its pilgrimage, and it lives a life of righteousness, based on this faith, having the attainment of that peace in view in every good action it performs in relation to God, and in relation to a neighbour, since the life of a city is inevitably a social life.

CRITIQUE

One of the great strengths of this Text and of the *City of God* generally is that it takes seriously the tension that the Christian must always feel between his vision of the transcendent and his expectations of the world. Whereas the modern NT exegete would tend to express this tension in terms of the Synoptic concept of the Kingdom of God – with its relevance to, but distance from, the temporal and its present and future references – most might maintain that some degree of tension is essential. On this understanding, it would be equally as wrong to identify the Kingdom of God wholly with some particular political programme, as to assert that it is totally without political relevance. Within these parameters, there are many variant positions, each subject to particular weaknesses.

The weakness of Augustine's position in this Text is, that the heavenly city is so marginally related to the earthly city, that it appears little interested in effecting changes within it. The pilgrim status of Christians effectively means that they may simply have to endure injustice rather than attempt to change it. So, finally, his advice to slaves is that, 'if they cannot be set free by their masters, they themselves may thus make their slavery, in a sense, free, by serving not with the slyness of fear, but with the fidelity of affection, until all injustice disappears and all human lordship and power is annihilated, and God is all in all' (IV.5). The individual Christian is not encouraged to oppose slavery or actively to combat injustice, but rather to endure it and wait for the time when 'God is all in all'. A radically different Christian interpretation is evident in Miranda's *Extract 12* and Bonino's *Extract 17*. In Augustine, the martyr understanding of Christianity is still apparent (see the last sentences of IV.9 and VII.8) and, indeed, in his battles with the Donatists in

North Africa he sometimes expected to be martyred himself (whilst, at the same time, rejecting the Donatist's own martyr-seeking attitude: cf Text X). Augustine was always more keen to combat what he regarded as Christian 'heresy' than to uphold social justice.

TEXT V
AQUINAS
On princely government

I. BACKGROUND

This Text comes from *De Regimine Principum*, XII-XIV (*On Princely Government*, from ed. A.P. D'Entrèves, *Aquinas: Selected Political Writings*, Blackwell, Oxford, 1948, trans. J.G. Dawson, pp. 67-77). The authentic parts of *De Regimine Principum* (mainly Book I from which this Text is taken) were written during Aquinas' time of teaching in Italy (1259-69) as specific advice to the King of Cyprus. Aquinas was not, of course, primarily a political theorist and his writings on political matters are thoroughly medieval, hierarchical and theocratic. He followed Aristotle in arguing that man is by nature a social and political animal and that Natural law requires rule by kings. Accordingly, he opened *De Regimine Principum* as follows:

'Our first task must be to explain how the term king is to be understood. Now whenever a certain end has been decided upon, but the means for arriving thereat are still open to choice, some one must provide direction if that end is to be expeditiously attained. A ship, for instance, will sail first on one course and then on another, according to the winds it encounters, and it would never reach its destination but for the skill of the helmsman who steers it to port. In the same way man, who acts by intelligence, has a destiny to which all life and activities are directed; for it is clearly the nature of intelligent beings to act with some end in view. Yet the diversity of human interests and pursuits makes it equally clear that there are many courses open to men when seeking the end they desire. Man, then, needs guidance for attaining his ends' (*ibid.* p.3).

On this basis, princely government rightly (according to

Natural law) directs individual lives, but it, in turn, is subordinate to Divine law and to the ecclesiastical ministers of this law. The latter crowns the former as grace crowns nature *(see above*, pp. 43f). In contrast to Luther's *Text IX*, Aquinas maintained that the tyrant need not always be obeyed:

> 'Tyrannical law, not being according to reason, is not law at all in the true and strict sense, but is rather a perversion of law. It does, however, assume the nature of law to the extent that it provides for the well-being of the citizens. Thus it bears some relationship to law in so far as it is the dictate to his subjects of some one in authority; and to the extent that its object is the full obedience of those subjects to the law. For them such obedience is good, not unconditionally, but with respect to the particular regime under which they live' *(ibid.* p.119, from *S.T.* I/II.92).

In so far as princely government promotes the well-being of individuals, it accords with Natural law and provides the basis on which grace can then act.

2. KEY ISSUES
Having attempted to establish that monarchy accords with nature and offers the best form of government, Aquinas now considers the duties of a king. He suggests a strong analogy between, on the one hand, God's control over the universe, and, on the other, reason's control over the individual and a king's control over society. If he is faithful to this analogy, a king should be guided by reason, justice, mildness and clemency (V.1). Whereas God is both creator and governor of the universe, usually a king is only governor of a city or kingdom. Yet, in governing, he ought to be aware of the purposes for which the city or kingdom was founded (V.2). Unlike God, the founder of a city or kingdom does not create from nothing, but chooses, from an existing place, a suitable site for his city or kingdom, plans the positions for his buildings, orders the people and provides for their needs – all functions which resemble the work of God as creator (V.3). The king, as governor – again analogous with God's work – must seek to

guide his people to their appointed end and not simply to preserve the status quo (V.4). The end of man is that final blessedness and enjoyment of God to be known after death (V.5) and not merely some perfection which already exists in man (V.6). Since this end cannot be attained alone by natural human virtue, but only through divine grace, it can only be divine rule, rather than a human government, which can lead man to it (V.7). This divine rule is entrusted to the Papacy and to the Church – to which all subordinate, temporal rulers must be subject (V.8).

3. ETHICAL ARGUMENTS

Analogical arguments, based upon Natural law, are apparent throughout this Text. Natural law provides the deontological basis for the discussion (see Text II). The world of nature reveals how human society should be ordered and how the king should behave. Yet the work of God himself can be used as the basic analogy for man's moral and social behaviour. For Aquinas, the concept of an analogy of being (*analogia entis*) between creator and created was crucial: indeed, precisely because the creature was the direct product of the creator, the former could be used to infer the existence and certain attributes of the latter, and the latter could be used to discover how the former should live. In much Reformed theology, sin is thought to have so distorted the creator/created relationship, that such analogical argument is impossible. But, for Aquinas, it is the key to his argument. The Aristotelian stress upon the end or 'telos' of man – seen here, though, in terms of the beatific vision (V.5) – gives the argument an eventual consequentialist or teleological bias.

4. BASES OF CHRISTIAN ETHICS

The quotation from Genesis (in V.3) plays an important role in this Text. Aquinas derives the principles for founding a city or kingdom analogically from it. This kind of analogical interpretation is obviously dependent on his overall understanding of theology and exegesis. The quotations from Paul, however, (in V.5 and V.7) are not used analogically, but rather to substantiate specifically theological points. Aquinas' assumption of ecclesiastical tradition and papal primacy is apparent in V.8: this tradition is simply presented prescriptively.

5. SOCIAL DETERMINANTS

Aquinas' discussion of political realities is, perhaps inevitably, deeply coloured by the social context of 13th Century Italy. Most obviously is this seen in his frequent mention of a king of 'a city or a kingdom': it reflects the world of relatively autonomous cities, or autocratic local leaders and of small-scale dynasties. It is also apparent in his assumptions about ecclesiastical tradition (cf *Text VIII. 7-12*) and about the structural unity of Church and State (see *above*, p. 46). Indeed, this particular Text is so evidently dependent on a specific social context that it may appear today as one of the most anachronistic of the Aquinas Texts.

6. SOCIAL SIGNIFICANCE

It is difficult to know whether or not *De Regimine Principum* had any serious influence upon politics. At the most, it provided a legitimation for the status quo of 13th Century Italy. Nonetheless, the specific way in which Aquinas attempted to derive the duties of political leaders, both from Natural law and from the concept of creation, has had a continuing influence upon Catholic political thought. This influence is clearly present in John XXIII's *Extract 11*, and even in Hastings' *Extract 24* and Temple's *Extract 10*.

FURTHER READING

The introduction by A.P. D'Entrèves to his *Aquinas: Selected Political Writing* is useful. However, reference should also be made to books concerned with Aquinas' understanding of war (see Section 3) and to those concerned with his notion of Natural law (see *above*, p.79).

TEXT V

AQUINAS

On princely government

The duties of a king; the similarity between royal power and the power of the soul over the body and of God over the universe.

V.1   To Complete what we have so far said it remains only
to consider what is the duty of a king and how he should
comport himself. And since art is but an imitation of
nature, from which we come to learn how to act
according to reason, it would seem best to deduce the
duties of a king from the examples of government in
nature. Now in nature there is to be found both a
universal and a particular form of government. The
universal is that by which all things find their place under
the direction of God, who, by His providence, governs
the universe. The particular is very similar to this divine
control, and is found within man himself, who, for this
reason, is called a microcosm, because he provides an
example of universal government. Just as the divine
control is exercised over all created bodies and over all
spiritual powers, so does the control of reason extend
over the members of the body and the other faculties of
the soul: so, in a certain sense, reason is to man what God
is to the universe. But because, as we have shown above,
man is by nature a social animal living in community,
this similarity with divine rule is found among men, not
only in the sense that a man is directed by his reason, but
also in the fact that a community is ruled by one man's
intelligence; for this is essentially the king's duty. A
similar example of such control is to be found among
certain animals which live in community, such as bees,
which are said to have a king. But in their case, of course,
the control has no rational foundation, but springs from
an instinct of their nature, given them by the supreme
ruler who is the author of nature. A king, then, should
realize that he has assumed the duty of being to his
kingdom what the soul is to the body and what God is to
the universe. If he thinks attentively upon this point he
will, on the one hand, be fired with zeal for justice, seeing
himself appointed to administer justice throughout his
realm in the name of God, and, on the other hand, he will
grow in mildness and clemency, looking upon the
persons subject to his government, as the members of his
own body.

Further development of this analogy and of the conclusions to be drawn from it.

V.2   We must now consider what God does in the universe, and thus we shall see what a king should do. There are, in general, two aspects of the work of God in the world. The first is the act of creation; the second His governance of it once He has created it. Similarly, the action of the soul upon the body presents two aspects. In the first place it is the soul which gives form to the body and secondly it is by the soul that the body is controlled and moved. It is the second of these two operations which pertains more particularly to the king's office; for all kings are bound to govern, and it is from this process of directing the government that the term king (rex) is derived. The former task, however, does not fall to all kings; for not every king founds the city or kingdom over which he rules; many fulfil their duties in cities or kingdoms which are already flourishing. It must not, however, be forgotten that if there had been no one in the first place to establish a city or a kingdom, there would be nothing to govern: so that the kingly office must also cover the founding of a city or a kingdom. Some kings have, in fact, founded the cities over which they afterwards ruled, as Ninus founded Nineveh, and Romulus Rome. It is furthermore the ruler's duty to protect what he governs and to make use of it for the ends for which it was intended: but he cannot be fully aware of the duties of his office if he fails to acquaint himself with the reasons for government. Now the reason for the foundation of a kingdom is to be found in the example provided by the creation of the world: in this we must first consider the creation of things themselves, and then their orderly distribution throughout the universe. Then we see how things are distributed in the various parts of the universe according to their different species; the stars in the heavens, birds in the air, fishes in the sea and animals upon the earth. Finally we note how abundantly divine providence furnishes each species with all that is necessary to it. Moses has described this orderliness shown in creation with great care and subtlety.

V.3 He first considers the creation of things by the words: 'In the beginning God created heaven and earth' (Gen. 1.1); then he notes that all things became, by divine command, distinct according to their appropriate order, as day from night, the heights from the depths, and the waters from dry land. Then he tells how the heavens were adorned with stars, the air with birds, the sea with fishes, and the earth with animals. Finally, he tells how dominion was given to men over the whole earth and the animals thereon. As for plant life, he says that it was given by providence for the use of both animals and men. Now the founder of a city or of a kingdom cannot create out of nothing the men or the dwelling places or all the other things necessary to life; he must use instead what nature has already provided. Just as all other arts find their materials from natural sources; the smiths working with iron and the builder with wood and stone. So one who is about to establish a city or a realm must, in the first place, choose a suitable site; healthy, to ensure the health of the inhabitants; fertile, to provide for their sustenance; one which will delight the eye with its loveliness and give natural security against hostile attack. Where any of these advantages are lacking, the site chosen will be the more suitable to the extent that such conditions, or at least the more indispensible of them, are fulfilled. Having chosen the site, the next task which confronts the founder of a city or of a kingdom is to plan the area to meet all the requirements of a civic life. When founding a kingdom, for example, one must decide where to build the towns and where tó leave the countryside open, or to construct fortifications: centres of study, open places for military training, and markets, all have to be taken into consideration: and similarly for every other activity which goes to make up the life of a kingdom. If it is a city which is to be established, sites must be asigned to churches, to administrative offices, and to the workshops of various trades. The citizens then have to be grouped in various quarters of the city according to their calling. Finally, provision must be made so that no person goes in want, according to his condition and calling: otherwise neither city nor kingdom would long endure. Such, very briefly, are the points a king must consider when establishing a city or a kingdom, and they can all be arrived at by analogy with the creation of the world.

Comparison between the priestly power and that of a king

V.4   Just as the creation of the world serves as a convenient model for the establishment of a city or a kingdom, so does its government allow us to deduce the principle of civil government. We must first have in mind that to govern is to guide what is governed to its appointed end. So we say that a ship is under control when it is sailed on its right course to port by the skill of a sailor. Now when something is ordered to an end which lies outside itself, as a ship is to harbour, it is the ruler's duty not only to preserve its integrity, but also to see that it reaches its appointed destination. If there were anything with no end beyond itself, then the ruler's sole task would be to preserve it unharmed in all its perfection. But though there is no such example to be found in creation, apart from God who is the end of all things, care for higher aims is beset with many and varied difficulties. For it is very clear that there may be one person employed about the preservation of a thing in its present state, and another concerned with bringing it to higher perfection; as we see in the case of a ship, which we have used as an example of government. Just as it is the carpenter's task to repair any damage which may occur and the sailor's task to steer the ship to port, so also in man himself the same processes are at work. The doctor sets himself to preserve man's life and bodily health; the economist's task is to see that there is no lack of material goods; the learned see to it that he knows the truth; and the moralist that he should live according to reason. Thus, if man were not destined to some higher end, these attentions would suffice.

V.5   But there is a further destiny for man after this mortal life; that final blessedness and enjoyment of God which he awaits after death. For, as the Apostle says (2 Corinthians 5.6): 'While we are in the body we are absent from God.' So it is that the Christian, for whom that blessedness was obtained by the blood of Christ, and who is led to it through the gift of the Holy Ghost, has need of another, spiritual, guide to lead him to the harbour of eternal salvation; such guidance is provided for the faithful by the ministers of the Church of Christ.

V.6   Our conclusion must be the same, whether we consider the destiny of one person or of a whole community. Consequently, if the end of man were to be found in any perfection existing in man himself, the final object of government in a community would lie in the acquisition of such perfection and in its preservation once acquired. So that if such an end, whether of an individual or of a community, were life and bodily health, doctors would govern. If, on the other hand, it were abundance of riches, the government of the community could safely be left in the hands of the economist. If it were knowledge of truth, the king, whose task it is to guide the community, would have the duties of a professor. But the object for which a community is gathered together is to live a virtuous life. For men consort together that they may thus attain a fullness of life which would not be possible to each living singly: and the full life is one which is lived according to virtue. Thus the object of human society is a virtuous life.

V.7   A proof of this lies in the fact that only those members may be considered part of the community who contribute jointly to the fullness of social life. If men consorted together for bare existence, both animals and slaves would have a part in civil society. If for the multiplication of riches, all who had common commercial ties would belong to one city. But it is those who obey the same laws, and are guided by a single government to the fullness of life, who can be said to constitute a social unit. Now the man who lives virtuously is destined to a higher end, which consists, as we have already said, in the enjoyment of God: and the final object of human association can be no different from that of the individual man. Thus the final aim of social life will be, not merely to live in virtue, but rather through virtuous life to attain to the enjoyment of God. If, indeed, it were possible to attain this object by natural human virtue, it would, in consequence, be the duty of kings to guide men to this end. We believe, however, that it is the supreme power in temporal affairs which is the business of a king. Now government is of a higher order according to the importance of the ends it serves. For it is always the one who has the final ordering of affairs who directs those who carry out what pertains to the attainment of the final aim: just as the sailor who must navigate the ship advises the shipwright as to the type of ship which will suit his purpose; and the citizen who is to bear arms tells the smith what weapons to forge. But the enjoyment of God is an aim which cannot be attained by human virtue alone, but only through divine grace, as the Apostle tells us (Romans, 6.23): 'The grace of God is eternal life'. Only a divine rule, then, and not human government, can lead us to this end. Such government belongs only to that King who is both man, and also God: that is to Jesus Christ, our Lord, Who, making men to be Sons of God has led them to the glory of heaven.

V.8   This, then, is the government entrusted to Him: a dominion which shall never pass away, and in virtue of which He is called in the Holy Scriptures, not only a priest but a king; as *Jeremias* says (23.5): 'A king shall reign and shall be wise'. It is from Him that the royal priesthood derives; and, what is more, all the Faithful of Christ, being members of Him, become thus, priests and kings. The ministry of this kingdom is entrusted not to the rulers of this earth but to priests, so that temporal affairs may remain distinct from those spiritual: and, in particular, it is delegated to the High Priest, the successor of Peter and Vicar of Christ, the Roman Pontiff; to whom all kings in Christendom should be subjects, as to the Lord Jesus Christ Himself. For those who are concerned with the subordinate ends of life must be subject to him who is concerned with the supreme end and be directed by his command. And because the pagan priesthood and everything connected with the cult of pagan gods was directed to the attainment of temporal benefits, which form part of the common weal of the community, and which lie within the king's competence, it was right that pagan priests should be subject to their kings. Similarly in the Old Testament, temporal benefits were promised to the people in reward for their faith, though these promises were made by the true God and not by demons; so that under the Old Law we read that the priesthood was subject to kings. But under the New Law there is a higher priesthood through which men are led to a heavenly reward: and under Christ's Law, kings must be subject to priests.

V.9   For this reason it came about by the admirable dispensation of divine providence, that in the city of Rome which God chose to be the main centre of Christendom, it gradually became the custom for the rulers of the city to be subject to the pontiffs.

CRITIQUE

The negative and dysfunctional side of Aquinas' understanding (and indeed medieval understanding generally) of government appears elsewhere in his writings. It was theocratic and thoroughly intolerant of any form of religious opposition. A.P. D'Entrèves pointed out:

'The theory of St. Thomas is the theory of the orthodox State. We are apt to forget it. We have grown so accustomed to the threat which comes from the State (D'Entrèves was writing in 1948), that we are only too ready to hail the Church as the champion of freedom. Medieval intolerance had at least one great advantage over modern totalitarianism. It subtracted entirely the definition of orthodoxy from the hands of the politician. It put a bar on Erastianism. It would never have allowed that 'the General Will is always right'. It was an intolerance of a different and more noble brand. But it was intolerance all right, and a thorough, totalitarian intolerance' (from his Introduction to *Aquinas: Selected Political Writings*, p. xxii).

As evidence of Aquinas' intolerance he cited his advice in *De Regimine Judaeorum* that Jews must not be harmed but must neverthless remain outcasts in the Christian community and should be forced to earn their living in non-usurious ways: 'Jews of both sexes and in all Christian lands should on all occasions be distinguished from other people by some particular dress' (*ibid.*, p.95: see further on *Luther's XII*). But, most of all, for Aquinas and his contemporaries, it was the Christian apostate who was to be treated harshly: 'if it be just that forgers and other malefactors are put to death without mercy by the secular authority, with how much greater reason may heretics not only be excommunicated, but also put to death, when once they are convicted of heresy' (*S. T.* II.II. Q.11.Art.3). This link, between theocratic and religiously intolerant attitudes, is particularly striking in someone, like Aquinas, who otherwise appears to have been a gentle and equable person (see further, *below*, pp.425-6). More positively, his stress upon the *duties* of kings and his admission that tyrants need not always be obeyed, contrast favourably with Luther.

TEXT VI
LUTHER
Trade and usury

I. BACKGROUND

This Text comes from *Trade and Usury* (from *Luther's Works*, vol. 45, Fortress Press, Philadelphia, 1966, trans. Charles M. Jacobs and rev. Walther I. Brandt, pp. 245-6, 247-254 & 255-60). Luther published this treatise in 1524 together with a re-print of his *Long Sermon on Usury* written earlier in 1520 (see *above*, p.89). Both works demonstrate his dislike of what he regarded as commercial greed (he was himself always disinterested in personal wealth) and his basic ignorance of economic realities. Luther accepted many of the medieval presuppositions about financial matters, notably Aristotle's notion that money does not produce money and the medieval ecclesiastical condemnation of usury. But he argued that contemporary practice failed to live up to these presuppositions and, indeed, failed to live up to biblical norms on wealth. In addition, he was unhappy about the failure of the diets of Nürnberg in 1522 and 1524 to deal effectively with the monopolistic practices of the trading companies. Luther was also reacting, in 1524, against the rigorist positions of the evangelical preachers Jacob Strauss and Wolfgang Stein, who maintained that a debtor is not even obliged to repay his debt to a usurer, for otherwise he would share in the usurer's guilt. The notion of surety or property insurance (VI.14) was first developed in the 14th Century and was held to be non-usurious, except when it was used to guarantee a loan. Despite the general advice to traders at the beginning of this treatise, it becomes clear (e.g. in VI.19) that Luther's primary concern here is with Christians in their relation to wealth and commercial activity. At this level, the treatise is arguably still relevant to contemporary Christian ethics.

2. KEY ISSUES

Even though he is pessimistic about his advice being heeded, Luther sets out what he considers to be the proper position of the Christian merchant (VI.1-2). The trade of essential commodities is necessary in the world (VI.3). But there are abuses (two of which are contained in this Text). Firstly, merchants can become greedy and try to sell their goods as expensively as possible (VI.5-6). Instead, they should sell them only at a price that is just and in a way that does no injury to others (VI.7). Differing circumstances render it difficult to make rules about just prices, but temporal authorities could appoint wise and honest men to do this or it could be left to market forces (VI.8-9). In this Christians must act according to their conscience (VI.10-11) and be prepared to confess any inadvertent sins resulting from trading (VI.12-13). The second abuse arises from merchants standing surety for individuals (VI.14). This practice is against Scripture (VI.14-15) and it puts a false trust in man rather than God (VI.16-18). In contrast, there are four specifically Christian ways of exchanging goods. First, Christians can simply let others steal their property (VI-19). Secondly, they can give to anyone in need (VI.20). Thirdly, they can lend expecting nothing in return (VI.21). But, if followed in a sinful world, these three ways would lead to the break-down of trade: in such a world, laws for non-Christians are essential (VI.23-4). Fourthly, Christians can buy and sell in cash alone, not relying upon credit or upon surety (VI.26).

3. ETHICAL ARGUMENTS

In contrast to Text III, this Text contains a variety of explicit forms of ethical argument. There is an appeal to Natural law (VI.5) and several to individual conscience (VI.7 and 10-11). Consequentialism is evident in VI.7 and the arguments in VI.13 are distinctly pragmatic. But there is an overall deontological basis to the positions maintained in the Text:- 'avarice', 'greed', 'robbing' and, indeed, 'injustice' (VI.5) are all assumed to be self-evidently wrong. Standing surety is also believed to be wrong primarily because it offends against Scripture (VI.14). Even popular German proverbs are used deontologically to reinforce his argument (VI.9 & 15). This Text is particularly important in illustrating the clear dichotomy that Luther often felt between the standards appropriate for the Christian and those to be required of the non-Christian.

4. BASES OF CHRISTIAN ETHICS

Both Old and New Testaments are used throughout this passage. Indeed, Scripture characteristically forms the basis and constant point of reference for Luther's contentions (cf Text III). This is particularly evident in his use of Proverbs (VI.14), Genesis (VI.18) and Matthew (VI.19). But there is also a strong doctrinal basis to his argument in VI.16-17 and the concept of the counsel of perfection for the clergy, in VI.19, is heavily dependent upon Christian tradition rather than the Bible. There is also an important reference to 'Christian love' in VI.6. It might even be possible to argue that Luther was a situationist as far as Christians were concerned: laws were considered necessary only because most people were not Christian: if the world consisted only of Christians, Christian love would be a sufficient guide for proper action. This position is most evident in the treatise of the previous year, *Temporal Authority: To What Extent It Should Be Obeyed*, that he refers to in VI.23, as the following excerpt demonstrates:-

'If all the world were composed of real Christians, that is, true believers, there would be no need for or benefits from prince, king, lord, sword, or law. They would serve no purpose, since Christians have in their heart the Holy Spirit, who both teaches and makes them to do injustice to no one, to love everyone, and to suffer injustice and even death willingly and cheerfully at the hands of anyone. Where there is nothing but the unadulterated doing of right and bearing of wrong, there is not need for any suit, litigation, court, judge, penalty, law or sword. . . because the righteous man of his own accord does all and more than the law demands. But the unrighteous do nothing that the law demands; therefore, they need the law to instruct, constrain, and compel them to do good. . . All who are not Christians belong to the kingdom of the world and are under the law. There are few true believers, and still fewer who live a Christian life, who do not resist evil and indeed themselves do no evil. For this reason God has provided for them a different government beyond the Christian estate and kingdom of God. He has subjected them to the sword so that, even though they would like to, they are unable to practice their wickedness, and if they do practice it they cannot do so without fear or with success and impunity. . . If this were not so, men would devour one another, seeing that the whole world is evil and that among thousands there is scarcely a single true Christian. No one could support wife and child, feed himself, and serve God. The world would be reduced to chaos. For this reason God has ordained two governments: the spiritual, by which the Holy Spirit produces Christians and right-eous people under Christ; and the temporal, which restrains the un-Christian and wicked so that – no thanks to them – they are obliged to keep still and to maintain an outward peace' (*Luther's Works, op.cit.,* Vol. 45, pp. 89-90).

This is one of Luther's clearest expressions of the notion of 'the two kingdoms'.

5. *SOCIAL DETERMINANTS*

The extent to which Luther was dependent upon medieval notions of finance has already been indicated and is particularly evident in his unworkable solution in VI.26. In addition, it might be argued that the sharp dichotomy that he made between the ethical requirements for Christians and those for non-Christians was exacerbated by his own particular social context. An accompaniment of the empirical phenomenon of conversion (see *above*, pp. 35-7) can be a subsequent tendency to exaggerate the depravity of the pre-conversion state and those associated with it. Certainly, in this Text Luther's estimate of 'non-evangelical Christians' appears very low. Doubtless, the excesses of parts of the 16th Century Catholic Church also contributed to the dichotomy that Luther drew (see *above*, p.91). Luther attempted to maintain a position mid-way between the Anabaptists' rejection of Christians participating in political and economic matters and the Church of Rome's assumption of all earthly authority within itself.

6. SOCIAL SIGNIFICANCE

It is ironic that, whilst Luther upheld the central convictions of medieval Christendom about the evils of usury, of unrestrained trade based upon maximum profit and of unjust and unjustifiable prices, he may have contributed indirectly to their propagation. Returning to Weber's thesis of *The Protestant Ethic and the Spirit of Capitalism* (see *above*, p.92), the very success of Luther's challenge to the Church of Rome's authority, may have helped to remove the sanctions enforced by this authority. Thus, on the issue of usury, Luther clearly despised it and tragically associated the Jew with it (see *Text XII*). Yet one of the social effects of his theological challenge may have been to promote a new individualism in Europe and the structural demise of effective sanctions against usury. It would be false to claim either that this was the sole factor in effecting economic change in Europe or that either Luther or Calvin were themselves directly and consciously responsible for the rise of the spirit of rational capitalism (the so-called 'work ethic'). Weber's thesis depends on neither claim. But it is possible to see Luther's challenge contributing significantly to changes already present in European society.

FURTHER READING

Luther's writings of the 1520's have been the subject of a considerable amount of books. Some of these have already been mentioned in relation to *Text III*. They can be compared fruitfully with Calvin's political writings in ed. John T. McNeill, *Calvin: on God and Political Duty*. On the issue of 'usury', J.T. Noonan, Jr., *The Scholastic Analysis of Usury* is useful.

TEXT VI

LUTHER

Trade and usury

VI.1   The holy gospel, now that it has come to light, rebukes and reveals all the 'works of darkness', as St. Paul calls them in Romans 13 (:12). For it is a brilliant light, which illumines the whole world and teaches how evil are the works of the world, and shows the true works we ought to do for God and our neighbor. As a result even some of the merchants have been awakened and become aware that in their trading many a wicked trick and hurtful financial practice is in use. It is to be feared that the words of Ecclesiasticus apply here, namely, that merchants can hardly be without sin (Ecclus. 26:29). Indeed, I think St. Paul's saying in the last chapter of the first epistle to Timothy fits the case, "The love of money is the root of all evils" (I Tim. 6.10), and again, "Those who desire to be rich fall into the devil's snare and into many useless and hurtful desires that plunge men into ruin and perdition" (I Tim. 6.9).

VI.2   I suppose that my writing will be quite in vain, because the mischief has gone so far and has completely gotten the upper hand in all lands; and because those who understand the gospel are probably able in such easy, external things to judge for themselves what is fair and what is not, on the basis of their own consciences. Nevertheless, I have been asked and urged to touch upon these financial evils and expose some of them so that, even though the majority may not wish to do right, at least some people – however few they are – may be delivered from the gaping jaws of avarice. For it must be that among the merchants, as among other people, there are some who belong to Christ and would rather be poor with God than rich with the devil, as Psalm 37 (:16) says, "It is better for the righteous to have a little than to have the great possessions of the wicked." For their sake, then, we must speak out.

VI.3   It cannot be denied that buying and selling are necessary. They cannot be dispensed with, and can be practised in a Christian manner, especially when the commodities serve a necessary and honorable purpose. For even the patriarchs bought and sold cattle, wool, grain, butter, milk and other goods in this way. These are gifts of God, which he bestows out of the earth and distributes among mankind. But foreign trade, which brings from Calcutta and India and such places wares like costly silks, articles of gold, and spices – which minister only to ostentation but serve no useful purpose, and which drain away the money of land and people – would not be permitted if we had [proper] government and princes. But of this it is not my present purpose to write, for I expect that, like overdressing and overeating, it will have to stop of itself when we have no more money. Until then, neither writing nor teaching will do any good. We must first feel the pinch of want and poverty. . .

VI.4   It is our purpose here to speak of the abuses and sins of trade, insofar as they concern the conscience. The matter of their detrimental effect on the purse we leave to the princes and lords, that they may do their duty in this regard.

VI.5   First. Among themselves the merchants have a common rule which is their chief maxim and the basis of all their sharp practices, where they say: "I may sell my goods as dear as I can." They think this is their right. Thus occasion is given for avarice, and every window and door to hell is opened. What else does it mean but this: I care nothing about my neighbor; so long as I have my profit and satisfy my greed, of what concern is it to me if it injures my neighbor in ten ways at once? There you see how shamelessly this maxim flies squarely in the face not only of Christian love but also of natural law. How can there be anything good then in trade? How can it be without sin when such injustice is the chief maxim and rule of the whole business? On such a basis trade can be nothing but robbing and stealing the property of others.

VI.6   When once the rogue's eye and greedy belly of a merchant find that people must have his wares, or that the buyer is poor and needs them, he takes advantage of him and raises the price. He considers not the value of the goods, or what his own efforts and risk have deserved, but only the other man's want and need. He notes it not that he may relieve it but that he may use it to his own advantage by raising the price of his goods, which he would not have raised had it not been for his neighbor's need. Because of his avarice, therefore, the goods must be priced as much higher as the greater need of the other fellow will allow, so that the neighbor's need becomes as it were the measure of the goods' worth and value. Tell me, isn't that an un-Christian and inhuman thing to do? Isn't that equivalent to selling a poor man his own need in the same transaction? When he has to buy his wares at a higher price because of his need, that is the same as having to buy his own need; for what is sold to him is not simply the wares as they are, but the wares plus the fact that he must have them. Observe that this and like abominations are the inevitable consequence when the rule is that I may sell my goods as dear as I can.

VI.7   The rule ought to be, not, "I may sell my wares as dear as I can or will," but, "I may sell my wares as dear as I ought, or as is right and fair." For your selling ought not to be an act that is entirely within your own power and discretion, without law or limit, as though you were a god and beholden to no one. Because your selling is an act performed toward your neighbor, it should rather be so governed by law and conscience that you do it without harm and injury to him, your concern being directed more toward doing him no injury than toward gaining profit for yourself. But where are there such merchants? How few merchants there would be, and how trade would decline, if they were to amend this evil rule and put things on a fair and Christian basis!

VI.8   You ask, then, "How dear may I sell? How am I to arrive at what is fair and right so I do not take increase from neighbor or overcharge him?" Answer: That is something that will never be governed either by writing or speaking; nor has anyone ever undertaken to fix the value of every commodity, and to raise or lower prices accordingly. The reason is this: wares are not all alike; one is transported a greater distance than another and one involves greater outlay than another. In this respect, therefore, everything is and must remain uncertain, and no fixed determination can be made, any more than one can designate a certain city as the place from which all wares are to be brought, or establish a definite cost price for them. It may happen that the same wares, brought from the same city by the same road, cost vastly more in one year than they did the year before because the weather may be worse, or the road, or because something else happens that increases the expense at one time above that at another time. Now it is fair and right that a merchant take as much profit on his wares as will reimburse him for their cost and compensate him for his trouble, his labor, and his risk. Even a farmhand must have food and pay for his labor. Who can serve or labor for nothing? The gospel says, "The laborer deserves his wages" [Luke 10:7].

VI.9   But in order not to leave the question entirely unanswered, the best and safest way would be to have the temporal authorities appoint in this matter wise and honest men to compute the costs of all sorts of wares and accordingly set prices which would enable the merchant to get along and provide for him an adequate living, as is being done at certain places with respect to wine, fish, bread, and the like. But we Germans have too many other things to do; we are too busy drinking and dancing to provide for rules and regulations of this sort. Since this kind of ordinance therefore is not to be expected, the next best thing is to let goods be valued at the price for which they are bought and sold in the common market, or in the land generally. In this matter we can accept the proverb, "Follow the crowd and you won't get lost." Any profit made in this way I consider honest and proper, because here there is always the risk involved of having to suffer loss in wares and outlay, and excessive profits are scarcely possible.

VI.10   Where the price of goods is not fixed either by law or custom, and you must fix it yourself, here one can truly give you no instructions but only lay it on your conscience to be careful not to overcharge your neighbor, and to seek a modest living, not the goals of greed. Some have wished to place a ceiling on profits, with a limit of one-half on all wares; some say one-third; others something else. None of these measures is certain and safe unless it be so decreed by the temporal authorities and common law. What they determine in these matters would be safe. Therefore, you must make up your mind to seek in your trading only an adequate living. Accordingly, you should compute and count your cost, trouble, labor, and risk, and on that basis raise or lower the prices of your wares so that you set them where you will be repaid for your trouble and labor.

VI.11   I would not have anyone's conscience be so overly scrupulous or so closely bound in this matter that he feels he must strike exactly the right measure of profit to the very *heller*. It is impossible for you to arrive at the exact amount that you have earned with your trouble and labor. It is enough that with a good conscience you make the effort to arrive at what is right, though the very nature of trade makes it impossible to determine this exactly. The saying of the Wise Man will hold good in your case too: "A merchant can hardly act without sin, and a tradesman will hardly keep his lips from evil" [Ecclus. 26:29]. If you take a trifle too much profit unwittingly and unintentionally, dismiss the matter in the Lord's Prayer where we pray, "Forgive us our trespasses" [Matt. 6:12]. After all, no man's life is without sin; besides, the time will come in turn when you get too little for your trouble. Just throw the excess in the scale to counterbalance the losses you must similarly expect to take.

VI.12   For example, if you had a business amounting to a hundred *gulden* a year, and you were to take – over and above all the cost and reasonable profit you had for your trouble, labor, and risk – an excessive profit of perhaps one or two or three *gulden*, that I would call a business error which could not well be avoided, especially in the course of a whole year's trading. Therefore, you should not burden your conscience with it, but bring it to God in the Lord's Prayer as another of those inevitable sins (which cling to all of us) and leave the matter to him. For it is not wickedness or greed, but the very nature and necessity of your occupation which forces you into this mistake. I am speaking now of goodhearted and God-fearing men, who would not willingly do wrong. It is like the marital obligation, which cannot be performed without sin; yet because of its necessity, God winks at it, for it cannot be otherwise.

VI.13　In determining how much profit you ought to take on your business and your labor, there is no better way to reckon it than by computing the amount of time and labor you have put into it, and comparing that with the effort of a day laborer who works at some other occupation and seeing how much he earns in a day. On that basis figure how many days you have spent in getting your wares and bringing them to your place of business, and how much labor and risk was involved; for a great amount of labor and time ought to have a correspondingly greater return. That is the most accurate, the best, and the most definite advice and direction that can be given in this matter. Let him who dislikes it, better it himself. I base my case (as I have said) on the gospel that the laborer deserves his wages [Luke 10:7]; and Paul also says in I Corinthians 9 [:7], "He who tends the flock should get some of the milk. Who can go to war at his own expense?" If you have a better ground than that, you are welcome to it.

VI.14　Second. A common error, which has become a widespread custom not only among the merchants but throughout the world, is the practice of one person becoming surety for another. Although this practice seems to be without sin, and looks like a virtue stemming from love, nevertheless it generally ruins a good many people and does them irreparable harm. King Solomon often forbade it, and condemned it in his proverbs. In Proverbs 6 [:1-5] he says, "My son, if you have become surety for your neighbor, you have given your hand on it; you are snared in the utterance of your lips, and caught in the words of your mouth. Then do this, my son, and save yourself, for you have come into your neighbor's power: Go, hasten and importune your neighbor. Give your eyes no sleep, and your eyelids no slumber. Save yourself like a gazelle from the hand, and like a bird from the hand of the fowler." Again. . . "Take a man's garment when he has given surety for another, and take a pledge from him for the stranger's sake" [Prov. 27:13].

VI.15   See how strictly and vehemently the wise king in Holy Scripture forbids one's becoming surety for another. The German proverb agrees with him, "Guarantors to the gallows;" as much as to say: It serves the surety right when he is seized and has to pay, for he is acting rashly and foolishly in becoming surety. Hence, it is decreed according to Scripture that no one shall become surety for another, unless he is able and entirely willing to assume the debt and pay it himself. Now it does seem strange that this practice should be wrong and be condemned, although a good many have learned by experience that it is a foolish thing to do, and have had subsequent misgivings about it. Why, then, is it condemned? Let us see.

VI.16   Standing surety is a work that is too lofty for a man; it is unseemly, for it is a presumptuous encroachment upon the work of God. In the first place, Scripture commands us not to put our trust and reliance in any man, but in God alone. For human nature is false, vain, deceitful, and unreliable, as Scripture says and experience daily teaches. He who becomes surety, however, is putting his trust in a man, and risking life and property on a false and insecure foundation. It serves him right when he fails, falls, and is ruined.

VI.17   In the second place, the surety is trusting in himself and making himself God (for whatever a man trusts in and relies upon is his god). But his own life and property are never for a single moment any more secure or certain than those of the man for whom he becomes surety. Everything is in the hand of God alone. God will not allow us a hair's breadth of power or right over the future, nor will he let us for a single moment be sure or certain of it. Therefore, he who becomes surety acts in an un-Christian way; he deserves what he gets, because he pledges and promises what is not his and not in his power, but solely in God's hands.

VI.18   Thus we read in Genesis 43 and 44, how the patriarch Judah became surety to his father Jacob for his brother Benjamin, promising to bring him home again or bear the blame forever [Gen. 43:8-9]. God nicely punished this presumption, and caused him to flounder and fail so that he could not bring Benjamin back until he gave himself up for him [Gen. 44:14-34] and then was barely freed by grace. The punishment served him right, for these sureties act as though they didn't even have to consult God on the matter or give thought to whether they are even sure of a tomorrow for their own life and property. They act without fear of God, as though they were themselves the source of life and property, and these were in their own power as long as they themselves willed it. This is nothing but a fruit of unbelief. . .

VI.19   Perhaps you will say, "How then are people to trade with one another if surety is improper? That way many would be left behind who might otherwise get ahead." Answer: There are four Christian ways of exchanging external goods with others, as I have said elsewhere. The first way is to let them rob or steal our property, as Christ says in Matthew 5, "If anyone takes away your cloak, let him have your coat as well, and do not ask it of him again." This way of dealing counts for nothing among the merchants; besides, it has not been held or preached as common teaching for all Christians, but merely as a counsel or a good idea for the clergy and the perfect, though they observe it even less than do the merchants. But true Christians observe it, for they know that their Father in heaven has assuredly promised in Matthew 6 [:11] to give them this day their daily bread. If men were to act accordingly, not only would countless abuses in all kinds of business be avoided, but a great many people would not become merchants, because reason and human nature flee and shun to the uttermost risks and damages of this sort.

VI.20   The second way is to give freely to anyone who needs it, as Christ also teaches in the same passage [Matt. 5:42; Luke 6:30]. This too is a lofty Christian work, which is why it counts for little among the people. There would be fewer merchants and less trade if this were put into practice. For he who does this must truly hold fast to heaven and look always to the hands of God, and not to his own resources or wealth, knowing that God will support him even though every cupboard were bare, because he knows to be true what God said to Joshua, "I will not forsake you or withdraw my hand from you" [Josh. 1:5]; as the proverb has it, "God still has more than what he ever gave away." But that takes a true Christian, and he is a rare animal on earth, to whom the world and nature pay no heed.

VI.21   The third way is lending. That is, I give away my property, and take it back again if it is returned to me; but I must do without it if it is not returned. Christ himself defines this kind of transaction in what he says in Luke 6 [:35], "Lend, expecting nothing in return." That is, you should lend freely, and take your chances on getting it back or not. If it comes back, take it; if it does not, it is a gift. According to the gospel there is thus only one distinction between giving and lending, namely, a gift is not taken back, while a loan is taken back – if it is returned – but involves the risk that it may become a gift. He who lends expecting to get back something more and something better than he has loaned is nothing but an open and condemned usurer, since even those who in lending demand or expect to get back exactly what they lend, and take no chances on whether they get it back or not, are not acting in a Christian way. This third way too (in my opinion) is a lofty Christian work; and a rare one, judging by the way things are going in the world. If it were to be practised generally, trade of all sorts would greatly diminish and virtually cease.

VI.22   These three ways of exchanging goods, then, observe in masterful fashion this matter of not presuming upon the future, and not trusting in any man or in oneself but clinging to God alone. Here all transactions are in cash, and are accompanied by the word which James teaches, "If God wills, so be it" [Jas. 4:15]. For here we deal with people as with those who are unreliable and might fail; we give our money freely, or take our chances on losing what we lend.

VI.23 Now someone will say "Who can then be saved? And where shall we find these Christians? Why, in this way there would be no trade left in the world; everyone would have his property taken or borrowed away, and the door would be thrown open for the wicked and idle gluttons – of whom the world is full – to take everything with their lying and cheating." Answer: I have already said that Christians are rare people on earth. That is why the world needs a strict, harsh temporal government which will compel and constrain the wicked to refrain from theft and robbery, and to return what they borrow (although a Christian ought neither to demand nor expect it). This is necessary in order that the world may not become a desert, peace vanish, and men's trade and society be utterly destroyed; all of which would happen if we were to rule the world according to the gospel, rather than driving and compelling the wicked by laws and the use of force to do and allow what is right. For this reason we must keep the roads safe, preserve peace in the towns, enforce law in the land, and let the sword hew briskly and boldly against transgressors, as St.Paul teaches in Romans 13 [:4]. For it is God's will that people who are not Christian be held in check and kept from doing wrong, at least from doing it with impunity. Let no one think that the world can be ruled without bloodshed; the temporal sword must and shall be red and bloody, for the world will and must be evil, and the sword is God's rod and vengeance upon it. But of this I have said enough in my little book on *Temporal Authority*.

VI.24 Borrowing would be a fine thing if it were practised between Christians, for every borrower would then willingly return what had been lent him, and the lender would willingly forego repayment if the borrower were unable to pay. Christians are brothers, and one does not forsake another; neither is any of them so lazy and shameless that he would not work but depend simply on another's wealth and labor, or consume in idleness another's goods. But where men are not Christians, the temporal authorities ought to compel them to repay what they have borrowed. If the temporal authorities are negligent and do not compel repayment, the Christian ought to tolerate the robbery, as Paul says in I Corinthians 6 [:7], "Why not rather suffer wrong?" But you may exhort, insist, and do what you will to the man who is not a Christian; he pays no attention because he is not a Christian and has no regard for Christ's doctrine.

VI.25   You still have a grain of comfort too in the fact that you are not obligated to make a loan except out of your surplus and what you can spare from your own needs, as Christ says of alms, "What you have left over, that give in alms, and everything is clean for you". Now if someone wishes to borrow from you an amount so large that you would be ruined if it were not repaid, and you could not spare it from your own needs, then you are not bound to make the loan. Your first and greatest obligation is to provide for the needs of your wife and children and servants; you must not divert from them what you owe them. The best rule to follow is this: If the amount asked as a loan is too great, just go ahead and give something outright, or else lend as much as you would be willing to give, and take the risk of having to lose it. John the Baptist did not say, "He who has one coat, let him give it away," but, "He who has two coats, let him give one to him who has none; and he who has food, let him do likewise" [Luke 3:11].

VI.26   The fourth way of exchanging goods is through buying or selling, but for hard cash or payment in kind. He who would use this method must make up his mind to rely not on something in the future but on God alone; also, that he will have to be dealing with men, men who will certainly fail and lie. Therefore, the best advice is this: whoever sells should not give credit or accept any security, but sell only for cash. If he wishes to lend, let him lend to Christians, or else take the risk of loss, and lend no more than he would be willing to give outright or can spare from his own needs. If the temporal government and regulations will not help him to recover his loan, let him lose it. Let him beware of becoming security for anyone; let him much rather give what he can. Such a man would be a true Christian merchant; God would not foresake him because he trusts properly in Him and cheerfully takes a chance in dealing with his untrustworthy neighbors.

VI.27   If there was no such thing in this world as becoming surety, if the free lending portrayed in the gospel were the general practice, and if only hard cash or wares on hand were exchanged in trade, then the greatest and most harmful dangers and faults and failings of trade and commerce would be well out of the way. It would then be easy to engage in all sorts of business enterprises, and the other sinful faults of trade could the more readily be prevented. If there were none of this becoming surety and this lending without risk, many a man would have to maintain his humble status and be content with a modest living who now aspires day and night to reach an exalted position, relying on borrowing and standing surety. That is why everyone now wants to be a merchant and get rich. From this stem the countless dangerous, and wicked devices and dirty tricks that have today become a joke among the merchants. There are so many of them that I have given up the hope that trade can be entirely corrected; it is so overburdened with all sorts of wickedness and deception that in the long run it will not be able to sustain itself, but will have to collapse inwardly of its own weight.

VI.28   In what has been said I wished to give a bit of warning and instruction to everyone about this great, filthy, widespread business of trade and commerce.

CRITIQUE

The limitations of some of Luther's medieval economic concepts have already been noted. Nonetheless, the central thrust of his treatise still has undoubted force. At a time, in the West, when the division between Christians and non-Christians, and between the churches and society at large, is often felt to be increasing, his argument assumes fresh relevance. Religious people, generally, may feel a requirement to distinguish more carefully than in a number of previous ages and societies, between what sort of behaviour is appropriate for them and what sort is to be enforced within society. In a number of areas of social ethics this problem may not be acute, but in the areas of personal ethics it often is. So, injunctions against murder and stealing, once socially defined, are expected to apply to all. But in areas of sexual morality any attempt at public enforcement has become considerably more controversial. It will be seen later (*below*, pp.417-8) that even this distinction (i.e. between social and personal ethics) is difficult to maintain consistently and that there are many issues that might claim to be both (e.g. marriage and abortion). Nonetheless, Luther's dilemma remains a real one. There is, indeed, a sense in which there would be no need of laws, courts, prisons etc, if everyone lived consistently by the rule of *agape*: all would tell the truth, respect the property and persons of others, and would be self-less and self-giving. Further, Luther is obviously and sadly correct in asserting that society is just not constituted by such agapeistic people – so laws, courts, prisons are essential if social chaos is to be avoided. He would have made an excellent critic of Fletcher's attempts to work out a system of ethics for all based solely upon *agape*. The dilemma for Christian business-men remains broadly as Luther depicted: they are not working in a society composed solely of sincere Christians and, if they were to follow the injunctions of the Sermon on the Mount literally, their business would probably collapse (as it would if they followed Luther's advice literally). Some present-day theologians, such as Miranda, would see this as good reason for the Christian business-man abandoning Western capitalism altogether. But for those who cannot accept this, tension seems inescapable. It is a tension evident in several of the Extracts in this Section.

Even if it is accepted that some dichotomy between Christian ethics and the ethical standards to be required of society is inevitable, Luther's depiction of this can still be criticised. His view of his contemporaries was bleak and he seemed to believe that if men could not be converted to Christianity they could only be restrained like beasts. Not only does this present a highly exclusive understanding of Christianity (see *above*, p.99), but it makes no allowance for transposed Christian values having an effect upon society at large (see *above*, pp.11-12).

EXTRACTS 7-12
BARTH, BERDAEV, NIEBUHR, TEMPLE,
JOHN XXIII, AND MIRANDA

I. *BACKGROUND*
Karl Barth's *Extract 7* comes from his commentary *The Epistle to the Romans* (OUP, 1929 edition, on Rmns 12.21 & 13.1), Nicolas Berdyaev's *Extract 8* from his *Freedom and the Spirit* (Geoffrey Bles Centenary Press, London, 1935, pp.x–xiv and xvi–xviii), Reinhold Niebuhr's *Extract 9* from his *Moral Man and Immoral Society* (Scribner's, New York, 1960 re-issue, pp.257–259 & 268–75), William Temple's *Extract 10* from his *Christianity and the Social Order* (Shepheard-Walwyn & SPCK, London, 1976 re-issue, pp.58–9, 60–2, 67–8, 69–71, 72-4, 75 & 77), Pope John XXIII's *Extract 11* from his Encyclical Letter *Pacem in Terris* (Catholic Truth Society, London, edition translated by Henry Waterhouse SJ, 1980, paras.80–96, 130–46 & 161–71) and José Porfirio Miranda's *Extract 12* from his *Marx and the Bible* (SCM, London, and Orbis Books, New York, 1977, trans. John Eagleson, pp.14–22). The first and third Extracts represent the views of the authors in their radical youth, whereas the next two represent those of Church statesmen at the end of their lives. *The Epistle to the Romans* represented Barth's radical break with Christian liberalism and proved to be the foundation-stone of the Neo-Orthodox movement in theology. Barth (1886–1968) wrote *Der Römerbrief* in the context of the revolutionary Europe of 1917–19 and, as a result of it, he was soon made a professor, first at Göttingen (1921), then at Münster (1925), then Bonn (1930) and, finally, on expulsion by Hitler, Basle (1935). Niebuhr (1892–1971) published *Moral Man and Immoral Society* in 1932, four years after becoming Professor of Applied Christianity at the Union Theological Seminary, New York, where he stayed until his retirement in 1960. He, too, wrote this work in the context of considerable social ferment, during the American Depression and, as a result of his pastoral experience

in industrial Detroit, prior to his appointment at UTS. Temple (1881-1944) wrote *Christianity and the Social Order* at the height of the Second World War, in 1941, twelve years after becoming Archbishop of York and a few months before becoming Archbishop of Canterbury. Unlike some of his more technical works, its style was designed for the non-theologian and, indeed, it sold some 150,000 copies when first published (re-issued 1956 and 1976). John XXIII (1881-1963) was Pope for five years, publishing *Pacem in Terris* in the year that he died and only months after convening the highly influential Second Vatican Council. *Extract 11* clearly reflects the liberal concerns of John XXIII and the social changes that characterised the 1960's. *Extract 12* reflects the present-day concerns of Latin American Liberation theology. Miranda, a Mexican Roman Catholic, was trained in both economics and biblical studies and has written, in addition, the influential *Marx Against the Marxists* (SCM, 1980). In contrast, Berdyaev (1874-1948) belongs fully to no theological movement and his writings are comparatively timeless. *Freedom and the Spirit* was written in 1927, in Paris, five years after his expulsion from his native Russia. Amongst his other important books are *The Meaning of History* (1923) and *The Destiny of Man* (1931). In his autobiography he describes his position as a Russian Orthodox Christian as follows: 'I confess a spiritual religion, I am a free Christian, who has not broken away from the church'. He died in Paris as a Russian expatriate and independent thinker and scholar.

2. KEY ISSUES

Barth argues that the existing orders in the political realm, whether democratic or not, appear as orders of man against God. Rulers and governments seem to be claiming falsely to possess a higher right over their fellow men. Even a theocracy would appear as supreme wrong-doing (7.1). Political revolution is born of the perception of the evil that lies in the very existence of governments of any sort. Yet, in the process of revolution, the revolutionary is himself overcome by evil, since he too confronts other men (often tyrannically) with a supposed right over them (7.2). True revolution involves forgiveness of sins and resurrection of the dead, whereas political revolutionaries bring hatred and demolition – mere reactions to the present order, rather than the intended new order (7.3). Thus, the revolutionary simply replaces one form of temporal power with another and may even make surviving elements of the previous order more dangerous. He attempts to substitute himself for God (7.4). But, since it is outside history, God's order cannot be established in this way (7.5-7). Indeed, God's order stands in permanent judgement on man's ecclesiastical and secular orthodoxies and -isms including legitimism [i.e. political theory concerned with establishing the legitimacy of particular regimes]. Judgement must be left to God alone (7.8). Powers are to be measured only by reference to God as God, who alone is judge, and the evil of the existing order is to be seen as really evil only in relation to God's order (7.9). Evil witnesses to the good and should be left for God alone to judge – vengeance is not ours, but God's (7.10).

Although both Barth and Berdyaev were, at times, highly active and committed in political affairs as individuals, as theologians they were equally apolitical. Berdyaev's apoliticism stems from his thoroughgoing stress on spitituality. He sees Christianity as undergoing a crisis in transition from an objective/collective form to a more subjective/individualistic one (8.1). For him, the collective/democratic and the individualistic/aristocratic types are evident throughout history. Socialists belong to the first type and tend to claim that a privileged minority have exploited the majority, whereas, in fact, they themselves have always persecuted the qualitative minority, favouring the 'average man' (8.2). Indeed, conservatives and monarchists also belong to this type, maintainting traditional institutions for the majority (8.3). As aristocrats of the spirit, saints, prophets and geniuses do not need conventional political structures (democratic or otherwise). Yet, they still ought not to separate themselves from the world, even if they are persecuted by the world (8.4). Democratic types may have greater talents than aristocratic types but they are less sensitive to the world's ugliness and barbarity (8.5). The Gnostic belongs mainly to the aristocratic type, clashing with democratic orthodox Christianity, but is in a sense closer to the present-day spiritually sensitive person and to the Russian concept of *sobornost* [a mystic concept often used by Russian theologians to denote the idea of oneness in togetherness] (8.6). But the Gnostic tended, proudly and wrongly, to separate himself from the carnal world and, in the process, proved unloving to his fellow men. Yet, the Church, in condemning the Gnostic, elaborated an inflexible system of theology (8.7). Nonetheless, there is still room in Christianity for people who can reach spritual heights, without boasting and separating themselves from the carnal world – despite the denial of this, at times, by both the Church and particular political regimes (8.8). The problem of the spirit and the spiritual life is the main problem confronting man today (8.9).

A distinction between the political and the religious appears, in a very different form, in Niebuhr's early *Moral Man and Immoral Society*. For Niebuhr, a sharp distinction must be made between individual and social ethics, the former requiring unselfishness as its ideal and the latter justice (9.1). They are not totally exclusive – for instance, insights from individual moral conscience are essential if society is fully to understand justice and without them justice would soon degenerate – but they cannot be fully harmonized (9.2). Whereas unselfishness is essential to individual morality, self-assertion may, at times, be essential for the survival of a particular society (9.3). Individual ethics has usually been cultivated by religion and appears thus as the antithesis of political morality (9.4). Attempts to apply such individual ethics to social groups have failed – whether in the case of the American blacks, Italian pacifist socialists, or pre-revolutionary Russians (9.5-7). It would be better to admit a moral dualism than to attempt to harmonize these two forms of morality. Just as we distinguish between moral judgements applied to self and those we apply to others, so, we must distinguish between those we apply to the individual and those we apply to society (9.8). The social group does not possess sufficient imagination for it to be amenable to pure love; particular groups are too selfish to allow themselves to subject their own interests to some inconclusive social ideal (9.9). But individuals, even those who are politically involved, ought still to be loyal to the highest canons of personal morality and, at times, may even have to dissociate themselves from their group

(9.10). And individuals, such as leaders of groups, must practise personal unselfishness if they are adequately to fulfill their social roles (9.11-12).

All of the next three authors believe that Christianity has a directly political role. For Temple, the Church, as the Church, must be concerned with general principles, whereas the individual Christian must seek to particularise these principles (10.1). Christian faith, by itself, cannot produce detailed political policies independent of economic and other factors, although it *can* point to relevant principles (10.2-3). The Church even has difficulties with the notion of the 'perfect social order' – not the least of which is that caused by man's imperfection (10.4-5). Political and economic systems must first provide for man's security even before providing for justice or expressing love (10.6). However, although Christianity does not suggest an 'ideal state', it does supply a number of general principles (10.7-8). So, it supplies the principle of respect for every person as a child of God and, as a result, people should come before societies and societies should be arranged to maximise the individual roles of its people (10.9-10). Again, it supplies the principle of freedom – understood, not simply as an absence of constraint, but, as self-determination (10.11-12). Law exists to preserve and extend this freedom (10.13). Freedom for the individual is freedom within the context of various social groups and man must be understood as social, in the sense of belonging to a variety of intermediate groups (10.14-17). The state which values freedom should be careful to give such groups freedom – and, indeed, Britain has derived many of its democratic habits from such groups as the Trade Unions, themselves owing much to the Chapels (10.18-20). Finally, there is a principle of fellowship leading to service; partly voluntary service by the individual and, partly, the individual seeing paid occupation as service (10.22-4).

John XXIII's discussion is also concerned with general principles which can be applied to political realities, although he views them in terms of rights and duties (a right entails a duty and a duty presupposes a right). In contrast to Niebuhr, he maintains that the Natural law notion of mutual rights and duties applies as much to the relationship between states as it does to that between individuals (11.1-3). This perspective involves recognising the reality of the moral order and the objectivity of truth, both by individuals and by states, in seeking to promote the common good (11.5-6). Granted such recognition, racial and ethnic discrimination and arrogance, based on superior talents or wealth, can play no part, either in individual or in communal behaviour (11.7-10: cf *Extracts 24*). The truth also requires fairness in the use of mass communication (11.11). States also have a duty to seek justice and not to seek their own advantage at the expense of others (11.12-13). When there is a clash of interests between states, peaceful and considerate means of resolving it should be sought, particularly when ethnic minorities are dealt with by states (11.14-17). States are becoming increasingly inter-dependent and it is vital that attention should be given to the universal common good (11.18-20). Present state structures are inadequate to deal with problems raised by such a universal common good (e.g. world peace) and this requires the establishment of some form of world government (11.21-5). Such a government should only come into being through universal consent – for otherwise it might favour one nation over others – and should be concerned with making sure that human rights are everywhere upheld (11.26-7). In addition, it should be concerned solely with questions related to the universal common good and not with those rightly belonging to individual states (11.28-9). UNO is a step in the direction of such a government (11.20-3). Individual Christians should be particularly concerned to offer themselves for public service and to seek to change society, not in terms of revolution , but gradually, in a spirit of duty and love (11.34-8). Peace will come only when individual hearts are changed and when it is built on the firm principles of God in Christ (11.39-45).

Amongst recent theologians it is, perhaps, the exponents of Liberation theology who have argued most strongly that Christianity has direct relevance to political issues. They are represented in this Section by Miranda and in the next by Bonino. Both are convinced that Marxist theory can illuminate the biblical understanding of man and that this understanding ought to inform our interpretation of political realities. Miranda is the Liberation theologian who has been at the greatest pains to demonstrate that the biblical understanding of wealth and poverty and the class divisions that have resulted from them, coincide at many crucial points with Marxist theory. In this Extract, he argues that in the Old Testament, particularly, 'almsgiving' and 'justice' are synonymous (12.1-3). Although this has frequently been forgotten by subsequent Christians, the early Church Fathers were clear that 'almsgiving' was really a restitution that someone makes for something that is not properly his (12.4-7). For Luke, the difference between 'rich' and 'poor' ('differentiating ownership', in Marxist terms) cannot be justified and, indeed, results from injustice and violence (12.8-9). Despite the attempts of some biblical critics to claim that such views are not authentic to Jesus himself, the evidence is overwhelming (12.10-12). Further, to regard the biblical position as 'primitive' is to make a highly suspect, Western value-judgement (12.13-14). The prophets were well aware of the injustice of differentiating ownership and it would be a mistake to explain their attitudes in terms of an anti-urban bias (12.14-20). Christianity must return to a fresh awareness of this injustice and even papal teaching must be interpreted afresh in its light (12.21-3).

3. ETHICAL ARGUMENTS

The clearest ethical arguments are contained in John XXIII's and Temple's Extracts. The first is thoroughly based upon Natural law and sees a straightforward continuum between the rights and duties of the individual and those of societies. These rights and duties must always be related to the 'commom good' and it is on this basis that, for example, he can argue that, 'the moral order itself demands the establishment of some sort of world government' (11.25). However, this deontological position is immediately followed by a number of consequential arguments – namely, that if such a government were imposed by force the 'efficacy of its action would thereby be imperilled' (11.26).

Temple's position, too, is dependent upon some notion of Natural law, albeit in a somewhat modified form. However, he also uses a mixture of deontological and consequential arguments. So, having enunciated a general principle of respect for persons, he argues, in a style owing something to utilitarianism, that 'society must be so arranged as to give to every citizen the maximum opportunity for making deliberate choices' (10.10). It is even possible that his radical stress upon the individual, his stress upon the 'primary principle' of respect for persons, and his avoidance of anything but general principles as absolutes, could be seen as a form of personalism.

Differing deontological positions are apparent in Niebuhr and Miranda. For the first, the notions of love and justice appear to be accepted deontologically, whereas, for Miranda, it is a strong moral identification (whether in Marxism or in the Bible) with the poor and the oppressed. However, Niebuhr's criticisms of those who have attempted to apply individual love to social situations, are predominantly consequentialist (9.4-7) and his defence of pacifism at this early stage of his career is entirely pragmatic (9.10).

Consequentialism is also apparent, sometimes, in the few ethical arguments of the, predominantly theological, Berdyaev and Barth Extracts. Berdyaev argues that absolute monarchies and socialist republics 'are alike necessary to the masses' (8.3), but only because they do not belong to the 'aristocracy of the spirit' (8.6). In a similar negative manner, Barth maintains that authoritarianism in politics leads to tyranny (7.1). Nonetheless, Barth's primary objection to such authoritarianism is theological – it usurps the position which should alone belong to God.

4. BASES OF CHRISTIAN ETHICS

Only three of the Extracts make any continuous use of the Bible and they differ significantly from each other in the way that they do this. Barth's Extract is obviously a part of his commentary on Romans, but it is quite unlike a scholarly, critical commentary. His remarks frequently have more to do with his own social context than to that of Paul (as in his discussion of political revolution) and have appeared to many as eisegetical rather than exegetical in character. John XXIII quotes both the OT and the NT (e.g. in 11.4, 43 & 44), but the central thrust of his argument does not depend upon them. As in Aquinas, the Bible is used to support a position which is first developed on the basis of Natural law. Although himself a Roman Catholic priest, Miranda's use of the Bible might seem more characteristic of the Reformed tradition: it is central to his argument, owes much to critical, non-Roman Catholic scholarship and ranges over both OT and NT.

Differing appeals to Christian tradition are also apparent in Miranda and John XXIII. The latter follows the traditional Roman Catholic approach (see further Welty's *Extract 14* and Paul VI's *Extract 23*) in seeking to substantiate particular positions from the Fathers or from the statements of previous Popes. So John XXIII quotes Augustine (11.13 & 39) and his predecessor Pius XII (11.6 & 36). However, Miranda mainly uses the Fathers to substantiate his position (12.4-7): papal statements provide him with obvious problems. As one still working within the Roman Catholic tradition, he is clearly concerned that he contradict, not direct papal teaching, but only papal 'suppositons' behind this teaching (12.22-3).

Differing theological bases are also apparent in these Extracts. Berdyaev and Barth are both emphatically theological in orientation, but the first emphasises the Spirit and a spiritual form of Christianity, whereas Barth's emphasis is upon the judgment of God and upon man's attempt to usurp God's position. John XXIII concludes his encyclical with christology (11.45), whereas Temple concludes his discussion with theological anthropology (10.26). In Miranda, it is the concept of 'justice', derived directly through Jesus from the Old Testament, which is central to his position. For all five theologians, it is clear that they believe that their distinctive approaches to political realities owe much to their initial theological positions. Only Niebuhr's Extract (in sharp contrast to the much later *Extract 2*) is relatively lacking in specifically Christian bases: indeed, religion appears in his analysis here as far more relevant to the individual than to society.

5.   SOCIAL DETERMINANTS

The influence of the particular socio-political contexts within which they wrote is especially evident in Barth, Niebuhr and Miranda. The background of revolutionary Europe of 1917-19 doubly influenced Barth. On the one hand, the specifically social repercussions convinced him (and many of his contemporaries) that revolution led to greater tyranny than it replaced. Throughout Europe there was considerable disillusionment with political attitudes of authoritarianism which had led, both to the Great War and to the Russian Revolution. On the other hand, Barth saw the theological liberalism of the pre-war period (which he had shared) as disastrously implicated with these attitudes. His rejection both of revolutionary politics and of theological liberalism and his espousal of Neo-Orthodoxy were clearly related to this European political context. Similarly, Niebuhr's ethical dualism can be related to the American Depression that followed this war. His experiences, in industrial Detroit, convinced him that liberal attempts to relate Christian concepts of love to social phenomena were misguided. The ineluctable forces of economic depression and the consequent feelings of helplessness of individuals caught within that depression and within the dehumanizing structures of contemporary industrialism, made a lasting impression on Niebuhr's mind. Similarly, the political and economic frustrations of South America, in the 1970's, has had an evident effect upon Miranda. He, too, rejects Western theological and political liberalism (12.6, 10 & 13) and declares emphatically that, 'the time has come for Christianity to break a long chain of hypocrisy and collusion with the established powers' (12.7). His stark contrasts between 'rich' and 'poor' and his close correlation of 'wealth' with 'violence and spoliation', may reflect the feudal, authoritarian and oppressive socio-political structures of parts of Central America, rather than what might be seen as the ambiguities of the mixed economies of the West.

Berdyaev stands in sharp contrast to these three theologians. His early espousal of Marxist theory is still partially evident in this Extract and his socialisation in Russian Orthodoxy also acts as a determinant of his position. Nonetheless, as has already been pointed out, despite the revolutionary context within which he lived, his writings, as a whole, still appear remarkably timeless.

John XXIII's Extract and Temple's Extract are not so timeless and clearly reflect the topical political interests of the contexts within which they were written. The issue of unemployment dominated much of Temple's political thought in the 1930's and occurs spontaneously as an illustration (10.2). In the period following Hiroshima and Nagasaki, peace became a very dominant concern, allied to a search for political stability in the developed and developing worlds. John XXIII's Extract clearly relates strongly to these concerns. Nonetheless, both Extracts are also characterised by a judiciousness and relative detachment, which may be the result, both of their authors' ecclesiastical positions and of their commitment to natural law theory.

6. SOCIAL SIGNIFICANCE

A number of the works from which these Extracts are taken had a real political influence. John XXIII was, perhaps, the most generally admired of recent Popes and his efforts to foster peace in the world received a wide audience, amongst both Roman Catholics and others. The issue of human rights has remained an important one in the Western world, even if the specific connection with Natural law articulated by John XXIII is now seldom discussed. In the 1940's and 1950's, Niebuhr was particularly influential in the United States. His ethical position changed considerably from *Moral Man and Immoral Society*, with his ethical dualism becoming less pronounced and a greater stress on 'political realism', but his central distinctions between love and justice remained highly influential. A number of key politicians and political theorists were directly influenced by his writings. Temple, in contrast, although he is often regarded as one of the most respected Archbishops of the Church of England in the 20th Century, seldom had the ear of prime ministers. His overt socialism and tendency to be outspoken on political issues tended to alienate him from politicians, such as Churchill. But, within church circles, his influence was very considerable and he played a major part in the *Life and Work Movement* which eventually became a central component of the *World Council of Churches*. Many of Temple's distinctions, between general principles, middle axioms (see *above* p. 62) and changing factors, were adopted by these two movements. Within present-day South America, Liberation theology now receives considerable political attention. It has radicalised a significant section of the Roman Catholic clergy there and provides a rare example of a theological movement acting as an independent social variable (i.e. as a social factor, such as 'class', which affects mass behaviour). The influence of Barth's *Der Römerbrief* upon theologians, rather than politicians, was very considerable. In fact, for many theologians it has proved to be one of the most seminal books of the first half of the 20th Century. However, Berdyaev's writings have seldom been known outside scholarly circles.

FURTHER READING

A number of the works of Barth, himself, are important for understanding his various approaches to political realities, including *How I Changed my Mind*, *Church Dogmatics* III.4 and *Ethics*. Of the many books written about Barth, the following are particularly useful: Charles West, *Communism and the Theologians*, H. Richard Niebuhr, *The Responsible Self* and R.E. Willis, *The Ethics of Karl Barth*. There have been a number of studies of Berdyaev, including Oliver Fielding Clarke, *Introduction to Berdyaev*, Donald A. Lowrie, *Rebellious Prophet: A Life of Nicolai Berdyaev*, E.L. Allen, *Freedom in God: A Guide to the Thought of Nicholas Berdyaev* and Michael Alexander Vallon, *An Apostle of Freedom: Life and Teachings of Nicolas Berdyaev*. For Niebuhr, see *above*, p.108. F.A.Iremonger's *William Temple: Archbishop of Canterbury* is still the definitive source for information about Temple: see also Ronald Preston's introduction to the 1976 edition of *Christianity and the Social Order*. For Liberation theology, see *below*, p. 355.

EXTRACT 7

BARTH

God's judgment on political revolutions

7.1   Be not overcome of evil, but overcome evil with good (Rmns. 12.21). The problem of the victory of right over wrong is presented to us in a far more essential form in the existence of human ordinances than in the existence of the *enemy* (12, 19, 20). Must not the existing order, the order that has already been FOUND, seem the very incarnation of triumphant unrighteousness to the man who is SEEKING after God and His Order? Is not the existing order a reinforcement of men against God, a safeguard of the normal course of this world against its disturbance by the great ambiguity and its defence against the pre-suppositon by which it is threatened on all sides? Are not the ordinances of men simply a conspiracy of the Many – far too many – against the One who manifests Himself, and can only manifest Himself, when the mature wisdom and authority of the Many crumbles in pieces? Rulers! What are rulers but men? What are they but men hypocritically engaged in setting things in order, in order that they may – cowards that they are – ensure themselves securely against the riddle of their existence? Are we not once again confronted by fools begging a few moments' delay before the sentence of death is pronounced upon them? The invectives that have been hurled against 'Governments' from the days of the Revelation of John to the fulminations of Nietzsche, from the Anabaptists to the Anarchists, have not been directed against defects in government but against the right of governments to *exist* at all. That men should, as a matter of course, claim to possess a higher right over their fellow men, that they should, as a matter of course, dare to regulate and predetermine almost all their conduct, that those who put forward such a manifestly fraudulent claim should be crowned with a halo of real power and should be capable of requiring obedience and sacrifice as though they had been invested with the authority of God, that the Many should conspire to speak as though they were the One, that a minority or a majority – even the supreme democratic majority of all against one – should assume that they are the community, that a quite fortuitous contract or arrangement should be regarded as superior to the solid organization of the struggle for existence and should proclaim itself to be the peace which all men yearn after and which all should respect; this whole pseudo-transcendence of an altogether immanent order is the wound that is inflicted by every existing government – even by the best – upon those who are most delicately conscious of what is good and right. The more successfully the good and the right assume concrete form, the more they become evil and wrong – *summum jus, summa injuria*. Supposing the right were to take the form of theocracy, supposing, that is to say, superior spiritual attainment were concreted into an ideal Church and all the peoples of the earth were to put their trust in it; if, for example, the Church of Calvin were to be reformed and broadened out to be the Church of the League of Nations; – this doing of the supreme right would then become the supreme wrong-doing. This theocratic dream comes abruptly to an end, of course, when we discover that it is the Devil who approaches Jesus and offers Him all the kingdoms of this world. It ends also with Dostoevsky's picture of the Grand Inquisitor. Men have no right to possess objective right against other men. And so, the more they surround themselves with objectivity, the greater is the wrong they inflict upon others. Others are, it is true, awaiting the right of the One. But when and where has the right of the Many really become the right of the One? Has it not been always and everywhere acquired fraudulently? Is there anywhere legality which is not fundamentally illegal? Is there anywhere authority which is not ultimately based upon tyranny?

7.2   There is a certain imperfection in the existing ordinances by which we are enabled to detect that their existence is, as such, evil. There is a certain uncontrollable tendency to freedom which causes both good and bad men to resent the chain which the Many – no doubt with the best intentions – put upon them. There is a certain strange and penetrating perception which sees through the fiction that lies behind our bondage. From this perception of the evil that lies in the very existence of the existing government, Revolution is born. The revolutionary seeks to be rid of the evil by bestirring himself to battle with it and to overthrow it. He determines to remove the existing ordinances, in order that he may erect in their place the new right. This is, of course, a wholly intelligible course of action, and one in which we might very well take part; it is, in fact, as intelligible as is hostility against the *enemy* (12.19) and conflict against our fellow men. (The revolutionary does not begin by betaking himself to the generally decried shedding blood. He begins by simply harbouring a certain secret poisonous resentment against the existing order – many indeed go no further than this; they detest the *Power*, and become wholly enslaved to feelings of resentment!) The revolutionary must, however, own that in adopting his plan he allows himself to be *overcome of evil*. He forgets that he is not the One, that he is not the subject of the freedom which he so earnestly desires, that, for all the strange brightness of his eyes, he is not the Christ who stands before the Grand Inquisitor, but is, contrariwise, the Grand Inquisitor encountered by the Christ. He too is claiming what no man can claim. He too is making of the right a thing. He too confronts other men with his supposed right. He too usurps a position which is not due to him, a legality which is fundamentally illegal, an authority which – as we have grimly experienced in Bolshevism, but also in the behaviour of far more delicate-minded innovators! – soon displays its essential tyranny. What man has the right to propound and represent the 'New', whether it be a new age, or a new world, or even a new – spirit? Is not every new thing, in so far as it can be schemed by men, born of what already *exists*? The moment it becomes a human proposition, must it not be numbered among the things that are? What man is there who, having proposed a novelty, has not proposed an evil thing? Far more than the conservative, the revolutionary is *overcome of evil*, because with his 'No' he stands so strangely near to God. This is the tragedy of revolution. Evil is not the true answer to evil. The sense of right which has been wounded by the existing order is not restored to health when that order is broken.

7.3   *Overcome evil with good.* What can this mean but the end of the triumph of men, whether their triumph is celebrated in the existing order or by revolution? And how can this end be represented, if it be not by some strange 'not-doing' precisely at the point where men feel themselves most powerfully called to action? The revolutionary has erred. He really means that Revolution which is the impossible possibility. He means forgiveness of sins and the resurrection of the dead. He means Jesus Christ – He that hath *overcome* – who is the true answer to the injury wrought by the existing order as such. But the revolutionary has chosen another revolution: he has adopted the possible possibility of discontent and hatred and insubordination, of rebellion and demolition. And this choice is not better, but much worse than choosing the possible possibility of contentment and satisfaction, of security and usurpation; for by it God is far better understood, but far more deeply outraged. The revolutionary aims at the Revolution by which the true Order is to be inaugurated; but he launches another revolution which is, in fact, reaction. The legitimist, on the other hand, himself also overcome of evil, aims at the Legitimism by which the true Revolution is inaugurated; but he maintains another legitimism which is, in fact, revolt! And so, as always, what men do is the judgement upon what they will to do (7.15, 19). When, however, the revolutionary becomes aware of the judgement, he is dispossessed of his well founded, concrete, justifiable action, and is turned towards the action of God. But how can he demonstrate the action of God save by dying where he was born? by dying, that is to say, where he first perceived the evil of the present order. What more radical action can he perform than the action of turning back to the original root of 'not-doing' – and NOT be angry, NOT engage in an assault, NOT demolish? This turning back is the ethical factor in the command, *Overcome evil with good*. There is here no word of approval of the existing order; but there is endless disapproval of every enemy of it. It is God who wishes to be recognized as He that *overcometh* the unrighteousness of the existing order. This is the meaning of the commandment; and it is also the meaning of the Thirteenth Chapter of the Epistle to the Romans.

7.4   Let every man be in subjection to the existing ruling powers (Rmns. 13.1a). Though subjection may assume from time to time many various concrete forms, as an ethical conception it is here purely negative. It means to withdraw and make way; it means to have no resentment, and not to overthrow. Why, then, does not the rebel turn back and become no more a rebel? Simply because the conflict in which he is immersed cannot be represented as a conflict between him and the *existing ruling powers*; it is, rather a conflict of evil with evil. Even the most radical revolution can do no more than set what *exists* against what *exists*. Even the most radical revolution – and this is so even when it is called a 'spiritual' or 'peaceful' revolution – can be no more than a revolt; that is to say, it is in itself simply a justification and confirmation of what already exists. For the whole relative right of what exists is established only by the relative wrong of revolution in its victory; wheras the relative right of revolution in its victory is in no way established by the relative wrong of the existing order. Similarly also, the power of resistance in the existing order is in no way broken by the victorious attack of revolution; it is merely driven backwards, embarrassed, and compelled to adopt different forms, and thus rendered the more dangerous; whereas the energy of revolution is dissipated and rendered innocuous – simply by its victory. And so the whole conduct of the rebel in no way constitutes a judgement upon the existing order, however much his act of revolution may do so. The rebel has thoughtlessly undertaken the conflict between God's Order and the existing order. Should he allow himself to appeal directly to the ordinance of God, 'should he boldly and confidently storm the heavens and bring down thence his own eternal rights which hang aloft inalienable, unbroken as the stars themselves' (Schiller), he betrays thereby perception of the true 'limit to the tyrant's power', but his bold storming of the heavens in no way brings about this limitation. He may be justified at the bar of history; but he is not justified before the judgement-seat of God. The sequel shows 'the return of the old natural order where men oppose their fellow men'. When men undertake to substitute themselves for God, the problem of God, His mind and His judgement, still remain, but they are rendered ineffective. And so, in his rebellion, the rebel stands on the side of the existing order.

7.5　　Let the existing order – state, Church, Law, Society, &c., &c. – in their totality be:

$$(a\ b\ c\ d)$$

7.6　　Let their dissolution by the Primal Order of God, by which their totality is contradicted, be expressed by a minus sign outside the bracket:

$$-(+a+b+c+d).$$

7.7　　It is then clear that no revolution, however radical, which takes place within the realm of history, can ever be identical with the divine minus sign outside the bracket, by which the totality of human ordinances is dissolved. Revolution can do no more than change the plus sign within the bracket – the plus, that is to say, which existing ordinances possess within the bracket because they exist – into a minus sign. The result of a successful revolution is therefore:

$$-(-a-b-c-d)$$

7.8　　And now we see that for the first time the great divine minus sign outside the bracket has transformed the anticipatory, revolutionary minus sign into a genuine plus sign. Revolution has, therefore, the effect of restoring the old after its downfall in a new and more powerful form. [Equally false, however, is the reckoning of the legitimists: false, because they consciously and as a matter of principle -- in their consciousness and in their appeal to principle lies the arrogant and titanic element in Legitim-ISM – add a positive sign to the terms within the bracket. But the divine minus sign outside the bracket means that all human consciousness, all human principles and axioms and orthodoxies and -isms, all *principality and power and dominion*, are AS SUCH subjected to the destructive judgement of God. *Let every man be in subjection* means, therefore, that every man should consider the falsity of all human reckoning as such. We are not competent to place the decisive minus sign before the bracket; we are only competent to perceive how completely it damages our plus and our minus. Accordingly, the subjection here recommended must not be allowed to develop into a new and subtle manner of reckoning, whereby we reintroduce once more an absolute right. It is evident that there can be no more devastating undermining of the existing order than the recognition of it which is here recommended, a recognition rid of all illusion and devoid of all the joy of triumph. State, Church, Society, Positive Right, Family, Organized Research, &c., &c., live off the credulity of those who have been nurtured upon vigorous sermons-delivered-on-the-field-of-battle and upon other suchlike solemn humbug. Deprive them of their PATHOS, and they will be starved out; but stir up revolution against them, and their PATHOS is provided with fresh fodder. No-revolution is the best preparation for the true Revolution; but even no-revolution is no safe recipe. To *be in subjection* is, when it is rightly understood, an action void of purpose, an action, that is to say, which can spring only from obedience to God. Its meaning is that men have encountered God, and are thereby compelled to leave the judgement to Him. The actual occurence of this judgement cannot be identified with the purpose or with the secret reckoning of the man of this world.]

7.9   Upon this background we are able to understand what follows – For there is no power but of God; and the powers that be are ordained of God (Rmns. 13.1b). Here a positive, affirmative authority seems to be assigned to the existing government. This would, however, directly contradict the basis of *subjection* which has been set forth above. It is therefore evident that the emphatic word 'God' must not be so interpreted as to contradict the whole theme of the Epistle to the Romans. We must not give to the word 'God' the value of a clearly defined, metaphysical entity. What will it profit us if a formal fidelity to the meaning of a word is purchased at the cost of complete infidelity to the Word? He of whom the *power* is and by whom every existing authority is ordained is God the Lord, the Unknown, Hidden God, Creator and Redeemer, the God who elects and rejects. This means that the mighty *powers that be* are measured by reference to God, as are all human, temporal, concrete things. God is their beginning and their end, their justification and their condemnation, their 'Yes' and their 'No'. If we adopt an attitude of revolution towards them – and this is the attitude adopted in the Epistle to the Romans, as is shown by the unmistakable fact that the passage dealing with human *rulers* follows immediately after the passage dealing with the *enemy* and is prefaced by the quite clear statement that men are to overcome *evil* – the attitude of revolution is, nevertheless, crossed by the reflection that it is only in relation to God that the evil of the existing order is really evil. God alone is the minus sign outside the bracket that is able to demolish the false plus signs within the bracket – and, moreover, the romanticists of the present order have also to learn as surely that genuine plus signs can exist only because of the minus sign of God.

7.10   We, therefore, have to remember that it is not for us to arm ourselves for action with the standard of the measurement of God – as though He acted through us! The revolutionary must also renounce the blue flower of romanticism. If then evil be evil in its relation to God, it is not a thing of which we can complain, any more than good is a thing about which we can boast. Therefore,

even the observer who has been directly hurt and
wounded by the evil of the existing order must bow
before Him who is so strong and wondrous a God, high
above all gods. If God be the Judge, who can share in His
judgement? And if God be the Judge, where is there then
not – righteousness? Where is there then evil which is not
pregnant with witness to the good? Where is there then
any concrete thing which is not pregnant with that which
is Primal and invisible? Is not, therefore, the existing
order a pregnant parable of the Order that does not *exist* –
*For the creature was subjected to vanity, not of its own will, but
by reason of him who subjected it in hope* (8.20)? The existing
order falls and passes to corruption because it *exists*. The
apprehension of this, however, has been, as we have
seen, the source of revolution. But the existing order is
justified against revolution precisely at this source; for
here the demand is made that the revolutionary should
not take the assault and judgement into his own hands,
but rather should recognize that the evil of the existing
order bears witness to the good, since it stands of
necessity as an order contrasted with THE ORDER.
Precisely in this contrast the existing order bears involuntary witness to THE ORDER and is the reflection of it.
The *powers that be* are, therefore, in the general course of
their existence – *of God*; and, in the particular form in
which they constitute a present urgent problem, especially for the revolutionary, they are – *ordained of God*. The
KRISIS to which the powers that be are subjected by God
renders the possibility of our revolting against them far
less advantageous to us than the possibility of our not
revolting. In any case revolution is thereby deprived of its
PATHOS, of its enthusiasm, of its claim to be a *high
place*; it is, in fact, deprived of all those factors which are
indispensable if the revolutionary is boldly and confidently and properly to 'storm the heavens'. *Vengeance
belongeth unto me* (12.19). Our subjection means, therefore, no more than that vengeance is not our affair. It
means that the divine minus before the bracket must not
be deprived of its potency by a series of anticipatory

negations on our part. [The supporters of the present order, who may perhaps feel encouraged by what has been said, must, however, be reminded that revolution has been *ordained* as evil, in order that they may bear witness to the good; and this means, in order that they may themselves be without justification and utterly unromantic, in order, in fact, that they too may turn and become from henceforth dis-ordered.]

EXTRACT 8
BERDYAEV
Politics and the spirit

8.1   The religious life passes through three characteristic stages. Firstly there is the stage of objective religion which is both popular and collective, natural and social. Secondly there is the subjective stage which is individualistic and psycho-spiritual. In the third stage the opposition between the objective and subjective is transcended and the highest degree of spirituality is reached. A condition of the emergence of Christianity is this movement from an objective and popular religion to one which is subjective and individual. But in actual practice Christianity has not developed in this way; it has crystallized into a religion which is at once objective and popular, social and collective. It is precisely this form of Christianity which is undergoing a crisis at the present time. Religious life is passing though a subjective and individualistic phase which cannot be final and which is bound, in its turn, to give way to something else.

8.2   There are two types which confront one another all through the course of man's history, and they are types which find it hard to enter into any mutual comprehension. The former belongs to the collective, to the majority of society, which outwardly predominates in history; the other belongs to the sphere of "spiritual individuality", to the elect minority, and its significance

in history is much harder to discover. These two types or
states of mind may be called, respectively, the "democratic" and the "aristocratic". Now socialists are in the habit
of affirming that throughout the course of history the
privileged minority has exploited the disinherited majority. But there is another truth which, though at first sight
less obvious, is more profound. The collective, the
"quantitative" majority, has always oppressed and persecuted in history the "qualitative" minority, that which
possesses the divine Eros and is composed of truly
spiritual individuals whose lives are directed towards the
highest aims. History works out habitually in favour of
the average man, and of the collective. It is for such that
the State, the family, the law, and our educational
institutions have been created, no less than the whole
fabric of custom and convention and the external
organization of the Church. It is for such that knowledge
and morality, dogma and cult have been adapted. It is the
average man, the typical product of the mass, who has
dominated history, and who has always insisted that
everything should be done for him and that everything
should be brought down to the level of his interests.

8.3   The right wing and the left, conservatives and revolutionaries, monarchists and socialists, all alike belong to
this collective "democratic" type. The conservatives and
the monarchists, who are the partisans of authority, are
not less "democratic" than those who actually bear the
name "democrats". For this social collective, for mankind in the mass, the hierarchy of authority is maintained
and ancient institutions are preserved. It is for them also
that they are abolished, and for them that revolutions are
made. Absolute monarchies and socialist republics are
alike necessary to the masses, and are equally well
adapted to the average man. It is, in fact, the average man
who has dominated among the nobility no less than
among the middle classes, the peasants, and the workers.
It is never for the aristocracy of the spirit that governments are established, constitutions elaborated, and
systems of learning or the technique of creation evolved.

8.4   Saints, prophets, geniuses, men, in short, who live on
the higher planes of the spiritual life and who are capable
of authentic creation, have no need of monarchy or
republicanism, conservatism or revolution, nor yet of
constitutions and educational establishments. For the
aristocracy of the spirit does not bear the burden of
history for itself. On the contrary it is made to submit to
institutions, reforms, and systems whether old or new, in
the name of the so-called people and of the collective, or,
in other words, of the happiness of the average man.
Evidently the aristocracy of the spirit, the elect who are
alive with the divine Eros, belong to the fallen race of
Adam and suffer in this way the consequences of the sin
which they have to expiate. They cannot isolate themselves from "the world" and must therefore bear its
burden, and serve the universal cause of freedom and of
civilization. One can only deplore the pride of men who,
while believing that they share in that which is highest,
regard with contempt lesser men, and will not help the
world to progress. But those who belong to the
aristocracy of the spirit, who are not responsible for the
qualities they possess, have in reality a bitter and tragic
destiny in the world, for they cannot adapt themselves to
any of the social conventions and systems of thought
which belong to average men. They are a race of men
who have always been oppressed and persecuted.

8.5   Those who are of the "democratic" type, whose
orientation is towards the masses and the organization of
the life of the collective, may be endowed with great
talents and may number among them great men, heroes,
geniuses, and saints. On the other hand those who are of
the "aristocatic" type, whose interests are centred on
other worlds and the creation of values which are of no
use to the average man, may be completely lacking in
genius and may be less powerful and talented than men of
the former type. Nevertheless they possess a different
spiritual organization which is at once more sensitive,
more complex, and more subtle than that of the
"pachyderms" of democratic breed. Such men suffer

more from the "world" and from its ugliness, barbarity, and decadence than the men whose attention is focussed upon the masses and the collective. Even the great men of the "democratic" type possess this simple kind of psychology, which places them under the protection of that very world which is so inimical to spiritual personalities less adapted to it. Cromwell and Bismarck belong to this type, as in a certain sense do all men of action, as well as the great statesmen and revolutionaries. This simple psychological make-up can also be found among many of the Doctors of the Church, who have often belonged to the democratic type.

8.6   From this point of view the Gnostics are of particular interest. A great number of them truly belong to the "aristocracy" of the spirit, but they seem to have been unable to reconcile themselves to the "democracy" of the Christian Church. The question is not whether they were in the right. The Church had profound reasons for opposing and condemning them, for had the Gnostics won the day Christianity would never have been victorious. It would have been transformed into an aristocratic sect. But the question which Gnosticism raises is a profoundly disturbing one which is always with us, and has its importance even to-day. Revelation and absolute truth are both distorted and assimilated, according to the make-up and spiritual development of the persons receiving them. Are we bound to consider as absolute and unchangeable that form of the Christian revelation which was intended for the average man? Must the more spiritual, complex, and subtle type of man, who has in some measure received the great gift of Gnosis, be brought down to a lower level and perforce rest content with a reduced spirituality for the sake of the masses, and in order that he may share in the fellowship of the whole Christian people? But is it possible to identify *sobornost* with the popular collective? Can the path which leads to the acquiring of the gifts of the Holy Spirit and to spiritual perfection and holiness be regarded as the sole criterion of spiritual life and the only source of religious Gnosis? . . .

8.7   The Gnostics did not understand the mystery of freedom, that is, of freedom in Christ, any more than they understood the mystery of love. There was in all this a hopeless dualism which upset the true hierarchy of values. The Gnostics were without a glimpse of the order of values upon which the world of the Christian rests, where the highest elements are organically linked with the lowest and thus assist the process of transfiguration and of universal salvation. Their interpretation of the hierarchic principle was a false one. The supreme Gnosis of "spiritual" persons is necessary for the salvation and transfiguration of those who are "carnal". "Spiritual" persons must not remain proudly upon the mountain-tops in separation from the "carnal" world, but they must devote their energies to its spiritualization and to raising it to the highest levels. Moreover the source of evil is spiritual and not carnal. The Church has rightly conde-mned the pride of the Gnostics, their hopelessly dualistic point of view, and the unbrotherly and unloving attitude which they displayed towards their fellow men and the world at large. But the consciousness of the Church was absorbed by preference with the problems of the average man, of the typical product of the mass. The Church was anxious to guide aright the ordinary man and was preoccupied with the task of effecting his salvation. In condemning Gnosticism, the Church in some measure affirmed and made lawful agnosticism. Even the problem which had given rise to such sincere and tormenting perplexity among the Gnostics was regarded as one which could not and indeed ought not to be raised. The highest aspirations of the spirit, the thirst for a deeper knowledge of divine and cosmic mysteries, were brought down to the level of average humanity. Not only the Gnosis of Valentinian but also that of Origen was regarded as inadmissible and dangerous, in the same way as that of Solovyov is today. A system of theology was elaborated which became an obstacle to the higher

Gnosis. Only the great Christian mystics succeeded in cutting their way through these well-nigh impregnable defences.

8.8   It must be recognized, however, that one of the difficulties connected with "the higher knowledge" in those days was that men could not disassociate it from its connection with the worship of demons, and here Christianity found itself entangled with pagan cults and with the "wisdom" of pagan religion. And yet it is possible for a higher Christian knowledge of spiritual things to exist which is at once more penetrating, less exoteric, and less moulded to the needs of the collective than that of the dominant systems of official theology. There is room in Christianity not only for St. Thomas Aquinas but also for Jacob Boehme, not only for the Metropolitan Philaret but also for Vladimir Solovyov. If spiritual persons ought not to boast of the heights they have reached, and to separate themselves from those of the "natural" and "carnal" order, it must not, on the other hand, be supposed that such men do not exist, nor must the aspirations of their spirit and their almost frenzied thirst for truth be denied satisfaction on the grounds that there is no such thing as "a higher spiritual knowledge". This would be equivalent, in an opposite direction, to that very destruction of the organic hierarchy of values which we have noticed already in Gnosticism. The world finds it easy to deny and despise every form of spiritual life, every aspiration of the spirit, and every sort of higher learning or knowledge. It readily asserts that such things are a clog upon the progress of the world towards its more complete organization and that they can perfectly well be left on one side. This is a point of view which is held and expressed by millions. Furthermore, nothing can be more heart-rending than to find the Church itself subscribing to that denial of the spirit which is professed by the State, a denial which at the opposite pole in atheistic Communism means the definite crushing out of the spirit and the extermination of every form of spiritual aristocracy.

8.9　　　　"Quench not the spirit" it has been said; but to deny
the problem presented to us by the Christian consciousness is to forget this command. The task which has as its
object the enlightenment of the world will ask for no
diminution in the quality of the spirit. Thus the problem
which above all is confronting us to-day is the problem of
the spirit and of the spiritual life.

EXTRACT 9

NIEBUHR

The conflict between individual and social morality

9.1　　　　A realistic analysis of the problems of human society
reveals a constant and seemingly irreconcilable conflict
between the needs of society and the imperatives of a
sensitive conscience. This conflict, which could be most
briefly defined as the conflict between ethics and politics,
is made inevitable by the double focus of the moral life.
One focus is in the inner life of the individual, and the
other in the necessities of man's social life. From the
perspective of society the highest moral ideal is justice.
From the perspective of the individual the highest ideal is
unselfishness. Society must strive for justice even if it is
forced to use means, such as self-assertion, resistance,
coercion and perhaps resentment, which cannot gain the
moral sanction of the most sensitive moral spirit. The
individual must strive to realise his life by losing and
finding himself in something greater than himself.

9.2　　　　These two moral perspectives are not mutually exclusive and the contradiction between them is not absolute.
But neither are they easily harmonised. Efforts to
harmonise them were analysed in the previous chapter. It
was revealed that the highest moral insights and achievements of the individual conscience are both relevant and
necessary to the life of society. The most perfect justice
cannot be established if the moral imagination of the
individual does not seek to comprehend the needs and

interests of his fellows. Nor can any non-rational instrument of justice be used without great peril to society, if it is not brought under the control of moral goodwill. Any justice which is only justice soon degenerates into something less than justice. It must be saved by something which is more than justice. The realistic wisdom of the statesman is reduced to foolishness if it is not under the influence of the foolishness of the moral seer. The latter's idealism results in political futility and sometimes in moral confusion, if it is not brought into commerce and communication with the realities of man's collective life. This necessity and possibility of fusing moral and political insights does not, however, completely eliminate certain irreconcilable elements in the two types of morality, internal and external, individual and social. These elements make for constant confusion but they also add to the richness of human life. We may best bring our study of ethics and politics to a close by giving them some further consideration.

9.3   From the internal perspective the most moral act is one which is actuated by disinterested motives. The external observer may find good in selfishness. He may value it as natural to the constitution of human nature and as necessary to society. But from the viewpoint of the author of an action, unselfishness must remain the criterion of the highest morality. For only the agent of an action knows to what degree self-seeking corrupts his socially approved actions. Society, on the other hand, makes justice rather than unselfishness its highest moral ideal. Its aim must be to seek equality of opportunity for all life. If this equality and justice cannot be achieved without the assertion of interest against interest, and without restraint upon the self-assertion of those who infringe upon the rights of their neighbors, then society is compelled to sanction self-assertion and restraint. It may even, as we have seen, be forced to sanction social conflict and violence.

9.4   Historically the internal perspective has usually been cultivated by religion. For religion proceeds from profound introspection and naturally makes good motives the criteria of good conduct. It may define good motives either in terms of love or of duty, but the emphasis is upon the inner springs of action. Rationalised forms of religion usually choose duty rather than love as the expression of highest virtue (as in Kantian and Stoic morality), because it seems more virtuous to them to bring all impulse under the dominion of reason than to give any impulses, even altruistic ones, moral pre-eminence. The social viewpoint stands in sharpest contrast to religious morality when it views the behavior of collective rather than individual man, and when it deals with the necessities of political life. Political morality, in other words, is in the most uncompromising antithesis to religious morality...

9.5   Every effort to transfer a pure morality of disinterestedness to group relations has resulted in failure. The negroes of America have practiced it quite consistently since the Civil War. They did not rise against their masters during the war and remained remarkably loyal to them. Their social attitudes since that time, until a very recent date, have been compounded of genuine religious virtues of forgiveness and forbearance, and a certain social inertia which was derived not from religious virtue but from racial weakness. Yet they did not soften the hearts of their oppressors by their social policy.

9.6   During the early triumphs of fascism in Italy the socialist leaders suddenly adopted pacifist principles. One of the socialist papers counselled the workers to meet the terror of fascism with the following strategy: "(1) Create a void around fascism. (2) Do not provoke; suffer any provocation with serenity. (3) To win, be better than your adversary. (4) Do not use the weapons of your enemy. Do not follow in his footsteps. (5) Remember that the blood of guerilla warfare falls upon those who shed it. (6) Remember that in a struggle between brothers those are victors who conquer themselves. (7) Be convinced that it is better to suffer wrong than to commit it. (8) Don't be impatient. Impatience is extremely egotistical; it is instinct; it is yielding to one's ego urge. (9) Do not forget that socialism wins the more when it suffers, because it was born in pain and lives on its hopes. (10) Listen to the mind and to the heart which advises you that the working people should be nearer to sacrifice than to vengeance." (Quoted by Max Nomad, *Rebels and Renegades*, p.294). A nobler decalogue of virtues could hardly have been prescribed. But the Italian socialists were annihilated by the fascists, their organisations destroyed, and the rights of the workers subordinated to a state which is governed by their enemies. The workers may live "on their hopes", but there is no prospect of realising their hopes under the present regime by practicing the pure moral principles which the socialistic journal advocated. Some of them are not incompatible with the use of coercion against their foes. But inasfar as they exclude coercive means they are ineffectual before the brutal will-to-power of fascism.

9.7   The effort to apply the doctrines of Tolstoi to the political situation of Russia had a very similar effect. Tolstoi and his disciples felt that the Russian peasants would have the best opportunity for victory over their oppressors if they did not become stained with the guilt of the same violence which the czarist regime used against them. The peasants were to return good for evil, and win their battles by non-resistance. Unlike the policies of Gandhi, the political programme of Tolstoi remained altogether unrealistic. No effort was made to relate the religious ideal of love to the political necessity of coercion. Its total effect was therefore socially and politically deleterious. It helped to destroy a rising protest against political and economic oppression and to confirm the Russian in his pessimistic passivity. The excesses of the terrorists seemed to give point to the Tolstoian opposition to violence and resistance. But the terrorists and the pacifists finally ended in the same futility. And their common futility seemed to justify the pessimism which saw no escape from the traditional injustices of the Russian political and economic system. The real fact was that both sprang from a romantic middle-class or aristocratic idealism, too individualistic in each instance to achieve political effectiveness. The terrorists were diseased idealists, so morbidly oppressed by the guilt of violence resting upon their class, that they imagined it possible to atone for that guilt by deliberately incurring guilt in championing the oppressed. Their ideas were ethical and, to a degree, religious, though they regarded themselves as irreligious. The political effectiveness of their violence was a secondary consideration. The Tolstoian pacifists attempted the solution of the social problem by diametrically opposite policies. But, in common with the terrorists, their attitudes sprang from the conscience of disquieted individuals. Neither of them understood the realities of political life because neither had an appreciation for the significant characterisics of collective behavior. The romantic terrorists failed to relate their isolated acts of terror to any consistent political plan. The pacifists, on the other hand, erroneously attributed political potency to pure non-resistance.

9.8 Whenever religious idealism brings forth its purest fruits and places the strongest check upon selfish desire it results in policies which, from the political perspective, are quite impossible. There is, in other words, no possibility of harmonising the two strategists designed to bring the strongest inner and the most effective social restraint upon egoistic impulse. It would therefore seem better to accept a frank dualism in morals than to attempt a harmony between the two methods which threatens the effectiveness of both. Such a dualism would have two aspects. It would make a distinction between the moral judgments applied to the self and to others; and it would distinguish between what we expect of individuals and of groups. The first distinction is obvious and is explicitly or implicitly accepted whenever the moral problem is taken seriously. To disapprove your own selfishness more severely than the egoism of others is a necessary discipline if the natural complacency toward the self and severity in the judgment of others is to be corrected. Such a course is, furthermore, demanded by the logic of the whole moral situation. One can view the actions of others only from an external perspective; and from that perspective the social justification of self-assertion becomes inevitable. Only the actions of the self can be viewed from the internal perspective; and from that viewpoint all egoism must be morally disapproved. If such disapproval should occasionally destroy self-assertion to such a degree as to invite the aggression of others, the instances will be insignificant in comparison with the number of cases in which the moral disapproval of egoism merely tends to reduce the inordinate self-assertion of the average man. Even in those few cases in which egoism is reduced by religious discipline to such proportions that it invites injustice in an immediate situation, it will have social usefulness in glorifying the moral principle and setting an example for future generations.

9.9   The distinction between individual and group morality is a sharper and more perplexing one. The moral obtuseness of human collectives makes a morality of pure disinterestedness impossible. There is not enough imagination in any social group to render it amenable to the influence of pure love. Nor is there a possibility of persuading any social group to make a venture in pure love, except, as in the case of the Russian peasants, the recently liberated Negroes and other similar groups, a morally dubious social inertia should be compounded with the ideal. The selfishness of human communities must be regarded as an inevitability. Where it is inordinate it can be checked only by competing assertions of interest; and these can be effective only if coercive methods are added to moral and rational persuasion. Moral factors may qualify, but they will not eliminate, the resulting social contest and conflict. Moral goodwill may seek to relate the peculiar interests of the group to the ideal of a total and final harmony of all life. It may thereby qualify the self-assertion of the privileged, and support the interests of the disinherited, but it will never be so impartial as to persuade any group to subject its interests completely to an inclusive social ideal. The spirit of love may preserve a certain degree of appreciation for the common weaknesses and common aspirations which bind men together above the areas of social conflict. But again it cannot prevent the conflict. It may avail itself of instruments of restraint and coercion, through which a measure of trust in the moral capacities of an opponent may be expressed and the expansion rather than contraction of those capacities is encouraged. But it cannot hide the moral distrust expressed by the very use of the instruments of coercion. To some degree the conflict between the purest individual morality and an adequate political policy must therefore remain.

9.10   The needs of an adequate political strategy do not obviate the necessity of cultivating the strictest individual moral discipline and the most uncompromising idealism. Individuals, even when involved in their communities, will always have the opportunity of loyalty to the highest canons of personal morality. Sometimes, when their group is obviously bent upon evil, they may have to express their individual ideals by disassociating themselves from their group. Such a policy may easily lead to political irresponsibility, as in the case of the more extreme sects of non-resisters. But it may also be socially useful. Religiously inspired pacifists who protest against the violence of their state in the name of a sensitive individual conscience may never lame the will-to-power of a state as much as a class-conscious labor group. But if their numbers grew to large proportions, they might affect the policy of the government. It is possible, too, that their example may encourage similar non-conformity among individuals in the enemy nation and thus mitigate the impact of the conflict without weakening the comparative strength of their own community.

9.11   The ideals of a high individual morality are just as necessary when loyalty to the group is maintained and its general course in relation to other groups is approved. There are possibilities for individual unselfishness, even when the group is asserting its interests and rights against other communities. The interests of the individual are related to those of the group, and he may therefore seek advantages for himself when he seeks them for his group. But this indirect egoism is comparatively insignificant beside the possibilities of expressing or disciplining his egoism in relation to his group. If he is a leader in the group, it is necessary to restrain his ambitions. A leadership, free of self-seeking, improves the morale of the whole group. The leaders of disinherited groups, even when they are avowed economic determinists and scorn the language of personal idealism, are frequently actuated by high moral ideals. If they sought their own personal advantage they could gain it more easily by using their abilities to rise from their group to a more privileged one. The temptation to do this among the abler members of disinherited groups is precisely what has retarded the progress of their class or race.

9.12   The progress of the Negro race, for instance, is retarded by the inclination of many able and educated Negroes to strive for identification and assimilation with the more privileged white race and to minimise their relation to a subject race as much as possible. The American Labor Movement has failed to develop its full power for the same reason. Under the influence of American individualism, able labor men have been more ambitious to rise into the class of owners and their agents than to solidify the laboring class in its struggle for freedom. There is, furthermore, always the possibility that an intelligent member of a social group will begin his career in unselfish devotion to the interests of his community, only to be tempted by the personal prizes to be gained, either within the group or by shifting his loyalty to a more privileged group. The interests of individuals are, in other words, never exactly identical with those of their communities. The possibility and necessity of individual moral discipline is therefore never absent, no matter what importance the social struggle between various human communities achieves. Nor can any community achieve unity and harmony within its life, if the sentiments of goodwill and attitudes of mutuality are not cultivated. No political realism which emphasises the inevitablity and necessity of a social struggle, can absolve individuals of the obligation to check their own egoism, to comprehend the interests of others and thus to enlarge the areas of co-operation.

EXTRACT 10

TEMPLE

Christianity and the social order

10.1   The method of the Church's impact upon society at large should be twofold. The Church must announce Christian principles and point out where the existing social order at any time is in conflict with them. It must then pass on to Christian citizens, acting in their civic capacity, the task of re-shaping the existing order in closer conformity to the principles. For at this point technical knowledge may be required and judgements of practical expediency are always required. If a bridge is to be built, the Church may remind the engineer that it is his obligation to provide a really safe bridge; but it is not entitled to tell him whether, in fact, his design meets this requirement; a particular theologian may also be a competent engineer, and, if he is, his judgement on this point is entitled to attention; but this is altogether because he is a competent engineer and his theological equipment has nothing whatever to do with it. In just the same way the Church may tell the politician what ends the social order should promote; but it must leave to the politician the devising of the precise means to those ends.

10.2   This is a point of first-rate importance, and is frequently misunderstood. If Christianity is true at all it is a truth of universal application; all things should be done in the Christian spirit and in accordance with Christian principles. 'Then,' say some, 'produce your Christian solution for unemployment'. But there neither is nor could be such a thing. Christian faith does not by itself enable its adherent to forsee how a vast multitude of people, each one partly selfish and partly generous, and an intricate economic mechanism, will in fact be affected by a particular economic or political innovation – 'social credit', for example. 'In that case,' says the reformer – or, quite equally, the upholder of the *status quo* – 'keep off the turf. By your own confession you are out of place here'. But this time the Church must say 'No; I cannot tell you what is the remedy; but I can tell you that a society of which unemployment (in peace time) is a chronic feature, is a diseased society, and that if you are not doing all you can to find and administer the remedy, you are guilty before God.' Sometimes the Church can go further than this point to features in the social structure itself which are bound to be sources of social evil because they contradict the principles of the Gospel.

10.3   So the Church is likely to be attacked from both sides if it does its duty. It will be told that it has become 'political' when in fact it has been careful only to state principles and point to breaches of them; and it will be told by advocates of particular policies that it is futile because it does not support these. If it is faithful to its commission it will ignore both sets of complaints, and continue so far as it can to influence all citizens and permeate all parties.

10.4   Before going on to state in outline the chief principles of Christian social doctrine, it may be wise, in the prevailing temper of our age, to add a further word of caution. For it is sometimes supposed that what the Church has to do is to sketch a perfect social order and urge men to establish it. But it is very difficult to know what a 'perfect social order' means. Is it the order that would work best if we were all perfect? Or is it the order that would work best in a world of men and women such as we actually are? If it is the former, it certainly ought not to be established; we should wreck it in a fortnight. If

it is the latter, there is no reason for expecting the Church
to know what it is. . .

10.5   The political problem is concerned with men as they
are, not with men as they ought to be. Part of the task is
so to order life as to lead them nearer to what they ought
to be; but to assume that they are already this, will
involve certain failure and disaster. It is not contended
that men are utterly bad, or that they are more bad than
good. What is contended is that they are not perfectly
good, and that even their goodness is infected with a
quality – self-centredness – which partly vitiates it, and
exposes them to temptations so far as they achieve either
freedom or power. This does not mean that freedom or
power should be denied to them; on the contrary, it is
fundamental to the Christian position that men should
have freedom even though they abuse it; but it is also to
be recognized that they certainly will abuse it except so
far as they are won by devotion to truth or to beauty to
that selfless outlook, which is only perfectly established
in men by love which arises in them in answer to the
redemptive love of God.

10.6   In any period worth considering, and probably to the
end of earthly history, statesmen will themselves be men,
and will be dealing with men, who abuse freedom and
power. Now the most fundamental requirement of any
political and economic system is not that it shall express
love, though that is desirable, nor that it shall express
justice, though that is the first ethical demand to be made
upon it, but that it shall supply some reasonable measure
of security against murder, robbery, and starvation. If it
can be said with real probability that a proposed scheme
would in fact, men being what they are, fail to provide
that security, that scheme is doomed. Christians have
some clues to the understanding of human nature which
may enable them to make a more accurate estimate than
others of these points. But they will not, if they are true
to their own tradition, approach the question with
rosy-tinted spectacles. Its assertion of Original Sin should

make the Church intensely realistic and conspicuously free from Utopianism.

10.7   There is no such thing as a Christian social ideal, to which we should conform our actual society as closely as possible. We may notice, incidentally, about any such ideals from Plato's *Republic* onwards, that no one really wants to live in the ideal state as depicted by anyone else. Moreover, there is the desperate difficulty of getting there. When I read any description of an Ideal State and think how we are to begin transforming our own society into that, I am reminded of the Englishman in Ireland who asked the way to Roscommon. 'Is it Roscommon you want to go to?' asked the Irishman. 'Yes,' said the Englishman; 'that's why I asked the way.' 'Well,' said the Irishman, 'if I wanted to go to Roscommon, I wouldn't be starting from here.'

10.8   But though Christianity supplies no ideal in this sense, it supplies something of far more value – namely, principles on which we can begin to act in every possible situation . . .

10.9   The primary principle of Christian ethics and Christian politics must be respect for every person simply as a person. If each man and woman is a child of God, whom God loves and for whom Christ died, then there is in each a worth absolutely independent of all usefulness to society. The person is primary, not the society; the State exists for the citizen, not the citizen for the State. The first aim of social progress must be to give the fullest possible scope for the exercise of all powers and qualities which are distinctly personal; and of those the most fundamental is deliberate choice.

10.10   Consequently society must be so arranged as to give to every citizen the maximum opportunity for making deliberate choices and the best possible training for the use of that opportunity. In other words, one of our first considerations will be the widest possible extension of personal responsibility; it is the responsible exercise of deliberate choice which most fully expresses personality and best deserves the great name of freedom.

10.11   Freedom is the goal of politics. To establish and secure true freedom is the primary object of all right political action. For it is in and through his freedom that a man makes fully real his personality – the quality of one made in the image of God.

10.12   Freedom is a great word, and like other great words is often superficially understood. It has been said that to those who have enough of the world's goods the claim to freedom means 'Leave us alone', while to those who have not enough it means 'Give us a chance'. This important difference of interpretation rests on a single understanding of freedom as absence of compulsion or restraint. But if that is all the word means, freedom and futility are likely to be so frequently combined as to seem inseparable. For nothing is so futile as the unhampered satisfaction of sporadic impulses; that is the sort of existence which leads through boredom to suicide. Freedom so far as it is a treasure must be freedom *for* something as well as freedom *from* something. It must be the actual ability to form and carry out a purpose. This implies discipline – at first external discipline to check the wayward impulses before there is a real purpose in life to control them, and afterwards a self-discipline directed to the fulfilment of the purpose of life when formed. Freedom, in short, is self-control, self-determination, self-direction. To train citizens in the capacity for freedom and to give them scope for free action is the supreme end of all true politics.

10.13   But man is a self-centred creature. He can be trusted to abuse his freedom. Even so far as he wins self-control, he will control himself in his own interest: not entirely; he is not merely bad; but he is not altogether good, and any fraction of self-centredness will involve the consequence that his purpose conflicts to some extent with that of his neighbour. So there must be the restraint of law, as long as men have any selfishness left in them. Law exists to preserve and extend real freedom. First, it exists to prevent the selfishness of A from destroying the freedom of B. If I am left untouched when I knock my neighbours on the head, their freedom to go about their duties and their pleasures may be greatly diminished. But the law which restrains any occasional homicidal impulse that I may have, by threatening penalties sufficiently disagreeable to make the indulgence of it not seem to be good enough, also protects my purpose of good fellowship against being violated by that same impulse. In such a case the restraint of the law increases the true freedom of all concerned . . .

10.14   No man is fitted for an isolated life; everyone has needs which he cannot supply for himself; but he needs not only what his neighbours contribute to the equipment of his life but their actual selves as the complement of his own. Man is naturally and incurably social.

10.15   Recent political theories have given ostensible emphasis to this truth and have then, as a rule, gone far to ignore it. Certainly our social organization largely ignores it. For this social nature of man is fundamental to his being. I am not first some one on my own account who happens to be a child of my parents, a citizen of Great Britain, and so forth. If you take all these social relationships away, there is nothing left. A man is talking nonsense if he says: 'Well, if I had been the son of some one else. . . etc' He *is* his parent's son; what he is supposing is not that *he* should be someone else's son, but that *he* should not exist and someone else should exist instead. By our mutual influence we actually constitute one another as what we are. This mutual influence finds its first field of activity in the family; it finds other fields later in school, college, Trade Union, professional association, city, country, nation, Church.

10.16   Now actual liberty is the freedom which men enjoy in these various social units. But most political theories confine attention to the individual and the State as organ of the national community; they tend to ignore the intermediate groupings. But that makes any understanding of actual liberty impossible; for it exists for the most part in and through those intermediate groups – the family, the Church or congregation, the guild, the Trade

Union, the school, the university, the Mutual Improvement Society. (Only in the nineteenth century could English people devise such a title as the last or consent to belong to a society so named; but the thing which that name quite accurately describes is very common and very beneficial.)

10.17 It is the common failing of revolutionary politics to ignore or attempt to destroy these lesser associations. They are nearly always the product of historical growth and do not quite fit any theoretical pattern. So the revolutionary, who is of necessity a theorist, is impatient of them. It was largely for this reason that the great French Revolution, which took as its watchword Liberty, Equality and Fraternity, degenerated into a struggle between Liberty and Equality wherein Fraternity was smothered and Liberty was judicially murdered. For the isolated citizen cannot effectively be free over against the State except at the cost of anarchy.

10.18 Liberty is actual in the various cultural and commercial and local associations that men form. In each of these a man can feel that he counts for something and that others depend on him as he on them. The State which would serve and guard Liberty will foster all such groupings, giving them freedom to guide their own activities provided these fall within the general order of the communal life and do not injure the freedom of other similar associations. Thus the State becomes the Community of communities – or rather the administrative organ of that Community – and there is much to be said for the contention that its representative institutions should be so designed as to represent the various groupings of men rather than (or as well as) individuals...

10.19 A democracy which is to be Christian must be a democracy of persons, not only of individuals. It must not only tolerate but encourage minor communities as at once the expression and the arena of personal freedom; and its structure must be such as to serve this end. That is the partial justification of Fascism which has made its triumphs possible. It sins far more deeply against true freedom than it supports it; yet in the materialist and mechanical quality of the democratic movement from Rousseau to Karl Marx and his communist disciples, it had real justification for reacting against them.

10.20   It is impossible to say how much we owe in our own country to the schooling in democratic habits provided, first by the old Trade Guilds, then, when the fellowship of trade had been broken up by the release of individualist acquisitiveness, by the Trade Unions, and ever since the seventeenth century by the dissenting congregations. Many of our most effective Labour leaders learned their art of public speech as local preachers; and the self-government of the local Chapel has been a fruitful school of democratic procedure. Our 'Left Wing' has by no means always maintained this close association of democratic principle with conscientious worship of God! But the historical root is there. And the British tradition of freedom has probably more of the element which consists of the claim to obey God rather than men and less of the element of mere self-assertiveness than has the democratic tradition in most other countries. The element of self-assertiveness is morally bad and politically disastrous; a freedom based upon it is only an opportunity for selfishness and will decline through anarchy to disruption of the State; the claim to obey God rather than men is a source both of moral strength, for it inspires devotion to duty, and of political stability, for such freedom may only be used in the service of the whole fellowship.

10.21   The combination of Freedom and Fellowship as principles of social life issues in the obligation of Service. No one doubts this in so far as it concerns the individual. Whatever our practice may be, we all give lip-service to this principle.

10.22   Its application to the individual is pretty clear. It affects him in two main ways – as regards work and leisure. In England we have depended a great deal on voluntary service given in leisure hours. We want a great deal more of it; and we have a right to expect more than we get from the Christian Churches. Yet it is certain that a very large proportion of the day-to-day drudgery of social service is done by Christian men and women in the inspiration of their Christian faith. We want more of them; but the greater part of what is done at all is done by Christian folk.

10.23 What is less often recognized in practice is the obligation to make of the occupation, by which a man or woman earns a living, a sphere of service. This may be done in two ways. Some young people have the opportunity to choose the kind of work by which they will earn their living. To make that choice on selfish grounds is probably the greatest single sin that any young person can commit, for it is the deliberate withdrawal from allegiance to God of the greatest part of time and strength...

10.24 It is not only individuals who must, if Christianity is the truth, guide their policy or career by the principles of service; all groupings of men must do the same. The rule here should be that we use our wider loyalties to check the narrower. A man is a member of his family, of his nation, and of mankind. It is very seldom that any one can render a service directly to mankind as a whole. We serve mankind by serving those parts of it with which we are closely connected... A man must chiefly serve his own most immediate community, accepting as the standard of its welfare that which its members are ready to accept (though trying, it may be, to lead them nearer to a fully Christian view), but always checking this narrower service by the wider claims, so that in serving the smaller community he never injures the larger.

10.25 But as a member of each small group – with a voice in determining its conduct and policy – e.g. as a Christian Trade Unionist or Managing Director, or as the Governor of a School – he will do all he can to secure that his own group accepts for itself the principle of service and sets its course in the way that will benefit not only its own members in their own self-interest, but also the larger community in which this group is a part.

10.26   Freedom, Fellowship, Service – these are the three
principles of a Christian social order, derived from the
still more fundamental Christian postulates that Man is a
child of God and is destined for a life of eternal fellowship
with Him.

EXTRACT 11

JOHN XXIII

Towards a world government

11.1   That inter-state relationships involve mutual rights and
duties has been frequently taught by our predecessors and
this we now confirm. These relationships, too, must
conform to the norms of truth, justice, friendship and
respect of freedom. For the same natural law which
governs the conduct of individual men applies with equal
force to the management of public affairs.

11.2   This will be clear to anyone who reflects that rulers
cannot discard their human dignity whilst they are acting
on behalf of the community and attending to its welfare.
They cannot, therefore, disregard the natural moral law
which binds them as men.

11.3   Nor is it to be imagined that men are driven to shed
their humanity by being elevated to the highest rank in
the state. On the contrary they have usually been chosen
because of their outstanding gifts and qualities.

11.4   We have seen, too, that it is the moral law which
provides for authority in the community. How then can
authority turn round and reject the moral law by which it
was constituted? It would lose its foundation and
collapse. We have God's own warning in the Book of
Wisdom:

Listen then kings and understand;
rulers of remotest lands, take warning;
hear this, you who have thousands under your rule,
who boast of your hordes of subjects.

For power is a gift to you from the Lord,
sovereignty is from the Most High;
he himself will probe your acts and scrutinise your
intentions (6.2-4)

11.5 All along the line, even when it comes to interstate relations, we have to maintain the principle that authority must seek to promote the common good of all, for that is the reason for its existence.

11.6 But one of the first rules for securing the common good is that the moral order be recognised and its precepts obeyed. 'If order amongst states is to be securely established it must rest on the bedrock of those unalterable standards of honesty which the Creator has made to appear in nature itself and established irremovably in the minds of men...These norms are guiding lights to show men and nations the way they should take. Their salutary and provident warnings must be observed if the attempts to build a new order in society are not to end in storms and ship-wreck.' (Pius XII, Christmas Broadcast, 1941).

11.7 First of all then the links between states must be forged in truth. Truth demands that in the creation of these links racial or ethnic discrimination should have no part: that all states be regarded as equal in their natural dignity. Each, in consequence, has the right to its existence, to its prosperity and to the aids which these make necessary, and the right to retain for itself the responsibility for securing all these. It can likewise legitimately demand to have its reputation respected and to be given the honours to which it is entitled.

11.8 We know that individual men differ greatly from one another in knowledge, strength of character, talents and the possession of wealth. But this is no reason why those who excel in such things should lord it over others. On the contrary the obligation that falls upon all and sundry to cooperate with others in striving for perfection lies more heavily on those with something extra to contribute.

11.9 In the same way some nations surpass others in scientific, cultural and economic development. But this superiority, far from permitting them an unjust domination over others, increases their obligation to contribute to the common welfare of all peoples.

11.10   In respect of their human dignity nature makes no men superior to others. Nor does it do so in the case of civil communities, for each of these is a body whose members are individual human beings. We know, too, well enough, how sensitive people are in matters that touch a nation's honour and with good reason.

11.11   Truth also calls for balance and fairness in the use of the means of communicating information which modern technology has put at men's disposal and which help nations to learn more about each other. This does not mean that a country is wrong in giving prominence to what can be said in its own favour. It does mean the rejection of any spreading of rumours which do violence to truth and justice and damage the reputation of another country.

11.12   Relations beween states must also accord with justice. This involves mutual recognition of rights, mutual fulfilment of obligations.

11.13   We have established that states have the right to exist, to prosper, to acquire the aids necessary for their development and to rely principally on their own efforts in so doing. They have the right also to protect their reputation and to insist on due honours being paid to them. It follows logically that there is a corresponding obligation on all of them to see that every one of these rights is safeguarded and that nothing is done to violate them. For, just as in private life men may not pursue their own interests in such a manner as to inflict unjust harm on others, in the same way states are guilty of criminal behaviour if they seek their own advantage at the expense of injuring others or unwarrantably oppressing them. How apt in this connection is St. Augustine's remark: 'Take away justice and what are kingdoms but gangs of robbers?' (*City of God*, IV.4.)

11.14   It can happen, and indeed does happen, that clashes of interests develop between states. The solution of these should be sought not in recourse to arms, nor in underhand and deceitful ways, but in a manner worthy of human beings: through mutual appreciation of arguments and attitudes, giving mature consideration to all points, weighing them in the balance of truth and resolving differences fairly.

11.15   This applies particularly to the problem of national consciousness. From the nineteenth century onwards there have been increasing attempts in various parts of the world to make political boundaries coincide with national ones, so as to give self-government to people of the same ethnic group. Since, for a variety of reasons, this cannot always be achieved, it often happens that minorities find themselves hemmed in within the frontiers of a nation comprised of people from another stock. This gives rise to serious problems.

11.16   It must be made quite clear that it is a gross violation of justice to do anything to reduce the vigour and growth of such minorities; all the more so if the abominable attempt is made to exterminate them.

11.17   The way to secure justice in such situations is for governments to take effective steps to improve the human conditions of these ethnic minorities, particularly as regards the use of their language, the preservation of their native genius, their ancient customs and their enterprises and activities in the economic field...

11.18   The latest advances in science and technology, exercising as they do such a profound influence on men's way of living, are causing people all over the world to come together and join in common enterprises. The interchange of goods and ideas and the amount of travel have all increased considerably. The result has been an extensive growth of contacts across national frontiers between individuals, families and intermediate bodies as well as between governments. All the time the economies of the various states are becoming so interdependent and gradually getting so inextricably interwoven that there already exists a sort of world economic order formed by the combination of the economies of the different nations. Added to this, the social progress, the order, the security and stability of each and every state are inevitably affected by what is happening in the others.

11.19   This being so, it is clear that individual states cannot properly develop and attend to their needs in isolation. For the prosperity and progress of any nation is part cause and part consequence of the prosperity and progress of the rest.

11.20   There is also a unity in the human race deriving from the human nature that men have perpetually in common and which demands that attention be given to the welfare of mankind as a whole: in other words to the universal common good.

11.21   In former times the governments of the various nations were considered capable of attending sufficiently to this universal common good. They did so either through their ambassadors or by congresses or by drawing up treaties and conventions. These were ways and means indicated by the natural law or the common law of all peoples or by positive international law.

11.22   In our day the customary relations between states have undergone a prodigious transformation. On the other hand the universal common good brings up for immediate attention serious and complex problems which have to do with security and peace on a world scale. On the other hand national governments, for the very reason that they all have equal status, are unable to impose a solution, however much they multiply their efforts to work out appropriate laws. It is not that they lack sufficient goodwill: it is simply that the authority they possess is inadequate for the purpose.

11.23   So it is that, in the circumstances in which human society finds itself today, both political organisations and political authority fall short of the standard required for attending properly to the universal common good.

11.24   Yet if we have a proper idea of the common good and a correct understanding of the nature and function of political authority we cannot help seeing that there must be perfect correspondence between the two. For the moral order which demands the existence of public authority for the common good of civil society must, in doing so, require also that it be equal to the task. This principle helps us to determine the form and the degree of competence with which to invest civil institutions. These institutions constitute the medium through which public authority is exercised and attains its purpose of promoting the common good. If they are to perform this function adequately they must have the form and the degree of competence which match contemporary circumstances at any given time.

11.25   Today, however, the common good of all nations involves problems which affect people all the world over: problems which can only be solved by a public authority which has the power, the form and the agencies competent to deal with them and whose writ covers the entire globe. We cannot therefore escape the conclusion that the moral order itself demands the establishment of some sort of world governemnt.

11.26   Such a world government, enjoying an authority extending to the farthest corners of the earth and having in its service agencies capable of advancing the universal common good, will need to come into being through universal consent and not be imposed by force. This is because authority of the kind we are speaking of must be able to operate effectively and this will involve being fair to all, devoid of favouritism and intent on the welfare of all peoples. If it were to be forcibly imposed on the rest by the more powerful nations, there would be good reason to fear that it would serve the interests of some few only or favour one nation unduly. The force and efficacy of its action would be thereby imperilled. For, though nations differ considerably in material wealth and military power, they all cling tenaciously to their claim for equal rights and for the excellence of their own way of life. They have good reason, therefore, to object to any rule imposed on them by force or arranged without their participation or to which they have not given a spontaneous assent.

11.27   Just as in the case of the common good of individual states so also in the respect of the interests of all states taken together, no proper judgment can be made without taking into consideration the human person. World government, therefore, has to be specially directed towards making sure that human rights are everywhere acknowledged, respected, protected and given ever wider scope. It can attend to this by its own direct intervention where the situation calls for it, or by creating the conditions which enable the governments of individual states to perform their functions more efficiently.

11.28   We must add that the relationships between the world government and the governments of individual nations must be regulated according to the principle of subsidiarity, in exactly the same way as the relationships within any country between the state government on the one hand and the citizens, families and intermediate bodies on the other. Thus it will be the province of such a world authority to consider and settle questions prompted by the universal common good, whether they touch on matters economic, social, political or cultural. We mean the sort of questions which, by reason of their gravity, their widespread nature and their extreme urgency cannot be dealt with satisfactorily by the governments of individual states.

11.29   To put it another way: the world authority must not arrogate to itself questions which rightly belong to individual member states. On the contrary it must see to it that all over the world those conditions prevail which give not only to national governments but to individual citizens and intermediate bodies a better opportunity to get on with their own business, fulfil their duties and vindicate their rights.

11.30   Everyone knows how, on 26 June 1945, there came into being the United Nations Organisation – UNO for short. Specialised agencies composed of members nominated by the governments to the various countries have been added to it since. To these are assigned projects of great importance and world-wide extent in social and economic matters and in the fields of science, education and public health. But the main purposes of the Organisation are declared to be: i. To maintain international peace and security; ii. To develop friendly relations among nations based on respect for the principle of equal rights; iii. To achieve international cooperation in solving international problems; iv. To be a centre for harmonising the actions of nations.

11.31   It is to this Organisation that we owe the Universal Declaration of Human Rights, approved by the UN General Assembly on 10 December 1948. In the Preamble to the

Declaration it is stated that 'the effective recognition and observance of the rights and freedoms' proclaimed in it are to be 'a common standard of achievement for all peoples and nations.'

11.32   We are well aware that some people are not entirely satisfied with some items in the Declaration, and with good reason. Nevertheless we think it is a step towards the creation of a legal and political system for the world as a whole, inasmuch as it enshrines a recognition of the dignity of the human person, asserts the right of every man on earth to seek truth in freedom, to observe moral norms, to do what justice demands, to live as befits a human being and to enjoy other rights consequent upon these.

11.33   It is therefore our earnest wish that the United Nations Organisation should go from strength to strength, perfecting its constitution and its agencies to meet the extent and grandeur of its tasks. May the time come soon when this Organisation will be able to give effective protection to human rights: rights which derive immediately from man's dignity as a person and which, for that reason, are all-embracing, on no account to be violated and never to be filched away. There is all the more reason for wanting this because men today are much more active in the public life of their own country, take a keener interest in international affairs and are becoming ever more conscious of belonging as living members to the whole family of mankind.

11.34   This is the place to repeat our exhortation that our sons should offer themselves readily for service in public life and should join with others in working for the good of the whole human race as well as that of their own country. Profiting by the guidance which their Christian faith provides and under the impulse of Christian love, they must work hard to ensure that whatever plans are formed to promote economic, social, political or cultural ends are such as will not hinder but will rather help men to develop in the supernatural order as well as the natural...

11.35   There are, indeed, generous souls who, when faced with a situation not completely or perhaps not at all consonant with justice, burn with a desire to put everything right at

once and who get carried away by such an ungovernable
zeal that their attempt at reform becomes a sort of
revolution.

11.36   To such people we would suggest that it is in the nature of
things for growth to be gradual and that in human
institutions no improvement can be looked for which does
not proceed step by step and from within. The point was
well put by our predecessor, Pius XII: 'Security and justice
lie in not completely overthrowing the old order but in well
planned progress. Uncontrolled passionate zeal always
destroys everything and builds nothing. It inflames cupid-
ity, never cools it. Since it does nothing but sow hate and
ruin, far from leading to reconciliation, it drives men and
political parties to the laborious undertaking of building
anew, on ruins left by discord, the edifice with which they
started.' [Address, 13/6/42]

11.37   Therefore, amongst the most urgent issues facing serious
thinkers today is that of working out a new pattern of
human relationships based on truth, justice, love and
freedom: relationships between man and man, between
citizen and state, between one country and another and,
finally, between individuals, families, intermediate bodies
and states on the one hand, and, on the other, the
community of the whole family of mankind. There is none,
surely, who will not esteem this as a service of the highest
order; for it is that which will render possible the building
up of true peace according to the pattern which God has
made.

11.38   Such thinkers, indeed, are all too few to accomplish
everything that requires to be done; but the whole of
mankind is deeply in their debt. It is fitting that we should
pay them a public tribute of praise and at the same time beg
them to press on with their beneficial efforts. It is our
constant hope that their numbers will be reinforced,
especially from the ranks of Christians inspired to join them
by a sense of duty and a spirit of love; for on those who have
enrolled under the standard of Christ there lies a special
obligation to bring vision and love to human society and to

act as leaven in the mass. They will succeed in this in the measure of their union with God.

11.39　For no peace can reign over the whole human family unless it has first gained sway in the hearts of individual men: that is to say unless each observes within himself the order which God has prescribed. Some words of St. Augustine are very appropriate here: 'Do you want your mind to be capable of controlling your passions? Let it bow to a superior power and it will conquer all beneath itself; and peace will come to you: true, certain and in right good order. What order? God commanding the mind and the mind the flesh. Nothing could be more in order'(*Miscellanea Augustiniana*)

11.40　It is our burning desire that such a peace should be established all over the world – a desire which is surely shared by all men of good will – which has led us to put forward these ideas on the problems which vex human society so sorely today and on the solution of which its future progress depends.

11.41　We do so knowing that, unworthy as we are of the office, we represent the One whom the divinely inspired prophet referred to as 'The Prince of Peace'. It is our bounden duty to dedicate ourselves to this work for the common good with all the strength of soul and body. But peace will remain a mere dream in men's minds unless it is built on the principles we have, with great hopes, sketched out in this letter: that is to say unless it is grounded on truth, given a framework of justice, raised to a lofty height and crowned by charity, and takes proper account of freedom.

11.42　To erect so wonderful an edifice is truly beyond the capacity of man, whatever his natural gifts, if he relies solely on his own powers. To construct human society in the image of the kingdom of God there is need of help from heaven.

11.43　So, during this Holy Week, we address our prayers to Him who, by His bitter Passion and Death, not only wiped away sin, the cause of all conflicts, miseries and inequalities, but led back with the human race to reconciliation with His heavenly Father through the shedding of His own blood;

thus winning for mankind the gift of peace. 'For he is the peace between us, and has made the two into one ... He came to bring the good news of peace, peace to you who were far away and peace to those who were near at hand.' [Eph. 2. 14–17]

11.44   This is a message which is echoed in the Liturgy of this sacred season: 'Jesus, our Lord, risen and standing in the midst of his disciples said "Peace be upon you, alleluia": the disciples saw the Lord and were glad.' Christ brought us peace and bequeathed it to us. 'Peace I bequeath to you, my own peace I give you, a peace the world cannot give, this is my gift to you.' [Jhn. 14.27]

11.45   It is this peace brought to us by our divine Redeemer which is the object of our entreaties in the prayers we address to Him. May He banish from the souls of men all that can undermine peace. May He mould them all to become witnesses of truth, justice and brotherly love. May He enlighten all who rule so that they provide for their subjects, together with commendable prosperity, the inestimable boon of impregnable peace. Finally, may Christ inspire all men with a determination to break down the barriers which keep men divided, to strengthen the bonds of mutual love which draw them together, to try to understand others and to find forgiveness for those guilty of wrongdoing. So that, following his plan and his guidance, all nations will arrive unfailingly at a union in brotherly concord in which will flourish and reign perpetually the peace for which men dream.

EXTRACT 12

MIRANDA

Justice and almsgiving

12.1   Since at least the sixth century A.D., a bald fact has been systematically excluded from theological and moral consideration: "To give alms" in the Bible is called "to do justice."

12.2   To cite a few of the passages which have resisted all misrepresentation, we mention Prov. 10:2; Tob. 4:10; 12:9; 14:11; Dan. 4:24; and Matt. 6:1-2. These are not the only ones, but these are unequivocal. When our Western translations say "almsgiving," they do not do so in bad faith. Indeed the reality involved is what we call today "almsgiving", and the translations are made for the people of today. But the original says *sedakah*, which signifies "justice." We might also add Ecclus. 3:30, 7:10 and 12:3, the original Hebrew of which we have only recently come to know. Previous centuries knew only the Greek translation, which, like our modern versions, is "almsgiving." With the same certainty we could also list Ps. 112:3,9; Artur Weiser and H.J. Kraus dogmatically interpret "justice" (*sedakah* in Hebrew) in these two verses as "fidelity-to-the-covenant," but they hold that the Bible treats no other theme but the covenant. As we shall see later, however, covenant theology belongs to a relatively late period in the Old Testament. In Ps. 112, as in the other passages we have cited, the Bible calls "justice" what we call "alsmgiving."

12.3   Some exegetes have tried to diminish the importance of this fact. They argue that the Greek translators of the Old Testament, the famous Seventy, caused some confusion by translating justice (*sedakah*) at times by *eleemosyne* 'almsgiving,' at other times by *eleos* 'compassion,' and at others by *dikaiosyne* 'justice.' But, in the first place, this characteristic of the translation should not distract us from the fact which is disconcerting for the West – that the works which we consider to be of charity and supererogation are in the original Bible text called works of justice. This is the same *sedakah* which the whole Bible considers transgressed when the worker does not receive his wage; see, for example, Jer. 22:13. In the second place, instead of minimizing the bald fact we have pointed out, the Greek translation exphasized it even more: It means that the translators of the Septuagint themselves were disconcerted.

12.4   The act which in the West is called almsgiving for the original Bible was a restitution that someone makes for something that is not his. The Fathers of the early Church saw this with great clarity: 'Tell me, how is it that you are rich? From whom did you receive your wealth? And he, whom did he receive it from? From his grandfather, you say, from his father. By climbing this genealogical tree are you able to show the justice of this possession? Of course you cannot; rather *its beginning and root have necessarily come out of injustice.*' 'Do not say, "I am spending what is mine; I am enjoying what is mine." In reality it is not yours but another's.'

12.5   Jerome comments in this way on Jesus' expression "money of injustice" (Luke 16:9): 'And he very rightly said, "money of injustice," for *all riches come from injustice.* Unless one person has lost, another cannot find. Therefore I believe that the popular proverb is very true: "The rich person is either an unjust person or the heir of one."' Basil the Great thinks the same way: 'When someone steals a man's clothes we call him a thief. Should we not give the same name to one who could clothe the naked and does not? The bread in your cupboard belongs to the hungry man; the coat hanging unused in your closet belongs to the man who needs it; the shoes rotting in your closet belong to the man who has no shoes; the money which you hoard up belongs to the poor.' Ambrose teaches the same thing in a formula of unsurpassable exactitude: 'You are not making a gift of your possessions to the poor person. *You are handing over to him what is his.*'

12.6   The defenders of private ownership have used wonders of subterfuge and misrepresentation to escape attack by such an unequivocal and constant tradition, which was only being faithful to Sacred Scripture. But no subtlety is able to whitewash these explicit teachings of Ambrose and Augustine: 'God willed that this earth should be the common possession of all and he offered its fruits to all. But avarice distributed the rights of possession (*Avaritia distribuit iura possessionum*).' '*Iustitia est in subveniendo miseris*: Assisting the needy is justice.'

12.7   Apologists for the status quo attribute this incontrovertible tradition to the imprecision of preachers. By
this standard however, we would also have to eliminate
not only the entire patristic tradition but the Bible as
well, for there is nothing imprecise about the statements
we have considered. On the contrary, they demonstrate
on the part of their authors the very clear intention of
formulating a well-deliberated idea. The time has come
for Christianity to break a long chain of hypocrisy and
collusion with the established powers and decide if its
message is or is not going to be the same as the Bible's.

12.8   It does us no good to think like the Greeks and say that
"money of injustice" cannot mean that injustice is
inherent in money like quality, like weight or color, and
that therefore we do not comprehend what Jesus means
by the term and should let the question rest. It is obvious
that Christ did not mean that, nor did Luke, for the
simple reason that neither of them was a disciple of
Aristotle. The expression in question should be understood in the context of a society divided between rich and
poor. "How happy are you who are poor" (Luke 6:20)
and "Alas for you who are rich" (Luke 6:24) are not
expressions which bless the physical fact of not having
money and condemn the physical fact of having money,
and neither are the numerous statements in the Psalter
and the prophets on behalf of the poor and against the
rich. The terms "rich" and "poor" are correlative, and
what the blessing and the corresponding curse attack is
precisely the difference between the two. It does not seem
to Luke (nor to Christ) that this difference can be
justified. It is "money of injustice" for, as Jerome
understood very well in the paragraph we have quoted,
"All riches come from injustice . . . . The rich person is
either an unjust person or the heir of one." Jesus ben
Sirach, who in Ecclus. 5:8 uses "unjust riches" with the
same sense as the term in Luke 16:9 (and not, certainly, in
a determinative sense, which would need the article" *tois
chremasin tois adikois*), with astonishing perspicacity provides the same explanation: 'Many have sinned for the

sake of profit; he who hopes to be right must be ruthless. A peg will stick in the joint between two stones, and sin will wedge itself between selling and buying.' (Ecclus. 27:1-2).

12.9   Let it not be said that the biblical authors did not understand economics; this is the same ben Sirach who in 3:30, 7:10, and 12:3 in the original Hebrew refers to "almsgiving" and "justice". The underlying conviction is that differentiating ownership, that which makes some rich and some poor within the same society, could not be achieved with the genuine acquiescence of those who were thereby disempowered; it could not and it cannot be achieved without violence and despoliation. The condemnation of the right in Luke 6:24 and the expression "money of injustice" in Luke 16:9 are based on the same conviction. If this were not so the programmatic battle cry which at the beginning of this Gospel Luke puts on the lips of Jesus' mother herself would be completely incomprehensible: 'He has filled the hungry with good things and sent the rich away empty' (Luke 1:53). This verse is generally classified among the incomprehensible, but such an alternative is not very scientific. It is obvious that the statement in question presupposes a definite conviction about the injustice of differentiating wealth, that is, the wealth which in the same society constitutes some people in one class and others in another. The underlying conviction can be none other than the one we have indicated: It is impossible for this wealth to have been acquired without violence and spoliation. To avoid this conclusion regarding what is at the basis of all these scriptural passages, it would be necessary to assert that they do not refer to every type of differentiating wealth, but only to that which was wrongly acquired. The passages would therefore imply that the wealth could have been rightly acquired. But the very strength of the texts is in the intentional universality of the statements, in the nondistinction, precisely in the fact that they do not allow distinctions: 'It is easier for a camel to pass through the eye of a needle than for a rich man to enter the kingdom of God' (Mark 10:25; Matt. 19:24; Luke 18:25). It is impossible to interpret this statement as directed against the distribution of differentiating ownership whch *de facto* prevails and not against *de jure* differentiating ownership as such. It is impossible to interpret it as directed aginst the abuses and not against differentiating ownership in itself.

12.10   The efforts of certain modern exegetes to negate the authenticity of this logion (Mark 10:25; Matt. 19:24; Luke 18:25) as the words of Christ himself only show how greatly the work of interpretation is influenced by the status which Western civilization bestows on the theologian and on Christianity itself as the official religion. Of this entire teaching they wish to retain as the original nucleus only Mark 10:26, which in substance says, "How difficult it is to be saved". They want us to believe that 10:25 is one example among many and that it was more or less invented by pre-Marcan community preaching, which does not have to be taken literally. But with this maneuver exegesis transgresses the methodological principles which it has scientifcally elaborated during many decades of meritorious work. In fact, the absolute impossibility of salvation for the rich is something which no primitive Christian community (before 70 A.D., as Mark's Gospel was written in 70 or 71) would have dared to assert if it were not basing its assertion on the authority of Christ himself. On the other hand, "how difficult it is to be saved" is a theological generality which could have been invented by any community or redactor of that time or any other. Therefore the most serious modern exegetes, from the accredited Joachim Jeremias and the authoritative Walter Grundmann to the very exigent Rudolf Bultmann and Norman Perrrin, hold that Mark 10:25 is an authentic saying of the historical Jesus.

12.11   Thus the statements of Luke 1:53, 6:24, and 16:9 could be, as regards their formulation, proper to Luke or to his preredactional tradition; as regards the content, however, they faithfully transmit to us the thinking of Christ himself, which we know from Mark 10:25 and many other equally authentic passages like Matt. 11:5-6 (Luke 7:22-23); Luke 6:20; etc.

12.12   Thus we can return to our starting point: The fact that differentiating wealth is unacquirable without violence and spoliation is presupposed by the Bible in its pointed anathemas against the rich; therefore almsgiving is nothing more than restitution of what has been stolen, and thus the Bible calls it justice. And we include here the New Testament. Matthew leaves no room for doubt when he explains and thematically attempts to delineate what justice is, that is, what makes some just and others not, in Matt. 25:31-46: "the just" (vv. 37 and 46); 'And they will go away to eternal punishment, and the just to eternal life' (v.46). It all has to do with giving food to the hungry, drink to the thirsty, a home to the stranger, clothing to the naked, etc. The list is given four times so that there can be no mistake. It would be difficult to establish with greater emphasis a definitive and single criterion to distinguish between the just and the unjust. And this justice cannot be reduced without misrpresentation to some kind of "virtue" or supererogation, as we see by the fate which awaits those who do not practise it: 'Go away from me with your curse upon you, to the eternal fire prepared for the devil and his angels' (v.41).

12.13   These are all works which the West calls charity, in contradistinction to justice. A frequent methodological error is to believe that the discrepancy is verbal or explicable by the alleged imperfection of biblical morality, which did not know how to distinguish between justice and charity. The discrepancy is a solid, unequivocal fact. To brand the biblical authors as primitive is a value judgment, not objective exegetical work. What is in question is precisely Western morality's alleged superiority to biblical morality. To base oneself on this superiority in order to reduce biblical thought to Western thought is an extraordinarily unscientific methodology for it prevents one from seeing the difference which exists between the thinking and wishing of the investigator and that of the authors being studied.

12.14   We have said that when the Bible calls "justice" what
Western culture calls "almsgiving" it is because the
private ownership which differentiates the rich from the
poor is considered unacquirable without violence and
spoliation; the Fathers of the Church also understood this
very clearly. The causal dependence which exists between the distribution of ownership and the distribution
of income had led us, by economics alone, to the same
conclusion. But it would be erroneous to think that this
economic fact escaped the biblical authors. Ecclus.
27:1-2, which we have cited, is exceedingly clear: It refers
to those who try to enrich themselves through profits,
and it points out how this profit occurs in buying and
selling. When in 3:30, 7:10, and 12:3 it refers to
"almsgiving" as "justice" (*sedakah*), the thinking is in
perfect congruence with the economic fact to which we
have alluded and which, to be sure, has escaped Western
moralist and jurists.

12.15   In 22:17 Jeremiah condemns this profit, after describing in v. 14 the luxurious home which King Jehoiakim
had built, undoubtedly with such profits. Thus in v. 13
the prophet could specify of what material the property
was made: 'Shame on the man who builds his house by
non-justice and completes its upstairs rooms by not-
right'. As economic theory demonstrates, profit is the
tangible concretization of the difference in incomes.
Jeremiah sees very clearly how private ownership arises
from this. We refer to the ownership which we have
called differentiating.

12.16   Amos is equally penetrating in the causal relationships
he draws. He, however, refers to no person in particular
but to the system itself: 'Well then, since you have
trampled on the poor man, extorting levies on his wheat
– those houses you have built of dressed stone, you will
never live in them; and those precious vineyards you have
planted, you will never drink their wine. "Assemble on
Samaria's mountain and see what great disorder there is
in that city, what oppression is found inside her." They
know nothing of fair dealing – it is Yahweh who speaks –

they cram their palaces full with violence and spoliation.'
(5:11; 3:9-10)

12.17   Here we have, despite all the appearances of elegance
and luxury, the true consistency of the property of the
rich: violence and spoliation. Their palaces and all that
which makes them into a class different from the rest of
the population are for Amos concretized oppression, the
accumulated materialization of violence and spoliation.
When he threatens punishment, Amos is aware that he is
proclaiming elementary justice. Because they trampled
on the poor and extorted from them levies of wheat, they
could build their houses of dressed stone, but they would
not inhabit them, for the day of justice is coming.

12.18   Micah (3:9-10) alludes to this same characteristic of
differentiating ownership as he contemplates the man-
sions and buildings of Jerusalem:
'You who loath justice and
pervert all that is right,
you who build Zion with blood,
Jerusalem with injustice.'

12.19   The second chapter of Habakkuk attacks profit in both
its second (vv. 6b-8) and third (vv. 9-11) stanzas. Then it
speaks of the cries of the walls and the beams of the
houses which were built with such materials:
'For the stone from the very walls cries out, and the
beam responds frm the framework.'
And it continues by taking up the words of Micah:
'Trouble is coming to the man who builds a town with
blood and founds a city on injustice.'(2:11; 2:12)

12.20   It is needless to draw out the list of biblical testimony.
Thirty years ago there were those who tried to explain
this unanimous understanding of the essence of differentiating ownership by the rural and antiurban origin
of the prophets. Today scientific exegesis rejects such
subterfuges of interpretation, of which the history of
Christianity is full. Any anecdotal or psychological
explanation is out of place here, for in the prophetic
anathemas there is a lucid understanding that inherited
wealth has its economic origin in profit. Moreover, Isaiah

and Hosea think the same way as the other prophets, and they are not peasants but city-dwellers. Isaiah is even from the capital, and proud of it.

12.21 Before Christianity became compromised with the prevailing social systems, that is, up to the fourth or fifth century A.D., there were never misrepresentations or evasions with regard to the biblical testimony concerning the inescapably unjust origin or differentiating ownership. The patristic passages which we have cited abundantly demonstrate this.

12.22 At the beginning of this chapter, I noted that the papal encyclicals' defense of private ownership cannot be quoted to brand as heterodox what I am sustaining. As Allaz and Bigo have demonstrated, the encyclicals understand ownership as something very different. I now wish to add, although I have already touched this in passing, that in their defense the popes obviously presuppose this provision: that the ownership has been legitimately acquired. Thus the papal doctrine on ownership is on a different level, onto which my considerations is no way enter. But the whole doctrine is conditioned by the implicit phrase: provided that the ownership has been legitmately acquired.

12.23 If it is objected that the popes presuppose that legitimately acquired ownership *de facto* does exist, I respond that in any case this notion is not the object of their teaching activity but is rather a supposition. Their teachings therefore do not prejudge the possibility of demonstrating that this supposition is false. Both the recent advances in economic science and the understanding that the Bible and the Church Fathers had of the matter demonstrate that the supposition is indeed false.

CRITIQUE

The critical attitude that one adopts towards the Extracts will partly depend upon the answer one gives to each of the questions that opened this Section: namely: (1) Can specific political structures, ideals or programmes be derived unambiguously from the Gospel?; (2) How far can the Church be identified with specific political regimes, ideals or programmes?; and (3) Should the individual Christian be totally obedient to specific political regimes, ideals or programmes? So, if one answers 'yes' to (1), the differing positions of Barth and Temple would be unacceptable. And if one answers 'yes' to the third only, that of Barth might be acceptable. Nonetheless, apart from these (vital) overall criticisms a number of more internal criticism of the individual Extracts can be made.

It has already been noted that, by the standards of critical exegesis, much of Barth's *Der Römerbrief* may appear eisegetical. However, the central difficulty is that this Extract seems to demand too rigid an obedience of the individual to government and acceptance of the political status quo (whether tyrannical or not). Such a position seems much more rigid than that of Calvin (see *above*, pp. 176-7) and, in practice, Barth later found it to be unsustainable in the face of Nazism. Nonetheless, as a theological corrective of facile revolutionary politics, Barth's contribution remains important – particularly since, as an individual, Barth was himself firmly committed to a left-wing political perspective.

Despite the equally important emphasis of Berdyaev on the spiritual in religion, his particular discussion of political realities will appear to many to be far too esoteric and elitist. His grudging allowance of political structures for 'the masses', combined with his avoiding any discussion of how these structures might be evaluated or improved, might seem both arrogant and ethereal. Yet, in response, Berdyaev might have claimed that, such attitudes are necessary, given man's persistent tendency to persecute or ignore the truly spiritual.

The central difficulty that is usually found in Niebuhr's *Moral Man and Immoral Soceity* involves the moral dualism that he frankly admitted and, yet, which he gradually modified during his life. As with Barth, it would seem that a sharply defined early position, which made obvious overall sense, could not be sustained in practice. Many critics have argued that such a sharp moral dualism would allow societies, governments and large corporations to act in highly immoral ways. On this argument, the prevarications of President Nixon's government would appear perfectly acceptable and only became wrong when they actually sought to obstruct justice. Although there is some force in this criticism, Niebuhr's early position was by no means as dualistic as, at first, it might appear, since he did insist that leaders of social groups must still adhere to 'the ideals of a high individual morality' (9.11).

Both Temple and John XXIII must face the difficulties confronting all Natural law theories (see *above*, pp. 86-8). The problems are, perhaps, less for Temple, since he only proposed general principles and was careful to show that these derive from general Christian doctrine. Provided one can accept the latter, then the former might seem to follow (although, even here, he showed his own bias in regarding respect for persons as the primary principle of Christian ethics). More important is the criticism that Temple appeared to believe that the specific application of general principles to political problems by politicians involves only 'technical knowledge' and 'judgments of practical expediency' (10.1). In fact, many political problems (as can be seen in the next Section) involve a whole range of smaller ethical, political and ideological decisions which divide Christians as much as anyone. Similarly, with John XXIII's *Pacem in Terris*, it is the avoidance of these sorts of decisions which may give it an air of generality and unreality. Precisely because both authors attempted to address as wide an audience as possible and sought a broad agreement in this audience, their discussions tend to lack the sort of specificity which might make them appear more realistic. The second part of Temple's *Christianity and the Social Order* attempted to remedy this by supplying a detailed and, admittedly, partisan (and now, of course, dated) series of political and economic proposals.

For many, Liberation theology appears as one of the most stimulating movements in recent theology. It has brought new insights and perspectives to the discipline and reminded many of the passion in the face of oppression which should characterise Christianity. Perhaps it would be unrealistic to expect it to be thoroughly defined and rigorously methodological whilst it is still developing. Nonetheless, the writings of, especially, Alredo Fierro in *The Militant Gospel*, Bonino and Miranda, demonstrate that it does not lack critical sophistication. Miranda's Extract supplies an important corrective to the medieval concept of 'almsgiving', which is undoubtedly still prevalent in the West. Yet, it is not itself without difficulties. Two, in particular, are crucial. The first is concerned with the adequacy of his exegesis. He concentrates upon the Old Testament criticism of wealth and tends to ignore the obvious limitations of this criticism and the existence of other and quite different strands within the OT. The (largely prophetic) stress upon 'justice' is, of course, only justice for the people of Israel: it seldom extends even to Israel's most immediate neighbours. And, even in the context of Israel, *sedakah* may be more concerned with maintaining a lawful society than achieving social equity or abolishing 'differentiating ownership.' Further, other strands in the OT (particularly in certain Psalms and in the prologue and postscript of Job) seem to regard 'wealth' as a reward for, or an indication of, 'righteousness'. Even in the NT, the various redactions contained in Luke do not all seem equally hostile to 'wealth' (see further, David Mealand's *Poverty and Expectation in the Gospels*). The second difficulty concerns Miranda's deliberate use of Marxist theory (e.g. 'differentiating ownership') to depict biblical concepts. However, this is a difficulty which will be discussed in the criticism of Bonino's *Extract 17*, since it is in that Extract that the issue is explicitly raised.

Looking for any points of unity between these Extracts is made more difficult by the polemical contexts from which they mostly derive. So, the contrasts between Barth and Miranda appear sharper because neither makes the sort of qualifications that they do in their less combative writings. Nonetheless, there might be broad agreement with the following points qualifying the three initial questions:

(1) Even if it is believed that specific political structures, ideals or programmes can be derived unambiguously from the Gospel, the latter cannot be *identified* with them. For the Christian, political realities must always be set in the context of transcendence. Even the theologian who is most often thought to have confused the Kingdom of God with political realities, Walter Rauschenbusch, was emphatic about this:

'The Kingdom of God is divine in its origin, progress and

consummation. It was initiated by Jesus Christ, in whom the prophetic spirit came to its consummation, it is sustained by the Holy Spirit, and it will be brought to its fulfilment by the power of God in his own time. The passive and active resistance of the Kingdom of Evil at every stage of its advance is so great, and the human resourses of the Kingdom of God so slender, that no explanation can satisfy a religious mind which does not see the power of God in its movements . . . The Kingdom of God, therefore, is not merely ethical, but has a rightful place in theology' (*A Theology for the Social Gospel*, pp. 139-40).

(2) If the Church's aims and aspirations cannot simply be identified with political realities, most Christians would also argue that neither can it be indifferent to them. A notion of the relative worth of political regimes, ideals and programmes (relative, that is, to the Kingdom of God), would suggest that they do serve an important function, but not one that should be absolutised. Whereas Christians have always differed with each other about the extent to which tyrannical regimes should be actively opposed, they might agree that some form of political reality is necessary to preserve peace and justice. Pure anti-nomianism has seldom been thought to be a justifiable Christian position.

(3) If political realities do have some relative worth for the well-being of society, then it would seem that individual Christians (enjoined, as they are, to love their neighbours) do have at least a general responsibility for obedience. There are still very real differences apparent between Christians about how far this obedience should go. But, again in the context of transcendence, this obedience can hardly be absolute. The theist, par excellence, should always be conscious that it is only to God that absolute obedience is properly given. However, for the present-day theologian, there is an additional reason for this position of relative obedience. In the light of critical, historical research, it should be evident that Christianity has subsisted in and adapted to a variety of socio-political contexts. It is one of the merits of South American Liberation theology, that it has

served to remind Western theologians that Christianity is not dependent upon any one single socio-political system. It should be a function of Western, critical theologians, in turn, to remind Liberation theologians that they too are engaged in a historically ralative, albeit vital, attempt to unravel the riches of the Gospel.

SECTION 3

WAR AND PEACE

SECTION 3

WAR AND PEACE

War presents the 20th Century with perhaps its most crucial moral problem. The scale, cost and potential destructiveness of modern warfare differentiate our own from all previous Centuries. In this Century alone, fifty million people may have died as a result of war: in a year, world arms expenditure is now equivalent to the total expenditure on basic foodstuffs and by AD 2000 may equal the total present wealth of the world: and man now has the capacity to destroy, many times, the present world population. If for no other reason, these horrific dimensions make it appropriate to have a whole Section devoted to the substantive issue of war and its opposite, peace.

However, there are other reasons for giving this Section to this single issue. Although the dimensions of warfare were previously quite different from those of the 20th Century, the issue of war has always raised crucial problems about the relationship of Christianity to society at large. Empirically, a clear pattern emerges in Christian responses to war and this indicates, more sharply than in most other moral issues, the degree to which these responses are socially determined. And ethically, divisions between Christian pacifists and militarists, on this issue, serve to highlight the pluralism within Christianity evident in all of the Sections of this Textbook.

These points – empirical and ethical – require some initial distinction between differing responses to war. Four 'ideal' types may be isolated (for these see further my *Theology and Social Structure*, p. 71f):

(A) *Thoroughgoing Militarism* – understood as a willingness to fight anywhere, at any time and for any cause.

(B) *Selective Militarism* – understood as a willingness to fight when one's country, or another, declares that the cause is just.

(C) *Selective Pacifism* – understood as a willingness to fight only when one is personally convinced that the cause is just.

(D) *Thoroughgoing Pacifism* – understood as an unwillingness to fight anywhere, at any time and for any cause.

These are ideal, not actual, types, so particular examples may be variants of them, but together they represent the range of options open to the individual, based upon his or her willingness or unwillingness to fight in war. The words 'in war' should be stressed: the responses are not primarily concerned with individual killing or violence, but rather with the issue of fighting or not on behalf of others (see Augustine's *Text VII.* 6-7). Not all thoroughgoing pacifists would admit this distinction – since for some of them it is killing in any form which is forbidden – but it is essential to most other Christian responses to war. This distinction will be examined further in the next Section (see *above*, pp. 417f.).

For most Christians, type A is not a Christian response to war, since only the non-idealistic or amoral mercenary belongs to it (though see Luther's *IX.26*). Further, a moral defence of fighting in war, whether in terms of type B or type C, requires some notion of a 'just war': the difference between the types depending on whether the individual concerned decides that the cause is just or whether he or she simply relies upon the judgement of the state or church. Since these two responses are the majority Christian responses to war, the importance of just-war theory can readily be seen. Naturally, individuals may not be thoroughly consistent in their responses to war: B and C may be mixed and many might even wish to avoid any notions of 'just' causes, regarding war as a mournful and ethically confused necessity. Nonethless, in so far as war is ever thought to be justifiable, some notion of justice is required and, in turn, differing responses on the part of the individual can be distinguished.

The fact that types B and C cover the majority of Christian responses to war today, serves to illustrate one of the central differences between the early and present-day churches. It is here that a key empirical observation can be made about the relationship between Christianity and society at large. A fundamental dichotomy can be seen between the pre-Constantinian and post-Constantinian churches: if, within the latter, types B and C constitute the majority of Christian responses to war, in the former it is type D which predominates. The historian Bainton even claims that, 'the age of persecution down to the time of Constantine was the age of pacifism to the degree that during this period no Christian author to our knowledge approved of Christian participation in battle': but, 'the accession of Constantine terminated the pacifist period in church history' (*Christian Attitudes Toward War and Peace*, pp. 66 & 85). In contrast with the early church, Christian pacifism, in its thoroughgoing sense, is today confined to a minority of Christians within churches and to a minority of sects, such as the Amish Mennonites, Anabaptists, Brethren, Jehovah's Witnesses and Quakers. Individual pacifist Anglicans, such as Raven (in *Extract 13*), tend to feel themselves to be relative outsiders in their own church and even the United Reformed Church group that produced *Extract 16* was a mixture of types C and D. Even the pacifism of present-day Quakers – with their characteristic avoidance of deontological moral stances, as in *Extract 22* – is by no means limited to type D.

Naturally there were differences of approach to war within the early church and it is sometimes difficult to decide whether it is warfare itself which was despised or the 'pagan' customs surrounding it. These differences range from the absolutism of Tertullian (c. 160–220), even before his conversion to the rigours of Montanism in middle-age, to the pragmatism of Origen (c. 185–254). Despite the undoubted presence of Christians in the Roman army in the late 2nd Century, Tertullian's attitude was uncompromising:

'Inquiry is made about this point, whether a believer may turn himself unto military service, and whether the military may be admitted unto the faith, even the rank and file, or each inferior grade, to whom there is no necessity for taking part in sacrifices or capital punishments. There is no agreement between the divine and the human sacrament, the standard of Christ and the standard of the devil, the camp of light and the camp of darkness. One soul cannot be due to two masters – God and Caesar. And yet Moses carried a rod, and Aaron wore a buckle, and John (Baptist) is girt with leather, and Joshua the son of Nun leads a line of march; and the People warred: if it pleases you to sport with the subject. But how will a Christian man war, nay, how will he serve even in peace, without a sword, which the Lord has taken away? For albeit soldiers had come unto John, and had received the formula of their rule; albeit, likewise, a centurion had believed; still the Lord afterward, in disarming Peter, unbelted every soldier' (*On Idolatry* 19, from *The Ante-Nicene Fathers*, 3).

Here, unambiguously, it is the sword itself and not simply military 'paganism' which Tertullian believed to be inconsistent with Christianity. Similarly, it will be seen later (*below*, pp. 418-9) that he took an absolutist stand against abortion and any form of individual homicide.

Like Tertullian, Origen probably just assumed that killing humans was contrary to the law of Christ. For him, Jesus forbade altogether 'the putting of men to death' and 'nowhere teaches that it is right for his own disciples to offer violence to anyone, however wicked' (*Against Celsus* 3.7). However, unlike Tertullian, Origen was determined to refute Celsus' charges that Christians were undermining the state through their pacifism:

'To this our answer is, that we do, when occasion requires, give help to kings, and that so to say, a divine help, "putting on the whole armour of God". And this we do in obedience to the injuction of the apostle, "I exhort, therefore, that first of all, supplications, prayers, intercessions, and giving of thanks, be made for all men; for kings, and for all that are in authority," and the more any one excels in piety, the more effective help does he render to kings, even more than is given by soldiers, who go forth to fight and slay as many of the enemy as they can. And to those enemies of our faith who require us to bear arms for the commonwealth, and to slay men, we can reply: "Do not those who are priests at certain shrines, and those who attend on certain gods, as you account them, keep their hands free from blood, that they may with their hands unstained and free from human blood offer the appointed sacrifices to your gods; and even when war is upon you, you never enlist the priests in the army. If that, then, is a laudable custom, how much more so, that while others are engaged in battle, these should engage as the priests and ministers of God, keeping their hands pure, and wrestling in prayers to God on behalf of those who are fighting in a righteous cause, and for the king who reigns righteously, that whatever is opposed to those who act righteously may be destroyed!" And we by our prayers vanquish all demons who stir up war, and lead to the violation of oaths, and disturb the peace, we in this way are much more helpful to the kings than those who go into the fields to fight for them. And we do take our part in public affairs, when along with righteous prayers we join self-denying exercises and meditations, which teach us to despise pleasures, and not to be led away by them. And none fight better for the king than we do. We do not indeed fight under him, although he require it; but we fight on his behalf, forming a special army – an army of piety – by offering our prayer to God' (*Against Celsus* 8.73, from *The Ante-Nicene Fathers* 4).

Even allowing for some special pleading here in the face of criticism, there are clear differences from Tertullian and, indeed, similarities with later Christian responses to war. Augustine, too, was concerned to defend Christianity against critics who thought it had undermined the state. Unlike Augustine, Origen developed no just-war theory, but he did admit to a 'righteous cause' in war. And there is a prefigurement of the medieval position, illustrated in Aquinas' VIII.7f that the clergy should be exempt from military service – a position with evident pre-Christian roots.

Nonetheless, the overall response of both Tertullian and Origen to war was on the opposite side of the pacifist/militarist divide to that of Ambrose and Augustine and to most subsequent theologians. First Ambrose and then Augustine, justified the full participation of Christians in war and sought to distinguish between 'just' and 'unjust' wars. At times, both men remained critical of the state (more critical than Aquinas in the theocratic 13th Century), but saw military service as a morally legitimate form of activity for the Christian. In contrast with Tertullian, Augustine saw the condemnation of Peter's use of the sword (in Mtt. 26.52-3) as a condemnation of acting 'in a hasty zeal' and 'without the sanction of the constituted authority', rather than as a condemnation of the sword as such (*VII.2*). And, in contrast with all other known theologians in the pre-Constantinian church, he interpreted the command to turn the other cheek (in Mtt. 5.39) as referring to 'an inward disposition' rather than to 'a bodily act' (*VII.8*). For the first time, even arguments from silence appear on the issue of war – for example, that Jesus did not actually condemn the centurion for being a soldier (*VII.6* see also *X.10*). Both Tertullian and Augustine were aware that the Old Testament often sanctions war (even wars of aggression), but their attitude to this evidence again contrasts. For Tertullian, Jesus' disarming of Peter revoked this sanction, whereas, for Augustine, Jesus' actions and commands were to be interpreted in such a way that they did not contradict the Old Testament evidence.

The legacy of Augustine can be seen quite clearly in this quotation from Welty (who had already pointed out that the Old Testament does not support pacifism):

Concerning war the New Testament must be considered in its entirety. Statements conditioned by the circumstances of the time cannot be regarded as universally valid and binding. Neither Christ nor the apostles condemned war or military service. Christ was sent into the world by the Father in order to establish the messianic kingdom of peace. But men rejected him and his Gospel, and thereby forfeited the promises that were directly linked with the coming of Christ (*A Handbook of Christian Social Ethics*, Vol. 2, p. 396).

In both Augustine and Welty it is the New Testament, rather than the Old, which is to be interpreted and contextualised and, in both, an argument from silence is adopted. Since both men can be literalistic in their understanding of other aspects of New Testament teaching, their uneasiness at this point is an important indication of a change in the socio-political context of the pre-Constantinian and post-Constantinian churches. In the first, the position of the church was, arguably, more that of sect, with a relatively exclusive understanding of its membership and doctrine and little feeling of responsibilty for society as a whole or for the working of government. In the second, it is the church type that seems to predominate: the church has a more inclusive understanding of itself and its boundaries with society, at large, are less clear-cut: now, for the first time, with the adoption of Christianity as a state religion by Constantine, it must come to terms with the moral dilemmas facing the state. If this explanation is accepted, the empirical dichotomy, in relation to this issue of war, appears less surprising. Indeed, it becomes difficult to see how a church, as a church, rather than as a sect, *can* systematically oppose a state on an issue as central to the latter as war: pacifism remains an option for the sect, particularly if it is already deeply estranged from society (as today with the Jehovah's Witnesses or the Exclusive Brethren), in a way that it is not an option for the church. In Luther's *Text IX*, with his high doctrine of the state, the church type position is well in evidence: his ecclesiological position precludes his espousing, either the revolutionary response of the peasants, or the radical pacifism of the Anabaptists.

This point leads naturally to a consideration of the ethical difficulties confronting the church type response to war. Some form of the just-war theory has usually been thought to be essential to it – as Augustine's *Text VII*, Aquinas' *Text VIII*, Welty's *Extract 14* and Ramsey's *Extract 15* all indicate – but it is a theory which faces very considerable difficulties. The first of these has already been noted – the difficulty of reconciling the Old and New Testament responses to war. Some theologians, like Raven in *Extract 13*, maintain that the whole tenor of the New Testament, as distinct from the Old, is in the pacifist direction and he is quick to point out the difficulties raised by arguments from silence in this context (*13.6*). The study by Macgregor, formerly of Glasgow University, to which he refers, is one of the fullest examinations of the New Testament evidence. Secondly, it has proved difficult to set out a just-war theory which is not tautological: characteristically, that in Welty (*14.12*) contains within it the concept of justice, as does that in Augustine (*VII.4*). Thirdly, the distinction between wars of aggression and wars of defence and the notion of a legitimate authority become particularly difficult to maintain in the context of wars of liberation (see *14.20f*). Since the latter have assumed a role of such great importance in the Third World and in Liberation theology, this difficulty is particularly troublesome in present-day Christian ethics. Fourthly, in the context of actual wars, it tends to become increasingly difficult consistently to apply just-war theories. So, in the light of progressive civilian bombing in World War 2, a just-war theorist, such as Temple, encountered very considerable problems in reconciling theory with actual practice. It may be a particular feature of modern wars that, as they intensify, so they become less susceptible to moral justificaton in any recognisably Christian form. Fifthly, nuclear warfare, or even the potential use, or threatened use, of nuclear weapons may, in themselves, exceed the bounds of any Christian just-war theory – a crucial point which Ramsey's *Extract 15* raises but does not resolve. This problem is exacerbated by the connection that is becoming increasingly apparent between nuclear weapons and nuclear power, by the proliferation of nuclear knowledge beyond the Western countries, by the possibility of nuclear terrorism and by strategical discussions of limited nuclear war. The dangers inherent in all of these 'developments' are so obvious and so immense that little further justification seems necessary for focusing this Section on the substantive issues of war and peace.

Amongst historical studies of Christian responses to war, the following are particularly important:

Roland H. Bainton, *Christian Attitudes Toward War and Peace*
Peter Brock, *Pacifism in Europe to 1914* and *Twentieth Century Pacifism*
C.J. Cadoux, *The Early Christian Attitude to War*

In addition, the following historical readers are very useful:

Arthur F. Holmes, *War and Christian Ethics*
Albert Marrin, *War and the Christian Conscience*

The sociological distinction between 'church' and 'sect' has been the subject of considerable debate (for a survey of the general typological debate see, for example, Betty Scharf's *The Sociological Study of Religion*). The following books, however, all interpret varying Christian responses to war in the light of the distinction:

Robin Gill, *Theology and Social Structure* and *Prophecy and Praxis*
David Martin, *Pacifism*
J. Milton Yinger, *The Scientific Study of Religion*

TEXT VII
AUGUSTINE
The just war

I. BACKGROUND

Reply to Faustus the Manichaean XXII. 69-76 (*The Nicene and Post-Nicene Fathers*, Vol. IV, Eerdmans, 1956, trans. R. Stothert). Augustine first met Faustus of Milevis in 383, when he was still himself a sympathiser with Manichaeism. But he was unimpressed by this largely self-taught leader of the Manichees: from his own classically educated, middle-class background, he wrote later that, 'I found at once that the man was not learned in any of the liberal studies save literature, and not especially learned in that, either' (*Confessions* V.vi.11). Faustus claimed to be living the life of a 'true' Christian, but Augustine came increasingly to distrust his attacks on Catholic orthodoxy and on the Bible, in so far as it diverged from Manichaeism. Augustine finally wrote his *Reply to Faustus* c. 397-8, at about the same time as his *Confessions* and shortly after becoming a bishop at Hippo. Augustine's sympathies with Faustus' understanding of sexual morality are still evident in his other writings of this time (see *below*, pp. 421f), but his doctrinal and exegetical antipathies to Faustus' views are well in evidence in this Text. Like Ambrose, his mentor at the time of his conversion, Augustine shows himself prepared to defend Old Testament militarism and to justify the notion of a just-war from a Christian perspective, even though, at the end of the Text, he still sees the importance of the witness of the response of many earlier Christians to war – martyrdom.

2. KEY ISSUES

The central issue which concerns Augustine is the difference between personally motivated, individual killing, on the one hand, and, on the other, killing on the authority of the monarch or of God himself. Moses' killing of the Egyptian (in Ex. 2.12) was wrong, because it was without any authority – as was Paul's killing of Christians or Peter's violent action in Gethsemane (VII.2). But, the spoiling of the Egyptians (in Ex. 7-14) was, in contrast, explicitly at God's command and, as command, was to be obeyed by Moses (VII.3). If it is objected that a good God could not give such a command, it can be replied that it is indeed only God who could do so: by implication, for man it would certainly be wrong to do so (VII.4). Thus act, agent and authority are all very important here (VII.5): for individual agents to act violently on their own authority and from passion is wrong, whereas, killing in war, in obedience to God or to some lawful authority, is not (VII.6). For Augustine, monarchs have a right to preserve peace through the use of warfare and soldiers have a duty to obey their monarchs, whether or not the latter are right actually to wage war in particular circumstances (VII.7). The final paragraph faces a fresh objection from Faustus and allegorically interprets Mtt. 5.39 in terms of 'an inward disposition' (for a similar stress upon intention, see X. 2-4).

3. ETHICAL ARGUMENTS

The central thrust of Augustine's ethical argument is clearly deontological – war is morally justifiable because, in parts of the Old Testament, God can be seen to command it. Faustus was no modern critical exegete, but his moral objections to Old Testament warfare would find a number of supporters today. However, Augustine increasingly adopted a literalistic acceptance of the Bible (see *above*, p.39) and was thus forced to defend and make sense of the evidence from Genesis and Exodus. As a result, an ethical position based upon the central criterion of obedience to God's commands (however unfathomable), seems the only one consistent with both Old Testament militarism and previous Christian pacifism/martyrdom. Apart from this central criterion, there are also a number of more minor Natural law types of argument apparent – e.g. in the crop analogy (VII.2), in the reference to natural order (VII.5) and in the reference to human peace (VII.7 – see also *Text IV*). Finally, Augustine's distinction between 'cowardly dislike' and the 'real evils in war' (VII.6) is important to his argument, although he gives no indication of its ethical basis. It is possible that the latter results, as much from his Roman, as from his Christian world.

4. BASES OF CHRISTIAN ETHICS

This last point raises important possibilities about the extra-Christian sources of Augustine's just-war theory. Again, it is clear that the central thrust of the argument in this Text, stems from his attempt to reconcile the Old Testament responses to war, with those confronting Christians at the end of the 4th Century. Augustine's appeals are, either to the Bible, or against Faustus and the Manichaeans. Nonetheless, he also makes assumptions (e.g. in VII.7) about political leadership and natural justice, which go beyond these appeals. At the end of the Text he also makes the specifically Christian allusion to the suffering of martyrs.

5. SOCIAL DETERMINANTS

If a church/sect typology is adopted, it is evident that Augustine reflected the transition of Christianity to a more church-type position in society. He remained uneasy about this position (see especially *Text IV*) and was well aware of Christianity's pacifist heritage (VII.8), but he did still sanction the full participation of Christians in war. Intellectually, Augustine characteristically reflected both the Graeco-Roman and the Hebraic world (cf *above*, p.66). To the latter, he owed his notion of war as obedience to God's commands, but, to the former, he owed his concepts of 'lawful authority', 'natural order' and 'justice': indeed the whole notion of a just-war theory is essentially classical, rather than biblical (even though 'justice' is certainly used in other contexts in OT prophets such as Amos). At the more personal level, it is possible that Augustine's crucial disappointment with Faustus may have owed something to their very different social class and educational backgrounds: it would have been difficult for someone, as socially and intellectually sophisticated as Augustine, to take seriously one such as Faustus.

6. SOCIAL SIGNIFICANCE

The importance of Augustine's position on war cannot be exaggerated. Again, in terms of church/sect typology, had he simply affirmed the pacifist tradition and convinced other Christians to do the same, a serious rift might have been made between 'church' (or,more accurately, 'sect') and society at large. It will be seen in *Text VIII* that, from his arguments, a just-war theory could be developed by later theologians and thus a way could be found to accommodate the awkwardness of the New Testament with the demands of the state. Here again Augustine's particular blend of Graeco-Roman and Hebraic notions has had a major effect upon both Western Christianity and society generally.

FURTHER READING

The primary sources for Augustine's understanding of war and peace are his *Reply to Faustus* and his later *The City of God* (see *Text IV*). For a survey of the relation of classical theories of just-war to Christian and non-Christian responses to war, John Ferguson's *War and Peace in the World's Religions* is useful. Fuller treatments can be found both in books already mentioned in the sectional introduction and in the following (though obviously they apply more to *Text VIII*):-Frederick H. Russell, *The Just War in the Middle Ages*; Joan D. Tooke, *The Just War in Aquinas and Grotius*.

TEXT VII

AUGUSTINE

The just war

VII.1   Moses . . . we love and admire, and to the best of our power imitate, coming indeed far short of his merits, though we have killed no Egyptian, nor plundered any one, nor carried on any war; which actions of Moses were in one case prompted by the zeal of the future champion of his people, and in the other cases commanded by God.

VII.2   It might be shown that, though Moses slew the

Egyptian, without being commanded by God, the action was divinely permitted, as, from the prophetic character of Moses, it prefigured something in the future. Now, however, I do not use this argument, but view the action as having no symbolical meaning. In the light, then, of the eternal law, it was wrong for one who had no legal authority to kill the man, even though he was a bad character, besides being the aggressor. But in minds where great virtue is to come, there is often an early crop of vices, in which we may still discern a disposition for some particular virtue, which will come when the mind is duly cultivated. For as farmers, when they see land bringing forth huge crops, though of weeds, pronounce it good for corn; or when they see wild creepers, which have to be rooted out, still consider the land good for useful vines; and when they see a hill covered with wild olives, conclude that with culture it will produce good fruit: so the disposition of mind which led Moses to take the law into his own hands, to prevent the wrong done to his brother, living among strangers, by a wicked citizen of the country from being unrequited, was not unfit for the production of virtue, but from want of culture gave signs of its productiveness in an unjustifiable manner. He who afterwards, by His angel, called Moses on Mount Sinai, with the divine commission to liberate the people of Israel from Egypt, and who trained him to obedience by the miraculous appearance in the bush burning but not consumed, and by instructing him in his ministry, was the same who, by the call addressed from heaven to Saul when persecuting the Church, humbled him, raised him up, and animated him; or in figurative words, by this stroke He cut off the branch, grafted it, and made it fruitful. For the fierce energy of Paul, when in his zeal for hereditary traditions he persecuted the Church, thinking that he was doing God service, was like a crop of weeds showing great signs of productiveness. It was the same in Peter, when he took his sword out of its sheath to defend the Lord, and cut off the right ear of an assailant, when the Lord rebuked him with something like a threat, saying, "Put up thy sword into its sheath; for he that taketh the sword shall perish by the sword." (Mtt. 26. 52-3). To take the sword is to use weapons against a man's life, without the sanction of the constituted authority. The Lord, indeed, had told His disciples to carry a sword; but He did not tell them to use it. But that after this sin Peter should become a pastor of the Church was no more improper than that Moses, after smiting the Egyptian, should become the leader of the congregation. In both cases the trespass originated not in inveterate cruelty, but in a hasty zeal which admitted of correction. In both cases there was resentment against injury, accompanied in one case by love for a brother, and in the other by love, though still carnal, of the Lord. Here was evil to be subdued or rooted out; but the heart with such capacities needed only, like good soil, to be cultivated to make it fruitful in virtue.

VII.3 Then, as for Faustus' objection to the spoiling of the Egyptians, he knows not what he says. In this Moses not only did not sin, but it would have been sin not to do it. It was by the command of God, who, from His knowledge both of the actions and of the hearts of men, can decide on what every one should be made to suffer, and through whose agency. The people at that time were still carnal, and engrossed with earthly affections; while the Egyptians were in open rebellion against God, for they used the gold, God's creature, in the service of idols, to the dishonor of the Creator, and they had grievously oppressed strangers by making them work without pay. Thus the Egyptians deserved the punishment, and the Israelites were suitably employed in inflicting it. Perhaps, indeed, it was not so much a command as a permission to the Hebrews to act in the matter according to their own inclinations; and God, in sending the message by Moses, only wished that they should thus be informed of His permission. There may also have been mysterious reasons for what God said to the people on this matter. At any rate, God's commands are to be submissively received, not to be argued against. The apostle says,

"Who hath known the mind of the Lord? or who hath been His counsellor?" (Rmns 11.34). Whether, then, the reason was what I have said, or whether in the secret appointment of God, there was some unknown reason for His telling the people by Moses to borrow things from the Egyptians, and to take them away with them, this remains certain, that this was said for some good reason, and that Moses could not lawfully have done otherwise than God told him, leaving to God the reason of the command, while the servant's duty is to obey.

VII.4   But, says Faustus, it cannot be admitted that the true God, who is also good, ever gave such a command. I answer, such a command can be rightly given by no other than the true and good God, who alone knows the suitable command in every case, and who alone is incapable of inflicting unmerited suffering on any one. . .

VII.5   According to the eternal law, which requires the preservation of natural order, and forbids the transgression of it, some actions have an indifferent character, so that men are blamed for presumption if they do them without being called upon, while they are deservedly praised for doing them when required. The act, the agent, and the authority for the action are all of great importance in the order of nature. For Abraham to sacrifice his son of his own accord is shocking madness. His doing so at the command of God proves him faithful and submissive. This is so loudly proclaimed by the very voice of truth, that Faustus, *eagerly* rummaging for some fault, and reduced at last to slanderous charges, has not the boldness to attack this action. It is scarcely possible that he can have forgotten a deed so famous, that it recurs to the mind of itself without any study or reflection, and is in fact repeated by so many tongues, and portrayed in so many places, that no one can pretend to shut his eyes or his ears to it. If, therefore, while Abraham's killing his son of his own accord would have been unnatural, his doing it at the command of God shows not only guiltless but praiseworthy compliance, why does Faustus blame Moses for spoiling the Egyptians? Your feeling of disapproval for the mere human action should be restrained by a regard for the divine sanction. Will you venture to blame God Himself for desiring such actions? Then "Get thee behind me, Satan, for thou understandest not the things which be of God, but those which be of men." Would that this rebuke might accomplish in you what it did in Peter, and that you might hereafter preach the truth concerning God, which you now, judging by feeble sense, find fault with! as Peter became a zealous messenger to announce to the Gentiles what he objected to at first, when the Lord spoke of it as His intention.

VII.6   Now, if this explanation suffices to satisfy human obstinacy and perverse misinterpretation of right actions of the vast difference between the indulgence of passion and presumption on the part of men, and obedience to the command of God, who knows what to permit or to order, and also the time and the persons, and the due action or suffering in each case, the account of the wars of Moses will not excite surprise or abhorrence, for in wars carried on by divine command, he showed not ferocity but obedience; and God, in giving the command, acted not in cruelty, but in righteous retribution, giving to all what they deserved, and warning those who needed warning. What is the evil in war? Is it the death of some who will soon die in any case, that others may live in peaceful subjection? This is mere cowardly dislike, not any religious feeling. The real evils in war are love of violence, revengeful cruelty, fierce and implacable enmity, wild resistance, and the lust of power, and such like; and it is generally to punish these things, when force is required to inflict the punishment, that, in obedience to God or some lawful authority, good men undertake wars, when they find themselves in such a position as regards the conduct of human affairs, that right conduct requires them to act, or to make others act in this way. Otherwise John, when the soldiers who came to be baptized asked, What shall we do? would have replied, Throw away your arms; give up the service; never strike, or wound, or disable any one. But knowing that such actions in battle were not murderous, but authorized by law, and that the soldiers did not thus avenge themselves, but defend the public safety, he replied, "Do violence to no man, accuse no man falsely, and be content with your wages." (Lk. 3.14). But as the Manichaeans are in the habit of speaking evil of John, let them hear the Lord Jesus Christ Himself ordering this money to be given to Caesar, which John tells the soldiers to be content with. "Give," He says, "to Caesar the things that are Caesar's," (Mtt. 22.21). For tribute-money is given on purpose to pay the soldiers for war. Again, in the case of the centurion who said, "I am a man under authority, and have soliders under me: and I say to one, Go, and he goeth; and to another, Come, and he cometh; and to my servant, Do this, and he doeth it," Christ gave due praise to his faith (Mtt. 8.9-10). He did not tell him to leave the service. But there is no need here to enter on the long discussion of just and unjust wars.

VII.7　A great deal depends on the causes for which men undertake wars, and on the authority they have for doing so; for the natural order which seeks the peace of mankind, ordains that the monarch should have the power of undertaking war if he thinks it advisable, and that the soldiers should perform their military duties on behalf of the peace and safety of the community. When war is undertaken in obedience to God, who would rebuke, or humble, or crush the pride of man, it must be allowed to be a righteous war; for even the wars which arise from human passion cannot harm the eternal well-being of God, nor even hurt His saints; for in the trial of their patience, and the chastening of their spirit, and in bearing fatherly correction, they are rather benefited than injured. No one can have any power against them but what is given him from above. For there is no power but of God (Rmns 13.1), who either orders or permits. Since, therefore, a righteous man, serving it may be under an ungodly king, may do the duty belonging to his position in the State in fighting by the order of his sovereign, – for in some cases it is plainly the will of God that he should fight, and in others, where this is not so plain, it might be an unrighteous command on the part of the king, while the soldier is innocent, because his position makes obedience a duty, – how much more must the man be blameless who carries on war on the authority of God, of whom every one who serves Him knows that he can never require what is wrong?

VII.8   If it is supposed that God could not enjoin warfare, because in after times it was said by the Lord Jesus Christ, "I say unto you, That ye resist not evil: but if any one strike thee on the right cheek, turn to him the left also," [Mtt.5.39] the answer is, that what is here required is not a bodily action, but an inward disposition. The sacred seat of virtue is the heart, and such were the hearts of our fathers, the righteous men of old. But order required such a regulation of events, and such a distinction of times, as to show first of all that even earthly blessings (for so temporal kingdoms and victory over enemies are considered to be, and these are the things which the community of the ungodly all over the world are continually begging from idols and devils) are entirely under the control and at the disposal of the one true God. Thus, under the Old Testament, the secret of the kingdom of heaven, which was to be disclosed in due time, was veiled, and so far obscured, in the disguise of earthly promises. But when the fullness of time came for the revelation of the New Testament, which was hidden under the types of the Old, clear testimony was to be borne to the truth, that there is another life for which this life ought to be disregarded, and another kingdom for which the opposition of all earthly kingdoms should be patiently borne. Thus the name martyrs, which means witnesses, was given to those who, by the will of God, bore this testimony, by their confessions, their sufferings and their death.

CRITIQUE

It would be unreasonable to criticise this Text as if it contained a fully developed just-war theory. Nevertheless, a number of tensions are evident within it, resulting from Augustine's attempt to reconcile the Old Testament with the New and with classical understandings of a 'just'war.

An immediate difficulty arises from the observation that, however sanctioned by Yahweh, a number of wars in the Old Testament, such as that against Canaan, appear, in classical terms, to be wars of aggression and not of defence. As a result, Augustine was prepared to concede an image of God which makes him, from the human perspective, morally vulnerable (VII.4). He would, of course, have pointed out, in this context, that it would indeed have been wrong for man, rather than for God himself, to have acted in such a way. This is an important point that is sometimes forgotten in discussions of the problem of evil or of the morality of particular images of God (see Don Cupitt's *Crisis of Moral Authority: the Dethronement of Christianity*). It is always dangerous to judge the Creator by the moral standards of the creature. Yet, Augustine's concession will still be difficult for many present-day Christians to accept.

A second difficulty arises from his judgement, that war may be fought on human as well as on divine authority (VII.7). Along with his classical sources, he admitted the possibility of 'some lawful authority' (VII.6) waging war, but gave few indications about what constituted a 'lawful authority'. This point will recur in relation to *Text VIII* and *Extract 14*, but it is important to note that Augustine did not resolve the issue. Further, his notion of civil obedience is dangerously unqualified in VII.7. Nürnberg, in the 20th Century, did not accept the notion of military obedience regardless of the perceived injustice of a situation.

Finally, Augustine's understanding of the authority of the Old Testament may appear pre-critical. Increasingly, he saw the only options as, either to accept the entire Bible literally, or to treat it in the highly selective way of Faustus. By opting for the first, he was inevitably forced to defend the moral behaviour of the Patriarchs, both in relation to polygamy (see *above*, pp.39-40) and here in relation to wars of aggression. However, a more critical understanding of the Old Testament would have avoided some of these problems.

TEXT VIII
AQUINAS
War, Christians and the clergy

I. BACKGROUND

This Text comes from *Summa Theologica*, 2a2ae, 40.1-2 (Vol. XXXV of the English Dominican translation, Blackfriars with Eyre & Spottiswoode, London and McGraw-Hill, New York, 1972). Taken from *Secunda Secundae* (see *above*, p.76), Question 40 considers the issue of war under four headings – 'Are some wars permissible?', 'May clerics engage in warfare?', 'May belligerents use subterfuge?' and 'May war be waged on feast days?' – of which the first two are reproduced here. Although there was no major war in northern Europe during Aquinas' life-time, there was a number of local wars and dynastic struggles, as well as a declining number of crusades. The struggle which led to the downfall of the Hohenstaufens and the establishment of Charles of Anjou in Naples, in 1268, directly affected Aquinas' own family: two of his brothers fought for the Emperor, but most of his family fought on the papal side. Yet, despite this existential involvement, the issue of war only played a very minor role in *Summa Theologica* and is handled very formally in this, the most extensive, discussion of it. The clerical interests of Aquinas and of his intended audience are clearly reflected in the four headings. Like many of his contemporaries, Aquinas seems to have accepted the inevitability of war and, perhaps as a result, discussed remarkably few of the ethical dilemmas that it raises. Other scholars, like Albert the Great, Bonaventure and Duns Scotus, did not discuss them at all.

2. KEY ISSUES

This Text focuses upon two questions:
 (a) Is it always a sin to wage war? Aquinas counters the

obvious New Testament quotations that are frequently used to support Christian pacifism (Mtt.26.52, 5.39 and Rmns 12.19) with a summary of Augustine's three criteria of a 'just' war: it must be undertaken on the authority of God or of the sovereign (VIII.3 & VIII.6.1); it must be for a just cause (VIII.4 & VIII.6.2); and it must be undertaken with a right intention, to promote the good and to avoid evil (VIII.5 & VIII.6.3-4).

(b) May clerics and bishops engage in warfare? He faces the objection that if warfare is just, *par excellence* it must be just for the clergy to participate fully in it. In reply, Aquinas considers that verses like Mtt.26.52, 2Tim.2.4, 1Cor.11.26 and 2Cor.10.4, either directly, or indirectly, preclude clergy from such action. For him, the contemplative and sacramental roles of the clergy are inconsistent with warlike pursuits (VIII.10-11): it is 'unbecoming their persons' (VIII.12.3): they must be concerned with 'works of higher merit' (VIII.12.4).

3. ETHICAL ARGUMENTS

This text provides an interesting example of Aquinas' attempt to combine an Aristotelian, consequentialist approach to ethics with a normative understanding of Augustinian and Biblical tradition. The notion of 'right intention' is explained in terms of his overall general principle of promoting the good and avoiding evil (VIII.5): positively, this entails serving 'the common good' (VIII.6.2) and, negatively, it risks eternal punishment (VIII.6.1). His consequentialism, based upon Natural law, is even more evident in his claims about naturally established role differentiation, as it affects the clergy (VIII.9). Once again, the *telos* of man provides the spur for his understanding of ethics (see *above*, p.78), even if this is combined with strong deontological assumptions about the legitimacy of war and of the tradition which justifies war.

4. BASES OF CHRISTIAN ETHICS

Aquinas' use of the Bible is also particularly interesting. He avoids Augustine's tendency to support a just-war position from the Old Testament and only uses Josh.6.4 late in his argument, against clerical participation in warfare (VIII.12.2). He does not resolve the awkward Mtt.5.39 and resolves Mtt.26.52 only by referring it to unauthorised, private violence (VIII.6). And he understands the quotations in VIII.8 – VIII.12.1 to be concerned only with the clergy. In general, his source of tradition is Augustine – albeit in a rather systematised and abbreviated form and often mediated through Gratian's *Decretum* (see *above*, p.76). Augustine appears as *the* authority to settle, beyond reasonable dispute, the ethical dilemma for Christians.

5. SOCIAL DETERMINANTS

Augustine, however, is used in a significantly (even if unintentionally) modified form. The socio-political context of Aquinas was quite different from that of Augustine and the former shows none of the latter's suspicions of the political order. As a result, the bones of Augustine's notion of a just war are adopted, but not the flesh of his overall distrust of the 'earthly city'. Further, the notions of guilt and just retribution that formed an important element in Augustine's understanding of war are reduced by Aquinas to a single sentence (VIII.4). The stylised format of the scholastic method is only partially responsible for these modifications. In part, they reflect a radically changed social context, in part, a very different religious psychology (see *above*, pp.35-6), and, in part, a culture which did not regard war as presenting particularly serious ethical problems. This final factor is clearly present in Aquinas' handling of the question of clerical participation in warfare: it was simply obvious, to him and to his contemporaries, that the clergy should not participate fully in warfare, that they were to be considered as ontologically different from the laity and that Petrine verses referred specifically to them (VIII.8). The early Christian, and, indeed, pre-Christian sources of these assumptions have already been noted in the sectional introduction.

6. SOCIAL SIGNIFICANCE

Aquinas' understanding of just-war theory has been the major influence in much subsequent Roman Catholic thinking on the issue of war – as can be seen in Welty's *Extract 14*. In effect, Aquinas re-inforced the church type response to war, established by Augustine and mediated through Gratian. Perhaps, because of this, any challenge to conventional militarist assumptions has, until very recently, come mainly from within non-Roman Catholic churches. In a nuclear age, however, it is now evident to a number of Roman Catholic moral theologians, that Aquinas' just-war theory cannot provide a sufficient basis for ethical decision-making on modern warfare.

FURTHER READING

There are scattered references to war and killing elsewhere in *Summa Theologica* and there are also implications that can be drawn from works like *De Regimine Principum* (see *Text V*) but *S.T.* 2a2ae.40 remains the most important source for his ideas. Frederick H. Russell's *The Just War in the Middle Ages* and Joan D. Tooke's *The Just War in Aquinas and Grotius* both provide excellent and detailed commentaries on Aquinas' notions. Thomas R. Heath's Appendix 2 to the English Dominican translation of *S.T.*, Vol. XXXV, also supplies important historical information. Recent Roman Catholic discussions of the extreme difficulty of reconciling Aquinas' just-war theory with the realities of nuclear warfare can be seen in the US Bishops' Pastoral Letter on War and Peace in the Nuclear Age, *The Challenge of Peace: God's Promise and Our Response* (1983) and Roger Ruston, *Nuclear Deterrrence – Right or Wrong?* (1981).

TEXT VIII

AQUINAS

War, Christians and the clergy

Is it always a sin to wage war?

VIII.1   OBJECTIONS: 1. It would seem that it is always a sin to wage war. Punishments are meted out only for sin.

But our Lord named the punishment for people who wage war when he said, *'All who draw the sword will die by the sword'* [Mtt.26.52]. Every kind of war then is unlawful.

2. Moreover, whatever goes against a divine command is a sin. But war does that. Scripture says, 'I say this to you, offer the wicked man no resistance' [Mtt.5.39]. Also, 'Not revenging yourselves, my dearly beloved, but give place unto wrath' [Rmns.12.19]. War is not always a sin then.

3. Besides the only thing that stands as a contrary to the act of virtue is a sin. Now war is the contrary of peace. Therefore it is always a sin.

4. Besides, if an action is lawful, practising for it would be lawful, as is obvious in the practice involved in the sciences. But warlike exercises which go on in tournaments are forbidden by the Church, since those killed in such trials are denied ecclesiastical burial. Consequently war appears to be plainly wrong.

VIII.2   ON THE OTHER HAND Augustine says, in a sermon on the centurion's son, 'If Christian teaching forbade war altogether, those looking for the salutary advice of the Gospel would have been told to get rid of their arms and give up soldiering. But instead they were told, "Do violence to no man, be content with your pay" [Lk.3.14]. If it ordered them to be satisfied with their pay, then it did not forbid a military career.'

VIII.3   REPLY: Three things are required for any war to be just. The first is the authority of the sovereign on whose command war is waged. Now a private person has no business declaring war; he can seek redress by appealing to the judgement of his superiors. Nor can he summon together whole people, which has to be done to fight a war. Since the care of the commonweal is committed to those in authority they are the ones to watch over the public affairs of the city, kingdom or province in their jurisdiction. And just as they use the sword in lawful defence against domestic disturbance when they punish criminals, as Paul says, 'He beareth not the sword in vain

for he is God's minister, an avenger to execute wrath
upon him that doth evil' [Rmns.13.4], so they lawfully
use the sword of war to protect the commonweal from
foreign attacks. Thus it is said to those in authority,
'Rescue the weak and the needy, save them from the
clutches of the wicked' [Psm.81.4]. Hence Augustine
writes, 'The natural order conducive to human peace
demands that the power to counsel and declare war
belongs to those who hold the supreme authority' [i.e.
Text VII.7 above].

VIII.4   Secondly, a just cause is required, namely that those
who are attacked are attacked because they deserve it on
account of some wrong they have done. So Augustine,
'We usually describe a just war as one that avenges
wrongs, that is, when a nation or state has to be punished
either for refusing to make amends for outrages done by
its subjects, or to restore what it has seized injuriously.'

VIII.5   Thirdly, the right intention of those waging war is
required, that is, they must intend to promote the good
and to avoid evil. Hence Augustine writes, 'Among true
worshippers of God those wars are looked on as
peace-making which are waged neither from aggrandise-
ment nor cruelty, but with the object of securing peace,
of repressing the evil and supporting the good.' Now it
can happen that even given a legitimate authority and a
just cause for declaring war, it may yet be wrong because
of a perverse intention. So again Augustine says, 'The
craving to hurt people, the cruel thirst for revenge, the
unappeased and unrelenting spirit, the savageness of
fighting on, the lust to dominate, and suchlike – all these
are rightly condemned in wars' [i.e. *Text VII.6 above*].

VIII.6   Hence: 1. Augustine writes, '"To draw the sword" is to
arm oneself and to spill blood without command or
permission of superior or lawful authority' [i.e. *Text
VII.2 above*]. But if a private person uses the sword by the
authority of the sovereign or judge, or a public person
uses it through zeal for justice, and by the authority, so to
speak, of God, then he himself does not 'draw the
sword', but is commissioned by another to use it, and

does not deserve punishment. Still even those who do use it sinfully are not always slain with the sword. Yet they will always 'die by the sword' since they will be punished eternally for their sinful use of it unless they repent.

2. These words, as Augustine says, must always be borne in readiness of mind, so that a man must always be prepared to refrain from resistance or self-defence if the situation calls for it. Sometimes, however, he must act otherwise for the common good or even for the good of his opponents. Thus Augustine writes, 'One must do many things with a kind of benign severity with those who must be punished against their will. Now whoever is stripped of the lawlessness of sin is overcome for his own good, since nothing is unhappier than the happiness of sinners. It encourages guilty impunity, and strengthens the bad will, the enemy inside us.'

3. Even those who wage a just war intend peace. They are not then hostile to peace, except that evil peace which our Lord 'did not come to send on the earth' [Mtt.31.34]. So Augustine again says, 'We do not seek peace in order to wage war, but we go to war to gain peace. Therefore be peaceful even while you are at war, that you may overcome your enemy and bring him to the prosperity of peace.'

4. Warlike exercises are not completely forbidden; only those which are excessive and dangerous and end in killing and looting. In olden times they presented no such danger. So, as Jerome writes, they were called 'practices of arms' or 'wars without blood.'

May clerics and bishops engage in war?

VIII.7   OBJECTIONS: 1. It would seem that clerics and bishops may engage in warfare. Now we have just agreed that wars are licit and just in so far as they protect the poor and the whole commonweal from an enemy's treachery. But this kind of activity above all is the duty of prelates. As Gregory writes, 'The wolf comes down on the sheep. That happens when any scoundrel or

maurauder tyrannizes faithful and humble people. And
the man who looked like a shepherd, but really was not,
abandoned the sheep and fled. He was frightened at the
danger to his own skin, and did not dare to stand up
against the injustice.' It is licit, therefore, for prelates and
clerics to fight.

2. Moreover Pope Leo writes, 'Since ominous news
had often come from the Saracen side, rumours were
circulating that they would come to the port of Rome
covertly and secretly. For this reason we ordered our
people to gather together and go down to the shore.'
Bishops, therefore, may go to war licitly.

3. Again, it would seem to come to the same thing
whether a man does something on his own or consents to
its being done by another. Scripture says, 'They who do
such things are worthy of death, and not only they that
do them, but they also that consent to them that do them'
[Rmns.1.32]. Now the fullest consent lies in persuading
others to do something; and bishops and clerics may
persuade others to fight. We read that 'Charlemagne
accepted war with the Lombards at the request and
entreaty of Adrian, Bishop of Rome.' Therefore they are
also allowed to fight.

4. Besides, whatever is virtuous and meritorious in
itself is not unlawful for prelates and clerics. Now war is
sometimes virtuous and meritorious. We read [in Gratian's *Decretum*] that 'if a man die for the true faith, to save
his country and to defend Christians, he will receive a
heavenly reward from God.'

VIII.8   ON THE OTHER HAND the words, 'Put your
sword back in its scabbard' [Mtt.26.52] were directed to
Peter as representing all bishops and clerics. Consequently, they may not fight.

VIII.9   REPLY: Many things are necessary for the good of
human society. Now the different functions are better
and more efficiently carried out by different peoples than
by one, as Aristotle shows. And certain occupations are
so inconsistent with one another that they cannot be
fittingly exercised together. Thus lesser jobs are forbid-

den those who are given major things to do. Human
laws, for example, forbid soldiers whose business it is to
fight to engage in commerce. Now fighting in war is
quite inconsistent with the duties of a bishop or a cleric,
and for two reasons.

VIII.10 First is general, namely that the operations of war are
totally upsetting; they seriously prevent the mind from
contemplating divine things, praising God, and praying
for people, which is what clerics are called to do. So just
as commercial enterprises are forbidden to clerics, since
they entangle the soul too much, so also are warlike
pursuits. 'No man being a soldier to God entangles
himself with secular business' [2 Tim.2.4].

VIII.11 The second reason is special. All holy Orders are
ordained for the ministry of the altar in which the passion
of Christ is represented sacramentally. 'Until the Lord
comes, therefore, every time you eat this bread and drink
this cup, you are proclaiming his death' [1 Cor.11.26].
Their office, then, is not to kill or to shed blood, but
rather to be ready to shed their own blood for Christ, to
do in deed what they portray at the altar. For this reason
legislation has been enacted making those who shed
blood, even if they have done so without sin, irregular.
Now no one given a duty to perform can lawfully do
anything which renders him unfit for the office. It is
altogether wrong, then, for clerics to fight in a war, since
that is aimed at shedding blood.

VIII.12 Hence: 1. Prelates ought to resist not only the wolves
who bring spiritual death on the flock but also pillagers
and oppressors who do physical harm to it. Their arms,
however, ought to be spiritual, not material, as Scripture
says, 'Our war is not fought with weapons of flesh, but
with spiritual weapons' [2 Cor.10.4]. Such are salutary
warnings and solemn pleas and, against the obstinate,
sentences of excommunication.

2. Prelates and clerics may make their presence felt at
war, not by taking up arms, but by spiritually helping
those who fight on the side of justice, exhorting,
absolving them, and giving other like spiritual assistance.

Thus in the Old Testament [i.e. Josh.6.4] the priests were commanded to sound the sacred trumpet in battle. This is why bishops or clerics were first allowed to go to the front. But for any of them to take up arms is an abuse of this permission.

3. We have said that every power, art or virtue directed towards an end has to prepare those elements useful for the achievement of that end. Now physical wars should be considered by Christian people as directed towards a divine spiritual good as their end, and to this end clerics are called. Accordingly they ought to prepare and urge others to fight in a just war. Clerics are forbidden to fight in war, not because it is a sin, but because it is unbecoming their persons.

4. Although to wage a just war is meritorious, nevertheless it is wrong for clerics because they are deputed to works of higher merit. The marriage act, for example, can be meritorious, but for those with a vow of virginity it becomes reprehensible since they are committed to a higher good.

CRITIQUE

Serious criticisms have been made of the two sets of answers that Aquinas gives to the questions raised in this Text:

(a) Is it always a sin to wage war? A number of modern just-war theorists have argued that: (i) Aquinas' three criteria for a 'just' war are inadequately expounded and (ii) he ignores other vital criteria. Aquinas' first criterion depends upon the 'authority of the sovereign' (VIII.3), but the problems that this form of authority raises are not discussed: 'it means, of course, in a general way, that war must be waged by the person or persons who hold appropriate political authority, but who, in the thirteenth century, such persons might be, was a rather delicate question needing serious discussion. To assume that the "prince" is meant, in a society so abounding with princes and petty rulers that they might from an international point of view be considered rather as private than as public entities, while in fact an emperor did exist, was paying tribute to, or at least acknowledging the existing state of affairs as ideal or acceptable rather than trying to outline a better one' (Joan D. Tooke, *The Just War in Aquinas and Grotius*, p.26). Similarly, the criteria of a 'just cause' and a 'right intention' are only very formally and abstractly set out. They have the additional problem of being tautological, since they already contain the ethical terms 'just' and 'right' in what purport to be requirements for determining whether or not a war is 'just'.

Tautology is also a problem in the following list of criteria for establishing the justice of a war. However, it does have the merit of supplying the additional criteria that are usually considered necessary by modern just-war theorists: 'For a war to be "just" it must (i) have been undertaken by a lawful authority; (ii) have been undertaken for the vindication of an undoubted right that has been certainly infringed; (iii) be a last resort, all peaceful means of settlement having failed; (iv) offer the possibility of good to be achieved outweighing the evils that war would involve; (v) be waged with a reasonable hope of victory for justice; (vi) be waged with right intention; (vii) use methods that are legitimate, i.e. in accordance with man's nature as a rational being, with Christian moral principles and international agreements' (from ed. T.R. Milford, *The Valley of Decision*, British Council of churches, 1961).

In Aquinas iii, iv, v and vii are notably absent. In the context of nuclear weapons, iv and vii have obviously become considerably more important than they could have been in the 13th Century (see *Extract 15*). But, in terms of iii, Aquinas shows no awareness of the importance of exhausting peaceful arbitration before going to war (see *Extract 16*), or even of the importance of determining whether victory is actually possible. Explicit reference to the differences between wars of aggession/ offence and wars of defence is absent from both Aquinas and the above list (see *Extract 14*). Whilst the latter does not answer all the difficulties facing just-war theorists mentioned in the sectional introduction, it is clearly more adequate than Aquinas' account.

(b) May clerics and bishops engage in warfare? Aquinas' defence of his position raises many exegetical, ethical and theological problems. Few, today, working in the context of critical biblical scholarship, would support his clerical interpretation of the New Testament quotations – even the Petrine quotations. It is notable that Mtt.26.52, for Tertullian, meant that Christians should be pacifists (see *above*, p.298); for Augustine, that unauthorised private violence was a sin (VII.2); and, for Aquinas, that the clergy should not participate fully in warfare (VIII.8). Ethically, Tooke argues that, 'Aquinas overwhelmed Christ's simple words with natural law morality' (*op.cit.*, p.123) and, indeed, as a result of the arguments he used, 'he came extraordinarily near to forbidding Christian participation in warfare completely when he forbade it outright to clerics' (p.171). Certainly if Luther's theological attack on the mediaeval priest/laity dichotomy is taken seriously, Christian pacifism, in some form, or, alternatively, the full participation of clergy in warfare, would seem more logical from Aquinas' position. Ironically, Luther accepted neither alternative: he condemned the Pope and his clergy for engaging in warfare and for forgetting their 'spiritual office' (e.g. in *On War Against the Turk*) and supported the right of the state to wage war and to compel its citizens to fight.

TEXT IX
LUTHER
Whether soldiers, too, can be saved

I. BACKGROUND

This Text comes from the treatise *Whether Soldiers, too, Can be Saved* of 1526 (from *Luther's Works*, Vol. 46, Fortress Press, Philadelphia, 1967, trans, Charles M. Jacobs and rev. Robert C. Schulz, pp. 96-9, 104-6, 107-11, 115-6 & 130-2). After years of rebellion against feudal Europe, the Peasants War broke out in 1525. A number of reformers, like Thomas Münzer, sided with the peasants and some of the latter appealed to Luther. He responded, at first, with the conciliatory *Admonition to Peace* – urging the princes to take the rebellion seriously and to acknowledge their part in causing it, and urging the peasants to avoid violence and to submit to authority – but then, in May of 1525, he wrote his notoriously violent *Against the Robbing and Murdering Hordes of Peasants*. Shocked by the violence of the peasants and by their insurrection, he urged the rulers to kill the rebellious peasants, 'for rebellion is not just simple murder; it is like a great fire, which attacks and devastates a whole land. . . Therefore let everyone who can, smite, slay, and stab, secretly or openly, remembering that nothing can be more poisonous, hurtful, or devilish than a rebel. It is just as when one must kill a mad dog . . . ' (*Luther's Works*, Vol. 46, p.50). The scandal that this created forced him, in July, to write *An Open Letter on the Harsh Book*, attempting to reconcile the views expressed in the two previous works. He was still convinced that the peasants needed suppressing through force, but maintained that this did not excuse the appalling cruelty of the rulers in putting the rebellion down. By 1526, he had considerably modified his tone, but not his attitude towards rebellion, submission to authority or the legitimacy of rulers using force. He wrote this Text in response to a request from Assa von Kram of Wittenberg, who was disturbed about reconciling his Christian faith with his profession as a soldier. The rebellion of the peasants and the radical innovations of the Reformation had opened up afresh the issue of legitimacy of war. Münzer, and Zwingli in Zurich, themselves adopted the sword: the Anabaptists renounced violence altogether as thoroughgoing pacifists. Luther, somewhere between the two, defended the right of rulers to use the sword and to command their subjects to do so and urged the latter to obey.

2. KEY ISSUES

This Text is concerned with two main moral issues – war and rebellion;

(a) War. Luther argues that war and soldiering are basically concerned with punishing wickedness and keeping peace (IX.1 & IX.8). Terrible though they may be, they serve to prevent more terrible things happening (IX.2). Indeed, it is God himself who institutes war (IX.3), as the Old Testament indicates (IX.6). The seeming contradiction suggested by Mtt. 5.39 is to be explained by the fact that, in the Spirit, Christians are subject only to Christ, but, in the body and in so far as their property is concerned, they are subject to worldly rulers and to their commands to fight in war (IX.9: i.e. Luther's classic notion of 'the two kingdoms', see *above*, pp. 207-8).

(b) Rebellion. Luther thoroughly condemns any attempt to depose rulers except in cases of real insanity (IX.12). The fact that a ruler is a tyrant is no reason for deposing him: he cannot hurt a man's soul (IX.16), his position is highly insecure in society (IX.20-1) and, in any case, it is for God to punish him (IX.19). Luther adds that he does not intend to flatter rulers, since he regards them as much 'subjects' as anyone else (IX.22-3). If, however, one is *certain* that a ruler is wrong, then one must follow God (IX.25).

Finally, Luther considers the question of a soldier's pay and concludes that, provided he is not greedy, he may work for pay and even sell his skills as a soldier to more than one ruler (IX.26).

3. ETHICAL ARGUMENTS

Luther was more acutely aware of the moral dilemmas created

by war than Aquinas, but he still seemed to regard war as an inevitable concomitant of government. Thus, because the individual is always required to obey his ruler, he is, at the same time, necessarily committed to war. Nonetheless, Luther did allow a conscience clause (IX.25). Further, he made a number of implicit (IX.12) and explicit (IX.21) appeals to Natural law. IX.8 also illustrates a tendency to consequentialism and to argue about the ethics of war from the ethics of individual behaviour: war is justified from the precedent of the punishment of wrongdoers and the paradigm of individual punishment, in turn, becomes the paradigm of social punishment.

4. BASES OF CHRISTIAN ETHICS

As with Augustine's *Text VII*, the Bible plays a crucial role in Luther's argument. He justifies war from Old Testament militarism (IX.6), from New Testament figures like John the Baptist and from commands to obey worldly rulers (IX.7). However, his exegesis of John 18.36 seems inverted (IX.6) and his interpretation of Mtt. 5.39 stands or falls with his notion of 'the two kingdoms' (IX.9 – see further, pp. 222-3 *above*). His argument, as a whole, is dominated by his theological conviction that obedience to rulers is demanded by God.

5. SOCIAL DETERMINANTS

Luther's general attitude towards war differed very little from the medieval Catholic position. War was regarded by him as an inevitable punishment at the disposal of rulers for wrongdoing – as, indeed, it was by Aquinas. But his own experiences, as a result of the Peasants War, have also clearly influenced the Text: they had served to convince him that rebellion brings more evils and suffering than even tyranny (IX.2 & 12). Further, he had clearly been stung by the very considerable criticism incurred as a result of writing *Against the Robbing and Murdering Hordes of Peasants*: for many, he was simply 'a friend of the rulers' (IX.22-3). His own upward social mobility may also have had an effect upon his attitudes here (see *above*, p. 34). On the other hand, the very fact of the Reformation meant that moral issues, like war, had to be reconsidered afresh, even though Luther's conclusions remained politically conservative.

6. SOCIAL SIGNIFICANCE

Luther's church type response to war had a major influence upon the history of Protestantism. He and other leading reformers ensured that the thoroughgoing pacifism of the Anabaptists remained a minority and sectarian response. Himself protected by the evangelical German rulers, he gave their use of force a new legitimacy and, at the same time, provided them with an important spur to developing German nationalism. The religious, political and, indeed, military power of Rome could be resisted with a clear Christian conscience. Nevertheless, scholars are divided as to how far the atrocities committed by some rulers, in suppressing the peasants in 1525, were influenced by Luther's writings.

FURTHER READING

The primary documents have all been mentioned under Background, except for Luther's *On War Against the Turk* of 1529. Reference should also be made to *Text VI*. The introductions and notes to these documents in *Luther's Works* Vol. 46 are an essential secondary source, as well as works on Luther already mentioned in the Introduction and in Section 1.

TEXT IX

LUTHER

Whether soldiers, too, can be saved

IX.1   Now slaying and robbing do not seem to be works of love. A simple man therefore does not think it is a Christian thing to do. In truth, however, even this is a work of love. For example, a good doctor sometimes finds so serious and terrible a sickness that he must amputate or destroy a hand, foot, ear, eye, to save the body. Looking at it from the point of view of the organ that he amputates, he appears to be a cruel and merciless man; but looking at it from the point of view of the body, which the doctor wants to save, he is a fine and true man and does a good and Christian work, as far as the work itself is concerned. In the same way, when I think of a soldier fulfilling his office by punishing the wicked, killing the wicked, and creating so much misery, it seems an un-Christian work completely contrary to Christian love. But when I think of how it protects the good and keeps and preserves wife and child, house and farm, property, and honor and peace, then I see how precious and godly this work is; and I observe that it amputates a leg or a hand, so that the whole body may not perish. For if the sword were not on guard to preserve peace, everything in the world would be ruined because of lack of peace. Therefore, such a war is only a very brief lack of peace that prevents an everlasting and immeasurable lack of peace, a small misfortune that prevents a great misfortune.

IX.2   What men write about war, saying that it is a great plague, is all true. But they should also consider how great the plague is that war prevents. If people were good and wanted to keep peace, war would be the greatest plague on earth. But what are you going to do about the fact that people will not keep the peace, but rob, steal, kill, outrage women and children, and take away property and honor? The small lack of peace called war or the sword must set a limit to this universal, worldwide lack of peace which would destroy everyone.

IX.3   This is why God honors the sword so highly that he says that he himself has instituted it (Rom. 13.1) and does not want men to say or think that they have invented it or instituted it. For the hand that wields this sword and kills with it is not man's hand, but God's; and it is not man, but God, who hangs, tortures, beheads, kills, and fights. All these are God's works and judgments.

IX.4   To sum it up, we must, in thinking about a soldier's office, not concentrate on the killing, burning, striking, hitting, seizing, etc. This is what children with their limited and restricted vision see when they regard a doctor as a sawbones who amputates, but do not see that he does this only to save the whole body. So, too, we must look at the office of the soldier, or the sword, with the eyes of an adult and see why this office slays and acts so cruelly. Then it will prove itself to be an office which, in itself, is godly and as needful and useful to the world as eating and drinking or any other work.

IX.5 There are some who abuse this office, and strike and kill people needlessly simply because they want to. But that is the fault of the persons, not of the office, for where is there an office or a work or anything else so good that self-willed, wicked people do not abuse it? They are like mad physicians who would needlessly amputate a healthy hand just because they wanted to. Indeed, they themselves are a part of that universal lack of peace which must be prevented by just wars and the sword and be forced into peace. It always happens and always has happened that those who begin war unnecessarily are beaten. Ultimately, they cannot escape God's judgment and sword. In the end God's justice finds them and strikes, as happened to the peasants in the revolt.

IX.6 As proof, I quote John the Baptist, who, except for Christ, was the greatest teacher and preacher of all. When soldiers came to him and asked what they should do, he did not condemn their office or advise them to stop doing their work; rather, according to Luke 3 (.14), he approved it by saying, "Rob no one by violence or by false accusation, and be content with your wages". Thus he praised the military profession, but at the same time he forbade its abuse. Now the abuse does not affect the office. When Christ stood before Pilate he admitted that war was not wrong when he said, "If my kingship were of this world, then my servants would fight that I might not be handed over to the Jews" (John 18.36). Here, too, belong all the stories of war in the Old Testament, the stories of Abraham, Moses, Joshua, the Judges, Samuel, David, and all the kings of Israel. If the waging of war and the military profession were in themselves wrong and displeasing to God, we should have to condemn Abraham, Moses, Joshua, David, and all the rest of the holy fathers, kings, and princes, who served God as soldiers and are highly praised in Scripture because of this service, as all of us who have read even a little in Holy

Scripture know well, and there is no need to offer further proof of it here.

IX.7   Perhaps someone will now say that the holy fathers were in a different position because God had set them apart from the other nations by choosing them as his people, and had commanded them to fight, and that their example is therefore not relevant for a Christian under the New Testament because they had God's command and fought in obedience to God, while we have no command to fight, but rather to suffer, endure, and renounce everything. This objection is answered clearly enough by St. Peter and St. Paul, who both command obedience to worldly ordinances and to the commandments of worldly rulers even under the New Testament (Rom. 13.1-4; 1 Pet. 2.13-14). And we have already pointed out that St. John the Baptist instructed soldiers as a Christian teacher and in a Christian manner and permitted them to remain soldiers, enjoining them only not to use their position to abuse people or to treat them unjustly, and to be satisfied with their wages. Therefore even under the New Testament the sword is established by God's word and commandment, and those who use it properly and fight obediently serve God and are obedient to his word.

IX.8   Just think now! If we gave in on this point and admitted that war was wrong in itself, then we would have to give in on all other points and allow that the use of the sword was entirely wrong. For if it is wrong to use a sword in war, it is also wrong to use a sword to punish evildoers or to keep the peace. Briefly, every use of the sword would have to be wrong. For what is just war but the punishment of evildoers and the maintenance of peace? If one punishes a thief or a murderer or an adulterer, that is punishment inflicted on a single evildoer; but in a just war a whole crowd of evildoers, who are doing harm in proportion to the size of the crowd, are punished at once. If, therefore, one work of the sword is good and right, they are all good and right, for the sword

is a sword and not a foxtail with which to tickle people.
Romans 13 (.4) calls the sword "the wrath of God."

IX.9   As for the objection that Christians have not been
commanded to fight and that these examples are not
enough, especially because Christ teaches us not to resist
evil but rather suffer all things (Matt. 5.39–42), I have
already said all that needs to be said on this matter in my
book *Temporal Authority*. Indeed, Christians do not fight
and have no worldly rulers among them. Their government is a spiritual government, and, according to the
Spirit, they are subjects of no one but Christ. Nevertheless, as far as body and property are concerned, they are
subject to worldly rulers and owe them obedience. If
worldly rulers call upon them to fight, then they ought to
and must fight and be obedient, not as Christians, but as
members of the state and obedient subjects. Christians
therefore do not fight as individuals or for their own
benefit, but as obedient servants of the authorities under
whom they live. This is what St. Paul wrote to Titus
when he said that Christians should obey the authorities
(Titus 3.1). You may read more about this in my book
Temporal Authority.

IX.10   That is the sum and substance of it. The office of the
sword is in itself right and is a divine and useful
ordinance, which God does not want us to despise, but to
fear, honor, and obey, under penalty of punishment, as
St. Paul says in Romans 13(.1-5) . . .

IX.11   Suppose that a people would rise up today or tomorrow and depose their lord or kill him. That certainly
could happen if God decrees that it should, and the lords
must expect it. But that does not mean that it is right and
just for the people to do it. I have never known of a case
in which this was a just action, and even now I cannot
imagine any. The peasants who rebelled claimed that the
lords would not allow the gospel to be preached and that
they robbed the poor people and, therefore, the lords had
to be overthrown. I answered this by saying that
although the lords did wrong in this, it would not
therefore be just or right to do wrong in return, that is, to

be disobedient and destroy God's ordinance, which is not ours to do. On the contrary, we ought to suffer wrong, and if a prince or lord will not tolerate the gospel, then we ought to go into another realm where the gospel is preached, as Christ says in Matthew 10 (.23), "When they persecute you in one town, flee to the next."

IX.12   It is only right that if a prince, king, or lord becomes insane, he should be deposed and put under restraint, for he is not to be considered a man since his reason is gone. "That is true," you say, "and a raving tyrant is also insane; he is to be considered as even worse than an insane man, for he does much more harm." It will be a little difficult for me to respond to that statement, for that argument seems very impressive and seems to be in agreement with justice and equity. Nevertheless, it is my opinion that madmen and tyrants are not the same. A madman can neither do nor tolerate anything reasonable, and there is no hope for him because the light of reason has gone out. A tyrant, however, may do things that are far worse than the insane man does, but he still knows that he is doing wrong. He still has a conscience and his faculties. There is also hope that he may improve and permit someone to talk to him and instruct him and follow this advice. We can never hope that an insane man will do this for he is like a clod or a stone. Furthermore, such conduct has bad results or sets a bad example. If it is considered right to murder or depose tyrants, the practice spreads and it becomes a commonplace thing arbitrarily to call men tyrants who are not tyrants, and even to kill them if the mob takes a notion to do so. The history of the Roman people shows us how this can happen. They killed many a fine emperor simply because they did not like him or he did not do what they wanted, that is, let them be lords and make him their fool. This happened to Galba, Pertinax, Gordian, Alexander, and others.

IX.13   We dare not encourage the mob very much. It goes mad too quickly; and it is better to take ten *ells* from it than to allow it a handsbreadth, or even a fingersbreadth in such a case. And it is better for the tyrants to wrong them a hundred times than for the mob to treat the tyrant unjustly but once. If injustice is to be suffered, then it is better for subjects to suffer it from their rulers than for the rulers to suffer it from their subjects. The mob neither has any moderation nor even knows what moderation is. And every person in it has more than five tyrants hiding in him. Now it is better to suffer wrong from one tyrant, that is, from the ruler, than from unnumbered tyrants, that is, from the mob . . .

IX.14   My reason for saying this is that God says, "Vengeance is mine, I will repay" (Rom. 12.19). He also says, "Judge not" (Matt. 7.1). And the Old Testament strictly and frequently forbids cursing rulers or speaking evil about them. Exodus 23 (22.28) says, "You shall not curse the prince of your people." Paul, in I Timothy 2 (.1-2), teaches Christians to pray for their rulers, etc. Solomon in Proverbs and Ecclesiastes repeatedly teaches us to obey the king and be subject to him. Now no one can deny that when subjects set themselves against their rulers, they avenge themselves and make themselves judges. This is not only against the ordinance and command of God, who reserves to himself the authority to pass judgment and administer punishment in these matters, but such actions are also contrary to all natural law and justice. This is the meaning of the proverbs, "No man ought to judge his own case," and, "The man who hits back is in the wrong."

IX.15   Now perhaps you will say, "How can anyone possibly endure all the injustice that these tyrants inflict on us? You allow them too much opportunity to be unjust, and thus your teaching only makes them worse and worse. Are we supposed to permit everyone's wife and child, body and property to be so shamefully treated and always to be in danger? If we have to live under these conditions, how can we ever begin to live a decent life?" My reply is this: My teaching is not intended for people like you who want to do whatever you think is good and will please you. Go ahead! Do whatever you want! Kill all your lords! See what good it does you! My teaching is intended only for those who would like to do what is right. To these I say that rulers are not to be opposed with violence and rebellion, as the Romans, the Greeks, the Swiss, and the Danes have done; rather, there are other ways of dealing with them.

IX.16   In the first place, if you see that the rulers think so little of their soul's salvation that they rage and do wrong, what does it matter to you if they ruin your property, body, wife, and child? They cannot hurt your soul, and they do themselves more harm than they do you because they damn their own souls and that must result in the ruin of body and property. Do you think that you are not already sufficiently avenged?

IX.17   In the second place, what would you do if your rulers were at war and not only your goods and wives and children, but you yourself were broken, imprisoned, burned, and killed for your lord's sake? Would you slay your lord for that reason? Think of all the good people that Emperor Maximilian lost in the wars that he waged in his lifetime. No one did anything to him because of it. And yet, if he had destroyed them by tyranny no more cruel deed would ever have been heard of. Nevertheless, he was the cause of their death, for they were killed for his sake. What is the difference, then, between such a raging tyrant and a dangerous war as far as the many good and innocent people who perish in it are concerned? Indeed, a wicked tyrant is more tolerable than a bad war, as you must admit from your own reason and experience.

IX.18   I can easily believe that you would like to have peace and good times, but suppose God prevents this by war or tyrants! Now, make up your mind whether you would rather have war or tyrants, for you are guilty enough to have deserved both from God. However, we are the kind of people who want to be scoundrels and live in sin and yet we want to avoid the punishment of sin, and even resist punishment and defend our skin. We shall have about as much success at that as a dog has when he tries to bite through steel.

IX.19   In the third place, if the rulers are wicked, what of it?

God is still around, and he has fire, water, iron, stone, and countless ways of killing. How quickly he can kill a tyrant! He would do it, too, but our sins do not permit it, for he says in Job (34.30), "He permits a knave to rule because of the people's sins." We have no trouble seeing that a scoundrel is ruling. However, no one wants to see that he is ruling not because he is a scoundrel, but because of the people's sin. The people do not look at their own sin; they think that the tyrant rules because he is such a scoundrel – that is how blind, perverse, and mad the world is! That is why things happened the way they did when the peasants revolted. They wanted to punish the sins of the rulers, as though they themselves were pure and guiltless; therefore God had to show them the log in their eye so they would forget about the speck in another man's eye (Matt. 7.3-5).

IX.20   In the fourth place, the tyrants run the risk that, by God's decree, their subjects may rise up, as has been said, and kill them or expel them. For here we are giving instruction to those who want to do what is right, and they are very few. The great multitude remain heathen, godless, and un-Christian; and these, if God so decrees, wrongfully rise up against the rulers and create disaster, as the Jews and Greeks and Romans often did. Therefore you have no right to complain that our doctrine gives the tyrants and rulers security to do evil; on the contrary, they are certainly not secure. We teach, to be sure, that they ought to be secure, whether they do good or evil. However, we can neither give them this security nor guarantee it for them, for we cannot compel the multitude to follow our teaching if God does not give us grace. We teach what we will, and the world does what it wills. God must help, and we must teach those who are willing to do what is good and right so that they may help hold the multitude in check. The lords are just as secure because of our teaching as they would be without it. Unfortunately, your complaint is unnecessary, since most of the crowd does not listen to us. The preservation of the rulers whom God has appointed is a matter that rests with God and in his hands alone. We experienced this in the peasants' rebellion. Therefore do not be misled by the wickedness of the rulers; their punishment and disaster are nearer than you might wish. Dionysius, the tyrant of Syracuse, confessed that his life was like the life of a man over whose head a sword hung by a silken thread and under whom a glowing fire was burning.

IX.21   In the fifth place, God has still another way to punish rulers, so that there is no need for you to avenge yourselves. He can raise up foreign rulers, as he raised up the Goths against the Romans, the Assyrians against the Jews, etc. Thus there is vengeance, punishment, and danger enough hanging over tyrants and rulers, and God does not allow them to be wicked and have peace and joy. He is right behind them; indeed, he surrounds them and has them between spurs and under bridle. This also agrees with the natural law that Christ teaches in Matthew 7 (.12), "Whatever you wish that men would do to you, do so to them." Obviously, no father would want his own family to drive him out of the house, kill him, or ruin him because he had done things that were wrong, especially if his family did it maliciously and used force to avenge themselves without previously having brought charges against him before a higher authority. It ought to be just as wrong for any subject to treat his tyrant in such a way . . .

IX.22   At this point I shall have to pause and listen to my critics, who cry, "See here, in my opinion you are flattering the princes. Are you now creeping to the cross and seeking pardon? Are you afraid? etc." I just let these bumblebees buzz and fly away. If anyone can do better, let him. I have not undertaken here to preach to the princes and lords. I think, too, that they will not be very happy to receive this flattery and that I will not have ingratiated myself with them, because it jeopardizes their whole class, as you have heard. Besides, I have said often enough elsewhere, and it is all too true, that the majority of the princes and lords are godless tyrants and enemies of God, who persecute the gospel. They are my ungracious lords and sirs, and I am not very concerned about that. But I do teach that everyone should know how to conduct himself in this matter of how he ought to act toward his overlord, and should do what God has commanded him. Let the lords look out for themselves and stand on their own feet. God will not forget the tyrants and men of high rank. God is able to deal with them, and he has done so since the beginning of the world.

IX.23	Moreover, I do not want anyone to think that what I have written here applies only to peasants, as though they were the only ones of lower rank and the nobles were not also subjects. Not at all! What I say about "subjects" is intended for peasants, citizens of the cities, nobles, counts, and princes as well. For all of these have overlords and are the subjects of someone else. A rebellious noble, count, or prince should have his head cut off the same as a rebellious peasant. The one should be treated like the other, and no one will be treated unjustly . . .

IX.24	A question: "Suppose my lord were wrong in going to war." I reply: If you know for sure that he is wrong, then you should fear God rather than men, Acts 4 (5:29), and you should neither fight nor serve, for you cannot have a good conscience before God. "Oh, no," you say, "my lord would force me to do it; he would take away my fief and would not give me my money, pay, and wages. Besides, I would be despised and put to shame as a coward, even worse, as a man who did not keep his word and deserted his lord in need." I answer: You must take that risk and, with God's help, let whatever happens, happen. He can restore it to you a hundredfold, as he promises in the gospel, "Whoever, leaves house, farm, wife, and property, will receive a hundredfold," etc. (Matt. 19.29).

IX.25	In every other occupation we are also exposed to the danger that the rulers will compel us to act wrongly; but since God will have us leave even father and mother for his sake, we must certainly leave lords for his sake. But if you do not know, or cannot find out, whether your lord is wrong, you ought not to weaken certain obedience for the sake of an uncertain justice; rather you should think the best of your lord, as is the way of love, for "love believes all things" and "does not think evil," I Corinthians 13 (.4-7). So, then, you are secure and walk well before God. If they put you to shame or call you disloyal, it is better for God to call you loyal and honorable than for the world to call you loyal and honorable. What good would it do you if the world thought of you as a Solomon or a Moses, and in God's judgment you were considered as bad as Saul or Ahab?

IX.26   The (next) question: "Can a soldier obligate himself to serve more than one lord and take wages or salary from each?" Answer: I said above that greed is wrong, whether in a good or an evil occupation. Agriculture is certainly one of the best occupations; nonetheless, a greedy farmer is wrong and is condemned before God. So in this case to take wages is just and right, and to serve for wages is also right. But greed is not right, even though the wages for the whole year were less than a *gulden*. Again, to take wages and serve for them is right in itself; it does not matter whether the wages come from one, or two, or three, or however many lords, so long as your hereditary lord or prince is not deprived of what is due him and your service to others is rendered with his will and consent. A craftsman may sell his skill to anyone who will have it, and thus serve the one to whom he sells it, so long as this is not against his ruler and his community. In the same way a soldier has his skill in fighting from God and can use it in the service of whoever desires to have it, exactly as though his skill were an art of trade, and he can take pay for it as he would for his work. For the soldier's vocation also springs from the law of love. If anyone needs me and calls for me, I am at his service, and for this I take my wage or whatever is given me. This is what St. Paul says in I Corinthians 9 (.7). "Who serves as a soldier at his own expense?" Thereby Paul approves the soldier's right to his salary. If a prince needs and requires another's subject for fighting, the subject, with his own prince's consent and knowledge, may serve and take pay for it.

CRITIQUE

Perhaps of all Luther's writings, those on war and rebellion have been subjected to some of the most severe criticism (his views on the Jews in *Text XII* did not receive the same publicity when published):

(a) War. Luther showed none of the abstractness of Aquinas on war. His writings show that he was well aware of some of the moral dilemmas and the suffering that war brings, particularly to non-combatants, women and children (IX.2). Nonetheless, he articulated none of the safeguards that Aquinas and, before him, Augustine, maintained in a just-war theory. If, in the light of modern warfare, Aquinas' theory is judged deficient, then Luther's writings must be judged to be even more deficient. Rulers were, indeed, warned of God's judgment (IX.19) and of the social insecurity of their position (IX.20-1), but they were given little advice on how they were to determine whether or not it would be right to wage war. On the other hand, individual conscience was allowed very clearly (IX.25) and Luther did attempt to come to terms with Mtt. 5.39 (although many today might reject his exegesis). Again, the professional soldier fighting for more than one ruler, was left with few guidelines, other than a prescription against greed (IX.26). Few medieval scholastics approved of mercenaries (see Frederick H. Russell, *The Just War in the Middle Ages*, p.277), but Luther, superficially at least, appeared to give them a degree of legitimation.

(b) Rebellion. It is interesting to debate how far a Lutheran like Bonhoeffer actually adhered to Luther's requirement that only insanity allowed one to depose a ruler. Did he regard Hitler as insane, when he became involved in his attempted assassination, or did he reject Luther at this point? There is probably no way of answering this question. In any case, it highlights the difficulty of following Luther literally – a difficulty that is particularly poignant in the social context of Bonino (*Extract 17*) or Miranda (*Extract 12*). Even though Luther did not intend to flatter rulers (IX.22-3), his position did require subjects to be remarkably subservient to them – dangerously subservient, as many might feel today.

EXTRACTS 13-18
RAVEN, WELTY, RAMSEY, URC GROUP,
BONINO AND GREGORIOS

I. *BACKGROUND*

Charles Raven's *Extract 13* comes from his Robert Treat Paine Lectures for 1950, *The Theological Basis of Christian Pacifism* (Fellowship of Reconciliation, 1952, pp. 19-22, 26-30 & 32-3). Ebehard Welty's *Extract 14* comes from *A Handbook of Christian Social Ethics*, Vol. 2 (Nelson, 1963, pp. 408-415 & 417-21, trans. Gregor Kirstein & rev. John Fitzsimons). Paul Ramsey's *Extract 15* comes from *The Limits of Nuclear War: Thinking About the Do-able and the Undo-able* (The Council on Religion and International Affairs, New York, 1963, pp. 41-2, 42-4, 45-8, 49-50, 50-1 & 53-4). The English United Reformed Church group's *Extract 16* comes from *Non-Violent Action: A Christian Appraisal* (SCM, 1973, pp. 44-9, 59-60, 61 & 62-3). José Míguez Bonino's *Extract 17* comes from his *Revolutionary Theology Comes of Age* (SPCK, 1975, pp. 107-9, 110-2, 112-4 & 114-8 American title, *Doing Theology in a Revolutionary Situation*, Fortress, 1975). Paulos Mar Gregorios' *Extract 18* comes from an article entitled 'Life from the Perspective of Science and the Christian Faith' from a series of studies for the 1983 World Council of Churches' General Assembly at Vancouver, ed. William H. Lazareth, *The Lord of Life* (WCC, 1983, pp. 34-6 & 39-43). Raven (1885-1965) served as an Anglican army chaplain in the First World War and only subsequently became a thoroughgoing pacifist. He was Regius Professor of Divinity at Cambridge University, writing up these lectures shortly after his retirement. One of the leading Christian pacifists in Britain during the crucial 1930's, he argued publicly against the selective militarism of Temple and others, writing a number of books on the theme of war, including *Is War Obsolete?* (1935) and *War and the Christian* (1938). *The Theological Basis of Christian Pacifism* thus reflects his thoughts after some 20 years of pacifism and, as one who witnessed two World Wars and the nuclear destruction of Hiroshima and Nagasaki. In this book he concludes that, 'atomic warfare makes nonsense of all the regularities defining a just war, and indeed should bring Christians to a radical revision of the traditional moral theology. . . if we are really prepared under any imaginable circumstances to murder the whole population of a hundred square miles by a single explosion, it becomes difficult to feel that our churchgoing and prayers, our duty toward our neighbours and our talk about love, service and sacrifice can be anything but cant and hypocrisy' (pp. 10-11). In the light of this experience, he was particularly bitter about Niebuhr's claim that Christian pacifists were merely 'utopians' (cf *Extract 2.17-19*). The Dominican Welty's *Handbook* was published originally in Freiburg in two volumes, with the title *Herders Sozialkatechismus: Grundfragen und Grundkräfte des sozialen Lebens* in 1952 (hence the focus given to Pius XII). It expresses clearly the traditionalist Roman Catholic approach to moral issues. Frequent use is made of papal pronouncements in the *Handbook* and Welty explains that, 'the quotations from papal documents are intended primarily as verifications of the actual answers given' (p.xvi). However, he also explains that, 'the use of the term "Handbook" does not imply that it is authoritative, but rather refers to the method of question and answer that has been used' (*ibid.*). Ramsey has had a longstanding interest in war ethics in addition to medical ethics (see *above*, p.101). He upheld selective militarism, in the context of American involvement in the Vietnam War, in *The Just War*, despite growing criticism and has always insisted that the Reformed tradition should take traditional just-war theory more seriously (even if nuclear weapons present it with grave problems). *Non-Violent Action* is a report commissioned for the United Reformed Church. The ecumenical, but predominantly URC, group that produced it were concerned to ask, 'whether civil and international tensions can be resolved by non-violent methods which are both morally right and effective in practical terms' (p.vii). Their 'rapporteur' was John Ferguson, then Dean and Director of Studies in Arts at the Open University and author of *The Enthronement of Love: Christ the Peacemaker*, (1952), *The Politics of Love* (1972) and *War* and Peace in the World's Religions (1977). Not all members of the group shared his thoroughgoing pacifism, but all took seriously the clause, in just-war theories, specifying that war must 'be a last resort, all peaceful means of settlement having failed'. Bonino, an Argentinian Methodist, presents a radical alternative from the perspective of Liberation theology. He was, until 1985, Dean of Postgraduate Studies of the Higher Evangelical Institute for Theological Studies in Buenos Aires. Paulos Mar Gregorios is a metropolitan of the ancient, pre-Chalcedonian Syrian Orthodox Church of Kerala, South India. As Paul Verghese he wrote *The Freedom of Man* (1972), whilst principal of the Orthodox Seminary at Kottayam, Kerala and, as a frequent contributor to the WCC, he is widely recognised as one of the most important present-day Indian theologians.

2. KEY ISSUES

For Raven, the theological basis of pacifism is the Cross (13.3), to the Jews a scandal and, to the Greeks and to a number of contemporary theologians, foolishness (13.4). He refutes 'arguments from silence' based on the NT (13.5) and argues that the model of *imitatio Christi* is an obligation for all Christians (13.9). He strongly criticises a Neo-Orthodox stress upon sin (including Niebuhr's understanding of sin) and sees it as a form of Apollinarianism (i.e. a view of Christ which denies him a sufficient humanity) (13.11). For him, Christian ethics is highly demanding (13.12-3) and is not a matter simply of calculating moral requirements (13.14): it is not about compromise, but about the victory of the Cross (13.15). Only the most serious of reasons should dissuade one from such an understanding of Christian ethics (13.16). Raven sees the dichotomy between the pre- and post-Constantinian Church as perhaps inevitable, but also as a serious distortion of Christianity (13.17f).

Welty responds to three questions in a style very reminiscent of the scholastic method adopted by Aquinas in *Summa Theologica*:- (i) Is war of aggression lawful? He maintains that it never is (14.1), but admits that it may be difficult to decide whether or not a particular war is a war of aggression or of defence: it is not even necessarily the State which opens hostilities that is the aggressor (14.3). The destructiveness of

modern wars presents particular moral problems (14.5), as do
the use of nuclear weapons as deterrents (14.8-11). (ii) Is
defensive war lawful? For Welty, self-defence of both the
individual and the State are legitimate, on condition that just-war
criteria are applied (14.12-15). However, this does not justify
preventive wars (14.16) or ruthless destruction (14.17). (iii) Can
a war of liberation be permissible? He maintains that it can be in
the instance of individual nations unjustly occupied and ruled by
another (14.20-1). In the instance of world imperialism, a war of
liberation may also be legitimate (14.26), but only if there is a
prospect of defeating this imperialism (14.28). However, the
appalling sacrifice of life involved in such a war raises serious
moral problems (14.29-31).

Of all the Extracts, it is that of Ramsey which most seriously
faces the particularly difficult dilemmas raised by nuclear
weapons. His aim, in *Extract 15*, is to establish what sort of
nuclear deterrence is morally justified. He maintains, at the
outset, that any notion of nuclear reprisal (such as a determination to destroy an enemy's cities if one's own are attacked – i.e. a
policy of 'city-exchange') contravenes natural justice, Christian
charity and any real purpose (15.3-7). If nuclear reprisal is
wrong in itself (*malum in se*), it cannot be 'made' right by other
considerations (15.6). To be morally justifiable, any notion of
nuclear deterrence involving city-exchange, must distinguish
carefully between the 'possibility' and the 'certainty' of such an
exchange, and between the 'appearance' and the 'actuality' of a
commitment to such an exchange. The position which Ramsey,
himself, defends is deterrence based only on an *apparent
possibility* of city exchange – i.e. it need only *appear* to an enemy
that one may *possibly* be prepared to act in this way (15.8-9). On
this basis, he has no difficulty in defending his position against
nuclear pacifists who maintain that deterrence rests upon an
unjustifiable intention to use nuclear weapons against cities:
Ramsey's position is rather based only on appearance: in reality
city-exchange would not be allowed (15.1013). However
irresolute one side may appear to another, nuclear weapons are
potentially so destructive as to act as deterrents simply by their
possession (15.14-20). In his earlier *War and the Christian Conscience* (1961), Ramsey argued that, 'an enemy cannot know

what he really has to fear unless he also knows what he has not to fear, and (what is more important) he cannot translate power into policy without letting him know. He will probe anyway, and find out. In politics, there is perhaps some usefulness in bluffing about the weapons we may or may not possess, but very little usefulness in bluffing about what we intend or are willing to do with the weapons we are known to have' (p.166). But now, he maintains that city-exchange bluff is both morally jusified (15.21-4) and empirically feasible (15.25-6).

The URC Group attempt to suggest how a government might put non-violence into practice (16.1). The very dimensions of modern war and its unacceptability to Christian conscience, make this attempt imperative (16.2-3). They argue that non-violent defence may be effective, if only in dismaying the aggressor (16.9), particularly in the area of political non-cooperation (16.10-15). For them, the Second World War helped neither the Polish people nor the Jews: non-violent action might not have produced worse results (16.18). They believe that a standing force of non-violent troups would be necessary (16.21-3) and considerable training in non-violent political activism (16.25-7). The way of non-violence will require the Christian virtues of persistence, patience, and, indeed, suffering (16.28-9).

Liberation theology has often been criticised in the West for its tacit, and sometimes explicit, support of violence in the cause of political revolution. In fact, Liberation theologians are themselves as divided as other Christians in their preparedness to sanction the use of violence (although all tend to point out that violence is already inherent in governments of oppression). Bonino's discussion of 'love' and 'peace' forms a particularly striking contrast to the other Extracts. He begins by claiming that Marxist theory is often misunderstood by Christians, who tend to see it as too materialistic and ignore the fact that the biblical understanding of man is materialistic (17.1-2). He sees an affinity between the Marxist concept of alienation and the Pauline dichotomy between works and faith (17.3): the biblical concept of 'the poor' is also illuminated by Marxism, although the latter's concept of the proletarian class is scientific and theoretical, whereas the former's is not (17.4-5) Further, 'love' in the New Testament is inextricably connected with socio-structural concepts (17.6). Peace can be understood in two ways. In the first, it is related to a conviction that the universe is rational and ordered and that violence threatens to disturb a divinely appointed order and, in the second, it is set in the context of man as liberator and creator, who must use some violence against the status quo (17.7-9). For the first, peace seen as order and lack of conflict, whereas, for the second, peace is dynamic and prophetic and sometimes necessitates conflict (17.10). The biblical notion is less concerned with abstract principles than with God's concrete acts and commands, wherein violence appears as a breaking out of unfree and unliberated conditions (17.11-12). This whole understanding must be related to the new humanity made known in Jesus Christ (17.13).

Gregorios is equally emphatic about relating socio-ethical issues of peace and justice to life in Christ. This passage and his other writings also show a strong concern about oppression and social injustice. Yet it is not so obviously written from the perspective of Liberation theology. He writes in the context of the Vancouver theme of 'Jesus Christ – the Life of the World' (18.1) which he relates to the threats to human life presented by the prospects of nuclear holocaust (18.2), dangers in biotechnology (18.3-9 – a long-standing concern of his), ecological misuse (18.10-11) and world poverty and injustice (18.12-13). 'Life', that is so threatened, Gregorios attempts to understand, first in terms of science, and then in terms of theology. The scientific answer to the question 'what is life' is presented here in summary form (18.20 – his excellent, but detailed, scientific account has been omitted because of lack of space). His theological discussion focuses upon the Assembly theme 'Life as a gift of God' (see below, pp. 547-9). He argues that this theme is directly relevant to a number of social issues concerning human life (18.22). For the Christian, life is 'created', not a product of 'nature' (18.23), and is thus dependent upon God, evoking in us a free response of love (18.24-9) and repentance (18.31). Gregorios maintains that both the whole of biological life and life in Christ are equally gifts of grace – biological life acting as the very basis and receptacle for eternal life (18.32-4). He views the spectrum of interconnected life in Orthodox terms (18.36) and sees the incarnation as affecting all levels of life and as overcoming the alienation of humanity from God (18.38-9). In the incarnation the gift is the Giver himself (18.41-2). But he argues that it is only small Christian communities that can act as adequate vehicles for this faith (18.43).

3. ETHICAL ARGUMENTS

Raven significantly avoids consequentialist arguments against militarism – for example, that war leads to appalling suffering or to greater misery than pacifism – and indeed criticises other pacifists for a 'negative abhorrence of war' (13.1 – and see also his earlier *Is War Obsolete?* p. 40). For him, consequentialism inevitably involves compromise (13.12). Instead, he maintains a deontological position, based upon an imitation of Christ (13.8). His claim that, 'ethics has become a matter of personal allegiance, not of statutory obligation' (13.12), might appear personalist, but it is primarily an attack upon uninvolved moral calculation (13.13).

Welty's approach, too, is deontological, standing firmly within the traditional Roman Catholic just-war position. However, there is also considerble evidence of pragmatism and consequential types of ethical argument in this Extract:- international tribunals are to be used as moral arbiters (14.3), the dimensions of modern warfare are considered to affect their morality (14.5), the risks of nuclear weapons are assessed consequentially (14.8) and, above all, the prospect of successful victory is treated as a central and essential criterion of a just war (14.12, 18, 28 and 30-1).

Ramsey resorts to a number of deontological and consequential approaches in his overall attempt to interpret just-war theory in the light of the general principles of 'natural justice' (15.3) and 'concrete Christian charity' or 'love-informed justice' (15.4 and 5.20). So, for Ramsey, city-exchange is deontologically *malum in se* (15.6), but it is also consequentially 'irrational' and 'purposeless' (15.7). His whole concept of apparent/possible commitment to city-exchange is highly pragmatic and leads him to a lengthy discussion of the morality of deception (15.24 – which is a much shortened version of this discussion).

URC Group, Gregorios and Bonino all demonstrate basic deontological commitments – the first to non-violence (though not necessarily, in all of its members, to thoroughgoing pacifism), and the others to the poor and oppressed. Clearly, Bonino shares the same basic commitment as Miranda in *Extract 12* - 'solidarity with the poor' (17.5). Even his relatively impartial analysis of the two concepts of 'peace', links the idea of 'liberation' with that of 'creation' itself. However, in *Non-Violent Action*, considerable pragmatism is also evident, particularly in its central contention that non-violence may be as effective as, or even more effective than, violence. Nonetheless, persistence and patience, even in the face of suffering, are prescribed deontologically (16.28-9).

4. BASES OF CHRISTIAN ETHICS

Raven uses the NT as his major source of appeal throughout this Extract. In part, his extensive use of the NT (and significantly not the OT) is explained by the fact that he wrote up these lectures whilst travelling and, 'sixty-five kilos of baggage for winter in Australia and New Zealand and summer in the United States left no room for any books except a Bible' (from the *Preface*). But, in part, it reflects his conviction that the main impetus of the NT supports thoroughgoing pacifism. As a result, he sees the post-Constantinian changes as being essentially departures from the Gospel. But for whichever reason, his use of the NT shows surprisingly little direct use of critical biblical scholarship. At the heart of his argument, there is also a doctrinal stress upon the Cross and an identification of the post-Constantinian 'departure' with Apollinarianism.

Welty's dependence upon Christian tradition is apparent at every point in his argument. His *Handbook* is punctuated throughout with long excerpts from papal pronouncements (as in 14.2., but reduced for brevity elsewhere in this Extract), yet with comparatively few biblical references (e.g. 14.13). Also clearly evident is his reliance upon traditional just-war theory.

Ramsey again shows considerable reliance upon rational/ philosophical argument (cf *Extract 5*) with an underlying conviction about love-transformed justice. The biblical basis of this conviction is not given here (though it is elsewhere – see *above*, p. 105) and, indeed, there is an underlying assumption that, on this issue at least, the overall values of 'natural justice' and Christian 'charity' coincide (see, particularly, 15.4 and 15.26). Even the arguments taken from the British Roman Catholics are not exclusively Christian (15.10f).

Like Raven, *Non-Violent Action* is based upon a doctrinal understanding of the Cross (16.6 & 28), but it also contains a strong appeal to Christian experience (16.29). It is interesting that the World Council of Churches' report, *Christians and the Prevention of War in an Atomic Age* (1958), which was so heavily criticised in Ramsey's *War and the Christian Conscience*, is treated here as an authority (16.3).

Bonino tends to be more critical in his citation of tradition – for example, in his analysis of the two theological understandings of 'peace' (17.10). Even his direct quotation from Barth – important as it undoubtedly was in the light of Barth's personal commitment to socialism – is selective. In Barth there was a much stronger sense of obedience to appointed powers (see *Extract 7*). However, as in Miranda, it is the Bible that is the basic authority in Bonino. Both men believe that a correlation can be made between certain fundamental Marxist concepts and biblical concepts. Miranda seeks to achieve this correlation by a detailed citation of particular biblical texts, whereas Bonino tends, rather, to refer to general biblical notions, such as that of the Kingdom of God (17.6 & 11) and that of poverty (17.4).

Gregorios, in contrast, makes no direct biblical references. In characteristic Orthodox style his argument rests upon doctrine and upon the received wisdom of tradition. Significantly, the latter can include the statement made by the joint Orthodox consultation which met to prepare for Vancouver (18.36). He also mixes this with his considerable knowledge of present-day science and sees the full Christian as a person of both culture and learning, on the one hand, and, on the other, of worship and faith (18.43). His strong liturgical stress is evident in the central position that he gives to eucharistic worship (18.39).

5.   SOCIAL DETERMINANTS
Of the five Extracts, that of Raven goes most against social context. At times, he found it difficult to reconcile his roles as a

thoroughgoing pacifist and as a senior clergyman within the Church of England. In 1945, he wrote in a private letter that, 'my faith isn't strong enough to survive the regular reading of Church papers;' (see, F.W. Dillistone, *Charles Raven: Naturalist, Historian and Theologian*, p. 437). And, in 1935, William Temple suggested, in *The Times*, that Raven's pacifism was 'heretical in tendency'. On the other hand, Ramsey and Welty both conform to church-type responses to war. Welty's *Handbook* is concerned throughout to accord with traditional Roman Catholic teaching (as his frequent citation of papal pronouncements indicates). Ramsey's defence of a just-war position is considerably more complex. In all his writings he is particularly critical of the position of 'nuclear pacifists'. Yet, at the same time, he increasingly stresses that a nuclear policy based upon the potential destruction of cities is unjustifiable. The specific stimulus for *The Limits of Nuclear War* was the American Secretary of Defense Robert McNamara's June 1962 speech. In this he defined American nuclear policy afresh: 'principal military objectives, in the event of a nuclear war stemming from an attack on the Alliance, should be the destruction of the enemy's forces, not of his civilian population' (p7). This change of policy, away from that of the 'mutual assured destruction' of the Dulles era, partly explains the differences already noted between Ramsey's writings on the morality of nuclear weapons. *Non-Violent Action* represents a minority position within the United Reformed Church, but it is significant that it avoids actual commitment to thoroughgoing pacifism, stressing, instead, the positive effectiveness of non-violence. Nevertheless, John Ferguson himself is a thoroughgoing pacifist, coming from a Quaker background. The politico-economic frustrations of both South America and India are evident in Bonino and Gregorios (see *above*, p. 233). Bonino's position is somewhat ambiguous, reflecting some of the tensions on this issue present in the movement. Gregorios, in contrast, reflects the equally strong Indian emphasis upon 'culture' and 'knowledge'. Whilst clearly concerned about poverty, the concept of 'liberation' itself is somewhat different in India, with the traditional notion of 'liberation' (*moksha*) referring rather to spiritual release and/or escape from the cycle of re-birth (*samsara*). Although Marxism

is strong in parts of India and espoused by some Roman
Catholic clergy, it is certainly not identical to Western Marxism.

6. SOCIAL SIGNIFICANCE

In the context of the 1930's, Raven's espousal of thoroughgoing
pacifism was particularly influential. Although not nearly so
well known to the general public as Dick Shepherd, the fact
that, as the Regius Professor of Theology at Cambridge, he was
an active supporter of the Peace Pledge Union, would have
served as a strong academic legitimation of the movement.
Certainly, Raven himself thought it important that academics
were involved in the peace movement of the time: 'Lord
Ponsonby, Lord Russell, Mr. Aldous Huxley, Mr. Gerald
Heard, Mr. Middleton Murray and the Bishop of Birmingham
are men whose intellectual power is probably greater than that
of any group in the public life of Britain... where they, each
from his special angle, have vindicated pacifism, they deserve a
fuller answer than the casual comment of ecclesiastics and
statesmen' (*War and the Christian*, p. 124). Doubtless to enhance
their influence, Raven usually presented his views on war in a
popular written style. Ramsey's influence as an exponent of
Christian ethics in America has also been fairly considerable,
although he has never achieved the political significance of
Reinhold Neibuhr. However, his support of a just-war theory
in relation to the Vietnam War did little to increase his influence.
Non-Violent Action has perhaps received less attention from
theologians and Christians generally than it deserves. The social
significance of Liberation theology has already been discussed
(see *above*, p. 234). Gregorios and his fellow metropolitan
Geevarghese Mar Osthathios (author of *Theology of a Classless
Society*, 1979, and *The Sin of Being Rich in a Poor World*, 1983) are
proving two of the most important present-day Indian theologians. The Syrian Orthodox Church of South India has
traditionally been somewhat conservative and socially isolated,
but recently has become far more active on socio-political
issues. The strongly Marxist state of Kerala does not show all of
the anti-clericalism of much Western Marxism and may in

principle be more open to the influence of an informed Christian minority.

FURTHER READING

I have analysed Raven's and Welty's positions on war further in *Theology and Social Structure*. F.W. Dillistone's biography *Charles Raven* is the most important source for further information about Raven. Gustafson often acknowledges his debt to Ramsey's writings and a number of the books cited earlier analyse his concepts (see *above*, p. 11). Liberation theology is still developing, but the readers edited by Alistair Kee, *A Reader in Political Theology* and *The Scope of Political Theology*, are useful guides to some of the different approaches apparent within it.

EXTRACT 13

RAVEN

The theological basis of christian pacifism

13.1   Christian pacifists derive their conviction not from the negative abhorrence of war nor from the utopian dream of a lotus-eater's world, but from the fact and significance of Jesus Christ. They concentrate attention on war because it is a typical symptom, and at this juncture the outstanding representative of evil. They believe that here is the concrete issue upon which today evil can be challenged most effectively, and that to challenge it here would ultimately involve a conflict over the whole field. Their confidence is grounded in the faith that peace on earth is God's will for his children and that man is in fact capable of fellowship. They cannot regard this hope as utopian without abandoning the Lord's Prayer and repudiating faith in its author.

13.2   But prior to these considerations is the historic event of the life and death of Jesus, the belief in the uniqueness and the validity of that event, and consequently the conviction that a new, final and authentic means for the overcoming of evil has been revealed to us. Far from agreeing that the progress of theological studies, or the development of human society, or the experience of recent happenings have shaken their position, they would maintain that the sophistries and propaganda and despair of their critics have in fact simplified the issue and strengthened their case. Amid the confusion and tragedy of the times the way of Christ stands out plainly for what it is, the hope of the world; but it is the way of the Cross. Considering the unanimity with which Christendom accepts the one symbol of its faith and the devotion with which individual Christians take it up daily, it is amazing that in the most urgent problem of our time they generally reject it and explain it away.

13.3 Jesus "came into the world to save sinners." He fulfilled his mission by a deliberate acceptance of death, and his martyrdom has proved the most momentous victory in history. Those are statements that underlie the whole substance of the New Testament. The earliest disciples proclaimed them as God's gift and message to the world. They also recorded and by their example attested that this way of the Cross was obligatory upon all who would follow. This was the will of God, and if it was rejected, the cry of "Lord, Lord" was a mere hypocrisy.

13.4 Such a brief statement is necessary if we are to appreciate the challenge and the novelty of the gospel. Adumbrated as we can see by the most profound of the prophets of Israel, vindicated to some degree at least by the experiences of that martyr-nation, it was yet a revelation running clean counter to the selfish instincts of men and nations, to the "common sense" of human wisdom, and to the traditional standards of human conduct and ambition. "To the Jews a scandal, to the Greeks a silliness": so the apostle Paul triumphantly admitted when he named it "the weakness and folly of God." "Utopian," decides Dr. Niebuhr; "not yet practicable," explained Dr. Temple; "mere suicide," say the politicians; "lily-livered treachery," cries the gutter-press; and in their various ways they "pass by on the other side." It is hard for one who realizes from many years of mental and spiritual struggle the difficulty of the decision and who has affectionate and grateful memories of his nonpacifist friends, to record that verdict, but the fact is plain.

13.5 Christ by his Cross presents to us his way of overcoming the sin of the world, and in this form at least the mass of mankind and even of Christians repudiate it. Twice in half a century the decision has been taken.

13.6 It is not necessary, in view of Professor G.H.C.Macgregor's full and unanswered study *The New Testament Basis of Pacifism*, to repeat at length the plain evidence from Gospels, Acts and Epistles, nor even to examine once more the exegesis of the few texts that are cited to suggest that Jesus and his immediate followers did not condemn the soldier's profession, or advocate invariable non-resistance. No one (except perhaps Dr. Malan of South Africa) would suggest that because the New Testament does not denounce slavery therefore slavery is a noble and sacred institution, or argue that because "ye have the poor always with you" therefore the effort to abolish poverty is a "soft utopianism." Yet this is precisely the line taken by those who quote "the strong man armed" or "not to bring peace but a sword" as giving the authority of Jesus for atomic warfare.

13.7 As part of the "humiliation" – the kenosis – of his incarnate life Jesus accepted the comradeship and circumstances of men and women imprisoned in the egotism and nationalisms of humanity. As the condition of his "teacher's" work among them he must somehow bridge the gulf between the wisdom of God and the follies and perversions of mankind. If he was to redeem them he must in some degree share their bondage. That he did so without disparaging his divinity is proof not only of the nature of God but of the fact that man is not totally alien and corrupt. But if the Creator can so stoop as to "take our nature upon him" we must yet recognize that "his ways are not our ways", and that if we are to become like him something more than compromise and accommodation to circumstances may well be expected of us. In any discipleship worthy of the name there must surely be room for martyrdom. If our Christian way of life can nowadays only be protected by the hydrogen bomb, may it not be time to examine afresh its claim to be Christian? "By their fruits you shall know them": do men gather such fruit from the vine of heaven?

13.8   The plain fact is that the Church since the First Century and with few exceptions has never, despite its protestations, taken Christ with complete seriousness. If it has not evaded the questions "Whom say ye that I am?" and "What think ye of Christ? Whose son is he?" it has given a credal answer but failed to endorse it or to act whole-heartedly upon it. "Let this mind be in you which was also in Christ Jesus"; "I live, yet not I; Christ lives in me"; – a multitude of such sayings proves that in the New Testament the *Imitatio Christi* was not a devotional aspiration but an admitted obligation. "In Christ" is the characteristic phrase of St. Paul. Its significance implies that such real identification of the believer with his Lord was a basic feature of discipleship, and its constant repetition underlines its primacy as the true constituent condition of human wayfaring . . .

13.9   The plain fact is that the antithesis of task and resources was resolved by Christ, but only at the inevitable breaking-point. Jesus himself overcame the world and accomplished the impossible when he cried, "My God, my God, why has thou forsaken me?" By accepting the Cross, by suffering dereliction, by surrendering everything without reserve, he revealed and released the infinite energies of God. He had already prepared his disciples by precept, warning them that they must be broken; now by example he sacrificed them with himself that they might be crucified with him and so be raised and glorified. Defeat for them as for him was in fact victory. From it flowed the consequences that changed not only their lives but the course of history. Throughout the centuries where men have experienced the full manifestation of exaltation and self-emptying, of adoration and abasement, they have attained a similar victory. But it must be confessed that the Church as a whole and most of its members have found the conditions too hard.

13.10   In so doing they have not been without excuse. Doctrinal and moral theology have both been so formulated as to enable us to remain contentedly orthodox and accept a comfortable.compromise, and although there has never in the past been any such general defeatism as characterizes Protestant neo-orthodoxy today, the distortion of the great doctrines of the faith and the approval of legalistic codes and minimum standards of conduct have for many centuries symbolized and intensified the measure of our apostasy. We shall deal in some detail with this subject hereafter, but if we are to set out the case fairly we must mention here and now the distortions that have excused our failure.

13.11   Put briefly, the changes are these. In the doctrine of Creation the fall and power of Satan have been so emphasized as to banish God from his world. The earth is represented as a province in rebellion. Its creatures have become totally corrupt. The witness of his works to their Maker, though it may not be wholly destroyed, is wholly unintelligible to mankind outside the scope of biblical or ecclesiastical salvation. In the Incarnation Apollinarian-sim, the belief that since all humanity is fallen there can be no full humanity in Jesus, has in fact even where Monophysitism is disavowed become the general Christology. Under the guise of belief in his impersonal manhood Christ has been removed from our species; he is the divine Intruder, and in consequence can no longer be in any but a mocking fashion our example, our inspiration. In consequence again, what he does, we cannot do. He must do it for us, and we can continue in our own way, forgiven but not seriously changed. We appreciate by faith what our Substitute has suffered; and to be crucified with Christ would be to replace faith by works and slip into Pelagianism. So too with the doctrine of the Holy Spirit, whose indwelling and energizing life was the proof of discipleship and the constitutent of the

Church. When the organic community of Pentecost was replaced by the organized and hierarchical empire of Catholicism the Gifts of the Spirit were identified with the supernatural and only too often magical effects of ritual acts in baptism, confirmation, penance, and the like, and these to be valid must be dispensed by special ministers who bestowed them not personally but officially and in such a manner that their own faith and character neither enriched nor impaired their efficacy.

13.12　So too in matters of morality. St. Paul had seen as the first consequence of Christ's triumph that the old way of legal and blinkered righteousness was superseded. "Ye are no longer under law but under grace" – that is, you live immediately in communion with God, not derivatively under obedience to his commands. Ethics has become a matter of personal allegiance, not of statutory obligation. In consequence, there can never be a time when we can say, "I have discharged my religious duties," nor, surely, any room for a doctrine of assurance or of bargaining for forgiveness. We cannot dare to "stand Paying a price at his right hand."

13.13　We dare not claim to be saved unless indeed we are saints and then we shall call ourselves the chief of sinners. God loves and forgives. Such convictions belong to a different world from all this calculation as to venial and mortal sins and the escape from years of purgatory. God guides and enables. Jesus never answered any question by rule of thumb or treated any questioner as a "case." What is one man's meat is another man's poison. "Hard cases make bad law" is the lawyer's (and the ecclesiastic's) maxim; to the Christian every case, his own included, is a hard case.

13.14　So the adventure of living, always exacting in its demands, has been tamed and harnessed and regulated by moralists and canonists. Instead of the delicate business of "perceiving and knowing what things we ought to do," we are told precisely where each fenced path leads us and at what points dangers are to be avoided and safety secured. It is all about as like the Christian life as exercise on a treadmill is to the ascent of a mountain in the company of an experienced guide.

13.15   But in spite of all this compromise and subterfuge the heart of the Christian gospel is not safety but victory – the victory over evil that was won by the way of the Cross. Jesus when he undertook his mission of deliverance was constantly tempted to use other methods: the reformer's road of material satisfactions; the statesman's road of armed rebellion and imperial rule; the ecclesiastic's road of awe and wonder and the fulfilment of prophecy and the role of the Lord's anointed. Even at the Mission's crisis in the last days at Jerusalem, he could still have appealed to the Zealots and fought, or he could have fled and taken refuge in Galilee. He chose to meet evil unarmed and unafraid, to let it do its worst with him, and to bear its wounds in his own body on the tree. So by death came life, and the twin sayings – "I am come that they may have life and have it abundantly" and "Whoso loveth his life shall lose it, whoso hateth his life in this world shall keep it unto life eternal" – are seen to be complementary.

13.16   Of course it is possible for us to say that we are incapable of following his example or else that the example is not one that ought to be followed. But if in this supreme lesson and achievement we are not to imitate him, either our discipleship becomes trivial or else his lordship is denied. To say, "This is too high a price for me to pay," is natural enough, but we ought surely not to make such a confession without shame. To say, "This was right for him, but it would be wrong for me," is to tear up those parts of his teaching in which he bade us follow and do his works and to assume that we can lightly disassociate ourselves from him whenever we think fit. In this matter of victory over evil – a matter fundamental to his whole ministry – what is not legitimate for us is to ignore his way or to replace it by some method of our own. But this is precisely what we do when we call pacifism a soft utopianism or decide that mass-killing is the lesser of two evils. And if we argue that all action is relative to its particular circumstances and that when Christ stood before Caiaphas or Pilate he acted in a way quite opposite from what Christians should take before a Hitler or a Stalin, we ought to support our disavowal of our Master by strong evidence and with grave hesitation, else it would seem obvious that we do not take Christ seriously. But in fact such evidence is not forthcoming and its place is too often taken by contempt or denunciation . . .

13.17   It may indeed be argued that in this matter, as in the case of slavery or of the subjugation of women, the world could not appreciate or adopt Christ's teaching until a long period of relapse and aspiration, compromise and tuition, had passed. We know as a fact of history that in the early and victorious years of Christendom pacifism was almost if not quite universal. Though this may be partly due to horror at the acts of allegiance to the genius of Caesar and of obedience to a persecuting magistracy which soldiering involved, yet the love and forgivingness and fortitude of the martyrs prove that the community that produced them had gone far toward overcoming the hatreds and ambitions and fears that are the springs of war. Indeed, the quality of their writings and the testimony of their enemies prove that they had entered richly into the mind of their victorious Lord. As he had overcome the world by refusing to fight or to flee so they also could face death with courage and joy, and by so doing could sow the seed of discipleship.

13.18   But when, in spite of the martyrs, the darkness fell upon the old world, it was perhaps inevitable that despair of the practicability of Christ's way should infect the Church. "Save thyself from the wrath to come" took the place of "Repent, for the Kingdom of Heaven is at hand," and the note of victory was replaced by that of redemption.

13.19   By creating through monasticism cells of religious life, taking over the responsibility and to some extent also the prestige of government, and elaborating an ecclesiastical system of duties and discipline and extending this to cover much of the domestic, social and political life of men, the Church succeeded not only in maintaining its own survival and influence but in baptizing and to some extent converting the new Europe. It is possible to argue that this was the best that could be done under the circumstances – and indeed the attempt to rewrite history or to distribute praise and blame is never profitable – but the contrast between the Christianity of the New Testament and that of the age of Charlemagne or even Hildebrand is too complete to be ignored. To regard as a legitimate descendant a system that departed from most of the fundamental principles of the gospel is to stretch the rules of inheritance to the breaking point. The triple tiara of the Papacy derives from the *Tu regere imperio populos Romane memento* much more than from the *Tu es Petrus* ...

13.20   If we argue, as the Reformed Churches are accustomed to do, that these "errors of Rome" were undone by Luther and Calvin, the plain reply must be that this is not true. The successful Reformers were men of their age who took over a large part of the system from which they broke away, and they persecuted more radical Christians almost as fiercely as Rome had persecuted the Albigenses. It was not until the Seventeenth Century, the epoch of the New Philosophy and Modern Science and of George Fox and Christian pacifism, that a real return to the ethos of the Apostolic Age made its appearance, and its leaders were seldom able to remain within the churches. From that time on we have witnessed a prolonged attempt on behalf of the older Christian denominations to decide whether truth or tradition shall prevail in their doctrine and life.

EXTRACT 14
WELTY
Wars of aggression and defence

Is war of aggression lawful?

14.1   'War of aggression, no matter on what grounds it is waged, today must be considered immoral and be rejected.'

14.2   PIUS XII (C.B., 1944; N.C.W.C., pp. 10,11).
"There is a duty, besides, imposed on all, a duty which
brooks no delay, no procrastination, no hesitation, no
subterfuge. It is a duty to do everything to ban once and
for all wars of aggression as a legitimate solution of
international disputes and as a means towards realizing
national aspirations. Many attempts in this direction have
been seen in the past. They have all failed. And they will
all fail always, until the saner section of mankind has the
firm determination, the holy obstinancy, like an obligation in conscience, to fulfill the mission which past ages
have not undertaken with sufficient gravity and resolution.

If ever a generation has had to appreciate in the depths
of its conscience the call: 'war on war', it is certainly the
present generation . . .

Unquestionably the progress of man's inventions,
which should have heralded the realization of greater
well-being for all mankind, has instead been employed to
destroy all that had been built up through the ages.

But by that very fact the immorality of the war of
aggression has been made ever more evident."

14.3   (1.) It is difficult to state exactly which wars should be
considered wars of aggression. Wars of aggression are
not confined to unjust, wilful attacks, for they may have
just causes, such as the infringement or the denial of
essential rights. Those who open hostilities cannot in
every case be described as the aggressors, for a State or a
group of States may be forced into a situation when it has
to anticipate the attack of the opponent. It is simplest to
consider as a war of aggression one that is declared to be
such by an international tribunal. But this definition is
strictly speaking of a merely formal nature; it states
nothing concerning the true nature of war of aggression.
Nevertheless, if the tribunal fulfils all the conditions for a
really unbiased and objective judgment, then its decisions
must be recognized as valid and be obeyed by all States
and by the community of nations. This seems the only
practical solution. In view of the new situation today

there would seem to be only one way of defining war of aggression; we must proceed from its opposite and say that today every war that is not forced on States or on the community of nations in order to protect themselves and their most sacred rights must be considered one of aggression. Thus we distinguish between the lawful, that is, the just war of defence and the unlawful war of aggression (no matter on what grounds it is fought).

14.4   Most Catholic moralists who have expressed an opinion on the matter agree in unreservedly condemning every modern war of aggression . . . The greatest difficulty lies in the question whether the so-called "war of liberation" is to be considered a war of aggression or of defence.

14.5   (2.) The reasons for the immorality of a war of aggression lie in the essential nature of modern warfare. The convulsions, losses and dangers are out of all proportion to the gain which a war of aggression may achieve. Of special consequence are: i. the terrible sacrifice and destruction on every side caused by weapons of destruction in a modern war; losses among the civilian population, as witness Hiroshima, Dresden, and Korea; the decay of morality; ii. the menace to world peace; every region today even in the most remote corner of the earth lies within the sphere of interest of the few big powers; the most senseless local conflict can easily develop into a world war. Even before an organized community of nations has been formed, the States are obliged in justice and charity to preserve the common good of mankind from being gravely endangered.

14.6   (3.) With the banning of wars of aggression States and nations are called on not only to refrain from all war of conquest, but even patiently to endure injustice rather than to seek redress by force. For it cannot be maintained that the customary international provocations constitute an extreme case of self-defence which alone may still justify war.

14.7   (4.) The question whether, and to what extent, modern weapons are controllable or uncontrollable is one of fact that can be answered only by the experts. Scientists are working with success on the production of "clean" bombs, the effects and after-effects of which could be controlled.

14.8 It is irresponsible and morally wrong to neglect the production of conventional weapons and to restrict rearmament to nuclear weapons "as a deterrent"; for the risk is that, when nuclear weapons are the only means of defence, States will be compelled to use them in order to repel an attack even by conventional weapons.

14.9 The decisive factor is not the scientific and technical but the "moral" control. What is to be defended must stand in some relation to the inevitable evil and losses. If the other conditions for waging just war are fulfilled, even unusually great damage can be justified.

14.10 We must distinguish between the moral justification of nuclear war and that of nuclear weapons. It is quite possible that certain types of nuclear weapons may be controllable and hence their employment justified for reasons of defence and on the conditions already mentioned. But a nuclear war cannot be justified if, and because, it is not restricted to these weapons, but includes the use of all, even uncontrollable, nuclear weapons.

14.11 States are strictly obliged, i. to agree to effective measures of control, that is to allow independent inspection of their own territory for this purpose; ii. to make timely provision for extensive measures of air-raid protection, so that as far as possible the danger to the population may be reduced; according to the latest scientific investigations a very considerable reduction of this danger is possible, though at great financial cost.

Is defensive war lawful?

14.12 'A purely defensive war is lawful even today under the following conditions:

1. There must be an unjust, actual attack that cannot otherwise be met.

2. The aggressor must not be harmed more than is necessary.

3. The defence must have a prospect of success, and no higher goods must be jeopardized than those which have to be defended.'

14.13 Catholic moralists are practically unanimous on this issue . . .

The right of self-defence exists not only for the individual, but also for nations and States. For brute force would otherwise be placed above right, and predatory war and armed aggression would have to be regarded as "just". In certain circumstances the State is even more obliged to resist than the individual who may be responsible only for his own life and conduct, whereas the State is entrusted with the protection of many individuals and groups, especially families, of goods and values such as justice, tradition, civilization. Moreover, it ought in the name of God to protect the sanctity of the moral order in the world against injustice and harm (cf. Rom. 13.4).

The conditions that apply to any just self-defence must be applied correspondingly to defensive war:

14.14 (1.) Defence in the form of armed resistance, which may involve heavy sacrifices in lives and property, is only permissible if an unjust attack is threatening or already in progress, and if all other means have been tried; in short, it must be a case of the ultimate resort.

14.15 What is essential is that the aggressor must be in the wrong, the defender in the right. A State that is attacked because of an injustice which it has itself committed and has not made good, must bow to the justice that is meted out to it. Pius XII expressly stated that there are some human values which would justify a defensive war even today. Such human values are the existence of an ordered political community and man's fundamental rights and liberties and especially Christian faith and morality. Before arms are taken up all other solutions must have been tried. Defensive war is only an *ultima ratio*, a last resort, if neither negotiations nor threats nor the intervention of other powers or of the community of nations are successful. Aggression must be actual; the

State must be "threatened with an unjust aggression, or already its victim" (Pius XII). Like an individual, the State need not wait until it is too late; "actuality" exists when it is morally certain that the aggressor is making final preparations for an attack and does not desist in spite of sufficient warning; usual indications are troop concentrations; suddenly increased press campaigns which suggests that a fitting cause for war is being invented etc.

14.16   It follows from what has been said that so-called preventive war is not permissible. A preventive war is waged in order to ward off a later, possible, perhaps probable attack. There is reason, or so it is thought, to fear that a State is preparing for war and will in the near future begin the war as soon as a favourable opportunity presents itself.

14.17   (2.) To defend, to repel, ought not to imply ruthless destruction. Self-defence does not entitle one to ruthless severity. Modern war in itself is hard and cruel enough. The one who has been unjustly attacked must do what he can to end the conflict as quickly as possible and not to inflict more wounds on the opponent than is necessary.

14.18   (3.) The third condition is that there must be a prospect of success, a solid probability (Pius XII, C. B. 1948, I.U.A., p. 96) that the defence will succeed in repelling the aggressor. The defenders may not jeopardize higher values in order to save lesser ones. Precisely in the case of a war of defence it is often difficult to forsee success, since the State attacked must often act with the utmost speed...

Can a war of liberation be permissible?

14.19   'If it is of defensive, not of aggressive character, a war of liberation is permissible and perhaps even a duty.'

This is one of the most delicate questions in the whole ethics of war. By war of liberation, including what is called war of invasion, is meant one that is undertaken in order to liberate countries from unjust foreign rule or occupation, or from an extremely grave menace. In some cases it may resemble a war of aggression or a preventive war, since it is begun in order to drive out a foreign power, or to prevent it from continuing the menace. Is such a war of liberation to be considered a war of aggression or a preventive war? The question has to be answered; for the totalitarian powers are not only causing widespread confusion by their completely unjust claims and methods, but also material and even worse intellectual and moral misery. May the free world turn the cold into a hot war if there is no other way out than slavery? Two possibilities will be dealt with here:

The liberation of individual nations

14.20   (1.) Let us suppose that a country is unjustly occupied and ruled by another. The occupation may take place in the course of an unjust war or for preventive reasons (for the "protection of neutrality"); authority is exercised without any consideration for right and justice: terror, suppression of the nation's individuality and self-government, political parties that are subservient to foreign dictators and parties, denial of human rights, suppression of liberty, etc.

14.21   (2.) Such a situation is clearly unjust; it is a continuous aggression against the nation, its existence, honour and most sacred rights. The methods of such a "system" or occupation are in fact not different from unjust military attacks. Certainly the principles governing just resistance to the State apply; for this is a matter of foreign interference, of usurpers invading foreign territory and coercing a foreign nation. Therefore it is clearly a case of self-defence against actual, unjust aggression.

14.22   The sense of mutual dependence among the nations ought to support the struggle for liberation of a people subjugated in this manner. The common good of the whole world may be involved; and apart from this there exists an obligation of the nations and states to help.

The war of liberation for peace and freedom in the world

14.23   (1.) Let us suppose that totalitarian power, completely materialist in outlook and consciously atheistic, in theory and practice professes world imperialism. This great power has such enormous resources in power and so many powerful supporters in satellite States and among its allies and followers in other countries that it constitutes *the* world danger. Its ideological basis is a ruthless collectivism recognizing no human dignity and rights. We are aware that this great power disturbs world peace wherever and whenever it can, and with all its strength is preparing an armed struggle for world domination; that wherever it has established its rule, the people are forcibly robbed of their most sacred rights by oppression and terror; education of youth to atheism; fight against God, Christ and the Church; uniformity of thinking, absence of any legal order and security.

14.24   This great power is at work enslaving other nations (adjoining territories and satellites) or undermining them, for example, by means of fifth columns, political parties influenced and commanded by the financial, intellectual support of the major power in question etc. There are occasional strikes, acts of sabotage, including political murder, and, above all, local wars are unleashed. These wars, as the major power openly admits or by its actions clearly shows, are in reality waged against the community of nations and against the free world; consequently they have the character of acts of aggression against world peace.

14.25   The question now is this: Under these circumstances has the world the right to armed self-defence, to a war of liberation? Or must humanity, that is, all the other nations as a whole, wait until the great power has struck? And if the nations foresee with certainty that due to the inequality of forces they might soon no longer be in a position to defend themselves, ought they to resign themselves to the inevitable fate of defeat later on and the enslavement to follow?

14.26   (2.) Some consider a war of liberation in these circumstances a defensive war imposed upon the free world and therefore lawful. They argue that since mankind has a natural, God-given right to its existence, fundamental freedoms, to peace and order, it has a right also to protect itself and its most sacred rights in good time against unjust attacks. It may not allow these rights to be flagrantly wrested from it. Unjust aggression by the other side against world peace and the most sacred right of mankind is already taking place with weapons not only of the cold, but also of the hot war; nations are held in subjugation, there is subversion, there are local wars etc.

14.27   This state of affairs has no precedent. The very existence not only of an individual nation but of mankind as a whole is at stake, and the case of self-defence in extreme necessity exists not only when the major armed offensive is already in progress, but already when this major offensive is inevitably approaching and through individual acts has already begun. Failure to act must not be allowed to lead to the loss of all rights. Responsibility for the resulting world war and its victims clearly lies with that great power which systematically aims at the enslavement of the world. In order that this great power should realize its reponsibility, and at the same time in order that everything possible may be done to avoid war, we demand that it should first be called upon to desist from its unlawful activities; otherwise the nations as a whole would consider themselves forced to take action. When the official organ of the community of nations has expressed this warning and has forbidden further preparations for war, the great power concerned may, and unless it submits, must be considered and treated as an unjust aggressor. When and where pressure can be exerted and is likely to be successful, it must be used, for example by breaking off diplomatic relations, imposing economic sanctions etc.

14.28   To be permitted such war of liberation too must have prospects of success. Since the good and ill of all humanity is at stake, all States and groups of States are obliged to participate if necessary, and the organized community of nations has undoubtedly the right to impose this obligation. Real interdependence among the nations should form the most effective defence and be most likely to avert such a war of liberation. Power that tends to disrupt can only be kept in check by the threat and the readiness for defence of a bigger power.

14.29 (3.) Others, in direct opposition to the first opinion, quite definitely deny that a war of liberation of the kind mentioned could be legitimate; they consider it an unlawful war of aggression or a preventive war. They would argue that a war of this kind, an unjust aggression involves the deliberate murder of innumerable innocent persons on both sides. We may never kill or harm for preventive reasons, not even when we fear that we might be attacked at some later time and would not then be strong enough to withstand it. In such a case, there is only one way out, which is to be cautious and to invoke the protection of a higher authority.

14.30 Such a war of liberation cannot compensate for the frightful sacrifices which it entails, and its prospects of success are too slight. In other words, we do not know if the conflict will be brought to a victorious conclusion, and even if it is, then it would be only at the price of proportionately great losses; and finally, what goods and institutions worth defending will the equally dechristianized and materialistic "liberators" bring in their train?

14.31 The fate of mankind must be entrusted to God in an heroic attitude of endurance and hope. God can so arrange things that the totalitarian power will listen to reason and abandon its aggressive plans, that the situation will in one form or another radically change, that new weapons will be invented which will deter the aggressor from his purpose. In short, it is possible, but not inevitable that the aggression will take place.

EXTRACT 15

RAMSEY

The justice of nuclear deterrence

15.1 I have argued that the No-Cities or Counterforce plus Avoidance (of civilian damage) policy is the only just and sensible way to conduct war; that weapons analysts have sometimes overlooked the distinction between the unthinkable that has simply not yet been thought and the unthinkable that is un-do-able when thought about; that war as a trial of wills disconnected from trials of strength becomes an abysmal and unlimited conflict of resolutions; that current discussions of "general" war or "limited strategic war" need to distinguish more clearly between long-range attacks on strategic forces and strategic attacks on cities; and finally I advanced tentatively a gradation of policy decisions designed to set "firebreaks" between the steps in increasing violence, up to the No-Cities or strategic Counterforce policy. We need now to take up the moral and practical questions involved in "deterrence during the war", which at every stage seems necessary to keep war limited.

15.2   I shall argue that none of the virtues of the limiting policy decisions for which a case can be made, or of war considered only in the context of constant massive deterrence, can invalidate the distinction between the do-able and the politically un-do-able.

15.3   It is frequently contended that "both prudence and international law" permit and make it "desirable to carry out reprisals in kind," and that the only question remaining once an enemy strikes one of our cities is how to determine the equivalence to be exchanged moment by moment in countervalue war. Whatever may be the rule of reprisal in international law today, this can hardly be said to settle the question of the justice – the natural justice – of reprisal in kind (or in *some* kinds). If it is unjust for an enemy to destroy our society, the fact that he does or tries to do so first cannot make it any less of an injustice for us to destroy his... Such a law of reprisals can only be described as a product of an age of legal positivism where justice has become something men and nations "make." No wonder they suppose they can make "just" an act that before was "unjust," or unjust when *first* done. With no sense of the difference between the do-able and the intrinsically un-do-able, the nations may well agree that a certain weapon or plan of war should never be used, unless, of course, it is. That excuse must today be called radically into question.

15.4   It can be shown that the traditional limits upon the "just" conduct of war were a product not so much of man's sense of justice as of "social charity" determining, in crucial situations in which the use of force cannot be avoided, how force can be directed to the saving of human life. From this point of view from the point of view of concrete Christian charity even more than in the context of the natural justice surrounding killing in war, this so-called law of reprisal in kind, if it is proposed as a sovereign and all-embracing rule for conduct, must itself always be condemned. Pure reprisal between persons or between nations will appear especially heinous to a just or Christian man. Neither in inter-personal nor in international relations will a Christian accept the reduction of moral and political agency to this attempt to gain an empty victory of one will over another. Instead, if he is properly instructed and sensitive to the requirements of a love-informed justice, he is apt to call such punishing reprisal of will against will the very epitome of sin and of injustice.

15.5   The injustice of the law of reprisal is perhaps hidden from view in impure cases where actually *doing* the reprisal in kind seems clearly connected with accomplishing some definite purpose. In this way an almost self-enforcing system of diplomatic immunity is maintained, and restrictions are imposed upon the travel of Soviet citizens in this country roughly equivalent to those imposed upon American citizens travelling in Russia. Almost all the laws of war in the past have been enforced, to the extent that they have been enforced, by creating the expectation of reprisal in kind. The race toward increasing irreconcilability between actions of nation-states seems to be slowed down by *doing*, on occasion, the expected reprisal in kind, even if in itself the action has no reconciling power.

15.6   But then, it ought to be observed that many of these enforcements, which seem to warrant reprisal in kind, involve actions which are not *malum in se*. In a great many kinds of action the nations can "make" right what they want to, and enforce rules they agree to by reprisals in these kinds. What was not inherently wrong when first done but only legally proscribed, can be legitimately done in reprisal. The possibility of massive nuclear retaliation against the society of an enemy who struck first has made clear that the rule of reprisal in kind was never an all-embracing rule for the conduct of men or nations. *This* kind of reprisal can only be justified by a very immoral "moral" system, or by a positivism that seeks to "make" right in the second place what was ruled to be wrong in the first.

15.7   To the argument from justice and the argument from charity may now be added a third argument against ever *doing* the reprisal in kind that is now in question. Today the irrationality and purposelessness of pure punishment is laid bare, and the spiritualization of war into a contest of resolves is exposed as the most *abysmal* of all wars we could contemplate. One can still contemplate it, but it cannot be done except as an act that no longer has political purpose. Such reprisal would be a choiceless choice, an act without a definite end to be attained. For it can no longer be said that reprisal in kind – the kind we are speaking about – will "restore the balance when one belligerent uses illegal means," or defend freedom or civilization, or hold back from destruction any life worth living, or even that it will enforce a lower limit of warfare . . .

15.8   Any politically viable solution of the problem of war today requires that we finally employ a distinction between the *possibility* and the *certainty* of illimitable city destruction; and in deterrence during the war that we carefully discriminate between the *appearance* and the *actuality* of being partially or totally committed to go to city exchanges . . . A nation ought never to be totally committed to action that is so irrational it can never be done by free, present decision; and even to *appear* to be totally committed may itself be altogether too dangerous. A nation ought not to communicate to an enemy that it might go to city exchanges without at the same time communicating some doubt about it, if it wants both to remain and to seem to remain a free agent with still some control over its destiny and the course of world politics. The *appearance* of *partial* commitment, or the *appearance* of *possible* commitment, may be enough of a commitment to deter an enemy.

15.9   I would be willing to consider adding to the stages of military decision set down in the previous section yet one more. A statesman might consider ordering one of the enemy's cities to be struck after a warning allowing time for civilians to be evacuated. That would be an act of countervalue warfare in which human beings have not been economized; and there may be some argument for it to be found in the changed nature of much property today in comparison with the period when both civilian property and civilian lives were surrounded with moral immunity from direct attack. Whatever be the correct judgment of this possibility, the arguments against ever actually engaging in a war of nerves by means of populated cities cannot be withdrawn. Deterrence will have to be accomplished by the deterrent effect of the *possibility* and the *appearance* of the possibility that the sanction of city exchanges will be invoked, or not accomplished at all.

15.10   I propose, first, to discuss the moral issues in preserving such a national posture, and to conclude with some remarks upon technical questions concerning the feasibility of limiting war under the deterrence of a possibility we do not intend to carry out. In approaching the moral issues involved in appearing to be willing to do something that is wrong, I shall make use of a volume of essays by British Roman Catholics (Walter Stein. ed.: *Nuclear Weapons and Christian Conscience*, London: Marlin Press, 1961) who follow the anatomy of the just war doctrine to a conclusion altogether different from mine, namely, nuclear pacifism.

15.11 It is never right to do wrong that good may come of it. Nuclear weapons have only added to this perennial truth the footnote: it can never do *any good* to do wrong that good may come of it. Neither is it right to *intend* to do wrong that good may come of it. If deterrence rests upon intending massive retaliatation it is clearly wrong no matter how much peace results. If weapons systems deter city exchanges only because and so far as they are intended to be used against cities, then deterrence involves a "conditional willingness" to do evil, and evil on a massive scale. Granting that deterrence deters before or during the war, and that it supports peace or the control of war, that alone cannot justify it. It would be justified "if, and only if, in employing this threat, we were not involved in . . . *immoral hypothetical decisions.*" The distinction between murder and killing in war, or between directly killing combatants and directly murdering non-combatants, posits an ethico-political principle that can only be violated, never abrogated. "Nothing, not even the alleged interests of peace, can save murderousness from evil", and nothing, not even the alleged interest in deterrence during war for the control of war can save the *intention* to commit murder from being evil. Does reliance on nuclear weapons for deterrence hypothetically commit us, here and now, to murder, there and then? If so, such deterrence is wrong, and can never be anything but wickedness. This conclusion would seem to follow from the comparatively simple moral truth that "if an action is morally wrong, it is wrong to intend to do it."

15.12 This is surely a correct "finding" as to the moral law. The authors of these chapters, however, intermix with this a certain "finding of fact" which may be questioned. They assert that "deterrence *rests*, in the end, on the intention to use nuclear weapons," not that in some or many of its forms it *may* or *might* rest on either present murderous intention or on a "conditional willingness" to do murder. No wonder the conclusion follows: if this is the case, deterrence "cannot but be morally repugnant for the same ultimate reason as is the use of the weapon held in reserve." The following statement of the case is a better one, and by accenting the first word the fact to be questioned can be stressed: "*If,* then, we find that 'having' nuclear weapons involves intending to explode them over predominantly civilian targets, no more need be said; this intention is criminal, just as the action is criminal." This is the matter of fact that needs to be determined – whether it *is* so, and must or should remain so if it is now the case – before we can know how the moral prohibition of intending to do wrong is to be applied in an assessment of deterrence policy.

15.13   The authors of these essays systematically fail to show that there can be no deterrent effect where there is no intention to use nuclear weapons. They underrate what is pejoratively called "the argument from bluff," while admitting that if this deterred and if this is what deters there would not be an implied "conditional commitment to total war"...

15.14   The technical possibility of deterrence before and during war can now be indicated, as can its compatibility with the moral prohibition of both the use and the intention to use nuclear (or any other) weapons in direct attacks on centers of population.

15.15   (1.) The collateral civilian damage that would result from counterforces warfare in its maximum form may itself be quite sufficient to deter either side from going too high and to preserve the rules and tacit agreements limiting conflict in a nuclear age. In that case, deterrence during the war and collateral civilian damage are both "indirect effects" of a plan and action of war which would be licit or permitted by the traditional rules of civilized conduct in war. To say that counterforce strikes over an enemy's own territory are licit or permitted is to say that one can morally intend and be "conditionally willing" to engage in such a war. Whether one positively should ever do so depends on the conditions. Collateral civilian damage is certainly an unavoidable indirect effect and, in the technical sense, an 'unintended' result of something a nation may and should make itself conditionally willing and ready to do. The deterrent effect, of which we are now speaking, is then, as it were, an indirect effect of the foreseeable indirect effects of legitimate military conduct.

15.16   One can certainly "intend" to deter in this fashion, and oneself be similarly deterred. Not knowing the tyrannies future history may produce one cannot say whether the one effect of successful resistance to them will justify the direct and the indirect costs. Still we foreknow that these costs may be very great indeed. This is to say that, at least to a very great degree, perhaps a sufficient degree, nuclear warfare is a design for war that is inherently self-limiting upon rational decision-makers without their having to intend to use these weapons directly to murder cities and civilians.

15.17   This is not at all a matter of "double-think about double effect." To justify "possession" for the sake of deterrence one does not have to invent possibly legitimate uses for nuclear weapons, such as their use against a ship at sea. Many a military installation in the nuclear age is fifty or more miles in diameter.

15.18   (2.) In respect to the nature of the weapons we possess, there are two possible uses which cannot be removed. The dual use the weapons themselves have – the fact that they may be used either against strategic forces or against centers of population – means that *apart from intention* their capacity to deter cannot be removed from them. This means that there may be sufficient deterrence in the subjectively unintended consequence of the mere possession of these weapons. No matter how often we declare, and quite sincerely declare, that our targets are an enemy's forces, he can never be quite *certain* that in the fury or in the fog of war his cities may not be destroyed.

15.19   This is so certainly the case that the problem of how to deter an enemy from striking our cities ought not for one moment to impede the shift to a counterforces policy and to the actual intention to use nuclear weapons only against forces. We should declare again and again, and give evidence by what we do, that our targets are his forces rather than his cities. Since it is morally repugnant to wage war without renouncing morally repugnant means, this should be speedily done, and communicated as effectively as possible to the enemy. Still, without any hesitation or ambiguity on our part, the weapons themselves will continue to have deterrent effect because they have ambiguous uses. They always *may* be used over cities; and no enemy can *know* that this will not be done.

15.20   Similar conclusions can be reached from an analysis of the "familiar spiral of reciprocal expectations" which is an important aspect of war in the nuclear age. This spiral not only threatens to be illimitable, but it serves as a built-in dampener, which no deliberate policy nor any intention can remove. This is the truth in T.C. Schelling's contention that in the nuclear age all forms of limited war raise the risk of general war, whether intended or not. The point here is not the "threat" of general war because of some technical or human failure or some mistaken calculation. The point is rather that in a nuclear age all war raises a risk of general war by an apparent *possibility* of a *politically irreversible trend.* War creates this risk which we share with the Russians. They can never "be confident that even the lack of resolution sometimes attributed to the United States could guarantee that general war would not result." "It is our sheer inability to predict the consequences of our actions and to keep things under control, and the enemy's similar inability [or our reciprocal doubt whether the other is in control], that can intimidate the enemy," and ourselves...

15.21   (3.) Only now do we come again to the suggestion that the distinction between the *appearance* and the *actuality* of being partially or totally committed to go to city exchanges may have to be employed in deterrence policy. In that case, only the appearance should be cultivated. If the first two points above do not seem to the military analyst sufficiently persuasive, *or able to be made so,* then an *apparent* resolution to wage war irrationally or at least an *ambiguity* about our intentions may have to be our expressed policy. This is a matter, not of the nature of the weapons themselves, but of the manner in which we possess them – the "having" of them that is necessary for deterrence during justifiably conducted war.

15.22 The moralist can certainly say to the decision-maker that it can never be right for him to do such a thing as attack an enemy's society, or for him actually to intend to do so, or under any conditions to be willing to match his resolution against that of the enemy by means of populated cities. He can point out to the statesman that it can never be right for him to contrive to "make" the un-do-able intention irrevocable, or to have the intention of doing so. He can even point out where the military analyst will be found saying the same thing about the irrationality of total committal to an irrational act of war, or even of appearing quite unambiguously to be totally and irreversibly committed.

15.23 But the moralist must be careful how he rushes in with his ethico-political principles mixed with an assortment of findings of fact and various arguments *ad horrendum*. He must be careful how he spells out his *moral* guidance for deterrence policy. For, on a sound solution of this problem the security of free societies may well depend in a nuclear age which is also an age of "megacorpses," "deracination from humanity," and of "unparalleled moral landslide." The moralist must be careful how he disparages the so-called "argument from bluff" to a morally licit form of deterrence; and he should examine whether the reasons *he* uses to dismiss this argument are telling *moral* ones or rather technical judgments he has gathered to fulfill a prejudice . . .

15.24 To say and to act as if we might go to city exchanges is certainly a form of deception. But, if this can be done without intending to make irrational immoral use of nuclear weapons, and even with the intention that our weapons be not so used and with the intention of revoking what had never even the appearance of total committal, such deception cannot be said to be based on the criminal intention or conditional willingness to do murder. The first thing to be said then, is that the intention to deceive is certainly a far cry from the intention to murder society, or to commit mutual homicide . . .

15.25   The military and political analysts I have consulted do *not* reject as infeasible the sort of "possession" of nuclear weapons for deterrence which we are now discussing. If it is thought to be infeasible now, then the "system" may have to be studied and perfected so that it can be done. For this may be one of those customarily "unthinkable" things which, the more you think about it, will prove to be technically and politically "do-able." If needed, it should be developed in many a scenario. It is on balance, I believe, morally "do-able," as city-busting is not, however much you think about it. Whether this ingredient in deterrence can be adopted and exercised by a democratic society is, of course, a serious question. It requires of a people a mature "ethic of restraint, limits and silence," not moral protest always, much less punitive fury or he-man morality; and a reliance on the morality and rationality of their political leaders not to be expected or (on any policy decision not so crucial) desired in a free society. For this reason, if for no other, all our attention and intention should doubtless be directed toward adopting, declaring and implementing a policy of counter-forces warfare, with the deterrence that policy affords. This is the doctrine which should form the consciences of free men today; and if their consciences are thus formed, it may then be possible to add to counter-force policy this last type of non-murderous deterrence.

15.26   Then it may be possible to put, not nuclear weapons as such, but the inter-city use of nuclear weapons into a category by itself, so that, while the capability still exists, the intention to attack cities will recede into the background so far as not to have actuality. Things as strange have happened before in the history of warfare. Tribes living close to death in the desert have fought cruel wars. They even used poisoned arrows, and certainly to a limited extent they fought one another by means of direct attack upon women and children. But they knew *not to poison wells*! That would have been a policy of mutual homicide, and a form of society-*contra*-society warfare that would have removed the possibility of any more bloody cruel wars, not to mention peacetime pursuits. In refraining from massive well-poisoning, or in keeping that ambiguous, did these tribes, in any valid or censorable sense of the word, still "intend" to poison wells?

EXTRACT 16

UNITED REFORMED CHURCH

Christians and non-violent action

16.1   Most people find it impossible to imagine how a non-violent resistance or non-violent attack would be organized by a government, and then go on to make the erroneous deduction that because they cannot imagine it, it therefore cannot be done. The same people would find it equally impossible to imagine the strategy in any future war fought by violent means, but that does not prove that a workable strategy for future wars does not exist.
But however difficult it is to imagine an alternative to violent struggle, we need an alternative to war for three reasons.

16.2   (a) Violence is now so violent it defeats its own purpose. It may have been possible in the past to win a war in some understandable sense of the word 'win', but not now. Soldiers see this. Thus General Eisenhower said: 'War in our time has become an anachronism. Whatever the case in the past, war in the future can serve no useful purpose.' Marshal of the RAF Sir John Slessor said: 'A world war in this day and age would be general suicide and the end of civilisation as we know it.' A third quotation is particularly apposite. 'Men are not looking for an alternative to a method which is still reasonably serviceable, but for an alternative to a method which has, in fact broken down. Civilization is not in the position of a man whose car is still going reasonably well, but just fancies a change. It is in the position of the man whose car has broken down beyond repair and who, for business reasons, must quickly buy another' (Ralph Bell, *Alternative to War*).

16.3   (b) Modern methods of warfare are increasingly unacceptable to the Christian conscience. The World Council of Churches report, *Christians and the Prevention of War in an Atomic Age* is clear on this.

'Although there are differences of opinion on many points, we are agreed on one point. This is that Christians have no alternative but openly to declare that the all-out use of these weapons (nuclear weapons) should never be resorted to. Moreover, we believe that Christians must oppose all policies which give evidence of leading to all-out war. Finally (although we would answer "No") we ask: "If all-out war should occur, does a Christian have any alternative but to accept a cease-fire, if necessary on the enemy's terms, and resort to non-violent resistance?" We purposely refrain from defining the stage at which all-out war may be reached.'

If Christians are to accept a cease-fire and resort to non-violent action, then the church needs to give time and effort to thinking out what non-violent resistance is and how it can be organized.

16.4   (c) But however inexpedient and immoral war may be, it will continue to be used because it is the only method we have at the present time of resolving certain crises which can and do arise in human affairs. Not all disputes can be deterred away or reconciled away. If your ultimate sanction is war when there is no possibility of a diplomatic solution to a dispute and you are faced with the choice – fight or submit to injustice – then you will end up fighting another war, because the sort of crises which have led to war in the past are certain to arise again in the future. We recognize that war is a method which can be abolished only if an alternative method is put in its place, and that wars and violent revolutions will continue to take place unless non-violent methods are discovered of fighting them out. The choice is between violent methods and non-violent methods – it is not an acceptable answer to say you don't like either – that you find violent methods immoral and non-violent methods impractical. A few may contract out, but the vast majority of men cannot do so, and certainly governments have to make a choice.

16.5 We also recognize that until an alternative to war is found, perparation for war will continue to take place, however much many may deplore it, and that there is every chance that in future wars it will be found expedient to use the most horrific of weapons. We are in a most dangerous position. But there is no hope of any sensible measure of disarmament until an alternative method of fighting is accepted. Those who negotiate at disarmament conferences are in the main men who honestly believe that their security and their ability to negotiate successfully (and therefore their ability to avert war) depend on the possession of more force than the other side and their ability to negotiate easily depends on possessing overwhelming force. As men on both sides believe that, it is highly unlikely that they will voluntarily consent to reduce the security in which they believe. Statesmen will not disarm before they can see another way of tackling their problem.

16.6 The problem is difficult but urgent. It is not our problem only, but the problem of the whole church. Can we believe that in the providence of God a method of resolving our crises and fighting our revolutions, which is both politically expedient and in agreement with the spirit and teaching of Jesus Christ, must exist, and that we are being called in this generation to find it?

16.7 Armed international conflict has involved action of three kinds – aggression, defence and intervention. Often there has been an element of all three in the same action:

in a power-conflict it is not easy to distinguish defence from aggression, and intervention in a third-party situation may be a cover for both.

16.8   (a) Aggression is ruled out for the Christian. Even those who have claimed that war may in certain circumstances be just have never allowed this of aggressive war. We are not therefore here concerned with the possibility of non-violent aggressive action, except in so far as the action involved (as opposed to the motivation) is indistinguishable from the action involved in defence or intervention.

16.9   (b) Action for defence is the most obvious field for non-violence. Such action is unlikely to prevent invasion, though even the most hardened invader is likely to be dismayed by the spectacle of waves of defenders ready to die but not to kill. It is to be insisted, time and again, that non-violent action will involve casualties, and heavy casualites, though they are never likely to be quite as heavy as those arising from violent action.

16.10   But the basic action of non-violent defence lies through various forms of non-co-operation: it is in fact no different from the action directed to non-violent social and political change [e.g. strikes, boycotts, civil disobedience etc.].

16.11   (c) The graver problems lie in intervening action: e.g. in resisting the Nazis before Britain is actually attacked, whether as anticipating a defence which must sooner or later be offered, or as responding to an unjust assault on Poland, or, even earlier, as revolutionary action against an immoral regime.

16.12   (i) It is doubtful whether one nation-state should intervene to overthrow the government of another: as long as nation-states remain, the precedents are dangerous. On the other hand concerned individuals and groups could properly dedicate themselves to changing an unjust regime; their methods will once again be those [in (b) above].

16.13   (ii) Plainly the more that can be done by international action the better: it is important that the world community recognizes a practical responsibility for righting injustice wherever it may be. Such action is better taken, when possible, by an international force than by a single nation.

16.14 (iii) The main non-violent weapon at present available is the severing of political, social and economic relationships. The sooner that the world community is such that severance of this kind (boycott, sanctions etc.) is a serious disability, the better.

16.15 (iv) Some of us have seen in addition the need for a strategy of pre-emptive non-violent strike, a *Blitzfreude*, the counterpart of *Blitzkrieg*. This would imply the use of non-violent invading forces in such numbers that it was impossible to hold them all in prison. Their action on landing would be to practise, and, more particularly, to foster civil disobedience. Not even a dictatorship can continue to function if a sufficient number of its citizens refuse to obey its orders . . .

16.16 The strategies of non-violent action will require long, careful and expert planning. Traditional wars have demanded the teamwork of considerable numbers of able and experienced staff officers trained for long periods and planning in advance to meet all manner of contingencies. Even so there is need for prompt response to unexpected developments, and no commander would predict all the action of a future war. Non-violent direct action will require no less careful planning, and no less expertise. The outlines which we have drawn will need working out in detail by experts.

16.17 In addition there are situations which are seemingly intractable to human wisdom. We do not 'have all the answers', any more than anyone else. It is at least a partial answer to the question 'How would you defend Hong Kong by non-violent means?' to ask the counter-question 'How would you defend Hong Kong by violent means?'

16.18 It is not easy to predict what would have happened had there been systematic non-violent resistance to the Nazis. The 1939 war was nominally fought in defence of Poland. It is not obvious that Poland is now freer. It did not save the Jews: the great massacres took place after war had broken out and under the stresses of war. It certainly checked the Nazis. But it did so at the cost of something between 25 and 50 million dead, a continent in ruins, a world divided into armed blocs, a legacy of starvation, crimes of violence, hatred, and, over the world, a habituation to war. If it is not obvious that non-violent acion would have had better results, it is equally not obvious that non-violent action would have had worse results.

16.19   We as Christians believe that because this is God's world, evil in it is by its nature unstable. Our task is to co-operate actively and constructively with the forces of good. We cannot always predict the results. We act by faith in God's power, not in our own cleverness...

16.20   It will already be plain that there is a variety of situations in which non-violent methods may be applicable, and that application of non-violent action within them will not be identical. For general purposes we may here identify five different types of situation:

(a) A nation confronted with invasion.

(b) A revolutionary situation in which the oppressed are challenging the oppressors.

(c) The same situation, in which an outside group seeks to intervene on the side of the oppressed.

(d) The resistance of lawfully constituted authority to a violent disaffected group.

(e) A conflict-situation in which there is need of outside mediation and peace-keeping operations.

16.21   Our first general proposal will no doubt seem surprising at first sight. It is for the training of the army in the attitudes, techniques and practice of non-violent action.

16.22   We have become increasingly aware of the need for a standing force trained in and disciplined to non-violence. In so far as the non-violent approach is valid, such a standing force is necessary to (a), (d) and (e) above, and perhaps to (c) where the outside group seeking to intervene is a nation-state. The army is by far the most obvious source of such a standing force.

16.23   This means that the army must get away from its
primary dependence on the rifle: the rifle must become an
instrument of the last resort, not the first resort. It means
educating the officers and the command structure in new
ways of thinking. It means a new kind of discipline,
greater not less, but sensible and sensitive, not 'Prussian';
it means that the soldier must continue to be trained to
unswerving obedience but must at the same time be
trained in responsible participation, must be ready to
operate on his own, must be prepared to practise an
exacting discipline. It means adding to army training, as
already indicated, conflict-analysis and other aspects of
social studies.

16.24   Alongside this we believe that it would be useful to
train as reservists a special force of civilians for non-
violent peacekeeping operations . . .

16.25   If the Christian churches take seriously the Christian
commitment to social justice they will forthwith sponsor
non-violent training-schools for political activists. Such
training would enable a more effective stand to be made
against injustice in this country; it would strengthen the
work of protest, whether against apartheid or nuclear
tests or war and violence in other parts of the world; it
might be of particular significance for concerned groups
working in Northern Ireland or Southern Africa. Training in non-violent action could well form an important
part of the churches' youth work.

16.26   Non-violent training of this sort should also be made
available through the churches to exiled African leaders
from white-dominated parts of Africa. Here (and indeed
elsewhere) it is important that the training should not
merely be training in non-violent action, but also training
in training for non-violent action.

16.27   It is important to see that successful non-violent action
is likely to need, if it does not absolutely depend on, the
following factors:

(a) A strongly committed and disciplined central
group.

(b) A substantial body of committed and disciplined

followers: the movement must not fall apart if the leaders are shot or imprisoned; there must always be a stream of volunteers to take the place of those who are eliminated.

(c) General support and sympathy from wide sections of the community . . .

16.28   Those who choose non-violence must not expect easy success or light casualties. Those who choose the way of war do not surrender after a single defeat or even a succession of defeats; those who choose non-violence must not feel that their campaign is a failure because it is not an immediate success. Persistence and patience are Christian virtues of essential importance to the practice of non-violence. Rondon's men, wedded to non-violence, had to pass through massacre to victory. Casualties in a non-violent campaign need not be less – on our side – than casualties in a campaign of violence. This is in accordance with our understanding of the way of the Cross. The blood of Christians is seed. It is through Good Friday that we pass to Easter.

16.29   And innocent people, and people who have not willed the way of non-violent resistance, will suffer. This is part of our human condition, that there is a solidarity of suffering; it is expressed in the New Testament in that the Incarnation had among its consequences the Massacre of the Innocents. The same is true of war. The bombs which fell on Coventry or Dresden or Hiroshima did not distinguish between guilty and innocent, sinners and saints, militarists and pacifists, adults and children. But in non-violent action we may expect a higher proportion of casualties to be among the volunteers. And though we may suffer Coventrys we shall not inflict Dresdens.

EXTRACT 17

BONINO

Liberation theology and peace

17.1   The ideas of confrontation, struggle, and violence seem particularly repugnant to the Christian conscience.

Before dealing with the area of ethical questions we must, nevertheless, dwell briefly on the concept of class. The phenomenon of classes in society is analyzed by Marx in relation to the way in which people relate to the productive process, particularly in the capitalist form of organizing production. It is well known that Marx finds the main distinction hinging on whether a man owns the means of production of whether he has to sell his labor to those who own them, i.e., the capitalist and the proletarian. Marx and his followers are, of course, aware that this particular configuration of classes is dependent on the existing forms of the capitalist economy, and therefore cannot be projected back to other societies. Moreover, they are aware that even in the capitalist industrial societies several forms of production and consequently different forms of social organization coexist and therefore that there are groups and segments of society that do not fit neatly into this dominant pattern. One could add that tribal societies in Africa or ethnic groups in Latin America as well as changes in the structure of capitalist production pose complex problems which may require rethinking certain elements in the Marxist conception of class. Both Marxist and non-Marxist sociologists are aware of these questions and there is at present a very significant literature dealing with the problem. There is no need for us to belabor this point. We are here dealing with the always provisional results of a scientific investigation. As such, a Christian need not accept it or question it except in terms of its scientific verifiability.

17.2   There are, nevertheless, two theological questions which deserve to be mentioned. The first has to do with Marx's point of departure (whether itself a result of his scientific analysis or not is at this point a moot question), namely, that man is to be basically and radically understood as a worker, as the being who appropriates, transforms, and humanizes the world through his work and who himself comes to his own identity, becomes man through this same work. If this is so, it is only to be expected that the forms of relationships and organizations in which man works will be the privileged means for understanding human life and society and that changes in one area will be closely related to changes in the other. Christian anthropology, on the other hand, has traditionally sought to understand man in terms of his intellectual, moral, and spiritual endowment or, in a more dynamic way, in terms of his relations to himself (self-understanding), to his neighbor, and to God. The theological understanding of man, therefore, has been predominantly – if not exclusively – philosophical, cultural, and religious. To such an approach, Marxist anthropology naturally smacks of materialism. Such an accusation is very widespread in Christian circles. But one may wonder whether it does not rest on a twofold misunderstanding. On the one hand, it reads Marx in terms of a mechanistic determinism which would see the spiritual life of man as a mere reflex of material conditions. There is no doubt that some Marxist thinkers, and particularly many popularizers, have amply justified such interpretation. In Marx himself, and in the best contemporary interpreters, the dialectical relations of material and cultural conditionings are much more subtly and carefully assessed. It may, nevertheless, be necessary to challenge and correct even more drastically Marx's conception at this point. I am, at the same time, more concerned with the other misunderstanding: the theological substitution of an idealist for the biblical understanding of man. Whether one deals with the creation stories, with the law, or with the prophetic message, there seems to be in the Bible no relation of man to himself, to his neighbor, or even to God which is not mediated in terms of man's *work*. His dignity is located in his mission to subdue and cultivate the world. His worship is related to the fulfillment of a law in which the whole realm of his economic and political activity is taken up (and not to an image or idol in which he could find a private and direct access to the deity) . . .

17.3   Marxism has understood the alienated character of work in our capitalist society, in which man is estranged from his work; work is objectified as something alien to him and bought through a salary. There is a striking similarity between this view and the Pauline rejection of "the works of the law" in which man's actions are also objectified as something "valuable in themselves," apart from the doer and the neighbor, as a "work" which can be merchandised in order to buy "justification." The work of faith, on the other hand, is never objectified – it is the believer himself in action in terms of love. The Christian will, therefore, understand and fully join the Marxist protest against the capitalist demonic circle of work-commodity-salary. But out of the justification by faith alone, he will have to ask whether alienation does not have deeper roots than the distortions of the capitalist society, even in the mysterious original alienation, in man's denial of his humanity (his attempt to know outside the relation of trust and work) which we call sin. This question, nevertheless, can only be asked in the context of a service (a *leitourgeia*, an *abodah*, a service, and a work which are at the same time worship) freely rendered, a work done "out of faith", outside the realm of worth and reward, in the anticipation of the realm of creative love which is the Kingdom!

17.4   If the biblical view of man's humanity as realized in work is recovered, and at the same time we are aware of the distortion introduced by sin into the life of society, the existence of classes and their conflict emerges as a possible major category for our understanding of history; a possible one, I say, because we must be concerned here with empirical observation and its interpretation and not with a philosophical or theological axiom. "Class" is a sociological concept and must be verified as such. All we have tried to indicate in the preceding pages is that the view of man which emerges in the Marxist discussion of class – namely, man as worker – is also fundamental for biblical anthropology. Another significant element appears in relation to the discussion of class: the biblical concept of "the poor." A number of studies have appeared recently, particularly in connection with the emphasis in Roman Catholic circles on "a Church of the poor." The result of biblical research on this point is aptly summarized by Gustavo Gutiérrez. The notion of poverty in the Scriptures is an ambivalent one. On the one hand it designates the weak, the destitute, the oppressed, and is as such "a scandalous situation" which must be redressed. On the other hand it indicates "spiritual childhood," humility before God, and as such it is a – perhaps *the* – basic virtue...

17.5   Now, is there a transition from the biblical idea of the poor to the Marxist view of an oppressed class? Can the Christian call to solidarity with the poor and the revolutionary convocation to class struggle be equated? There seems to be both a genuine and sound discernment but also some dangerous misunderstandings and short-cutting in these indentifications. As to the first, there seems to be no serious possibility to argue on biblical and theological grounds against Karl Barth's dictum: "God always takes his stand unconditionally and passionately on this side and on this side alone: against the lofty and on behalf of the lowly..." The misunderstandings arise from an insufficient recognition of the necessary analytical mediations between the Marxist category of the "proletarian class" and the biblical one of "the poor." This latter one – insofar as it refers to the oppressed and disinherited – is a pre-scientific, simply empirical designation arising out of direct observation of a situation of oppression and injustice. When Christians in Latin America (or elsewhere) denounce the hard and moving realities of hunger, unemployment, premature death, exploitation, repression, and torture, they are - as Old Testament prophets – moving at the level of empirical observation and ethical and religious (quite justified) judgment. This is no doubt also present, although in a humanist form, in Marxism. A revolutionary theory, nevertheless, moves at least two steps further: (1) It purports to give a rational, verifiable, and coherent account of the causes, dynamics, and direction of the process and (2) it offers a correspondingly rational, calculated, organized, and verifiable strategy for overcoming the present situation. We have already noted that the theory must be constantly checked and corrected. But, quite apart from these corrections, its existence poses theological questions which we dare not evade if we aim to overcome mere good will and irrelevant generosity.

17.6   One theological issue which claims our attention in this respect is the question of efficacious love. Two points need to be mentioned briefly. The first is that the commandment of love must evidently be read in the context of Jesus' proclamation of the Kingdom of God. It cannot, therefore, be reduced to a purely interpersonal or intersubjective dimension, but must be set in relation to the eschatological and cosmic scope of the Kingdom. This means that love is inextricably interwoven with hope and justice. The second point follows. Love is not exhausted in the area of intentionality and demonstration but it is other-directed and demands efficacy. It is not content to express and demonstrate, it intends to accomplish . . .

17.7   A second theological issue that needs to be clarified is the background of the concept of peace as it is commonly used and the problem of violence. At the risk of oversimplification, I want to sketch the two theological perspectives which seem to me to find expression in the current discussion of these issues. One of them is built on the principle of the rationality of the universe – the conviction that a universal order penetrates the world. Heaven and earth, nature and society, moral and spiritual life seek the equilibrium that corresponds to their rational place, and the preservation of this order is the supreme value. Whatever perturbs it becomes "a trampling of reason." In its most crass form, this concept simply becomes an ideological screen (to use Ricoeur's expression) to hide the injustice of the status quo by identifying it with cosmic rationality. Violence is understood in the light of this order: whatever disturbs it is irrational and evil and ought to be countered through a rational use of coercion. This logic, undoubtedly plagued with fallacies, nevertheless, flourishes in the "Christian" rhetoric of the right. The will of God coincides with the ordering of things, which in turn coincides with the present order, threatened by "the violent ones." To resist the threat is to obey God.

17.8   This is not the place to engage in a detailed analysis of this theological point of view. It can, of course, be formulated in a more guarded way, avoiding a direct identification of the rational order of things with the existing one and positing a normative order – such as the concept of a natural law in its various older and newer forms – which can even justify a certain "subversive violence." Nevertheless, the question remains as to the historical roots of both the idea and the content of such natural law. As to the former, it seems to me possible to trace it to the philosophical rationalization of a mythology of the "cosmos" which in turn sacralizes a static and stratified society. As to the contents of such natural law, it has often been noted that it reproduces some set of historical conditions – whether of the past or of the present. The historically undeniable fact that this theological perspective came to dominate Christianity at the time when this latter was co-opted as the religious undergirding and sanction of the empire is in itself a very significant comment.

17.9   The other perspective conceives man as a project of liberation that constantly emerges in the fight against the objectifications given in nature, in history, in society, in religion. Man is a creator, and creation is always, in some measure, a violence exerted on things as they are. It is an affirmation of the new against "that which is"; it is an eruption that can only make room for itself by exploding the existing systems of integration. Violence plays a creative role in this scheme as the "midwife" (even though I don't think that Marx's famous dictum can be totally interpreted in this perspective). This conception can also be escalated to the extreme, elevating violence as an ultimate principle of cration, valid in itself because it is, par excellence, the destruction of all objectifications. Only in the destruction of everything that limits him – nature, social order, ethical norm, divinity – can man find his freedom, i.e., his humanity. But even without looking for these extreme formulations, it is possible to conceive history as a dialectic in which the negation through which the new can emerge implies always a certain measure of violence.

17.10   As theological positions, both perspectives find support in the biblical and ecclesiastical tradition. They are frequently identified respectively with the priestly and prophetic streams and it would not be difficult to trace both currents in the history of Christian theology. They have given rise to two different understandings of peace which deserve mention in connection with our subject. The first one equates peace with order, lack of conflict, harmonious integration – one would almost say "ecological balance in nature and society." The German theologian Hans P. Schmidt finds its roots in the Babylonian myth of society as a living organism and thinks that it finds expression in the wisdom tradition in the Bible. It dominates the Graeco-Roman conception of peace and has shaped the theological tradition since Augustine. The other view of peace is typically represented by the prophets but can be shown, I think, to be the predominant one in the Bible. Peace is a dynamic process through which justice is established amid the tensions of history. The Catholic Latin American Conference of bishops at Medellin (1968) has summarized well this view of peace as a work of justice, an ever renewed task, and a fruit of active love. It is quite evident that the possibility of conflict will be differently viewed in these two conceptions. For the first it will be in itself negative, a rupture in harmony; for the second it may be a positive manifestation of the situation which requires righting. Violence in the more specific sense of physical compulsion or destruction may be accepted or rejected in either of the two views, but acceptance or rejection will be viewed in a different way. In the first it will be judged in terms of order; in the second, in terms of the struggle for justice.

17.11   Recent discussions tend to be polarized along these two theological traditions. While I think that they represent significant dimensions of Christian thought, I want to suggest that their approach is seriously distorted and needs correction. In making order and rationality on the one hand or freedom and conflict on the other the basic starting points for theological refection, they miss, I think, the biblical starting point, which is never an abstract notion or principle, but a concrete situation. The Bible does not conceive man and society as a function of reason or freedom but in concrete historical relations of man-things-God. Even if we try to understand the basic biblical notions of justice, mercy, faithfulness, truth, peace, we are always thrown back to concrete stories, laws, invitations, commandments; they are defined as an announced action or commandment of God in a given historical situation. This does not mean, to be sure, that these words are empty sounds covering a number of capricious and heterogeneous events but it does mean that ethical criteria are not defined a-temporally but in relation to the concrete conditions of existence of men historically located. These facts taken together do represent a direction – the Kingdom of God – in terms of which one may speak of worthy or unworthy actions. But this direction cannot be translated into a universal principle – reason, order, liberty, conflict.

17.12   Against this background, violence appears in the Bible, not as a general form of human conduct which has to be accepted or rejected as such, but as an element of God's announcement-commandment, as concrete acts which must be carried out or avoided in view of a result, or a relation, of a project indicated by the announcement-commandment. Thus, the law forbids certain forms of violence to persons and things and authorizes and even commands others. There are wars that are commanded – even against Israel – and wars that are forbidden – even on behalf of Israel. If one tries to find some coherence in these indications, a first and simple formulation might be that the invitation to exercise or renounce conflict and violence tends to open the space in which men (concretely as foreigner, widow, orphan, poor, family) can be and do, on earth, that which belongs to their particular humanity. In general, it seems possible to say that conflict and violence are means to break out of conditions (slavery, vengeance, arbitrariness, oppression, lack of protection, usurpation) that leave a man, a group of people, or a people unable to be and act as a responsible agent ("as a partner in the covenant") in relation to the others, to things, to God. If this is so, it will not be surprising that, in general terms, peace is preferable to hostility, generosity to vindictiveness, production to destruction, trust and harmony to threat and fear. At this point, the idea of order and rationality has its significant place in Christian reflection. But, given the conditions in which – according to Scripture – human life develops, it is also not surprising that God's announcement-commandment comes almost always as a call to the creation of a new situation, to a transformation and righting of the status quo. This is the priority to which the insistence on liberation legitimately points. Nevertheless, liberation and order, conflict and integration are not conceptual keys for a philosophy of history but heuristic elements for a reflection on God's Word in a given historical situation. They are not, moreover, symmetrical elements; the biblical perspective, centered in the person and work of Jesus Christ, always incorporates order, rationality, preservation in a dynamics of transformation and not the reverse.

17.13   If we try to bring together the two theological themes developed in the last pages – efficacious love and the conditions of peace and conflict – in order to return to our specific problem of class struggle, we can say that this question cannot be debated abstractly, but in relation to God's accouncement-commandment in Jesus Christ of a new man and a new humanity which must be witnessed to and proleptically anticipated in history.

EXTRACT 18

GREGORIOS

Nuclear war and human life

18.1   The Sixth Assembly of the World Council of Churches has good reasons to choose as its theme: "Jesus Christ – the Life of the World." We live in a world where life itself is imperilled; not only human life, but all life.

18.2   The four perils that face life can be summarized as follows:

(1.) *The nuclear peril*: A holocaust, or burnt offering, of practically the whole earth, has been a distinct possibility for humanity, for the past twenty years or more. We can be grateful that we have actually refrained from burning the planet up in the last twenty years. But we can do so any time, by the pressing of one or more buttons. There may be human and animal survivors immediately after a nuclear war. But whether they or their progeny can survive for very long in a radiation-filled biosphere seems in doubt. Even the peaceful use of nuclear energy poses hazards to life on our planet.

18.3   (2.) *The peril of biotechnology*: This is difficult to assess. Some five years ago, the biological community in the West took the initiative to express public alarm about the possible disastrous consequences of new biotechnology.

18.4   The DNA molecule, the basic component of genes, had been decoded. There was hope that particular characteristics of an organism could be located in particular genes or their components. This hope has now receded. But the new technology of gene-splicing, or putting together differing elements of different genes, raises the possibility that human personal and social characteristics can be altered by genetic manipulation. The possibility can also be conceived of creating new breeds of monsters by splicing genes. Experts spoke about the possibility of creating crosses between humans and, say, gorillas, in order to create a new breed of semi-humans who could be conscripted to do docile mechanical labour without the risk of their organizing themselves into trade unions, demanding their rights or going on strike.

18.5   Fear was expressed that new micro-organisms, developed in the research laboratory, may escape by accident into the biosphere, and cause diseases in humans and other animals and plants, diseases against which they had no immunity.

18.6   It is now an established fact that highly poisonous micro-organisms have been developed through biotechnology, and stored by the great powers as a possible weapon to be used in war. The international convention against biological weapons forbids their use, but not their manufacture or stockpiling.

18.7   Despite recent assurances from the biological community that safe-guards against the bio-peril are adequate, the general public remains unassured and insecure. They have learned from experience that the previous assurances of experts about the adequacy of safeguards against the hazards of peaceful use of nuclear energy have subsequently been proved to be false. The experts, even if sincere, could be wrong about the safety of the new research in biotechnology.

18.8   There is much wisdom in the statement by Dr. Erwin Chargaff, professor emeritus of biochemistry at Columbia: "Anyone affirming immediate disaster is a charlatan. But anyone denying the possibility of its occuring is an even greater one."

18.9   Even if the danger is a long-term one, the churches have to be alert to the consequences of developments in this field, and the theme chosen provides a platform for dealing with the issues and educating the common people.

18.10   (3.) *The ecological peril*: The indiscriminate burning of fossil fuels (coal, gas and oil) for energy, and the irresponsible misuse of the limited resources of the planet, have posed a threat to the biosphere – that fragile envelope around the earth which makes life possible. Besides the pollution of air, water and food, the very balance of the eco-system can be imperilled by industrial development, energy consumption and waste disposal.

18.11   Some measures have recently been taken by some governments to lower the level of pollution. But no international agreements have yet been reached to keep the pollution level low, or to regulate the process of exploitation of the limited resources of the earth. The risk that the eco-balance may be seriously upset by our industrial civilization is still great. The churches have a responsibility to continue to alert people to this real danger to life on earth.

18.12   (4.) *The peril of global injustice*: The resources and the technology necessary to ensure a decent standard of living to all human beings are now at the disposal of humankind. And yet the number of the millions who do not have access to the means for a life worthy of human beings continues to increase. While enormous amounts of resources and technology are being wasted on pointless military weapons, millions perish from hunger and malnutrition, ignorance and disease. The lack of political will to remedy this evil frightens thinking people. Nations make pious resolutions on cutting down weapons and devoting resources to development, but little actually happens.

18.13   The desperation of the poor and the powerless can imperil life on earth, for power does not remain for ever with the mighty. Injustice unremedied soon explodes in destructive revolt.

18.14   The Central Committee of the World Council of Churches had all these four perils in mind when it settled on the theme "Jesus Christ – the Life of the World".

18.15   But the question of *how* Jesus Christ can be the life of the world and save it from these four perils remains basically unanswered. It is to that question that the Assembly and its preparatory process must pay adequate attention. And it is a contribution to that preparatory process that this paper is offered.

18.16   *What is life? A scientific answer*
Any answer to the question: What is life? must depend

upon the category structure that one chooses for the question as well as the answer.

Is it a theological question? Or is it a scientific question? If the latter, then we must say that the answer can only be in terms of a label applied to a common class of properties which can be investigated scientifically. We can say what properties or functions all living beings have in common. It is an arbitrary label created by human beings for the sake of convenience in thinking. The definition may not include all life, and the boundaries may be quite fuzzy. This is the case with scientific concepts like species, animals, insects, etc., for example, but they are useful shorthand.

18.17 That is all one can hope for in any scientific treatment of what constitutes life. But a theological answer to such a question has to take into account both what science has to say about life, and also go farther into questions like origin, purpose, etc., which do not properly fall within the domain of science.

18.18 In treating the theme, "Jesus Christ – the Life of the World", we must deal with life, both in terms of the understanding of life in the sciences, and in terms of the Christian understanding of life, which need not be in conflict with the scientific understanding, but must necessarily go beyond.

18.19 Let us begin, therefore, with science, keeping in mind the possibility that any answer in science may be no more satisfying than the answer to a similar question: What is electricity? How do we define life? The definition must apply to all of life – human, animal and plant . . .

18.20 From a scientific perspective, therefore, one can say:

(a) There is no agreed definition of life, nor is the boundary between life and non-life clear, e.g. a virus, the heart of a frog that has been vivisected in the laboratory, or a person in terminal illness whose life has been artifically prolonged, etc.

(b) Living beings exhibit negative entropy, which offsets, at least temporarily, the positive entropy which characterizes all matter.

(c) Each living being is in itself an organized community with differentiation and coordination of functions controlled by genetic structure.

(d) Life is an open system, self-regulating, orderly, dependent on other reality, receptive, relational.

(e) Life – at least at higher levels – is characterized by consciousness, awareness, will, choice and freedom, though these are characteristics difficult to explain in terms of physics and chemistry alone.

As has been stated, life cannot be understood, at least for Christians, in terms of science alone. We should, therefore, consider the theme, along with the four sub-themes chosen for the Assembly in a more specifically theological context.

18.21   *What is life? A theological answer*

The Assembly main theme, "Jesus Christ – the Life of the World", has now been broken up into four themes: Life a gift of God; Life confronting and overcoming death; Life in its fullness; Life in unity. The consideration of these four sub-themes should bring out some of the aspects of life in Jesus Christ which lie beyond the competence of science. Our considerations here will be limited to the first sub-theme, on the basis of the faith of the Christian community and its understanding of reality.

18.22   (1.) *The gift and the Giver* All life is a gift from God. This should not be regarded as a mere preacher's platitude. To acknowledge one's life, as well as that of others, as a sacred gift has enormous consequences for the way we make our decisions on many issues – suicide, war, poverty, injustice, nuclear weapons, and so on. This claim, however, constitutes one of the dilemmas of our modern civilization which affirms itself, at least at the state level, as secular. In a secular society, what is the basis for affirming the sacredness of life or of its gift character? If there is no God, whose gift is life? Nature's? But what is nature? Something which exists by itself?

18.23   The concept of nature is of pagan origin and has no basis in the Christian understanding of reality. Neither nature nor we exist from ourselves, or on our own. We come from God, So does nature. Both are creation – not nature. It is important for Christians to acknowledge ourselves and the world as created – not as existing by nature.

18.24   To be created means several things. First, when we acknowledge ourselves and the world as created, we confess that all created reality is contingent and dependent upon God's creative will for its very existence and functioning. We are not our own. Our very existence we owe to God as a gift. Once we acknowledge the gift, we acknowledge also our responsibility to the Giver. But it is not a legal responsibility of which we speak. For accepting a free gift does not entail any legal responsibility to the Giver. If we confess, however, that it is a gift of love, given in freedom, then there has to be a *response* - rather than a burdensome *responsibility*. It is a response of love – a free response.

18.25   It cannot be a response arising from the fear of consequences of not responding in love. For a response arising from fear that God will punish us is neither a loving response nor a free one. The Giver does not *demand* any response, for love does not make demands, but gives itself freely. The Giver rejoices when there is a free response in love, but cannot command it or ask for it.

18.26   Much has been written about Christian ethical responsibility, quite often in a contractual or covenantal understanding of the relationship between God and humanity. Much less has been said about responsiveness, as distinct from responsibility. There is a world of difference between response and responsibility. The very ethos is different. Responsibility is due and can be demanded – a legal obligation. Response is free; it can be given or withheld. There can be penalty or punishment for not fulfilling one's responsibility. For failing to respond, there may be consequences – disastrous ones at that; but no punishment as such.

18.27   Life is God's gift – a gift of grace, an offering of love, the creative love of the Creator. And the response to love is not only not demanded, but it is not even prescribed. There is no such thing as a single appropriate response to any given gift of love. The reponse itself is an occasion for creativity on the part of the responder.

18.28   There is no logic by which we can deduce from the recognition that life is God's gift what the proper response to that gift is. There are some aspects of that response which seem common – gratitude, for example, and the turning to God in repentance. But those are aspects which are permanent features of any adequate response to God.

18.29   The response we make does not depend so much on the gift as on the Giver. It is important to know the nature of the gift of life, for otherwise it would be difficult to make the right use of the gift. But is it not more significant to know the Giver and to enter into a loving relationship with that Person?

18.30   Knowing God, however, is not a matter of theology. In theology we have concepts about God – right or wrong – but no real knowledge of God as a Person.

18.31   The first aspect of knowing God as Giver of life must be repentance. Repentance means turning away from our idle, trivial, foolish and sinful preoccupations towards the One who has endowed us with life. Turning towards God as Giver of life thus implies also a recognition of the folly of turning towards and pursuing other things and goals; the recognition that we have made a mess of the gift of life by not turning towards the Giver and responding to the love that prompted the gift; recognition also that my life is not my own, but a loving gift, to be cherished and fulfilled.

18.32   (2.) *Life and life eternal.* At this point we should recognize the two different but related kinds of life we have received as a gift: the gift of biological life by creation, and the gift of life in Christ through the incarnate Lord Jesus Christ. Both are gifts of grace. Neither is ours by right. Without the first the second is hardly possible. Frequently it is said: there is no question of the first one – that is, biological life, being by nature and the second one, i.e. life in Christ, alone as being by grace. That is the kind of error into which false theologies often plunge us. All life is a gift of grace, biological life and eternal life, plant life and animal life.

18.33   Biological life is certainly a gift to us – including plant and animal life. We live from plant and animal life. The plants are especially a gift of grace, for without them there is no photosynthesis, no grain or fruit, no animals, no food for humans. Without plants and trees who will absorb all the carbon-dioxide we breathe out, and assure our continuous supply of oxygen? We should be grateful for God's gracious gift of plants and trees and animals.

18.34   Biological life, ordinary life, is the basis and receptacle for eternal life. Any attempt to glorify eternal life at the expense of biological life should be resisted as a temptation. True, biological life is temporary. It is subject to death. But without it can we receive eternal life? And how can we say that biological life is ours by nature and only eternal life is a gift of grace? It is a fact that eternal life is a far superior gift. But that does not make ordinary life any less a gift of God's grace. Failure to recognize this fact lies at the base of our ecological peril, of our social injustice, of our making a mess of our ordinary life. Christians especially need to recognize more readily the nature of ordinary life, of the life of all, as the gracious gift of God's creation. That would provide them with a basis for an understanding and a way of life that is more Christian. That would help them understand science and technology, culture and the arts, politics and economics, family and society, education and health, and everything else in a truly Christian light.

18.35   (3.) *The gift and the Giver are one!* Biological life is a gift from God, gratefully to be acknowledged and faithfully to be cherished. That is not, however, to diminish the distinction between biological life and life eternal in Christ.

18.36   A consultation of some Orthodox theologians, meeting in Damascus in 1982, drew up a distinction between the different kinds of life we know... We restate that distinction as follows:

(a) *God's life:* self-derived, self-sustaining, self-giving, eternal, infinite, not subject to death or disintegration, unmixed with evil, true being, the ground and source of all being, in itself incomprehensible.

(b) *Angelic life:* created, not mixed with evil and therefore not subject to death, and experiencing the presence of God unhindered by the screen of sin.

(c) *Human life:* created, other-derived, other-dependent, mortal, finite, always mixed with evil.

(d) *Sub-human life on earth:* also created and therefore other-derived and other-dependent, mortal, finite, but integrally related to human life.

(e) *Anti-God life:* created, but in rebellion against the purposes of God, interfering with the affairs of humans, discomfited in Christ, but still allowed to be active as a testing ground for freedom, though doomed to destruction.

18.37   All these five levels of life are interconnected and interacting. Any attempt to understand human life in isolation from the other four levels is bound to be both superficial and misleading.

18.38   But the gospel of Jesus Christ announces to us a new fact – that all levels of life are affected by an event which took place in time and space – in Palestine 2000 years ago. The Second Person of the Holy Trinity has now permanently and inseparably united levels one and three in the only Begotten Son of God, overcome sin and death as a divine human person, and is to unite all forms of life and non-life, after testing in the fire of judgment, to become a harmonious but differentiated whole in the risen Jesus Christ.

18.39   This is the astounding new gift of God's grace proclaimed in the gospel by the church and acknowledged in the believing community.

There is no scientific proof possible for this declaration. To those who believe, it is more certain than any so-called scientific fact.

It is this supreme gift which we celebrate with joy in the eucharistic liturgy and which we proclaim with confidence to all creation.

The alienation of humanity from God has now been overcome. God and humanity have become inseparably one. There is no more a gap of separation. God is at one with us. Immanuel! With us, God!

18.40   This gift is such that to respond to it is simply to surrender oneself totally to such infinite love – of course, to find oneself confirmed and revitalized by that infinite love! In the utter trust of faith, we mortal humans surrender ourselves to such love without any reservation, without any fear about what will happen to our freedom and identity. Our trust is so complete in his love, that it drives out all fear – including fear of loss of freedom and identity, fear of condemnation and punishment, fear and anxiety about our personal destiny.

18.41   Here, the gift is the Giver himself. And our response can be nothing less than to surrender our paltry and feeble self into those loving hands. There is no question now of taking the gift and walking away from the Giver, for the gift is the Giver himself. In accepting the gift in humble repentance and perfect trust we ourselves become one with the Giver. The Giver, the gift, and the receiver are united in that life-giving embrace of the Supreme Lover.

18.42   It is as we experience this supreme gift that we recognize fully that all life, all things, all that exists, with all the suffering and pain, the struggles and conflicts, the beauty and the joy, the fears and the hopes, are a gift of grace from the Supreme Lover. In that experience we see that what we regarded wrongly as nature is also a gift of grace – not ours by right; as we are possessed by the Great Lover, possession itself becomes meaningless. We no longer seek to possess, for we are God's, and God is ours, and there is nothing to possess further. This is freedom – the freedom of love in which God and humanity are united in one, and all things with us in God!

18.43   It is idle to hope that the present church structures can truly become communities of faith, living the life that overcomes death and transmitting life to the world around. What is more practical is to seek to found smaller pioneering communities – of Christians who have overcome their fear of death, who really believe that Jesus Christ is risen indeed, and who work out the implications of that faith.

Such a community must be deeply rooted in two worlds – the modern world of science and technology, of poverty and injustice, of rootlessness and lovelessness on the one hand, and on the other, the life-giving powers of the Spirit operating in a genuine community of faith and worship.

If the Sixth Assembly can lead to the founding of such pioneer communities, the theme will have served some purpose.

CRITIQUE

One of the problems involved, in comparing the Texts with the Extracts in this Section, is that their perceptions of war are radically different. For the Twentieth Century, war involves the possibility of man's total self-destruction: nuclear weapons present Christian ethics with horrific dimensions, quite beyond the concepts of Augustine, Aquinas or Luther. In this sense, there is a crucial hiatus between the Texts and the Extracts, despite the attempts of Welty and Ramsey to understand modern warfare in terms of traditional just-war concepts. Ramsey is particularly aware of this problem and, as a result, concludes ambivalently – for him just-war theory is both essential to and inadequate for a moral understanding of modern war. *Non-Violent Action* suggests a radical alternative and, indeed, raises the crucial question, in terms of a just-war theory, of whether it can ever be said that all peaceful means have been exhausted, in conflict situations, before recourse is made to violence. But the overall problem remains whether this document or Raven present a serious alternative to nuclear deterrence.

On this point, Raven's Extract is particularly vulnerable. He is clearly sensitive to Niebuhr's charge of 'utopianism' (cf 2.19) but, for some, he does not fully resolve it. They might argue that, given the existence of nuclear weapons in the possession of secretive and totalitarian military authorities (weapons that can, at best, be destroyed, but not 'disinvented') their precipitate disposal might make the world more, rather than less, dangerous. Unilateral disposal of nuclear weapons need not necessarily be 'precipitate', but it does require safeguards which are absent from this Extract. Further, Raven's *imitatio Christi* atonement model may appear particularly vulnerable, as may his less than critical treatment of the New Testament. This model is certainly not the only way of understanding atonement. Nonetheless, this Extract does have a purity of moral vision rare in Christian ethics.

Welty's reliance upon international tribunals to determine whether or not particular wars are wars of aggression (14.3) may itself be somewhat utopian. Further, his central notions of 'justice', 'defence' and 'liberation' remain difficult to objectify: it is, indeed, no casy task to set out a just-war theory which is not, at some point, tautological. Finally, his style of argument – dependent as it is on papal authority – too severely limits its usefulness to a traditional Roman Catholic context.

Of all the Extracts, that of Ramsey meets the most critical dilemmas of modern war, yet it still shows many of the weaknesses noted earlier (see *above*, p.167). Its arguments are often tortuous (a number of his side-arguments have been omitted to aid clarity) and relatively uncoordinated. So, it is an obvious weakness of the Extract that, having admitted that *any* possession of nuclear weapons carries the risk of unintended city destruction (15.18-19), he still believes that a position based only on nuclear bluff is sustainable and justifiable (15.21f). The very possession seems to involve a risk that the morally 'un-do-able' might actually be done. Indeed, since Ramsey wrote this passage, nuclear weapons have so proliferated vertically and horizontally that their accidental, or even intentional, use might appear to be a greater possibility than before. Serious doubts have also been raised about the stability of existing nuclear weapons' systems and about their military coherence as systems of 'deterrence' – see further, my *The Cross Against the Bomb*, 1984. In addition, Ramsey's earlier objections to nuclear bluff (see *above*, p. 347) are not properly answered in *The Limits of Nuclear War*. In particular, the point that an enemy 'will probe anyway, and find out' that the nuclear threat is merely bluff, seems convincing, given other similar security leaks in the West. Another argument, sometimes encountered, might be open to Ramsey: i.e. if nuclear weapons have the capacity always to deter, their possession should not be regarded as immoral when such possession in effect guarantees their non-use. However, proponents of this argument tend to ignore irrational or accidental uses of nuclear weapons. It is these uses, especially, which render ineffective any fool-proof 'deterrent' value involved in the possession of nuclear weapons.

Non-Violent Action, too, leaves a number of crucial questions unresolved:- (a) Can nuclear threats be averted through the systematic use of non-violent action? The examples that the URC Group give of the effectiveness of non-violent action tend to be at a rather low level of potential warfare. (b) Can a determined and thoroughly immoral aggressor be affected by non-violent action? One of the few world leaders systematically to practise Christian non-violent action in order to effect political change, Kenneth Kaunda, has now concluded, as a result of his war with, what was at the time, Rhodesia, that it cannot (see his, *Kaunda on Violence*). He argues that non-violence can only be fully effective against a morally sensitive opponent: if one sits down in front of the tanks of an opponent who is not, one is simply run over! cf Niebuhr's criticism of the Italian pacifists, who were 'ineffectual before the brutal will-to-power of fascism' (9.6). Gandhi's active non-violence in India, on the other hand, he saw as more 'realistic' (9.7) – a highly significant concession.

A number of crucial difficulties also face Bonino. Like Miranda, he claims that 'scientific', Marxist concepts can be used to clarify biblical concepts. Some of the points that they both make, in defence of Marxism and against simplistic attacks by other Christians, are convincing and, in the context of the economic and political oppression that has, at times, characterised South America, the central focus of Liberation theology is highly important. Nonetheless, Bonino's contention that, there is 'a striking similarity' between Paul's notion of 'works' and the Marxist concept of 'alienation' requires far more analysis and justification (17.3). It is also difficult to accept, without further evidence, that the Marxist concept of the 'proletariat', derived as it is from an urban industrial context, has much to do with the biblical concept of the 'poor' (see *above*, p. 289). Further, there is a certain lack of clarity in the concept of 'peace' that Bonino proposes to replace the two traditional theological concepts.

Gregorios provides a link with the next Section. His principle of regarding human life as a 'gift' from God has important implications for personal as well as social ethics (see *below*, pp. 547-9). Few outside the Orthodox theological world may accept all of his assumptions (e.g. 18.36), but he does distinguish clearly the overall way in which a theological perspective differs from a purely empirical understanding of human life. If a Christian is true to this perspective, threats to human life should always be viewed with horror.

Despite the very real differences of opinion between these Exracts, it is possible to identify a number of points which most Christians hold in common. All the Extracts would agree that, if modern warfare is to be justified at all, it is only to be justified with extreme reluctance and as a very last resort. Even the possession of a nuclear deterrent is a concession to an evil world. And, in the context of liberation struggles, violence is only to be justified because it is already implicit in an oppressive status quo. This present-day reluctance represents an important return to Augustine's position. It has already been seen that, in Aquinas' writings, Augustine's reluctance in condoning warfare at all, is often absent. The justifiability or otherwise of wars becomes a matter of formal presentation. However, faced with the horrific dimensions of modern warfare, most Christians today might agree that war is in principle evil and is to be resisted, either with a very reluctant use of violence, or with a use of non-violent means. There are two important elements here which might differentiate present-day Christianity from certain other religious or secular positions. Firstly, war *is* regarded as evil: there is no concept here of a 'holy war'. Secondly, it is an evil which is to be resisted (violently or otherwise): there is no sanction for acquiescence or refusing to take notice. Christianity is seen as eirenic, but not quietistic: it involves an uneasy tension between 'peace' and 'justice'.

SECTION 4

HUMAN LIFE AND INTERPERSONAL RELATIONSHIPS

SECTION 4

HUMAN LIFE AND INTERPERSONAL RELATIONSHIPS

The distinction between social and personal ethics is, at best, approximate. In personal ethics, the focus is more upon the individual and, in social ethics, it is more upon society. But it is only a relative difference of focus, since many issues in personal ethics have a social dimension and many issues in social ethics involve individual decision-making. So, for most ethicists, there is an important distinction to be made between killing in the context of war and individual homicide. War involves societies as a whole and individuals who kill within this context, usually do so on the authority of their society and without personal malice against the particular individuals they kill (in modern warfare, killing at a distance is even less personal). Depending on whether they are selective militarists or selective pacifists (see *above*, p. 296), they may or may not believe that it is for them personally to decide on the actual justifiability of the particular war in which they are engaged. However, individual homicide, whether of self or of another, raises the most crucial problems of individual decision-making, social authorisation and often personal malice. It has already been seen, that Augustine saw a clear distinction, between participation in war and the sort of violence Peter displayed at Gethsemane. Peter acted 'in a hasty zeal' and 'without the sanction of the consituted authority' (Text *VII.2*). Similarly, he sanctioned war in specifiable circumstances, but not individual suicide (Text

X.10). But, even in this instance, the distinction between personal and social ethics is difficult to sustain. As Augustine implies, capital punishment has more in common with war than individual homicide, since the executioner usually acts without personal malice and upon the decision and authority of society at large. And issues, such as abortion, involve both personal and social dimensions, since they are the object both of intense personal decision-making and of social legitimation. Even suicide, although seldom socially sanctioned, is regarded as a criminal activity in some societies, but not in others.

This Section consists of three broad themes in personal ethics. The first of these is the issue of individual homicide. Augustine's Text on suicide is balanced by Fletcher on euthanasia and Gustafson and Clément on abortion. The second is the issue of sexual morality. Aquinas' Text on pre-marital sexual activity and marriage is contrasted with the Quaker Group's understanding of the 'new morality' and Paul VI's encyclical on birth control. The third is the issue of sexual and racial stereotypes. Luther's late views on the Jews are compared with Hastings' Extract on the theology of race and Ruether's Extract on feminist theology and ecology. The scope of this Section is intentionally broad to demonstrate some of the range of approaches in these somewhat diffuse ethical areas. At the same time, it is intended in this Section to raise some of the most crucial substantive dilemmas facing present-day Christian ethics.

The issue of individual homicide forms a natural bridge and a contrast with the previous Section. The dichotomy between the pre-Constantinian and post-Constantinian churches (see *above*, p. 297f), is evident, but is not nearly so clear-cut. Bainton argues that: 'the early Church saw an incompatibility between love and killing. In later times the attitude and the act were harmonized on the ground that the destruction of the body does not entail the annihilation of the soul. The early Church had an aversion to bloodshed' (*Christian Attitudes Toward War and Peace*, p.77). So Tertullian, on the basis of Acts 15.20, maintained that the three irremissible sins were idolatry, adultery and homicide (*De Pudicitia, XII*). His general conviction, both before and after his conversion to Montanism, was that, for the Christian,

homicide in any form is forbidden; that, if necessary, the
Christian must suffer persecution rather than retaliate; and that
the Christian, by enduring violence, can look for a reward
beyond this world. This is evident in the following pre-
Montanist quotation:

> Which is the ampler rule, to say, "Thou shalt not kill", or
> to teach, "Be not even angry"? Which is more perfect, to
> forbid adultery, or to restrain from even a single lustful
> look? Which indicates the higher intelligence, interdicting
> evil-doing, or evil-speaking? Which is more thorough, not
> allowing an injury, or not even suffering an injury to be
> repaid? . . . Think of these things, too, in the light of the
> brevity of any punishment you can inflict – never to last
> longer than till death... No doubt about it, we, who
> receive our awards under the judgement of an all-seeing
> God, and who look forward to eternal punishment from
> him for sin, – we alone make real effort to attain a
> blameless life' (*The Apology*, 44-5, from *The Ante-Nicene
> Fathers*, 3).

Abortion he regarded simply as murder. Similarly, the Council
of Elvira (c.300) in the West, decreed that a woman guilty of an
abortion be refused Holy Communion, even on her death-bed:
and the Synod of Ancyra (314) in the East, ordained a penalty of
ten years' penance for the woman who had an abortion.

In the post-Constantinian church some changes become
apparent. Although he retained a rigorous position on suicide,
Augustine's attitude to abortion was more qualified than that of
previous theologians. In discussing the distinction between an
embryo without a soul (*informatus*) and an embryo with a soul
(*formatus*), he maintained that the abortion of the first should be
punished only by a fine, whereas that of the second should be
treated as murder (*Quaest. in Exodus 21,80*; *Quaest. Vet. et Nov.
Test*, 23). In one form or another, a distinction between an
animated and an unanimated foetus was not finally refuted by
the Roman Catholic Church until 1869, when Pius IX affirmed
that the ensoulment of the foetus commences at conception and
set excommunication as the penalty for those seeking to procure

an abortion. On the issue of abortion, the comparative rigour of the contemporary Roman Catholic and Orthodox Churches, evident in Paul VI's *Extract 23* and Clément's *Extract 21*, represents a partial return to the position of the pre-Constantinian church.

Until recent times, Augustine's rigorist position on.suicide remained that of most Christians. Further, recent discussions of certain forms of euthanasia have much in common with early debates on suicide. Voluntary direct euthanasia, in particular, might be seen as a form of suicide and it is for this reason that Fletcher's *Extract 19* can be compared directly with Augustine's *Text X*. Of course, other forms of euthanasia raise different ethical dilemmas which were not discussed by the classical authors. This can be seen if one distinguishes between the following positions, based upon the two variables of the doctor's intention and the patient's will, in a situation in which the latter's life is shortened or terminated:

Eventual death of patient caused by . . .
(a) Direct treatment by doctor of willing patient
(b) Direct treatment by doctor of non-willing patient
(c) Indirect effects of treatment by doctor of willing patient
(d) Indirect effects of treatment by doctor of non-willing patient
(e) Non-treatment by doctor of willing patient
(f) Non-treatment by doctor of non-willing patient

Naturally, if direct, or even indirect, treatment were to be applied to the *un*willing (rather than a non-willing) patient this might constitute murder rather than euthanasia. The concept of 'willingness' on the part of the patient is not without considerable difficulties – e.g. is a comatose patient, who has previously favoured euthanasia, 'willing' or 'non-willing'? – but these six 'ideal' types (see above, p. 296) show something of the range of the issue in contemporary medical ethics. In type (a), the doctor agrees to the patient's request to end or shorten his or her life. In type (b), the doctor acts in the same way, but the patient is unable to will this (perhaps because he or she is comatose, senile, or mentally undeveloped). In types (c) and (d), it is not the primary intention of the doctor to shorten the life of the patient, whether or not the latter wills this. Instead, it may be the primary intention of the doctor to lessen the pain of the patient, whilst being aware that in the process he or she may shorten the life of that patient (i.e. the ethical notion of 'double effect'). In types (e) and (f) it is withholding treatment that shortens the life of the willing or non-willing patient. For many type (e) hardly constitutes an example of euthanasia at all, since it is often considered to be a right of a mature, rational individual to decide whether or not to receive treatment. Nonetheless, it is logically related to the other types. Further complications are raised by the difficulties of defining 'treatment' in this context – e.g in type (f), is intensive nursing, without which a comatose patient might die, to be regarded as 'treatment'?

If this analysis is adopted, straightforward support for, or rejection of, 'euthanasia' will appear difficult for many contemporary Christians. Only those who approve, or, conversely, those who disapprove, of euthanasia in *all* of the above forms, will be able to adopt such a straightforward approach. Perhaps, for most, even Augustine's absolutist position on suicide is unacceptable.

Yet, if there is a dilemma apparent amongst contemporary Christians on this issue, even greater perplexity is evident in contemporary attitudes towards human sexuality. There is also a sharp contrast to be drawn between the views of Augustine on sexuality and those of many Christians today. It is sometimes held that Augustine steered a mid-path between the Manichaean rejection of the flesh as evil and the Pelagian rejection of any notion of original sin. Against the Pelagians he insisted that marriage involves a sacramental bond and is good only in so far as it enables procreation. And, against the Manichaeans, he insisted that God had blessed man with the words 'Be fruitful and multiply': it was not procreation itself which was sinful, but lust. But here lay Augustine's problem: marriage is for procreation and this is good, yet procreation is impossible without lust and this is sinful. It is this element in his thinking which suggests that Augustine never wholly escaped his own early Manichaeism. Unfortunately it is an element which had a profound effect on much subsequent Christian thought on sexuality. In his anti-Pelagian treatise, *On Marriage and Con-*

cupiscence, he justified his belief in the sinfulness of sexual desire, even within marriage, with the following Natural law argument:

> How significant is the fact that the eyes, and lips and tongue, and hands, and feet, and the bending of the back, and neck, and sides, are all placed within our power – to be applied to such operations as are suitable to them, when we have a body free from impediments and in a sound state of health; but when it must come to man's great function of the procreation of children, the members which were expressly created for this purpose will not obey the direction of the will, but lust has to be waited for to set those members in motion, as if it had legal right over them, and sometimes it refuses to act when the mind wills, while it often acts against its will! Must not this bring the blush of shame over the freedom of the human will, that by its contempt of God, its own Commander, it has lost all proper command for itself over its own members? Now, wherein could be found a more fitting demonstration of the just depravation of human nature by reason of its disobedience, than in the disobedience of those parts whence nature herself derives subsistence by succession . . . This, then, was the reason why the first human pair, on experiencing in the flesh that motion which was indecent because disobedient, and on feeling the shame of their nakedness, covered these offending members with fig-leaves (*De Nuptiis et Concupiscentia*, VII, from *The Nicene and Post-Nicene Fathers*, 5).

The influence of this view can be seen in Aquinas' *Text XI* and Paul VI's *Extract 23* and a strong reaction against it is evident in the Quaker Group's *Extract 22*.

Augustine's justification of monogamous marriage was only relative. He defended the polygamy of the patriarchs against both the Manichaeans and the Pelagians (see *above*, p.39-40 and *De Nuptiis et Concupiscentia*, IX), since he believed their motives to have been procreative rather than lustful. He attacked those pagan monogamous marriages which were, in his opinion, based solely upon lust. And, apparently like Paul, he valued celibacy much higher than marriage.

Some of these elements are still present in Luther's writings on sexuality and marriage. He, too, justified the polygamy of the patriarchs (see *above*, p.39), had a low opinion of his contemporaries' sexual behaviour and supported Paul's justification of marriage as 'a remedy of sin':

> To unaided human nature, as God created it, chastity apart from matrimony is an impossibility. For flesh and blood remain flesh and blood, and the natural inclination and excitement run their course without let or hindrance, as everyone's observation and experience testify. Therefore that man might more easily keep his evil lust in bounds, God commanded marriage, that each may have his proper portion and be satisfied; although God's grace is still needed for the heart to be pure (*The Large Catechism* of 1528, on the sixth commandment).

'Lust' is still seen as evil, marriage still appears as a concession for frailty and there are some (although few) who, 'by reason of extraordinary gifts...have become free to live chaste lives' (*ibid.*). But, in contrast to Augustine and Aquinas, monasticism is no longer regarded as a higher state than marriage. Indeed, he claimed of marriage that, 'God blessed this institution above all others and made everything on earth serve and spring from it. It is not an exceptional estate but the most universal and noblest, pervading all Christendom, yea, extending through the whole world' (*ibid.*). As the Reformation established itself and doubtless as a reflection of his own happy marriage, Luther increasingly came to see the family as the proper focus (replacing the monastery) of Christian socialisation. In his less formal moments, he could write: 'Ah, dear God, marriage is not a thing of nature but a gift of God, the sweetest, the dearest, and the purest life above all celibacy and all singleness, when it turns out well, though the very devil if it does not. For although women have the art, with tears, lies and snares to beguile a man, they can also be superb and say the very best . . . A great thing is this bond and communion between man and wife' (*T.R.* 4786).

Despite the real affection for women and appreciation of marriage evident in this quotation, it also provides a clear example of sexual stereotypes. Personal and social prejudices occur frequently in Luther's writings and few are more shocking than those contained in *Text XII*. Both he and Augustine, in their different ages and social contexts, were inveterate polemicists, so it is not surprising that their prejudices are so often in evidence. Just as Luther supported the princes in violently supressing the peasants, so Augustine in later life came to support the, at times violent, coercion of Donatists in North Africa. In a letter to the Donatist Bishop, Vincentius, in 408, Augustine conceded that, 'originally my opinion was, that no one should be coerced into the unity of Christ, that we must act only by words, fight only by arguments, and prevail by force of reason, lest we should have those whom we knew as avowed heretics feigning themselves to be Catholics' (*Letters* XCIII). But his increasing pessimism about his fellow men and bitter experiences of North African polemics, convinced him otherwise:

> In some cases, therefore, both he that suffers persecution is in the wrong, and he that inflicts it is in the right. But the truth is, that always both the bad have persecuted the good, and the good have persecuted the bad: the former doing harm by their unrighteousness, the latter seeking to do good by the administration of discipline; the former with cruelty, the latter with moderation; the former impelled by lust, the latter under the constraint of love. For he whose aim is to kill is not careful how he wounds, but he whose aim is to cure is cautious with his lancet; for the one seeks to destroy what is sound, the other that which is decaying. The wicked put prophets to death; prophets also put the wicked to death. The Jews scourged Christ; Christ also scourged the Jews (*ibid.*).

The tone of this is considerably more moderate than that of Luther's *Against the Robbing and Murdering Hordes of Peasants* (see above, p. 327), but its dangers are just as great. Augustine has moved far from the plea of his fellow countryman, Tertullian, to suffer persectuion without retaliation, and already one can see the beginnings of a position which was to result in the Inquisition. Again, there is nothing in Augustine to match Luther's vitriol against the Jews, but they are identified as a group that was specifically scourged by Christ. And elsewhere he could argue that the Jewish Dispersion was a direct result of their idolatry and finally of their 'putting Christ to death' (*City of God*, IV, 34).

It is a measure of the extent to which prejudice and intolerance are besetting weaknesses of much Christian theology, that the otherwise mild-mannered Aquinas simply assumed that women were less rational than men (XI.8) and that discrimination against Jews and violent persecution of 'heretics' were appropriate positions for the church to adopt (see *above*, p. 204). In examining Luther's *Text XII*, it will be important to ask whether or not these forms of prejudice and intolerance arc intrinsic features of Christian theology. Clearly, Hastings' *Extract 24* maintains that they are not. But, in arguing such a position, it must be frankly admitted that much of the history of Christian theology contains these features both implicitly and even sometimes quite explicitly.

Full awareness of sexual stereotypes is a comparatively recent phenomenon. Although both Augustine and Luther supported marriage and were appreciative of and gained much from women (for Augustine it was his mother and for Luther it was his wife), each adhered to what they would have regarded as a thoroughly Pauline understanding of the role and position of women. Augustine was emphatic that wives should be subordinate to husbands:

> Nor can it be doubted, that it is more consonant with the order of nature that men should bear rule over women, than women over men. It is with this principle in view that the apostle says, "The head of the woman is the man"; and, "Wives, submit yourselves unto your own husbands" (*De Nuptiis et Concupiscentia*, X).

And, even more significantly, at one point he exclaimed: 'Whether it is in a wife or a mother, it is still Eve (the temptress) that we must beware of in any woman' (*Ep.* 243, 10).

For most of its history, theology has been primarily a male pursuit, so it is perhaps not surprising that recent female theologians have found much of it redolent with male assumptions and prejudices. Ruether's *Extract 25* stands as an important corrective to this and it is to be hoped that future textbooks will contain many more Extracts from female theologians. Those who stand outside the social situation within which particular stereotypes and social prejudices are formed, are far more likely to be able to identify them for what they are. In part, even Augustine was aware that this is so. At several points in *The City of God*, he argues that, although something may seem repugnant, it is really only so by convention or custom. Taking the story of Adam and Eve literally, he maintained that the human race resulted from what his contemporaries would have regarded as incestuous relationships:

> It was indeed generally allowed that brothers and sisters should marry in the earliest ages of the human race; but the practice is now so utterly repudiated that it might seem that it could never have been permitted. For custom is the most effective agent in soothing or shocking human sensibilites (XV.16).

And, against those 'male chauvinists' who argued that, at the resurrection, all women will turn into men, he insisted (with his characteristic repudiation of the mechanisms of sexual intercourse):

> For my part, I feel that theirs is the more sensible opinion who have no doubt that there will be both sexes in the resurrection. For in that life there will be no sexual lust, which is the cause of shame... Thus while all defects will be removed from their bodies, their essential nature will be preserved. Now a woman's sex is not a defect; it is natural. And in the resurrection it will be free of the necessity of intercourse and childbirth. However, the female organs will not subserve their former use; they will be part of a new beauty, which will not excite the lust of the beholder (XXII.17).

To the modern reader it may seem extraordinary (and perhaps suspicious!) that he should single out women for this inquisitive treatment. But for a Roman Christian, now in his early seventies, it was progressive indeed!

TEXT X
AUGUSTINE
Suicide

I. BACKGROUND

This Text comes from *The City of God* I.17–18, 19b–22 & 27 (Pelican Classics, trans. Henry Bettenson and ed. David Knowles, Penguin, 1972, pp.26–8, 30–4 & 38–9). This initial part of *The City of God* was written c. 413 and was a part of Augustine's attempt to praise Christian beliefs and virtues at the expense of 'pagan' ones (see *above*, p.64). In the classical world, suicide was sometimes seen as virtuous and heroic, particularly by the Cynics and, to a lesser extent, by the Stoics. On the other hand, Neo-Platonists, whose position strongly influenced Augustine (see *above*, p.37), generally disapproved of it. His conflicts with the Manichaean rejection of killing in any form are still evident in this Text (*X.9*, see *above*, p. 304).

2. KEY ISSUES

Augustine's central proposition in this Text is that suicide is murder, albeit of oneself rather than of another. No one has a private right to kill someone – not even themselves (X.1). And, since 'purity' is a virtue of the mind and not of the body, even a fear of 'pollution', as a result of rape, does not justify suicide (X.2–4). The difference between Christians and others is illustrated by the classical example of Lucretia: she murdered herself after an adulterer had embraced her, whereas a Christian would not have done so (X.5–6). The Bible does not sanction suicide, but enjoins people not to kill (X.7–8). This command applies to humans alone, not to animals and certainly not to plants (X.9). The only exceptions to the commands not to kill are those forms of killing which are prescribed by a just law or are specifically prescribed by God himself (X.10). Contrary to classical belief, suicide does not show 'greatness of spirit', but rather weakness in the face of oppression (X.11) and is not supported by the Judaeo-Christian tradition (X.12). If it were to be allowed that people should kill themselves to avoid succumbing to sin, then all should commit suicide immediately after absolution (X.13-4)!

3. ETHICAL ARGUMENTS

Augustine's overall position is undoubtedly deontological. It is sufficient for him to show that suicide transgresses the command not to kill. There are important exceptions to this command, but suicide is not one of them – unless it is divinely commanded (as in the instance of Samson). However, there are also two remarkable features of this Text relating to his mode of ethical argument. The first is his stress upon intention in X.2-4 (cf. VII.8). Sexual purity is a product of intention and is not destroyed by forcible rape. Moral virtue is to be assessed by the intention of the moral actor and not by what happens to his or her body. The second is the *reductio ad absurdum* in X.13-4. With his characteristic waspish humour, Augustine ridicules those who recommend suicide as a means to avoid some evil.

4. BASES OF CHRISTIAN ETHICS

As part of the polemic of the *City of God*, Augustine compares classical virtues with Christian ones. For the Graeco-Roman world, suicide may appear to be a defence of 'honour' (X.5) or a sign of 'greatness of spirit' (X.11), but not for Christians. The Decalogue forbids this form of killing and, since they were commanded directly by God, Old Testament examples of Abraham attempting to commit murder or of Samson committing suicide, do not contravene this (X.10). Thus, the Bible is treated literally and deontologically. Nevertheless, Augustine introduces an argument from silence, supposing that Samson must have been 'secretly ordered' by the Spirit (cf VII.6). There is also an interesting contrast between 'the pure light of a good conscience' of the individual with the 'darkness of the error' of the mob (X.11).

5. SOCIAL DETERMINANTS

This Text, like *Text I*, shows the dependence of Augustine upon both the Graeco-Roman and the Hebraic worlds. He consciously reacts against the former in his rejection of 'heroic' suicide. Yet his style of argument is still heavily dependent upon this world. In true classical style, his concern is for the 'man of purity and high principle', for 'what he will mentally accept or repudiate' and for 'qualities which make up the moral life' (X.2). Further, whilst rejecting the Manichaean repudiation of all killing, his implicit assumption that 'lust' is inherently sinful may derive from his own earlier Manichaeism. At the same time, the Decalogue clearly plays a central role in his attitude towards suicide. In addition to these cognitive determinants, certain social structures are relevant to the issue of suicide. In his seminal study, *Suicide*, the pioneer French sociologist, Émile Durkheim, claimed that suicide is more prevalent in societies which lack social cohesion or integration. For him, religion could be an important factor in supplying a moral integration for particular societies (he maintained that Catholicism was far more successful at doing this than Protestantism and that, as a result, suicide was twice as prevalent amongst Protestants as amongst Catholics). *The City of God* was written in response to the 'pagan' challenge that conversions to Christianity had led to the moral deterioration and subsequent sacking of Rome in 410. In such a situation, if Durkheim's thesis is followed, it is not surprising that the issue of suicide was particularly relevant in 413 and that it was an issue of moral conflict between 'pagans' and Christians.

6.   SOCIAL SIGNIFICANCE

Until very recent times, Augustine's deontological rejection of suicide was the established position within Christianity. By the Middle Ages it was forbidden for suicides to have a Christian burial. Aquinas believed that suicide contravened Natural law, since it was contrary to the natural desire of man to live. Only with the rise of rationalist philosophy did suicide receive any legitimation. So, David Hume, rejecting the notion of an immortal soul, argued that a person might quite rationally commit suicide. And within non-Roman Catholic churches, it is only within the last two or three decades that there has been a growing belief that suicide should not be treated as a criminal activity and that 'parasuicides' require pastoral care rather than censure (indeed, the term 'parasuicide' was invented to replace the traditional term 'attempted suicide' partly to suggest that it may have more to do with seeking help and attention than death). Only in 1961 did suicide cease to be treated as a crime in Britain.

FURTHER READING
Augustine's chief discussion of the issue of suicide is in Book I of *The City of God*. Hugh Trowell's *The Unfinished Debate on Euthanasia* contains a useful, brief history of Christian attitudes towards suicide and its relation to euthanasia and a bibliography. In addition, there have been a number of church reports on suicide/euthanasia, including the Church of England's *On Dying Well* and the Roman Catholic, Linacre Centre's *Euthanasia and Clinical Practice*.

TEXT X
AUGUSTINE
Suicide

The question of suicide caused by fear of punishment or disgrace.

X.1   Some women killed themselves to avoid suffering anything [like rape] and surely any man of compassion would be ready to excuse the emotions which led them to do this. Some refused to kill themselves, because they did not want to escape another's criminal act by a misdeed of their own. And anyone who uses this as a charge against them will lay himself open to a charge of foolishness. For it is clear that if no one has a private right to kill even a guilty man (and no law allows this), then certainly anyone who kills himself is a murderer, and is the more guilty in killing himself the more innocent he is of the charge on which he has condemned himself to death. We rightly abominate the act of Judas, and the judgment of truth is that when he hanged himself he did not atone for the guilt of his detestable betrayal but rather increased it, since he despaired of God's mercy and in a fit of self-destructive remorse left himself no chance of a saving repentance. How much less right has anyone to indulge in self-slaughter when he can find in himself no fault to justify such a punishment! For when Judas killed himself, he killed a criminal, and yet he ended his life guilty not only of Christ's death, but also of his own; one crime led to another. Why then should a man, who has done no wrong, do wrong to himself? Why should he kill the innocent in putting himself to death, to prevent a guilty man from doing it? Why should he commit a sin against himself to deprive someone else of the chance?

The question of violence from others, and the lust of others suffered by an unwilling mind in a ravished body.

X.2   'But', it will be said, 'there is the fear of being polluted by another's lust.' There will be no pollution, if the lust is another's; if there is pollution, the lust is not another's. Now purity is a virtue of the mind. It has courage as its companion and courage decides to endure evil rather than consent to evil. A man of purity and high principle has not the power to decide what happens to his body, but only what he will mentally accept or repudiate. What sane man will suppose that he has lost his purity if his body is seized and forced and used for the satisfaction of a lust that is not his own? For if purity is lost in this way, it follows that it is not a virtue of the mind; it is not then ranked with the qualities which make up the moral life, but is classed among physical qualities, such as strength, beauty, and health, the impairment of which does not in any way mean the impairment of the moral life. If purity is something of this sort, why do we risk physical danger to avoid its loss? But if it is a quality of the mind, it is not lost when the body is violated. Indeed, when the quality of modesty resists the indecency of carnal desires the body itself is sanctified, and therefore, when purity persists in its unshaken resolution to resist these desires, the body's holiness is not lost, because the will to employ the body in holiness endures, as does the ability, as far as in it lies.

X.3   The body is not holy just because its parts are intact, or because they have not undergone any handling. Those parts may suffer violent injury by accidents of various kinds, and sometimes doctors seeking to effect a cure may employ treatment with distressing visible effects. During a manual examination of a virgin a midwife destroyed her maidenhood, whether by malice, or clumsiness, or accident. I do not suppose that anyone would be stupid enough to imagine that the virgin lost anything of bodily chastity, even though the integrity of that part had been destroyed. Therefore while the mind's resolve endures, which gives the body its claim to chastity, the violence of another's lust cannot take away the chastity which is preserved by unwavering self-control.

X.4   Now suppose some woman, with her mind corrupted and her vowed intention to God violated, in the act of going to her seducer be defiled. Do we say that she is chaste in body while she is on her way, when the chastity of her mind, which made the body chaste, has been lost and destroyed? Of course not! We must rather draw the inference that just as bodily chastity is lost when mental chastity has been violated, so bodily chastity is not lost, even when the body has been ravished, while the mind's chastity endures. Therefore when a woman has been ravished without her consenting, and forced by another's sin, she has no reason to punish herself by a voluntary death. Still less should she do so before the event lest she should commit certain murder while the offence, and another's offence at that, still remains uncertain . . .

Lucretia's suicide.

X.5   Her killing of herself because, although not adulterous, she had suffered an adulterer's embraces, was due to the weakness of shame, not to the high value she set on chastity. She was ashamed of another's foul deed committed *on* her, even though not *with* her, and as a Roman woman, excessively eager for honour, she was afraid that she should be thought, if she lived, to have willingly endured what, when she lived, she had violently suffered. Since she could not display her pure conscience to the world she thought she must exhibit her punishment before men's eyes as a proof of her state of mind. She blushed at the thought of being regarded as an accomplice in the act if she were to bear with patience what another had inflicted on her with violence.

X.6   Such has not been the behaviour of Christian women. When they were treated like this they did not take vengeance on themselves for another's crime. They would not add crime to crime by committing murder on themselves in shame because the enemy had committed rape on them in lust. They have the glory of chastity within them, the testimony of their conscience. They have this in the sight of God, and they ask for nothing more. In fact there is nothing else for them to do that is right for them to do. For they will not deviate from the authority of God's law by taking unlawful steps to avoid the suspicions of men.

Christians have no authority to commit suicide in any circumstance.

X.7   It is significiant that in the sacred canonical books there can nowhere be found any injunction or permission to commit suicide either to ensure immortality or to avoid or escape any evil. In fact we must understand it to be forbidden by the law 'You shall not kill', particularly as there is no addition of 'your neighbour' as in the prohibition of false witness, 'You shall not bear false witness *against your neighbour.*' But that does not mean that a man who gives false witness against himself is exempt from this guilt, since the rule about loving one's neighbour begins with oneself, seeing that the Scripture says, 'You shall love your neighbour as yourself.'

X.8   Moreover, if anyone who gives false witness against himself is just as guilty as if he did so against a neighbour – although the prohibition forbids false witness against a neighbour and might be misunderstood as implying that there is no prohibition of false witness against oneself – then it is the more obvious that a man is not allowed to kill himself, since the text 'Thou shall not kill' has no addition and it must be taken that there is no exception, not even the one to whom the command is addressed.

X.9   Hence some people have tried to extend its scope to wild and domestic animals to make it mean that even these may never be killed. But then why not apply it to plants and to anything rooted in the earth and nourished by the earth? For although this part of creation is without feeling, it is called 'living', and is hence capable of dying and consequently of being killed, when violence is done to it. And so the Apostle, speaking of seeds of this kind, says, 'What you sow does not come to life unless it dies'; (1 Cor. 15.36) and it says in one of the psalms, 'He killed the vines with hail,' (Psm. 78.47). But do we for this reason infer from 'Thou shall not kill' a divine prohibition against clearing away brushwood, and subscribe to the error of the Manicheans? That would be madness. We reject such fantasies, and when we read 'You shall not kill' we assume that this does not refer to bushes, which have no feelings, nor to irrational creatures, flying, swimming, walking, or crawling, since they have no rational association with us, not having been endowed with reason as we are, and hence it is by a just arrangement of the Creator that their life and death is subordinated to our needs. If this is so, it remains that we take the command 'You shall not kill' as applying to human beings, that is, other persons *and* oneself. For to kill oneself is to kill a human being.

All homicide is not murder

X.10   There are however certain exceptions to the law against killing, made by the authority of God himself.

There are some whose killing God orders, either by a law, or by an express command to a particular person at a particular time. In fact one who owes a duty of obedience to the giver of the command does not himself 'kill' – he is an instrument, a sword in its user's hand. For this reason the commandment forbidding killing was not broken by those who have waged wars on the authority of God, or those who have imposed the death-penalty on criminals when representing the authority of the State in accordance with the laws of the State, the justest and most reasonable source of power. When Abraham was ready to kill his son, so far from being blamed for cruelty he was praised for his devotion; it was not an act of crime, but of obedience. One is justified in asking whether Jephtha is to be regarded as obeying a command of God in killing his daughter, when he had vowed to sacrifice to God the first thing he met when returning victorious from battle. And when Samson destroyed himself, with his enemies, by the demolition of the building, this can only be excused on the ground that the Spirit, which performed miracles through him, secretly ordered him to do so. With the exception of these killings prescribed generally by a just law, or specially commanded by God himself – the source of justice – anyone who kills a human being, whether himself or anyone else, is involved in a charge of murder.

Is suicide ever a mark of greatness of soul?

X.11   Those who have committed this crime against themselves are perhaps to be admired for greatness of spirit; they are not to be praised for wisdom or sanity. And yet if we examine the matter more deeply and logically, we shall find that greatness of spirit is not the right term to apply to one who has killed himself because he lacked strength to endure hardships, or another's wrongdoing. In fact we detect weakness in a mind which cannot bear physical oppression, or the stupid opinion of the mob; we rightly ascribe greatness to a spirit that has the strength to endure a life of misery instead of running away from it, and to despise the judgement of men – and in particular the judgement of the mob, which is so often clouded in the darkness of error – in comparison with the pure light of a good conscience. If suicide is to be taken as a mark of greatness of spirit, then Theombrotus will be a shining example of that quality. The story is that when he had read Plato's book which discusses the immortality of the soul, he hurled himself from a wall and so passed from this life to a life which he believed to be better. There was no kind of misfortune, no accusation, true or false, which led him to do away with himself under an intolerable load. It was only greatness of spirit which prompted him to seek death and to 'break the pleasant bonds of life'. But Plato himself, whom he had been reading, is witness that this showed greatness rather than goodness. Plato would have been first and foremost to take this action, and would have recommended it to others, had not the same intelligence which gave him his vision of the soul's immortality enabled him to decide that this step was not to be taken – was, indeed, to be forbidden.

X.12   'But many people did away with themselves to avoid falling into the hands of the enemy.' The question is not only whether they did, but whether they ought to have done so. Sound reason is certainly to be preferred to examples. Some examples are in full harmony with sound reason, and they are the more worthy of imitation as they are more eminent in their devotion to God. Neither the patriachs nor the prophets acted thus; nor did the apostles, since the Lord Christ himself, when he advised them to escape from one town to another in case of persecution, could have advised them to take their own lives to avoid falling into the hands of their persecutors. If he did not order or advise this way of quitting this life, although he promised to prepare eternal dwellings for them after their departure, it is clear that this course is not allowed to those who worship the one true God, whatever examples may be put forward by 'the Gentiles who have no knowledge of him' (1 Thes. 4.5). . .

Should one commit suicide to avoid sin?

X.13   There remains one situation in which it is supposed to be advantageous to commit suicide; I have already begun to discuss the question. It arises when the motive is to avoid falling into sin either through the allurements of pleasure or through the menaces of pain. If we agree to allow this motive we shall not be able to stop until we reach the point when people are to be encouraged to kill themselves for preference, immediately they have received forgiveness of all sins by washing in the waters of holy regeneration. For that would be the time to forestall all future sins – ,the moment when all past sins have been erased. If self-inflicted death is permitted, surely this is the best possible moment for it! When a person has been thus set free why should he expose himself again to all the perils of this life, when it is so easily allowed him to avoid them by doing away with himself? And the Bible says, 'A man who is fond of danger will fall into it.' (Ecclus. 3.26). Why are men so fond of all these great dangers, or at any rate are willing to accept them, by remaining in this life, when they are allowed to depart from it? If a man has a duty to kill himself to avoid succumbing to sin because he is at the mercy of one man, who holds him prisoner, does he suppose that he has to go on living so as to endure the pressures of the actual world, which is full of temptations at all times, temptations such as that which is dreaded under one master, and innumerable others, which are the necessary accompaniment of this life? Has perverse silliness so warped our judgement and distracted us from facing the truth? For on this assumption, why do we spend time on those exhortations to the newly baptized. We do our best to kindle their resolve to preserve their virginal purity, or to remain continent in widowhood, or to remain faithful to their marriage vows. But there is available an excellent short cut which avoids any danger of sinning; if we can persuade them to rush to a self-inflicted death immediately upon receiving remission of sins, we shall send them to the Lord in the purest and soundest condition!

X.14   But in fact if anyone thinks that we should go in for persuasion on these lines, I should not call him silly, but quite crazy. Then how could anyone justify saying to any human being: 'Kill yourself, to avoid adding more serious sin to your small shortcomings, living, as you do, under a master with the manners and morals of a savage', if he cannot say, without being a complete criminal, 'Kill yourself, now that all your sins have been absolved, to avoid committing such sins again, or even worse, while you are living in a world full of the allurements of impure pleasures, so maddened with all its monstrous cruelties, so menacing with all its errors and terrors'? To say this would be monstrous; it follows that suicide is monstrous. If there could be a valid reason for suicide one could not find one more valid than this; and since this is not valid, a valid reason does not exist.

CRITIQUE

It would be a mistake to assess Augustine's contentions on suicide as if they were modern contentions and to forget that they derive from a very specific polemical context. Nonetheless, because of their social significance in shaping Christian, and indeed secular, attitudes towards suicide, their strengths and weaknesses should be noted.

Positively, Augustine's stress upon intention in Christian ethics has proved to be extremely important. Although it is difficult for most victims of rape not to feel guilt and remorse, Augustine placed rape into a more adequate ethical context. Impurity lies in intention, not in involuntary action. It is the rapist and not the one who is raped who is impure, so it would be wholly inappropriate for the Christian to recommend suicide as a means of escaping rape. Further, even today, most Christians might agree that what Durkheim termed 'altruistic suicide' (whereby people commit suicide because their religion or society tell them that it is their duty – *Suicide*, pp. 217f.) is seldom justifiable. Most might support Augustine's attacks on the martyr-seeking attitudes of the Donatists.

Negatively, Augustine showed little awareness of, or sym-

pathy for, other reasons for suicide or 'parasuicide'. For
Durkheim there were two other categories of suicide – egoistic
and anomic. The first results from lack of integration of the
individual into society: the more an individual is left to his or
her resources, the more likely that individual is to commit
suicide. The second results from lack of regulation of the
individual by society: so, the chaos ensuing from divorce can
render men (more than women) especially vulnerable to suicide.
A greater awareness of these specifically social determinants of
suicide has inclined many today towards a more sympathetic
attitude to those who commit, or appear to attempt, suicide.
Indeed, in the West today, suicide/parasuicide is far more likely
to be thought of as a medical, rather than as a moral or religious,
problem.

Even though attitudes towards suicide have changed amongst
both Christians and non-Christians, at least one theological
point links the former with Augustine. For Christians (and
theists generally) life is ultimately God-given and, as a
consequence, should never be taken casually or for selfish
motives. So convinced, individuals may be hesitant about
usurping for themselves what they regard as a function of God,
or treating functionally the life that God has given. Whether or
not this precludes the Christian from voluntary, direct euthanasia or rational, calculated suicide, will be discussed in relation to
Fletcher's *Extract 19*. But, clearly, it may at least make one
cautious (for a discussion of this 'adeodatic axiom', see *below*,
pp. 547-9).

TEXT XI
AQUINAS
Fornication and marriage

I. BACKGROUND

This Text comes from *Summa Contra Gentiles* 3.2.122-4 & 126 (University of Notre Dame Press, London, and Doubleday, New York, 1975, trans. Vernon J. Bourke, pp. 142-51 & 155-6). Unlike *Summa Theologica* (see *above*, p. 76) *Summa Contra Gentiles* was explicitly written for a non-Christian audience and, hence, characteristically it argues initially from reason rather than from Christian revelation – the latter is normally used only to demonstrate its consonance with the former. It is the earlier of the two works, being started after Aquinas went to Paris in 1256 and continued after his return to Italy. The intellectual system of Christianity in the 13th Century was facing major challenges, both from the Islamic world and from the naturalism of secular culture. Aquinas wrote *Summa Contra Gentiles* as an attempt to demonstrate the reasonableness of Christianity in the face of this Graeco-Islamic intellectual threat. Accordingly, he devoted the first book of the work to the existence and attributes of God, the second to Creation, the third (from which this Text comes) to Providence and man's relation to God, and only the fourth to the specifically Christian doctrines of Salvation (which can be known fully, not through unaided reason, but through revelation). Immediately before this Text, Aquinas sought to refute some of the central claims of astrology and notions of fate and to defend the Christian notions of providence, prayer, miracles and divine law, and, immediately after it, he considered the question 'In What Way Poverty is Good'. Throughout these various discussions, a number of Aristotelian Natural law principles are evident (see also, *Text V*). So, he assumed that the virtue of something must always be related to the end of man (XI.4), that man is a social animal (X.6) and that the virtue of something ought to be assessed by whether or not it contributes to the overall well-being of the society or simply to the well-being of a particular individual (X.7). The Text shows that Aquinas was well aware of secular promiscuity and of Islamic polygamy and divorce. However, for him, they were contradicted by Natural law (and, in turn, also by Divine law and by the Bible). More positively, he was concerned to refute the Platonic (and, significantly, with it the Augustinian) notion that the sexual act was in itself, or in its association with 'lust', evil: within the context of a stable, monogamous marriage, sexual intercourse is both natural and in accord with divine providence. Nonetheless, he shared with Augustine the beliefs that procreation is the *sine qua non* of sexual intercourse and that celibacy is a higher state than marriage. Aquinas' debt to Aristotle rather than to Plato, is also apparent in *XI.8*, in the notion that the socialisation of children necessarily involves the correction of their natural passions.

2. KEY ISSUES

Aquinas' initial concern is to counter those who maintain that, as long as it harms no one, 'fornication' is not sinful (XI.1-3). For him, the proper end for the emission of semen is the propagation of the species (XI.4). As a result, any deliberate emission in situations where, either generation cannot result, or proper upbringing of resulting children is impossible, is sinful (XI.5-6). Children need both parents to bring them up and to instruct them in reason (XI.7-8). Properly ordered emission of semen is both required for the preservation of the species and is prescribed by the Bible (XI.9.12). For the same reasons, marriage should be life-long (XI.13-16). Infidelity in marriage goes against the natural wish of fathers to know their offspring (XI.17), whereas the greater the friendship in marriage the more long-lasting it will be (XI.18). Marriage is in accordance with natural promptings for the common good and with Divine law (XI. 19-22). Sexual promiscuity contravenes Natural law (XI.23-4). On the other hand, sexual intercourse which is directed to the generation and upbringing of children is not sinful but reasonable (XI.25). Sexual intercourse is a natural and God-given phenomenon and therefore cannot be evil in itself (XI.26-30).

3. ETHICAL ARGUMENTS

This Text provides one of the clearest examples of Aquinas' use of Natural law. The position which is established in theory in Text II, is here used as the main mode of ethical argument. Aquinas first establishes what is 'natural', in the sense of being in accord with nature, in either human or animal form. From this he derives ethical prescriptions, which are then related to biblical norms. Thus, deontological assumptions are made both about the natural order and about biblical revelation. Further, he characteristically uses consequential ethical arguments: sexuality is to be related to its end (procreation) and this end is to be related to the common good of man. So, promiscuity is thought to be wrong deontologically (because it contravenes the natural order and biblical revelation) and consequentially (because it does not contribute to the common good). On the other hand, properly directed sexual intercourse and even sexual inclinations are not considered to be evil or sinful: it is the use to which sexual intercourse is put that determines whether or not it is sinful. Similarly poverty or wealth are not virtuous or wrong in themselves. For Aquinas virtue may be seen as a mean: 'The goodness of everything that comes under measure and rule consists in its being conformed to its rule. Consequently, evil in these things lies in departure from rule or measure either by excess or defect. And therefore it is clear that the good of moral virtue consists in being up to the level of the measure of reason... in the mean between excess and defect' (*S. T.* I.II, Q.64, Art.1). Measured against the rule of reason, both poverty and wealth may appear evil if taken to excess. But if they conform to the rule of reason – which, 'measures not only the size of a thing that is used, but also the circumstances of the person, and his intention, the fitness of place and time, and other such things' (*S.C.G.*, 3.2.134) – they can both be virtuous.

4. BASES OF CHRISTIAN ETHICS

In keeping with the method of *Summa Contra Gentiles*, Aquinas introduces biblical quotations only at the end of each argument. (XI.10-11, 18-22 & 29). Perhaps it is not surprising that most of these quotations are taken from the Pentateuch and Pauline epistles. However, underlying much of the arguments is a notion of Creation: the natural order can supply man with indications of how he should behave, precisely because it is a God-given order (XI.12 – see *above*, p. 195).

5. SOCIAL DETERMINANTS

Aquinas wrote within the constraints of 13th Century Christendom. Although he was clearly aware of other sexual patterns, he was confident that heterosexual, exclusive monogamy (or, somewhat illogically, celibacy) alone conformed to reason and that this was wholly consonant with the Bible. Today both of these assumptions have been challenged. Following Augustine, he regarded procreation as the essential function of sexual intercourse and, although he wrote about husbands and wives as 'an association of equals' (XI.16), yet, along with many of his contemporaries, he regarded men as the more rational. Since 'reason' and 'virtue' were so closely linked in his thought, this last assumption is particularly problematic.

6. SOCIAL SIGNIFICANCE

It will be evident in Paul VI's *Extract 23* that Aquinas' view of procreation as an essential function of all occasions of sexual intercourse has proved especially significant. Indeed, this mediated position still plays a crucial role in present-day Roman Catholic moral teaching. On this account, not only are homosexuality and prostitution alike condemned, but also all forms of sexual intercourse which involve wholly effective contraception, both within marriage as well as outside of marriage. However, Aquinas has also proved influential in his divergence from Augustine, since many Christians today (Roman Catholic and non-Roman Catholic) would insist that sexual intercourse and sexual desire are not in themselves evil. It is their abuse (however defined) which is considered evil.

FURTHER READING

Important discussions of sexuality and marriage are contained in both *Summa Theologica* (e.g. I.II.77) and *Summa Contra Gentiles*. In addition to the secondary commentaries on Aquinas already mentioned, Roland H. Bainton's *Sex, Love and Marriage: A*

Christian Survey provides a useful, brief survey of historical attitudes and a bibliography. In addition, V.A. Demant's *An Exposition of Christian Sex Ethics* and Helmut Thielicke's *The Ethics of Sex* offer Anglican and Reformed approaches respectively.

TEXT XI

AQUINAS

Fornication and marriage

> *The reason why simple fornication is*
> *a sin according to divine law,*
> *and that matrimony is natural*

XI.1 From the foregoing we can see the futility of the argument of certain people who say that simple fornication is not a sin. For they say: Suppose there is a woman who is not married, or under the control of any man, either her father or another man. Now, if a man performs the sexual act with her, and she is willing, he does not injure her, because she favors the action and she has control over her own body. Nor does he injure any other person, because she is understood to be under no other person's control. So, this does not seem to be a sin.

XI.2 Now, to say that he injures God would not seem to be an adequate answer. For we do not offend God except by doing something contrary to our own good, as has been said. But this does not appear contrary to man's good. Hence, on this basis, no injury seems to be done to God.

XI.3 Likewise, it also would seem an inadequate answer to say that some injury is done to one's neighbor by this action, inasmuch as he may be scandalized. Indeed, it is possible for him to be scandalized by something which is not in itself a sin. In this event, the act would be accidentally sinful. But our problem, is not whether simple fornication is accidentally a sin, but whether it is so essentially.

XI.4   Hence, we must look for a solution in our earlier considerations. We have said that God exercises care over every person on the basis of what is good for him. Now, it is good for each person to attain his end, whereas it is bad for him to swerve away from his proper end. Now, this should be considered applicable to the parts, just as it is to the whole being; for instance, each and every part of man, and every one of his acts, should attain the proper end. Now, though the male semen is superfluous in regard to the preservation of the individual, it is nevertheless necessary in regard to the propagation of the species. Other superfluous things, such as excrement, urine, sweat, and such things, are not at all necessary; hence, their emission contributes to man's good. Now, this is not what is sought in the case of semen, but, rather, to emit it for the purpose of generation, to which purpose the sexual act is directed. But man's generative process would be frustrated unless it were followed by proper nutrition, because the offspring would not survive if proper nutrition were withheld. Therefore, the emission of semen ought to be so ordered that it will result in both the production of the proper offspring and in the upbringing of this offspring.

XI.5   It is evident from this that every emission of semen, in such a way that generation cannot follow, is contrary to the good for man. And if this be done deliberately, it must be a sin. Now, I am speaking of a way from which, *in itself*, generation could not result; such would be any emission of semen apart from the natural union of male and female. For which reason, sins of this type are called *contrary to nature*. But, if by accident generation cannot result from the emission of semen, then this is not a reason for it being against nature, or a sin; as for instance, if the woman happens to be sterile.

XI.6   Likewise, it must also be contrary to the good for man if the semen be emitted under conditions such that generation could result but the proper upbringing would be prevented. We should take into consideration the fact that, among some animals where the female is able to take care of the upbringing of offspring, male and female do not remain together for any time after the act of generation. This is obviously the case with dogs. But in the case of animals of which the female is not able to provide for the upbringing of offspring, the male and female do stay together after the act of generation as long as is necessary for the upbringing and instruction of the offspring. Examples are found among certain species of birds whose young are not able to seek out food for themselves immediately after hatching. In fact, since a bird does not nourish its young with milk, made available by nature as it were, as occurs in the case of quadrupeds, but the bird must look elsewhere for food for its young, and since besides this it must protect them by sitting on them, the female is not able to do this by herself. So, as a result of divine providence, there is naturally implanted in the male of these animals a tendency to remain with the female in order to bring up the young. Now, it is abundantly evident that the female in the human species is not at all able to take care of the upbringing of offspring by herself, since the needs of human life demand many things which cannot be provided by one person alone. Therefore, it is appropriate to human nature that a man remain together with a woman after the generative act, and not leave her immediately to have such relations with another woman, as is the practice with fornicators.

XI.7 Nor, indeed, is the fact that a woman may be able by means of her own wealth to care for the child by herself an obstacle to this argument. For natural rectitude in human acts is not dependent on things accidentally possible in the case of one individual, but, rather, on those conditions which accompany the entire species.

XI.8 Again, we must consider that in the human species offspring require not only nourishment for the body, as in the case of other animals, but also education for the soul. For other animals naturally possess their own kinds of prudence whereby they are enabled to take care of themselves. But a man lives by reason, which he must develop by lengthy, temporal experience so that he may achieve prudence. Hence, children must be instructed by parents who are already experienced people. Nor are they able to receive such instruction as soon as they are born, but after a long time, and especially after they have reached the age of discretion. Moreover, a long time is needed for this instruction. Then, too, because of the impulsion of the passions, through which prudent judgment is vitiated, they require not merely instruction but correction. Now, a woman alone is not adequate to this task; rather, this demands the work of a husband, in whom reason is more developed for giving instruction and strength is more available for giving punishment. Therefore, in the human species, it is not enough, as in the case of birds, to devote a small amount of time to bringing up offspring, for a long period of life is required. Hence, since among all animals it is necessary for male and female to remain together as long as the work of the father is needed by the offspring, it is natural to the human being for the man to establish a lasting association with a designated woman, over no short period of time. Now, we call this society *matrimony*. Therefore, matrimony is natural for man, and promiscuous performance of the sexual act, outside matrimony, is contrary to man's good. For this reason, it must be a sin.

XI.9   Nor, in fact, should it be deemed a slight sin for a man to arrange for the emission of semen apart from the proper purpose of generating and bringing up children, on the argument that it is either a slight sin, or none at all, for a person to use a part of the body for a different use than that to which it is directed by nature (say, for instance, one chose to walk on his hands, or to use his feet for something usually done with the hands) because man's good is not much opposed by such inordinate use. However, the inordinate emission of semen is incompatible with the natural good; namely, the preservation of the species. Hence, after the sin of homicide whereby a human nature already in existence is destroyed, this type of sin appears to take next place, for by it the generation of human nature is precluded.

XI.10 Moreover, these views which have just been given have a solid basis in divine authority. That the emission of semen under conditions in which offspring cannot follow is illicit is quite clear. There is the text of Leviticus (18:22-23): "thou shalt not lie with mankind as with womankind . . . and thou shalt not copulate with any beast." And in I Corinthians (6:10): "Nor the effeminate, nor liers with mankind . . . shall possess the kingdom of God."

XI.11 Also, that fornication and every performance of the act of reproduction with a person other than one's wife are illicit is evident. For it is said: "There shall be no whore among the daughters of Israel, nor whoremonger among the sons of Israel" (Deut. 23:17); and in Tobias (4:13): "Take heed to keep thyself from all fornication, and beside thy wife never endure to know a crime"; and in I Corinthians (6:18): "Fly fornication."

XI.12 By this conclusion we refute the error of those who say that there is no more sin in the emission of semen than in the emission of any other superfluous matter, and also of those who state that fornication is not a sin.

That matrimony should be indivisable

XI.13 If one will make a proper consideration, the preceding reasoning will be seen to lead to the conclusion not only that the society of man and woman of the human species, which we call matrimony, should be long lasting, but even that it should endure throughout an entire life.

XI.14 Indeed, possessions are ordered to the preservation of natural life, and since natural life, which cannot be preserved perpetually in the father, is by a sort of succession preserved in the son in its specific likeness, it is naturally fitting for the son to succeed also to the things which belong to the father. So, it is natural that the father's solicitude for his son should endure until the end of the father's life. Therefore, if even in the case of birds the solicitude of the father gives rise to the cohabitation of male and female, the natural order demands that father and mother in the human species remain together until the end of life.

XI.15   It also seems to be against equity if the aforesaid society be dissolved. For the female needs the male, not merely for the sake of generation, as in the case of other animals, but also for the sake of government, since the male is both more perfect in reasoning and stronger in his powers. In fact, a woman is taken into man's society for the needs of generation; then, with the disappearance of a woman's fecundity and beauty, she is prevented from association with another man. So, if any man took a woman in the time of her youth, when beauty and fecundity were hers, and then sent her away after she had reached an advanced age, he would damage that woman contrary to natural equity.

XI.16   Again, it seems obviously inappropriate for a woman to be able to put away her husband, because a wife is naturally subject to her husband as governor, and it is not within the power of a person subject to another to depart from his rule. So, it would be against the natural order if a wife were able to abandon her husband. Therefore, if a husband were permitted to abandon his wife, the society of husband and wife would not be an association of equals, but, instead, a sort of slavery on the part of the wife.

XI.17   Besides, there is in men a certain natural solicitude to know their offspring. This is necessary for this reason: the child requires the father's direction for a long time. So, whenever there are obstacles to the ascertaining of offspring they are opposed to the natural instinct of the human species. But, if a husband could put away his wife, or a wife her husband, and have sexual relations with another person, certitude as to offspring would be precluded, for the wife would be united first with one man and later with another. So, it is contrary to the natural instinct of the human species for a wife to be separated from her husband. And thus, the union of male and female in the human species must be not only lasting, but also unbroken.

XI.18   Furthermore, the greater that friendship is, the more solid and long-lasting will it be. Now, there seems to be the greatest friendship between husband and wife, for they are united not only in the act of fleshly union, which produces a certain gentle association even among beasts, but also in the partnership of the whole range of domestic activity. Consequently, as an indication of this, man must even "leave his father and mother" for the sake of his wife, as is said in Genesis (2:24). Therefore, it is fitting for matrimony to be completely indissoluble.

XI.19   It should be considered, further, that generation is the only natural act that is ordered to the common good, for eating and the emission of waste matters pertain to the individual good, but generation to the preservation of the species. As a result, since law is established for the common good, those matters which pertain to generation must, above all others, be ordered by laws, both divine and human. Now, laws that are established should stem from the prompting of nature, if they are human; just as in the demonstrative sciences, also, every human discovery takes its origin from naturally known principles. But, if they are divine laws, they not only develop the prompting of nature but also supplement the deficiency of natural instinct, as things that are divinely revealed surpass the capacity of human reason. So, since there is a natural prompting within the human species, to the end that the union of man and wife be undivided, and that it be between one man and one woman, it was necessary for this to be ordered by human law. But divine law supplies a supernatural reason, drawn from the symbolism of the inseparable union between Christ and the Church, which is a union of one spouse with another (Eph.5:24-32). And thus, disorders connected with the act of generation are not only opposed to natural instinct, but are also transgressions of divine and human laws. Hence, a greater sin results from a disorder in this area than in regard to the use of food or other things of that kind.

XI.20   Moreover, since it is necessary for all other things to be ordered to what is best in man, the union of man and wife is not only ordered in this way because it is important to the generating of offspring, as it iş in the case of other animals, but also because it is in agreement with good behavior, which right reason directs either in reference to the individual man in himself, or in regard to man as a member of a family, or of a civil society. In fact, the undivided union of husband and wife is pertinent to good behavior. For thus, when they know that they are indivisibly united, the love of one spouse for the other will be more faithful. Also, both will be more solicitous in their care for domestic possessions when they keep in mind that they will remain continually in possession of these same things. As a result of this, the sources of disagreements which would have to come up between a man and his wife's relatives, if he could put away his wife, are removed, and a more solid affection is established among the relatives. Removed, also, are the occasions for adultery which are presented when a man is permitted to send away his wife, or the converse. In fact, by this practice an easier way of arranging marriage with those outside the family circle is provided.

XI.21   Hence it is said in Matthew (5:31) and in I Corinthians (7:10): "But I say to you . . . that the wife depart not from her husband."

XI.22   By this conclusion, moreover, we oppose the custom of those who put away their wives, though this was permitted the Jews in the old Law, "by reason of the hardness of their hearts" (Matt. 19:8); that is, because they were ready to kill their wives. So, the lesser evil was permitted them in order to prevent a greater evil.

That matrimony should be between one man and one woman

XI.23   It seems, too, that we should consider how it is inborn in the minds of all animals accustomed to sexual reproduction to allow no promiscuity; hence, fights occur among animals over the matter of sexual reproduction. And, in fact, among all animals there is one common reason, for every animal desires to enjoy freely the pleasure of the sexual act, as he also does the pleasure of food; but this liberty is restricted by the fact that several males may have access to one female, or the converse. The same situation obtains in the freedom of enjoying food, for one animal is obstructed if the food which he desires to eat is taken over by another animal. And so, animals fight over food and sexual relations in the same way. But among men there is a special reason, for, as we said, man naturally desires to know his offspring, and this knowledge would be completely destroyed if there were several males for one female. Therefore, that one female is for one male is a consequence of natural instinct.

XI.24   But a difference should be noted on this point. As far as the view that one woman should not have sexual relations with several men is concerned, both the afore-mentioned reasons apply. But, in regard to the conclusion that one man should not have relations with several females, the second argument does not work, since certainty as to offspring is not precluded if one male has relations with several women. But the first reason works against this practice, for, just as the freedom of associating with a woman at will is taken away from the husband, when the woman has another husband, so, too, the same freedom is taken away from a woman when her husband has several wives . . .

That not all sexual intercourse is sinful

XI.25   Now, just as it is contrary to reason for man to perform the act of carnal union contrary to what befits the generation and upbringing of offspring, so also is it in keeping with reason for a man to exercise the act of carnal union in a manner which is suited to the generation and upbringing of offspring. But only those things that are opposed to reason are prohibited by divine law, as is evident from what we said above. So, it is not right to say that every act of carnal union is a sin.

XI.26   Again, since bodily organs are the instruments of the soul, the end of each organ is its use, as is the case with any other instrument. Now, the use of certain bodily organs is carnal union. So, carnal union is the end of certain bodily organs. But that which is the end of certain natural things cannot be evil in itself, because things that exist naturally are ordered to their end by divine providence, as is plain from what was said above. Therefore, it is impossible for carnal union to be evil in itself.

XI.27   Besides, natural inclinations are present in things from God, Who moves all things. So, it is impossible for the natural inclination of a species to be toward what is evil in itself. But there is in all perfect animals a natural inclination toward carnal union. Therefore, it is impossible for carnal union to be evil in itself.

XI.28   Moreover, that without which a thing cannot be what is good and best is not evil in itself. But the perpetuation of the species can only be preserved in animals by generation, which is the result of carnal union. So, it is impossible for carnal union to be evil in itself.

XI.29   Hence it is said in I Corinthians (7:28): "if a virgin marry, she hath not sinned."

XI.30   Now, this disposes of the error of those who say that every act of carnal union is illicit, as a consequence of which view they entirely condemn matrimony and marriage arrangements. In fact, some of these people say this because they believe that bodily things arise, not from a good, but from an evil, source.

CRITIQUE

Because of their particular influence upon present-day Roman Catholic moral theology, it is important to subject Aquinas' views on sexuality and marriage to critical attention. It may be anachronistic to accuse him of propagating damaging sexual stereotypes or restrictive notions of the role of sexual intercourse, but it is still important to assess his overall arguments.

Positively, his writings on sexual issues offer much moral sense. In a more technological age, it is easier to miss the obvious fact that, whatever other functions it performs, human sexuality does have a primary function in reproduction. Further, within a Christian context, the upbringing of children in the most responsible manner remains a primary duty for all Christian parents. Most Christians might agree that the monogamous, exclusive family remains the most responsible context in which to carry out this duty. Sexuality often does entail procreation and procreation should involve responsible upbringing. Further, there is obvious sense in Aquinas' notion of sexual sin. Not only did he insist that the sexual act, or the desire that leads to this act, is not inherently sinful, but he also maintained that: 'Every act of sin proceeds from an inordinate craving after some temporal good. This again proceeds from an inordinate love of self; for to love anyone is to wish him good. Therefore inordinate love of self is the cause of all sin' (S.T. I.II.Q.77, Art. 4).

Negatively, his arguments illustrate some of the most crucial weaknesses of Natural law arguments. Many of the assumptions that Aquinas made about sexuality and sexual differentiation will appear to 20th Century readers as owing more to custom and convention than to Natural law. For example, he could assume that homosexuality and homosexual inclinations were indeed 'unnatural' and the consequence of sin or distortion. To many today this is not so clear: whatever the complex determinants of homosexuality might be, a homosexual predisposition does seem to be the 'nature' of some. Further, non-procreative, nocturnal emissions of semen, infertility at certain points in the menstrual cycle, and abortions in the form of miscarriages, all happen spontaneously and frequently and thus might be regarded as 'natural'. The very notion of the 'natural' in this area of sexuality seems to encourage value-judgements from its supposedly neutral users. Aquinas was no exception.

Supposing a Natural law theory of human sexuality could be established (it *is* surprisingly prevalent in popular, secular discussions of sexual morality) it would still face problems. Even if it is conceded that procreation is the obvious function of sexuality, it is far from clear that it *should* be the *only*, or the *indispensable*, function of human sexuality (this point will be made further in relation to *Extract 23*). Further, on Aquinas' own argument (XI.5), if a couple knows that one of them is spontaneously sterile, are they on that account to refrain from all further sexual intercourse? Many might argue that, particularly today in an over-crowded world, it would be irresponsible and unrealistic to restrict the function of sexual intercourse to reproduction and to proscribe it outside this function. But, even in the context of 13th Century Europe, Aquinas' logic was still faulty: to derive an exclusive moral prescription from an empirical observation of function was to commit an extraordinary category error. With the benefit of hind-sight, it has turned out to be a particularly troublesome error for many present-day Roman Catholics.

TEXT XII
LUTHER
On the Jews and their lies

I. *BACKGROUND*

This Text comes from *On the Jews and Their Lies* of 1543 (from *Luther's Works*, Vol. 47, Fortress Press, Philadelphia, 1971, pp. 137–42, trans. Martin H. Bertram). This virulent treatise, written three years before Luther's death, was unavailable in English translation until 1971 and is reproduced here only after considerable hesitation. Luther was always capable of violent swings of mood – as can be seen by comparing his two letters to the rebellious German peasants in 1525 (see *above*, p. 327) – but none is more startling or shocking than that represented here. The swing can be seen most fully if this treatise is compared with his treatise of 1523, *That Jesus Christ Was Born a Jew*. There he criticised the Roman Church for its crude attacks upon the Jews; 'They have dealt with the Jews as if they were dogs rather than human beings; they have done little else than deride them and seized their property' (*Luther's Works*, Vol. 45, p. 200). In contrast, Luther maintained the following position:

> If the Jew should take offence because we confess our Jesus to be a man, and yet true God, we will deal forcefully with that from Scripture in due time. But this is too harsh for a beginning. Let them first be suckled with milk, and begin by recognizing this man Jesus as the true Messiah; after that they may drink wine, and learn also that he is true God. For they have been led astray so long and so far that one must deal gently with them... So long as we thus treat them like dogs, how can we expect to work any good among them?. . . If we really want to help them, we must be guided in our dealings with them not by papal law but by the law of Christian love . . . If some of them should prove stiff-necked, what of it? After all, we ourselves are not all good Christians either (p. 229).

The tone is evidently patronising but not virulent. A number of Luther's contemporaries were dismayed by the later work, although fortunately it sold far fewer copies than the 1523 treatise. Luther wrote the present treatise in response to a Jewish apologetic pamphlet. In the first section (which starts with this Text) he examined the 'false boasts' of the Jews: in the second he examined a number of key biblical texts: in the third he returned to specific and, of course, much exaggerated, criticisms of the Jews: and in the final section he advised the authorities to let Jewish synagogues and houses be burnt and to deprive them of their prayer books and means of making a living:

> I wish and I ask that our rulers who have Jewish subjects exercise a sharp mercy towards these wretched people . . . they must act like a good physician who, when gangrene has set in, proceeds without mercy to cut, saw, and burn flesh, veins, bone, and marrow. Such a procedure must also be followed in this instance. Burn down their synagogues, forbid all that I enumerated earlier, force them to work, and deal harshly with them, as Moses did in the wilderness, slaying three thousand lest the whole people perish . . . If this does not help we must drive them out like mad dogs, so that we do not become partakers of their abominable blasphemy and all their other vices and thus merit God's wrath and be damned with them. I have done my duty. Now let everyone see to his. I am exonerated (*Luther's Works*, Vol. 47, p. 292).

2. KEY ISSUES

Luther was convinced by the time that he wrote this Text, that Jews are too 'venomous', 'embittered' and 'blind' to be converted into Christians and that, as a result, Christians should not trouble themselves to argue with them (XII.1-8). Further, their proud boasts about being descended from the patriarchs and of being a holy people (in contrast with 'we Gentiles'), are simply 'stupid folly' (XII.10-12). They even boast and thank God that they are male rather than female – just as Plato did (XII.12). Both the Old Testment prophets and Jesus and John the Baptist condemned the Jews for their pride (XII. 13).

Indeed, if the Jewish Messiah did come, they would reject, blaspheme and crucify him (XII. 14-15).

3. ETHICAL ARGUMENTS

There is an overall deontological basis to Luther's attack upon Jews (cf. *Text VI*). He labelled the Jews as 'miserable and accursed' (XII.1), 'embittered, venomous, blind' (XII.8) 'raving, mad, and stupid' (XII.12) and 'arrogant' and guilty of 'pride' (XII.13). These rhetorical labels or pejorative stereotypes are applied sweepingly (as are all racist notions) to Jews as a whole and, of themselves, are thought sufficient to condemn them. More consequentially, Luther also maintained that 'the terrible distress that has been theirs for over fourteen hundred years in exile' (XII.4) was also evidence of their condemnation.

4. BASES OF CHRISTIAN ETHICS

This Text illustrates how secular and religious anti-Semitism are often interconnected. Luther regarded the Bible as confirming his general condemnation of Jews. Ignoring the obvious Jewish context of the Bible and, indeed, the sayings of Jesus, he applied notions like that of the 'brood of vipers' and the 'devil's children' to contemporary Jews. In his earlier treatise he had reminded his readers 'that Jesus Christ was born a Jew', but in this Text Jesus is depicted simply as condemning all Jews. There is also a doctrinal basis to the anti-Semitism of Luther and of many of his contemporaries. For them, the Jew represented a permanent symbol of unredemption. Along with 'heretics' and 'apostates', they had been confronted by Christ, but had rejected him and had remained unconverted: all three groups were essentially unredeemed 'blasphemers' upholding an anti-Christian religion (cf. Aquinas, p. 204, *above*).

5. SOCIAL DETERMINANTS

By the 16th C, anti-Semitism was deeply embedded into European culture. Despite the relatively small number of Jews actually living in Europe at the time, they were frequently treated as scapegoats for sexual crimes, for plagues and even for natural disasters. In the 1490's they were driven from Spain and

Portugal and were often the object of discrimination in Luther's Germany. The statues of the virtuous, virginal, triumphant Church and the blinded, licentious, defeated Synagogue outside Strasbourg Cathedral typify medieval attitudes towards Jews. Nonetheless, since the virulence of *On the Jews and Their Lies* shocked even some of Luther's contemporary Reformers, it requires additional explanation. There is still debate about whether Luther was always inclined to be anti-Semitic and merely disguised this for tactical reasons in *That Jesus Christ Was Born a Jew*, or whether he became more so in embittered old age. Gordon Rupp argues for this second position:

> We remember the context of the last five years of Luther's life. They were clouded by many physical ills. In these writings, he refers to his gall-stones and to bleeding ulcers, while the sight of one eye was impaired and he had a disease of the middle ear and, probably, angina . . . Ancient foes were on the wing. The Counter Reformation was under way, and a great Papal Council had been summoned at last. For twenty-five years the Emperor had been unable to drive home that Edict of Worms which had declared Luther an outlaw. In his last days, Luther was aware that armies were gathering . . . So like an old lion, he roared, he bared his teeth and turned at bay against them all (*Martin Luther and the Jews*, p.16).

Further, as Rupp points out, Luther's wife appears to have been even more anti-Semitic than he was and may have influenced his later views. On a journey in 1546, he wrote to her: 'My poor old darling, I was taken faint before Eiselben. My fault, but if you had been here you would have blamed it on the Jews . . . when we have settled our main business I must do something about those Jews – Count Albert is for it, but nobody does anything and I shall have to give him a word of support from the pulpit' (*Weimarer Ausgabe*, Br. II, 286.1).

6. SOCIAL SIGNIFICANCE
Even though *On the Jews and Their Lies* did not itself circulate widely, its social significance must be assessed together with

other expressions of medieval and post-medieval anti-Semitism by Christians. Whereas it may not be possible to establish a direct causal relationship between them and 20th Century Nazi atrocities (particularly since Nazi ideology was, in part, explicitly anti-Christian), the persistence of European anti-Semitism is now widely seen as connected with certain Christian attitudes and convictions. Within recent years, a number of sociologists have tried to assess whether or not there is a causal relationship between present-day Christian attitudes and anti-Semitism. One of the most celebrated studies, by Charles Glock and Rodney Stark, concludes:

We have searched for a religious basis for anti-Semitism. It was suggested that commitment to traditional Christian ideology predisposed persons to adopt a particularistic conception of religious legitimacy, narrowly to consider their own religious status as the only acceptable faith. These features of Christianity were then linked with historical images of the Jews as apostates from true faith and as the crucifiers of Jesus. Subsequently it was shown that orthodoxy, particularism, and a negative image of the historic Jew, combined with a rejection of values of religious libertarianism, overwhelmingly predicted a hostile *religious* image of the contemporary Jew' (*Christian Beliefs and Anti-Semitism*, p. 130).

FURTHER READING
E. Gordon Rupp's Robert Waley Cohen Memorial Lecture to the Council of Christians and Jews, *Martin Luther and the Jews*, contains a full discussion of all of the main Luther Texts on the Jews. There is also an important introduction to *On The Jews and Their Lies* in *Luther's Works*, Vol. 47. An excellent, critical review of the considerable amount of sociological research that has been conducted (mainly in America) on a possible causal relationship between Christianity and anti-Semitism/racial prejudice, is by R.L. Gorsuch and A. Aleshire. 'Christian Faith and Prejudice: Review of Research', *Journal for the Scientific Study of Religion*, Sept. 1974,. 13.3. The article is less confident than Glock and Stark about being able to establish such a rela-

tionship. Important theological and historical discussions of Christianity and anti-Semitism can be found in Gregory Baum's *The Jews and the Gospel* and *Religion and Alienation*, Rosemary Ruether's *Faith and Fratricide* and Charlotte Klein's *Anti-Judaism in Christian Theology*.

TEXT XII

LUTHER

On the Jews and their lies

XII.1   I had made up my mind to write no more either about the Jews or against them. But since I learned that these miserable and accursed people do not cease to lure to themselves even us, that is, the Christians, I have published this little book, so that I might be found among those who opposed such poisonous activities of the Jews and who warned the Christians to be on their guard against them. I would not have believed that a Christian could be duped by the Jews into taking their exile and wretchedness upon himself. However, the devil is the god of the world, and wherever God's word is absent he has an easy task, not only with the weak but also with the strong. May God help us. Amen.

XII.2   Grace and peace in the Lord. Dear sir a good friend, I have received a treatise in which a Jew engages in dialogue with a Christian. He dares to pervert the scriptural passages which we cite in testimony to our faith, concerning our Lord Christ and Mary his mother, and to interpret them quite differently. With this argument he thinks he can destroy the basis of our faith.

XII.3   This is my reply to you and to him. It is not my purpose to quarrel with the Jews, nor to learn from them how they interpret or understand Scripture; I know all of that very well already. Much less do I propose to convert the Jews, for that is impossible. Those two excellent men, Lyra and Burgensis, together with others, truthfully described the Jews' vile interpretation for us two hundred and one hundred years ago respectively. Indeed they refuted it thoroughly. However, this was no help at all to the Jews, and they have grown steadily worse.

XII.4   They have failed to learn any lesson from the terrible distress that has been theirs for over fourteen hundred years in exile. Nor can they obtain any end or definite terminus of this, as they suppose, by means of the vehement cries and laments to God. If these blows do not help, it is reasonable to assume that our talking and explaining will help even less.

XII.5   Therefore a Christian should be content and not argue with the Jews. But if you have to or want to talk with them, do not say any more than this: "Listen, Jew, are you aware that Jerusalem and your sovereignty, together with your temple and priesthood, have been destroyed for over 1,460 years?" For this year, which we Christians write as the year 1542 since the birth of Christ, is exactly 1,468 years, going on fifteen hundred years, since Vespasian and Titus destroyed Jerusalem and expelled the Jews from the city. Let the Jews bite on this nut and dispute this question as long as they wish.

XII.6   For such ruthless wrath of God is sufficient evidence that they assuredly have erred and gone astray. Even a child can comprehend this. For one dare not regard God as so cruel that he would punish his own people so long, so terribly, so unmercifully, and in addition keep silent, comforting them neither with words nor with deeds, and fixing no time limit and no end to it. Who would have faith, hope, or love toward such a God? Therefore this work of wrath is proof that the Jews, surely rejected by God, are no longer his people, and neither is he any longer their God. This is in accord with Hosea 1 (:9), "Call his name Not my people, for you are not my people and I am not your God." Yes, unfortunately, this is their lot, truly a terrible one. They may interpret this as they will; we see the facts before our eyes, and these do not deceive us.

XII.7   If there were but a spark of reason or understanding in them, they would surely say to themselves: "O Lord

God, something has gone wrong with us. Our misery is too great, too long, too severe; God has forgotten us!" etc. To be sure, I am not a Jew, but I really do not like to contemplate God's awful wrath toward this people. It sends a shudder of fear through body and soul, for I ask, What will the eternal wrath of God in hell be like toward false Christians and all unbelievers? Well, let the Jews regard our Lord Jesus as they will. We behold the fulfillment of the words spoken by him in Luke 21 (:20, 22f.): "But when you see Jerusalem surrounded by armies, then know that its desolation has come near . . . for these are days of vengeance. For great distress shall be upon the earth and wrath upon this people."

XII.8   In short, as has already been said, do not engage much in debate with Jews about the articles of our faith. From their youth they have been so nurtured with venom and rancor against our Lord that there is no hope until they reach the point where their misery finally makes them pliable and they are forced to confess that the Messiah has come, and that he is our Jesus. Until such a time it is much too early, yes, it is useless to argue with them about how God is triune, how he became man, and how Mary is the mother of God. No human reason nor any human heart will ever grant these things, much less the embittered, venomous, blind heart of the Jews. As has already been said, what God cannot reform with such cruel blows, we will be unable to change with words and works. Moses was unable to reform the Pharaoh by means of plagues, miracles, pleas, or threats; he had to let him drown in the sea.

XII.9   Now, in order to strengthen our faith, we want to deal with a few crass follies of the Jews in their belief and their exegesis of the Scriptures, since they so maliciously revile our faith. If this should move any Jew to reform and repent, so much the better. We are now not talking with the Jews but about the Jews and their dealings, so that our Germans, too, might be informed.

XII.10   There is one thing about which they boast and pride themselves beyond measure, and that is their descent from the foremost people on earth, from Abraham, Sarah, Isaac, Rebekah, Jacob, and from the twelve patriachs, and thus from the holy people of Israel. St. Paul himself admits this when he says in Romans 9 (:5): *Quorum patres*, that is, "To them belong the patriarchs, and of their race is the Christ," etc. And Christ himself declares in John 4 (:22), "Salvation is from the Jews." Therefore they boast of being the noblest, yes, the only noble people on earth. In comparison with them and in their eyes we Gentiles (*Goyim*) are not human; in fact we hardly deserve to be considered poor worms by them. For we are not of that high and noble blood, lineage, birth, and descent. This is their argument, and indeed I think it is the greatest and strongest reason for their pride and boasting.

XII.11   Therefore, God has to endure that in their synagogues, their prayers, songs, doctrines, and their whole life, they come and stand before him and plague him grievously (if I may speak of God in such a human fashion). Thus he must listen to their boasts and their praises to him for setting them apart from the Gentiles, for letting them be descended from the holy patriarchs, and for selecting them to be his holy and peculiar people, etc. And there is no limit and no end to this boasting about their descent and their physical birth from the fathers.

XII.12   And to fill the measure of their raving, mad, and stupid folly, they boast and they thank God, in the first place, because they were created as human beings and not as animals; in the second place, because they are Israelites and not *Goyim* (Gentiles); in the third place because they were created as males and not as females. They did not learn such tomfoolery from Israel, but from the *Goyim*. For history records that the Greek Plato daily accorded God such praise and thanksgiving – if such arrogance and blasphemy may be termed praise of God. This man, too, praised his gods for these three items: that he was a human being and not an animal; a male and not a female; a Greek and not a non–Greek or barbarian. This is a fool's boast, the gratitude of a barbarian who blasphemes God!

Similarly, the Italians fancy themselves the only human beings; they imagine that all other people in the world are non-humans, mere ducks or mice by comparison.

XII.13   No one can take away from them their pride concerning their blood and their descent from Israel. In the Old Testament they lost many a battle in wars over this matter, though no Jew understands this. All the prophets censured them for it, for it betrays an arrogant, carnal presumption devoid of spirit and of faith. They were also slain and persecuted for this reason. St. John the Baptist took them to task severely because of it, saying, "Do not presume to say to yourselves. 'We have Abraham for our father'; for I tell you, God is able from these stones to raise up children to Abraham" (Matt. 3:9). He did not call them Abraham's children, but a "brood of vipers" (Matt. 3:7). Oh, that was too insulting for the noble blood and race of Israel, and they declared, "He has a demon" (Matt. 11:18). Our Lord also calls them a "brood of vipers"; furthermore, in John 8 (:39,44) he states: "If you were Abraham's children, you would do what Abraham did . . . You are of your father the devil." It was intolerable to them to hear that they were not Abraham's but the devil's children, nor can they bear to hear this today. If they should surrender this boast and argument, their whole system which is built on it would topple and change.

XII.14   I hold that if their Messiah, for whom they hope, should come and do away with their boast and its basis they would crucify and blaspheme him seven times worse than they did our Messiah; and they would also say that he was not the true Messiah, but a deceiving devil. For they have portrayed their Messiah to themselves as one who would strengthen and increase such carnal and arrogant error regarding nobility of blood and lineage. That is the same as saying that he should assist them in blaspheming God and in viewing his creatures with disdain, including the women, who are also human beings and the image of God as well as we; moreover, they are our own flesh and blood, such as mother, sister, daughter, housewives, etc. For in accordance with the afore-mentioned threefold song of praise, they do not hold Sarah (as a woman) to be as noble as Abraham (as a man). Perhaps they wish to honor themselves for being born half noble, of a noble father, and half ignoble, of an ignoble mother. But enough of this tomfoolery and trickery.

XII.15 We propose to discuss their argument and boast and prove convincingly before God and the world – not before the Jews, for, as already said, they would accept this neither from Moses nor from their Messiah himself – that their argument is quite empty and stands condemned.

CRITIQUE

The debate about whether or not there is a causal connection between certain Christian attitudes and beliefs and the phenomenon of anti-Semitism is yet to be resolved. However, in Luther's later writings there *is* a clear connection between his religious convictions, his mode of biblical exegesis and his appalling attitude towards the Jews. His convictions and prejudices appear mutually reinforcing. His growing intolerance of all but evangelical Christians, his increasing conviction that Jews are unconvertible, and therefore unredeemable, his penchant for quoting 'anti-Semitic' (!) biblical passages, and his adoption of popular stereotypes about Jews, need not be related to each other in any single causal sequence. They provide legitimation for each other.

It is for this reason that a number of theologians today believe that it is essential for Christians to find less exclusive ways of expressing their faith than was often the case in the past (I have argued this further in *Prophecy and Praxis*). In all three classical authors, but especially here in Luther, religious intolerance inclined them, on occasions, to civil totalitarianism. Rupp's conclusion is judicious:

But, as we follow Luther through the years, we find a signal instance of how we become like what we hate. We see a growing obstinacy, a hardening of heart, a withering of compassion, a proneness to contemptuous abuse – the very things he thought were the marks of judgment on the Jews . . . What if not pure doctrine, but suffering be a hall-mark of the People of God? And if, as Luther thought, Jew and Gentile may be bound together in a solidarity of guilt, have we perhaps begun to understand what is the greater solidarity of promise? May not Jew and Christian together explore this more excellent way, in penitence and compassion (*Martin Luther and the Jews*, p.22).

EXTRACTS 19-25
FLETCHER, GUSTAFSON, CLEMENT, QUAKER GROUP, PAUL VI, HASTINGS AND RUETHER

I. BACKGROUND

Joseph Fletcher's *Extract 19* comes from his *Morals and Medicine* (Gollancz, London, 1955, pp. 190-7 & 207-10), James M. Gustafson's *Extract 20* from an article entitled a 'A Protestant Ethical Approach' in ed. John T. Noonan, Jr., *The Morality of Abortion* (Harvard University Press, Cambridge, Massachusetts, 1970, pp. 107, 110-4, 116-7 & 119-22), M. Olivier Clément's *Extract 21* was an article for *Episkepsis* (No. 78, 29th May, 1973) published by the Orthodox Center of the Ecumenical Patriarchate, Geneva, entitled originally, 'Some Observations on Abortion by an Orthodox', the Quaker Group's *Extract 22* comes from ed. Alastair Heron, *Towards a Quaker View of Sex: An essay by a group of Friends* (Friends Home Service Committee, London, revised edition, 1964, pp. 43-8 & 50-2), Pope Paul VI's *Extract 23* from his Encyclical Letter *Humanae Vitae* (Catholic Truth Society, London, revised edition, 1970, pp. 6-8 & 10-19), Adrian Hastings' *Extract 24* from ed. Clifford S. Hill and David Mathews, *Race: a Christian Symposium* (Gollancz, London, 1968, pp. 139-43) and Rosemary Radford Ruether's *Extract 25* from her *New Woman/New Earth* (Seabury, New York, 1975, pp. 186, 187-90 & 204-11). Fletcher (see *above*, pp. 101) wrote *Morals and Medicine* in 1954 on basis of the Lowell lectures he gave at Harvard University in 1949. The book reflects his long-term interest in medical ethics and his controversial support for the legalization of voluntary euthanasia. In the Preface, he admits that the book is 'at the most only a modest contribution to the ethics of medicine, not to its theology', but nonetheless hopes that 'the ethical judgments I have reached are within the range and provision of Christian theology' (p.xi). Adopting an explicitly personalist position in the book (it was written before he developed the notion of 'situation ethics'), he maintains that it is based upon his personal experiences, 'gained through a quarter of a century in the ministry, fifteen of them concentrated in the teaching and clinical supervision of theological students exploring human needs in parishes, hospitals, social agencies, and homes' (p.xiii). Gustafson's *Extract 20* and Clément's *Extract 21* present very different Reformed and Orthodox approaches to the issue of abortion. Together they also provide an interesting contrast with the liberal Anglican position of Fletcher in *Extract 4*. James M Gustafson, a professor of Christian ethics, first at Yale and now at Chicago University, is the author of a number of works attempting to compare Roman Catholic and Reformed approaches to Christian ethics – including *Can Ethics be Christian?*, *Protestant and Roman Catholic Ethics* and *Theology and Ethics*. Clément is a professor at St. Sergius Orthodox Institute in Paris. *Extract 22* and *Extract 23* provide a similar contrast and illustrate the pluralism apparent in this area of Christian ethics. The group of Quakers that produced *Towards a Quaker View of Sex* included three psychiatrists, two headmasters, a barrister, a psychologist, a teacher of educationally subnormal children, a research zoologist and a marriage guidance counsellor. The group started to meet in 1957 as a response to 'problems brought by young Quaker students, faced with homosexual difficulties, who came to older Friends for help and guidance': for them it 'appeared that the Society of Friends as such had little to say to people troubled sexually, and that at the same time many Friends were in serious doubt whether the Church's traditional view spoke to this condition' (first edition, p.5). Originally published in the same year as John Robinson's *Honest to God* (SCM, 1963), it caused considerable interest and was re-printed several times within a few months. By 1968, it was widely expected in the West that Paul VI would seek to liberalise the official Roman Catholic positions on contraception and, possibly, even on abortion. Vatican II had contributed to these expectations, as had a general concern about the over-population for the world. However, after agonising over the issues for several months, Paul finally published his Encyclical *Humanae Vitae*, re-inforcing the traditionalist positions of Pius XII. Hastings, in contrast, belongs to a much more radical form of Roman Catholicism and has been an outspoken critic of traditionalist Roman Catholic understandings of both sexuality and priestly celibacy. In *Extract 24*, he writes on one of his most central interests, having worked for many years in various parts of Africa and written a number of important books on contemporary Christianity there including *A History of African Christianity 1950-75* (CUP, 1975). He is currently a professor of religious studies at Leeds University. Rosemary Ruether also comes from a Roman Catholic background and is now recognised as one of the leading feminist theologians. She is professor of historical theology at Howard University and her books include *Liberation Theology* (Paulist Press, 1972) and *Faith and Fratricide: The Theological Roots of Anti-Semitism* (Seabury, 1974). She regards feminism as a means to overcome a number of 20th Century forms of 'alienation': 'In Nazism the reactionary drive against the libertarian tradition culminated in a virulent revival of racism, misogynism, elitism, and military and national chauvinism. Its victims were Jews, Communists, Social Democrats and libertarians of all kinds – and finally, the nascent women's movement' (*Liberation Theology*, pp. 117-8). Whilst Christianity was not actually the originator of these forms of alienation, it 'took over this alienated world view of late classical civilisation' (p. 122). But now, 'women must be the spokesmen for a new humanity arising out of the reconciliation of spirit and body' (p. 124).

2. KEY ISSUES

Fletcher defends voluntary medical euthanasia for patients enduring incurable and fatal physical suffering. He argues that it should not be confused with eugenics, but rather be seen as choosing a peaceful death (19.11-12). He realises that euthanasia might be seen as a form of suicide (and, therefore, following *Text X*, as wrong), but he maintains that men do have a right to die and that suicide, as such, is not necessarily egoistic (19.1). Indeed, it would be wrong to prolong mere life at the expense of an individual's personality (19.2). For him, euthanasia is not 'murder', since it involves no malice on the part of the doctor (19.3), nor need it infringe the Decalogue, since it is *unlawful* killing which is prohibited (19.7-8). Further, some objections to euthanasia – e.g. the notion that God alone should decide when someone should die, or the belief that suffering should be accepted as part of the divine plan (19.4 & 9) – can be seen to be objections to *any* form of medical intervention.

Gustafson's approach to abortion is considerably more complex than that of Fletcher in *Extract 4*. Like Fletcher, he starts with a case-study of a rape victim (in some respects it is a more difficult case than that of Fletcher since it involves the concept, which is often denied by legal systems, of 'marital rape'). But, unlike Fletcher, he takes moral rules and 'legalism' very seriously. He points out that there are considerable medical and legal complications in this case (20.3-4). Nonetheless, there are strong financial and spiritual/emotional reasons for the victim wishing to seek an abortion (20.5-6). At the same time, there are also three competing moral considerations in the case – based upon the inviolability of life, the evils of rape and the keeping of civil laws against abortion (20.7-8). (This Extract was clearly written before the American Supreme Court ruling disallowing particular State laws against abortion). One of the crucial difficulties of such a case is that, for the Christian, it involves factors other than straightforward beliefs, principles and logic – such as notions of love (20.9-11). Together these make the case highly ambiguous (20.1214). Although he is aware that some will disagree, Gustafson concludes that he would favour an abortion in this case (20.15). He sees the case as consisting of a number of competing values (20.16-17), but insists that compassion is vital (20.18). Whilst he is concerned to differentiate his Reformed position from a traditionalist Roman Catholic position on abortion, he is aware that *in practice* the two positions may not be that different (20.21-3 – a recurring theme in his writings). Finally, he differentiates his position from situationists or contextualists such as Paul Lehmann (in *Ethics in a Christian Context* - 20.24).

Clément attempts to set out a 'spiritual approach' to the problem of abortion and then to examine its social implications. In an Orthodox perspective, the human beings exists from the moment of conception (21.3) and belongs, not to the parents, but to God (21.4). Women who have abortions risk destroying their own spiritual natures (21.5). Yet Christians can properly affirm all of this only if they are prepared to care physically and spiritually for women who are tempted to have abortions (21.6-9). This does not mean that Christians must impose their views on others by law – they must insist upon the spiritual foundation of their views. But, in pluralistic societies at least, Christians can support measures to educate the young and warn legislators of the psychological and spiritual dangers of abortion, without at the same time victimising women seeking abortions (21.10). Even if legislators conclude that they must allow limited abortion, the Christian must continue to stress the tragedy of abortion and the real meaning of love (21.11).

The Quaker Group's approach is much closer to that of Fletcher (see also *Extract 4*). Throughout the report the argument is against what is seen as the traditional, codified, prescriptive approach of the 'organised churches'. This latter approach has been tainted by a literalistic understanding of the Adam and Eve myth, viewing sexual intercourse as inherently sinful (22.1-8). In rejecting this approach, it is maintained that sexual activity is essentially neither good nor bad: it can be indulged in destructively or constructively (22.9). For neither homosexuals nor heterosexuals can love be codified (22.11-12). Positively, some form of morality is essential, since all acts have an impact upon society; marriage and family life should be preserved, at least to provide a loving context for children; and sexual exploitation of any sort is sin (22.14). Morality should be creative, as God himself is creative, and should be grounded in personal experience rather than in some external authority (22.16-19). To avoid misinterpretation, the Group insists that, at an individual level, the traditional Christian code can be enriching if it comes from the heart (22.20-24) and that this approach should not be seen as a justification of permissiveness or of sexual exploitation – marital or extra-marital – heterosexual or homosexual (22.29-33). True chastity should be regarded as a standard of human relationships and as a quality of the spirit, not as a physical act (22.29-33).

For Paul VI (as for Clément) such a divorce between the physical and the spiritual is unacceptable. Whilst not viewing sexual activity as inherently sinful, but rather as 'honourable and good' (23.24), he does insist that, if it involves the 'direct interruption of the generative process', it thereby becomes sinful (23.28). All sexual intercourse must allow both its unitive and procreative functions to operate. It is on this principle that both induced abortion and certain forms of contraception are condemned. He is aware of the population explosion and the changed economic structure of the present-day world (22.1-3) and that this has led many to argue for an acceptance of medicinal contraception (22.4-6). He argues that marital love is fully human and should be total, faithful and creative (23.10-17). Within marriage, responsible parenthood requires couples to recognise that they have duties towards God, to themselves, to their families and to human society (27.18-22) and that one of these duties – based upon Natural law – involves obedience to the principle of always allowing *both* of the functions of sexual intercourse to operate (23.23-4). Sexual intercourse which is deliberately contraceptive, direct sterilization and induced abortion are all intrinsically wrong (27.27-31). Spacing births, for good reasons, by taking advantage of a woman's natural cycles is allowable, since this is indeed natural and does not tempt people to marital infidelity or allow Governments to abuse the situation (22.34-8). Paul VI is aware that this position will not be acceptable to all, but still insists that the Church must not betray its responsibility to expediency (23.39-41).

Hastings is more conscious of the fallibility of the historical Church and of the need for Christians 'to admit it without circumlocution' (24.4). Nonetheless, like Paul VI, he lays much stress upon the Created Order and believes that moral implications can be derived from this Order. In this instance, it is the phenomenon of racism which is antithetical to Creation (24.1:cf. *Extract 11.7-10*). The Christian Gospel is fundamentally opposed to contemporary forms of racism (i.e. racial theories and labels) and racialism (i.e. active racial discrimination) and has universalism built into it (24.2-3). So, even though racial discrimination is often a blatant feature of contemporary Christianity, it is condemned by the majority of Catholic and non-Catholic Christians (24.4-5). The Church cannot teach 'a spiritual unity and admit a physical separation' (24.7) but is rather the sacrament of unity, the unity of all men (24.8). In the Eucharist, Christians are one body, the very negation of apartheid (24.9-10). Without this unity the Church is not the Church (24.11-12).

Ruether is also passionately concerned about the unity of humans. Elsewhere she has written extensively upon various forms of racism and racialism and of their links with certain forms of Christian belief. In this passage she is more concerned with sexist divisions and their links with differing understandings of nature. She argues that divisions between mind and body and between society and nature belong, not to the Old Testament, but to the Greek and Christian traditions (25.1-4). In these latter traditions, nature and the bodily are typically regarded as inferior; and women are regarded as belonging more to them than to the transcendent spiritual realm of males (25.5-7). Outside the sphere of redemption, Christianity typically regarded nature as demonic and the lusty female as the stereotype of the demonic (25.8). To escape these two dominations – of women and of nature – Ruether argues that society must change its world-view away from concepts of domination, possession, conquest and accumulation (25.9). This must be achieved, not through escapist, romantic primitivism (25.10), but through a communitarian socialism in which work-home and male-female dualities are overcome (25.11-14). She then outlines a number of practical ways in which this might be achieved by reviewing the traditional functions and structures of the nuclear family (25.16-8). Thus, 'society would have to be transfigured by the glimpse of a new type of social personality' (25.19).

3. ETHICAL ARGUMENTS

It is noticeable here, that those writing from a Roman Catholic or Orthodox background tend to argue deontologically, whereas both Fletcher and the Quaker Group are primarily personalists, and even Gustafson shows signs of a tendency towards personalism (20. 8-12 & 15). So, even though both Hastings and Ruether represent radical perspectives emerging from Roman Catholic tradition (perspectives which in many respects are highly critical of this tradition), their ethical arguments are closer in kind to those of Paul VI and Clément than they are to those of Fletcher and the Quaker Group. Certainly, both Paul

VI (23.7 & 24) and Hastings (24.3) make explicit use of Natural law and both are emphatic that the precepts derived from Natural law *are* to be obeyed (23.24 & 24.6). Ruether makes no explicit use of Natural law, but the deontological character of her overall argument is evident from the way that she regards concepts, such as 'alienation' (25.3), 'subjugation' (25.5), 'repression' (25.6), etc., as self-evidently wrong. The force of her argument depends almost entirely upon these deontological convictions. On their basis she can make such emphatic claims as, for example, that 'an ecological revolution must overthrow all the social structures of domination' (25.9). Clément's argument, too, appears to be based upon a deontological conviction – in this case, that life, from the moment of conception, is God-given and fully human and therefore that abortion is wrong.

Fletcher adopts a consciously personalist position (19.2 & 19.10f.) and is critical of positions which refuse 'to allow for anything but the consequences of a human act' as ethical criteria (19.3). This personalism does not contain all the features of his later 'situation ethics' (e.g. in 19.3 he seems prepared to accept the precept that 'murder is wrong' and writes more about 'mercy' than '*agape*') but it is clearly related to situationism. Similarly, the Quaker Group's rejection of a tradition which 'knows precisely what is right and what is wrong' and their insistence that 'love cannot be confined to a pattern' (22.11) belong to the personalist position. More specifically, Ramsey identified their position as one of act-agapism (see *Extract 5.4*). To this position they add the Quaker emphasis upon personal experience as the main source of authority on moral and religious issues (22.16).

Nonetheless elements of other ethical approaches are also evident in the Extracts. Paul VI appears at first to reject consequentialism (23.31), but then uses consequential arguments to justify 'natural' methods of contraception (23.36-7). The Quaker Group justify the institution of marriage consequentially (22.14) and finally assess sexual activity by the criterion of whether it is 'destructive' or 'constructive' (22.25f.). Clément, too, is influenced in his argument about what he believes to be the psychological and spiritual damage caused by abortion (21.5). At times, Fletcher appears to assume a deontological concept of 'rights' (19.1). And Gustafson, whilst finally rejecting situationism or contextualism (20.24) seems to accept a modified Natural law position similar to that of Ramsey or Niebuhr (see *above*, p. 105).

4. BASES OF CHRISTIAN ETHICS

The Bible has a fairly central place in all except Gustafson, but in none is it treated as the only source of authority. Fletcher tends to use the Bible to corroborate positions that he has already reached (19.13 – cf 4.9) or to form objections to his own position (19.7-8). Other theologians are used by him in a similar way (19.4-5). It seems likely that it is the notion of 'mercy' which is most instrumental to his position on euthanasia (19.4 & 14). For Clément and Hastings, general Biblical concepts are crucial to their positions (21.3 & 24. 1-2). Yet for both theologians, tradition appears to be equally important. So, Clément makes characteristic, authenticating references to Orthodox tradition (21.3 & 5) and to liturgy (21.3 & 8-9), whereas Hastings refers to papal teaching (24. 3-5 & 8). Significantly, Hastings also uses a pronouncement from the WCC as a similar authority to be cited (24.4-5). Again, for both, doctrine is extremely important. Clément's position is governed by his Orthodox emphasis upon the 'spiritual' (cf Berdyaev's *Extract 8*), whereas Hastings' understanding of the unity of man is interpreted in sacramental and eucharistic terms. For Gustafson, too, doctrine is crucial. Even though he argues that his case cannot be resolved solely through theological principles or Natural law precepts (20.9), his argument is strongly shaped by his notions of God (20.10-11).

For Paul VI, it is tradition and, particularly, consistency with previous papal teaching, that appears to be the most important influence upon his position (e.g. 23.7, 17, 27 & 39). His use of the Bible tends to be illustrative (23.10 & 39). The Quaker Group's and Ruether's use of the Bible tends to be illustrative in a different sense. Both Extracts have, in common, a desire to show that previous Christian approaches to their respective moral issue are wrong and destructive. Either as a result of misusing the Bible or as a result of prejudices already within the

Bible, Christianity has hitherto misled people in the areas of sexuality or sexism. In neither Extract does either the Bible or Christian tradition appear to play a significant role in forming their own positions. For the Quakers, it is personal experience which is thought to be crucial (22.16f): a moral code must have 'its roots in the depths of our being' (22.21). For Ruether, the present-day feminist critique might seem to be the strongest influence upon her concept of 'communitarian socialism' (25.11-14).

5. SOCIAL DETERMINANTS

Secular influences are evident in all of these Extracts. This is even true of those Extracts by Paul VI and Clément which are consciously written to counter what they regard as prevailing secular assumptions. So, although Clément emphasises the 'spiritual' throughout – in terms, both of the unity of spirit and body in the embryo and of the spiritual health of the mother – he concedes that Western Christians live in pluralistic societies (21.10). In such societies, illegal abortion is already a reality (he was writing before the legalisation of abortion in France) and he is aware that absolutist Christian positions may end up damaging the situation still further. His theology requires an absolutist rejection of abortion, but his experiences within Western society militate against this. Similarly, Paul VI's position would have been more consistent had he rejected all methods of contraception. But, in response to the social changes that he himself indicates (23.1-3), the concession had already been made, that 'natural' methods of contraception are allowable. In the debate that followed, it soon became apparent that, the distinction between 'natural' methods (themselves often requiring thermometers, ovulation charts etc.) and 'artificial' methods, is difficult to sustain or justify.

The social factors influencing the other Extracts are recognised by each of them. Fletcher believes that his pastoral experience in hospitals and his continued medical contacts whilst teaching, contributed directly to his concern about euthanasia. Gustafson's recent work is all characterised by a concern to take social factors very seriously (19.1-6). More than most Christian ethicists, he often uses sociology. The Quakers believe that their position is a direct response to young people, particularly homosexuals, coming to each of them for pastoral help at a time of social transition on sexual issues. Hastings uses his own widespread experience of human contact with differing peoples in Africa. And Ruether shows the clear influence of the women's movement of the 1970's. All provide clear and self-aware illustrations of one of the central contentions of this Textbook – that theology generally, and Christian ethics in particular, must always be related to the social context from which it derives.

6. SOCIAL SIGNIFICANCE

Only Paul VI's *Humanae Vitae* has had a widespread influence upon society at large. When it was first published, *Towards a Quaker View of Sex* was considered controversial. It was attacked by Paul Ramsey in his *Deeds and Rules in Christian Ethics*, but defended by more radical theologians such as John Robinson. The fact that it was first published within months of the latter's *Honest to God*, contributed to its impact upon the contemporary churches. Fletcher's *Morals and Medicine* was first published in the previous decade and before the emergence of 'secular theology'. Nonetheless, Fletcher's continued support of voluntary euthanasia has often been cited by its American defenders: at a time when most churches were opposed to it, his social significance may have resided in the legitimation he could provide for the movement. And Ruether is proving one of the most influential feminist theologians today. Yet, it was Paul VI's encyclical which directly affected the lives of ordinary Roman Catholics and it effectively ensured continued official opposition by the Roman Catholic Church both to induced abortion and to medicinal contraception. Even though there appears to be a difference in the West between the actual practice of Roman Catholic laity (who *do* resort to induced abortion and medicinal contraception in commensurate numbers to non-Roman Catholics) and the official position of the Church, the latter continues. It seems likely that the effect of this continuing difference amongst articulate Roman Catholics, has been to lead them to be more critical of authority within the Church. If this suggestion is correct, it provides an interesting illustration of the way in which theology may sometimes by socially significant in ways unintended by theologians themselves.

FURTHER READING

The expanded version of Paul Ramsey's *Deeds and Rules in Christian Ethics* (1967) provides an important critique of both Fletcher and the Quaker Group. Fletcher's own *Moral Responsibility* continues the debate about euthanasia. Gustafson's *Protestant and Roman Catholic Ethics* sets *Humanae Vitae* into its theological and social context in recent debate. A number of other Reformed and Roman Catholic contributors to ed. John T. Noonan Jr.'s *The Morality of Abortion* - including Noonan himself, Paul Ramsey and Bernard Häring – make important contributions to the ethical debate. Further, Noonan's study *Contraception* provides a useful history of Roman Catholic and Canonist attitudes to contraception. Long's studies (see *above*, p.11) provide overall commentaries. For studies of racism and theology, see *above*, p. 416.

EXTRACT 19

FLETCHER

Euthanasia

19.1   (A.) It is objected that euthanasia, when voluntary, is really suicide. If this is true, and it would seem to be obviously true, then the proper question is: have we ever a right to commit suicide? Among Catholic moralists the most common ruling is that "it is never permitted to kill oneself intentionally, without explicit divine inspiration to do." Humility requires us to assume that divine inspiration cannot reasonably be expected to occur either often or explicitly enough to meet the requirements of medical euthanasia. A plea for legal recognition of 'man's inalienable right to die' is placed at the head of the physicians' petition to the New York State Assembly. Now, has man any such right, however limited and imperfect it may be? Surely he has, for otherwise the hero or martyr and all those who deliberately give their lives are morally at fault. It might be replied that there is a difference between the suicide, who is directly seeking to end his life, and the hero or martyr, who is seeking directly some other end entirely, death being only an undesired by-product. But to make this point is only to raise a question as to what purposes are sufficient to justify the loss of one's life. If altruistic values, such as defense of the innocent, are enough to justify the loss of one's life (and we will all agree that they are), then it may be argued that personal integrity is a value worth the loss of life, especially since, by definition, there is no hope of relief from the demoralizing pain and no further possibility of serving others. To call euthanasia egoistic or self-regarding makes no sense, since in the nature of the case the patient is not choosing his own good rather than the good of others.

19.2 Furthermore, it is important to recognize that there is no ground, in a rational or Christian outlook, for regarding life itself as the *summum bonum*. As a ministers' petition to buttress the New York bill puts is, "We believe in the sacredness of *personality*, but not in the worth of mere existence or 'length of days.'. . . We believe that such a sufferer has the right to die, and that society should grant this right, showing the same mercy to human beings as to the sub-human animal kingdom." (The point might be made validly in criticism of this statement that society can only recognize an "inalienable right," it cannot confer it. Persons are not mere creatures of the community, even though it is ultimately meaningless to claim integrity for them unless their lives are integrated into the community.) In the personalistic view of man and morals, asserted throughout these pages, personality is supreme over mere life. To prolong life uselessly, while the personal qualities of freedom, knowledge, self-possession and control, and responsibility are sacrificed is to attack the moral status of a person. It actually denies morality in order to submit to fatality. And in addition, to insist upon mere "life" invades religious interests as well as moral values. For to use analgesic agents to the point of depriving sufferers of consciousness is, by all apparent logic, inconsistent even with the practices of sacramentalist Christians. The point of death for a human person *in extremis* is surely by their own account a time when the use of reason and conscious self-commitment is most meritorious; it is the time when a responsible competence in receiving such rites as the viaticum and extreme unction would be most necessary and its consequences most invested with finality.

19.3   (B.) It is objected that euthanasia, when involuntary, is murder. This is really an objection directed against the physician's role in medical euthanasia, assuming it is administered by him rather than by the patient on his own behalf. We might add to what has been said above about the word "murder" in law and legal definition by explaining that people with a moral rather than a legal interest – doctors, pastors, patients, and their friends – will never concede that malice means only premeditation, entirely divorced from the motive and the end sought. These factors are entirely different in euthanasia from the motive and the end in murder, even though the means – taking life – happens to be the same. If we can make no moral distinction between acts involving the same means, then the thrifty parent who saves in order to educate his children is no higher in the scale of merit than the miser who saves for the sake of hoarding. But, as far as medical care is concerned, there is an even more striking example of the contradictions which arise from refusing to allow for anything but the consequences of a human act. There is a dilemma in medication for terminal diseases which is just as real as the dilemma posed by the doctor's oath to relieve pain while he also promises to prolong life. As medical experts frequently point out, morphine, which is commonly used to ease pain, also shortens life, i.e., it induces death. Here we see that the two promises of the Hippocratic Oath actually conflict at the level of means as well as at the level of motive and intention.

19.4 (C.) What of the common religious opinion that God reserves for himself the right to decide at what moment a life shall cease? Koch-Preuss says euthanasia is the destruction of "the temple of God and a violation of the property rights of Jesus Christ." As to this doctrine, it seems more than enough just to answer that if such a divine-monopoly theory is valid, then it follows with equal force that it is immoral to lengthen life. Is medical care, after all, only a form of human self-assertion or a demonic pretension, by which men, especially physicians, try to put themselves in God's place? Prolonging life, on this divine-monopoly view, when a life appears to be ending through natural or physical causes, is just as much an interference with natural determinism as mercifully ending a life before physiology does it in its own amoral way.

19.5 This argument that we must not tamper with life also assumes that physiological life is sacrosanct. But as we have pointed out repeatedly, this doctrine is a form of vitalism or naturalistic determinism. Dean Sperry of the Harvard Divinity School, who is usually a little more sensitive to the scent of anti-humane attitudes, wrote recently in the *New England Journal of Medicine* that Albert Schweitzer's doctrine of "reverence for life," which is often thought to entail an absolute prohibition against taking life, has strong claims upon men of conscience. Perhaps so, but men of conscience will surely reject the doctrine if it is left unqualified and absolute. In actual fact, even Schweitzer has suggested that the principle is subject to qualification. He has, with apparent approval, explained that Gandhi "took it upon himself to go beyond the letter of the law against killing . . . He ended the sufferings of a calf in its prolonged death-agony by giving it poison." It seems unimaginable that either Schweitzer or Gandhi would deny to a human being what they would render, with however heavy a heart, to a calf. Gandhi did what he did in spite of the special sanctity of kine in Hindu discipline. In any case Dr. Schweitzer in his African hospital at Lambaréné is even now at work administering death-inducing-because-pain-relieving drugs. As William Temple once pointed out, "The notion that life is absolutely sacred is Hindu or Buddhist, not Christian," He neglected to remark that even those Oriental religionists forget their doctrine when it comes to *suttee* and *hari-kari*. He said further that the argument that it cannot ever be right to kill a fellow human being will not stand up because "such a plea can only rest upon a belief that life, physiological life, is sacrosanct. This is not a Christian idea at all; for, if it were, the martyrs would be wrong. If the sanctity is *in* life, it must be wrong to give your life for a noble cause as well as to take another's. But the Christian must be ready to give life gladly for his faith, as for a noble cause. Of course, this implies that, *as compared with some things*, the loss of life is a small evil; and if so, then, *as compared with some other things*, the taking of life is a small injury" (*Thoughts in War Time*, 1940, pp. 31-2).

19.6   Parenthetically we should explain, if it is not evident in these quotations themselves, that Dr. Temple's purpose was to justify military service. Unfortunately for his aim, he failed to take account of the ethical factor of free choice as a right of the person who thus loses his life at the hands of the warrior. We cannot put upon the same ethical footing the ethical right to take our own lives, in which case our freedom is not invaded, and taking the lives of others in those cases in which the act is done against the victim's will and choice. The true parallel is between self-sacrifice and a merciful death provided at the person's request; there is none between self-sacrifice and violent or coercive killing. But the relevance of what Dr. Temple has to say and its importance for euthanasia is perfectly clear. The non-theological statement of the case agrees with Temple: "Are we not allowing ourselves to be deceived by our self-preservative tendency to rationalize a merely instinctive urge and to attribute spiritual and ethical significance to phenomena appertaining to the realm of crude, biological utility?"

19.7   (D.) It is also objected by religious moralists that euthanasia violates the Biblical command, "Thou shalt not kill." It is doubtful whether this kind of Biblicism is any more valid than the vitalism we reject. Indeed, it is a form of fundamentalism, common to both Catholics and reactionary Protestants. An outspoken religious opponent of euthanasia is a former chancellor to Cardinal Spellman as military vicar to the armed forces, Monsignor Robert McCormick. As presiding judge of the Archdiocesan Ecclesiastical Tribunal of New York, he warned the General Assembly of that state in 1947 not to "set aside the commandment 'Thou shalt not kill.'" In the same vein, the general secretary of the American Council of Christian Churches, an organization of fundamentalist Protestants, denounced the fifty-four clergymen who supported the euthanasia bill, claiming that their action was "an evidence that the modernistic clergy have made further departure from the eternal moral law."

19.8   Certainly those who justify war and capital punishment, as most Christians do, cannot condemn euthanasia on this ground. We might point out to the fundamentalists in the two major divisions of Western Christianity that the beatitude "Blessed are the merciful" has the force of a commandment too! The medical profession lives by it, has its whole ethos in it. But the simplest way to deal with this Christian text-proof objection might be to point out that the translation "Thou shalt not kill" is incorrect. It should be rendered, as in the responsive decalogue of the *Book of Common Prayer*, "Thou shalt do no murder," i.e., unlawful killing. It is sufficient just to remember that the ancient Jews fully allowed warfare and capital punishment. Lawful killing was also for hunger-satisfaction and sacrifice. Hence, a variety of Hebrew terms such as *shachat*, *harag*, *tabach*, but *ratsach* in the Decalogue (both Exodus 20:13 and Deut. 5:17), clearly means *unlawful* killing, treacherously, for private vendetta or gain. Thus it is laid down in Leviticus 24:17 that "he who kills a man shall be put to death," showing that the lawful forms of killing may even be used to punish the unlawful! In the New Testament references to the prohibition against killing (e.g., Matt. 5:21, Luke 18:20, Rom. 13:9) are an endorsement of the commandments in the Jewish law. Each time, the verb *phoneuo* is used and the connotation is *unlawful* killing, as in the Decalogue. Other verbs connote simply the fact of killing, as *apokteino* (Luke 12:4, "Be not afraid of them that kill the body") and *thuo* which is used interchangeably for slaughter of animals for food and for sacrifice. We might also remind the Bible-bound moralists that there was no condemnation either of Abimelech, who chose to die, or of his faithful sword-bearer who carried out his wish for him.

19.9   (E.) Another common objection in religious quarters is that suffering is a part of the divine plan for the good of man's soul, and must therefore be accepted. Does this mean that the physicians' Hippocratic Oath is opposed to Christian virtue and doctrine? If this simple and nfering were a valid one, then we should not be able to give our moral approval to anesthetics or to provide any medical relief of human suffering. Such has been the objection of many religionists at every stage of medical conquest, as we pointed out in the first chapter in the case of anesthetics at childbirth. Here is still another anomaly in our mores of life and death, that we are, after much struggle, now fairly secure in the righteousness of easing suffering at birth but we still feel it is wrong to ease suffering at death! Life may be begun without suffering, but it may not be ended without it, if it happens that nature combines death and suffering . . .

19.10   There are three schools of thought favoring euthanasia. First, there are those who favor voluntary euthanasia, a personalistic ethical position. Second, there are those who favor involuntary euthanasia for monstrosities at birth and mental defectives, a partly personalistic and partly eugenic position. Third, there are those who favor involuntary euthanasia for all who are a burden upon the community, a purely eugenic position. It should be perfectly obvious that we do not have to endorse the third school of thought just because we favor either the first or the second, or both. Our discussion has covered only the first one – voluntary medical euthanasia – as a means of ending a human life enmeshed in incurable and fatal physical suffering. The principles of right based upon selfhood and moral being favor it.

19.11   Defense of voluntary medical euthanasia, it should be made plain, does not depend upon the superficial system of values in which physical evil (pain) is regarded as worse than moral evil (sin) or intellectual evil (error). On the contrary, unless we are careful to see that pain is the least of evils, then our values would tie us back into that old attitude of taking the material or physical aspects of reality so seriously that we put nature or things as they are *out there* in a determinant place, subordinating the ethical and spiritual values of freedom and knowledge and upholding, in effect, a kind of naturalism. C.S. Lewis has described it by saying that, "Of all evils, pain only is sterilized or disinfected evil." Pain cannot create moral evil, such as a disintegration or demoralization of personality would be, unless it is submitted to in brute fashion as opponents of euthanasia insist we should do.

19.12   We repeat, the issue is not one of life or death. The issue is which kind of death, an agonized or peaceful one. Shall we meet death in personal integrity or in personal disintegration? Should there be a moral or a demoralized end to mortal life? Surely, as we have seen in earlier chapters, we are not as persons of moral stature to be ruled by ruthless and unreasoning physiology, but rather by reason and self-control. Those who face the issues of euthanasia with a religious faith will not, if they think twice, submit to the materialistic and animistic doctrine that God's will is revealed by what nature does, and that life, *qua life*, is absolutely sacred and untouchable. All of us can agree with Reinhold Niebuhr that "the ending of our life would not threaten us if we had not falsely made ourselves the center of life's meaning." One of the pathetic immaturities we all recognize around us is stated bluntly by Sigmund Freud in his *Reflections on War and Death*: "In the subconscious every one of us is convinced of his immortality." Our frantic hold upon life can only cease to be a snare and delusion when we objectify it in some religious doctrine of salvation, or, alternatively, agree with Sidney Hook that "the romantic pessimism which mourns man's finitude is a vain lament that we are not gods." At least, the principles of personal morality warn us not to make physical phenomena, unmitigated by human freedom, the center of life's meaning. There is an impressive wisdom in the words of Dr. Logan Clendenning: "Death itself is not unpleasant. I have seen a good many people die. To a few death comes as a friend, as a relief from pain, from intolerable loneliness or loss, or from disappointment. To even fewer it comes as a horror. To most it hardly comes at all, so gradual is its approach, so long have the senses been benumbed, so little do they realize what is taking place. As I think it over, death seems to me one of the few evidences in nature of the operation of a creative intelligence exhibiting qualities which I recognize as mind stuff. To have blundered onto the form of energy called life showed a sort of malignant power. After having blundered on life, to have conceived of death was a real stroke of genius" (*The Human Body*, 1941, pp. 442-3).

19.13   As Ecclesiastes the Preacher kept saying in first one way and then another, "The living know that they shall die" and there is "a time to be born and a time to die, a time to plant and a time to pluck up that which is planted." (Eccl. 9.5 & 3.2). And in the New Covenant we read that "all flesh is as grass" and "the grass withereth, and the flower thereof falleth away." Nevertheless, "who is he that will harm you, if ye be followers of that which is good?" (1.Pet. 1.24 & 3.13).

19.14   Medicine contributes too much to the moral stature of men to persist indefinitely in denying the ultimate claims of its own supreme virtue and ethical inspiration, mercy.

EXTRACT 20

GUSTAFSON

Abortion – a reformed perspective

20.1   The pregnant woman is in her early twenties. She is a lapsed Catholic, with no significant religious affiliation at the present time, although she expresses some need for a "church." Her marriage was terminated by divorce; her husband was given custody of three children by that marriage. She had an affair with a man who "befriended" her, but there were no serious prospects for a marriage with him, and the affair has ended. Her family life was as disrupted and as tragic as that which is dramatically presented in Eugene O'Neill's *Long Day's Journey into Night*. Her alcoholic mother mistreated her children, coerced them into deceptive activity for her ends, and was given to periods of violence. Her father has been addicted to drugs, but has managed to continue in business, avoid incarceration, and provide a decent income for his family. The pregnant woman fled from home after high school to reside in a distant state, and has no significant contact with her parents or siblings. She has two or three friends.

20.2   Her pregnancy occurred when she was raped by her former husband and three other men after she had agreed to meet him to talk about their children. The rapes can only be described as acts of sadistic vengeance. She is unwilling to prefer charges against the men, since she believes it would be a further detriment to her children. She has no steady job, partially because of periodic gastro-intestinal illnesses, and has no other income. There are no known physiological difficulties which would jeopardize her life or that of the child. She is unusually intelligent and very articulate, and is not hysterical about her situation. Termination of the pregnancy is a live option for her as a way to cope with one of the many difficulties she faces . . .

Salient Facts in One Christian Moralist's Interpretation

20.3   In the personal situation under discussion, it is clear that if medical factors alone were to be considered grounds for an abortion, none would be morally permissible. The woman had three pregnancies that came to

full term, and the children were healthy. To the best of
her knowledge there are no medical problems at the
present time. Periodic gastro-intestinal illnesses, which
might be relieved with better medical care, would not be
sufficient medical grounds. Although the present pregnancy is disturbing for many reasons, including both
the occasion on which the pregnancy occurred and the
future social prospects for the woman and the child, in
the judgment of the moralist the woman is able to cope
with her situation without serious threat to her mental
health. The medical factors insofar as the moralist can
grasp them, would not warrant a therapeutic abortion.

20.4   Legal factors potentially involved in this situation are
serious. First, and most obvious, the woman resides in a
state where abortion of pregnancies due to sexual crimes
is not at present legally permissible. Since there are not
sufficient grounds for a therapeutic abortion, a request to
a physician would put him in legal jeopardy. Even if
abortion was permissible because of the rapes, this
woman was unwilling to report the rapes to the police
since it involved her former husband and had potential
implications for the care of her children. To report the
rapes would involve the woman in court procedures
which seem also to require time and energy that she needs
to support herself financially. To seek an abortion on
conscientious moral grounds would be to violate the law,
and to implicate others in the violation. Not to press
charges against the rapists is to protect them from
prosecution. Disclosure of the rapes would make the
abortion morally justifiable in the eyes of many, but it
might lead to implications for her children. The legal
factors are snarled and are complicated by social factors.

20.5   The moralist has to reckon with the financial plight of
the woman. She is self-supporting, but her income is
irregular. There are no savings. Application for welfare
support might lead to the disclosure of matters she wishes
to keep in confidence. If a legal abortion was possible, the
physician would receive little or no remuneration from
the patient. There are no funds in sight to finance an

illegal abortion, and the medical risks involved in securing a quack rule that out as a viable prospect. The child, if not aborted, could be let out for adoption, and means might be found to give minimum support for the mother during pregnancy. If she should choose to keep the child, which is her moral right to do, there are no prospects for sufficient financial support, although with the recovery of her health the woman could join the work force and probably with her intelligence earn a modest income.

20.6   The spiritual and emotional factors involved are more difficult to assess. While the moralist is impressed with the relative calm with which the woman converses about her predicament, he is aware that this ability is probably the result of learning to cope with previous inhumane treatment and with events that led to no happy ending. Socially, she is sustained only by two or three friends, and these friendships could readily be disrupted by geographical mobility. She has no significant, explicit religious faith, and as a lapsed Catholic who views the Church and its priests as harsh taskmasters, she is unwilling to turn to it for spiritual and moral sustenance. She has a profound desire not merely to achieve a situation of equanimity, of absence of suffering and conflict, but also to achieve positive goals. Her mind is active, and she has read fairly widely; she expresses the aspiration to go to college, to become a teacher, or to engage in some other professional work, both for the sake of her self-fulfillment and for the contribution she can make to others. She has not been defeated by her past. She can articulate the possibility of keeping the child, and see the child as part of the world in which there would be some realization of goals, especially since she has been deprived of her other children. She has confidence, she has hope, and she seems to be able to love, though she wonders what else could happen to make her life any more difficult than it is. She carries something of a guilt load; the courts gave custody of her three children to the husband because of adultery charges against her. Yet, her interpretation of that marriage in her youth was that it freed her from her parental home, but that the marriage itself was a "prison." She responds to the rapes more in horror than in hatred, but is too close to that experience to know its long-range impact on her.

20.7   The more readily identifiable moral factors are three, though in the ethical perspective of this paper, this constitutes an oversimple limitation of the "moral" and of the nature of moral responsibility. One is the inviolability of life, the sanctity of life. My opinion is that since the genotype is formed at conception, all the genetic potentialities of personal existence are there. Thus it is to be preserved unless reasons can be given that make an exception morally justifiable. A second is rape – not only a crime, but a morally evil deed. The sexual relations from which the pregnancy came were not only engaged in against the woman's will, but were in her judgment acts of retaliation and vengeance. The third is the relation of morality to the civil law. If abortion were considered to be morally justifiable, to have it done would be to break the civil law. It would be an act of conscientious objection to existing laws, and is susceptible to scrutiny by the moral arguments that pertain to that subject in itself.

20.8   All of these factors in isolated listing, and others that could be enumerated, do not add up to a moral decision. They are related to each other in particular ways, and the woman is related to her own ends, values, and to other beings. And the moralist's relationship is not that of a systems analyst sorting out and computing. His relationship is one of respect and concern for the person; it is colored by his perspective. It is necessary, then, to state what seem to be the factors that are present in the perspective of the moralist that influence his interpretation and judgment.

Salient Aspects of the Moralist's Perspective

20.9   The perception and the interpretation of the moralist are not a simple matter to discuss. It would be simpler if the author could reduce his perspective to: (a) theological and philosophical principles; (b) moral inferences drawn from these; and (c) rational application of these principles to a narrowly defined case. But more than belief, principles, and logic are involved in the moral decision. A basic perspective toward life accents certain values and shadows others. Attitudes, affections, and feelings of indignation against evil, compassion for suffering, and desire for restoration of wholeness color one's interpretation and judgment. Imagination, sensitivity, and empathy are all involved. For Christians, and many others presumably, love is at work, not merely as a word to be defined, and as a subject of propositions so that inferences can be drawn from it, but love as a human relationship, which can both move and inform the other virtues, including prudence and equity (to make a reference to St. Thomas). All of this does not mean that a moral judgment is a total mystery, it does not mean that it is without objectivity.

20.10   The perspective of the Christian moralist is informed and directed by his fundamental trust that the forces of life seek the human good, that God is good, is love. This is a matter of trust and confidence, and not merely a matter of believing certain propositions to be true. (I believe certain statements about my wife to be true, including the statement that she wills and seeks my good, but the reasons for my trust in her cannot be described simply by such a statement.) Yet the way in which I state my convictions about this trust defines in part my moral perspective and my fundamental intentionality. (What I know *about* my wife sustains my trust in her, and in part sets the direction of our marriage.) Life, and particularly human life, is given to men by God's love: physical being dependent upon genetic continuity; the capacity of the human spirit for self-awareness, responsiveness, knowledge, and creativity; life together in human communities, in which we live and care for others and others live and care for us.

20.11   God wills the creation, preservation, reconciliation, and redemption of human life. Thus, one can infer, it is better to give and preserve life than to take it away; it is better to prevent its coming into being than to destroy it when it has come into being. But the purposes of God for life pertain to more than physical existence: there are conditions for human life that need delineation: physical health, possibilities for future good and meaning that engender and sustain hope, relationships of trust and love, freedom to respond and initiate and achieve, and many others. The love of God, and in response to it, the loves of men, are particularly sensitive to "the widow, the orphan, and the stranger in your midst," to the oppressed and the weak.

20.12   These brief and cryptic statements are the grounds for moral biases: life is to be preserved, the weak and the helpless are to be cared for especially, the moral requisite of trust, hope, love, freedom, justice, and others are to be met so that human life can be meaningful. The bias gives a direction, a fundamental intention that does not in itself resolve the darkness beyond the reach of its light, the ambiguities of particular cases. It begins to order what preferences one would have under ideal conditions and under real conditions. One would prefer not to induce an abortion in this instance. There is consistency between this preference and the Christian moralist's faith and convictions. But one would prefer for conception to arise within love rather than hate, and one would prefer that there would be indications that the unknowable future were more favorably disposed to the human well-being of the mother and the child . . .

Pertinent Principles That Can Be Stipulated for Reflection

20.13   Neither the moralist nor the woman comes to a situation without some convictions and beliefs that begin to dissolve some of the complexity of the particularities into manageable terms. Perhaps the traditional Catholic arguments simply assume that one can begin with these convictions and principles, and need not immerse one's self in the tragic concreteness. The pertinent ones in this case have already been alluded to, but here they can be reduced to a simpler scheme.

1. Life is to be preserved rather than destroyed.
2. Those who cannot assert their own rights to life are especially to be protected.
3. There are exceptions to these rules.

Possible exceptions are:

a. "medical indications" that make therapeutic abortion morally viable. Condition not present here.

b. the pregnancy has occurred as a result of sexual crime. (I would grant this as a viable possible exception in every instance for reasons imbedded in the above discussion, if the woman herself were convinced that it was right. In other than detached academic discussions I would never dispatch an inquiry with a ready granting of the exception. If the woman sees the exception as valid, she has a right to more than a potentially legal justification for her decision; as a person she has the right to understand why it is an exception in her dreadful plight.)

c. the social and emotional conditions do not appear to be beneficial for the well-being of the mother and the child. (In particular circumstances, this may appear to be a justification, but I would not resort to it until possibilities for financial, social, and spiritual help have been explored.)

20.14   In the short-hand of principles this can be reduced to an inconsistency between on the one hand the first and second, and on the other hand 3.b. and perhaps 3.c. While I am called upon to give as many reasons for a decision between these two as I can, the choice can never be fully rationalized.

The Decision of the Moralist

20.15   My own decision is: (a) if I were in the woman's human predicament I believe I could morally justify an abortion, and thus: (b) I would affirm its moral propriety in this instance. Clearly, logic alone is not the process by

which a defence of this particular judgment can be given;
clearly, the facts of the matter do not add up to a
justification of abortion so that one can say "the situation
determines everything." Nor is it a matter of some
inspiration of the Spirit. It is a human decision, made in
freedom, informed and governed by beliefs and values, as
well as by attitudes and a fundamental perspective. It is a
discernment of compassion for the woman, as well as of
objective moral reflection. It may not be morally "right"
in the eyes of others, and although we could indicate
where the matters of dispute between us are in discourse,
and perhaps even close the gap between opinions to some
extent, argument about it would probably not be
persuasive. The judgment is made with a sense of its
limitations, which include the limitations of the one who
decides (which might well result from his lack of
courage, his pride, his slothfulness in thinking, and other
perversities) . . .

20.16   In place of the determination of an action as right or
wrong by its conformity to a rule and its application, I
have stressed the primacy of the person and human
relationships and the concreteness of the choice within
limited possibilities. There can be no guarantee of an
objectively right action in the situation I have discussed,
since there are several values which are objectively
important, but which do not resolve themselves into a
harmonious relation to each other. Since there is not a
single overriding determination of what constitutes a
right action, there can be no unambiguously right act.

20.17   Whereas the moral theology manuals generally limit
discussion to the physical aspects of the human situation,
I have set those in a wider context of human values,
responsibilities, and aspirations. While this does not
make the physical less serious, it sets it in relation to other
matters of a morally serious nature, and thus qualifies the
way one decides by complicating the values and factors to
be taken into account.

20.18   I find it difficult in discussing possible abortions to
limit the personal relationships as exclusively to the

physician and the patient as do the manual discussions, and to limit the time span of experience to the fact of pregnancy and action pertaining to it alone. Most significantly in the instance discussed, the conditions under which the pregnancy occurred modify the discussion of the abortion.

20.19   The role of compassion and indignation, of attitudes and affections in the process of making a decision is affirmed in my discussion to a degree not admitted in traditional moral theology. Indeed, I indicated the importance of one's basic perspective, and the way in which one's perception of a situation is conditioned by this perspective. Situations cannot be reduced to discrete facts; one's response to them is determined in part by one's faith, basic intentions, and dispositions, as well as by analysis and the rational application of principles.

20.20   Although I have only sketched most briefly the theological convictions that inform the perspective, they perhaps have a more central place in the ways in which I proceed than is the case in traditional moral theology. I wish not to suggest that there is a deposit of revelation, supernaturally given, which I accept on authority as a basis of moral perspective; such a position is not the alternative to natural law. Ampler elaboration of this, however, is beyond the bounds of this paper.

20.21   Although the structure I have used as a model differs from that model used by the Roman Catholic manuals of moral theology, in a specific instance a Catholic moralist might reach a conclusion not strikingly dissimilar from my own in counselling the woman. He could do so by means of the classic Catholic doctrine of "good faith." As expounded by Alphonsus Liguori, a confessor is not to disturb the good faith of the penitent if he believes that telling the penitent he is committing a sin will not deter him from his course of action, but will merely put him in "bad faith," that is, in a state of mind where he is aware that what he is doing is opposed to the will of God. There are exceptions to this doctrine where the penitent must be informed of what is necessary to salvation, or where the common good is endangered by the proposed actions. These exceptions, however, do not seem applicable to the special kind of case I have outlined. Consequently, a Catholic moralist faced with a woman who believes she is doing what is right in seeking an abortion, and who in all probability would not be deterred by advice to the contrary, might well conclude that his responsibility was not to put the woman in bad faith.

20.22   This Catholic approach to a particular case accords with mine in recognizing a principle of personal responsibility which the moralist must honor. He cannot coerce the person; in some sense each person must decide for himself. This approach differs from mine, however, in the analysis of the act of abortion, which is treated in a special sense as a sin. Elucidation of this difference would require extensive discussion of the relation of religion and morality in the two approaches, in the uses of the concept of sin, and other matters too large to be developed here. This Catholic approach also differs from mine in the limits it would impose on cooperation with the act by the counsellor.

20.23   A Catholic moral theologian, if he approved of the outcome of the discussion presented here, might compliment it by indicating that it is an example of prudence informed by charity at work, or that it is an exercise in the virtue of *epikeia*, applying principles to particular cases. If such generosity were shown, I would not be adverse to being pleased, for it would indicate that some of the polarizations of contemporary moral theology between ethics of law and situational ethics are excessively drawn. I would also suggest, however, that there is a different valence given to prudence and equity, indeed, to the moral virtues, in the order of ethical analysis here than is the case in the treatises on medical ethics. There is a sense in which the present discussion subordinates law to virtue as points of reliance in making moral decisions.

20.24   Since there is no fixed position called "situation ethics," it would be futile to distinguish the approach taken here from what cannot be readily defined. I would say in general that in comparison with Paul Lehmann's ethics of the theonomous conscience, with its confidence in a renewed sensitivity and imagination to perceive what God is doing in the world to make and keep human life human, the approach of this paper is more complex, and ultimately less certain about its answer. Further, the weight of responsibility for reflection and for action rests heavily upon the actor, since no perceptive powers I have enable me to overcome the distance between God and the action that I respond to. I cannot claim to perceive what *God* is doing. The polemical force with which Lehmann attacks "absolutist ethics" is foreign to this approach; while I clearly believe that abstract principles and logic alone do not contain the dynamics of suffering and evil, or of love and good, their utility in bringing clarity to discussion is much treasured.

20.25 As the morally conscientious soldier fighting in a particular war is convinced that life can and ought to be taken, "justly" but also "mournfully," so the moralist can be convinced that the life of the defenceless foetus can be taken, less justly, but more mournfully.

EXTRACT 21

CLEMENT

Abortion – an Orthodox perspective

21.1 It is difficult to speak dispassionately about abortion because it has to do with love and death, in other words, with things which are of the utmost consequence for the human condition. And also because it concerns woman in all her carnal "mystery", wherein are mingled life, death, and blood, as if in a particularly disturbing form of the sacred. It should be added, moreover, that sometimes woman experiences in every fibre of her being a weariness, a sense of solitude, an anguish before which the reactions of men are somewhat superficial.

21.2 In spite of all this, I should like to try to set up a few guideposts for a spiritual approach to the problem. Then

I shall suggest a possible role for Christians in relation to this question in civic life.

To whom does the embryo belong?

21.3   It is certain that, from an Orthodox point of view, the human being, that is, the potential person, exists from the moment of conception. Western Scholastics, influenced by the thought of pagan antiquity, believed that the soul is the determinant principle of the body and that therefore the embryo becomes truly human only when, after several weeks, it assumes a human form. But the Bible does not divide the soul from the body. For it, as for the Fathers and the liturgy (which celebrates the "conception" of John the Baptist and of Mary), the human being exists from conception. And science today emphasizes that the genetic program of the individual is established from the moment of fusion of the two parent cells.

21.4   Therefore the child does not belong to either the father or the mother – it belongs to God. During the first weeks when its very presence remains a secret, it must be received somehow in faith. It is at this time that abortion seems to raise few problems. The woman who rejects the child does not acknowledge that this particle of flesh, which is an extension of herself, is in reality another person. What is killed has no face, no human form, and so little solidity. Yet is not this unknown one, defenceless, undisclosed, whose presence is unobtrusive, like an image of God, who also took "the form of a servant", and who cannot be present with us unless we welcome him in love? In any case, in a Christian perspective, the argument of advocates of abortion that the embryo "belongs" to its mother makes no sense.

21.5   Moreover, woman seems to be constituted for this welcoming, this maturation in secret. As far as the body is concerned, abortion can be a relatively harmless operation. But it can never be harmless for the profound sensitivities of a woman, for her "bowels of mercy", in the uterine sense, to use the very beautiful biblical expression which is used to describe the tender mercy of our God. If, as Maximus the Confessor says, the body and soul are symbols of each other, it can be said that the true essence of woman is this capacity for spiritual maternity which is so well represented in the icons by the loving faces of the Virgin, this capacity to "bring God to birth in desolate souls", as Paul Evdokimov has written. As a result, a woman who resorts to abortion, and particularly if she makes a practice of doing so, runs the risk of destroying her own spiritual nature.

Succouring the woman who "descends into hell"

21.6 But we have the right to say all this only if we are ready in our communities to accept material and moral responsibility for those women who, driven to despair, in the grip of anguish and fatigue, see no other solution than abortion. How many women, who at least the first time sense deeply the unnatural character of abortion, would renounce this "solution", if they would find in us, in our churches, a little selfless love, a welcome which makes no judgment upon them, and if they could also have the certitude that, for a man who is a Christian, there is no problem in marrying a woman whom the bourgeois world labels in a strangely blasphemous way a "virgin-mother", if he truly loves her.

21.7 Are we ready to welcome also a woman who has had an abortion, who has made this descent into hell (even if it is the gleaming, and to all appearances cordial, hell of an ultra-modern hospital)? Are we ready to help her find release, to offer her reconciliation, to make clear to her the import of her act – this is necessary if she is to be truly healed, but also the even greater import of the love which God and her fellows bear her?

21.8 The prayer in the Byzantine rite for a woman who has had an abortion is worth quoting here: 'Master, Lord our God, who wast born of the Holy God-bearing and ever-virgin Mary, and as a babe wast laid in a manger (and as a tiny embryo in a mother's womb!), do thou thyself according to thy great mercy, have mercy upon this thine handmaid, who today is in sin, having fallen even unto . . . murder . . . Heal her suffering, and grant unto her, O lover of mankind, health and strength of body and soul . . . Cleanse her from bodily defilement, and from diverse inward travail befalling her . . . For we . . . are all defiled before thee, O Lord.'

21.9   This prayer says everything: there is the acknowledgement of the tragic nature of abortion – and it is precisely here that penitence plays a therapeutic role – and also the reminder that spiritually we are all aborted, that our lives are miserable abortions, and that therefore penitence is also for us. For us too the great joy is the pardon God offers those who repent and "turn their hearts". "Go, and sin no more."

The role of Christians in civic life

21.10   In civic life it is not the role of the Church to impose a law either to forbid or to legalize abortion. In the countries of Eastern Europe, where the Church has been silenced and abortion has been more or less legalized, everything is reduced to a problem of evangelism. In France, we live in a pluralistic society where Christians can speak out, where they are even urged to do so. Let us guard against setting out in detail our "ethical principles" in an effort to impose them on others; let us rather insist upon their spiritual foundation, that is, always and forever, the Good News. The message of the Gospel, however, is not something foreign to the depths of human nature, to the authentic human conscience, since man is made in the image of God. The Good News revives, stimulates the conscience of man, reminds him of what fundamentally is required of him – a personal life lived together with others in communion and in responsibility freely assumed – and makes it fully possible for him to meet this requirement. We shall find a response if we maintain the irreducible character of personal existence, and that this existence in the form of an embryo is only entrusted to a woman and – let us not forget – to a man. We will support legislation to make available to young people information on responsible parenthood, on the condition that this information (related to sexual education and family planning) does not make sexuality into an object in itself but places it always in the context of the mystery of an encounter between persons and mutual responsibility. We will remind the law-maker that legalization pure and simple, that is, the making of abortion a normal practice, would have the gravest psychological (and spiritual) consequences, for men, who would be encouraged in irresponsible sexuality, and especially for women who, finding in abortion the most convenient method of birth control, would end up ravaged, wounded in the very essence of their being. But this has a unilateral aspect (since it ignores the responsibility of the man), and that, in the present circumstances, it is even futile, since it leads on the woman either to destructive guilt feelings or to arrogant rebellion, which is no better, for it fails to recognize the true dimensions of human existence. In our society, which cannot – or does not wish to – call itself Christian, too many unfortunate women, because they have neither the money nor the necessary contacts to make possible the trip to London or Geneva, fall victim to the black – and traumatic – magic of the abortionist.

21.11   The law-maker who seeks the lesser evil and must take into account the actual spiritual temper of society, will probably be led to tolerate abortion in certain limit-conditions of great distress. It seems to me that Christians must admit, at least for others, this "necessary accommodation" for exceptional situations, without ceasing – indeed quite the contrary – to stress the tragic nature of abortion and the real meaning of love. It remains for the law-maker, as for all of us, to support in the society all efforts – some of which may originate with Christians – to multiply those milieux which offer a haven, assistance, and reconciliation, communities wherein humanity is the criterion, wherein not only the sexual role but also the personhood of "the other" is recognized. Here the example and influence of the church can carry much weight.

21.12   To conclude: May our own spiritual life become a little less "aborted", and there will then be fewer abortions.

EXTRACT 22

QUAKER GROUP

A new morality needed

The Church and Sexuality

22.1   It will be relevant at this point to refer to the history of the Church's attitude to sexuality throughout the centuries, and to elements in that attitude that seem inconsistent with some of the deepest insights in the Bible.

22.2   Throughout nearly all its history and in some sections of the Church today, the myth of Adam and Eve (called without justification the Fall of Man) is treated as though it were historical fact on which logical arguments can be built. It this way, sexuality came to be regarded as necessarily polluted with sin in that event. Even when rejected as historical fact, this myth still has its effect upon the attitude of some Christians to sexuality; it will therefore be wise to think more about it. First, this, like other myths, had an earlier Babylonian origin and was used for religious purposes by the Jewish teachers. Further, like all myths, it is a poetic and symbolic representation of the condition and predicament of man. It is not exclusively or even primarily concerned with sexuality. It is a myth representing the transition of man, either in his racial history (phylogenesis) or his development for babyhood (ontogenesis) from an unreflective obedience to instinct to a condition in which he is responsible for his actions, in which he can reflect on them and make judgments and moral choices, weighing up possible courses of action in the light of a concept of good and evil.

It is a story, not of man's fall, but of man's growing up, and of the pain that growing up involves. It is significant that God is recorded as saying (Gen. 3.22): "Behold, the man is become as *one of us*, to know good and evil." To recognize and love what is good is to know also what is evil, to fear it and to be tempted by it. To know the good is to know joy, but it is also to experience pain, to be tempted to pride and presumption.

22.3   It is unfortunate that sexual intercourse takes place btween Adam and Eve only after the expulsion from the Garden; this perhaps provides an excuse for thinking that sexual intimacy is associated with a sinful and disobedient state. But this is not given in the text nor it is a necessary implication. Indeed Eve claims the help of God in the matter. The shame associated with nakedness immediately after the eating of the fruit of the tree of knowledge need not imply that sex became tainted there and then with sin: it may imply a recognition that our sexuality more than anything else in us can lift us to the heights of self-realization or plunge us into degradation; it is the focus of our self-awareness. The awareness of nakedness may further be a symbol of the awareness of vulnerability, of exposure to pain that must come with self-consciousness.

22.4   No doubt from the earliest days of Christianity there have been men and women for whom the sexual relationship was illumined and deepened by the Christian message of love, for whom it expressed a true equality, an equal-sided valuation and respect, for whom coitus was an expression of tenderness and unity, not merely the gratification of animal urges. But it is one of the great tragedies of history that not until recent times had this implication of Christianity found public expression.

22.5   Dr. Sherwin Bailey, a leading Anglican authority on this subject, can find no evidence of this expression in any theological writing before the appearance in the seventeenth century of *Holy Living*, by Jeremy Taylor, a married bishop of the English Church who owed much to the support and companionship of his wife. In that book coitus is for the first time referred to as an act that relates two people in togetherness. It was an experience "to lighten the cares and sadness of household affairs, and to endear each other." Dr. Bailey writes, "Taylor maintains that marriage is the queen of friendships, and husband and wife the best of all friends; the love that binds them together is a 'union of all things excellent'; it contains in it proportion and satisfaction and rest and confidence" (Bailey, 1959).

22.6   In contrast to this, for the previous fifteen hundred years almost every writer and leader in the Church, both Catholic and Reformed, regarded sexuality as unavoidably tainted with sin, and the sex-relationship in marriage (apart from procreation) as a licensed outlet for the bestial impulses in man. This latter concept of marriage is overwhelmingly repulsive to many of us now, yet it is no exaggeration to say that it has lingered in the Church almost to the present day, and only recently has it become possible to be married in church without hearing an echo of it in the marriage service.

22.7   Dr. Sherwin Bailey, writing of earlier centuries, says: ". . . the general impression left by the Church's teaching upon simple and unlearned people can only have been that the physical relationship of the sexes was regarded by religion as unworthy, if not as shameless and obscene. The effect of such teaching must necessarily have been grave; it caused a distortion of principles and values which has left an indelible mark upon Christian sexual thought and we can only guess at the psychological disturbances and conflicts which it has produced in the lives of individuals" (Bailey, 1959).

22.8   Only in the present century have Christians dared in any general way to follow in the steps of Jeremy Taylor and to accept that, irrespective of any other purpose, coitus can be justified and dignified as the expression of a deep relation between two persons. We do not blame Christianity and Christians of earlier centuries; we can seek the origin of misconceived attitudes in the compromise between pagan and Christian thought and in the social conditions of the Dark Ages.

22.9   We have then to reject the idea that there is anything necessarily sinful about sexual activity. A better understanding of the nature and value of myth, and a more scientific approach to problems of human behaviour, have delivered many Christians from this oppressive and destructive idea. Sexual activity is essentially neither good nor evil; it is a normal biological activity which, like most other human activities, can be indulged in destructively or creatively.

22.10   Further, if we take impulses and experiences that are potentially wholesome and in a large measure unavoidable and characterize these as sinful, we create a great volume of unnecessary guilt and an explosive tension within the personality. When, as so often happens, the impulse breaks through the restriction, it does so with a ruthlessness and destructive energy that might not otherwise have been there. A distorted Christianity must bear some of the blame for the sexual disorders of society.

A Way Forward

22.11   In trying to summarize the feelings and judgments that have come to us in the course of our several years' deliberations, we must keep this historical survey in mind. It supports us in rejecting almost completely the traditional approach of the organized Christian church to morality, with its supposition that it knows precisely what is right and what is wrong, that this distinction can be made in terms of an external pattern of behaviour, and that the greatest good will come only through universal adherence to that pattern. Nothing that has come to light in the course of our studies has altered the conviction that came to us when we began to examine the actual experiences of people the conviction that love cannot be confined to a pattern. The waywardness of love is part of its nature and this is both its glory and its tragedy. If love did not tend to leap every barrier, if it could be tamed, it would not be the tremendous creative power we know it to be and want it to be.

22.12   So we are concerned with the homosexuals who say to each other "I love you" in the hopeless and bitter awareness of a hostile criminal code and hypocritical public opinion, and also with the anguish of men and women who know they love one another when marriage is impossible and only suffering can be envisaged. We recognize that, while most examples of the "eternal triangle" are produced by boredom and primitive misconduct, others may arise from the fact that the very experience of loving one person with depth and perception may sensitize a man or woman to the lovable qualities in others.

22.13   We think it our duty, not to stand on the peak of perfectionism, asking for an impossible conformity while the tide of human life sweeps by us, but to recognize, in compassion, the complications and bewilderment that love creates and to ask how we can discover a constructive way in each of an immense variety of particular experiences. It is not by checking our impulse to love that we keep love sweet. The man who swallows the words "I love you" when he meets another woman, may in that moment and for that reason begin to resent his wife's existence; but it is also true that love may be creative if honestly acknowledged though not openly confessed. We need to know much more about ourselves and what we do to our inner life when we follow codes or ideals that do not come from the heart.

22.14   Those who have read so far will recognize how difficult it has been for us to come to definite conclusions as to what people ought or ought not to do. But although we cannot produce a ready-made external morality to replace the conventional code, there are some things about which we can be definite. *The first is that there must be morality of some sort to govern sexual relationships.* An experience so profound in its effect upon people and upon the community cannot be left wholly to private judgment. It will never be right for two people to say to each other "we'll do what we want, and what happens between us is nobody else's business." However private an act, it is never without its impact on society, and we must never behave as though society – which includes our other friends did not exist. *Secondly, the need to preserve marriage and family life has been in the forefront of our minds throughout our work.* It is in marriage that sexual impulses have their greatest opportunity for joyful and creative expression, and where two people can enter into each other's lives and hearts most intimately. Here the greatest freedom can be experienced – the freedom conferred by an unreserved commitment to each other, by loving and fearless friendship, and by openness to the world. In marriage, two people thus committed can bring children into the world, provide them with the security of love and home and in this way fulfil their sexual nature. *Finally, we accept the definition of sin given by an Anglican broadcaster, as covering those actions that involve exploitation of the other person.* This is a concept of wrongdoing that applies both to homosexual and heterosexual actions and to actions within marriage as well as outside it. It condemns as fundamentally immoral every sexual action that is not, as far as is humanly ascertainable, the result of a mutual decision. It condemns seduction and even persuasion, and every instance of coitus which, by reason of disparity of age or intelligence or emotional condition, cannot be a matter of mutual responsibility.

22.15   It is clear that we need a much deeper morality, one that will enable people to find a constructive way through even the most difficult and unpredictable situations – a way that is not simply one of withdrawal and abnegation. There are many who say that when people find themselves in a situation where it is difficult to be consistently moral, they must practise self-denial and "bear their cross". This is often the right way; but it is a serious misconception of the Cross to suggest that it is related only to self-denial.

22.16   Morality should be creative. God is primarily Creator, not rule-maker. Quakerism from the beginning rejected the idea of particular observances, rituals or sacrament, and instead regarded the whole of life's activities as potentially sacramental. The Quaker movement arose in a time of spiritual stirring. By rejecting all authority save that of the Holy Spirit and the headship of Christ, its vital witness was to an authority which begins in personal experience, in the encounter of man and God in the human spirit and mind. Quakersim begins with a search and its method is experimental.

22.17   Every true Christian, of whatever branch of the Church, accepts that the whole of his life must be brought before God. The Society of Friends places particular emphasis on our individual and personal responsibility. We cannot accept as true a statement that is given us merely because it is given with the authority of tradition or a Church. We have to make that truth our own – if it is a truth – through diligent and prayerful search and a rigorous discipline of thought and feeling. Man is intended to be a moral being. That is not to say that he should accept a formal morality, an observance of *mores*, but that his actions should come under searching scrutiny in the light that comes from the Gospels and the working of God within us.

22.18   There have been periods in our Quaker history when the effort to achieve consistency and integrity toppled over into a humourless scrupulosity, leading to a restricted life in which a pattern of conduct was secured at the expense of warmth and joy and creativeness. Friends, if they keep in mind the need to avoid this error, could help to discover that kind of conduct and inner discipline through which the sexual energy of men and women can bring health of mind and spirit to a world where man's energy always threatens to become destructive. We need a release of love, warmth and generosity into the world, in the everyday contacts of life, a positive force that will weaken our fear of one another and our tendencies toward aggression and power-seeking. We need to recognize fearlessly and thankfully the sexual origin of this force.

22.19 This search is a move forward into the unknown; it implies a high standard of reponsibility, thinking and awareness – something much harder than simple obedience to a moral code. Further, the responsibility that it implies cannot be accepted alone; it must be responsibility within a group whose members are equally committed to the search for God's will.

22.20 Perhaps our last words should be to those, equally aware of the tragedy, who may be distressed and put off by our rejection of a morality that has seemed to them a product of Christianity. We do know, from the intimate experience of several of us, that it is possible to give substance to the traditional code, to live within its requirements, enriched by an experience of love at its most generous and tender, and conscious of our debt to Christ in showing us what love implies. We would ask those who cannot easily follow our thoughts to recognize what has driven us – Christians and Friends, trying to live up to the high standard of integrity that our religious society asks of us – to our insistent questioning.

22.21 It is the awareness that the traditional code, in itself, does not come from the heart; for the great majority of men and women it has no roots in feeling or true conviction. We have been seeking a morality that will indeed have its roots in the depths of our being and in our awareness of the true needs of our fellows.

22.22 We believe that there is indeed a place for discipline, but that it can only be fully healthy as well as fully Christian when it is found in application to the *whole* of life. The challenge to each of us is clear: accustom yourself to seeking God's will and to the experience of his love and power, become used in your daily life to the simple but tremendous spiritual fact that what God asks he enables, provided only and always that we want to do his will.

22.23   Men and women thus accustomed will not be less
exposed to sexual difficulties – heterosexual or homosexual – than others whose lives are not "under discipline" in
this way. As we see it, the difference lies in their response
to the claims of sexual urges. Whereas the emotional or
"moral" response focusses attention on the control of the
sexual urge in isolation, the way of life we have described
makes it likely that the particular sexual problem will be
seen in the full context of ordinary daily living, and thus
be kept in perspective as something for which God has
not only a solution but a positive purpose.

22.24   Such positive purpose may – and often does – involve
the acceptance of suffering by the person concerned. We
have no unity with those who regard all tension and all
frustration as being by definition bad or unhealthy: such a
view is utterly without psychological foundation. The
mental and spiritual well-being of a person depends
rather on his or her developed capacity to deal with
tensions and frustrations as and when they arise. The
Christian cannot escape the implications of the Cross. In
the power of the Holy Spirit, there are no dangers from
which strength cannot be gained, no apparent disaster
which cannot be transformed into spiritual opportunities
. . .

22.25   There is a danger that any compassionate view that is
published – like this present essay – may be misread. A
reader here and there may accept *some* of our ideas, and
then proceed to put his interpretation of them into action
– imposing on his victims the consequences of a
permissiveness that we appear to support. It must
therefore be said that at no point does our approach
approve of mere permissiveness. To the question "May
we do what we like?" we do *not* answer "Yes, you may".
We have been led to ask what may be the actual and
ultimate result in the persons concerned of love affairs
involving coitus, and have implied that the result is not
necessarily or invariably destructive. We do not, however, encourage anyone to think that it would be "perfectly

all right" to make love with a casual friend who equally desires the experience.

22.26   The true answer to our open question might prove to be as critical of "free love" as of mere obedience to an external morality. Sexual actions can never be primitively "innocent". We are not in the Garden of Eden. We are a complex race of people with the imprint of a long history on our spirits. Sexual actions stir us far below the level of consciousness, and may do more than we know to shape our future. There is an almost overwhelming urge throughout society towards the trivializing of sexual actions and the separating of them from the rest of life. A young man, whose whole working life is given to preparation for a responsible career, may nevertheless think it all right to propose "going to bed" to a girl he has only just met and whose surname is unknown to him. We think it probable that to use one's capacity for love-making in so tenuous a relationship is to reduce ultimately one's capacity for any depth of feeling or commitment. For in many such liaisons there is a deliberate intention to steer clear of being involved, to have fun without commitment.

22.27   In trying to work out the implications of the high stasay, we have been unable to avoid the continual challenge of the questions – *when is it right to have sexual intercourse?* and, *is it ever right outside marriage?* The problem of sexual behaviour outside marriage is everywhere under discussion at the present time, and the needs of many who want guidance are not met by the simple statement that chastity is right and un-chastity wrong. Such a statement leaves many untouched and some desperate.

22.28   We condemn exploitation in any form. Exploitation is using the partner to satisfy a physical or an emotional need without considering the other as a person. There are many forms of exploitation from the extreme of prostitution for material gain to exploitation in marriage. It is exploitation if the insecure boy enhances his sense of masculine adulthood by sexual adventures, without considering the girl's feelings. It is equally exploitation if the girl leads the young man into marriage by using her attraction as a bait without thinking about his welfare. Exploitation can also happen in non-sexual relationships when the stronger character accepts adoration from the weaker and the less mature, or when one person uses the other to enrich his or her status or self-confidence. This can occur not only between unequal, but also between equal partners. In marriage it is also exploitation if the man uses the woman to show his masculine prowess or the woman uses the man to establish her social status as a married woman, or as one who is attractive and valued. Neither partner has stopped to consider the other's value.

22.29   In seeking to find a truly Christian judgment of this problem, we have again and again been brought to the quality of human relationships as the only final criterion. To base our judgment on whether or not the sex-act has taken place is often to falsify that judgment fantastically. Is the girl who remains chaste, but leaves would-be lovers stimulated to the point where desire would almost certainly seek relief elsewhere, more or less blameworthy than the girl who surrenders, whether in mistaken generosity or in the pathetic desire to "keep her boy"? *The Christian standard of chastity should not be measured by a physical act, but should be a standard of human relationship, applicable within marriage as well as outside it.*

22.30   Moreover, the problem of what to say to the early developing, over-stimulated youth of the present time is not the same as the problem of what to say to the responsible young men and women equipped by experience and education to analyse and evaluate a situation in which they find themselves. A simple "thou shall not" meets the needs of neither.

22.31   When human relationships are judged by this criterion, it is found to result in an assessment of behaviour not very different from that of conventional Christian morality, but it brings us to a new realization of the true nature of chastity. True chastity is a quality of the spirit: it entails the deepest respect and a profound value for human relationships. It involves the most generous giving, which may mean the restraint of withholding, but it is not solely measured in physical terms. Further, there are lives which are being lived unconventionally with more true chastity than some lived in obedience to conventional codes.

22.32   If chastity means respect for oneself and others, then promiscuity is the final denial of it. It denies the importance of personality, and those who seek relief in this way of life imprison their true selves – they are sexual deviants damaging both themselves and their transitory partner by divorcing the physical from the spiritual and keeping impersonal what should involve the whole personality. Yet wherever the most transient relationship has, as it may have, an element of true tenderness and mutual giving and receiving, it has in it something of good.

22.33   Promiscuity cannot be countered by the mere statement that it is sinful: its causes need to be sought and understood. It is often the expression of loneliness and insecurity, born of a lack of experience of real relationships with others. Promiscuity is exploitation – one-sided or mutual but the wrongfulness of exploitation cannot be realized unless the significance of personality is perceived, until it is recognized, as Von Hügel put it, that "caring is the greatest thing, caring matters most."

EXTRACT 23
PAUL VI
Birth control

23.1   The changes that have taken place are in fact of considerable importance and concern different problems. In the first place there is the question of the rapid increase in population which has made many fear that world population is going to grow faster than available resources, with the consequence that many families and developing countries are being faced with greater hardships. This fact can easily induce public authorities to be tempted to take radical measures to avert this danger. There is also the fact that not only working and housing conditions, but the greater demands made both in the economic and educational field require that kind of life in which it is frequently extremely difficult these days to provide for a large family.

23.2   It is also apparent that, with the new understanding of the dignity of woman, and her place in society, there has been an appreciation of the value of love in marriage and of the meaning of intimate married life in the light of that love.

23.3   But the most remarkable development of all is to be seen in man's stupendous progress in the domination and rational organization of the forces of nature to the point that he is endeavouring to extend this control over every aspect of his own life – over his body, over his mind and emotions, over his social life, and even over the laws that regulate the transmission of life.

23.4   This new state of things gives rise to new questions. Granted the conditions of life today and taking into account the relevance of married love to the harmony and mutual fidelity of husband and wife, would it not be right to review the moral norms in force till now, especially when it is felt that these can be observed, only with the gravest difficulty, sometimes only by heroic effort?

23.5   Moreover, if one were to apply here the socalled principle of totality, could it not be accepted that the intention to have a less prolific but more rationally planned family might not transform an action which renders natural processes infertile into a licit and provident control of birth? Could it not be admitted, in other words, that procreative finality applies to the totality of married life rather than to each single act? It is being asked whether, because people are more conscious today of their responsibilities, the time has not come when the transmission of life should be regulated by their intelligence and will rather than through the specific rhythms of their own bodies.

23.6   This kind of question required from the teaching authority of the Church a new and deeper reflection on the principles of the moral teaching on marriage – a teaching which is based on the natural law as illuminated and enriched by divine Revelation.

23.7   Let no Catholic be heard to assert that the interpretation of the natural moral law is outside the competence of the Church's Magisterium. It is in fact indisputable, as Our Predecessors have many times declared, that Jesus Christ, when he communicated his divine power to Peter and the other apostles and sent them to teach all nations his commandments, constituted them as the authentic guardians and interpreters of the whole moral law, not only, that is, of the law of the gospel but also of the natural law, the reason being that the natural law declares the will of God, and its faithful observance is necessary for men's eternal salvation.

23.8   The Church, in carrying out this mandate, has always provided consistent teaching on the nature of marriage, on the correct use of conjugal rights, and on all the duties of husband and wife. This is especially true in recent times . . .

23.9   The questions of the birth of children, like every other question which touches human life, is too large to be resolved by limited criteria, such as are provided by biology, psychology, demography or sociology. It is the whole man and the whole complex of his responsibilities that must be considered, not only what is natural and limited to this earth, but also what is supernatural and eternal. And since in the attempt to justify artificial methods of birth control many appeal to the demands of married love or of 'responsible parenthood', these two important realities of married life must be accurately defined and analyzed. This is what We mean to do, with special reference to what the Second Vatican Council taught with the highest authority in its Pastoral Constitution *Gaudium et Spes.*

23.10   Married love particularly reveals its true nature and nobility when we realize that it derives from God and finds its supreme origin in him who 'is Love', the Father 'from whom every family in heaven and on earth is named' (Eph. 3.15).

23.11   Marriage, then, is far from being the effect of chance or the result of the blind evolution of natural forces. It is in reality the wise and provident institution of God the Creator, whose purpose was to establish in man his loving design. As a consequence, husband and wife, through that mutual gift of themselves, which is specific and exclusive to them alone, seek to develop that kind of personal union in which they complement one another in order to co-operate with God in the generation and education of new lives.

23.12   Furthermore, the marriage of those who have been baptized is invested with the dignity of a sacramental sign of grace, for it represents the union of Christ and his Church.

23.13   In the light of these facts the characteristic features and exigencies of married love are clearly indicated, and it is of the highest importance to evaluate them exactly.

23.14   This love is above all fully *human*, a compound of sense and spirit. It is not, then, merely a question of natural instinct or emotional drive. It is also, and above all, an act of the free will, whose dynamism ensures that not only does it endure through the joys and sorrows of daily life, but also that it grows, so that husband and wife become in a way one heart and one soul, and together attain their human fulfilment.

23.15   Then it is a love which is *total* - that very special form of personal friendship in which husband and wife generously share everything, allowing no unreasonable exceptions or thinking just of their own interests. Whoever really loves his partner loves not only for what he receives, but loves that partner for her own sake, content to be able to enrich the other with the gift of himself.

23.16   Again, married love is *faithful* and *exclusive* of all other, and this until death. This is how husband and wife understood it on the day on which, fully aware of what they were doing, they freely vowed themselves to one another in marriage. Though this fidelity of husband and wife sometimes presents difficulties, no one can assert that it is impossible, for it is always honourable and worthy of the highest esteem. The example of so many married persons down through the centuries shows not only that fidelity is co-natural to marriage but also that it is the source of profound and enduring happiness.

23.17 And finally this love is *creative of life*, for it is not exhausted by the loving interchange of husband and wife, but also contrives to go beyond this to bring new life into being. 'Marriage and married love are by their character ordained to the procreation and bringing up of children. Children are the outstanding gift of marriage, and contribute in the highest degree to the parents' welfare.' (*Gaudium et Spes*, pp. 1070–72).

23.18 Married love, therefore, requires of husband and wife the full awareness of their obligations in the matter of responsible parenthood, which today, rightly enough, is much insisted upon, but which, at the same time, should be rightly understood. Hence, this must be studied in the light of the various inter-related arguments which are its justification.

23.19 If first we consider it in relation to the biological processes involved, responsible parenthood is to be understood as the knowledge and observance of their specific functions. Human intelligence discovers in the faculty of procreating life, the biological laws which involve human personality.

23.20 If, on the other hand, we examine the innate drives and emotions of man, responsible parenthood expresses the domination which reason and will must exert over them.

23.21 But if we then attend to relevant physical, economic, psychological and social conditions, those are considered to exercise responsible parenthood who prudently and generously decide to have a large family, or who, for serious reasons and with due respect to the moral law, choose to have no more children for the time being or even for an indeterminate period.

23.22   Responsible parenthood, moreover, in the terms in which we use the phrase, retains a further and deeper significance of paramount importance which refers to the objective moral order instituted by God, – the order of which a right conscience is the true interpreter. As a consequence the commitment to responsible parenthood requires that husband and wife, keeping a right order of priorities, recognize their own duties towards God, themselves, their families and human society.

23.23   From this it follows that they are not free to do as they like in the service of transmitting life, on the supposition that it is lawful for them to decide independently of other considerations what is the right course to follow. On the contrary, they are bound to ensure that what they do corresponds to the will of God the Creator. The very nature of marriage and its use makes this clear, while the constant teaching of the Church affirms it.

23.24   The sexual activity, in which husband and wife are intimately and chastely united with one another, through which human life is transmitted, is, as the recent Council recalled, 'honourable and good'. It does not, moreover, cease to be legitimate even when, for reasons independent of their will, it is foreseen to be infertile. For its natural adaptation to the expression and strengthening of the union of husband and wife is not thereby suppressed. The facts are, as experience shows, that new life is not the result of each and every act of sexual intercourse. God has wisely ordered the laws of nature and the incidence of fertility in such a way that successive births are already naturally spaced through the inherent operation of these laws. The Church, nevertheless, in urging men to the observance of the precepts of the natural law, which it interprets by its constant doctrine, teaches as absolutely required that *in any use whatever of marriage* there must be no impairment of its natural capacity to procreate human life.

23.25   This particular doctrine, often expounded by the Magisterium of the Church, is based on the inseparable connection, established by God, which man on his own initiative may not break, between the unitive significance and the procreative significance which are both inherent to the marriage act.

23.26   The reason is that the marriage act, because of its fundamental structure, while it unites husband and wife in the closest intimacy, also brings into operation laws written into the actual nature of man and of woman for the generation of new life. And if each of these essential qualities, the unitive and the procreative, is preserved, the use of marriage fully retains its sense of true mutual love and its ordination to the supreme responsibility of parenthood to which man is called. We believe that our contemporaries are particularly capable of seeing that this teaching is in harmony with human reason.

23.27   For men rightly observe that to force the use of marriage on one's partner without regard to his or her condition or personal and reasonable wishes in the matter, is no true act of love, and therefore offends the moral order in its particular application to the intimate relationship of husband and wife. In the same way, if they reflect, they must also recognize that an act of mutual love which impairs the capacity to transmit life which God the Creator, through specific laws, has built into it, frustrates his design which consititutes the norms of marriage, and contradicts the will of the Author of life. Hence, to use this divine gift while depriving it, even if only partially, of its meaning and purpose, is equally repugnant to the nature of man and of woman, strikes at the heart of their relationship and is consequently in opposition to the plan of God and his holy will. But to experience the gift of married love while respecting the laws of conception is to acknowledge that one is not the master of the sources of life but rather the minister of the design established by the Creator. Just as man does not have unlimited dominion over his body in general, so also, and with more particular reason, he has no such dominion over his specifically sexual faculties, for these are concerned by their very nature with the generation of life, of which God is the source. For human life is sacred –

all men must recognize that fact, Our Predecessor, Pope John XXIII, recalled, 'since from its first beginnings it calls for the creative action of God' (*Mater et Magistra* 1961).

23.28   Therefore we basee first principles of a human and Christian doctrine of marriage when we are obliged once more to declare that the direct interruption of the generative process already begun and, above all, direct abortion, even for therapeutic reasons, are to be absolutely excluded as lawful means of controlling the birth of children.

23.29   Equally to be condemned, as the Magisterium of the Church has affirmed on various occasions, is direct sterilization, whether of the man or of the woman, whether permanent or temporary.

23.30   Similarly excluded is any action, which either before, at the moment of, or after sexual intercourse, is specifically intended to prevent procreation – whether as an end or as a means.

23.31   Neither is it valid to argue, as a justification for sexual intercourse which is deliberately contraceptive, that a lesser evil is to be preferred to a greater one, or that such intercourse would merge with the normal relations of past and future to form a single entity, and so be qualified by exactly the same moral goodness as these. Though it is true that sometimes it is lawful to tolerate a lesser moral evil in order to avoid a greater or in order to promote a greater good, it is never lawful, even for the gravest reasons, to do evil that good may come of it – in other words, to intend positively something which intrinsically contradicts the moral order, and which must therefore be judged unworthy of man, even though the intention is to protect or promote the welfare of an individual, of a family or of society in general. Consequently it is a serious error to think that a whole married life of otherwise normal relations can justify sexual intercourse which is deliberately contraceptive and so intrinsically wrong.

23.32   But the Church in no way regards as unlawful

therapeutic means considered necessary to cure organic diseases, even though they also have a contraceptive effect, and this is forseen – provided that this contraceptive effect is not directly intended for any motive whatsoever.

23.33   However, as We noted earlier, some people today raise the objection against this particular doctrine of the Church concerning the moral laws governing marriage, that human intelligence has both the right and the responsibilty to control those forces of irrational nature which come within its ambit and to direct them towards ends beneficial to man. Others ask on the same point whether it is not reasonable in so many cases to use artificial birth control if by so doing the harmony and peace of a family are better served and more suitable conditions are provided for the education of children already born. To this question we must give a clear reply. The Church is the first to praise and commend the application of human intelligence to an activity in which a rational creature such as man is so closely associated with his Creator. But she affirms that this must be done within the limits of the order of reality established by God.

23.34   If therefore there are reasonable grounds for spacing births, arising from the physical or psychological condition of husband or wife, or from external circumstances, the Church teaches that then married people may take advantage of the natural cycles immanent in the reproductive system and use their marriage at precisely those times that are infertile, and in this way control birth, a way which does not in the least offend the moral principles which we have just explained.

23.35   Neither the Church nor her doctrine is inconsistent when she considers it lawful for married people to take advantage of the infertile period but condemns as always unlawful the use of means which directly exclude conception, even when the reasons given for the latter practice are neither trivial nor immoral. In reality, these two cases are completely different. In the former married couples rightly use a facility provided them by nature. In the latter they obstruct the natural development of the generative process. It cannot be denied that in each case married couples, for acceptable reasons, are both perfectly clear in their intention to avoid children and mean to make sure that none will be born. But it is equally true that it is exclusively in the former case that husband and wife are ready to abstain from intercourse during the fertile period as often as for reasonable motives the birth of another child is not desirable. And when the infertile period recurs, they use their married intimacy to express their mutual love and safeguard their fidelity towards one another. In doing this they certainly give proof of a true and authentic love.

23.36　　Responsible men can become more deeply convinced of the truth of the doctrine laid down by the Church on this issue if they reflect on the consequences of methods and plans for the artificial restriction of increases in the birth-rate. Let them first consider how easily this course of action can lead to the way being wide open to marital infidelity and a general lowering of moral standards. Not much experience is needed to be fully aware of human weakness and to understand that men – and especially the young, who are so exposed to temptation – need incentives to keep the moral law, and it is an evil thing to make it easy for them to break that law. Another effect that gives cause for alarm is that a man who grows accustomed to the use of contraceptive methods may forget the reverence due to a woman, and, disregarding her physical and emotional equilibrium, reduce her to being a mere instrument for the satisfaction of his own desires, no longer considering her as his partner whom he should surround with care and affection.

23.37　　Finally, grave consideration should be given to the danger of this power passing into the hands of those public authorities who care little for the precepts of the moral law. Who will blame a Government which in its attempt to resolve the problems affecting an entire country resorts to the same measures as are regarded as lawful by married people in the solution of a particular family difficulty? Who will prevent public authorities from favouring those contraceptive methods which they consider more effective? Should they regard this as necessary, they may even impose their use on everyone. It could well happen, therefore, that when people, either individually or in family or social life, experience the inherent difficulties of the divine law and are determined to avoid them, they may be giving into the hands of public authorities the power to intervene in the most personal and intimate responsibility of husband and wife.

23.38 Consequently, unless we are willing that the responsibility of procreating life should be left to the arbitrary decision of men, we must accept that there are certain limits, beyond which it is wrong to go, to the power of man over his own body and its natural functions – limits, let it be said, which no one, whether as a private individual or as a public authority, can lawfully exceed. These limits are expressly imposed because of the reverence due to the whole human organism and its natural functions, in the light of the principles, which we stated earlier, and according to a correct understanding of the so-called 'principle of totality', enunciated by Our Predecessor, Pope Pius XII.

23.39 It is to be anticipated that not everyone perhaps will easily accept this particular teaching. There is too much clamorous outcry against the voice of the Church, and this is intensified by modern means of communication. It should cause no surprise that the Church, any less than her divine Founder, is destined to be a 'sign of contradiction' (Lk. 2.34). She does not, because of this, evade the duty imposed on her of proclaiming humbly but firmly the entire moral law, both natural and evangelical.

23.40 Since the Church did not make either of these laws, she cannot be their arbiter – only their guardian and interpreter. It can never be right for her to declare lawful what is in fact unlawful, because this, by its very nature, is always opposed to the true good of man.

23.41 By vindicating the integrity of the moral law of marriage, the Church is convinced that she is contributing to the creation of a truly human civilization. She urges man not to betray his personal responsibilities by putting all his faith in technical expedients. In this way she defends the dignity of husband and wife. This course of action shows that the Church, loyal to the example and teaching of the divine Saviour, is sincere and unselfish in her regard for men whom she strives to help even now during this earthly pilgrimage 'to share as sons in the life of the living God, the Father of all men'.

EXTRACT 24

HASTINGS

The theology of race

The Divisions of Mankind

24.1   The Bible begins with Adam and the genealogy of Jesus too is taken in Luke's gospel back to Adam, son of God (Luke 3. 38). Here again we have the basic concern for all mankind. It is that which descent from Adam signifies – unity of all men in nature and need. All exist in the image of God, all are subject to work and suffering, all die. Cousins in nature, all are called to be brothers in Christ: Parthians, Medes, Elamites, . . . the Roman centurion, the Ethiopian minister. One of the most evident implications of the New Testament is then the total unimportance of race. Racialism is just self-evidently non-Christian, even though time and again Christians have indeed become racialists – often by thinking themselves back from the New to a twisted version of the Old Testament situation. Is not the Faith Europe, and Europe Christendom? Have the natives of America souls? Is not Britain the true Israel? God's own people and God's own land – God has chosen *us*, has given *us* this land, has made *them* different, hewers of wood, drawers of water.

24.2   Today the psychological division between "us" and "them" may often take, in the world at large, a more manifestly racial character than in the past. But it often tended that way: English and foreigners; Greeks and barbarians; Aryans and Jews; White and coloured. The building up of a situation of this kind and its segregationalist responses is all too characteristic of human society, but the Gospel has its response: a more explicit response than it has for almost any other social problem, and that just because the Church had to face such a situation – although one couched in particularly theological terms – right from the beginning. Despite hesitations countenanced by authority and deviationist groups with their very apartheid line – they refused to eat with the Gentiles and *separated* themselves (cf. Galatians 2. 12) – the Church's considered response was uncompromising: "God shows no partiality". The wall is down between "us and them".

Christian Universalism

24.3   Thus the Christian Church by the most striking facts of her mission and her earliest crisis in self-awareness has universalism built into her. The mediaeval tradition, which turned the wise men of the Epiphany – the very first Gentiles to worship Christ – into three kings, black, white and brown, expressed in its simple, popular, grass-roots way, the essential equality of men and of race in the light of Christ, which is something utterly to be taken for granted within the Church. She has always accepted her mission as one to all nations and has never admitted racial differences as a barrier to the Christian or human community. But only since the sixteenth century has she been faced with situations of continuous inter-racial contact on a large scale. It must be admitted that the result was in many ways not encouraging. Massacres of Indians, the organized slave trade, even the denial that these were really men at all. But the Church's voice did not hesitate. Not only champions like Bartholomew de Las Casas but the Pope himself spoke out with clarity: "The Indians, though still not received into the bosom of the Church, must not be deprived of their freedom or possessions, *for they are men*" (Paul III in 1537). It was the position of the great theologian of natural law, Francisco de Vitoria: natural rights belong to men because they are men, members of a single universal society. They admit of no racial distinction.

24.4   Rome's first "Vicar Apostolic" for Africa was a young Congolese, Prince Henry, consecrated bishop in 1518. Likewise the first vicar apostolic in India was a Brahman convert, Mathew de Castro, appointed in 1637. These were fine gestures, the instinctive movements of the Christian mind. They did, alas, remain little more. Further African and Indian bishops were not appointed in the Catholic Church until the twentieth century. The official position of the Church was one thing, the pragmatic attitudes and prejudices of most Christians another, and in practice the latter widely prevailed. Racial discrimination, even of a blatant kind, has been a notable feature of Christian life in many places in modern times – a discrimination which has penetrated even within churches and ecclesiastical institutions of all kinds. It is not the function of this article to study history, neither to excuse, nor to blame. Certainly in this matter, as in many others, we have sinned and need to admit it without circumlocution. Today the World Council of Churches, the Popes and the Vatican Council have all expressly condemned racial discrimination and that is certainly sincerely endorsed by the great majority of convinced Christians.

24.5   "The Church rejects, as foreign to the mind of Christ, any discrimination against men or harassment of them because of their race, colour, condition of life or religion" (Vatican II, 1965). "When we are given Christian insight the whole pattern of racial discrimination is seen as an unutterable offence against God, to be endured no longer, so that the very stones cry out" (W.C.C., Evanston 1954).

24.6   Life and property, all the exigencies of the human condition, fellowship with other men, the highest things and the lowest, the grace of God, the communion of the Church – all these things are offered to men without exception because they are men united in the solidarity of their common divine image, their common human parentage, their common redemption.

The Sacrament of Unity

24.7   That is the witness of the Christian Church and it always will be so. There can be no walls of separation. The Church does not teach a doctrine of invisible and spiritual things alone. On the contrary, she witnesses to the Incarnation – to God being with us. We saw him and touched him and ate and drank with him. Christians are the disciples of Jesus of Nazareth, those of his company who ate and drank together in fellowship and must still continue to do so. This living, human, physical being-together is the sign and sacrament of all she teaches and means. She cannot teach a spiritual unity and admit a physical separation. She does not even start with the spiritual unity; she started with the physical togetherness of a common board, supper with the Lord.

24.8   In the fine words of St. Cyprian, repeated and stressed by the Vatican Council (e.g. in the Constitution on the Church, no. 9 and the Liturgy constitution, no. 26), the Church is the "sacrament of unity". A sacrament is a visible signpost, a credible manifestation, a showing forth in place and time such as men can understand. And this unity is a human one, a unity of men, of the men whom the Lord loves, of all men. To deny the spiritual unity and equality of men is utterly to deny the Bible; while to deny that this unity is and must be manifest in the visible Church, to admit apartness in the visible Church though not in the Spirit, would be equally to deny the Incarnation, that the Son of God lived among men, his Church a fellowship of men on earth, an eating and drinking society, a physical cum spiritual communion.

24.9   The basic physical element linking the initial company of Christians has always to continue. The Eucharist supper is the permanent centre and cause-of-being of the Church. Do *this* as a memorial of me. Eat, drink, together. We are one body for we share in the one bread. The absolute heart and essence of Christian living is the negation of apartheid: not uniform belief in the existence of God, but common drinking from a shared cup – the sacrament of unity. It is the unity of men as men in their very animality, and that is made the sign of the union of the spirit. The most earthly communion, the sign of the most divine: the bread we bless and break and eat together is it not a sharing in the body of Christ?

24.10   It is a sign with meaning. It really implies unity with God and unity among men. To eat together in church and to remain on principle apart in the seven-day-a-week life whose meaning has to be signed in the Sunday Eucharist would be utter nonsense. It would make of it an empty sign, a farce. Far better not to go to church at all than to participate in that contradiction-in-terms a segregated eucharist or even in a eucharist for the segregated.

24.11   The Church of the Word made flesh is for all men, Jew and Greek, Roman and Ethiopian, and its membership involves physical fellowship. The life and unity she offers cannot just be a subject for belief, it must be lived, and lived in the flesh. Otherwise the Church is not the Church.

24.12   Man matters, and the universal brotherhood of man; race does not. That is not only a judgment of philosophical conviction or religious faith. When one has lived for years with people of another race, worked and played and argued and disagreed with them, when one has read together Antigone and Hamlet and St. Joan, and shared their struggles and triumphs and emotional crises, and shared one's own with them, then one knows indeed with the conviction of the deepest human experience that men are one, and differences of race slip away into the fringes of insignificance. The death of Socrates is no more mine than theirs. It belongs to all whose humanity is sufficient to share in it and the experience of this joins us together inseparably as men, just as communicating in a common eucharist presenting the death of Jesus Christ joins us utterly as Christians.

EXTRACT 25
RUETHER
Feminist theology and ecology

25.1 Since women in western culture have been traditionally identified with nature, and nature, in turn, has been seen as an object of domination by man (males), it would seem almost a truism that the mentality that regarded the natural environment as an object of domination drew upon imagery and attitudes based on male domination of women . . .

25.2 The social and symbolic roots of this view of the world as "rapine" are not easily sorted out. Since Lynn White's essay on "The Religious Roots of our Ecological Crisis," (in *Science* 155, 1967), it has been common to trace this view back to the Old Testament mandate that "man" subdue the earth and have dominion over the animals (Gen. 1:28). But this interpretation incorporates the Genesis language too directly into Christian and secular views of domination, based on splits between mind and body, society and nature, and is insensitive to the residue of earlier nature religion that still influences the view of nature found in the Old Testament. Unlike Christianity, Hebrew religion, especially in its pre-exilic period, is not a religion of alienation that views nature as inferior or evil. Like the Canaanite religion, which the Hebrews partly overthrew and partly assimilated, it is a religion of socionatural renewal.

25.3 Society and nature cohere in a single created community under the sovereignty of God. The breaking of the covenant with God results both in a devastation of the social covenant (social injustice), and in a devastation of

the covenant with nature (drought, pollution, blight –
see, for example, Isa. 24). A restoration of fidelity to God
brings a restoration of the conditions of social justice in
human relations and of benign relations between society
and nature. The social and the natural languages are so
intimately integrated that it is something of a distortion
even to speak of them as two different relations, rather
than as parts of a single socionatural covenant that binds
the creation into one community. Humanity, not nature,
is the contrary element from whence arises disobedience.
Old Testament religion concentrates on restoring
humanity to the sovereignty of God, as the discordant
element that breaks the community of creation.

25.4   Unlike the Greek and Christian traditions, the Old
Testament is patriarchal without linking this to an
alienated view of creation. Indeed the hostile actions of
the natural environment are often identified with the
activity of God in punishing Israel for "her" wayward
(harlot) activity. The language of God toward Israel is
modelled on patriarchal domination of males over
females, fathers over children. But the natural world
remains an autonomous sphere of God's dominion and
the revelation of divine power and glory that God can use
for or against Israel. Only in the context of Israel's
fidelity to God does nature become benign toward the
human community. It is not a neutral sphere upon which
ruling males can impose their own desires.

25.5   Two important elements which unite class and sexist
languages to a view of nature as a sphere of human
domination and repression are absent from the psalms
and the prophets. One element is that view which regards
consciousness as transcendent to visible nature, while the
bodily sphere is seen as ontologically and morally
inferior, to be subjugated by the superior principle
represented by the mind. The second element absent
from the Old Testament is the reading of the spirit-nature
split into class and sexist relations, so that women, slaves,
and lower classes are seen as analogous to the inferior

realm of bodily "nature," while ruling-class males identify themselves with transcendent spirit.

25.6   These two elements, absent from pre-exilic Old Testament religion, are typical of classical philosophy. Here the authentic self is regarded as the soul or transcendent rationality, over against bodily existence. As we have seen, the relation of spirit to body is one of repression, subjugation, and mastery. Material existence is ontologically inferior to mind and the root of moral evil. Moreover, the language of hierarchical dualism is identified with social hierarchy. The hierarchy of spirit over body is expressed in the dominion of males over females, freed-men over slaves, Greeks over "Barbarians." Domination is "naturalized," so that the inferior ontological and moral characteristics of body in relation to mind are identified with the inferior psychobiological "natures" of women and subjugated classes.

25.7   After the fourth century B.C. the more optimistic ideal of Hellenic culture of harmony of body and spirit gave way to a pessimistic world alienation. Plato was the precursor of a quest for salvation viewed as flight from activity and material existence. Aristotle gave explicit form to the implicit misogynism of Plato's ontological hierarchicalism. Later Platonism fused elements from the two into an ascetic, misogynist world fleeing religious philosophy. This mood of world alienation – again, as detailed above – links with developments in Judaism in the Hellenistic period. In the apocalyptic writings (ca. 200 B.C. to A.D. 130), the "world" is seen as having slipped out of the sovereignty of God. Not God, but diabolic powers exercise immediate mastery over the world. The prophetic split between apostasy and future hope has become dualistic and otherworldly. Salvation now requires the destruction of the present created world and the creation of a new spiritual universe where Israel can be redeemed and God reign. Human hopes and the absolutism of God's demands have split apart what earlier biblical faith had held together in dialectical unity. Transcendent hope and commandment demand an infinite and immortal world that shatters the limits of the original created order of God. Gnostic radicals did not hesitate to suggest that the creator of the present world, the God of the Old Testament, was not the true God, but a demon.

25.8   Christianity was born through a fusion of apocalyptic Judaism and Platonic dualism. Despite the efforts of the Church Fathers to knit back together the God of creation and the God of eschatological redemption, cosmic alienation and spiritual dualism triumphed in classical Christian spirituality. But the Christian theological synthesis, which reigned from the patristic era through seventeenth-century Protestant orthodoxy, was hardly a theology that secularized the world as a sphere of neutral human domination. The Christian view of nature split creation into two opposite possibilities: sacramentality and demonization. Nature, restored to the sovereignty of God through Christ, was exemplified in the sacraments. Here, in the sacral sphere conquered by the Church, nature once more shone forth as the image and incarnate presence of God. But, outside this sphere of redemption, nature was demonic and alien to God, an outer darkness where Satan and his evil host abounded. A secular science that would seek to free itself from ecclesiastical control would be regarded as falling into this demonic sphere and tantamount to the Faustian alliance with the devil. For classical Christianity, nature could be sacramental or demonic, but never secular, i.e., never neutral and "value-free." Classical Protestantism, just as vehemently as Catholicism, would see "fallen" nature as demonic, while assaulting and shrinking the sense of nature as sacramental. Again, it is not accidental that renewed demonology and witch hunts abounded in the era of religious warfare between Catholics and Protestants, and both saw their stereotypic victim as an evil, lusty female . . .

25.9   Women must see that there can be no liberation for them and no solution to the ecological crisis within a society whose fundamental model of relationships continues to be one of domination. They must unite the demands of the women's movement with those of the ecological movement to envision a radical reshaping of the basic socio-economic relations and the underlying values of this society. The concept of domination of nature has been based from the first on social domination between master and servant groups, starting with the basic relation between men and women. An ecological revolution must overthrow all the social structures of domination. This means transforming that world-view which underlines domination and replacing it with an alternative value system. It is here that the values and development learned in the patriarchal family and in the local community are of great importance. How do we change the self-concept of a society from the drives toward possession, conquest, and accumulation to the values of reciprocity and acceptance of mutual limitation? It is hard even to imagine a coherent alternative beyond the present horizons of crisis and impending disaster. Even when reasonable and possible alternatives can be sketched, the practical power to counteract the systems which perpetuate the world of global exploitation and war escape us. We seem to be awaiting a planetary rebirth which can come about only when massive catastrophe decisively discredits the present systems of power. We scarcely know whether either the physical or the spiritual resources exist to make such a creative leap beyond disaster. So it is with fear and trembling that we even try to dream of new things.

25.10   First of all, harmony between the human community and natural systems has nothing to do with anti-intellectual or anti-technological primitivism. The human capacity for technological rationality is itself the highest gift of nature. It needs to be freed from its captivity to ruling-class domination and not be regarded as inherently evil. Escapist, romantic primitivism tends to be the response of alienated children of the elite. It has little to offer those left out of the present affluence. What is needed is democratization of decision-making over technological development and equalization of its benefits. It must become impossible for a small ruling class to monopolize the wealth from world resources, while transferring the social costs to the people in the form of poisoned air, water, and soil. This also demands the development of new ecological technology oriented toward preservation of the earth.

25.11   Some obvious changes are necessary. High on the agenda is a total overhaul of the present method of transportation that is based on the private auto and the freeway system. The gasoline auto will have to be phased out, to be replaced by public mass transit between urban centers, and bicycles and electric cars and buses within local areas. Congested areas should be cleared of trucks or cars entirely, to allow only bicycles or pedestrians. We are fully capable of designing such an alternative, but lack of coordinated planning and commitment of politicians to the present automobile, trucking, and oil interests keeps us tied to a transportation system that is heading for disaster. There must be a general shift from energy sources which are polluting and limited to those which are nonpolluting and renewable, such as sun, wind, water, electricity, and perhaps nuclear energy, if ways can be found to handle its wastes. Clearly an ecological technology will demand great scientific imagination, but an imagination directed toward the common good of the entire world community and one which seeks to integrate the human sociosphere into the biosphere of nature in a positively reinforcing relationship.

25.12   It seems possible that, as disasters mount from the present unregulated system, there may come a time when the major systems of power in the United States, Russia, and perhaps even China would move together to create a global planned society. This will be called a "socialist revolution," and many well-meaning liberals will be convinced that democracy must be sacrificed for human survival. Even persons such as Henry Kissinger have been free to suggest that democracy's days are numbered. One can well imagine a sudden unanimity about this among right-wing and left-wing world leaders, all of whom are basically fascists. Some unified management of world resources is needed, so that national rivalries cease to keep the planet in a permanent state of economic and military warfare. The destruction of our resources in war technology and its threat to survival must be ended. But if that government is to be other than totalitarian, managed for the benefit of a world ruling class, socialist communities must be built from the bottom up.

25.13 A democratic socialism has to be a communitarian socialism. This means the economic and political sectors of local communities are run on the principles of subsidiarity, self-ownership, and self-management. Planning, distribution, and enforcement of standards need to be ceded to larger units: metropolitan regions, states, nations, and international bodies. But these levels of government must be rooted in strong self-governing local communities, with representatives elected from the base. Only in this way can socialism be kept from becoming total alienation of the atomized individual in huge impersonal corporatisms. An urgent task for those concerned about the society of the future is the development of viable forms of local communalization on the level of residential groups, work places, and townships that can increase our control over the quality of our own lives.

25.14 It is on the level of the local community that socialism can change the dependency of women by transforming the relationship among power, work, and home. The nuclear family cannot overcome the caste status of women because it is the victim of a rigid complementarity of work-home, male-female dualities. As we saw earlier, Marxist or state socialism has tended to solve this by giving over female work to state agencies in order to integrate women into productive labor. The stratagey of a communitarian socialist society is different. It would bring work back into an integrated relationship to self-governing living communities. Women's work is still communalized and professionalized, but control over these functions remains with families themselves who band together in groups on the level appropriate for particular functions. For example, a residential group would develop communal shopping, cooking, child care, cleaning, or gardening by collectivizing its own resources. The child is not taken out of the family into an impersonal state agency to free the mother for other activity. Rather, it gains a tribe while remaining rooted in the family.

25.15   Communalization of functions of local groups should not be confused with what is called a commune in contemporary America, i.e., eight or ten young adults in a house built for a nuclear family. This is an unstable unit at best. What we are talking about is the principle of the kibbutz, but applied in a diversity of forms to different living and working patterns. Communalized living requires a new architecture which balances private and corporate dimensions of life. It calls for new urban planning to integrate living with work. Clear, objective political forms that maximize personal participation need to be developed. Short-term committees with rotating membership who bring propositions before a direct primary assembly would be my own preference. Models for such communities are not beyond our reach. We have a long tradition of Christian communitarianism to draw from. Even residential colleges, although not fully democratic, are a well-accepted example of a self-governing community for work and living.

25.16   I will outline a few of the ways in which socialized local communities could greatly alter the traditional role of women. Communalization of child-raising in residential groups or even in work places could change the child-bearing patterns in nuclear families. The isolated family tries to have several children in order to create a mini-community. In a communal family, children would grow up with a sense of a large group of "brothers and sisters." A bonding of children of a group of families would develop, extending the child's own peer group and also gaining relations with a large group of other adults who are personally concerned with her or him. The personal child-parent relationship would not be destroyed, but it would be supplemented by a larger group of siblings, mothers and fathers, and older brothers and sisters, much as is the case today where the family is still rooted in clan and tribe. Adults who do not have their own children would also have an opportunity to nurture and develop the lives of children. Children would have a sense of a variety of other adults, older children and peers to whom they could turn for resources that might not exist in their immediate families. Fifty adults might have between them about twenty or twenty-five children, which would still afford a bountiful community of children, but rapidly return the population to a level which the earth would be better able to support.

25.17   The tasks of housekeeping, child-raising, food procurement and preparation would be communalized and spread between men and women. One sexual group would no longer be structured into exclusive responsibility for this type of work, isolated from each other and from the work places. Those who chose to be managers of these functions would be skilled professionals and suitably rewarded. Dimensions of private life and control over personal needs would still be retained, allowing for individual choice in relating private and communal aspects of life. The communalization of much of the equipment of daily life – such as communal kitchens, communally owned vehicles and tools signed out on need – could drastically reduce the present patterns of consumption, waste, and duplication of equipment in nuclear families. A decentralized economy would return much of the production to small factories, workshops, and farms owned and run by the local community. Materials would be made to be long-lasting. The shoddy goods made to decay and be replaced rapidly in the profit economy would lose their rationale. There would also return a pride in craftsmanship essential to the dealienation of labor. Home and work, production and consumption, field and factory would be related organically, making each human group aware of the ecological relations of its own material life with that of nature. Human society, patterned for a balance through diversity, would be consciously integrated into its environment. The key to this integration is the use of wastes. In an ecologically balanced society, there should be no real "waste." In effect, the wastes of each system should become converted into being the fuel or food of another system in a recycling process that continually renews and beautifies the environment.

25.18   Since local communities would make many of the decisions that affect their immediate lives, self-government would counteract much of the present sense of alienation and powerlessness of the atomized individual. The interrelationship of home and work would allow men and women to take an equal hand in both nurturing and supportive roles and also in work and political life. The split between alienated work life and shrunken domesticity, which segregates women on one side of this divide, would be overcome by bridging the gap between the two, rather than by abolishing and devaluing the roles of family life. Not only would women be allowed the participaion in the larger social processes that they have historically been denied, but men also would recover the affective and nurturing roles with children and other people historically denied them, which has repressed the gentle, humane side of males and shaped the male personality into that hyper-aggressivity and antagonistic combativeness that has been called "masculine." Without sex-role stereotyping, sex-personality stereotyping would disappear, allowing for genuine individuation of personality. Instead of being forced into a mold of masculine or feminine "types," each individual could shape a complex whole from the full range of human psychic potential for intellect and feeling, activity and receptivity. A richer pattern of friendship could also develop among adults, diffusing the often over-exclusivism of the nuclear marriage that makes two married adults each other's sole personal nurturers of personal intimacy over a lifetime.

25.19 The center of such a new society would have to be not just the appropriate new social form, but a new social vision, a new soul that would inspire the whole. Society would have to be transfigured by the glimpse of a new type of social personality, a "new humanity" appropriate to a "new earth." One might call this even a "new religion," if one understands by this the prophetic vision to shape a new world on earth, and not an alienated spirituality. A society no longer bent on "conquering the earth" might, however, also have more time for the cultivation of interiority, for contemplation, for artistic work that celebrated being for its own sake. But such interiority would not be cultivated at the expense of the community, as in monastic escape from "the world." It would be a cultivation of the self that would be at one with an affirmation of others, both our immediate neighbors and all humanity and the earth itself, as that "thou" with whom "I" am in a state of reciprocal interdependence.

25.20 Such solidarity is not utopian, but eminently practical, pointing to our actual solidarity with all others and with our mother, the earth, which is the actual ground of our being. Perhaps this also demands a letting-go of that self-infinitizing view of the self that culminates in the wish for personal immorality. One accepts the fact that it is the whole, not the individual, which is that "infinite" out of whose womb we arise at birth and into whose womb we are content to return at death, using the human capacity for consciousness, not to alienate ourselves from nature, but rather, to nurture, perfect, and renew her natural harmonies, so that earth might be fair, not only for us and our children, but for all generations of living things still to come.

CRITIQUE

Once again radical differences over moral issues are apparent amongst Christians. For some, abortion, contraception, euthansia and suicide are inherently sinful. For others, they are sinful in some contexts, but not in others. For some, it is only heterosexual activity, within the context of monogamy, that is permissible for the Christian. For others it is wrong to prejudge individuals' sexual relationships – marital or extra-marital: heterosexual or homosexual – without knowing the particularities of a specific loving relationship. For some, the maxims of the women's movement and presumptions of a multi-racial society are still anathema. For others, they are prerequisites of a satisfactory, present-day Christian moral code. By now, the reader will not need reminding that the moral responses of Christians to issues concerned with personal relationships divide them as much as they might unite them. The Extracts intentionally illustrate some of these divisions. Before seeking any points of unity between them, it is important to identify some of their individual weaknesses.

One of the central difficulties in the Fletcher Extract is that it shifts from one concept of euthanasia to another to suit the argument. In terms of the six-fold typology offered in the introduction (see *above*, p. 420), he sometimes seems to envisage type a (19.1), sometimes type b (at the beginning of 19.3), sometimes c or d (at the end of 19.3), and sometimes e or f (19.4). Although there is a relationship between these various types, the ethical issues that they raise are often quite distinct and to fail to identify them only confuses the argument. Another crucial difficulty that many Christians have had with Fletcher's arguments on euthanasia concerns legislation. It is one thing to admit that at least types c to f should be allowed to the doctor if he or she is convinced that, in particular situations, they are right. It is quite another to suggest that there should be legislation to support this decision. To most legislators the difficulties of definition and the dangers of abuse have been obvious.

The evident strength of Gustafson's Extract is that it does attempt to take into consideration all the variables in the particular case-study in question. So, he is concerned to set out the medical, legal, financial, spiritual, emotional and, finally, the theological factors that are relevant. Further, in 20.13 he shows that he is well aware that the issue of abortion raises conflicting moral principles. Unlike Fletcher, he does not simply dismiss 'legalism' and set aside any notion of moral principles or rules. Nonetheless, he shares with Fletcher a concern for the 'concreteness' of ethical decision-making. Indeed, in the article from which this Extract is taken, he insists that the moralist: 'is obligated to assist, if necessary, in finding competent medical care . . . Second, financial resources are needed. To put her on her own in this regard would be to resign responsibility prematurely for a course of action in which the moralist concurred, and might jeopardize the woman's health and welfare. Third, the woman needs continuing social and moral support in her efforts to achieve her aspirations for relief from anguish and for a better human future . . . Fourth, the moralist is under obligation, if he is convinced of the propriety in this human situation of an abortion, to seek reform of abortion legislation which would remove the unjust legal barrier to what he believes to be morally appropriate' (ed. John T. Noonan, Jr., *The Morality of Abortion*, pp. 117-8). The weakness of the Extract is that, despite his awareness of the similarity between Roman Catholic and non-Roman Catholic attitudes to abortion *in practice*, he still regards the former as tied *in theory* to a juridicial and inflexible approach. Perhaps Enda McDonagh is more accurate when he writes, at the end of the same decade, that, 'no longer free to reach for his manual to find the answer to a particular problem, the Catholic student of moral theology finds himself confronted with a bewildering range of information, analysis and opinion on an increasing range of problems' (*Doing the Truth*, p. 14). Certainly, in this Textbook, pluralism is as apparent amongst Roman Catholics as it is amongst non-Roman Catholics.

Many, within the West, may feel that Clément presents too idealised and too 'spiritual' an understanding of the embryo and of the woman (especially in 21.5) and that his unequivocal identification of abortion with murder is too harsh (21.8-9). In part, this may represent a clash between Eastern and Western forms of Chrisitan understanding. More specifically, there is a certain ambiguity in his expression at a particularly crucial point. In 21.3 he claims that, 'the human being, that is, the potential person, exists from the moment of conception'. The force of his argument implies that one should regard the embryo as *fully* human from conception, but the qualifying concept of 'potential person' introduces doubt. On this point, Western thought in general is very ambivalent – and herein lies the central, ethical dilemma over abortion – yet Clément himself appears ambiguous.

The Quaker Group's report has been subject to a good deal of criticism. It is not the work of professional theologians, so perhaps it is not surprising that its theological conclusions have often been contested. It has already been seen that the link between sexuality and sin, that they suppose to be typical of Christian tradition (22.1-7), is actually more typical of Augustine than Aquinas. And many have suggested that their distinction between the physical and the spiritual (22.29-33) does not do justice to the Christian concept of man. Other difficulties result from their attempt to present a thoroughgoing personalism. As with Fletcher's account of situation ethics (see *above*, p. 167) it may be doubted whether, in fact, they have based all of their contentions upon the single standard of 'love'. Other concepts, such as 'exploitation' and 'destructiveness', are introduced without explanation. And it might be doubted whether this really is an account of ethics for all people, and not simply for the strong, intelligent and middle-class. Ramsey was emphatic in his opposition to this report:

> How can Christians nourish the seeds of a wider social responsibility while seeming to praise only acts and never rules that embody personal responsibility between the two parties to sexual relations? Plainly, the waywardness of the human heart works against any *ethos*, customs, or laws that are generally good for all, and not only against "the traditional code". . . . only some form of rule-agapism, and not act-agapism, can be consistent with the elaboration of a Christian's social responsibilities. No social morality ever was founded, or ever will be founded, upon a situation ethic (*Deeds and Rules in Christian Ethics*, p. 20).

Because of its social significance, Paul VI's Extract has been subjected to more criticism than any of the other Extracts. Even within Roman Catholicism, it has been widely disputed – although, of course, it remains a part of official teaching. Quite apart from *overall* judgments about its validity and the extent to which it is thought to be appropriate or not for present-day society, several internal weaknesses can be noticed. Firstly, it shares the same weakness as Aquinas' *Text XI*. A stress upon responsible parenthood is certainly vital to Christian ethics (and too easily ignored in situations of liberalised divorce and abortion). And a clear understanding that sexuality *is* concerned with procreation and not simply with individual pleasure, is also vital (and again too easily ignored). But, even if it is conceded that procreation is the obvious function of sexuality (Aquinas' position), or that sexuality has both a procreative and a unitive function (Paul VI's position), it does not follow that procreation, or even potential procreation *should* be the *only*, or the *indispensable*, function of human sexuality. This point illustrates one of the central difficulties facing Natural law theories (see *above*, p. 86) – the validity of attempting to derive man's moral end from man's 'natural' tendencies. The second weakness within the Extract is linked to this point. It appears that both abortion (spontaneous abortion) and sterility (primary infertility) are 'natural' phenomena which divorce sexual activity from procreation. Further, sexual activity is 'naturally' not exclusively heterosexual, since forms of individualised sexual activity occur spontaneously in sleep and for some homosexual predispositions are increasingly seen as 'natural'. Nature, then, would appear to be more ambiguous than either Aquinas or Paul VI suppose. The latter shows himself aware of some of these ambiguities (23.24), but he regards them only as natural forms of spacing births, instituted by God, which are not to be interfered with by man. It is this contention which makes him vulnerable to a third criticism. Fletcher might have pointed out to him that, in a sense, the whole of modern medicine is 'a form of human self-assertion or a demonic pretension, by which men, especially physicians, try to put themselves in God's place' (19.4). Few would wish to use this argument to justify *every* conceivable act of medical intervention, but many have asked why barrier and hormonal methods of contraception should be singled out as being particularly intrusive.

Hastings also works within the Natural law tradition (although less centrally than Paul VI) and, as a result, shares in some of its weaknesses. There is an inherent philosophical difficulty involved in attempting to derive 'natural rights' from the fact that men are 'members of a single universal society' (24.3). Suppose that scientists had been able to establish the opposite – i.e. that 'race' is a biological, not simply a social, fact. This would not in itself justify racialism on moral grounds. However, the main bases of Hastings' arguments are biblical and doctrinal. Both of these bases present further difficulties. It is possible to maintain that biblical concepts of the 'unity of man' were as much particularistic as universalistic. So, it has already been argued that the prophetic stress upon 'justice' was mainly, with important exceptions such as Amos, concerned with justice for the people of Israel and not even for Israel's most immediate neighbours (see *above*, 290). And it is an open question how far Paul's notion of being one 'in Christ' can really be interpreted in universalistic terms: distinctions between Jew and Greek and between male and female may be broken down 'in Christ', but remain for outsiders and, indeed, between outsiders and those 'in Christ'. The point of contention is removed to christology and, doubtless, Hastings presupposes a universalistic understanding of this. Similarly, he presupposes a unitive understanding of the eucharist, whilst he must be aware that, in practice, Christians have often made the eucharist a manifest symbol of division. In the ecumenical movement Christians clearly have been divided on whether to regard the eucharist as a means to unity or as a fruit of unity. This is far from seeing it as a symbol of unity. But again his remarks are less descriptive than teleological. And this may be their strength.

The feminist critique of theology is still emerging and it would be wrong to dismiss it on the basis of positions that are evidently in process of developing. The second half of Ruether's Extract is conscious of being thought-in-process. Within the same paragraph she can alternate between apparent confident conviction ('an ecological revolution must overthrow all the social structures of domination') and tentativeness ('it is hard even to imagine a coherent alternative beyond the present horizons of crisis and impending disaster' 25.9). Further, she tends to write at a high level of generality which avoids scholarly qualifications (so, although Aquinas' *Text XI. 8* assumes that males are more rational than females, it would be rash to categorise all Christians thus). And, it is possible that the concept of communitarian socialism that she sketches *is* utopian, despite her protestations (25.20). All of these features may result from the broad canvas and experimental style that she adopts. Yet, at one crucial point in her argument, they have a misleading effect. She has a tendency to introduce concepts like 'alienation' and 'domination' as if they were self-explanatory. In fact, the literature on 'alienation' in the social sciences is extensive and hardly unified and, as a political label, it has been used with equal emphasis by quite opposing factors (see also *above*, p. 412). Even the highly influential concept of 'liberation' has been used equally emphatically by otherwise quite opposing political factions. Labels, especially emotively charged labels, are seldom self-explanatory. Yet, the force of Ruether's argument depends heavily upon them.

Despite these very real weaknesses within each of the Extracts and, despite the obvious differences of moral belief between them and between the Texts, two points of unity might be suggested. They depend upon two axioms – these might be termed the adeodatic axiom and the agapistic axiom. The first is a general theistic axiom based upon the presupposition that all life is God-given, whereas the second is a specifically Christian presupposition that *agape* should be intrinsic to all personal relationships. Unambiguous and incontrovertible sets of moral prescriptions for specific issues cannot be supplied by either of these axioms. It seems likely that Christians will continue to disagree with each on many issues within social and personal ethics. But both can set parameters within which most Christian thought on ethical issues might be happy to operate.

The adeodatic axiom would suggest that the theist can accept that life is entirely neither sacred nor profane. Surely, Fletcher, through Temple, is right to insist that, for the Christian, sanctity is not *in* human life (19.5). Indeed, for the theist generally, a notion of God-givenness implies a clear distinction between Creator and creature. If man, as creature, is to be regarded in any sense as holy, it is only a holiness derived wholly from God. From the philosophical perspective, the adjective 'holy' is unique in religious language: all other adjectives are primarily human characteristics, applied only analogically to God, whereas 'holy' is primarily a divine characteristic, applied only analogically to man. Thus, for the theist, any 'rights' that might go with this life, are God-*given*, not inherent possessions. As a result, many theists will continue to be cautious about agreeing that people have 'an inherent right to take their own lives' or that women have an inherent right to abortion. Because life is viewed in the transcendent context of God-givenness it cannot be regarded either as entirely profane. It is a divine gift and, therefore, cannot be regarded casually. Any action or behaviour which treats human life casually undermines the adeodatic axiom. Casual sexual relationships, abortion on demand, irresponsible parenthood, legalised direct forms of euthanasia, sexism and racialism, all have a tendency to do just this. So, it is hardly surprising that theists tend to be cautious about agreeing to them. Even though amongst theists there are obvious differences on all of these issues, a degree of caution would seem to be suggested by the notion of adeodasis. If all human life is a gift from God, man's appropriate response might best be depicted as gratitude (cf. Gregorios in 18.28).

The agapistic axiom would suggest that, for the Christian, an appropriate response to human life is also *agape*. Because of the debates generated by Situation ethics, it is possible to miss this unifying feature of Christian personal ethics. Since the debates of the 1960's, most exponents of Christian ethics might agree that pure-act-agapism is inadequate. They might also agree that *agape* is not the only principle that can be derived from the Gospel. But neither of these agreements invalidates the contention that *agape* is crucial to a Christian understanding of personal relationships. Many might agree with Niebuhr that individualised understandings of *agape* cannot resolve political complexities. Nevertheless, Niebuhr was the first to admit that, at least on personal ethical issues, *agape* is crucial. In Christian understandings of man and God, *agape* denotes both God's relationship to men and the relationship that God requires men to have with their fellow men. Within the context of Christian ethics, all sexual relationships should be, not just non-casual, but agapistic. *Agape* should be the characteristic of all of our interpersonal behaviour, whether this behaviour is between sexes or between 'races'. Christians will still disagree with each other on dilemmas such as abortion. But if their eventual decisions are judged to be un-agapistic, they will thereby also be judged to be un-Christian. On such issues, pure pragmatism, for example, is not a defensible Christian approach. Whilst *agape* might not be the whole of Christian ethics, it is nonetheless fundamental to it.

Neither axiom is sufficient in itself. For most of the exponents of Christian ethics surveyed in this textbook, *agape* is held in tension with justice and, in the Synoptic picture of Jesus, with moral indignation and anger at men's sin and wrong-doing. The adeodatic axiom is also held in tension with the sinfulness of much of the human 'given', and may even at times be in tension with *agape* (as Gustafson's Extract shows). An adequate understanding of Christian ethics must never seek to ignore or eliminate this tension. Rather it should regard it as one of the most creative features of Christian ethics. For the Christian this world is always a mixture of the 'now' and the 'not yet', of 'signs of the Kingdom' but not 'the Kingdom all in all'. Creative tension may indeed be the hall-mark of Christian ethics at its best.

BIBLIOGRAPHY

(This is an English language bibliography: for recent German language books in Christian ethics, see Fairweather & McDonald, 1984, and Gustafson, 1978 and 1981).

Ethics

ADKINS, A.W.H., *Merit and Responsibility*, Oxford University Press, Oxford, 1960.

ATKINSON, R.F., *Conduct: An Introduction to Moral Philosophy*, Macmillan, London, 1969.

BAIER, K., *The Moral Point of View: A Rational Basis of Ethics*, Cornell University Press, Ithaca, New York, 1958.

BRADLEY, F.H., *Ethical Studies*, Oxford University Press, Oxford, Second Edition, 1927.

BROAD, C.D., *Ethics and the History of Philosophy*, Routledge & Kegan Paul, London, 1952.

CAMPBELL, A.V., *Moral Dilemmas in Medicine*, Churchill Livingstone, Edinburgh and London, 1972.

CARRITT, E.F., *Theory of Morals*, Oxford University Press, Oxford, 1928.

DEVLIN, Patrick, *The Enforcement of Morals*, Oxford University Press, Oxford, 1965.

DEWEY John, *Theory of the Moral Life*, ed. Arnold Isenberg, Holt, Rinehart & Winston, New York, 1960.

DOWNIE, R.S. and TELFER, E., *Respect for Persons*, Allen & Unwin, London, 1969.

DOWNIE, R.S., *Roles and Values*, Methuen, London, 1971.

EMMET, Dorothy, *Rules, Roles and Relations*, Macmillan, London, 1966.

EWING, A.C., *The Definition of Good*, Routledge & Kegan Paul, London, 1952, and The Free Press, New York, 1965.

FLEW, A.G.N., *Evolutionary Ethics*, Macmillan, London, and St. Martins, New York, 1967.

FOOT, Philippa, ed. *Theories of Ethics*, Oxford University Press, Oxford and New York, 1967.

FRANKENA, W.K., *Ethics*, Prentice-Hall, N.J., Second Edition, 1973.

FRANKENA, W.K. and GRANROSE, J.R., eds., *Introductory Readings in Ethics*, Prentice-Hall, N.J., 1974.

GARNER, R.T. and ROSEN, Bernard, *Moral Philosophy*, Macmillan, New York, 1967.

GERT, Bernard, *The Moral Rules*, Harper & Row, New York, 1970.

HARE, R.M., *The Language of Morals*, Clarendon Press, Oxford, 1952.

HARE, R.M., *Freedom and Reason*, Clarendon Press, Oxford, 1963.

HARE, R.M., *Moral Thinking: Its Levels, Methods and Point*, Oxford University Press, Oxford and New York, 1981.

HARMAN, Gilbert, *The Nature of Morality: An Introduction to Ethics*, Oxford University Press, Oxford and New York, 1977.

551

HART, H.L.A., *Law, Liberty and Morality*, Oxford University Press, Oxford and New York, 1963.

HART, H.L.A., *Punishment and Responsibility*, Oxford University Press, Oxford and New York, 1968.

HASTINGS CENTER, *The Teaching of Ethics in Higher Education*, series of books on ethics in a variety of disciplines, Hastings Center, Hastings-on-Hudson, NYS, 1980.

HEARN, T.K., ed. *Studies in Utilitarianism*, Meredith, New York, 1971.

HOSPERS, J., *Human Conduct*, Hart–Davis, London, 1963.

HUDSON, W.D., ed. *The Is-Ought Question*, Macmillan, London, 1969.

HUDSON, W.D., *Modern Moral Philosophy*, Doubleday, New York, 1970, and Macmillan, London, rev. 1984.

KAMENKA, E., *Marxism and Ethics*, Macmillan, London and New York, 1969.

KENNY, A., *Action, Emotion and Will*, Routledge & Kegan Paul, London, 1963.

KENNY, A., *Will, Freedom and Power*, Oxford University Press, Oxford, 1975.

LYONS, D., *Forms and Limits of Utilitarianism*, Clarendon Press, Oxford, 1975.

MACINTYRE, Alasdair, *A Short History of Ethics*, Macmillan, New York, 1966 and Routledge & Kegan Paul, London, 1967.

MACINTYRE, Alasdair, *Against the Self-Images of the Age*, Duckworth, London, 1971.

MACKIE, J.L., *Ethics: Inventing Right and Wrong*, Penguin, London, 1977.

MOORE, G.E., *Principia Ethica*, Cambridge University Press, Cambridge, 1903 and Oxford University Press, London and New York, 1966.

MOORE, G.E., *Ethics*, Williams & Norgate, London, 1912.

MURDOCH, Iris, *The Sovereignty of the Good*, Routledge & Kegan Paul, 1970.

NOWELL-SMITH, P.H. *Ethics*, Blackwell, Oxford, 1957.

PRICHARD, H.A., *Moral Obligation: Essays and Lectures*, Clarendon Press, Oxford, 1949.

PRIOR, A.N., *Logic and the Basis of Ethics*, Oxford University Press, Oxford, 1949.

RAWLS, John, *A Theory of Justice*, Oxford University Press, Oxford and New York, 1973.

ROSS, W.D., *The Right and the Good*, Clarendon Press, Oxford, 1930.

ROSS, W.D., *Foundations of Ethics*, Clarendon Press, Oxford, 1939.

SCHLICK, M., *The Problems of Ethics*, Prentice Hall, New York, 1938.

SEN, A. and WILLIAMS B., eds. *Utilitarianism and Beyond*, Cambridge University Press, Cambridge, 1982.

SIDGWICK, H., *Methods of Ethics*, Macmillan, London, 1907.

SINGER, M.G., *Generalisation in Ethics*, Eyre & Spottiswoode, London, 1963.

SMART, J.J.C., and WILLIAMS, B., *Utilitarianism for and Against*, Cambridge University Press, Cambridge, 1973.

STEVENSON, C.L., *Ethics and Language*, Yale University Press, New Haven, 1945.

STEVENSON, C.L., *Facts and Values: Studies in Ethical Analysis*, Yale University Press, New Haven, 1963.

WARD, Keith, *The Development of Kant's View of Ethics*, Blackwell, Oxford, 1972.

WARNOCK. G.J., *Contemporary Moral Philosophy*, Macmillan, London, 1966 and St. Martin's Press, New York, 1967.

WARNOCK, G.J., *The Object of Morality*, Methuen, London, 1971.

WARNOCK, Mary, *Existentialist Ethics*, Macmillan, London, 1967.

WARNOCK, Mary, *Ethics Since 1900*, Oxford Unviersity Press, Oxford and New York, Third Edition, 1978.

Christian Ethics

ACCM, *Teaching Christian Ethics*, SCM Press, London, 1974.

BAELZ, Peter, *Ethics and Belief*, Sheldon, London, 1977.

BAILEY, D.S., *Homosexuality and the Western Christian Tradition*, Longmans, London, 1955.

BAILEY, D.S., *The Man/Woman Relation in Christian Thought*, SCM Press, London, 1959.

BAINTON, Roland H., *Sex, Love and Marriage: A Christian Survey*, Fontana, London, 1958.

BAINTON, Roland H., *Christian Attitudes Toward War and Peace: A Historical Survey and Critical Re-evaluation*, Abingdon, New York, 1960, and Hodder & Stoughton, London, 1961.

BARTH, Karl, *Ethics*, T & T Clark, Edinburgh, 1981.

BEACH, Waldo and NIEBUHR, H. Richard, *Christian Ethics: Sources of the Living Tradition*, Ronald Press, New York, Second Edition, 1973.

BENNETT, John C., *Christian Ethics and Social Policy*, Scribner's, New York, 1946.

BENNETT, John C., ed. *Storm Over Ethics*, Bethany Press, Philadelphia, 1967.

BENNETT, John C., *The Radical Imperative*, Westminster, Philadelphia, 1975.

BERDYAEV, Nicolas, *Christianity and Class War*, Sheed & Ward, London, 1931.

BERDYAEV, Nicolas, *The Destiny of Man*, Scribner's, New York, and Geoffrey Bles, London, 1935.

BERDYAEV, Nicolas, *Freedom and the Spirit*, Scribner's, New York, and Geoffrey Bles, London, 1935.

BERDYAEV, Nicolas, *The Meaning of History*, Scribner's New York, and Geoffrey Bles, London, 1936.

BERDYAEV, Nicolas, *The Realm of Spirit and the Realm of Caesar*, Gollancz, London, 1952, and Harper, New York, 1953.

BONHOEFFER, Dietrich, *Sanctorum Communio*, Collins, London, 1963.
BONHOEFFER, Dietrich, *No Rusty Swords*, Harper & Row, New York, and Collins, London, 1965.
BONHOEFFER, Dietrich, *The Cost of Discipleship*, SCM Press, London, 1978.
BONHOEFFER, Dietrich, *Ethics*, Macmillan, New York, 1955, and SCM Press, London, rev. ed. 1978.
BROWN, David, *Choices: Ethics and the Christian*, Blackwell, Oxford, 1983.
BRUNNER, Emil, *The Divine Imperative*, Macmillan, New York, and Lutterworth, London, 1937.
BRUNNER, Emil, *Justice and the Social Order*, Harper, New York, and Lutterworth, London, 1945.

CADOUX, C.J., *The Early Christian Attitude to War*, London, 1919.
CHILDRESS, James F., ed. *A Dictionary of Christian Ethics*, Westminster, Philadelphia, and SCM Press, London, 1985.
CHURCH OF ENGLAND, Board for Social Responsibility, *Homosexual Relationships*, Church Information Office, London, 1979.
CHURCH OF ENGLAND, Board for Social Reponsibility, *On Dying Well*, Church Information Office, London, 1975.
CHURCH OF ENGLAND, Board for Social Responsibility, *The Church and the Bomb*, Hodder & Stoughton, London, 1982.
CHURCH OF SCOTLAND, Reports to the General Assembly, *God's Will for the Church and Nation*, (The Baillie Report), SCM Press, London, 1946.
COOK, David, *The Moral Maze*, SPCK, London, 1983.
CUPITT, Don, *Crisis of Moral Authority: The Dethronement of Christianity*, Westminister, Philadelphia, and Lutterworth, London, 1972.
CURRAN, Charles E., *Catholic Moral Theology in Dialogue*, Fides, Notre Dame, Indiana, 1972.
CURRAN, Charles E., *Ongoing Revision: Studies in Moral Theology*, Fides, Notre Dame, Indiana, 1975.
CURRAN, Charles E., ed. *Absolutes in Moral Theology?*, Greenwood Press, Westport, 1975.
CURRAN, Charles E., *Issues in Sexual and Medical Ethics*, University of Notre Dame, Notre Dame, 1978.

DEMANT, V.A., *Religion and the Decline of Capitalism*, Faber & Faber, London, 1952.
DEMANT, V.A., *An Exposition of Christian Sexual Ethics*, Hodder, London, 1963.
D'ÉNTREVES, A.P., *Natural Law*, Hutchinson, 1951.
DUNSTAN, G.R., *The Artifice of Ethics*, SCM Press, London, 1974.
DUNSTAN, G.R., ed. *Duty and Discernment*, SCM Press, London, 1975.

FAIRWEATHER, Ian C.M. and MCDONALD, J.I.H., *The Quest for Christian Ethics*, Handsel Press, Edinburgh, 1984.

FLETCHER, Joseph, *Morals and Medicine*, Princeton University Press, NJ, 1954 and Gollancz, London, 1955.

FLETCHER, Joseph, *Situation Ethics*, Westminster, Philadelphia, and SCM Press, London, 1966.

FLETCHER, Joseph, *Moral Responsibility,: Situation Ethics at Work*, Westminster, Philadelphia, and SCM Press, London, 1967.

FLETCHER, Joseph, *Humanhood: Essays in Biomedical Ethics*, Prometheus Books, Buffalo, 1979.

FORELL, George Wolfgang, ed. *Christian Social Teachings: A Reader in Christian Social Ethics from the Bible to the Present*, Augsburg, Minneapolis, 1971.

FORELL, George Wolfgang, *History of Christian Ethics*, Augsburg, Minneapolis, 1979.

FORRESTER, Duncan B., *Christianity and the Future of Welfare*, Epworth, London, 1985.

GILL, Robin, *The Social Context of Theology*, Mowbrays, Oxford, 1975.

GILL, Robin, *Theology and Social Structure*, Mowbrays, Oxford, 1977.

GILL, Robin, *Prophecy and Praxis*, Marshall, Morgan & Scott, London, 1981.

GILL, Robin, *The Cross Against the Bomb*, Epworth, London, 1984.

GREEN, Ronald M., *Religious Reason: The Rational and Moral Basis of Religious Belief*, Oxford University Press, New York, 1978.

GUSTAFSON, James M., *Christ and the Moral Life*, Harper & Row, New York, 1968.

GUSTAFSON, James M., *The Church as Moral Decision-Maker*, Pilgrim, Philadelphia, 1970.

GUSTAFSON, James M., *Can Ethics Be Christian?*, University of Chicago Press, Chicago, 1975.

GUSTAFSON, James M., *Protestant and Roman Catholic Ethics*, University of Chicago Press, Chicago, and SCM Press, London, 1978.

GUSTAFSON, James M., *Theology and Ethics*, Oxford University Press, Oxford and New York, 1981.

HÄRING, Bernard, *The Law of Christ*, 3 vols. Newman Press, Westminster, Md., 1961-6.

HÄRING, Bernard, *Medical Ethics*, Fides, Notre Dame, Indiana, and St. Paul, Slough, 1972.

HÄRING, Bernard, *Free and Faithful in Christ*, 3 Vols. Seabury, New York, and St. Paul, Slough, 1978.

HARNED, David Baily, *Grace and Common Life*, University of Virginia, VA, 1971.

HARNED, David Baily, *Faith and Virtue*, Pilgrim, Philadelphia, 1973.

HARRIS, P., ed., *On Human Life: An Examination of Humanae Vitae*, Burns & Oates, London, 1968.

HAUERWAS, Stanley, *Vision and Virtue: Essays in Christian Ethical Reflection*, Fides, Notre Dame, Indiana, 1974.

HAUERWAS, Stanley, *Character and the Christian Life: A Study in Theological Ethics*, Trinity University Press, San Antonio, 1975.

HAUERWAS, Stanley, *The Peaceable Kingdom*, SCM Press, London, 1984.

HEBBLETHWAITE, Brian, *The Adequacy of Christian Ethics*, Marshall, Morgan & Scott, London, 1981.

HOULDEN, J.L., *Ethics and the New Testament*, Mowbrays, Oxford, 1973.

HOLMES, Arthur, F., *War and Christian Ethics*, Baker, New York, 1975.

HOLMES, Arthur, F., *Ethics: Approaching Moral Decisions*, Downers Grove, Ill. 1984.

HUGHES, Gerard J., *Authority in Morals*, Sheed & Ward, London, 1983.

KIRK, Kenneth E., *Some Principles of Moral Theology*, Longmans, Green, London, 1920.

KIRK, Kenneth E., *Conscience and its Problems: An Introduction to Casuistry*, Longmans, Green, London, 1927.

KIRK, Kenneth E., *The Vision of God: The Doctrine of the Summum Bonum*, Longmans, Green, London, 1931.

KNOX, John, *The Ethic of Jesus in the Teaching of the Church: Its Authority and Its Relevance*, Abingdon, New York, 1961, and Epworth, London, 1962.

LEHMANN, Paul, *Ethics in a Christian Context*, Harper & Row, New York, and SCM Press, London, 1963.

LEHMANN, Paul, *The Transfiguration of Politics*, Harper & Row, New York, 1975.

LINACRE CENTRE, *Euthanasia and Clinical Practice*, Linacre, London, 1982.

LITTLE, David and TWISS, Sumner B., *Comparative Religious Ethics: A New Method*, Harper & Row, New York, 1978.

LONG, Edward LeRoy, Jr, *Conscience and Compromise: An Approach to Protestant Casuistry*, Westminster, Philadelphia, 1954.

LONG, Edward LeRoy, Jr, *A Survey of Christian Ethics*, Oxford University Press, New York and Oxford, 1967.

LONG, Edward LeRoy, Jr., *A Survey of Recent Christian Ethics*, Oxford University Press, New York and Oxford, 1982.

MCDONAGH, Enda, *Invitation and Response: Essays in Christian Moral Theology*, Gill & Macmillan, Dublin, 1972.

MCDONAGH, Enda, *Gift and Call*, Gill & Macmillan, Dublin, 1975.

MCDONAGH, Enda, *Doing the Truth*, Gill & Macmillan, Dublin, 1979.

MACGREGOR, G.H.C., *The New Testament Basis of Pacifism*, James Clarke, London, 1936.

MACQUARRIE, John, ed. *A Dictionary of Christian Ethics*, SCM Press, London, 1967 (see CHILDRESS for rev. ed.).

MACQUARRIE, John, *Three Issues in Ethics*, Harper & Row, New York, and SCM Press, London, 1970.

MAHONEY, John *Seeking the Spirit*, Sheed & Ward, London and New York, 1982.

MANSON, T.W., *Ethics and the Gospel*, ed. R.H. Preston, SCM Press, London, 1960.

MARRIN, Albert, ed. *War and the Christian Conscience: From Augustine to Martin Luther King, Jr.*, Henry Regnery, Chicago, 1971.

MITCHELL, Basil, *Law, Morality and Religion*, Oxford University Press, London and New York, 1967.

MITCHELL, Basil, *Morality: Religious and Secular*, Oxford University Press, Oxford and New York, 1980.

NIEBUHR, H. Richard, *Christ and Culture*, Harper, New York, 1951.

NIEBUHR, H. Richard, *The Responsible Self*, Harper & Row, New York, 1963.

NIEBUHR, Reinhold, *Moral Man and Immoral Society*, Scribner's, New York, 1932 and 1960, and SCM Press, London, 1963.

NIEBUHR, Reinhold, *An Interpretation of Christian Ethics*, Harper, New York, 1935, and SCM Press, London, 1936.

NIEBUHR, Reinhold, *The Children of Light and the Children of Darkness*, Scribner's, New York, 1944.

NIEBUHR, Reinhold, *The Nature and Destiny of Man*, 2 Vols, Nisbet, London, 1943, and Scribner's, New York, 1949.

NIEBUHR, Reinhold, *Faith and History*, Scribner's, New York, 1949.

NIEBUHR, Reinhold, *Christian Realism and Political Problems*, Scribner's, New York, 1953, and Faber & Faber, London, 1964.

NOONAN, John T., Jr., *The Scholastic Analysis of Usury*, Harvard University Press, Cambridge, MS, 1957.

NOONAN, John T., Jr, *Contraception: A History of Its Treatment by the Catholic Theologians and Canonists*, Harvard University Press, Cambridge, MS, 1965.

NOONAN, John T., Jr, ed. *The Morality of Abortion: Legal and Historical Perspectives*, Harvard University Press, Cambridge, MS, 1970.

NYGREN, Anders, *Agape and Eros*, SPCK, London, 1953.

OGLETREE, Thomas W., *The Use of the Bible in Christian Ethics*, Blackwell, Oxford, 1985.

OPPENHEIMER, Helen, *The Character of Christian Morality*, Faith Press, London, 1965.

OPPENHEIMER, Helen, *The Hope of Happiness*, SCM Press, London, 1983.

OSBORN, Eric, *Ethical Patterns in Early Christian Thought*, Cambridge University Press, Cambridge, 1976.

OUTKA, Gene H. and RAMSEY, Paul, *Norm and Context in Christian Ethics*, Scribner's, New York, 1968, and SCM Press, London, 1969.

OUTKA, Gene H., *Agape: An Ethical Analysis*, Yale University Press, New Haven, 1973.

OUTKA, Gene H. and REEDER, John D. Jr, *Religion and Morality*, Anchor, New York, 1973.

PANNENBERG, Wolfhart, *Ethics,* Search Press, London, and Westminster, Philadelphia, 1981.

PIERCE, C.A., *Conscience in the New Testament,* SCM Press, London, 1955.

PRESTON, Ronald H., ed. *Technology and Social Justice,* SCM Press, London, 1971.

PRESTON, Ronald H., ed. *Industrial Conflicts and their Place in Modern Society,* SCM Press, London, 1974.

PRESTON, Ronald H., ed. *Perspectives on Strikes,* SCM Press, London, 1975.

PRESTON, Ronald H., *Religion and the Persistence of Captialism,* SCM Press, London, 1979.

PRESTON, Ronald H. *Explorations in Theology,* Vol. 9, SCM Press, London, 1981.

PRESTON, Ronald H. *Church and Society in the Late Twentieth Century: The Economic and Political Task,* SCM Press, London, 1983.

RAMSEY, I.T., ed, *Christian Ethics and Contemporary Philosophy,* SCM Press, London, 1966.

RAMSEY, Paul, *Basic Christian Ethics,* Scribner's New York, 1951, and University of Chicago Press, Chicago, 1980.

RAMSEY, Paul, *War and the Christian Conscience: How Shall Modern War be Conducted Justly?,* Duke University Press, Durham, NC, 1961.

RAMSEY, Paul, *Nine Modern Moralists,* Prentice-Hall, NJ, 1962.

RAMSEY, Paul, *The Limits of Nuclear War: Thinking About the Do-able and the Undo-able,* Council on Religion and International Affairs, New York, 1963.

RAMSEY, Paul, *Deeds and Rules in Christian Ethics,* Oliver & Boyd, Edinburgh, 1965: rev. Scribner's New York, 1967.

RAMSEY, Paul, *Who Speaks for the Church?,* Abingdon, New York, 1967.

RAMSEY, Paul, *The Just War: Force and Political Responsibility,* Scribner.s, 1968.

RAMSEY, Paul, *Fabricated Man: The Ethics of Genetic Control,* Yale University Press, New Haven, 1970.

RAMSEY, Paul, *The Patient as Person,* Yale University Press, New Haven, 1970.

RAMSEY, Paul, *The Ethics of Fetal Research,* Yale University Press, New Haven, 1975.

RAMSEY, Paul, *Ethics at the Edges of Life,* Yale University Press, New Haven, 1978.

RAUSCHENBUSCH, Walter, *Christianity and the Social Crisis,* Macmillan, New York, 1907.

RAUSCHENBUSCH, Walter, *Christianizing the Social Order,* Macmillan, New York, 1916.

RAUSCHENBUSCH, Walter, *A Theology for the Social Gospel,* Macmillan, New York, 1918.

ROBINSON, N.H.G., *The Groundwork of Christian Ethics*, Collins, London, 1971.

SANDERS, Jack T., *Ethics in the New Testament*, SCM Press, London, 1975.

SCHILLEBEECKX, Edward, *Marriage: Human Reality and Saving Mystery*, 2 Vols, Sheed & Ward, London, 1965.

TAYLOR, A.E., *The Faith of a Moralist*, 2 Vols, Macmillan, London, 1932.

TEMPLE, William, *Nature, God and Man*, Macmillan, London, 1934.

TEMPLE, William, *Citizen and Churchman*, Eyre & Spottiswoode, London, 1941.

TEMPLE, William, *Christianity and the Social Order*, Penguin, London, 1942, and Shepheard-Walwyn & SPCK, London, 1976 (with Introduction by Ronald Preston).

THOMAS, G.F., *Christian Ethics and Moral Philosophy*, Scribner's, New York, 1955.

THIELICKE, Helmut, *The Ethics of Sex*, James Clarke, London, 1964, and Baker, Grand Rapids, Michigan, 1975.

THIELICKE, Helmut, *Theological Ethics*, 3 Vols, Eerdmans, Michigan, 1979.

TILLICH, Paul, *Love, Power and Justice*, Oxford University Press, New York, 1954.

TILLICH, Paul, *Morality and Beyond*, Harper & Row, New York, 1963, and Fontana, London, 1969.

TROWELL, Hugh, *The Unfinished Debate on Euthanasia*, SCM Press, 1973.

WARD, Keith, *Ethics and Christianity*, Allen & Unwin, London, 1970.

WARD, Keith, *The Divine Image: The Foundations of Christian Morality*, SPCK, London, 1976.

WELTY, E. *A Handbook of Christian Social Ethics*, 2 Vols, Nelson, Edinburgh, 1960-63.

WINTER, Gibson, *Elements for a Social Ethic*, Macmillan, New York, 1966.

WOODS, G.F., *A Defence of Theological Ethics*, Cambridge University Press, Cambridge, 1966.

YODER, John Howard, *The Politics of Jesus*, Eerdmans, Michigan, 1972.

Additional Relevant Books

ALLEN, E.L., *Freedom in God: A Guide to the Thought of Nicolas Berdyaev*, London, 1950.

BAINTON, Roland H., *Here I Stand: A Life of Martin Luther*, Abingdon, New York, 1950.

BARNSLEY, John H., *The Social Reality of Ethics*, Routledge & Kegan Paul, London and Boston, 1972.

BARR, James, *The Bible in the Modern World*, SCM Press, London, 1973.

BARROW, R.W., *Introduction to St. Augustine: The City of God*, London, 1950.

BARTH, Karl, *How I Changed My Mind*, T & T Clark, Edinburgh, 1969.

BARTH, Karl, *Church Dogmatics*, Vols I-IV, T & T Clark, Edinburgh, 1936-69.

BAUM, Gregory, *The Jews and the Gospel*, Bloomsbury, 1961.

BAUM, Gregory, *Religion and Alienation: A Theological Reading of Sociology*, Paulist Press, New York, 1975.

BAUM, Gregory, *The Social Imperative: Essays on the Critical Issues that Confront the Christian Churches*, Paulist Press, New York, 1979.

BERGER, Peter L. and LUCKMANN, Thomas, *The Social Construction of Reality*, Doubleday, New York, 1966, and Penguin, London, 1971.

BERGER, Peter L., *The Sacred Canopy*, Doubleday, New York, 1967: British title, *The Social Reality of Religion*, Faber & Faber, 1969.

BERGER, Peter L., *A Rumor of Angels*, Doubleday, New York, and Pelican, London, 1969.

BERGER, Peter L., *The Heretical Imperative*, Anchor/Doubleday, 1979, and Collins, London, 1980.

BETHGE, Eberhard, *Dietrich Bonhoeffer: Theologian, Christian, Contemporary*, Collins, London, 1970.

BONINO, José Míguez, *Doing Theology in a Revolutionary Situation*, Fortress, Philadelphia, 1975: British title, *Revolutionary Theology Comes of Age*, SPCK, London, 1975.

BOFF, Leonardo, *Liberating Grace*, Orbis, New York, 1979.

BOFF, Leonardo, *Way of the Cross – Way of Justice*, Orbis, New York, 1982.

BROCK, Peter, *Pacifism in the United States from the Colonial Era to the First World War*, Princeton University Press, NJ, 1968.

BROCK, Peter, *Twentieth-Century Pacifism*, Van Nostrand Reinhold, 1970.

BROCK, Peter, *Pacifism in Europe to 1914*, Princeton University Press, NJ, 1972.

BROWN, Peter, *Augustine of Hippo: A Biography*, University of California, Berkeley, and Faber & Faber, London, 1967.

BROWN, Peter, *Religion and Society in the Age of Saint Augustine*, Faber & Faber, London, 1972.

CLARKE, Oliver Fielding, *Introduction to Berdyaev*, Bles, London, 1950.

COPLESTON, F.C., *Aquinas*, Penguin, London, 1955, and Harper & Row, New York, 1976.

COX, Harvey, *Secular City*, Macmillan, New York, and SCM Press, London, 1965,

CURTIS, J.E. and PETRAS, J.W., *The Sociology of Knowledge: A Reader*, Duckworth, London, 1972.

DILLISTONE, F.W., *Charles Raven: Naturalist, Historian and Theologian*, Hodder & Stoughton, 1975.

DODD, C.H., *The Authority of the Bible,* Nisbet, London, 1929: rev. Fontana, London, 1960.

DODD, C.H., *Gospel and Law,* Cambridge University Press, Cambridge,1951.

DUNN, James D.G., *Unity and Diversity in the New Testament,* SCM Press, London, 1977.

DURKHEIM, Émile, *Suicide: A Study in Sociology,* (1897) Routledge & Kegan Paul, London, 1970.

FERGUSON, John, *The Politics of Love,* James Clarke, London, 1973.

FERGUSON, John, *War and Peace in the World's Religions,* Oxford University Press, Oxford and New York, 1978.

FIERRO, Alfredo, *The Militant Gospel: An Analysis of Contemporary Theologies,* Orbis, New York, and SCM Press, London, 1977.

FORELL, George Wolfgang, *Faith Active in Love: An Investigation of the Principles Underlying Luther's Social Ethics,* Augsburg, Minneapolis, 1954.

FREEMANTLE, Anne, ed. *The Social Teachings of the Church,* Mentor-Omega, New York, 1963.

GLOCK, Charles and STARK, Rodney, *Christian Beliefs and Anti-Semitism,* Harper, New York, 1966.

GODSEY, John D., *The Theology of Dietrich Bonhoeffer,* SCM Press, London, 1960.

GOTTWALD, N.K., ed. *The Bible and Liberation,* Orbis, New York, 1983.

GUTIÉRREZ, Gustavo, *A Theology of Liberation,* Orbis, New York, 1973, and SCM Press, London, 1974.

GUTIÉRREZ, Gustavo, *The Power of the Poor in History: Selected Writings,* Orbis, New York, and SCM Press, London, 1983.

HABERMAS, J., *Knowledge and Human Interests,* Beacon Press, Boston, 1971.

HAMILTON, Peter, *Knowledge and Social Structure,* Routledge & Kegan Paul, London, 1974.

HILL, Michael, *A Sociology of Religion,* Heinemann, London, 1973.

IREMONGER, F.A., *William Temple: Archbishop of Canterbury,* Oxford University Press, Oxford 1948.

KAUNDA, Kenneth, *Kaunda on Violence,* Collins, London, 1980.

KEE, Alistair, ed. *Reader in Political Theology,* SCM Press, 1974.

KEE, Alistair, ed. *The Scope of Political Theology,* SCM Press, London, 1978.

KEGLEY, Charles W., and BRETALL, Robert W., *Reinhold Niebuhr: His Religious, Social, and Political Thought,* Macmillan, New York, 1961.

KLEIN, Charlotte, *Anti-Semitism in Christian Theology,* SPCK, London, 1978.

KÜNG, Hans, *Infallible?,* Fount, London, 1971.

KÜNG, Hans, *On Being a Christian,* Doubleday, New York, and Collins, London, 1977.

LEWIS, H.D., *Philosophy of Religion*, English Universities Press, London, 1965.

LOWRIE, Donald A., *Rebellious Prophet: A Biography of Nicolas Berdyaev*, Gollancz, 1960.

MCNEILL, John T., ed. *Calvin On God and Political Duty*, Bobbs-Merrill, Indianapolis, 1950.

MANNHEIM, Karl, *Ideology and Utopia*, Routledge & Kegan Paul, London, 1936.

MARTIN, David, *Pacifism: An Historical and Sociological Study*, Routledge & Kegan Paul, London, 1965.

MARTIN, David, ORME MILLS, John, and PICKERING, W.S.F., edd. *Sociology and Theology: Alliance and Conflict*, Harvester, Sussex, 1980.

METZ, J.B., *Theology of the World*, Herder & Herder, New York, 1969.

METZ, J.B., *Christianity and the Bourgeoisie*, Concilium, 1979.

MEYER, D, *The Protestant Search for Political Realism*, Berkeley, California, 1960.

MILFORD, T.R., ed. *The Valley of Decision: The Christian Dilemma in the Nuclear Age*, British Council of Churches, London, 1961.

MIRANDA, José Porfirio, *Marx and the Bible*, Orbis, New York, and SCM Press, London, 1977.

MIRANDA, José Porfirio, *Marx Against the Marxists*, Orbis, New York, and SCM Press, London, 1980.

NIEBUHR, H.Richard, *The Social Sources of Denominationalism*, Holt, New York, 1929.

NINEHAM, D.E., *The Use and Abuse of the Bible*, SPCK, London, 1976.

O.CONNOR, D.J., *Aquinas and Natural Law*, Macmillan, London, 1967.

OSSOWSKA, Maria, *Social Determinants of Moral Ideas*, Routledge & Kegan Paul, London 1971.

OSTHATHIOS, Geervarghese Mar, *Theology of a Classless Society*, Orbis, New York, and Lutterworth, London, 1979.

OSTHATHIOS, Geevarghese Mar, *The Sin of Being Rich in a Poor World*, Christian Literature Society, Madras, 1983.

RAVEN, Charles E., *Is War Obsolete?*, Allen & Unwin, London, 1935.

RAVEN, Charles E., *War and the Christian*, London, 1938

RAVEN, Charles E., *The Theological Basis of Christian Pacifism*, Fellowship of Reconciliation, London and New York, 1952.

ROBINSON, John A.T., *Honest to God*, SCM Press, London, 1963.

RUETHER, Rosemary Radford, *Liberation Theology*, Paulist Press, New York, 1972.

RUETHER, Rosemary Radford, *Faith and Fratricide: The Theological Roots of Anti-Semitism*, Seabury, New York, 1974.

RUETHER, Rosemary Radford, *New Woman/New Earth*, Seabury, New York, 1975.

RUPP, E.Gordon, *Martin Luther and the Jews*, Council of Christians and Jews, London, 1972.

RUSSELL, Frederick H., *The Just War in the Middle Ages,* Cambridge University Press, Cambridge and New York, 1975.

RUSTON, Roger, *Nuclear Deterrence – Right or Wrong?,* Commission for International Justice and Peace of England and Wales, Catholic Information Services, Abbots Langley, Herts, 1981.

SCHNACKENBURG, Rudolf, *The Moral Teaching of the New Testament,* Burns & Oats, 1964, and Herder & Herder, New York, 1965.

SHAW, D.W.D., *The Dissuaders,* SCM Press, London, 1978.

SMART, Ninian, *The Science of Religion and the Sociology of Knowledge,* Princeton University Press, NJ, 1975.

SOLLE, Dorothee, *Political Theology,* Fortress, Philadelphia, 1974.

STARK, Werner, *The Sociology of Knowledge,* Routledge & Kegan Paul, London, 1958.

TAWNEY, R.H., *Religion and the Rise of Capitalism,* John Murray, London, 1926.

TAWNEY, R.H., *Equality,* Allen & Unwin, London, 1931.

TOOKE, Joan, *The Just War in Aquinas and Grotius,* SPCK, London, 1965.

TROELTSCH, Ernst, *The Social Teaching of the Christian Churches,* (1919) Allen & Unwin, London, 1931, and Harper, New York, 1960.

US BISHOPS, *The Challenge of Peace: God's Promise and Our Response,* Pastoral Letter on War and Peace in the Nuclear Age, US Catholic Conference, Washington, DC, and CTS/SPCK, London, 1983.

VALLON, Michael Alexander, *An Apostle of Freedom: Life and Teaching of Nicolas Berdyaev,* London, 1960.

VERGHESE, Paul, *Joy of Freedom,* Lutterworth, London, 1967.

VERGHESE, Paul, *Freedom of Man,* Westminster, Philadelphia, 1972: rev. and expanded as *Freedom and Authority,* Christian Literature Society, Madras, 1974.

WEBER, Max, *The Protestant Ethic and the Spirit of Capitalism,* (1901) Allen & Unwin, London, 1930.

WEBER, Max, *The Sociology of Religion,* (1920) Beacon Press, Boston, 1963, and Methuen, London, 1965.

WEST, Charles C., *Communism and the Theologians: Study of an Encounter,* Westminster, Philadelphia, and SCM Press, London, 1958.

WILLIS, R.E., *The Ethics of Karl Barth,* Leiden, 1971.

WILSON, Bryan, *Religion in Sociological Perspective,* Oxford University Press, Oxford and New York, 1982.

WINGREN, Gustav, *Luther on Vocation,* Muhlenberg Press, Philadelphia, 1957.

WINGREN, Gustav, *The Christian's Calling,* Oliver & Boyd, Edinburgh, 1958.

WORLD COUNCIL OF CHURCHES, *Christians and the Prevention of War in an Atomic Age,* SCM Press, London, 1961.

YINGER, J.Milton, *The Scientific Study of Religion,* Collier-Macmillan, New York, 1970.

INDEX OF BIBLICAL REFERENCES

OLD TESTAMENT

APOCRYPHA

NEW TESTAMENT

GENERAL INDEX

566